Social
Research
Methods

Social Research Methods

JUBILEE
CAMPUS
LRC

Alan Bryman

Edward Bell

Jennifer Reck

Jessica Fields

New York   Oxford
OXFORD UNIVERSITY PRESS

Oxford University Press is a department of the University of Oxford.
It furthers the University's objective of excellence in research, scholarship,
and education by publishing worldwide. Oxford is a registered trade mark of
Oxford University Press in the UK and certain other countries.

Published in the United States of America by Oxford University Press
198 Madison Avenue, New York, NY 10016, United States of America.

For titles covered by Section 112 of the US Higher Education
Opportunity Act, please visit www.oup.com/us/he for the latest
information about pricing and alternate formats.

Library of Congress Cataloging-in-Publication Data
Names: Bryman, Alan, author.
Title: Social research methods / Alan Bryman, Edward Bell, Jennifer Reck,
    Jessica Fields.
Description: New York, NY : Oxford University Press, [2022] | Includes
    bibliographical references and index.
Identifiers: LCCN 2021015474 (print) | LCCN 2021015475 (ebook) | ISBN
    9780190853662 (paperback) | ISBN 9780190853686 (epub)
Subjects: LCSH: Social sciences—Methodology.
Classification: LCC H61 .B698 2022 (print) | LCC H61 (ebook) | DDC
    300.72/1—dc23
LC record available at https://lccn.loc.gov/2021015474
LC ebook record available at https://lccn.loc.gov/2021015475

9 8 7 6 5 4 3 2 1
Printed by LSC Communications, United States of America

Brief Contents

PART I
Principles of Research

PART II
Concepts and Cases

PART III
Modes and Practices of
Inquiry

PART IV
Gathering Information

PART V
Making Sense and Sharing What We've Learned

Contents

PART I
Principles of Research   1

PART II
Concepts and Cases   48

PART III
Modes and Practices of Inquiry 94

5 How Can Researchers Understand Meaning, Process, and Experience in the Social World?
Qualitative Research 96

6 How Can Researchers Enumerate and Examine Broad Patterns to Social Life?
Quantitative Research 120

7 Where Do Principles and Practice Meet in Research?
Study Design 144

PART IV
Gathering Information 166

8 How Do Researchers Study Patterns that Span Populations and Categories of Experience?
Questionnaires and Structured Interviews 168

9 How Do Researchers Learn about People's Perspectives and Lives?
Qualitative Interviewing   194

10 How Can Researchers Study the Patterns of People's Lives?
Participant Observation and Ethnography   218

11 How Do Researchers Study the Ways Meanings Are Communicated in Everyday Life?
Content Analysis   241

12 What Can Researchers Learn from Information Others Collected?
Existing Data   267

PART V

Making Sense and Sharing What We've Learned   294

Guide to the Book

Who Would Benefit from Reading This Book?

We wrote this book for undergraduate students taking a research methods course, most often in sociology departments but also in other social science disciplines, such as health studies, social work, and education. We cover a wide range of methods and approaches to study design, data collection, and analysis.

Research methods are not tied to any particular nation, and the principles underlying them transcend national boundaries. The same is true of this book. Alan Bryman wrote the original text on which ours is based with the needs of British postsecondary students in mind, but instructors across Europe and Canada adopted it as well. Edward Bell later adapted Bryman's textbook for Canadian instructors and students. He preserved the qualities that contributed to the book's initial success—its clarity, comprehensiveness, and presentation of social research methods in an international context—while expanding the discussion of Canadian and, more broadly, North American examples, sources, and research studies.

We, Jen Reck and Jessica Fields, adapted Bryman and Bell's Canadian text for a US audience. We were initially drawn to the text as a foundation for ours not only because of its clarity and comprehensiveness but also for its attention to qualitative and quantitative methods. The text took differences between qualitative and quantitative research seriously, but did not assume that those differences are either inevitable or insurmountable. We've tried to preserve these qualities in this adaptation while bringing concerns and commitments of special importance to American readers. We emphasize research methods as a tool to understand and address social problems, divisions, and inequities with which the United States and other countries struggle. We approach research as a collection of decisions to be made thoughtfully: having considered one's options and with implications and consequences in sight. And we highlight the work of scholars from historically marginalized communities in an effort to broaden and deepen the available picture of sociological research. Our hope is that this book, first, elevates the work already underway to address historical inequities and, second, welcomes a new generation of scholars into the sociological project of seeking understanding as way to promote justice.

Features of the Text

The book has several features that represent our approach to research and our priorities as teachers. As instructors who have taught research methods for many years, we wrote this book as a teaching tool. Students are often uncertain about and even resistant to learning research methods, so we maintained the original text's accessible and clear approach and wrote in a student-focused voice. We encourage students to imagine themselves as researchers, foregrounding questions that motivate them to consider choices researchers make, how they make them, and what they mean.

We also link research to a social justice agenda and foreground examples from studies employing an intersectional analysis and engaging meaningfully with discussions of race, class, gender, sexuality, and disability. We depart from perspectives that might position quantitative methods as the preferred research strategy, and qualitative and quantitative work as conflicting orientations. Instead, the text will allow students to understand the unique knowledge each type of research can produce and grapple with the questions that different methods can explore. To that end, we emphasize research as a way of asking and answering questions about the world, and the book provides information about the ways we can pursue that inquiry in different ways depending on the methods we choose. All of these book features will be useful for teachers encouraging their students to become complex thinkers about decisions researchers make in their work.

Additional material that works towards this goal includes our in-depth research examples and discussion of mixed methods approaches throughout the book. Chapters include boxes called *Mixed Methods in Action* that introduce examples of mixed methods research. These features help highlight the chapter's focal topic and emphasize the ways qualitative and quantitative methods complement one another. We also include in-depth empirical examples to engage students in key topics contemporary researchers explore and share information about their research process. In these boxes, titled *Methods in Motion*, we help students understand the choices researchers make and demonstrate how they develop knowledge about pressing social issues.

The book also emphasizes writing as a thinking tool. At the end of each chapter, we include a writing prompt we call *Portfolio Exercise*. These exercises guide students through all the steps of devising an individual research project, and each Portfolio prompt directs them to think and write about their own chosen research topic in relation to the chapter's concepts. The prompts are a scaffolded set of exercises that could support a student writing a research proposal. Chapter 15, which focuses specifically on writing and dissemination, introduces writing as a practice, supporting students to see themselves as writers and fostering more understanding of the writing process.

Approach to Language and Terminology

Our social justice-oriented approach in the book also extends to the language and terminology we have used. We use gender-inclusive language ("people of all genders" rather than "men and women"; "they" versus "he/she"). The text also emphasizes person-first language ("people with disabilities" instead of "disabled people"; "person experiencing homelessness" instead of "homeless person") and non-stigmatizing language ("incarcerated person" versus "inmate" or "criminal"; "learning difference" versus "learning disability").

The book also includes race, gender, and sexuality terminology that is gender-neutral and preferred among the communities described. We use the acronym LGBTQIA2S+ (Lesbian, Gay, Bisexual, Transgender, Queer, Intersex, Asexual, Two-Spirit, Plus) as more inclusive than lesbian/gay or LGBT. We also use the term BIPOC (Black, Indigenous, people of color) rather than "people of color." BIPOC is a term meant to encourage solidarity among Black, Indigenous, and other communities of color and highlight the particular experiences Black and Indigenous people have within the system of White supremacy. We use the gender-neutral term Latinx rather than the gender-binary options Latino and Latina or "Hispanic," an umbrella term originating from colonial definitions and governmental attempts to enumerate the population. We also use the term Black rather than African American to encompass the diverse origins and backgrounds in the Black community. Indigenous is used as a term that encompasses a variety of groups who were first inhabitants of what is now the United States and many other places around the world. Rather than using homogenizing umbrella terms, we include specific terminology when it is applicable—for instance, "Filipino" or "Chinese American" rather than "Asian American." Following the suggestions of the National Association of Black Journalists and others, we have chosen to capitalize terms used to denote a race, such as Black, White, and Brown.

However, we also include the terminology used by the researchers we cite in this book when it refers to their research focus, population, and sample studied. Thus, in a single discussion you might see us use the term Latinx (to refer to the overall community) and Hispanic (to refer to the researchers' terminology used to describe their sample).

We do not claim that all of these language choices are preferred or used by everyone in the communities about which we speak, and we recognize that language is constantly transforming and contested. These choices reflect our perspectives (at the time of completing the manuscript) on current conversations about how to use language to respectfully present people's lives and identities.

Structure of the Book

PART I comprises two scene-setting chapters that deal with basic ideas about the nature of social research and a chapter on research ethics.

- **Chapter 1** sets the stage with an exploration of *research as a way to make sense of the world*. We consider the role research plays in creating knowledge and building and testing theory, and explore qualitative and quantitative research as *research orientations* that offer different approaches to studying people and society. This chapter includes a discussion of *research questions*: what they are, why they are important, and how they are formulated. We discuss abstract concerns—the place of values and politics in social research—as well as practical concerns, like time and other resources required to conduct research.
- **Chapter 2** considers *research ethics*, including the history of professional standards to guide research and the role of institutional review boards in overseeing research practice. We outline key ethical principles, interrogate power imbalances between researchers and participants, and explore ethical considerations particular to different research strategies.

PART II chapters address two fundamental concerns that span social research approaches and methods: how to work with concepts (*measurement*) and how to select the cases we will study (*sampling*).

- In **Chapter 3**, we turn to *measurement*. The focus includes general approaches to measuring concepts, strategies of operationalization and conceptualization, and the role of previous research and theory in measurement. After examining measurement in qualitative and quantitative research, we consider the path from concepts to variables, levels of measurement, and the reliability and validity of measurement.

- **Chapter 4** addresses *sampling*, including principles of representativeness and types and principles of probability and nonprobability sampling. We explore sources of sampling error, decisions regarding sample size, and the relationship between sample size, on one hand, and reliability and validity on the other.

PART III turns readers' attention to modes and practices of inquiry—qualitative and quantitative inquiry and possible study designs.

- The focus of **Chapter 5** is *qualitative research*. The chapter describes the emergence of qualitative inquiry as a recognized methodology and establishes qualitative research as a distinct perspective. The chapter identifies steps in qualitative research and introduces how the methodology approaches the task of understanding the social world.
- We turn in **Chapter 6** to *quantitative research*. As in the previous chapter, we discuss the history of quantitative social science and introduce its distinct perspective and approach. The chapter outlines the aims and steps of quantitative work and its orientation towards knowledge.
- **Chapter 7** introduces the idea of *study design*, along with the basic frameworks within which social research is carried out (experimental, cross-sectional, longitudinal, and case study designs). The discussion also explores theoretical, ethical, and feasibility considerations when selecting a study design.

PART IV chapters explore qualitative and quantitative data collection methods.

- **Chapter 8** focuses on *structured interviewing and questionnaires*. The chapter posits survey research generally as a sort of interaction and suggests that the framework of interaction can guide question writing, overall design, and the implementation of survey research.
- **Chapter 9** examines *qualitative interviewing*, whether semi-structured or unstructured one-on-one interviews or focus groups. The chapter

focuses on how to prepare for, conduct, and record one-on-one interviews and focus groups. Our discussion considers the particular opportunities and challenges in online interviewing and focus groups, and explores the differences between qualitative interviewing and related methods.

- **Chapter 10** discusses *ethnography and participant observation*. We explore strategies for selecting and then gaining and maintaining access to a site as well as relationships with participants: how to learn from key informants, roles researchers can assume in the field, and ways to complete a study and leave the field. We also discuss how to write field notes.
- **Chapter 11** examines approaches to *content analysis*, a method used in the study of print, online, and other "texts." We discuss how researchers identify materials for content analysis, qualitative and quantitative approaches to analyzing content, and the unique promise and challenges of this method.
- The focus of **Chapter 12** is *existing data*, including large surveys, official statistics, official government documents, oral histories, and big data. We identify special considerations of working with data others collected, and we describe secondary analysis of existing data.

PART V presents strategies for analyzing and sharing findings.

- **Chapter 13** takes up *qualitative analysis*. Our discussion ranges from practical concerns like organizing data and the use of computer-assisted qualitative data analysis software to more abstract considerations like the role of theory and intersectional analysis in qualitative analysis.
- In **Chapter 14**, we discuss *quantitative analysis*, describing univariate, bivariate, and multivariate analyses. We offer an introduction to the logic of statistical analysis, noting the ways quantitative researchers can understand the world with increasing complexity as they analyze the relationships among variables.
- **Chapter 15** explores *writing and dissemination*. We emphasize that writing spans the entire research process and encourage students to think of themselves as writers. We explore practices like feedback and revision, describe the usual sections of a paper or presentation, and offer suggestions for effectively disseminating one's research.

Teaching and Learning Support

Oxford University Press offers instructors and students a comprehensive teaching and learning package of support materials for adopters of *Social Research Methods*.

Oxford Learning Link

The Oxford Learning Link (OLL) at www.oup.com/he/bryman-reck-fields1e is a convenient destination for all teaching and learning resources that accompany this book. Accessed online through individual user accounts, the OLL provides instructors with up-to-date ancillaries while guaranteeing the security of grade-significant resources. In addition, it allows Oxford University Press to keep users informed when new content becomes available. The OLL for *Social Research Methods* contains a variety of materials to aid in teaching:

- **Instructor's Resource Manual**: Our robust and innovative Instructor's Resource Manual includes chapter overviews, learning objectives, suggested class activities and assignments, and a sample syllabus.
- **Test Bank**: The test bank contains a variety of question types (multiple-choice, true/false, and short-answer) for use in student quizzes and exams, and can be uploaded into various learning management systems.
- **Lecture Slides**: PowerPoint slides for every chapter can be customized to help you enhance your classroom presentation, whether you teach in person or online.

Digital Learning Tools

Social Research Methods comes with an array of digital learning tools to ensure your students get the most out of your course:

- **Enhanced Ebook and Premium Resources:** The enhanced ebook offers students a richer, more dynamic experience than the print textbook by incorporating premium digital resources that are carefully curated and thoughtfully inserted at meaningful points to enhance the learning experience. Quizzes, videos, and other activities are all available directly through the ebook or via an access code that comes with every new copy of the print book.
- **Learning Management System Integration**: Oxford University Press offers the ability to integrate OUP content directly into currently supported versions of Canvas, D2L, or Blackboard. Contact your local rep or visit us at learninglink.oup.com/integration for more information.

Format Choices

Oxford University Press offers cost-saving alternatives to meet the needs of all students. This text is offered in a loose-leaf format at a 30 percent discount off the list price of the text, and as an enhanced ebook, through RedShelf, at a 50 percent discount. Instructors can also customize Oxford textbooks to create the course material you want for your class. For more information, please contact your Oxford University Press representative, call 800.280.0280, or visit us online at www.oup.com/he.

Acknowledgments

Our thanks go first to Alan Bryman and Edward Bell, the earlier authors of *Social Research Methods*. Professor Bryman wrote the original UK version, and Professor Bell adapted that volume for a Canadian audience. This volume, adapted for US readers, rests on the exceptional work of our predecessors.

Those who contributed to the US adaptation include Oxford University Press's Executive Editor, Sherith Pankratz. Her intelligence, enthusiasm, and vision are legendary, and her editorial decisions have helped to create a generation of critical and incisive sociological thinkers. We are beyond honored to count ourselves among the sociologists she has published. We worked with a number of talented editors at Oxford—that will happen when you take four years to complete a project—and we are grateful to each of them for their contributions to the US adaptation of *Social Research Methods*. Janice Evans, Janna Green, Eric Sinkins, and Maeve O'Brien all demonstrated extraordinary patience, editorial elegance, and care for our aims in this text. Suzanne Copenhagen's copyediting was invaluable. Several anonymous reviewers provided detailed feedback on this adaptation. Their generous suggestions and comments improved the quality of the final product immensely by helping us avoid omissions and errors; any remaining shortcomings of the book are ours alone.

For many years, Jen and Jessica were colleagues in the Sociology Department at San Francisco State University. We came to know each other as we taught undergraduate courses on research methods to talented students, many of whom balanced their commitment to school with significant commitments to family and community. This textbook—its commitment to careful analysis and to sociology's role in understanding and re-imagining the world—is rooted in the ethics and practices of SF State. In fact, the book wouldn't be possible without that grounding. We thank all of our colleagues in the SF State Sociology Department for years of support and inspiration, and we offer special thanks to Chris Bettinger and Alexis Martinez for early conversations about this textbook. Chris Bettinger also created this book's Appendix on computer-assisted data analysis; we are grateful that readers will benefit, as we have, from his insightful and student-centered approach to teaching research methods.

Jen and Jessica also benefitted from the support of talented and committed student research assistants. Undergraduate Sociology students at San Francisco State University worked as research assistants and interns: Jamie Goloyugo, Jerry Iremia, Austin Leong, Eddie Ochoa, Ian Roorda, Bernadette Stafford, Tiffany Villaro-Kwak, and Sara Yun. MA students in the SF State Sexuality Studies Department provided invaluable research assistance: Tina Coyne, Donna Cruz, Asako Hanafusa, Brandon Igarta, Ginger Mueller-Testerman, Siri Nybakk, and Nikki Van Wagner. Ali Greey, a PhD student in the University of Toronto Sociology Department, was instrumental to our completing the final manuscript and accompanying materials. We send our deepest thanks and respect all of these students.

Jen thanks her brother, Brian Reck, and SF State colleagues Chris Bettinger and Alexis Martinez, for their insights and expertise on chapter drafts focused on statistical methods. To my writing-together group (A. Ikaika Gleisberg, Valerie Francisco-Menchavez, Maxine Lee, and Rebekah Edwards), I appreciate you for helping me make space to write in the final stages of this manuscript. Alecia Burley, thank you for your love and generous care. And to Olivia Cicoletti-Reck, thank you for taking my attention away from this book with bike rides, Steven Universe, and cat habitat construction projects, and for asking all the good questions about the world.

Jessica offers thanks to her writing group (Chlöe Brushwood Rose, Jen Gilbert, and Sue Winton) and to her Summer 2020 National Center for

Faculty Development and Diversity Faculty Success Program peer group (Michele Cooke, Erin Furtak, Jimmie Manning, and Ankeny Weitz). She is grateful also to her new colleagues at the University of Toronto for providing new sources of methodological inspiration and creativity. Finally, Jen and Max, thank you for all of the questions you raise about social life—both the obdurate injustices that trouble us and the paths to new possibilities that inspire. I love you both.

Jessica and Jen are grateful to live, work, and write this book on the traditional and occupied territories of many First People and Nations. Jessica writes in Toronto, Canada, which is the traditional land of the Anishinabewaki ᐊᓂᔑᓈᐯᐎᐦᐠ, the Huron-Wendat, the Seneca, and most recently, the Mississaugas of the Credit River. Jen writes in the San Francisco Bay Area, on land that is occupied territories of the Ohlone people, including the Chochenyo and the Karkin (East Bay), the Ramaytush (San Francisco), the Yokuts (South Bay and Central Valley), and the Muwekma tribe throughout the region.

Jen Reck
Jessica Fields

List of Reviewers

The authors and Oxford University Press would like to thank the following reviewers who provided valuable feedback at various stages throughout the development of this adaptation:

Sofya Aptekar, University of Massachusetts Boston
James Bany, Hanover College
Diane C. Bates, The College of New Jersey
Brittany Battle, Rutgers University, New Brunswick
Rebecca Brooks, Ohio Northern University
Jan Buhrmann, Illinois College
Jeffrey Chin, Le Moyne college
Joyce Clapp, University of North Carolina Greensboro
Jason T. Eastman, Coastal Carolina University
Brenda I. Gill, Alabama State University
Brian K. Gran, Case Western Reserve University
Tina Granger, Nicholls State
Wendi Johnson, Oakland University
Sandra Loughrin, University of Nebraska, Kearney
Dr. Patricia Maloney, Texas Tech University
Dr. James N. Maples, Eastern Kentucky University
Michelle Meyer, Louisiana State University
Hien Park, Vanguard University
Kathrin Parks, Loras College
JoEllen Pederson, Longwood University
Seth Pipkin, University of California Irvine
David J. Rioux, University of Houston
Karen Robinson, CSU San Bernardino
Norman Rose, Kent State University
Gabriella Sanchez, University of Texas – El Paso
Juan Sandoval, Saint Louis University
Monica Solinas-Saunders, Indiana University
Jeffrey Stone, California State University Los Angeles
Hollie Tripp, UNC Charlotte
Carey Usher, Mary Baldwin University
Stephanie Whitehead, Indiana University East
Anita Zuberi, Duquesne University

Social Research Methods

PART I
Principles of Research

Research is a way to make sense of the world. As we design studies, collect and analyze data, and share our findings, we create knowledge, building and testing theories about how the world works (and doesn't work). The research questions we pose, values we hold, and political context in which we study, as well as the practical concerns we navigate—limitations of time, money, and other resources—shape the research experience. So, too, do ethical considerations, including the institutional standards to which researchers are held and the history of ethical abuses in social research. The ethical principles of social research are crucial to addressing power imbalances between researchers and participants and to designing research strategies that do no harm to those involved.

1

What Is Social Research?
A Particular Way of Knowing

▲ Photo by JORGE GUERRERO, SEBASTIEN BOZON, JOSE SANCHEZ, KIRILL KUDRYAVTSEV, SAJJAD HUSSAIN, CHANDAN KHANNA, JOSEPH EID, VLADIMIR ZIVOJINOVIC, MONEY SHARMA, MIGUEL MEDINA, ARUN SANKAR, PEDRO PARDO, ANDY BUCHANAN, ADEK BERRY, BULENT KILIC, CHARLY TRIBALLEAU, JEAN-CHRISTOPHE VERHAEGEN, JAIME REINA, DIMITAR DILKOFF, JUAN MABROMATA, NIKOLAY DOYCHINOV, PAUL FAITH/AFP via Getty Images

Research offers a systematic way of learning about the world. Whether we become researchers our-selves, read the research other people produce, or see our worlds change because of new insights from research, an understanding of research methods helps us ask and answer crucial questions about the world in which we live.

Reading this chapter will help you to

- describe the role of empirical research in the creation of knowledge;

- discuss the place of theory in social research, including theory-testing and theory-building;

- explain the value of and difference between deductive and inductive reasoning;

- explore qualitative and quantitative approaches to research;

- identify qualities of strong research questions;

- discuss the role of values, politics, and practical considerations in the research process; and

- appreciate the importance of social research to making sense of the world.

People conduct social research for many reasons. Often the goal is to test a particular understanding of the world; in other cases, the aim is to gather information in order to generate a new understanding. For example, a sociologist may spend time at the United States–Mexico border to understand how broad debates about immigration shape everyday interactions between migrants and government agents. Sometimes researchers engage in "fact-finding" or exploratory work—they may wonder, for example, how many people are stopped at the border and how many cross the border without incident. Other times, researchers are driven by what they consider a pressing social problem—for example, family separations or inadequate enforcement of refugee and asylum policies. Yet another stimulus for research is personal experience: having grown up near a border, a researcher may wonder if the experience of living near the border in Texas is similar to that of people who live along it in New Mexico or those living along contested borders in Europe. Still other researchers may want to address a practical concern: for example, how best to train volunteers working with families at the border.

The discipline of sociology emerged in the eighteenth and nineteenth centuries in part as a way of understanding the social crises associated with modern life, and that tradition continues to this day. Though the crises and conditions of contemporary life have changed over the last centuries, what has remained constant in sociology is a curiosity about the world and a commitment to conducting **empirical research** to better understand the world.

That curiosity often takes the shape of a **sociological imagination**. In 1959, American sociologist C. Wright Mills asserted that the sociological imagination involved an "awareness of the relationship between personal experience and the wider society" (Mills 1959, 3). According to Mills, this awareness would allow people to recognize that "personal troubles" reflect broader "public issues" (8). One example could be unemployment. Understood through the sociological imagination, a person's unemployment would be the product not simply of inadequate motivation or poor qualifications or preparation; the sociological imagination calls on us instead to look at broader employment opportunities and social norms around employability. Efforts to increase employment would focus not only on candidates' qualifications but also on opportunities and

empirical research   A way of studying and understanding the world through systematic and direct observation.

sociological imagination   The practice of linking people's experiences to social conditions—for example, connecting personal troubles to public issues or individual biography to social history.

obstacles in the broader job market. Mills argued that a sociological imagination prepared people to understand and respond to social injustice.

An understanding of research methods gives shape and direction to our curiosity, commitments, and responses—that is, to our sociological imaginations. A grasp of research methods has practical rewards: we gain a set of skills that are likely to make us more successful as students and even more employable when looking for a job. An understanding of research methods also invites us into a conversation among researchers seeking to illuminate the world: it helps us understand what's required to produce knowledge, and we are better positioned to make sense of the ideas that other researchers offer and to generate empirical insights of our own. Whether we become researchers ourselves, read the research other people produce, or see our worlds change because of new insights from research, an understanding of research methods helps us ask and answer crucial questions about the world in which we live.

Introduction: Reasons to Study Research Methods

In all likelihood you are reading this book as part of your first research methods course. Because you are going to spend considerable time and effort doing something new, it makes sense to consider some existential questions: Why am I here? Why should I study social research methods? What is the point?

If you're like most college and university students, you are here, at least in part, because you have to be. Methodology is fundamental to sociology; research methods is a required course in most sociology departments; and you have to read this book to complete course assignments and do well on quizzes and exams. But what if there were more to social research methods than those requirements and incentives? What if this book—and research methods—helped you explore topics that are important to you?

For example, does it matter to you that billions of human beings struggle to survive on less than $2 per day, while others are so wealthy that they would be hard pressed to ever spend all of their money? Do you have an interest in gender equality, environmental sustainability, crime, single motherhood, ethnic tensions, labor relations, racism, the living conditions of Indigenous people, changing notions of the family, or sexual mores? Do you wonder how you might test your hunch that it's an effective strategy for students who live off campus to use their commuting time to do homework? Or maybe you wish that you better understood the methods used to chart rates of Covid-19 infection and testing in your community during the first wave of the 2020 pandemic.

To come up with informed, thoughtful analyses of these and other social issues, and to be capable of evaluating the claims made by others on these topics, it is crucial to be familiar with the various **research methods** used to generate knowledge in sociology and other social sciences. It is also important to understand the terms used to discuss research methods. As you've probably noticed, in this book we will highlight important terms in bold and define them where they first appear. All of the key terms are compiled in a glossary at the end of this book.

Knowledge Creation

We often hear that "knowledge is power," and in many ways that is true. Dictators know this best: they try to limit access to knowledge in order to preserve their power over others. But the maxim leaves several questions unanswered. What is knowledge? How can it be acquired? How do we tell the difference between a sound idea and one that should be ignored? How can we gather information that will help us understand our subject matter, and what sorts of information should we seek? How should that information be analyzed and evaluated? Are there some things that we will never fully understand, regardless of how hard we try?

---

research methods Tools and practices used to gather and analyze information about topics of interest to the researcher and the broader community.

Knowledge is *created*, much like statues, paintings, bridges, music, and loaves of bread are. In most sociology courses, students spend their time absorbing, and sometimes challenging, claims made about the social world. For example, you may learn in one of your sociology courses that men are more likely than women to commit violent crimes. You may come to understand the conditions that push people into homelessness. Perhaps you'll encounter a theory explaining why some countries are rich and powerful while others are not. Learning about and reflecting on claims to knowledge is deeply valuable endeavor, but we will turn our focus just slightly in this course to questions of methods and methodology—in other words, *how* those claims about gender and violence, homelessness, and global power are created and gain acceptance as knowledge.

Methodology

To create knowledge, we need a **methodology**—a way of producing knowledge. If you accept the premise that knowledge is power, learning about research methods means learning how to gain and wield a form of power. How could methodology be power? For one thing, if you know how knowledge is created, you won't be fooled as easily as someone who doesn't know. Learning how clothes are made can help you tell the difference between a good pair of jeans and a shoddy pair; similarly, understanding where social knowledge comes from will help you distinguish between valid claims and fatuous ones.

Improving your critical thinking skills this way has many benefits. Having a solid grasp of social research methods will help you make sense of the material you will be expected to understand in your sociology courses. At various points in your university or college career, you will probably be called on to conduct small research projects. The knowledge you gain in this course can put you at an advantage for these assignments and could provide a starting point for more sophisticated research if you go on to graduate school or become a professional social scientist.

Methodology ultimately can make you a producer of ideas. Start thinking of yourself as someone who not only absorbs ideas and evaluates them but also projects them onto the world. You're a student, yes, but you can also be a researcher: someone who has the skills to ask questions about the world, examine social behavior, and contribute to our understanding of it.

Types of Understanding—and Research

Research generally falls into four categories:

- **exploratory**,
- **descriptive**,
- **explanatory**, and
- **evaluative**.

Each category yields a particular understanding of the world (Table 1.1).

A single study may generate multiple and overlapping understandings. For example, a researcher might include exploratory questions about changes in the undergraduate sociology curriculum and evaluative questions about course grades and completion. A study's purpose or purposes will vary according to the researcher's interests and what we already know about a topic. Eventually, we will likely know quite a bit about the ways Covid-19 and physical distancing changed campus life. For now, though, there's a need for exploratory and descriptive studies that document the new world we live in.

---

methodology The theory, justification, and assumptions behind the selection and use of research methods.

---

exploratory research Research conducted to generate questions and hypotheses about emerging or not-yet-defined phenomena.

---

descriptive research Research conducted to provide descriptive accounts of people, situations, and settings.

---

explanatory research Research conducted to explain and predict future conditions for people, situations, and settings.

---

evaluation research Research undertaken to assess the impact of real-life interventions, including policy changes and social programs.

TABLE 1.1 | Four Categories of Research

	Purpose	Possible Research Question
Exploratory	Generate questions and hypotheses about an emerging or not-yet-defined phenomenon	How have measures taken during the Covid-19 outbreak changed college education?
Descriptive	Respond to guiding questions to provide an account of people, situations, and settings	How did the way sociology courses are taught change during the periods of physical distancing?
Explanatory	Explain and predict future conditions for people, situations, and settings	How is remote instruction affecting students' loyalty to their campus?
Evaluative	Assess and improve effectiveness of interventions and policies	What is the impact of remote teaching and learning on course completion rates?

Beginning in August 2020, masked students in college classrooms became a familiar scene. Do a quick search online to see if you can find some exploratory studies of Covid-19's impact on campus life.

Methodologists draw another important distinction is between **applied research** and **basic research**. Applied research aims to find an answer or solution to a practical problem faced by a community or organization. The goal is to gain an insight that can be immediately applied to a particular context. For example, a long-term care facility might work with an applied researcher to study workers' use of personal protective equipment in order to understand and address obstacles to workers' using gloves, masks, gowns, and other equipment consistently. Basic research is not driven by such immediately practical concerns. A sociologist might study shifting social norms around wearing masks in public spaces in the United States. While the findings may have practical applications and may speak to the needs of a community or organization, basic research focuses on the production of insight, theory, and knowledge.

Epistemology and Ontology

Whether applied or basic, all research involves a claim to understanding and knowledge. One of the most profound questions to ask someone making any claim to knowledge about Covid-19, college education, or any other topic is, "How do you *know*

---

applied research   Research conducted to address practical problems.

---

basic research   Research conducted with the goal of advancing knowledge.

that?" That simple question is at the heart of any consideration of research methods and, like so many of its kind, has no simple answer. The branch of philosophy that addresses such issues—what the nature of truth is, what sorts of things can be known, what should be accepted as knowledge, how knowledge is to be sought—is called **epistemology**. A related division of philosophy, **ontology**, is concerned with the nature of reality and existence, what "reality" means, and what should be considered real. There is no shortage of positions among social scientists—and among sociologists especially—about what is real.

Ways of Knowing

Questions of how we know what we know (epistemology) and what constitutes reality (ontology) shape the ways we understand the social world. Tradition, intuition, authority, and common sense all inform these epistemological and ontological positions. For example, tradition may dictate in some communities that we celebrate a girl's coming of age when she turns fifteen, and we may intuit that this age of maturity—fifteen—has something to do with the start of puberty. In the eyes of the law, a girl may not reach maturity in the United States until the age of eighteen, when she is allowed to vote, or the legal drinking age of twenty-one. A person's common sense may invoke an entirely different set of criteria to determine maturity: the ability to care for oneself, sensible decision making, and growing economic independence.

All of these ways of knowing inform our everyday movement through the world as well as the research process. A researcher conducting a study of the relationship between maturity and safe driving will have to sort through the various definitions of maturity. Are they interested in legal or cultural standards of maturity? Do they want to consider physical maturation (brain development, for example), or are they more interested in emotional and social maturity?

In today's world we are inundated with traditional, legal, common-sense, and intuitive claims about people, society, and global affairs: how men and women are different (or the same), whether a binary understanding of gender is sufficient, why people marry and why they divorce, how schools both promise advancement through education and reproduce entrenched social inequalities, and so on. The

knowledge and skills you can acquire through learning about various social research methods will be useful when you have to assess those types of claims in order to make decisions in your life. And you may not be the only beneficiary of what you will learn: the people who are affected by your decisions could benefit as well.

Theory Building and Testing

Regardless of the motivation for doing research, the data gathered are usually viewed in relation to **theory** of some kind. Theories are attempts to "make sense of it all," to find order and meaning in what may sometimes feel like an infinite mass of information. Theories are not the same as opinions, which are based on personal beliefs. Unlike opinions, theories can be tested through empirical research; they represent the best available explanation of a phenomenon given the evidence at hand.

Deductive versus Inductive Reasoning

What is the relationship between building social theory and conducting empirical research? Generally, we can identify two approaches. **Deductive research** centers on theory testing, while **inductive research** is committed to theory building. Each represents a different method for acquiring knowledge.

The deductive method starts when researchers come up with a theory to try to explain a particular

---

epistemology The philosophical field concerned with how we know what we know.

---

ontology The philosophical field concerned with nature of being and reality.

---

theory An idea or system of ideas that provides logical explanations of social phenomena, behavior, and change.

---

deductive research An approach to inquiry that begins with a statement of theory from which hypotheses may be derived and tested.

---

inductive research An approach to inquiry that begins with the collection of data, which are used to develop theories, hypothesis, and concepts.

BOX 1.1 Deductive Study of Early Childhood Sexuality Education

In what ways could conversations between mothers and sons reflect social factors beyond gender—for example, race, mother's age, and social class?

Karin A. Martin and Katherine Luke (2010) wondered whether the lessons about sexuality that young children in the United States receive from their parents is as heavily gendered as what is available to adolescents. The existing research on sexuality education in the home focuses on parents' relationships with their adolescent children and does not take up the more sensitive question of lessons learned in early childhood, even though common sense suggests that parents begin teaching their children about sexuality and gender—both explicitly and implicitly—from a young age.

The existing research indicates (1) mothers do the bulk of sharing information about sex and sexuality with their children, and (2) mothers generally talk more with their adolescent daughters than with their adolescent sons about most issues, including their bodies and puberty, relationships, and sexual violence. However, (3) mothers talk more with their adolescent sons about masturbation and condom use. The difference in openness may lie in mothers being more comfortable talking with their daughters because of shared experiences of gender and sexuality.

phenomenon and then deduce a specific **hypothesis** or hypotheses from that theory. Researchers test hypotheses with empirical data (Figure 1.1), and if the data gathered do not support the hypotheses, the theory needs to be revised or rejected.

When the deductive approach is put into operation, the researcher does not always follow the exact sequence of steps shown in Figure 1.1. For example, a new hypothesis may come to mind during the data-gathering stage, or the relevance of the data for a second theory may become apparent after the data have been collected. Although the sequence outlined in the figure is common, it is only a general model. Furthermore, this notion of research as essentially "theory testing" does not provide a complete picture of what all social researchers do.

Inductive research does not adhere to the sequence outlined in Figure 1.1. Rather than test theory against collected data, theory may also follow or arise from the collection and analysis of data—in other words, theory can be the *outcome* of inductive

---

hypothesis A tentative assertion that draws on existing research, designed to be tested against empirical findings.

Martin and Luke wondered whether these patterns begin in early childhood—on one hand, a time of intense gender socialization and, on the other, a time in which children are often cast as sexually innocent. Maybe this separation between gender and sexuality means that learning can and does look a little different in early childhood?

Martin and Luke designed a deductive study in which they would test six hypotheses (Hs) about the conversations mothers have with their children aged 3 to 6:

> Mothers talk more with daughters about relationships (H1), reproductive bodies (H2), sexual abuse (H3), and morality (H4), and more with boys about the explicit topics of intercourse and pleasure (H5). . . . [I]f H1–H4 are supported, mothers will report being more comfortable and at ease with their daughters as opposed to their sons regarding sexual issues (H6).

The researchers' analysis of data collected through an online survey of US mothers of young children supported hypotheses H1, H2, and H4: mothers do talk more with young daughters about relationships, reproductive bodies, and morality. Their analyses did not support H3 or H5;

they found no difference in how mothers talk with their daughters and sons about sexual abuse or pleasure. Instead, mothers talk little about pleasure with both girls and boys, and they report discussing the risk of sexual victimization with all their children. The authors attribute this finding to, among other things, increased visibility of the sexual abuse of children, including boys. Martin and Luke's testing of H6 did not point to any difference in how comfortable mothers feel talking to their daughters and sons. However, they did find that mothers feel less comfortable allowing their sons to see them undressed (while, for example, changing clothes). This finding suggests that adults don't perceive young children as entirely asexual.

Tackling the sensitive issue of children and sexuality, Martin and Luke's deductive analysis challenges existing theories about patterns of gender socialization in the family and assumptions of children's sexual innocence. The authors also generate a new theoretical possibility to be tested in later research: that gender socialization is shaped by a cluster of influences, including gendered double standards, ideas about children's sexual innocence, and the social worlds that children and their families inhabit.

research. (See Figure 1.2 for the difference between deduction and induction and Box 1.2 for an example of the latter.) In inductive research, data are gathered not to test a theory but to come up with the information required to construct a theory. Data gathering comes first, and the effort to create concepts and theories out of it comes later. After some theoretical reflection, a researcher may decide to collect more data to establish the conditions under which the theory does or does not hold. This strategy of shifting between data and theory is often described as *iterative*, meaning the process is repeated several times to

develop and refine the theory. We will discuss these ideas further when we explore qualitative analysis in Chapter 13.

In practice, few, if any, studies are purely deductive or inductive. Just as deduction always entails an element of induction (theories do not emerge from a pristine mind unaware of previous findings), so does the inductive process always entail some degree of deduction (no researcher will be totally unaware of theories that might be applicable to the phenomenon being observed). Some combination of both can be found in the same research.

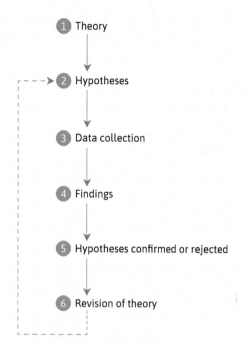

FIGURE 1.1 **The process of deduction**

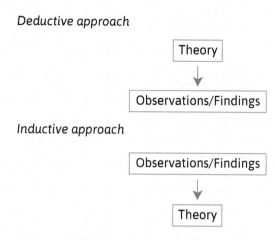

FIGURE 1.2 **Deductive and inductive approaches to the relationship between theory and research**

Middle-Range Theories and Grand Theories

Many social theories fall into what sociologists describe as the "middle range" (Merton 1967). Middle-range theories are limited in scope and can be tested directly by gathering empirical evidence. For instance, Émile Durkheim's theory of suicide is a theory of the middle range. It maintains that the people at greatest risk of dying by suicide are those who feel the most loosely connected to society. One way to test Durkheim's theory of suicide would be to compare suicide rates for married people with those for single, divorced, or widowed people. Robert Merton's (1938) anomie theory, which suggests that crime is more common when a society instils a desire for wealth in everyone but provides insufficient means for all to achieve it, is another example of a middle range theory. Such theories represent attempts to understand and explain a well-defined aspect of social life.

Grand theories, by contrast, are general and abstract. They include theories you may have encountered in other sociology courses, including structural functionalism, symbolic interactionism, critical theory, poststructuralism, and feminism.

Grand theories do not offer many direct indications of how to collect evidence to test them; instead they serve as frameworks for study design, data collection, and analysis. These frameworks can shape not just a single study but an entire field of study. For example, Patricia Hill Collins ([1990] 2002), Dorothy Smith (1987), and others developed standpoint theory from a general feminist perspective. This theory maintains that the way we view and make our way through the world is largely determined by our placement in various hierarchies of status and power. One offshoot of standpoint theory has been an increased willingness to consider how researchers' social positions shape the insights they achieve in empirical research. As Elizabeth Hordge-Freeman writes, Collins and other standpoint theorists have claimed that "shared experiences of oppression among Black women offered those who occupied this marginalized identity access to certain understandings about the nuances of oppression" (2018, 3). Hordge-Freeman thus draws on her experiences as a Black woman to examine the everyday entanglement of love, power, and race in Black Brazilian families.

Qualitative and Quantitative Inquiry

Scholars writing about research methods usually distinguish between qualitative and quantitative research. We will discuss these modes of inquiry at length in Chapters 5 and 6, respectively. In this

BOX 1.2 An Inductive Study of Regional Patriarchy

As part of a larger study of the sexual lives and life histories of adult Mexican immigrants living in Los Angeles, Gloria González-López (2004) asked 20 men about their feelings on virginity, premarital sex, and their daughters' futures. By relying on inductive analysis, González-López was able to meet one of her goals: namely to explore stereotypes about Mexican men as "rigid and authoritative macho men controlling their families" (2004, 1118).

González-López found that the fathers

In what ways could conversations between fathers and daughters reflect social factors beyond gender—for example, race, father's age, and social class?

she interviewed did not prioritize virginity as much as they valued "sexual moderation" that would allow their daughters to "take care of themselves" and prepare to enter college and secure economic stability. Those fathers who were born and raised in Mexico's urban centers also affirmed their daughters' sexual autonomy, while those born and raised in rural contexts were less permissive. All fathers' fears for their children reflected the dangers they recognized in their new homes. The fathers felt that Los Angeles was unsafe for young women, and in their interviews, they described fearing for their

daughters in ways that they had not while living in Mexico.

The interviews suggest that masculinity and fatherhood are variable experiences, and González-López coins the term "regional patriarchies" to describe "the distinctive types of patriarchies that women and men construct in diverse geographical regions of Mexican society" (2004, 1119). Her inductive analysis suggests a new theoretical understanding of patriarchy as something that shifts across urban and rural contexts and across national borders, with these regional differences producing different experiences of masculinity and fatherhood.

chapter, we will highlight the most basic distinction: **qualitative research** relies mainly on words and other non-numerical symbols in the collection and analysis of data, while **quantitative research** uses numbers and statistics. Qualitative research is often inductive, while quantitative research is frequently deductive.

qualitative research Inquiry that uses mainly words, images, and other non-numerical symbols as data and involves little or no quantification.

quantitative research Inquiry using numerical data and statistical analysis.

Another main difference between the two types is that qualitative researchers engage in interpretive work, while quantitative researchers rely on mathematical measurement and numerical analysis techniques. However, many researchers contend that the differences are deeper than merely the amount of quantification. For example, the methods differ in their epistemological foundations. Much of the distinction between qualitative and quantitative research lies in their relationship to **positivism**, the theory that authentic knowledge rests in empirical observations that are subject to the rational and scientific analysis.

Quantitative research

- incorporates the practices and norms of positivism;
- usually entails a deductive approach to the relationship between theory and research, in which theory testing is a prime objective; and
- generally embodies a view of society as an external, objective reality subject to social laws much like natural laws governing the physical world.

Qualitative research, on the other hand,

- replaces positivist models of social research with methodologies that seek to determine how people interpret their social world;
- takes a predominantly inductive approach to the relationship between theory and research, in which generating theories and interpretations is a goal; and
- approaches social reality as a constantly shifting and emergent property of people's creations.

Debates over the merits and usefulness of qualitative versus quantitative approaches is a longstanding one in sociology, much like the debate over whether positivism is the preferred approach to knowledge. Positivists generally adhere to principles and practices of the scientific method, as depicted in Figure 1.3.

---

positivism   An epistemological position that advocates using empirical methods and logic to study of social reality.

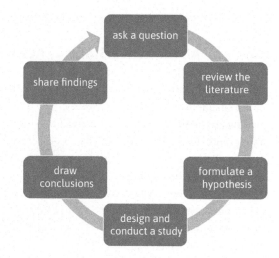

FIGURE 1.3   **The scientific method**

The scientific method supports the positivist pursuit of deductive understanding emanating from the testing of hypothesis and rooted in systematic and logical practices. Qualitative researchers, who pursue inductive understandings of subjective meanings grounded in data, are less wedded to the scientific method. Like quantitative researchers, they raise questions, engage with previous literature, and design, conduct, and share findings from their studies. However, qualitative research does not involve the assertion and testing of hypotheses, and, as we will discuss in Chapter 5, qualitative inquiry does not always unfold in the order or logic that the scientific method requires.

While we will spend time discussing and contrasting the general orientations of qualitative and quantitative research in this textbook, we do not want hammer a wedge between them. There are notable exceptions to the general rule that qualitative research is inductive and quantitative is deductive. And while quantitative researchers may be more accountable to the principles of the scientific method, both qualitative and quantitative research involve systematic inquiry—methodical, logical, and consistent practices of gathering and making sense of data. Discussing the nature of social research is just as complex as conducting research. We can outline the typical philosophical assumptions and research practices of the two general orientations, but the reality

Mixed Methods in Action

As we explore qualitative and quantitative research methods throughout this textbook, we will also highlight *mixed methods approaches*. This type of research draws on multiple methods, often both qualitative and quantitative. Researchers might use survey data to measure the extent of a social pattern that interests them and then use interview data to explore the meaning and experience behind that pattern. For example, in his study of color-blindness in the contemporary United States, *Racism without Racists*, Eduardo Bonilla-Silva used surveys to get a sense of broad racial attitudes and interviews to see how racial ideology is "produced and reproduced in communicative interaction" (2006, 11). That is, in qualitative interviews, Bonilla-Silva explored how the racist ideas and attitudes documented in survey research are expressed in discussions with liberal White people who assert they are not racist. In interviews, White study participants invoked "color-blindness" as an explanation for their opposition to affirmative action and other remedial programs that would address the racism that the participants claim to oppose. The interviews provide insight into how the rhetoric of color-blindness allows White people to inhabit this contradiction. We will discuss this example at greater length in Chapter 5.

Another researcher might bring together interviews and participant observation, as Laurie Olsen did in *Made in America: Immigrant Students in Our Public Schools* (1997). Olsen spent time observing the experiences of immigrant students on a high school campus and then interviewed students and teachers to learn more about the experiences of being new to a US community and then becoming part of—or not a part of—that community. Analysis of the observation and interview data reveals to Olsen that becoming "American" comes to mean becoming White, Christian, and English-speaking. Like Bonilla-Silva, Olsen finds that the ideology of color-blindness allows educators to celebrate the diversity of their student bodies without interrupting the tracking and other institutional sorting that marginalize and stifle immigrant students.

We highlight mixed-methods research for a couple reasons. First, mixed methods are increasingly practiced in social research. Second, this approach resists the divide researchers often assert between qualitative and quantitative methods. For researchers exploring mixed methods, the question is, what methods will best help me reach the understanding I seek? The answer often involves reaching across a qualitative/quantitative divide.

---

is messier than those neat categories would suggest. As we discuss in the Mixed Methods in Action feature, the categories are inevitably and productively blurred in **mixed-methods research**. Issues become more complicated the deeper we delve into them, as we will see in Chapters 5 and 6.

Formulating Questions

The formulation of your **research question** will profoundly affect what you can accomplish in a study and how you will accomplish it. The question you ask will eventually guide

- the literature search;
- the design of the study;
- the decisions about what data to collect and from whom;

---

mixed-methods research An approach to inquiry that draws on multiple tools and procedures—often both qualitative and quantitative—to collect and analyze data.

---

research question An answerable question that organizes data collection and analysis, determines study design, and otherwise provides a foundation for research.

- the analysis of the data; and
- the presentation of findings.

A research question states the purpose of the study in the form of a question. This approach is useful because a question is often more evocative and stimulating than a simple declarative statement. A question arouses curiosity and challenges the researcher to find ways to answer it. A well-stated research question in a final paper or presentation also helps readers understand what answers the study will provide.

In what ways might responses to TV portrayals vary across genders and sexualities?

The process of formulating and assessing research questions can feel like something of an art. Nevertheless, some general principles and practices can guide you toward a strong sociological question. Social research often starts with the choice of a general area of interest. At this stage, a general research question might be

> How do people feel about lesbian, gay, bisexual, transgender, queer, intersex, asexual, Two-Spirit, plus (LGBTQIA2S+) families?

This broad curiosity has to be narrowed down, for example, to

> How does the population of American adults react to the portrayal of LGBTQIA2S+ parents on television dramas?

or

> Are LGBTQIA2S+ families welcome in local school communities?

But even those questions are too broad. The next level of specification might yield something like

> Do young, straight men react differently than young, straight women to the portrayal of LGBTQIA2S+ romance on television program *X*? If so, do those differences reflect different ideas about sexual identity among young women compared with young men?

or

> How do self-described progressive parents in heterosexual relationships respond to school-based sex education that addresses the experiences of LGBTQIA2S+ families?

The first question could be linked to larger theories of sex roles, the development of sexual identity, and socialization. The second question could be linked to questions of social inclusion and exclusion and the tolerance of difference in society.

No single study can answer all the research questions that occur to the researcher. A single study will satisfy only a piece of the researcher's curiosity. Nevertheless, researchers must narrow their broad interest into a clear, researchable question in order to work within practical considerations, including the time and funding available.

The research question may change as the study progresses. The focus may change with the discovery of a new data source or the analysis of the initial findings. For instance, if the researchers in our example find that having an LGBTQIA2S+ relative in the immediate family makes a large difference in people's attitudes, their research question, methodology, and theoretical orientation may change. The research question may also shift because of limitations in time and

---

BOX 1.3 Considerations for Developing Research Questions

A good research question will

- be clear, specific, and understandable to others;
- be researchable, allowing for the development of a study design and the collection of data;
- relate in some way to established theory and research that suggest how to approach your question and how your research can contribute to knowledge and understanding; and

- have the potential to make a contribution to the existing knowledge about the topic.

If you are unsure about how to formulate research questions (or about other aspects of research), look at journal articles or research monographs to see how other researchers state them. Which examples do you find most compelling? What strategies (for wording and phrasing, for example) seem most effective when stating a research question?

---

other resources available to the researcher. Box 1.3 offers some tips on developing research questions.

Research questions set realistic boundaries for research. A poorly formulated question can result in unfocused and substandard research. No matter how well designed a questionnaire is or how skilled the interviewers are, clear, specific research questions that are grounded in existing theory and research help prevent studies going off in unnecessary directions or tangents.

Perceptions, Values, and Practicalities

The norm of **objectivity** is familiar to most lay readers of science, who generally believe that values and preconceptions skew study results. Yet neither researchers nor research practices exist in a vacuum, sealed off from values and philosophical and political debates. Beliefs, preconceptions, and convictions follow us into the classroom and into our research, determining our commitments and interests as students, and shaping our experience of learning about all aspects of social life—including research methods.

The Objective Ideal

The ideal of an objective researcher dominates lay and academic discussions of research, and many sociologists agree that research that reflects its practitioners' personal views is biased and invalid. Émile Durkheim (1858–1917), a founding figure in

sociology, aspired to study social facts, which he defined as objects whose study requires that all "preconceptions must be eradicated" ([1897] 1952, 31). Many sociologists agree with Durkheim and strive to ensure that their research adheres to this standard. Others ask whether this is possible. Max Weber, another of sociology's founding figures, argued that values are inherent to sociology and the social sciences more broadly. Sociologists in this tradition advocate an interpretive model of social research that Weber called *verstehen*, a German term we can translate as "meaningful understanding." Interpretive sociology attends to the meanings people attach to social life and understands social reality to be constructed through those meanings.

Weber strove toward objectivity, even as he waded into the murkier waters of interpretation and meaning. He urged researchers to suspend their assessments of the meanings people attached to behaviors and contexts: it should not matter whether the researcher shares or agrees with those positions—their task is just to study the positions. Some social researchers contest this call for the suspension of values. They argue that sociologists and others do not work in a moral or evaluative void: values and other

---

objectivity The ontological position that approaches social phenomena as if they exist independent of social actors or their perceptions and that calls on researchers to draw conclusions based on fact and not influenced by values, bias, or preconceptions.

Methods in Action | The Art of Reflexivity

Ruth Behar made a significant contribution to social researchers' thinking about reflexivity with her book *The Vulnerable Observer* (1996). Behar argues for social research in which the researcher refuses to always "stay behind the lens of the camera, switch on the tape recorder, keep pen in hand" (1996, 2). She asserts that, by allowing themselves to be vulnerable, researchers also allow readers to better understand who will guide them through the social world they're exploring. She encourages researchers to consider seriously who they are in relationship to the people they study and how that relationship shapes the insights they are able to achieve. Behar also cautions her readers,

> Writing vulnerably takes as much skill, nuance, and willingness to follow through on all the ramifications of a complicated idea as does writing invulnerably and distantly. I would say it takes yet greater skill.... To assert that one is a "white middle-class women" or a "black gay man" or a "working class Latina" ... is only interesting if one is able to draw deeper connections between one's personal experience and the subject under study. That doesn't require a full-length autobiography, but it does require a keen understanding of what aspects of the self are the most important filters through which one perceives the world and, more particularly, the topic being studied. (Behar 1996, 13)

For Behar, then, the task in reflexivity is to recognize not simply who we are but also how our identities and biographies shape the research we conduct and the conclusions we achieve.

---

preconceptions are always present and can intrude at any or all points in the process.

Sometimes values are an obstacle to empirical research and impede the research process. Researchers may develop affection or sympathy for the people they are studying, making it difficult to disentangle their work as empirical researchers from their concern for the participants' well-being. Researchers may also be frustrated or angered by the people they study, making it difficult to produce an analytical but sympathetic account of what they witness during data collection.

The objective ideal leaves social researchers with something of a conundrum: should we strive to attain this lofty standard, knowing it can never be reached, or should we abandon the standard altogether, conceding that our research can never be free of bias? Feminist researchers have introduced a third option, known as the reflexive ideal.

The Reflexive Ideal

One tenet of feminist research is that we best respond to these challenges to objectivity by, first, recognizing that research cannot be value-free and, second, trying to ensure that values are acknowledged and made explicit. This practice of **reflexivity**, or self-reflection, can help researchers ensure that their values do not undermine their ability to achieve meaningful interpretations of their findings. Reflexive researchers forewarn readers of their biases and assumptions and explain how these may have influenced their conclusions. Since the mid-1970s many have published "insider" accounts of what doing research is really like. Our next Methods in Action feature provides an example.

Researchers who adopt a reflexive approach may go so far as to embrace consciously value-laden research. For example,

- Some people conducting **feminist research** consider it inappropriate (even impossible) to do research on women in an objective, value-neutral

---

reflexivity   The practice of and commitment to considering how one's beliefs, experiences, and presence shapes insights gained through empirical research.

feminist research   A mode of inquiry informed by principles of feminist social movement and committed to addressing power imbalances in the research process and gendered social inequalities.

way because it would be incompatible with their values. Rather than shed their values, they conduct research that exposes the conditions of women's disadvantage in a patriarchal society. Some feminist writers claim that only research on women intended for women is consistent with women's wider political needs.

- Similarly, researchers informed by **critical race theory** (CRT) will bring to any study a commitment to challenging institutional racism and promoting social change. CRT research topics might include hate crimes, racist speech, affirmative action and university admissions, mass incarceration, and employment discrimination—all topics that reflect and affirm CRT commitments.

- Researchers use **intersectional theory** to examine the ways multiple identities and social differences combine—that is, *intersect*—to magnify the oppression of members of marginalized communities. Intersectional theory is grounded in efforts to explain and address Black women's intersecting experiences of racism and sexism, and intersectional researchers continue to investigate interlocking types of violence in an effort to transform them.

Each of these theoretical positions reflects values that shape researchers' questions, mode of inquiry, and more.

Disinterest and Methodological Decisions

Though not all researchers reject the ideal of value-free research, most writers today recognize the limits of objectivity. Categorical pronouncements like Durkheim's have fallen into disfavor. At the same time, most researchers resist the idea of giving free rein to one's political beliefs and value positions. Researchers continue to struggle with the all-too-human propensity to reject research findings summarily when the researcher's ideological or moral positions are not compatible with their own.

Political Positions and Conditions

If values and moral positions can influence sociological research, so too can politics. Social researchers sometimes take sides from the very beginning of a study.

Feminist researchers may, for example, focus on the disadvantages that women face and the possibilities for improving their position. Anti-racist researchers may design a study that interrogates disciplinary policies and practices in US schools, concerned that Black students are subject to unfair suspensions and expulsions. Political positions may vary: some researchers may favor government intervention in economic affairs, while others may defend the free market.

Politics lie not only in researchers' stances but also in the institutions and relationships they navigate. Students may find themselves choosing a study design or topic they think will appeal to their teachers and supervisors. The research grants and fellowships that many students rely on to cover the costs of their education and research often prioritize topics with political currency; these might include, for example, how the Covid-19 pandemic affected employment patterns, the organization of public space, and participation in social protest. Researchers—student and faculty—may decide to tailor their research to funders' priorities in order to secure available resources. Some social research is commissioned by private firms, foundations, or government agencies with vested interests in the outcomes of the research. As public funding for research constricts, social researchers increasingly turn to external funding sources. These organizations naturally have their own priorities and may be more likely to invest in studies that will be useful to them or supportive of their operations and worldviews.

Each of these funding and support contexts represents political terrain that a researcher must navigate. While contending with these multiple and sometimes contentious influences, researchers' responsibility is to strive for a stance of disinterest and to allow themselves to be surprised by what they learn in a study. Researchers cannot permit their preconceptions to preclude certain findings

---

critical race theory A theoretical perspective, emerging from legal studies, that focuses on race and power in social life.

---

intersectional theory A theoretical perspective that considers multiple and overlapping systems of discrimination in marginalized and oppressed communities.

BOX 1.4 Feminist Methods and Values

Feminist methodology and research are not immune to hierarchical relationships in data collection and analysis. Feminist interviewers routinely design interviews that allow participants to interject their ideas, correct researchers' misconceptions, and claim some role in the production of knowledge. Focus groups have been an appealing method because they allow participants to meet one another, build understanding together, and engage in a collective process of knowledge production.

The research setting often involves a power imbalance between the researcher and the research subject. What are some ways to address this imbalance in interviews?

Feminist survey researchers often commit themselves to documenting profound gendered inequalities in order to advance the goals of the feminist movement. What marks feminist research may not be the specific method chosen but the commitment to ensuring that the chosen method resonates with the researcher's feminist values.

In the early 1980s, several feminist social researchers proposed that quantitative research is incompatible with feminist ideals. For writers such as Annie Oakley (2013), quantitative research is bound up with patriarchal power, as seen in the researcher's control of the respondent and the research context. Oakley and some other feminists consider qualitative and quantitative research a one-way affair in which researchers extract information from participants and give little in return. For many feminists, conventional research borders on exploitation and is incompatible with the value that feminism attributes to non-hierarchical relationships.

or conclusions—even those that challenge deeply held beliefs. Disinterest requires us to suspend our emotional, political, and intellectual investments in a study's outcome long enough, well enough, and systematically enough to allow unexpected and even unwelcome results to emerge. Only with a commitment to disinterest can we ensure reliable and independent thinking in social research.

Gaining access to respondents can also be political. Access to organizations and institutions is usually mediated by formal and informal gatekeepers concerned not only about the researcher's motives but also about what the organization stands to gain from the investigation, what it will lose in terms of staff time and other costs, and the potential risks to its image. Often, gatekeepers

Imagine you want to study the effect of live music performance on a concert crowd. What are some of the obstacles you would face as a researcher? How might you overcome these obstacles?

seek to influence how the investigation will take place: what kinds of questions can be asked; who can and cannot be a focus of study; how much time will be spent with each research participant; how the findings will be interpreted; and what form the reports will take, even to the point of asking to approve drafts.

Public institutions such as police departments, schools, and hospitals, as well as many commercial firms, are concerned with how they are going to be represented in publications. Consequently, gaining access is almost always a matter of negotiation. The product of such negotiations is often referred to as "the research bargain," and in many cases there is more than one deal to strike. Once granted, access does not ensure a smooth passage in subsequent dealings with the people to be studied. Researchers

may find subgroups attempting to enlist them in advancing a particular goal. Research participants who doubt the utility of social research may even try to obstruct the process.

Practical Considerations

Practical issues—time, money, and logistics—also shape social research. A study of live music performance may involve paying steep ticket fees: does the researcher have the funds to cover those costs? Concerts are often in the evening, presenting a challenge for students who are parenting or who have to work evenings. Students with disabilities may have to consider whether the venue is accessible; other students may wonder whether their clothing, hair, and gender presentation will allow them to move comfortably through the concert venue.

Other practicalities are more about the topic and people being investigated. Researchers who want to study people involved in illicit activities—for example, price fixing, shoplifting, or drug dealing—may find it difficult to develop a rapport with the group if they don't share those experiences. Regardless of the topic, researchers will have to gain access to a study setting, and participants will have to consent to participate in the planned study. And regardless of the method researchers choose, they should have the skills required to conduct the study, as well as the support of teachers and colleagues who can answer questions and help them navigate unexpected challenges.

Practical considerations are those mundane realities that can make the difference between a successful and unsuccessful project. All researchers should ask themselves if they have the time, money, support, and skills necessary to complete the study. Ultimately, research is a balance of the ideal and the feasible—a commitment to pursuing our curiosity about the social world systematically and, as we discuss in the next chapter, ethically.

Key Points

Introduction: Why Study Research Methods?

- A knowledge of research methods gives practical shape to our sociological imaginations and better positions us to secure employment, consume and produce research, and engage in public debate about important social issues.

Knowledge Creation

- Methodological decisions and practices guide the way we produce knowledge of the world.
- Research serves four general purposes: exploration, description, explanation, and evaluation.
- Research may be applied (aiming to address or solve a practical problem) or basic (conducted in pursuit of insight, theory, or knowledge).
- Epistemological considerations, regarding how we know what we know, and ontological considerations, regarding the nature of reality, play significant roles in the choice of a research strategy.

Theory Building and Testing

- In empirical research, theory can either precede data collection and analysis (deduction) or emerge from data collection and analysis (induction).

- Empirical research generally engages with theory of the middle range: testable theories with limited scope. Grand theories generally provide larger frameworks that guide empirical research.
- Social investigation occurs through quantitative and qualitative research, separate approaches that come with distinct epistemological and ontological assumptions.
- Research questions shape the whole of a study, from conceptualization to implementation to dissemination.

Perceptions, Values, and Practicalities

- Sociologists hold a range of positions on the place of values in social research, with some advocating objectivity and others promoting reflexivity.
- The political dimensions of research shape the positions researchers take on social issues as well as funding and other institutional conditions researchers navigate.
- Researchers must strike a balance between the interests motivating their study and practical considerations like time, money, and logistics.

Questions for Review

1. What is empirical research?
2. What is the difference between research methodology and research methods?
3. What distinguishes the four types of research?
4. What are the different aims of applied and basic research?
5. What is the relationship between theory and deductive research? Between theory and inductive research?

6. How do grand and middle theories figure in the research process?
7. How do qualitative and quantitative modes of inquiry relate to the scientific method?
8. Though much of this chapter focuses on differences between modes of inquiry and epistemological positions, what value is there in blurring methodological boundaries through, for example, mixed-methods approaches?
9. How do research questions shape the overall research process?
10. What are some characteristics of a good research question?
11. Discuss and contrast objective and reflexive approaches to the role of values in social research.
12. In what ways do political positions and conditions shape social research?
13. What are some practical concerns to consider when designing and conducting research?

Portfolio Exercise

At the end of each chapter, we have included a portfolio exercise that will encourage you to apply the ideas from that chapter to your own research interests. These exercises can be completed in a methods course that meets in person, online, or some combination of the two. Together, the fifteen exercises will constitute a semester-long engagement with research methods, culminating in a research proposal.

This chapter's exercises encourage you to generate a first draft of your research question and to reflect on various influences shaping your research interests.

We encourage you to begin this exercise with paper and pen or pencil. Set a timer for 2–3 minutes and brainstorm a list of topics that interest you (for example, public perceptions of dog breed aggression, gendered experiences of online gaming, coffee consumption and external stressors, or activism on campus). Don't think too much about getting the list perfect; just keep brainstorming topics and allow yourself to be surprised by what you write. When the timer goes off, trade your pen for a highlighter or colored pencil and read through the list, highlighting or circling 2–3 topics that you'd like to examine using the tools of social research.

Begin drafting questions for the selected topics. (You may want to complete this step on a computer, if you find that more comfortable.) First, referring as necessary to our discussion of these research purposes earlier in Chapter 1, try to draft an exploratory, descriptive, explanatory, and evaluative question for each topic. Notice which questions appeal most to you and thus which purpose your question positions you to pursue. Notice whether your question seems to call for deductive or inductive reasoning and qualitative and/or quantitative inquiry. These are hunches at this point; don't worry too much about getting it right.

Review the drafted questions and choose one to develop for now. Remember that you're likely to revise your research question as the semester progresses, so you only need to think of your question as a rough draft; the point here is to get your portfolio started and to practice writing researchable questions. To that end, make sure your question

- addresses something you want to know,
- is clear and specific,
- reflects a sociological imagination,
- can be answered through empirical research, and
- speaks to the research and broader communities that matter to you.

Write a final (for now) version of your question and share it with others for feedback. You will revisit—and revise—this question again in later Portfolio Exercises.

Interactive Activities

1. Working in small groups in class or online, select a social phenomenon, human behavior, or experience on a particular topic. Write a research question—for example, "What causes eating disorders?" or "What is it like to be a survivor of domestic violence?" or "What influences students'

decisions to enroll in summer courses?" Next assess the quality of your question:

a. Is it clear, specific, and understandable?

b. Is it researchable?

c. What is its relationship to established theory and research?

d. How would an answer to the question contribute to understandings about that topic?

Next, consider the role values and politics may play in your group's question:

e. Does your question imply an objective researcher? A reflexive researcher? What would be required for you to achieve objectivity or reflexivity in answering your research question?

f. What personal values make this question interesting to you?

g. How does your question resonate with or challenge the political conditions in which you study and live?

h. Finally, think through some practical considerations: what time, money, and other resources would you need to answer this research question well?

2. Divide into four breakout groups that meet (1) synchronously in person or online or (2) asynchronously. Groups 1 and 3 build a case for position "a" below, while Groups 2 and 4 argue for position "b":

a. The social researcher's most important duty is to *explain* the social world, not to change it. The search for practical applications such as positive social change may create political bias, such as when researchers ignore or reject findings that do not align with their political views.

b. The social researcher's most important duty is to *make the world a better place* by ridding society of things such as racism, economic inequality, and sexism. Research that does not have positive social change as its primary goal is not worth doing.

Reconvene, so each group can make its case. The reconvening may happen synchronously online or in person, or your instructor may create an online space where students contribute asynchronously. After each group presents its argument, the class as a whole identifies the most compelling arguments from each group and votes on which group made the strongest case overall.

Online Resources

A good way to become familiar with the research process is to read articles published in academic journals, such as the following general sociology journals. You may need to use your school's library server or institutional account to access some of them.

American Journal of Sociology
www.journals.uchicago.edu/toc/ajs/current

American Sociological Review
https://journals.sagepub.com/home/asr

British Journal of Sociology
www2.lse.ac.uk/BJS/Home.aspx

International Journal of Sociology
www.tandfonline.com/loi/mijs20#.VVtagIVhBc

Qualitative Sociology
www.springer.com/social+sciences/journal/11133

Social Forces
http://sf.oxfordjournals.org

For more resources please visit
www.oup.com/he/bryman-reck-fields1e

2

What Principles and Standards Guide Research?
Research Ethics

▲ AP Photo/Hassan Ammar

Before research with people as participants can begin, researchers must demonstrate that their work will be ethical. This is no small task, given that ethical considerations pertain to *all* research methods and come into play at *every stage*, from the recruitment of participants to the publishing of results. This chapter examines some general ethical principles and their applications to real research situations.

Reading this chapter will help you to

- describe the history and development of shared professional guidelines for ethical research;

- grasp the role of institutional review boards (IRBs) in providing oversight on research;

- outline key ethical principles guiding research, including informed consent and voluntary participation, confidentiality and anonymity, and ensuring participants' well-being and safety;

- understand how power imbalances between researchers and participants affect ethical choices; and

- recognize unique ethical considerations in different forms of research.

Imagine you've been assigned to do preliminary research on a topic that could be the focus of your semester-long research study. You've recently joined a study group with some classmates and have become fascinated by the group dynamic: some people collaborate, others dominate, and there seems to be a romantic triangle developing. You decide to study social dynamics in academic environments, and to observe the interactions in your study group as a way to refine your research question. Because you feel that telling the others could alter their behavior, you take notes secretly for a few weeks.

During this time, two members go out on a bad date, leading one to quit the group. The other gossips about the person at the next meeting and reveals personal details about the date. Some members seem uncomfortable with the information and try to focus on studying for the

upcoming quiz, but you all eventually leave feeling unprepared. One of the members tells you, "My friend took this class last semester. I might just study from his test."

How are you supposed to write your paper when your notes include details on romantic conflicts, gossip, group tension, and possible cheating—especially when you never told your group mates you were studying them? Should you have asked their permission earlier? Should you ask it now? Should you throw out all your notes and do something else rather than risk exposing their private business? Or is it possible to hide their identities so the professor won't know whom you're talking about? The decisions you made, the questions that came up, and the dilemmas you encountered in this scenario relate to a fundamental issue all researchers grapple with: research ethics.

Introduction: The Importance of Research Ethics

As we saw in Chapter 1, researchers normally choose a general research orientation and a **research design** early in the process. Another issue they should address in a study's initial stages, and

keep in mind throughout the project, is **research ethics**—the moral and professional standards that guide research decisions and define what choices are acceptable or unacceptable. Even if a researcher is seeking knowledge that will benefit everyone, the welfare of the individuals and groups under

research design A framework for collecting and analyzing data, which outlines a researcher's approach, procedures, and goals.

research ethics The moral and professional standards that guide decisions and actions taken during the research process and define what choices are considered acceptable or unacceptable.

Defendants in the Nuremberg trials stand accused of Nazi war crimes during World War II. What social conditions continue to make it necessary to develop guidelines to protect vulnerable populations? What responsibility should governments and professional organizations hold for overseeing the ethical choices researchers make?

study is of paramount importance. Understanding research ethics is crucial: how researchers handle this area affects the integrity of the project as well as the reputation of the social sciences as a whole. Professional organizations define the core ethical principles, and university review boards oversee researchers' projects; individual researchers are responsible for putting these principles into action and responding thoughtfully to ethical issues that emerge during the research process. Having read the first chapter of this book, you are in a good position to grasp the ethical dilemmas that researchers typically face.

The History of Research Ethics

Guidelines for ethical research were first developed after the 1946 Nuremberg trials, when the horrific experiments perpetrated by Nazi doctors during World War II came to light. These trials resulted in the **Nuremberg Code**, a 10-point memorandum stating that research should benefit society, that it

---

Nuremberg Code A 10-point ethical code, developed as a result of the Nuremberg trials, that focuses on gaining participant consent, doing no harm, and offering social benefit.

should not cause harm, and that participants must freely consent. Many in the scientific community viewed the code as applying only to those who would purposefully engage in barbaric research practices, but others believed that all research should be governed by some set of professional standards. While the code was not directly adopted as a practice by professional organizations, it did later inspire groups to develop their own expectations about ethics and research.

In the United States, the first official set of principles governing research ethics did not come until the late 1970s, after a reporter exposed the details of the **Tuskegee Syphilis Experiment**. This was a deeply unethical and racist study that was funded by the US Public Health Service and made possible by the researchers' disregard for the health and welfare of Black communities that were vulnerable to extreme exploitation. From the 1930s to the 1970s, the researchers collected data on 399 low-income African American men with syphilis to study how the disease would progress if left untreated. Anti-Black racism influenced the study at every stage. First, the population was targeted because the researchers believed that Black men were more prone to sexually transmitted infections and uninterested in treatment. Then the participants were falsely told they were receiving treatment for the disease during the study. In 1945, when it was discovered that penicillin

---

Tuskegee Syphilis Experiment An unethical study of untreated syphilis in Black men conducted from the 1930s to 1970s in the United States; the exposure of participant abuses led to the release of the Belmont Report.

Belmont Report A document outlining three main ethical principles—respect for persons, beneficence, and justice—published in 1979 by The National Commission for the Protection of Human Services of Biomedical and Behavioral Research.

Common Rule The system used currently in the US to protect human participants in research studies; also known as the Federal Policy for the Protection of Human Subjects.

could treat syphilis, they were denied treatment. By the study's end, over 30% of the participants had died of syphilis or complications from syphilis. Moreover, 40 wives of participants had been infected, and 19 of their children had been born with syphilis (Jones 1993).

After these abuses were revealed, the US government settled a lawsuit filed by participants and their descendants, paying them a mere $10 million in 1974 and providing free medical care to participants and family members who had been infected with syphilis due to the study. In response to the revelations about the Tuskegee study abuses, Congress in 1974 passed the National Research Act, which created the National Commission for the Protection of Human Services of Biomedical and Behavioral Research. The Commission produced the **Belmont Report** (National Commission for the Protection of Human Subjects of Biomedical and Behavioral Research 1979), which outlined three main ethical principles to protect research participants:

1. Respect for Persons: Participants must be treated as autonomous agents, and those with diminished autonomy must be protected.
2. Beneficence: Researchers must ensure participants' well-being, maximizing benefits and reducing potential harms.
3. Justice: Both the possible risks and the benefits of research must be fairly distributed. (National Commission for the Protection of Human Subjects of Biomedical and Behavioral Research)

While the Belmont Report influenced research practices and professional discussions about ethics, it was not until 1991 that the US government outlined an official policy guiding ethical research undertaken by government agencies. The Federal Policy for the Protection of Human Subjects, known as the "**Common Rule**," is the current system used to ensure protection of human research participants. It took the government another six years to acknowledge fully and publicly the atrocities of the Tuskegee Experiment and its lasting historical trauma. In 1997, President Bill

Clinton officially apologized to the remaining survivors, their families, and the African American community.

The American Psychological Association (APA) adopted its first code of ethics in 1953, and the American Anthropological Association (AAA) followed in 1967. The American Sociological Association (ASA) began developing a set of shared ethical principles for the discipline in the 1960s (Schuler 1969) and approved its first Code of Ethics in 1970. Currently, the ASA Committee on Professional Ethics (COPE) reviews and updates the code as needed every five years (ASA 2019). This document includes six general guidelines for professional conduct:

1. professional competence,
2. integrity,
3. professional and scientific responsibility,
4. respect for people's rights, dignity, and diversity,
5. social responsibility, and
6. human rights (ASA 2018, 4–5).

In the next sections, we review some common ways researchers think about such principles and put them into practice.

Institutional Oversight and Research Ethics

Each college and university has an **institutional review board (IRB)**, a committee that is responsible for overseeing all research involving human participants proposed by members of their academic community. Before such a project begins—even before potential participants are approached—an IRB must review and approve it. Generally, the boards are made up of researchers from a variety of disciplines and include at least one community member from outside the institution (typically a college or university) under whose auspices the research will take place. When the researcher plans to study uniquely vulnerable populations, such as incarcerated people, a person with specific knowledge about that population must sit on the committee. The board membership is constituted this way

to provide a balanced and diverse perspective on the ethics of proposed studies.

IRBs may approve a research project, request modifications, or reject it outright. If the research is to be conducted over an extended timeframe, the committee may also hold periodic reviews, or at least require that the researchers file an annual report. Thus, the IRB considers ethics in an important procedural way. The overall goal is to protect research participants' well-being and the well-being and reputation of the institution. It is not in a university's best interest, for instance, for a researcher affiliated with it to conduct unethical research for which the institution may be considered culpable. Certain types of research are exempt from IRB review, such as research examining routine activities in educational settings that doesn't interfere with the learning environment and observation of public behavior in which participants cannot be identified. These proposals still must be submitted to the IRB to determine whether they are actually exempt from full review, and researchers must still consider the ethics of these studies.

Some researchers express concern about how IRB guidelines have become increasingly stringent over time (Newmahr and Hannem 2016). This trend stemmed from some cases in the 1990s (mostly in medical research) where privacy and informed consent violations led to increased liability concerns and more scrutiny. Yvonna Lincoln and William Tierney (2004) argue that this scrutiny most affects unconventional methodologies, such as postmodern and qualitative methods.

Ethical questions specific to certain methodologies are not always easy to translate into traditional IRB requirements, which could be barriers to approval. For example, Nazilla Khanlou and Elizabeth Peter (2005) argue that some IRBs unfamiliar with participatory action research (PAR) inappropriately evaluate their ethics using criteria identical to that which they apply to traditional research projects.

---

institutional review board (IRB) A committee that oversees proposed research involving human participants to ensure ethical practices.

In participatory action research, which we will examine in Chapter 7, professional researchers work collaboratively with community members to create and carry out research projects that are meant to be mutually beneficial. Collaboration and mutual benefit often require PAR researchers to approach their projects using unconventional research designs and methods, and Khanlou and Peter find that this variety is not always understood by IRB boards. PAR projects also face unique ethical challenges: projects constructed in collaboration with community members to create positive social change often cannot avoid political implications. And since these

are collaboratively developed and carried out, the typical "researcher" and "researched" roles can be blurry. Khanlou and Peter (2005) state that IRBs should be trained to guide PAR researchers through ethical questions particular to PAR, such as whether the community was actually integral to creating and carrying out the project and if the research is designed to maximize the emancipatory potential of the work.

Ethnographic research is another common methodology with complicated ethical considerations that make it difficult for IRB panels to assess it. Staci Newmahr and Stacey Hannem (2016) describe **ethnographic research** as "relationship work." Because ethnographers' research hinges so much on developing relationships with people in the field, it is difficult to assess ahead of time what risks or vulnerabilities their participants might encounter in that process. Further, ethnographers cannot anticipate all of the

---

ethnography (or ethnographic research)   A method in which researchers immerse themselves in social settings for an extended period of time, observing behavior and interacting with study participants in order to understand people's culture and experiences.

BOX 2.1 Approaches to Ethical Questions: Mindfulness

While undertaking a study on incest in Mexico, Gloria González-Lopez (2011) became aware that she needed to approach ethical concerns in an unconventional way, which she describes as becoming "mindful." For her, this meant "becom[ing] keenly aware of and present in the social contexts and circumstances surrounding the everyday life experiences of the people who participate in my research" (González-Lopez 2011, 448). This reflection first arose when she realized that requiring her participants to sign and keep a copy of the university-branded official consent form could put them at risk. Although the IRB required this form, González-Lopez concluded she had to rethink this plan in order to protect her participants "from the potential consequences of complying with an institutional procedure paradoxically designed to protect them" (448). She found that ethical questions more often emerge after IRB approval and in the process of conducting the research, particularly when studying sensitive subjects.

González-Lopez recommends that researchers practice "mindful ethics" and approach ethics not as a rigid checklist of what to do or not to do but as a commitment to "be alert to the urgency of being present at the moment and being cautious about what we take for granted" (449). In her study of family incest, González-Lopez needed to consider her participants' emotional well-being, be prepared to support them as they shared deeply personal information, know how to notice and respect their boundaries, and offer necessary resources to them as needed. She concludes, "to the extent that we are ethically aware, we will always have concerns and questions regarding the implications of our research and how it's perceived. These are likely to be thorny questions with no simple answers" (459). For González-Lopez, ethical research hinges on researchers' engaging in a process in which they acknowledge and grapple with those hard questions.

people they will encounter in the field or the information that will emerge during the process, so drawing up a list of everyone from whom they will need informed consent ahead of time for IRB approval is not realistic. IRBs are most effective when they are acquainted with the particular ethical issues that might arise in ethnography, PAR, and other designs and methods and when they have the expertise necessary to guide researchers through these situations.

IRB panels perform a valuable function in protecting research participants' rights and the integrity of researchers' work, so having a community of scholars provide oversight on proposed research benefits all stakeholders. Many social researchers argue that this role should take the form of collaboration and conversation rather than top-down, hierarchical supervision and decision making.

Gloria González-Lopez (2011) encourages researchers not to view IRB approval as evidence that all ethical questions have been resolved. While such approval is an important first step, researchers should also reflect upon their ethical decisions throughout the entire process. Box 2.1 explores some of González-Lopez's suggestions for thinking about these issues throughout a study.

Key Ethical Principles in Research

When researchers conduct studies, they must determine what decisions they define as ethical and unethical and make choices they feel comfortable with. However, because not everyone has the same threshold for defining an act unethical, debates about ethics and ethical dilemmas are inevitable. Further, unique ethical questions may arise depending on the type of research or the communities involved, including children, people with social privilege, or people in vulnerable situations.

In the following sections, we define three key ethical principles—informed consent/voluntary participation, confidentiality, and protection from harm—and explore debates and unique considerations about each one. While these principles address distinct concerns, they also share core considerations. In many ways, the Belmont Report's "Respect for Persons" stipulation forms the basis of many ethical choices and is fundamental to all the principles.

Informed Consent and Voluntary Participation

A core principle of ethical research is the stipulation that people must give **informed consent** to participate in the study. Potential research participants must not only be asked for their permission before they are placed in a study but also be informed of all the risks and benefits involved. To assess these elements and provide informed consent, prospective participants need a basic idea of what the study will entail.

In most studies, potential participants receive an information sheet or read an orienting paragraph that outlines what the research is about, how it will be conducted, and what risks and benefits of participation they can anticipate. The document or paragraph normally includes the names of the people in charge of the research, their institutional affiliations, and their contact information. Typically it also contains assurances of confidentiality, along with a description of how the data will be stored and how the results will be published (Figure 2.1).

Prospective participants should be encouraged to ask questions and seek clarification if necessary. If they have all the information required and are willing to participate, they sign a *consent form*, which may include a brief synopsis of the study and states explicitly that research participants are free to exit the study at any time without penalty. Sometimes the consent form and the information document are merged into one, as illustrated in Figure 2.1.

Only people competent to make an informed decision about participation should be asked for their consent. Most adults are considered able to provide informed consent, although for reasons of illness, other incapacitation, or language differences, some may not be capable of making an informed decision. In this case, they must have a person considered competent to decide on their behalf or support them as they decide. Similarly, children are not ordinarily

---

informed consent A core principle of ethical research, stipulating that participants must agree freely and with full understanding to participate in any study.

Letter of Information: A study of personality in adult twins

Dear _____ :

You recently completed a number of questionnaires for a research project conducted by Dr. _____ at _____ College. We are very grateful for your participation in our research. At this time, we would like to in invite you to take part in a further research study examining relationships between different measures of personality.

If you agree to participate in this study, you will be asked to complete the following questionnaires: the TAS-20 Alexithymia Test, the Deadly Sins Scale, the AQ-9 (a measure of attitudes toward mental illness), the Moral Foundations Questionnaire, the Political Issues Questionnaire, and the Self-Report Altruism Scale. Each of these is a paper-and-pencil personality questionnaire, and each will take approximately 5 to 15 minutes to complete.

Most of the items in the questionnaires require you to indicate the extent to which different statements are descriptive of you or your twin. Please feel free to complete the items at your own pace, in your own home. It is not necessary to fill out all of the questionnaires in one sitting. We do, however, ask that you fill out the questionnaires by yourself rather than with your twin, as we are interested in your unique responses.

There are no known risks involved in participating in this study. Participation is voluntary. You may refuse to participate, and to not answer any questions that you do not feel comfortable addressing. You may withdraw from the study at any time.

Once you have completed as many of the questionnaires as you wish to complete, please mail them back to us in the provided self-addressed stamped envelope. The questionnaires will then be stored in a locked cabinet in Dr. _____ 's office until they have been scored. At that point, they will be shredded. Only Dr. _____ and her research assistant will have access to the questionnaires and to the response sheets. Your name will never be given out, nor will it appear in any written report about the study. All of your responses will be kept completely confidential.

Once we have processed your questionnaires, you will be sent $50.00 and your name will be entered into a draw for a chance to win one of ten $250.00 prizes. At the completion of the study, we will send you a summary of the study's findings, if you so request.

If you have questions regarding any aspect of this study, you are welcome to contact Dr. _____ by telephone (xxx-xxx-xxxx) or by email (xxxxxx@xxx.edu). If you have any further questions about the manner in which this study is being conducted or about your rights as a research participant, you may contact the Director of the Office of Research Ethics at _____ College by telephone (xxx-xxx-xxxx) or by email (xxxxxx-@xxx.edu).

Completion and return of the questionnaires indicates your consent to participate in the study.

Thank you for your interest in this study. This letter is yours to keep for future reference.

Dr. _____ , Professor of _____ , _____ College

FIGURE 2.1 A sample information letter and consent form

considered capable of giving informed consent. Parents or legal guardians are usually given the information sheet as well as an opportunity to ask questions and seek clarifications about the research before signing the consent form on behalf of the child. Quite often a parent/guardian must be present when the child interacts with the researcher. This does not mean that the adults hold all the decision power, as the youth also must assent. Parent/guardian permission is referred to as *consent* and child/youth permission as *assent*. Researchers should secure both the consent of the parent/guardian and the assent of the youth unless the IRB waives the assent requirement; this happens if the child is incapable of giving assent or if the research is determined to be of direct benefit of the child (US Department of Health and Human Services 2020).

Researchers must not coerce or pressure people into participating. Thus, it is particularly important to inform participants of their *right to withdraw from the study at any time*—and to honor that right. Another issue related to participant coercion and voluntary choice concerns payment for participation, also known as providing an incentive. Ronit Dinovitzer, John Hagen, and Patricia Parker (2003) conducted a quantitative analysis assessing the factors that contribute to high educational attainment among immigrants to Canada. They offered their participants five dollars to participate. It seems unlikely that anyone answered the questionnaire simply for the small amount of money involved. Still, some IRBs do not allow participants to be paid, except to cover logistical costs (transportation, parking, etc.). In general, it is considered unethical to offer payment if it would lead participants to take risks they would not otherwise accept.

Deception and the Milgram Experiments

In experiments, researchers commonly use some degree of deception in order to avoid the **reactive effects** that occur when people know they are being observed. Participants may not behave naturally and authentically when they are fully informed of the experiment's purpose and know what the researchers are looking for. This gives rise to an ongoing debate in the social sciences about whether the benefits of using deception ever outweigh the importance of obtaining fully informed consent.

A famous debate about deception and informed consent concerns Stanley Milgram's (1963) obedience experiments. Milgram designed his studies in an effort to understand the brutality of the Nazi concentration camps. In particular, he wanted to know how a person could cause an innocent human being extreme harm and whether being ordered to do so by an authority figure has anything to do with it. He devised a laboratory experiment in which a supposedly reputable researcher (the authority figure) had participants act as "teachers" who would ask "learners" questions and punish them for incorrect answers by giving them increasingly severe electric shocks. In all instances, the teachers were told that the shocks were part of the study and would not cause any permanent harm, despite the cries of pain. The participants did not know that the learners—who were actually confederates of Milgram—were not being shocked and that the cries were actually recordings. The experiment continued until the teacher refused to administer more shocks.

In the version of the study in which they could not see the learners, a substantial majority (62 percent) of participants administered the strongest shocks possible. In a variation of the experiment, participants were given the option of ordering another person (a confederate) to administer the shocks; in this situation, more than 90 percent of participants ordered the greatest shocks possible. Many of the participants were visibly upset as they carried out the experimenter's orders, but they were told that it was essential that they continue and that they had no other choice. As a result, the participants did what they were told.

Milgram saw these results as evidence that people were willing to inflict serious harm on innocent others if ordered to do so by an authority figure—a finding that may help us understand human atrocities and how they may be prevented. But the study involved a number of ethically questionable elements. One was deception: aside from being led to believe that the shocks were real, the participants were told that the experiment was

---

reactive effects (or reactivity) The impact on research when participants know that they are being studied, which may result in atypical or inauthentic behavior.

investigating how people learn, not how people come to commit cruel acts. To the extent that they were not informed of the experiment's purpose, they were lied to, although they were *debriefed* (informed of the deception and the reason for it) afterward.

On one hand, most people would agree that in everyday life, lying and deception should be avoided. On the other hand, Milgram's experiment would have failed had the participants known the truth. Imagine the outcome had the participants been told, "We're going to see whether you are willing to inflict severe pain on an innocent person." But does that justify the deception? Was the knowledge gained worth the psychological discomfort? This is the sort of difficult question that researchers and IRB members must ponder.

Deception can be a controversial issue in observational research as well. Some writers claim that if all **covert research** were disallowed, studying certain populations—cults, drug dealers, people who commit white-collar crime, and others—would be impossible (see Box 2.2). Some social reformers believe that exposing the misdeeds of the powerful is an acceptable use of deception, but this view raises the question of what amount is acceptable in other situations. Would it be appropriate to use deception to expose the transgressions of marginalized people and the less powerful?

Questions Surrounding Informed Consent

Purposeful deception, like that used in Stanley Milgram's obedience experiments, is often cited as the prime example in questions around informed consent procedures. However, it is not a typical situation. In most research, deliberations about informed consent occur in a more routine and regular manner. We ask ourselves, *who can truly give free consent?* For instance, at what age should young people be in charge of their own informed consent? Or if prison officials approve a research study, might the incarcerated people feel obligated to grant consent lest they be punished for refusing?

Researchers also think about *how to approach getting consent*. We offer information about the study

---

covert research   Research conducted without informing the participants that the study is taking place.

when getting consent, yet researchers also avoid giving too many details about the research for fear of contaminating people's responses. If you approached Tinder users and asked them to complete your survey, might their answers be different if you told them you were studying misogynistic behavior on dating apps versus saying the study focused on interactions across genders on dating apps?

Elizabeth Murphy and Robert Dingwall (2007) note that the question of informed consent can be complicated in ethnography. It can be challenging to determine from whom informed consent is required when conducting research in semi-public settings, like hospitals, businesses, or social and political organizations. Ethnographers typically get consent from the main people regularly in the location they are studying. For example, in a hospital, staff, volunteers, and people who work in hospital retail kiosks are regulars. Patients, visitors, and people making deliveries are not: they move in and out of the setting. A researcher must decide when to get consent from such non-regulars, which can be complicated when the researcher is in the field for a long period of time and encounters many people for brief stints.

A similar situation occurs in public settings, where ethnographers encounter many people. In public settings like malls, parks, or public streets, there is not the expectation of privacy that one would have in spaces like a place of worship or in people's homes (or semi-public spaces like hospitals). Murphy and Dignwall (2007) point out that in many public and semi-public settings, securing informed consent from every person who moves through or within the space is impossible. If a researcher were required to acquire individual consent from everyone in this kind of setting, they argue, ethnographers would be "so occupied with negotiating consent [they] would have no time to carry out the research and would destroy the setting as an object of study" (2007, 2229–2230).

In some field research settings, providing information sheets and consent forms may be impractical; it might even defeat the purposes of the study. Overly formal agreement between the researchers and the informants might signal a lack of trust; in this case, less formal approaches may be used. Imagine you were interested in how regulars at a local dive bar engage as a community. How might they respond if you talked with them about your study, getting their permission for your observation in a more conversational way? How would they react if you approached them with printed-out permission forms for them to read and sign?

Confidentiality and Anonymity

Keeping participants' identities and records private is an important element of research, as it can prevent embarrassment and harm, especially to people's reputations and personal

What are some appropriate ways to gain access and develop trust within different social settings? Imagine if you wanted to observe drinking behavior at parties: How would you approach getting access to study a small, intimate party like this one compared to a large, public gathering?

BOX 2.2 What Are the Boundaries of Informed Consent?

Sudhir Venkatesh's *Gang Leader for a Day: A Rogue Sociologist Takes to the Streets* (2008) sparked much debate around informed consent and other ethical issues. As a graduate student, Venkatesh did ethnographic research on drug dealers and other tenants in a south-side Chicago public housing project, the Robert Taylor Homes. To get access to the residents, he was not fully honest about his research. He told people in the field he was a student researcher, but he also convinced one of his key informants and a focus of the book—J. T., who was a gang leader and crack dealer—that he was writing a biography about him. Stretching the truth in this way helped Venkatesh gain admittance into J. T.'s world. He also shared information from tenants with J. T.,

who then extorted the people for money. This "informing-on-the-informants-moment" (Waterston 2012) had consequences in the residents' daily lives and diminished their faith in Venkatesh while it increased J. T.'s trust in him.

Venkatesh's controversial work raised much debate about ethical boundaries and professional standards. Did J. T. fully understand what the research was about, and did the other residents know that their information might be shared with their neighbors? Would disclosing to J. T. confidential information on the neighbors fall into the category of causing harm? Were Venkatesh's choices necessary to gain entry to an underground economy that many researchers cannot access? Were his decisions worthwhile?

relationships. Protecting participants' identities can make them feel more comfortable in giving honest answers.

This injunction means that the research participants should not be identifiable when the findings are published, although exceptions may occasionally be made in the case of historical work or of studies dealing with public figures. **Confidentiality** means participants' identities are kept private, and the researcher ensures that the information cannot be linked to an individual identity. When identities are **anonymous**, it is impossible for anyone, even the researcher, to link data to a particular respondent. In quantitative research, participants are usually identified by code numbers rather than names when the data are processed; their actual identities are stored in a secure location. They are normally told on the information sheet that their data will form part of a statistical aggregate (e.g., "50% of respondents expressed some dissatisfaction with their romantic partner's listening skills") and therefore they will not be personally identifiable. Qualitative researchers will often give participants a **pseudonym**—a different name used in documents and reports—and keep the data secure so no one else can link the data to any particular person.

The issues that arise with privacy and confidentiality in qualitative research—especially when it involves in-depth analysis of a small number of people—are different from the issues that come up in quantitative studies. Pseudonyms are typically used to protect people's identities, but the detailed

---

confidentiality The protection of the identities of research participants, arising from measures taken by the researcher to ensure that information provided by individual participants cannot be linked back to them.

---

anonymity The practice of ensuring that participants' identities are unknown to the researcher, thus ensuring that information provided cannot be linked back to individual participants.

---

pseudonym A made-up name given to a research participant to protect their privacy by concealing their identity in documents and reports related to the research.

description of the physical and social setting, which qualitative researchers usually include to provide needed context for the study, frequently offer enough clues to identify some of the participants. Arthur Vidich and Joseph Bensman's (1968) study of a US town they called "Springdale, New York" is instructive in this regard. The researchers studied class dynamics, religious traditions, and political struggles among town residents, seeking to understand how the characteristics of the rural village reflected broader societal trends. In the published results, the researchers were uncomplimentary about the town and many of its leaders, and many people felt that the researchers' tone was patronizing. The residents felt their town had been misrepresented, and that the town was easy to identify. Once the citizens recognized the real town behind the "Springdale" pseudonym, it was easy to identify many of the people described in the book. The town's citizens responded with a Fourth of July parade where many wore badges citing their book pseudonyms, and an effigy of Vidich was set up so that it peered into manure. The townspeople also announced their refusal to cooperate in any more social research.

In quantitative research, maintaining participants' confidentiality is often a straightforward endeavor. Even if a survey researcher is aware of the identities of individual members of their sample, questionnaires are usually returned anonymously and cannot be connected to individual people. Study samples are often quite large, and the presentation of aggregate data does not have the potential to reveal people's responses. Some ethical considerations particular to quantitative research, including how ethics relates to sampling, are discussed in Box 2.3.

Covert Research Controversies

In covert research, people are not informed that they are part of a study. Clearly, researchers engaging in this type of research have not obtained informed consent. Covert studies raise concerns that they infringe upon people's privacy and compromise confidentiality.

One of the most famous and controversial cases of covert research is Laud Humphreys' *Tearoom Trade* ([1970] 2017). Humphreys observed sexual

BOX 2.3 What Ethical Considerations Are Unique to Quantitative Research?

A. T. Panter and Sonya K. Sterba (2011) describe quantitative research integrity as an ethical concern. On the surface, it can appear that mathematical information presented using statistics offers an unbiased description of reality. Panter and Sterba remind us that numbers are another communication tool and can be used just as deceptively as any other form of communication. They argue that quantitative researchers must consider ethical issues particular to statistical work in order to conduct valid, ethically sound studies.

One example they cite involves sampling strategy. A cornerstone of statistical work is random sampling. As we will see in Chapter 4, random sampling means that every element in a population has an equal chance of being selected. This allows statisticians to use data from their random sample to estimate trends in the broader population. Panter and Sterba point out that a statistical researcher must systematically (and honestly)

collect a sample that is not biased to guarantee the kinds of findings the researcher is hoping for. They also note that sometimes researchers are unsatisfied with the estimates that come from the sample they collected. In such cases, they remind us, the researcher must not "shop around" for the results they'd hoped for by using different methods of analyzing the sample (Panter and Sterba 2011, 24).

Overall, Panter and Sterba state that statistical researchers must be fully transparent about their choices, outlining their decisions around how and why the data were collected, their reasons for choosing certain variables, their strategy for measuring the variables, their sampling process, and their explanations for any missing data. Conducting research with integrity is a key ethical consideration, and ethical questions come into play with every research methodology, whether quantitative or qualitative.

---

encounters between men in public toilets ("tearooms"), taking the role of a "watch queen"—a person who looks out for possible intruders, including police, while other men meet and engage in sexual activity. Humphreys recorded some of the men's license plate numbers and later used them to track down names and addresses—thus further compromising confidentiality and privacy—to create a sample of 100 active tearoom participants. To reduce the risk of being recognized, he waited a year before contacting anyone and changed his hairstyle. He then visited the homes of some of the men, posing as a public health officer. He asked the men about their health issues (a ruse), including some questions about marital sex. He did not reveal that he knew about their sexual experiences with men, nor did he debrief them when the study was finished.

Humphreys learned that many of the men he observed were heterosexually married and integrated

members of the straight community. These findings allowed him to challenge popular stereotypes of the day, which framed gay attraction as a mental illness and cast gay desires as invariably leading to a gay life and identity.

Was Humphreys' research ethical? Some argue that covert research was his only option because few people engaging in gay sex in those days were willing to talk about it. In fact, sexual acts between men were against the law; offenders were subject to prison sentences and could be committed to mental hospitals against their will. Humphreys' supporters also maintain that his studies led to a better understanding of human sexuality and the treatment of stigmatized people. Humphreys' choices to observe the men, follow them to get their license plate numbers, and then track them down in their homes raised concerns about risks to the men's confidentiality, however. His detractors argue that the knowledge gained did not justify deceiving the men or invading their privacy. The debate continues to this day.

In spite of the widespread insistence on informed consent and privacy rights, and the recognition that covert observation is especially prone to violations of those principles, researchers continue to conduct covert studies. Virtually all codes of ethics allow covert research as a last resort, but most state that it should be avoided "as far as possible." This guideline acknowledges that covert research may be acceptable in rare instances and emphasizes that the benefits of the research should outweigh any harm.

Protecting Participants from Harm

As is implied by the ethical guidelines of informed consent and confidentiality, a social researcher's priority should be to ensure that the people being studied are not harmed by their participation. All researchers should assign paramount importance to the physical, mental, emotional, spiritual, social, and economic well-being of the person, group, or community affected by the research. The welfare of research participants should take priority over everything else, *including the acquisition of knowledge*, even if it would expand our understanding of humanity or lead to improvements in the human condition.

Determining Harm

It may seem obvious that participants should not be harmed by taking part in research activities, whether they be surveys, field research studies, or any other kind of social scientific investigation. As with many moral rules, however, knowing how to practice this principle is anything but simple. We all know that research participants should not be physically harmed in the process of being studied, but are any and all harms unjustifiable? What about milder forms, such as short-term anxiety or embarrassment? Is it morally acceptable to subject people to temporary discomfort if the research has the potential to improve our understanding of society or human behavior in general?

Researchers should do their best to anticipate and guard against harmful or disturbing consequences for participants, but it's not always easy to know

where to draw the line. Robert Rosenthal and Lenore Jacobson (1968) studied how teacher expectations affect their treatment of students. In an experiment they randomly selected a group of students and told their teachers that the academic performance of these students was expected to excel quickly the following year (they called these students "spurters"). They noticed the teachers paid more attention to this group of students compared to the ones identified as "non-spurters." A question arises: were the non-spurters adversely affected in their intellectual development by the increased attention given to the other group? After all, teachers have limited time and energy; the more they spent with the spurters, they less they had for everyone else. Was that a violation of research ethics? Was potential harm suffered by the non-spurters outweighed by the knowledge gained by the researchers?

Sometimes a researcher may feel obliged to disregard some ethical concerns as they prioritize doing no harm. For instance, they may be less worried about privacy and confidentiality if the research uncovers evidence of serious harm or criminal activity. In his ethnographic research, Mark Totten (2001) wanted to know how youth gang members interpreted the violence they perpetrated against their girlfriends and how they accounted for their racist and homophobic activities. One underlying factor he observed was their rather limited mental construction of masculinity. Most had lived on the street, were victims of severe child abuse and neglect, and had witnessed their mothers being beaten. They saw their own violence as affirming their masculinity.

That was the sociology, but what about the welfare of the people concerned? Totten was compelled to act in some instances. By law, he had to report any abuse suffered by children under the age of 16, regardless of whether they were gang members or their victims. In 18 US states and Puerto Rico, any person who suspects child abuse or neglect is required to contact the authorities. In this study, those deemed at risk of suicide had to be referred to mental health providers. Finally, some of the gang members were on probation or living in treatment facilities, so the authorities there also had to be informed. To ensure he did not break the confidentiality of his participants,

Totten informed the boys ahead of time what situations would require him to report what he learned to authorities. He studied only the boys who agreed to participate after learning about those boundaries.

There is always a risk that members of disadvantaged groups will be abused, mistreated, or disrespected by the researchers who study them. People accessing social services might resent an implication, however subtle, that they need "help" of some kind or the assumption that the researcher has a superior sort of wisdom or political insight. Some Western anthropologists have been barred from re-entering the countries where they did their fieldwork because the locals found them to be intrusive and disrespectful. This need to consider equity and to avoid unfair treatment of disadvantaged people reflects the Belmont Report's principle of justice, which emphasizes that the risks and benefits of research must be distributed equitably. Harm must not outweigh the potential benefits of the research, but as our examples show, harms and benefits can be difficult to judge correctly, and assessments of them ultimately involve value judgments, consideration of social inequality, as well as scientific decisions.

Mixed Methods in Action | Different Methodologies, Different Ethical Considerations

Martin Tolich (2016) observes that mixed methods research involves unique ethical considerations. Researchers follow the same ethical guidelines whether their research is qualitative or quantitative, yet their chosen methodology affects the specific way they approach research ethics. For instance, qualitative researchers maintain participant confidentiality just as quantitative researchers do, but a quantitative method such as a survey more often allows for respondent anonymity than an in-depth qualitative interview would.

Surveys are often anonymous, but what different ethical considerations might come up if the researcher conducts a structured interview, directly reading the questionnaire to the participant and filling out their answers?

Survey researchers usually ask their respondents to sign a consent form before they fill out the questionnaire, thus securing informed consent before participation. In qualitative research, consent can be an ongoing process, as researchers often conduct long or multiple interviews and ethnographers immerse themselves in field sites for long periods. Thus, researchers using mixed methods must recognize the unique ethical issues raised in the different methodologies they use and confront them throughout the study's duration.

BOX 2.4 Safety in Research

Just as you should ensure that no harm comes to participants, you should assess whether your studies could put you, the researcher, in potentially dangerous circumstances. Be sure to do a thorough risk assessment of the research environment before you undertake your project.

Janina Pawelz (2018) discussed the ways female researchers studying male-dominated spheres must build safety plans into their research strategies. She cites her own work on gangs in Southeast Asia and the Caribbean. For example, she never conducted research after dark, did not reveal where she lived, lived with a host family (rather than alone) and kept in regular contact with them, was honest about her research at all times, did not carry valuables, avoided riding alone in cars with research participants, and dressed and presented herself conservatively.

Even in seemingly safe conditions, a researcher can face a sudden outburst of abuse or threatening behavior; you cannot always predict how people will react to a particular trigger, such as a survey topic or interview question. If the researcher sees signs that trouble is imminent (e.g., through body language), the best response is to withdraw from the situation.

Once sure that you will not be placing yourself in harm's way, you may also need to convince your university, advisor, or IRB that your safety will not be compromised. Will Small, Lisa Maher, and Thomas Kerr (2014), who did ethnographic research with intravenous drug users in Vancouver, were told by their IRB to consult with local police about safety issues and provide them with the ethnographers' names. The researchers had to go to great lengths to convince the board that proper precautions would be taken, that they would be safe, and that police involvement would make it difficult to recruit participants and ensure the confidentiality of the results. After a prolonged review process, the board relented, and the study went ahead as planned.

Balancing Harms and Benefits

One challenge in trying to balance harms and benefits lies in identifying all the circumstances in which harm is likely. Might a questionnaire on relationship satisfaction lead some respondents to question and eventually leave their partners? Could asking an eighth-grade student athlete about steroid use encourage experimentation with the drug? Some people filling out a survey may be uncomfortable answering certain personal questions; some may find a focus group discussion stressful, especially if they inadvertently reveal more than they had intended. Does it follow that such studies should not be conducted? Probably not. Instead, most ethical codes maintain that if there is any prospect of harm to participants, and if the risks of the research are greater than the risks of everyday life, informed consent is a minimum requirement.

One challenge in assessing benefit in the social sciences is that it is typically indirect; in most cases it follows from an increase in knowledge. However, direct benefits can accrue, such as when research findings inspire positive social reform or contribute to beneficial societal change. One way to maximize the benefit of social research is to conduct it in a methodologically sound manner. Participants should not be put through the rigors of the study if it is not designed or conducted properly and therefore is of little or no value. Researchers can disagree over what constitutes a sound methodology. Nonetheless, each perspective assumes that there are optimal ways of doing the research; if these are ignored it's doubtful that anyone, including the researcher, will get the maximum benefit.

Ethics as a Question of Power and Social Justice

All of the main ethical principles outlined above recognize that researchers often occupy a position of power over the people they research. At base, a researcher should consider what power differentials might exist between them and the people they research and how these could affect their participants'—and their own—choices and actions.

For instance, researchers should consider what factors could affect people's participation in a study. What if the research takes place in a hierarchical organization or setting in which the participants hold little power? Low-wage employees discussing work practices at their company, student athletes sharing information about professors and coaches, or early-career dancers in a local company could all encounter challenges due to their power status in the setting. Employees might feel that company authorities are invested in the research and worry they will face retaliation if they refuse to participate. They may worry that sharing information could anger their superiors or reflect badly on the organization. If an employee willingly participates in a study, a researcher must protect them from consequences of participation.

Some participants' **positionality** can make it difficult to successfully ensure confidentiality. Carol Robinson (2020) encountered such dilemmas when she studied incarcerated people with terminal illnesses. Intense surveillance in prison institutions made it difficult—and sometimes impossible—to ever speak to anyone (incarcerated people and staff) privately. Some incarcerated people are not allowed to have one-to-one meetings without staff present or can meet only in more "public" prison spaces where they can be seen and overheard. Robinson worked collaboratively with incarcerated participants to determine where and when to do an interview with the most privacy. Prison staff face other challenges: their offices are often not private, and staff may have to reveal that they are speaking to the researcher in order to arrange for someone to cover for them during the time they are away. Robinson worked with the prison's staffing organizers to

ensure staff could meet with her without disclosing that they were meeting with a researcher.

Wider cultural and political power dynamics may also influence the ways researchers carry out their studies. Jennifer Hales (2006) points out that a colonialist mentality often pervades research conducted on subordinated peoples. Where there is a power inequity between the researcher and those being studied, she advises, one should ask the following questions: "Why is the research done? How is it done? Who defines, initiates, and conducts the research? On/with/for whom is the research carried out? What topics are addressed? Who benefits and how? Who interprets for whom and who represents whom?" (Hales 2006, 243).

Often, researchers hold graduate degrees and high prestige. Thus, researchers must ask themselves: How might power dynamics make my respondent feel compelled to share information with me or feel uncomfortable doing so? What does it mean to tell this person's story in my research? What limitations might I confront in my ability to represent this person's experiences?

Black feminist writer bell hooks (1989) considers the relationship between power dynamics and knowledge production when White women write about Black women's lives. hooks encourages readers to "seriously question the racist and sexist politics which determine who is an authority" (hooks 1989, 45); that is, how structures of power might enable certain people—White women, in this example—to be seen as authorities on a community that they are not a part of and that they have heightened structural privileges over (Black women). hooks states, "When we write about the experiences of a group to which we do not belong, we should think about the ethics of our action, considering whether or not our work will be used to reinforce and perpetuate domination" (1989, 43). hooks's argument suggests that when White researchers write about BIPOC

---

positionality The way in which social and structural contexts impact a person's identity, status, and perspectives and affect the amount of power and authority someone holds within interpersonal and institutional interactions.

BOX 2.5 **Power, Positionality, and Representation in Research**

For over six years, Alice Goffman (2014) did ethnographic research on how young Black men and their families in a West Philadelphia neighborhood she called "Sixth Street" routinely faced punitive social control and criminalization. Her research demonstrated that the neighborhood men experienced repeated cycles of incarceration. She detailed their day-to-day attempts to avoid police and survive within an environment imposing many barriers upon them. After completing the research, she destroyed thousands of pages of field notes to protect her participants from any police inquiries; this was particularly important to her because her participants had become close friends to her, confidants, and even roommates.

When Goffman's study was first published, it garnered extensive mainstream attention and accolades. The academic community quickly began to debate Goffman's ethics and the appropriateness of her methods, writing style, and analysis. Critics felt that Goffman got too close to her participants and wrote about them in a lurid and sensationalistic tone more akin to journalism than ethnography; many felt this approach was particularly problematic for a White woman writing about Black people's lives. Some related the controversy over her research choices and representation of her participants to broader debates over the ethics of ethnography as a method and notorious examples like Humphreys' *Tearoom Trade* (Kaufman 2015; Zussman 2016). Victor Rios (2015) asserted that Goffman's melodramatic tone created an analytical problem: the "sensationalist stories of crime and violence in the book distract the reader from the stated objective of understanding police and mass incarceration" (307). He argued that Goffman created archetype characters rather than presenting a nuanced analysis of the systems of criminalization and hyper policing surrounding Black communities. Goffman's depiction of her informants employed what Rios called a "Jungle Book narrative" that reified problematic stereotypes.

Rios's critique suggests that social researchers have an ethical responsibility to represent their participants in ways that challenge rather than reinforce the social conditions that disadvantage them. Like hooks, Rios emphasizes positionality, asserting that Goffman wrote herself into the story in an autobiographical manner that was neither self-reflexive nor sociological (307). Goffman responded to some critiques about her work's accuracy but gave little response to the representation questions. She didn't feel it necessary to apologize for her writing style and choices; she felt allegiance to earlier ethnographers who emphasized deep involvement with and detailed description of their informants' lives with little emphasis on researcher role and positionality. For Goffman, telling the story of Sixth Street residents was more important than the question of whether and how *she* should tell their story (Lewis-Kraus 2016).

All these debates represent longstanding questions about what type of effects social research can have on public discourse, academic knowledge, and participants' everyday lives. How might it be important to consider these issues a matter of ethics?

(Black, Indigenous, and People of Color) communities, heterosexual researchers write about LGBTQIA2S+ (Lesbian, Gay, Bisexual, Transgender, Queer and/or Questioning, Intersex, Asexual, Two-Spirit, and the countless affirmative ways in which people choose to self-identify) experiences, or cisgender men write about women's lives, they should discuss the position from which they write

What's the role of research in affecting the outcomes of contentious public debates? Do you feel there are unique ethical responsibilities when conducting research that might be used to inform social policy?

and speak, interrogate how privilege influences their perspective, and resist claiming they are more of an authority than members of the community about which they write (1989, 47–48). Box 2.5 discusses a recent debate over these issues.

Conversations about power and research ethics are relevant also to the political motivations and consequences of research. In 2012, Mark Regnerus published a study concluding that young adults raised by parents who had a same-sex relationship grew up to have poorer social, emotional, and relationship outcomes than their peers raised by parents in heterosexual relationships. These findings sparked a significant controversy among scholars who questioned the ethics of his study design and his integrity as an autonomous researcher (Cheng and Powell 2015; Manning et al. 2014;

Perrin, Cohen, and Caren 2013; Rosenfeld 2015; Schumm 2016). A key criticism focused on Regnerus's measurement strategy and classification of family structures. The heterosexual parents in his study tended to be in intact relationships, whereas the parents who had a same-sex relationship were in mostly unstable family structures. Further, a large number of the people he claimed had been "raised by" parents who had a same-sex relationship (which Regnerus defined as lesbian or gay parents whether or not they identified as lesbian or gay) had not lived with them for any significant period of time. Of the 236 respondents in the sample who had been raised by parents who had a same-sex relationship, only 51 had lived in such households for at least a year. Analysis of data from this smaller group showed comparable outcomes with kids raised by people in a heterosexual relationship.

Questions and disagreements about how researchers measure their variables are common in academic debates about methodological choices and ethical concerns. However, discussion of the Regnerus study gained an additional layer as some critics expressed concern regarding the study's political ramifications. Some of Regnerus's peers expressed concerns about the study's potential misuse by parties looking to draw conclusions about children with LGBTQIA2S+ parents and to defend arguments against gay marriage and LGBTQIA2S+ parenting (Gates et al. 2012; Perrin et al. 2013). Multiple scholars (including Regnerus) countered that the results could not be used for such purposes, as the study was retrospective, focused on young adults and not children, and did not offer conclusions about the impact of same-sex marriage on children.

Nevertheless, when the US Supreme Court reviewed the constitutionality of laws restricting marriage equality in 2013, Regnerus supported the continued denial of marriage rights for LGBTQIA2S+ couples, arguing that heterosexual parents are best for children and that too many questions remain about whether children develop as well in LGBTQIA2S+ households. For many, these actions confirmed suspicions that Regnerus pursued research that would support an anti-gay political agenda. In addition, the study was funded by the Witherspoon Institute, a conservative think tank linked to several religious political organizations with a history of fighting against LGBTQIA2S+ rights. This raised questions about Regnerus's ethics and the degree to which the funding organization influenced his autonomy as a researcher and affected his choices.

Another recent example of the intersection of research, politics, and ethics is work by Domenico "Mimmo" Parisi, a Mississippi State University sociology professor and director of the National Strategic Planning and Analysis Research Center (NSPARC). NSPARC collects government data in Mississippi, including education data, information on people accessing state resources such as human services and public assistance, and economic information. The agency secures people's confidentiality by assigning them a 10-digit number—that way, it can track their participation in different state agencies but protect their identities. Although NSPARC takes important measures to protect people's privacy, the way Parisi presents the data has been ethically controversial.

NSPARC receives government funding, and Parisi has collaborated with state government officials to attract more investment in the state while countering claims that the quality of life in Mississippi is poor. Other researchers, lawmakers, and state agency representatives claim that Parisi and his team mine the data for the most positive figures so they can present a view of Mississippi that is better than reality. In one example, the state economists' office questioned the accuracy of Mississippi workforce data that NSPARC reported. NSPARC published a report of the state's economic outlook that estimated the workforce participation rate of people aged 25 to 55 was 2 percentage points higher than the official estimate of state economists. NSPARC claimed that their workforce participation rate of 80 percent was in line with the national rate of 82.1 percent. The state economists' office noted the rate was actually 78.2%, which is the fifth-worst level in the United States (Wolfe 2019).

In another example, NSPARC published a fact sheet citing census data showing that 10 percent of millennials were leaving the state—a figure that was generally in line with the national average (Parisi 2018, 17). When critics argued that Mississippi was actually experiencing a "brain drain" because so many millennials were leaving the state, Parisi wrote a special report to the governor that reinterpreted the data to place a more positive spin on the trends. Parisi emphasized that the outmigration levels were low by presenting the raw numbers of millennials who had left (rather than the percentages as previously reported) and then compared these raw numbers to those in all other states, even though many states have much larger populations. This downplayed the extent to which millennials were leaving the state and presented

BOX 2.6 What about Research Using the Internet?

A great deal of social research is now done online. All the ethics guidelines discussed in this chapter apply to online research, with a handful of exceptions. One involves material that is publicly available and protected by law, such as Census Bureau public-use files or data in public archives. In such cases, researchers are not required to obtain informed consent, although they must obey the relevant laws and regulations. Another exception applies to online information that is publicly accessible and does not involve any expectation of privacy. This usually includes videos, social media posts, newspaper materials, political or commercial publications, third-party interviews, and any other online materials that can be collected without direct interaction with or attribution to research participants.

How should researchers approach consent and confidentiality in online environments? What unique ethical considerations should researchers make when doing online research?

In their study of expressions of hostility between Black urban youth and police, Desmond Upton Patton et al. (2016) examined Twitter posts, replies, and retweets between a young Chicago gang member, Gakirah Barnes, and her followers. Their research showed that Barnes and her followers found an outlet on Twitter for their grief, anger, and disdain after police shot and killed a friend of theirs. The researchers debated whether they should protect the users' identities by anonymizing their handles when publishing the research. They decided to use Barnes's real handle and name because the mainstream news coverage had already extensively discussed her online statements, but to anonymize her followers' handles to protect their identities.

Any situation that involves direct contact with research participants, including online surveys and interviews, is subject to the same ethics protocols as in-person research. The same goes for gaining access to online materials where there is a reasonable expectation of privacy, as in the case of internet chat room discussions, email, and the postings of organizations with restricted memberships, such as self-help groups. In these situations, both researchers and research participants have to be especially vigilant, as it is relatively easy to conduct covert research online. A researcher could quite easily pose as a regular participant in a self-help chat room for people who engage in self-harm, and then use the material as data for a qualitative study. But doing so would be equivalent to joining an in-person discussion group and not revealing one's identity as a researcher. The ethical implications of covert research discussed earlier in this chapter apply to such a situation.

a more positive picture of what was going on in Mississippi (Wolfe 2019). As this and other examples suggest, researchers can influence public understandings of important social trends, and their methodological choices reflect a range of motivations.

Considering Ethics in Research

As we have discussed in this chapter, researchers should reflect upon ethics at every stage of the research process. Early instances of exploitative research led to the development of shared professional agreements outlining characteristics of ethical research. These principles are brought to life as researchers plan for how to do ethical research. Professional bodies, such as IRBs, offer oversight to ensure researchers are accountable to their participants and the institutions (often colleges and universities) under whose authority they conduct their work. Researchers must ensure that their participants voluntarily consent to participate, take measures to protect their participants' privacy, and be certain that benefits of participation outweigh potential harms. Professional organizations, such as the American Sociological Association and university IRBs, have guidelines to advise researchers on taking ethics into account, but it is typical for ethical dilemmas to arise. In order to ensure they conduct ethical studies, researchers must reflect on ethics at every stage of the process, consider ethical challenges unique to their particular methodologies or study population, and be mindful of how power differences might influence their conduct and their participants' experiences.

In the following chapters of the book, we turn to the parameters that researchers consider in early stages of their research: deciding how they will measure the variables and concepts they intend to study (measurement) and how to choose the people who will participate in their study (sampling).

Key Points

Introduction: Why Are Research Ethics Important?

- Research ethics are the standards that guide researchers' decisions and define what choices are considered acceptable and unacceptable.
- The ethical considerations enacted on behalf of the researcher reflect the integrity of a study and the reputation in the social sciences as a whole.
- Ethical considerations should be updated and maintained throughout the research process.

The History of Research Ethics

- Early examples of abusive and unethical research, such as Nazi medical experiments and the Tuskegee syphilis study, inspired the development of professional ethical standards.
- The Belmont Report, which was written after the mistreatment of participants in the Tuskegee Syphilis study was exposed, outlines three ethical principles to uphold when conducting research with human subjects: Respect for Persons, Beneficence, and Justice.

Institutional Oversight and Research Ethics

- An institutional review board (IRB) is a committee responsible for overseeing all research involving human participants conducted through a particular college or university.
- Some research methodologies have unique ethical concerns that are not always easy to assess using strict institutional rules of the IRB; these call for more specific understanding and consideration.

Key Ethical Principles in Research

- There are three core ethical principles researchers must follow: informed consent/voluntary participation, confidentiality, and harm protection.

- It is necessary that research participants participate voluntarily, that they not be coerced into participating, and that they be made aware of any risks and benefits of their participation.
- Purposeful deception is a controversial research tactic, and examples like the Milgram experiment studying authority raise questions about informed consent procedures.
- Keeping participants' identities and records private is an important element of research ethics.
- A researcher's primary concerns should be to ensure that the people being studied are not harmed by their participation and to remember that their participants' well-being is of paramount importance.

Ethics as a Question of Power and Social Justice

- When planning and carrying out studies, researchers must think about their positionality and how it could affect the participants' experiences and possibly reinforce oppressive social conditions.

- Material that is publicly available and protected by law (e.g., official publications, third-party interviews, newspapers, whether online or in print) can be used for research without having to obtain informed consent, provided the researcher follows relevant laws and regulations.

Considering Ethics in Research

- Professional organizations help determine whether a study follows key ethical principles and offer support for researchers during the research process.
- Even when following agreed-upon ethical principles, it is common for ethical dilemmas to arise during research.
- Researchers must consider ethics at every stage of the process and consider unique power dynamics or experiences of their participants that might affect their experiences.

Questions for Review

1. How are ethical issues relevant to social research?
2. What was the Nuremberg Code? Why was it developed, and how did it impact research ethics?
3. How did anti-Black racism factor into the Tuskegee syphilis study? What resulted from the study being exposed?
4. What are the three main tenets of the Belmont Report?
5. What is an IRB, and what does it regulate?
6. What are some unique ethical considerations in different types of research, and how might an IRB deal with those?
7. What are the three key ethical principles researchers must follow?
8. What are some of the difficulties involved in implementing the principle of informed consent when doing ethnographic research?

9. Under what conditions might deception in social research be justified?
10. Why are privacy and confidentiality so important in research? What consequences could arise if these cannot be guaranteed?
11. What is meant by "harm to participants"?
12. What is meant by "balancing harms and benefits"?
13. How can Milgram's "electric-shock" experiment and Humphreys' *Tearoom Trade* study be used to illustrate issues of research ethics?
14. How are power differences related to ethics?
15. Describe some of the controversies over power and social research, and how these relate to ethical principles.
16. How might researchers best deal with ethical dilemmas they face during the research process?

Portfolio Exercise

Imagine that as part of your research topic, you decided to conduct a study using human participants. Consider how you might ethically invite people to participate in your study. Write a short letter to inform potential research participants about your research, how it will be conducted, and what the potential risks and benefits of participation are. Be sure to include assurance of confidentiality, a depiction of how their data will be stored, and how you intend to write about what you learn (for example, writing a class paper or publishing a journal article).

Interactive Activities

1. Divide into small breakout groups that meet either (1) synchronously in person or online or (2) asynchronously. The groups should discuss 2–3 of the controversial studies described in this chapter (Milgram, Humphreys, Goffman, Venkatesh, Regnerus, Parisi). Half the groups will support claim "a" below, and half should support claim "b."

   With your group, discuss and write down supports for your assigned claim, making reference to the key points raised in the chapter:

   a. This study was, on balance, ethical.
   b. This study was, on balance, unethical.

   After your discussion, present your group's argument to the class, either in person or online. The class as a whole will then identify compelling points that each group presented and decide which group has made the strongest case. Reflect on your conclusions about the studies' ethics and the challenges involved in designating each example as simply ethical or unethical.

2. Divide into breakout groups. Each should focus on one of the main ethical principles: informed consent/voluntary participation, confidentiality, and harm protection.

   With your group, gather information about your assigned principle by using the questions below and prepare a presentation in which you explain the principle to the class. In a synchronous online or in-person class with a larger number of students, presentations can take place with multiple breakout groups created (each with all three principles represented), or groups who have been assigned the same ethical principle can be guided by the instructor as to which information they should present on to the whole class group. In an asynchronous environment, multiple discussion groups can be created that each have all three subgroups included. The presentation should address these questions:

   a. How would you define this principle? What are the overall definition and characteristics of this ethical principle? Why is it important for researchers to follow this principle?
   b. How do researchers follow this principle? What measures should researchers do to ensure they follow the principle? What specific actions should they take, and what general things should they think about and consider?
   c. What are examples of dilemmas researchers face when trying to follow this principle? What challenges, complexities, and concerns might come up when researchers attempt to follow the principle?

3. Watch the documentary on the Zimbardo–Stanford Prison Experiment (www.youtube.com/watch?v=yUZpB57PfHs). In class or online, discuss the following questions:

   a. To what degree did the study follow the key ethical principles of informed consent/voluntary participation, confidentiality, and harm protection?
   b. What are your reflections on the issue of power differentials as an ethical concern in this study? Think about how the study was carried out, how the findings were reported, and any conflicts of interest the researcher had.

Online Resources

- Thomas Blass's Stanley Milgram website provides information on the famous psychologist: **http://www.stanleymilgram.com**

- The University of Southern Indiana provides examples of IRB submissions and reviewer checklists. **https://www.usi.edu/ospra/institutional-review-board-irb/irb-examples/**

For more resources please visit
www.oup.com/he/bryman-reck-fields1e

PART II
Concepts and Cases

Two concerns span all social research approaches: What concepts and ideas will the researcher work with, and what events, objects, people, or cases will they study? These are questions of measurement and sampling—methodological issues that involve a lot of terms. For example, discussions of measurement usually include talk of concepts, operationalization, conceptualization, reliability, and validity; sampling involves discussions of probability and nonprobability, error, and sample size. While it will be important to be able to recognize and define these terms, it's more important that you understand the bigger question: How can researchers best translate our abstract notions about the world into precise and clearly defined ideas that we can systematically observe in the social world? The precision of researchers' concepts and observations help make their research findings more convincing and compelling to the audiences they're trying to reach.

◀ *Moods and Modes*, by Ellie Balk, www.elliebalk.com. The mural captures the moods of Brooklyn high school students based on their social interactions over a 10-day period. Each square in the mural represents a person. The frame color identifies the age group. The inside circle identifies the different modes of communication, and the background colors represent the emotions associated with interactions. Used with permission of the artist.

3

How Do Researchers Identify and Evaluate Social Concepts?
Measurement

▲ Photo by STR/AFP via Getty Images

To ensure that their observations reflect something meaningful about social life, researchers create and rely on systems of measurement. This term reflects a commitment to defining social phenomena, even when they—and social life in general—are complex and ambiguous. Through measurement, researchers strive to clarify the ideas that drive a study, specify and define concepts to describe those ideas, and develop strategies for observing these concepts in the real world.

Reading this chapter will help you to

- understand general approaches to measuring concepts in social research;

- apply strategies for defining and implementing concepts (i.e., conceptualization and operationalization);

- describe the role of previous research and theory building in developing concepts;

- recognize measurement concerns specific to qualitative and quantitative research;

- chart the path from concepts to variables;

- identify levels of measurement; and

- evaluate the reliability and validity of measures.

You have probably encountered online quizzes that will tell you, for example, which Disney character you most resemble or what career best suits you. You probably sense that these quizzes are silly; however, you might also suspect that you're much more like Elsa than Anna or you'd make a better lawyer than veterinarian.

Your faith in such quizzes—as shaky or as strong as it may be—indicates your confidence that they reveal something about you, your personality, and your future. As you consider whether the questions are meaningful and the results are accurate, you are assessing whether the questions collectively capture the elusive idea of "suitability" or "personality." You may also wonder whether retaking the test would yield the same results.

As we raise questions about the meaning of these tests or even dismiss them outright, we are doing more than deciding to take or not to take an online quiz. We are also asking about measurement—how we define the ideas, experiences, and outcomes that interest us and the integrity of the tools we use to capture the relationships among them.

Introduction: The Task of Measurement

Measurement is the process of defining, observing, and recording ideas, experiences, and outcomes of interest—such as an online quiz that promises to describe your personality or identify a suitable profession. The term suggests precision, for example, a measuring tape determining the length of a piece of fabric down to 1/16th of an inch. Like tailors, social researchers strive for accuracy, but their tools and units of measurement are often less fixed. Researchers are interested in abstractions like social norms, opportunity and stratification, and unintended consequences. To measure these ideas, researchers develop conceptual definitions of them, look for indicators of their existence in the real world, and ask questions. The measurement tools required to answer those questions involve as much ambiguity as precision due to the complexities of the social world—how do we capture the many factors that make up a personality or contribute to an occupational outcome? For social researchers, the task is fourfold: to be as accurate as

---

measurement   The process of defining, observing, and recording ideas, experiences, and outcomes of interest.

Although social researchers, like tailors, strive for accuracy in measurement, why might the precision of a tape measure be inappropriate when studying social life?

possible, to recognize potential ambiguities, to guard against mismeasurement, and to understand how ambiguities and mismeasurement may shape a study's results.

Identifying and Measuring Concepts

Social research is a science of abstractions. Let's think through a hypothetical study that asks, "Do students generally have enough money to pay off-campus rent?" This seemingly straightforward question is complicated: What's the best way to find out how much money students have? Should we get details about their personal income or that of anyone supporting them? Maybe we should also consider whether they have savings, expect to inherit money or property, or rely on student loans. And we might want to ask about their monthly expenses so we understand how rent fits into a broader financial picture. Once we decide *what* to measure, the question of *how* to measure remains. Should we ask study participants to report their incomes and expenses? Or should we ask for copies of their tax returns, financial aid forms, pay stubs, or monthly bills? Maybe we should consult public records or existing data on housing trends or the cost of living, if they're available. Even these precise measures may not fully capture how students fare in an expensive rental market. We may want to ask similarly complicated questions about the quality of the housing they find or the stress they endure while looking for a home.

The success of this study—like any other—depends on the practical strategies that researchers develop for observing and analyzing the abstractions that interest them. These strategies are methods of measurement. Researchers must be clear about what abstract dynamics they want to study and specifically define them. This process is necessary for devising a plan for observing these dynamics in the real world. The credibility of the study's findings rests on the appropriateness of its measurement strategies— that is, the extent to which the methods of observing and making sense of the world offer consistent and meaningful accounts of the topics that interest us. Several methods are available to help researchers assess and ensure the usefulness of their measurement tools, as we will discuss in this chapter.

Why Measure?

As our discussion suggests, there are many reasons to pay careful attention to measurement.

First, measurement helps researchers *describe and determine the relationship between concepts*. If we accurately measure income, rent, and other monthly expenses, we should have a compelling picture of the financial constraints that students face when housing costs rise. We will have a sound measure of their income and expenses and will understand costs in their local rental market. Measurement will allow us to describe accurately the relationship between the broader economy and students' ability to secure housing. As we chart this relationship across different income levels and a range of housing markets, we will begin to understand that cost of living may compromise students' ability to complete a post-secondary degree.

Second, measurement allows researchers to *delineate meaningful differences between people*. Although researchers may easily distinguish between people in terms of broad categories, finer distinctions are often more difficult to recognize. As we consider our hypothetical study, we may want to distinguish between not only annual incomes but also the cost of living in different cities and neighborhoods. We may also want to note the different demands faced by students whose families offer financial support and those who are financially independent.

Third, measurement *provides a consistent device for gauging such distinctions*. A measure's results should not be affected by either the time at which it is administered or the person who administers it. The measure should generate consistent results *unless* the phenomenon or characteristic being studied has changed. Across our hypothetical study, measures of rent and other living expenses should come from a consistent source. In other words, if we decide to ask people to report their rent and other expenses, we need to use that strategy with everyone—not ask some students about their housing costs, use university records to ascertain the cost for other students, and then compare those figures. Similarly, those measures and the data they produce should be consistent regardless of who is using them; two researchers working independently to understand the rent–income relationship should arrive at similar numbers. Consistency allows researchers to trust that the variations they witness are due to real changes in the social phenomena they observed, not to faulty measurement.

What Is a Concept?

Concepts describe the ideas, phenomena, people, and patterns that interest researchers. These terms provide the foundation of any measurement strategy and the building blocks for the analysis and theory that emerge from social research. We have already introduced several concepts in this chapter, including income, housing, off-campus, and monthly expenses. We have encountered others in previous chapters, such as

> anti-Black racism,
> borders,
> educational attainment,
> gangs,
> harm,
> mindfulness,
> sexuality education,
> terminal illness.

Each term represents a concept chosen by researchers to describe elements of the social world that are significant to the phenomena they hope to understand.

---

concept A general or abstract idea that describes observations and ideas about some aspect of the social world.

In Box 3.1, we identify concepts at the core of Adia Harvey Wingfield's (2009) research on the glass escalator phenomenon, a counterpart to the glass ceiling. Wingfield is one of many researchers interested in what factors might facilitate or inhibit professional advancement and success. Responding to Christine Williams' research findings that men are frequently on an invisible stairway moving steadily upward when they work in feminized or female-dominated occupations (1992), Wingfield considered whether *all* men

As an analogy for career advancement, the glass escalator suggests that not everyone is moving up. What might cause the professional escalator to bring some employees down?

experience this advantage. Examining the racial identities of men doing what's often considered "women's work," she found that the effect was inconsistent. The glass escalator, she argues, is "a function not only of gendered advantage but of racial privilege as well" (2009, 6). In other words, Whiteness and masculinity account for white men's ability to "ride a glass escalator to success" (2009, 13) in feminized occupations; BIPOC men do not have the same opportunities. We will return to Wingfield's article throughout this chapter's discussion of measurement.

---

conceptualization The description or clarification of a concept's meaning, often in the form of a dictionary definition.

---

operationalization An explanation outlining the process through which a researcher will observe the presence, absence, or degree of a concept's existence.

Conceptualization and Operationalization

Like any researcher, Wingfield had to break her abstract formulations into more specific elements in order to study them. To do so, she followed a specific set of principles researchers employ in the measurement process. She **conceptualized** and **operationalized** the terms at the center of her research.

Conceptualization

Sometimes researchers can rely on everyday understandings of the concepts that interest them. For example, readers can understand Wingfield's concept of "minority men" to point broadly to BIPOC men. The implicit definition resonates with common-sense understandings and does not seem to require further explanation. Many concepts are anything but straightforward to define, however, and a researcher might look to ideas from previous theory or research to aid in their conceptualization.

BOX 3.1 Identifying Concepts

The following abstract—with main concepts highlighted—is from Wingfield's article, "Racializing the Glass Escalator: Reconsidering Men's Experiences with Women's Work":

> Many men who work in women's professions experience a glass escalator effect that facilitates their advancement and upward mobility within these fields. Research finds that subtle aspects of the interactions, norms, and expectations in women's professions push men upward and outward into the higher-status, higher-paying, more "masculine" positions within these fields. Although most research includes minority men, little has explicitly considered how racial dynamics color these men's encounters with the mechanisms of the glass escalator. In this article, the author examines how intersections of race and gender combine to shape experiences for minority men in the culturally feminized field of nursing and finds that the upward mobility implied by the glass escalator is not uniformly available to all men who do "women's work." The author concludes that the glass escalator is a racialized concept and a gendered one and considers the implications of this for future studies of men in feminized occupations (Wingfield 2009, 5).

These concepts fall into three categories: *people*, *locations*, and *processes*. People include men and minority men. In other studies, locations might mean national, city, or institutional boundaries; here, they are more abstract and refer to women's professions and masculine positions. Processes are often even more abstract, as they relate to how people interact with and adjust to the social forces and conditions that shape their exchanges with other people and institutions. Processes that interest Wingfield relate to social influences and their outcomes, including

- the glass escalator effect;
- advancement and upward mobility;
- interactions, norms, and expectations; and
- intersections of race and gender.

Across the three categories, the concepts grow increasingly abstract. Defining processes like advancement and upward mobility may be especially difficult. Nevertheless, all concepts involve some complexity and thus require careful definition, as we discuss in the next section.

Conceptualization Using Theory and Research

When we define concepts, we might employ something akin to a dictionary definition. If we conceptualize "work," we might define it as labor one does for compensation. Yet Wingfield was interested in *feminized* work—a more specific term than the overall concept of "work."

One way to approach defining such abstract terms is to look to social theory, which presents ideas about the social world that can help researchers better understand the abstract concepts they're studying. Sociologists analyzing work and gender have crafted useful theories about the experiences of workers who are the numerical minority in their fields. Kanter (1977) theorized about the experiences of those she termed "tokens," highly visible workers who constitute the numerical minority in their field and who face isolation and stereotyping from co-workers that compromise their success. This theory has influenced a great deal of research in the sociology of work, and many researchers have utilized this conceptualization in their analyses of women in male-dominated jobs.

Wingfield similarly looked to previous research in her conceptualizations. She uses the concept "women's professions" interchangeably with "feminized professions" in her abstract and offers a definition in her opening paragraph: "jobs predominantly filled by women [that] require 'feminine' traits such as nurturing, caring, and empathy" (2009, 5). This definition is Wingfield's own, but she draws on decades of research on work and gender that argues sex segregation is important to people's occupational experiences. Similarly, she describes advancement and upward mobility as "entry into better paying, higher status positions" (2009, 6).

As discussed in Chapter 1, the feedback loop between theory and research is a cornerstone of empirical work; this dialogue also helps researchers develop stronger, more accurate measurement strategies. Researchers who use Kanter's "tokens" concept could test the degree to which this theory was useful in explaining people's experiences at work. Though the concept often rings true when women are the tokens in male-dominated professions, Williams found that white men are fast-tracked to leadership in feminized professions because they easily form relationships with supervisors and mentors, are perceived to be natural leaders, and can distance themselves from the stigma of femininity. Being a token was a disadvantage for women and offered men an advantage. Williams developed her glass escalator concept to describe this phenomenon, which she conceptualizes as the "subtle mechanisms in place that enhance [men's] positions in [women's] professions" (Wingfield, citing Williams 1995, 108).

Wingfield wondered how gendered advantage might be racialized. She defined gendered racism as the ways in which "racial stereotypes, images, and beliefs are grounded in gendered ideals" (2009, 9), citing other theorists and researchers as instrumental in helping her develop this conceptualization. The new concept and conceptualization she offered meant that her measurement strategy had to account for the ways that interactions, norms, and expectations at work are not only gendered but also racialized. With a general understanding of these terms in hand, she was poised to detail how gender and race influence access to the glass escalator.

---

indicator Something that points to, provides evidence of, or otherwise measures a concept.

But how does Wingfield's conceptualization of gendered racism allow her to document this dynamic in the real world? To understand how this concept plays out in people's lives requires the next step in the measurement process: operationalization.

Operationalization

With the move from conceptualization to operationalization, measurement becomes more concrete and focused as we specify what procedures we will use to measure the existence of the concept. Let's return to our earlier tailor analogy. A tailor might design an elegant suit that fits the client well and is appropriate to the particular occasion. When the time comes to make the suit, other details become important. What fabric is available? How do the colors look against the client's complexion? Does it hang well on the client's body? Can the client afford the fabric the tailor has chosen? The concept of the suit begins to take practical shape—it is operationalized.

Similarly, measurement strategy takes practical shape as the researcher moves from conceptualization to operationalization. With her concepts in place, Wingfield next needs to determine how to observe the phenomena that interest her. Will she observe BIPOC men from a range of racialized and Indigenous categories? Which feminized professions will she consider? How will she define advancement and upward mobility in her study? How will she recognize interactions, norms, and expectations? This is an empirical study; these abstract ideas need to become clearly named characteristics that the researcher can observe in the real word. Figure 3.1 demonstrates how a term moves from the abstract to the concrete in the measurement process.

In the operationalization process, researchers choose what observable characteristics will indicate the existence of their abstract concept in the real world. The specific pieces of evidence in the real world are described as **indicators** of the concept; these are factors that show the presence, absence, or degree to which the concepts exist. Sometimes indicators are simple measures: the total income reported on a tax return is an indicator of a person's annual salary, and registration as a Republican, Democrat, Green, Libertarian, or Independent is an indicator of a political

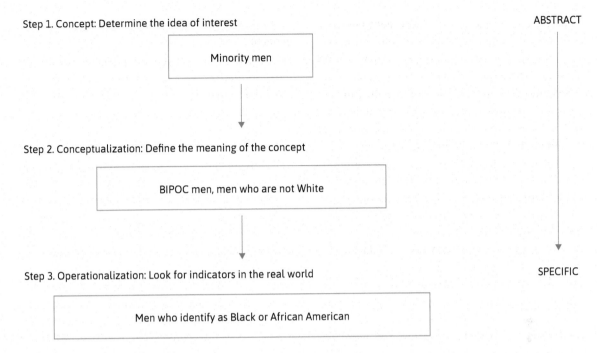

Step 1. Concept: Determine the idea of interest

Minority men

ABSTRACT

Step 2. Conceptualization: Define the meaning of the concept

BIPOC men, men who are not White

Step 3. Operationalization: Look for indicators in the real world

SPECIFIC

Men who identify as Black or African American

FIGURE 3.1 **The process of measurement.**

Methods in Motion | Proposition 54

In October 2003, California's statewide ballot included Proposition 54, officially known as the Racial Privacy Initiative, which intended to

> Amend [the state] Constitution to prohibit state and local governments from using race, ethnicity, color, or national origin to classify current or prospective students, contractors or employees in public education, contracting, or employment operations.

Advocates heralded the proposition as a step toward a "colorblind society." In some ways, it resonated with some researchers' claims that race is a biological fallacy and social construction, not a social reality. However, the American Sociological Association (ASA) issued a formal statement against the initiative. The ASA argued that such research "allows scholars to document how race shapes social ranking, access to resources, and life experiences; and advances understanding of this important dimension of social life, which in turn advances social justice" (2003, 4). Race may not be a biological fact, but "when a concept is central to societal organization, examining how, when, and why people in that society use the concept is vital to understanding the organization and consequences of social relationships" (2003, 1).

Without studies of race, the ASA argued, we cannot understand how race organizes a host of social relations, including whom we marry, parent, and form political alliances with. If we don't collect data about race, we also can't notice how people's access to resources—education, health care, housing, and more—are stratified according to race. Race doesn't cause social disparities, but disparities are often racialized. Measurement allows us to document and address those patterns.

affiliation. In other cases, an indicator refers to an indirect measure of a concept. For example, concerns about money expressed in an interview may be used as an indirect measure of financial security. Declared income may be a direct measure of personal income but becomes indirect if used as an indicator of social class. Political party affiliation would be considered an indirect indicator of political attitude.

Table 3.1 outlines the conceptualization and operationalization of terms in Wingfield's study. As you look over this chart, note a key aspect of operationalization: we often ask questions when we operationalize concepts and look for their indicators in the real world. Because Wingfield focused her study on Black and African American men's experiences, she asked, "How would you describe your racial identity?" A response of Black and/or African American indicates belonging to that racial category. Wingfield defines the more abstract term "advancement and upward mobility" to mean entry into better-paying, higher-status positions. She measured Black men's advancement and upward mobility in nursing by asking questions about their work histories, current experiences, and career goals.

Although Wingfield used single indicators, some concepts are more complex and require multiple indicators. For instance, simply stating a political party affiliation does not capture all the relevant meaning in the underlying concept and may even lead to mismeasurement—the absence of a party affiliation does not indicate the absence of a political attitude. Many concepts have multiple ways of manifesting themselves in the real world and would be considered multidimensional. If you were interested in student satisfaction with school and simply asked "How satisfied are you in school?" you might miss the complexity of the situation. Students who describe themselves as not satisfied may like some parts of school, just as those who claim to be satisfied may dislike specific aspects. Yet specificity does not always make measurement more effective: asking students how satisfied they are with their grades would give only partial insight because it would miss satisfaction with friendships, the educational experience itself, or campus safety. In such cases, social researchers note that many concepts consist of multiple facets, which are described as dimensions. Researchers use multiple-indicator measures to capture multiple dimensions. To put it simply, when researchers ask a number of questions, they can explore a wider range of issues covered by the concept. Table 3.1 has examples of operationalization using single and multiple indicators.

Our discussion of Wingfield's work has focused on conceptualization and operationalization in a qualitative interview study. Wingfield has provided an important starting point because her research is conceptually important, complicated, and clear. However, many

How might racialized and gendered notions of care affect access to the glass escalator?

TABLE 3.1 | Concepts, Conceptualization, and Operationalization in Wingfield's "Racializing the Glass Escalator"

Concept	Conceptualization	Operationalization Using a Single Indicator
Minority men	BIPOC men, men who are not white	Men who identify as Black or African American
Women's professions	Jobs predominantly filled by women and requiring "feminine" traits (e.g., nurturing, caring, and empathy)	Employment in nursing

Concept	Conceptualization	Operationalization Using Multiple Indicators
Advancement and upward mobility	Entry into better-paying, higher-status positions	Participants' responses to questions about work histories, current experiences, and career goals as nurses
Interactions, norms, and expectations	Relationships with colleagues and supervisors; suitability for nursing and higher-status work; establishing distance from femininity	Participants' descriptions of patients' and colleagues' responses to and perceptions of them at work and their own gendered behavior at work

researchers who work with qualitative data find that conventional measurement standards are ill-suited to their work. The language of measurement connotes numbers (remember the tailor's measuring tape), which often feels more suitable to quantitative analysis. Nevertheless, principles of accuracy hold in both qualitative and quantitative research: all researchers must systematically define, observe, and record ideas, experiences, and outcomes of interest.

BOX 3.2 Measuring Space

Technology increasingly allows researchers to measure abstractions, including the spatial organization of social life. Alexis N. Martinez, Jennifer Lorvick, and Alex H. Kral (2014) considered questions of how people live in and move through cities when they studied the implementation and accessibility of health promotion programs and services. To better understand injection drug users' (IDUs') access to HIV- and overdose-prevention services, Martinez et al. used geographic information systems (GIS) software to map intersections between IDUs' activity spaces and the locations of syringe exchange programs (SEPs) in San Francisco. The authors conceptualized activity spaces as "the local areas within which people move or travel in the course of their daily activities" and operationalized the term by determining where participants slept at night, hung out during the day, and used drugs over a 6-month period (2014, 517). Analysis of the GIS suggested that large activity spaces may mean that IDUs are more likely to have an HIV- and overdose-prevention service within their activity. However, those IDUs who move in relatively small activity spaces with SEPs are most likely to have access to and use the services. Martinez et al. helped answer a pressing question: how can we ensure the people who need health services have access to them?

Measurement in Quantitative Research

In quantitative research, concepts are usually described as variables. They may be possible *causes* of a certain aspect of the social world (**independent variables**) or be *caused* (or *influenced*) *by* another variable (**dependent variables**). A single concept may be an independent variable in one context and a dependent variable in another. For example, social mobility might provide an explanation (How does being either upwardly or downwardly mobile affect Asian American men's political attitudes?) or be something to be explained (What conditions lead some Asian American men to be upwardly mobile and others not?). Concepts may also be used for descriptive or comparative purposes. A researcher

---

independent variable A characteristic, social condition, or behavior that a researcher considers likely to affect other characteristics, conditions, or behaviors.

---

dependent variable A measured behavior, characteristic, or condition that a researcher considers likely to be affected by other aspects of the social world.

---

might be interested in describing changes in the degree of social mobility among Asian American men over time or in comparing variations among levels of social mobility among different communities of BIPOC men.

The same care that Wingfield demonstrated in the conceptualization and operationalization of her concepts goes into quantitative measurement when working with variables. Quantitative researchers must define the broad phenomenon of interest to them and then ensure that the operationalization resonates with that conceptualization. For example, Catherine Taylor (2010) shares Wingfield's interest in the support available to men and women in occupations dominated by another gender. Taylor has studied this availability in mixed-sex, female-dominated, and male-dominated occupations. Because the conceptualization of "occupations" is crucial to her study, she drew a distinction between gender-dominated workplaces and occupations: while a woman may be one of relatively few women surgeons nationally, she might work in an all-women surgical practice. Though there may be many women in a particular workplace, ideas about women's limited capacities as physicians might still compromise their access to support in the occupation as a whole, beyond the walls of their everyday workplace (2010, 190–191).

With this understanding in mind, Taylor had to determine how to measure occupational sex segregation. She created a measure, drawing on existing survey data. As she explains, "The proportion of women in the participant's occupation is coded as the actual proportion of women, according to nationally representative data" (2010, 197). She linked the occupation of

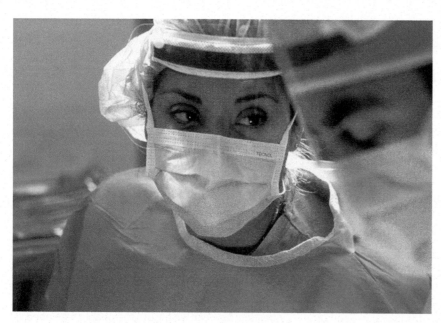

How could the gender composition of a hospital's surgical team affect a surgeon's experiences of collegiality and isolation at work?

each participant in the 1995 National Survey of Midlife Development in the United States to the number of women who reported being in that occupation in the 1995 Current Population Survey. Taylor concludes, "The resulting measure was used to compute the proportion of women in each participant's occupation in 1995" (2010, 197). This operationalized concept adheres to her conceptual definition by focusing on the actual national gender composition of the occupation, not on the individual workplace or the perceived gender composition of the occupation.

Levels of Measurement

In quantitative research, operational measures often involve assigning numbers to the different values the measure might yield. (These numbers help make quantitative analysis possible, as we discuss in Chapter 14.) Suppose that a researcher constructing a survey decides that the concept "gender" will have four possible values: woman, man, nonbinary, and other. Once the survey data are collected, the researcher needs to code the answers by entering them into a statistical analysis software package. It's time to assign numbers, and the researcher decides on the following:

0 = woman
1 = man
2 = nonbinary
3 = other

Levels of measurement help us understand what sense to make of those numbers. Do the numbers 0–3 suggest a hierarchy of categories, the possibility of "zero gender"? Or are the numerical categories simply convenient names for longer terms? Notions of nominal, ordinal, interval, and ratio level measurement clarify the situation, as we will see in the following sections.

How would you write survey questions that recognize gender diversity and make a research interview a good experience for respondents?

No matter what the level, measurement should be mutually exclusive and exhaustive. To be **mutually exclusive**, categories should not overlap; each instance of the variable should fit into one category only. In our example, those who are women are not men or nonbinary; each of these gender categories

---

mutually exclusive   The quality of measurement categories for which each case fits into only one response or variable category.

---

exhaustive   The quality of measurement categories that anticipates and meaningfully sorts all possible responses to a survey item and thus all potential units of analysis.

---

nominal measurement   The measurement level in which categories only name phenomena and do not rank order or assign any consistent numerical value.

is distinct and someone who identifies with one of them does not fit into the others. The categories are **exhaustive** if they represent all possibilities and thus allow every case to be categorized. Every participant in our study should be able to state their gender identity using the options we present. The "other category," as you may suspect, is crucial to our measure of gender being exhaustive. Box 3.3 discusses the ways measuring gender using only these four categories would be limiting and suggests alternatives.

Nominal Measurement

In **nominal measurement**, the categories are simply names. "Woman, man, nonbinary, and other" describe a range of responses to a question about gender identities. The numbers assigned to them suggest no rank order or other difference in value.

BOX 3.3   **Measuring Gender and Sexual Fluidity**

J. E. Sumerau et al. (2017) call on social researchers to develop measures of gender and sexuality that reflect fluidity. As they note, "Queer Theory called for scholarship to move beyond binary categorizations into an exploration of the variation and nuance of contemporary and historical bio-social-psychological existence" (2017, 645). A starting point would be unpacking gendered identities that some see in overly binary or simplistic terms. For instance, in Wingfield's research, a conceptualization of "men" might be people who live and identify as men, whether they were assigned male at birth or not. This queering of measurement calls attention to the ways sex and gender are assumed to be binary and recognizes the complexity of people's lived genders. While qualitative researchers have begun to embrace this approach, quantitative researchers have been slower to answer the call. Sumerau and colleagues suggest quantitative researchers heed the call and consider expanding

- gender response categories on surveys to include, for example, woman, man, transgender, cisgender, agender, gender fluid, bigender, androgynous, and other, or an open-ended question for which participants write in their answers, and
- sexualities measurements beyond heterosexual, lesbian, gay, and bisexual to include, for example, romantic, gendered, racialized, monogamous, and polyamorous desires and pleasures.

These suggestions may be challenging, but the authors also believe that such practices "may help quantitative sociology 'come out of the closet' and reclaim its empirical and methodological rigor" (2017, 654). If a researcher included gender and sexuality as important concepts in a study and did not measure all these various identities and experiences, what might be misunderstood or ignored in the analysis?

Ordinal Measurement

In **ordinal measurement**, the categories can be rank ordered. For example, Taylor included a measure of education in her study, with the following categories:

- some grade school to some high school
- GED or graduated high school
- some college (no bachelor's degree)
- graduated college or other professional degree

These categories fall into an order—from completing some grade school to earning a degree. However, the distance between categories is neither consistent nor meaningful. The distance from some grade school or high school to completing high school is not necessarily the same as that between completing high school and completing some college. Quantitative researchers working with survey data often create ordinal variables by using **Likert scales** to ask questions (see Box 3.4).

---

ordinal measurement The measurement level in which named categories place observed cases and variation into rank order.

Likert scale A widely used format in which respondents are typically asked their degree of agreement with a series of attitude statements that together form a multiple-indicator measure. The scale is designed to measure the intensity of respondents' feelings about an issue.

BOX 3.4 Using Likert Questions when Measuring Attitudes

Investigating attitudes is a prominent area in survey research. One of the most common techniques for this investigation is the Likert scale. Named after its developer, Rensis Likert, this scale is a multiple-indicator measure of the intensity of feelings about a particular topic. Usually, the scale comprises a series of statements (known as "items") on an issue or theme, and participants indicate their level of agreement with each, using a five-point gauge from "strongly agree" to "strongly disagree" (seven-point and other formats are also used). There is normally a middle position of "neither agree nor disagree" or "undecided," indicating neutrality on the issue. A participant's reply on each item is scored, and the scores are then aggregated.

Variations on the typical format are scales referring to evaluation (for example, "very poor" to "very good") and frequency. Sandy E. James et al. (2016) used this setup in their comprehensive survey about transgender people's lives in the United States. For example, participants were presented with several items about how frequently leaders or members of their spiritual/religious communities had done such things as "Tell you that your religion/faith accepts you as a trans person," "Ask you to stop coming to services or faith community functions," "Accept you for who you are as a trans person," or "Ask you to meet with spiritual/religious leaders to stop you from being trans." Participants chose "Never," "Once or twice," "A few times," or "Many times."

There are several principles to remember when creating Likert items:

- Items are often phrased as statements, not questions.
- Items must all relate to the same object (in our example, experiences with one's religious community).
- Items that make up the scale should be interrelated and use varied phrasing so that some imply a positive view of the phenomenon of interest and others a negative one. For example, Michelle Fine et al. (2003) used 12 Likert scale questions to measure young people's attitudes toward police, including "When I go out, my family worries that I may have problems with the police" and "Most police are just trying to protect the public." The first implies a more negative and mistrustful view of police, the second a more positive one.

Interval and Ratio Measurement

By contrast, the distance between categories in **interval** and **ratio measurement** is meaningful and consistent. IQ and temperature are classic examples of interval measurement: the distance between 32 and 33 degrees Fahrenheit is equal to that between –5 and –6 degrees, and the 1-degree distance is meaningful. That is, we can make logical sense of the differences between the distances. A zero category is arbitrary: a temperature of 0 degrees does not indicate an absence of temperature; it is an arbitrarily named point in a range of possibilities.

Ratio measurement includes the possibility of a meaningful and non-arbitrary zero. Height and weight are ratio measurements because true zero values are possible; negative values are not.

When creating a measurement scheme for their variables, researchers have choices to make around levels of measurement (see Table 3.2 for a summary). Concepts can be measured at multiple levels of measurement, and multiple measures may be crucial to quantitative data analysis (see Chapter 14).

---

interval measurement   The measurement level in which distance between named categories is meaningful and consistent, zero categories are arbitrary, and negative values are possible.

---

ratio measurement   The measurement level in which distance between named categories is meaningful and consistent, a true zero category is possible, and negative values are not possible.

---

reliability   The research criterion concerned with the degree to which the measure of a concept is stable or consistent.

Reliability and Validity

The credibility of a study's findings rests on the reliability and validity of its measurement strategies—that is, the extent to which the methods of observing and making sense of the world offer consistent and accurate accounts of the topics that interest us. Both are essentially concerned with how adequately concepts have been measured.

Reliability

Reliability is concerned with the *consistency* of measures. Would repeatedly applying the same measurement technique to a research subject yield the same results? If the answer is yes, the measure is reliable. For example, if engineers' accounts of their work vary when asked on different occasions or if different findings are produced when different researchers use the test on the same people, the measure may be unreliable.

The reliability of a measurement strategy should be evident in three domains: stability over time, internal reliability, and inter-observer consistency.

Stability over Time

"Stability" refers to whether the results of a measure fluctuate as time progresses, assuming that what is being measured is not changing. If one administers a measure to a group and then repeats it, say, an hour, week, or month later, there should be little variation in the results. The most obvious way of testing a measure's stability is the *test–retest* method, which involves administering a test or measure on one occasion and re-administering it to the same sample on another occasion. That is,

---

TABLE 3.2 | Levels of Measurement

Level	Description
Nominal	Names only, with no rank order or other value (e.g., gender or sexual identity)
Ordinal	Rank-ordered named categories (e.g., level of education)
Interval	Named categories with meaningful and consistent distances, arbitrary zero categories, and possibly negative values (e.g., temperature)
Ratio	Named categories with meaningful and consistent distance and true zero category but no negative values (e.g., height)

Time 1 (T$_1$)   Time 2 (T$_2$)

Observation 1   Observation 2
(Obs$_1$)   (Obs$_2$)

One would expect to find a high correlation between Obs$_1$ and Obs$_2$. Those who score high on the first observation should also score high on the second, and those who score low on the first should score low on the second. If the correlation is low, the measure is unstable, implying that it cannot be relied upon.

Internal Reliability

A more common test for reliability is to determine whether multiple measures that are administered in *one sitting* are consistent—in other words, whether participants' scores on any one indicator tend to be related to their scores on the others. For example, on a scale created to measure attitudes toward climate change, people who agree with the statement that it is a significant threat will also likely agree it is important to make changes in how we affect the environment.

Two common tests of **internal reliability** are *Cronbach's alpha coefficient* and the *split-half*

method, measures of reliability that are computed mathematically in quantitative research. The former is a scale of 1 (perfect internal reliability) to 0 (no internal reliability); 0.80 is typically considered the minimum acceptable level, although many researchers accept 0.60. The latter test ensures that all parts of the test reliably measure what they are intended to by dividing it in half and comparing the results of each. The scores should be similar—a perfect positive correlation (complete internal consistency) would yield a correlation coefficient of 1; no correlation (no internal consistency) would produce a coefficient of 0.

Inter-Observer Consistency

When more than one researcher takes part in an activity involving subjective judgment—for example, recording observations or translating data into categories—their conclusions may differ. This problem can arise in a number of research contexts, including when answers to open-ended questions have to be categorized or in structured observation when observers

---

internal reliability The degree to which items that make up a scale or index are consistent or correlated.

Mixed Methods in Action | Workplace Discrimination Experienced by University Faculty

The research on workplace advancement consistently points to the prevalence of race and gender discrimination. In light of this finding, Ruth Enid Zambrana et al. (2017) explored the degree to which Mexican American faculty in research universities were encouraged early in life to pursue higher education and the quality of the mentorship available to them. They conducted a mixed method study—using an online survey, individual and group qualitative interviews, and a post-interview survey—and relied on multiple strategies to measure anti-Mexican bias, including a Perceived Gender, Race/Ethnicity, and Class Bias scale and open-ended interview questions. They used inter-observer consistency to ensure reliable coding of the interview data, so "each

interview was coded independently, line by line, by two trained qualitative coders; disagreements in coding were reconciled by a third independent coder" (2017, 462).

Every participant in this study reported discrimination. Isolation, stereotypes, and their colleagues' failure to address racial and gender equity all contributed to the discrimination that Mexican American faculty face. Early and active mentoring was a source of important support and guidance, and those faculty members whose mothers had more than a high school education had the greatest success securing mentorship. The team's finding highlights the importance of social capital—networks of relationships with positive and productive benefits for people.

have to decide how to classify participants' behavior. Is the person under observation "afraid," "concerned," or "just thinking" when reading about plans to decrease access to health care? Problems arise if observers classify a particular behavior differently. The Mixed Methods in Action box featuring Ruth Enid Zambrana and colleagues' research (2017) describes how researchers assess reliability using inter-observer consistency.

Validity

Validity is concerned with the *integrity* of a study's conclusions. Measurement validity refers to whether an indicator (or set of indicators) devised to gauge a concept actually does so. When people argue about whether an IQ score really measures intelligence levels, they are raising questions about the test's measurement validity in relation to the concept of intelligence.

Researchers use a variety of techniques to determine whether they have measured what they wanted, with some considering internal validity and others external validity.

Internal validity relates to causality (see Chapter 6) and asks the following questions: Could the cause be something else? Might there be a network of causes? In discussing issues of causality, it is common to refer to proposed causes as independent variables and the corresponding effect as the dependent variable. Internal validity raises the issue of how confident you can be that the independent variable impacts the dependent variable.

External validity involves whether a study's findings are applicable in settings outside the research

---

validity The research criterion concerned with the integrity of a study's conclusions.

---

face validity The type of validity achieved if, on inspection, an indicator appears to measure the concept in question.

---

concurrent validity The type of validity indicated by relating a measure to existing criterion or a different concept indicator to see if one predicts the other.

environment, particularly everyday or natural social settings. Sometimes the research setting is so artificial or so different from real life that we may question whether the results tell us anything about what people typically experience. The more the social scientist creates realistic settings, the greater the chance that the findings will be externally valid. Qualitative research tends to fulfill the requirement of external validity because it relies on data collected in naturally occurring situations and environments—for example, by spending months with people to observe their behavior or conducting open-ended interviews that allow in-depth exploration of ideas framed in cooperation with the participant.

Internal and external validity are addressed through tests of *face validity, concurrent validity, construct validity,* and *convergent validity.*

Face Validity

At a minimum, a researcher who develops a new measure should establish that it has **face validity**—that is, that the measure appears to reasonably reflect the content of the concept in question. Face validity can be established by asking those with expertise in the field to judge whether the measure seems to reflect the concept concerned. Alternatively, researchers can assess their own measures. Establishing this sort of validity is essentially an intuitive process; it is usually a first step for quantitative researchers concerned with the validity of their measures.

Concurrent Validity

Researchers can also seek to gauge a measure's **concurrent validity**. To do this, they explore a *criterion* that is relevant to the concept in question but that can differ from case to case (for example, from person to person). For example, as students' school satisfaction decreases, their days of missed school are assumed to increase. Thus, a researcher seeking to establish the concurrent validity of a new measure of school satisfaction might determine if students who are satisfied with school are less likely to be absent compared

BOX 3.5 A Case of Convergent Invalidity: Crime Statistics

Official reports about crime and victimization studies often provide different indications of the amount of crime in society. Two main sources of US crime statistics are the FBI's annual description of crimes reported in 18,000 jurisdictions across the country and the annual Bureau of Justice Statistics (BJS) survey of 90,000 US households. The latter asks participants 12 and older if they have been crime victims (even if they did not report the crimes). Such victimization data rou-

Police gather evidence at a murder scene. The crime will definitely be entered into the official crime statistics. Why will it become part of the official record while other crimes might not?

tinely indicates more crime than official police reports because many people do not report their experiences (due to inconvenience, embarrassment, mistrust of police, etc.).

This fact can help explain why these two sources show different information. Looking at the years 1993-2016, FBI data indicate that violent crimes decreased by 48% and the BJS shows a drop of 74%. In the same period, property crime was reported to decrease by 48% (FBI) and 66% (BJS; Gramlich 2018). Given that the BJS data include unreported crimes, this implies that both crime rates decreased even more significantly than FBI statistics suggest.

to those who are not satisfied. If there is no difference in absenteeism between the two groups, it is doubtful that the new measure gauges school satisfaction.

Construct Validity

When using **construct validity**, researchers note whether the way concepts relate to each other is consistent with what their theories would predict.

Suppose that a researcher wants to establish the construct validity of a measure of job satisfaction. Drawing on a theory that job satisfaction is influenced by the stimulation that comes from performing several

---

construct validity The type of validity established by determining whether concepts being measured relate empirically in the manner that relevant theories predict.

different activities, the researcher may anticipate that people who do routine jobs are less satisfied with their work than those who have greater opportunities for variety, complexity, and creativity. If these variables correlate in the expected manner, the measure in question has construct validity. But if those who do routine jobs are just as satisfied as those with more varied positions, the theorized relationship is weak or non-existent. In this situation, the measures used may be invalid, the deduction made from the theory may be misguided, or the theory may need revision. Whatever the problem, the researcher should probably seek another measure and try again.

Convergent Validity

Some researchers prefer to use **convergent validity** to determine a measure's validity. They compare the measure of a concept developed using one method to the measure of the same concept developed using another. For instance, if a questionnaire asks activists how much time they spend on various activities (such as attending meetings or participating in direct protest), its validity may be determined by directly observing the activists to see how much time they actually spend on them.

---

convergent validity The type of validity established by comparing two differently developed measures of one concept.

An interesting instance of convergent invalidity is described in Box 3.5. Crime surveys were consciously devised to serve as a check on official police statistics. The two sets of data are collected in different ways: official crime statistics are gathered as part of processing offenders in the criminal justice system, whereas crime victimization surveys provide data from interviews with members of the general public. Victimization surveys measure the crimes that people experience, as well as some experiences that may not be legally defined as crimes; they also omit certain crimes (for example, when someone presumes a stolen item is simply "lost"). Police statistics measure the crimes that people report, plus those that the police discover or choose to document. Moreover, not all crimes end up in official police statistics. In any case, the "true" volume of crime at any one time is almost always a contested notion (Reiner 2000).

Qualitative sociologist Howard S. Becker describes the measurement process as ideally a dialogue—a constant back and forth between ideas and data (1998, 152; see also Ragin (1992) 2014). That dialogue keeps researchers thinking regularly and repeatedly about their goals, their decisions, and their outcomes: what did we hope to measure, and what have we in fact measured? Engaged in that back and forth and with an eye to validity and reliability, researchers can offer study results with confidence.

Key Points

Introduction: What Is Measurement?

- The term "measurement" describes the systems used by social researchers to classify observations and ideas, reflecting their commitment to being precise and accurate in the face of the ambiguity of social life.

- Researchers are interested in abstractions like social norms, opportunity and stratification, and unintended consequences, and they must develop strategies to observe and analyze these abstractions.

Identifying and Measuring Concepts

- Researchers not only decide what to measure but also consider how they will measure it.

- Measurement allows researchers to determine relationships between concepts, delineate meaningful differences between people, and work as consistent devices for gauging distinctions.

- Concepts can be sorted into categories.

Conceptualization and Operationalization

- Researchers conceptualize and operationalize terms before using them in their research.
- Building on previous research and theorizing can strengthen conceptualizations and the credibility of measurement strategies.
- Observable characteristics of abstract concepts are called indicators.
- Social researchers use multiple-indicator measures to capture multiple dimensions or facets of a concept.

Measurement in Quantitative Research

- In quantitative research, concepts are described as variables, which are either independent or dependent.
- Operational measures often involve assigning numbers to the different values the measure might yield, simplifying the analysis process.
- Levels of measurement include nominal, ordinal, interval, and ratio.

Reliability and Validity

- The credibility of a study's findings rests on the reliability and validity of its measurement strategies.
- The reliability of a measurement strategy should demonstrate stability over time, internal reliability, and inter-observer consistency.
- Measurement validity refers to whether or not an indicator (or set of indicators) devised to gauge a concept works.
- Validity can be internal or external; tests of both include face validity, concurrent validity, construct validity, and convergent validity.

Questions for Review

1. What is the relationship between researchers' ideas about the world and the concepts they work with?
2. How do researchers contend with ambiguity and complexity in the social world?
3. In what ways are multiple indicators of a concept preferable to a single indicator?
4. What are the dangers of relying on a single indicator to measure a concept?
5. What role can theory play in conceptualization?
6. Describe the move from abstract to specific in the move from conceptualization to operationalization.
7. What role do indicators play in operationalization?

8. What does it mean for measurement categories to be both mutually exclusive and exhaustive?
9. Name and describe the different levels of measurement.
10. What is the test-retest method, and what is it used for?
11. What is the importance of inter-observer reliability in measurement?
12. What determines the external validity of a measure or concept?
13. What must a researcher compare to test convergent validity?
14. Discuss the following: "Whereas validity presupposes reliability, reliability does not presuppose validity."

Portfolio Exercise

Write your research question or hypothesis and highlight the concepts. Which ones will you measure and how will you measure them? To generate ideas, create a mind-map using pen and paper or an online platform. Consider the following concepts as they relate to your potential measures and research topic:

a. people/population,
b. behaviors,
c. locations,
d. opinions, and
e. processes.

Next, consider the specifics and select your research topic (this may change slightly over the course of your research). Then, create a second mind-map focusing on your topic and the concepts you've generated. Consider the following:

a. What are you measuring? Be specific.
b. How will you measure it?
c. Is your topic best suited for quantitative, qualitative or mixed methods research?
d. How can you test the validity of your measures?

e. What single or multiple indicators might you observe?
f. What conceptualized and operationalized terms might you use in relation to your research?

Interactive Activities

1. Find an online quiz, like the ones described at the beginning of this chapter. In a group, in person or online, answer the following questions:
   a. What concepts is the quiz claiming to illuminate or explain?
   b. How does the quiz define (or conceptualize) those concepts?
   c. What are the concepts' operational definitions?
   d. What are some indicators of the concepts?
   e. Name any specific problems with the reliability of the quiz's measurement strategy.
   f. Name any specific problems with the validity of the quiz's measurement strategy.
   g. Are the categories exhaustive and mutually exclusive? Explain your answer.

2. Answer the following questions about the ASA's statement regarding Proposition 54 (see the "Methods in Motion" box).
   a. How does a social understanding of race differ from biological understandings?
   b. According to the ASA, what are some of the risks of not collecting racial data?
   c. What evidence do the statement authors present that race is "central to societal organization" (4)?
   d. According to the ASA, how does collecting data on race and studying race contribute to both scientific and public agendas?

Online Resources

- William M. K. Trochim's website Research Methods Knowledge Base (2020) includes a discussion, with examples, of Likert scaling.
  www.socialresearchmethods.net/kb/scallik.php

- MacGrercy Consultants present a video on the basics of making a mind map.
  www.youtube.com/watch?v=wLWV0XN7K1g

- Tony's Buzan's discussion of how to make a mind map is also worth watching.
  www.youtube.com/watch?v=u5Y4plsXTV0

For more resources please visit
www.oup.com/he/bryman-reck-fields1e

4

How Do Researchers Select the People, Places, and Things to Study?
Sampling

▲ Ringo Chiu via AP

This chapter is devoted to principles of sampling and researchers' considerations about which people or entities to include in their studies. It examines why researchers engage in sampling, what issues are involved in choosing a sample, and why qualitative and quantitative researchers choose different sampling strategies.

Reading this chapter will help you to

- understand the role of sampling in the overall research process;

- appreciate why generalizable findings require a representative sample;

- distinguish between probability and non-probability sampling techniques, the reasons researchers choose them, and their main principles;

- define the main types of probability sampling: simple random, systematic, stratified random, and multistage cluster;

- describe different types of non-probability sampling: convenience, purposive, snowball, and quota;

- identify potential sources of sampling error in research and their effects; and

- recognize the main issues involved in deciding sample size and how sampling strategy can affect reliability and validity.

Suppose a friend tries a new apple pie recipe and asks for your opinion. How do you decide if the pie's good? You consider eating the whole thing in one sitting, but you probably couldn't finish it, at least not without feeling sick afterward. You realize that you need to just eat *part* of the pie to test the recipe. But which part? If you try only the filling or the crust, you won't get the full picture: you need to eat both together. You might take a bite of crust and filling from the middle or the outer edge, but this won't give you a sense of the whole, especially if the middle is undercooked and the edges are burnt. You might try some of the crust around the edge so that you can compare it with others, but you still won't be able to assess the entire pie. You realize that you should cut a wedge that includes parts in the middle, moves toward the edge, and also includes the outside crust. Once you eat this slice, you can feel comfortable with your conclusion about how the pie tastes overall and whether your friend should keep using this recipe.

Just like your pie dilemma, researchers have to determine what people or elements will give the most accurate sense of the topic being studied. Because it is too costly, time consuming, or logistically impossible to study every single person or element in the universe of possibilities, they choose a smaller subset to study (as you tried a slice of the pie rather than eating the whole thing). This process is known as sampling.

Introduction: How Researchers Rely on Sampling

Imagine a researcher is studying the experiences children with divorced parents have in school and their families' involvement in supporting their education. It would be difficult, if not impossible, to gather information from every single child who has divorced parents. Although researchers are often interested in the entirety of cases they're studying, being able to gather data from the whole **population** is rare. For this reason, researchers engage in **sampling**—gathering a subset of a population (a *sample*) to study.

Sampling has an impact on virtually all the research discussed in this book. Researchers' questions, study focus, and goals influence how they conduct their sampling. The strategy used determines what information they acquire and influences their interpretation of the results. In this chapter, we begin with a discussion of the main sampling strategies that researchers use and why they use them, then consider how to reduce error and increase response rates, and conclude with some considerations for researchers during the process.

Sampling in the Research Process

One of the first steps in developing a sampling plan is to clarify what **elements** you are studying. Suppose you are wondering about students' experiences with your school's on-campus advising resources. In this case the elements (and thus the members of your sample) are individual students at your school. In the social sciences, an element is often a person; but nations, cities, regions, schools, media sources, and many other things can be sampled as well. For example, the elements in a study exploring how media coverage might affect public perception about opioid use were individual news stories focused on opioid use (Webster, Rice, and Sud 2020). In our example of children with divorced parents, the elements could be individual family units; the sampling strategy would consist of recruiting families for participation.

Another core aspect to sampling is approaching it in a thoughtful and systematic way in order to reduce bias. To learn about experiences of your fellow students, in-depth interviews or questionnaires could be useful ways to collect data. However, let's say that there are nine thousand students at your university. The time and energy required to conduct that many interviews and the money needed to distribute all those questionnaires are prohibitive. Studying a sample of students would have to suffice.

But would any sample do? What if you gave questionnaires to everyone in your classes? Or stood in a busy location on campus and interviewed anyone who agreed to speak with you? If your goal is to get some experience in data gathering and analysis, or to

conduct a pilot study, the samples might be fine. But these strategies can also introduce some problems:

- If you distribute questionnaires in your classes, anyone not taking a course with you will be excluded. How many music or chemistry majors take sociology?
- If you interview people between your classes, your sample will exclude anyone who happens to be somewhere else at that particular time. Some students will be at work, others will have skipped classes that day, and many will have a timetable different from yours. Some students may never need to pass by where you are standing.
- Your decisions about which people to approach may be influenced by your judgments about how friendly or cooperative they seem. Gender, race, and age are only a few of the factors that could impact your selection of prospective respondents.

The problem with these sampling strategies is that the choice of possible participants depends on non-universal criteria (availability and personal judgment). The sample would not represent the population from which it was selected (a situation we discuss more later). In addition, you would have selected the sample somewhat haphazardly, following your whims rather than a methodical process. Introducing these biases means you can't draw conclusions that reflect the overall experience of students at your school.

Generalizability and Representativeness

When determining sampling strategy, researchers should identify specific research goals and then determine how to gather data that speak to those goals.

---

population All cases or people covered by a theory or explanation; the universe of units from which a sample is selected.

---

sampling The process in which a researcher selects a subset of a population to study.

---

element A single case (person, city, etc.) in a population.

Why is it important to gather a representative sample? What if you were studying children's physical activity levels and only recruited study participants from the playground?

Maybe your aim is to develop research findings that capture a snapshot of the entire population to be able to make conclusions about trends and patterns of experience. When researchers can make inferences about the populations they're studying, they can obtain a "big picture" understanding and develop information about broad patterns and wide-scale social dynamics. If your aim is **generalizability**, it would be vital to gather a **representative sample**. Returning to our advising resources example, this means your sample must accurately reflect the nine

---

generalizability   The ability to make inferences about a population by using sample data.

---

representative sample   A sample that is a microcosm of the population and similar to the population in all essential respects.

---

probability sampling   The process of using a randomly selected sample in which each unit in the population has a known and equal probability of being selected.

---

sampling frame   A list of all the units in a population from which a sample is to be selected.

---

sampling error   Differences between the characteristics of a random sample and the population from which it is selected.

---

thousand students on your campus. A representative sample is most likely when a researcher uses probability samples (see the next section). Many researchers prefer the representative approach because they want to generalize their findings to a population. While the sample and population characteristics may not be exactly the same, the first can be used to estimate the second with a known probability of error.

Probability Sampling

Probability sampling relates to probability theory, a branch of mathematics focused on determining the basic patterns of observations and predicting the frequency of a particular outcome. A simple example is flipping a coin: the flipping is the observation and the outcome is heads or tails. A probability theorist would try to figure out the likelihood of getting heads or tails in any single flip, as well as in repeated flips. As long as the coin flipper doesn't cheat, the result is random.

These principles apply here in that probability samples are chosen randomly, so every member of the population has a known and equal chance of being selected (just as heads or tails does in each coin flip). Statisticians can determine the probability of each population member being selected for the sample and the probability researchers can be confident in the inferences they're making about the population. If you continue in your statistics education after this class, you'll learn a lot more about this process. For now, you only need to know that probability sampling enables a researcher to predict how well their sample aligns with trends in the overall population, thus helping to ensure results are generalizable.

To use probability sampling techniques, researchers need a **sampling frame**, an accurate list of population members from which the sample will be drawn. For the study on students' experiences of advising resources, the sampling frame would be the university's list of all full-time, enrolled students. Thus, probability sampling depends on the existence of a sampling frame. If it is inadequate, such as excluding some cases, a **sampling error** can occur: the sample may not represent the population, even if a researcher employs a **random sampling** method.

Types of Probability Sampling

Simple Random Sampling

Simple random sampling is the most basic form of probability sampling. This type is like picking names out of a hat: each element in the population is included in a list, and the researcher chooses the sample by removing one element at a time without looking. Because it is typically unrealistic to pick names from a hat to select a sample, researchers usually randomly assign numbers to population members to maintain confidentiality and use a table of random numbers (found in many statistics books) or a computer program that generates random numbers.

Two points are worth noting here. First, there is almost no opportunity for bias, since the selection process is entirely random and selection does not depend on availability. Second, the selection process takes place without the potential participants' knowledge; no one knows they will be asked to be part of a study until they are contacted by someone associated with it.

Sometimes researchers use a combination of sampling techniques to gather their samples. You'll notice that some of the following descriptions of other probability sampling techniques include gathering a simple random sample.

Systematic Sampling

In **systematic sampling**, the sample is selected directly from the sampling frame, without using random numbers. Instead, elements are selected using a *sampling interval*. Suppose you want a sample size of 450 students for your advising resources study. Recalling that the population of your school is nine thousand students, the probability that any individual student will be chosen can be computed in this way:

Sample size/Population Size = 450/9,000 = 0.05

Thus, each student's probability of being included in the sample is 5 percent (0.05 x 100), or 1 in 20. This

value is called the *sampling ratio,* and is expressed through the formula

$$n/N$$

where n is the sample size and N is the population size.

This sampling ratio means that the sampling interval is 20, and you would select every 20th person from the sampling frame. However, it wouldn't be truly random if you began at the first name and chose every 20th student after that. A *random start* begins the process, which in this case can be achieved by randomly selecting a number from 1 to 20. Say the chosen number is 16. Your first case is number 16 and you select every 20th case following it.

For systematic sampling to be effective, there should be no inherent ordering or pattern in the sampling frame, a feature called *periodicity*. For example, if the sampling frame was set up such that case 1 was a first-year student, case 2 a second-year, case 3 a third-year, and case 4 a fourth-year, with that pattern continuing throughout, the sample would be unrepresentative. If there is any pattern to the list, researchers much arrange the cases in random order or choose a different sampling method.

Nicole Bedera and Kristjane Nordmeyer (2015) used systematic sampling in their content analysis study of how college websites advise students on reducing their risk of sexual assault. They selected every 22nd school on a list of 907 colleges, collecting a final sample of 40. They found that 25 schools had no rape prevention tips or discussion of sexual assault on their websites. The remaining 15 sites conveyed that

---

random sampling The form of sampling in which the sample is selected randomly and all units of a population have an equal chance of being selected.

---

simple random sample A probability sampling method in which each unit selected from the population, and each combination of units, has an equal probability of being included.

---

systematic sampling A probability sampling method in which units are selected from a sampling frame at fixed intervals (e.g., every fifth unit).

BOX 4.1 Studying Populations

A Census is supposed to count everyone in a population. What are the benefits of doing that? What problems arise if not everyone is counted, or the count does not accurately represent people's experiences and identities?

Although researchers usually study samples, they sometimes strive to study entire populations. An attempt to collect data from all elements in the population rather than from a sample is described as a census. The phrase "the census" typically refers to the enumeration of all (or nearly all) members of a nation-state's population. An example is the United States Census, in which the government attempts to collect data about all the members of the US population every 10 years. The US Census began in 1790; the most recent version was completed in 2020. Due to constraints in resources, however, censuses are rare.

The extent to which a census measures the population reflects the political climate and understandings of the historical moment in which it is conducted. Consider "Mexican" as a racial category. The US government added "Mexican" as a racial category in the 1930 Census, a move that was protested by both the Mexican government and the League of the United Latin American Citizens (LULAC). Both argued that people of Mexican descent living in the United States should legally be considered White, based on the terms of the treaty signed when the United States annexed the Southwest, which pledged that all Mexicans in the region would be treated as full American citizens. Given that only White people could then be citizens of the United States, the argument made sense. Why was it so important? At the time, being racialized as non-White was dangerous, and "passing for" (trying to be seen as) White was a way to avoid risk and fit into the dominant culture (Dowling 2014). The US government would use information collected in the 1930 Census to round up Mexicans during the Depression, just as they used Census information to locate, arrest, and incarcerate Japanese Americans during the 1940s. "Mexican" was removed as a racial category after the 1930 Census, and no Latinx group has been listed as a race on the Census questionnaire since (Dowling 2014).

In the US Census, people have only been able to select their own race since 1960; prior to that, census takers judged respondents' races. Only since 2000 have multiracial people been permitted to describe themselves as belonging to more than once racial group, and in 2020 people selecting "Black" or "White" could, for the first time, include more detail about their ethnic or national backgrounds (for example, Haitian or Irish; Brown 2020).

This still may not fully capture people's identities, however. According to the Census Bureau's definition, "White" describes someone tracing their origins to any of the original peoples of Europe, the Middle East, or North Africa; and the 2020 Census specifies German, Irish, English, Italian, Lebanese, Egyptian, Polish, French, Iranian, Slavic, Cajun, and Chaldean as belonging to the White race. Thus, people of Middle Eastern and North African descent are constrained in their choices on the US Census to "White," "Black," or "some other race." A US Census Bureau study (Mathews et.al. 2017) found that if "Middle Eastern and North African" (MENA) were given as an option, people with backgrounds from those regions who identified as White dropped to 20 percent from 85.5 percent (2017, 59).

There has also been a long controversy over the use of "Hispanic" as a category to describe people of Latinx descent. As noted, no Latinx category has been included as a race since the 1930 Census. Beginning in 1970, respondents could indicate that they were of Hispanic origin, tracing their background to Spanish-speaking Latin American countries, yet they would still have to identify the race with which they most closely identified—typically White, Black, or American Indian. A Census Bureau study done after the 2010 Census found that over half of the Latinx people who selected "White" as their racial category did so not because they thought of themselves as White but because they felt there was no other accurate choice. The Census

Bureau tested a combined question that permitted people to select all options that applied to their identified race or ethnic origin, including "Hispanic or Latino" along with "White," "Black," "American Indian," "Asian," and other racial categories. This increased the number of Latinx people who chose solely "Hispanic or Latino" and decreased the number who selected "White." Julie A. Dowling (2014) argues that this difference reflects the fact that Latinx people relate to the category "Hispanic" in different ways, some as a race and some as an origin. Dowling's interviews in New Mexico and Texas, for instance, revealed that the largely Mexican American population there defines "Hispanic" specifically as someone of Mexican origin who was born in the United States.

While questions about LGBTQIA2S+ identity were proposed to be included for the first time in the 2020 Census, the Trump administration removed them from both the Census and the American Community Survey (ACS). Instead, the 2020 Census asked only about the relationships between people who share a home—providing options for people to note if they live with a married or unmarried partner they identify as "same-sex." Though this was the first time same-sex cohabiting partners were counted in the Census, the question does not measure the population of people who identify as LGBTQIA2S+, those who do not live with a same-sex partner, or those who do not identify their partnership as "same-sex" (which could include transgender, Two-Spirit, or non-binary people, asexual people, or others in the community). Thus, while the Census measures the entire US population, limits remain to the characteristics the Census measures and what we can learn about the United States from Census data.

it's women's ultimate responsibility to increase their safety and reduce their assault risk. They concluded the websites' advice suggested "a paradox for women in which they are always vulnerable to attack, yet expected to prevent their own sexual assaults" (540).

Stratified Random Sampling

Some populations contain subgroups (known as strata) where the numbers vary a great deal. For instance, if you were interested in studying the occupation of nursing, which the Census Bureau estimates is 90.4 percent women and 9.6 percent men (Landivar 2013), a simple random sample would be unrepresentative. It would be preferable to use **stratified random sampling**, which involves dividing the population into subgroups by a criterion (in this case, gender) and selecting either a simple random or systematic sample from each of the resulting strata. You might divide your sample into two strata—woman-identified and man-identified nurses—and then take a random sample of each group until your final sample matches the Census percentages. So long as the relevant data are available, it's possible to ensure your sample is exactly representative in terms of the proportion of woman-identified and man-identified nurses in the population. This is described as **proportionate stratified random sampling**.

Jennifer K. Benz et al. (2011) utilized stratified random sampling in their study examining people's awareness about racialized health disparities in the United States. They did structured telephone interviews with a random national sample of 3,159 people aged 18

---

stratified random sampling A probability sampling method in which units are randomly sampled from a population that has been previously divided into subgroups (strata).

---

proportionate stratified random sampling A probability sampling method in which units are randomly sampled from strata in numbers equal (proportionate) to their representation in the overall population.

---

disproportionate stratified random sampling A probability sampling method in which units are randomly sampled from strata in numbers not equal (disproportionate) to their representation in the overall population.

---

and over. They stratified their sample by race, including the groups White, African American, Latinx, and Asian American/Pacific Islander (AAPI). As is sometimes the case, the researchers wanted to carry out a detailed analysis of subgroups that are a small proportion of the overall population—here, AAPIs. They conducted **disproportionate stratified random sampling**, in which they oversampled this group to include a larger proportion than it is in the overall US population. Sampling this way allowed the researchers to collect data enabling a robust statistical analysis about this group's opinions. They found that awareness of health disparities disproportionately affecting African Americans and Latinx people had increased in all racial groups. Interestingly, the former was the group most aware of the differences and also knowledgeable about the effects on their community as well as other BIPOC communities. AAPIs and African Americans were equally as likely to perceive a health disparity between AAPIs and Whites, when overall the AAPI community was perceived as doing just as well as White people.

The advantage of stratified sampling is that it ensures the sample is distributed in the same way as the population in terms of the stratifying criterion (or differently if that contributes to the researcher's analysis in meaningful ways). Other sampling methods might not always capture elements that may be a small proportion of an overall population. For example, 2 percent of the US population identify as Indigenous alone or in combination with other ethnic identities. Just 0.8 percent of the population identify as solely Indigenous. Without an explicit strategy to include Indigenous people in a sample, it would be quite easy for a sample to exclude this group; stratified sampling can help prevent this omission.

On the other hand, this strategy requires that the relevant criteria be known in advance of the research, which is not always the case. Stratified sampling is feasible only when it is relatively easy to identify and allocate units to strata (such as five job titles at a company). Setting up five strata based on physical activity level, from "competitive athletes" to "couch potatoes," would be difficult because it would require an initial study just to get the population data needed to create them. Furthermore, multiple stratifying criteria can be used at the same time. In your advising resources study, you could stratify by college/academic unit and gender or by college/academic unit, gender, and level of study (i.e., undergraduate or postgraduate), etc., so long as the criteria are relevant to the research question and data on the stratifying criteria are available for the population.

Multistage Cluster Sampling

No more than local travel would be required in your advising resources study because the students to be

Imagine you wanted to compare the profile of people getting tested for Covid in different states or different countries. How might cluster sampling be more practical than other sampling strategies? How would you approach the sampling?

interviewed all attend the same university. This is not the case when interviewing a national sample of students or even people in a large city; the travel involved might add a great deal to the time and cost of the research. Another problem with large populations is the general lack of an adequate sampling frame. There is no master list of all students registered at US universities. Without a sampling frame, it's impossible to select a simple random or systematic sample.

One way to deal with these issues is to employ **multistage cluster sampling**. In this method, the primary sampling unit (the first stage of the process) is an aggregate of the population's individuals or units, known as a *cluster*. The second stage involves sampling units within the clusters. José Miguel Cruz, Rosario Queirolo, and María Fernanda Boidi (2016) used this approach in their comparative study of factors affecting support of marijuana legalization in El Salvador, the United States, and Uruguay. They administered their survey to a sample of 3,740 individuals, recruited in three stages: they separated each nation into clusters of regions and randomly selected regions in each country; listed the urban and rural areas in the selected regions and randomly

chose areas; and noted different population sizes of municipalities and randomly selected municipalities of different population sizes.

If the clusters in this form of sampling are not created judiciously, the chances of having an unrepresentative sample may increase. A number of technical requirements must be satisfied when selecting clusters and subunits, but the process can be effective when done properly. It is also more economical than simple random or systematic sampling because of the reduced travel costs.

Cluster sampling solves the problem of an inadequate sampling frame. Cruz and colleagues' study does not require a list of all people in El Salvador, the United States, and Uruguay, which would be hard to come by. Quite often, cluster sampling also entails stratification. For example, the researchers stratified areas in terms of whether they were urban and

---

multistage cluster sampling A probability sampling method in which the researcher first samples sets of cases (clusters) and then samples units within them, usually using a probability sampling method.

BOX 4.2 Non-Probability Sampling: Sampling Frames and Marginalized Populations

There are many examples of populations for which it's impossible to gather a probability sample because there is no sampling frame. Because the existence of sampling frames of marginalized populations depends on the political climate and dynamics of inequality, a non-random sample is often necessary.

For example, when studying the population of Covid-positive people in a state, the state's testing organizations would have a list of those people. However, testing is not available equally across many states, some people might be asymptomatic

and not get tested, and there is evidence that economically marginalized people might have less testing access. So, this does not provide a complete sampling frame. There is also no sampling frame of all college students eligible for the Deferred Action for Childhood Arrivals (DACA) program. Many undocumented students have felt it is too risky to apply for the program, given the mass deportations that have occurred since the Obama administration. In both of these cases, a non-probability sample may be a more reasonable choice, whether the research is qualitative or quantitative.

---

rural and municipalities that were of different population sizes. They grouped areas and municipalities along these criteria first and then selected from each stratum.

Non-Probability Sampling

Conventional wisdom may suggest that the more random the sample, the more trustworthy the conclusions. However, researchers do not necessarily adhere to such ideas when assessing sampling strategies. Instead, they base their decisions on methodological orientations. For instance, qualitative researchers often do not have the ultimate goal of their sample being generalizable to, or representative of, the overall population (this will be discussed further in Chapter 5). They generally employ **non-probability sampling**, a non-random sampling method.

What unique information might be gleaned using a non-random sampling method? Laura Abrams

---

non-probability sampling The process of using a non-random (but still systematic) sampling method, in which some units in the population are more likely than others to be selected.

(2010) argues that qualitative research questions are best explored using non-probability sampling techniques:

> In qualitative studies, researchers usually have no basis to assume a "normal distribution" of the experiences, interactions, or settings that are of interest to them. Moreover, random sampling assumes that one person is 'as good as the next' as a data point so long as they contribute to representing the larger population. Qualitative researchers, on the other hand, recognize that some informants are better situated to provide key insight and understandings than others. Similarly, while random sampling tends to discard outliers, qualitative research is often interested in extreme or "negative cases" for their unique insights. (537–538)

Howard Becker (1998) also argues that researchers should include outliers or unique cases in their samples. He claims that researchers should "confront ourselves with just those things that would jar us out of the conventional categories, the conventional statement of the problem, the conventional solution" (85). To Becker, this necessitates selecting cases to study that may be unusual, represent a range of experience, or may not be recognized in typical "hierarchies of credibility" (90).

Many qualitative researchers aim for what could be described as conceptual generalization—to build their understanding of experiences by gathering in-depth and personal data through methods such as qualitative interviewing or long-term observation. For example, you might want to explore students' experiences with time management. In this case, you could recruit a sample that represents people who embody attributes typical of the overall population or perhaps experiences that offer

Imagine you decided to take a convenience sample of people lining up at this New York City Apple Store on the day a new phone was released. How would you recruit people in a way that made sure you didn't bias the sample?

a unique snapshot of student experience, such as first-generation college students. In that way, your focus would be to develop a deeper conceptual understanding of this dynamic by exploring people's real-life experience (see Chapters 5 and 13).

Types of Non-Probability Sampling

Non-probability sampling includes all forms that are not conducted according to the canons of probability sampling. It covers a wide range of different sampling strategies, including convenience, purposive, snowball, and quota.

Convenience Sampling

Convenience sampling is used because the elements are readily available and people are willing to participate. Imagine you are interested in the types of people who are early adopters of the newest technological devices. You might go to the nearest Apple store on the release day of the latest iPhone and survey the people lining up to buy one. The advantages of this method are that you can quickly and easily access the type of

people you're interested in, you don't have to pay travel costs, and you don't have to do much preparation to recruit people. However, it is impossible to generalize the findings to technology fans as a whole: the fact that you chose the customers at your local store makes them likely different from phone customers in general. Although you chose this location because it was convenient and aligns with your research interest, it doesn't mean that you gather the sample casually. As mentioned earlier, the researcher must be systematic and resist approaching people for participation in a way that introduces bias, such as only recruiting those who seem friendly or particularly willing.

The inability to generalize from findings collected through convenience sampling does not mean the method should always be avoided. In fact, they are used more often than you might think. For instance, Lauren Haack, Theresa Kapke, and Alyson Gerdes (2016) used convenience sampling to explore young Latinos'

---

convenience sampling A non-probability sampling method that is selected because of its availability to the researcher.

specific mental health outreach needs. They followed the National Institute of Health (2002) multicultural sampling guidelines on reaching Latinx populations. The guidelines inspired them to gather a good sample by developing a relationship with a local charter school that offered benefits for both their study and the school and to recruit students by participating in school functions and engaging with students' families.

Often, researchers use this type of sampling when undertaking pilot studies or testing the reliability of scales they propose to use in their research. Imagine an education professor is interested in the leadership qualities that teachers want in their principals and has several classes made up of teachers working part-time toward master's degrees. The professor could give them a questionnaire—recruiting a sample of convenience—to help develop a battery of queries to measure teachers' leadership preferences. Since it is highly desirable to pre-test such a research instrument before actually using it, administering it to a group that is not part of the main study is a legitimate way of exploring issues such as whether respondents will reply honestly to questions on sensitive topics and whether the questions are clear. A convenience sample may be used to test new scales for reliability and/or generate ideas for further research.

Purposive Sampling

Researchers using **purposive sampling**, sometimes called judgmental sampling, choose their sample based on attributes that they feel would be most appropriate for their study. They are often studying a particular domain and deem certain people

---

purposive sampling A non-probability sampling method in which researchers choose attributes that are most appropriate to the study; also called judgmental sampling.

---

snowball sampling A non-probability sampling method and form of convenience sampling in which the researcher makes initial contact with a small group of people connected to the research topic and then uses them to establish contact with others.

---

or cases as ideal for their purposes (Tongco 2008). For example, researchers interested in the ways formerly incarcerated people transition to post-prison life might interview a group of people recently released from prison living in a transitional housing program. Since sample members are chosen based on study needs, a researcher may use a screening system to determine who will be recruited for the sample. In a study on people with disabilities involved in adaptive athletics, a researcher might canvas participants in local organizations for people with disabilities and ask, "Have you ever been involved in sports or athletic activities adapted for people with disabilities?" Anyone answering "no" would be excluded from the study.

In purposive sampling, researchers may choose samples based on those who can give them the most information on the study topic or who have particular expertise in the issue. They may choose a case study of the people or elements they view as most typical representatives of the issue or include people or situations that they see as an outlier or extreme case. Valerie Francisco-Menchavez (2018) used purposive sampling to meet participants for her study on the care work Filipina migrants do to maintain their extended family and kin connections across vast distances and with long separations. She worked with a New York Filipinx community organization for Filipina domestic workers, Kabalikat Domestic Workers Support Network. A significant percentage of Filipina migrants are employed in domestic work, so this organization was an appropriate venue for meeting potential participants.

Snowball Sampling

Snowball sampling is a form of convenience sampling that has attracted a lot of attention over the years and is especially useful for recruiting hard-to-reach populations. With this approach, the researcher makes initial contact with a small group of people who are relevant to the research topic and then relies on them to establish contact with others. Box 4.3 describes Becker's (1963) generation of a snowball sample of marijuana users for what is often regarded as a classic study of drug use.

Mixed Methods in Action | Sampling Strategies to Reach Specific Populations

Purposive sampling can be a useful recruitment strategy when you desire to recruit participants that align specifically to your study's aims. In their mixed-methods study of how food environments around tribal lands might affect health disparities among American Indian, Gwen M. Chodur, et al. (2016) explored the hypothesis that Indigenous people living on tribal land face both geographic and economic barriers to accessing healthy food. They used purposive sampling in both phases of their study.

To analyze the food environments around tribal land, the researchers gathered a purposive sample of California census tracts within counties containing at least one tribal land, which was 29 of the 58 counties in the state. Relying on a dataset called InfoUSA, they were able to identify the food establishments within each geographic area (determining number of supermarkets, fast food and sit-down restaurants, convenience stores, etc.), which they then categorized as healthy, intermediate, or unhealthy establishments. They measured the mean distance to the closest food retailers and the density of food establishments in tribal lands compared to non-tribal areas, controlling for variables such as income and urbanicity.

In the qualitative portion of their study, the researchers interviewed 24 tribal members and asked them questions about their food environment, food acquisition, tribal culture, and tribal environment. They used purposive sampling to recruit interview participants, sending fliers to all of the California tribal health clinics. They also used quota sampling, which they describe as stratified purposive sampling. To determine the members of their final sample, they included strata such as

various tribal sizes, different geographic areas, and presence of a casino (this research was part of a larger study about how having a tribal casino related to health).

The research team found that there was not a significant difference between the density of unhealthy food vendors in tribal and non-tribal areas, but that tribal areas have much fewer healthy food vendors than do non-tribal areas. This quantitative finding corresponded to findings from the qualitative interviews, in which participants reported challenges in easily accessing healthy food options.

Interestingly, although there were fewer healthy food vendors near tribal lands, healthy vendors were no farther away from the tribal lands than they were from non-tribal lands. The comparison of quantitative and qualitative data introduced the important point that the distance to a healthy food vendor was not the only influence on people's access to healthy food. Having a healthy food vendor nearby did not mean that healthy food felt accessible to people living on tribal land. Factors such as high prices for organic food, limited availability of preferred food items, and rural roads making travel more difficult affected people's access to the healthy food vendors.

Thus, using mixed methods enabled these researchers to assess the geographic distribution of food establishments on tribal lands and also to explore what this means in people's everyday lives. Because the researchers used purposive quota sampling to recruit their interviewees, they were able to consider how living in different environments might affect people's food access and perceptions about the availability of healthy food options.

Becker writes, "The sample is, of course, in no sense 'random'; . . . it would not be possible to draw a random sample, since no one knows the nature of the universe from which it would have to be drawn" (Becker 1963, 46). In other words, there is no accessible sampling frame for the population. The difficulty

BOX 4.3 A Snowball Sample

Becker (1963, 45–46) described how he generated a sample of marijuana users:

> I had been a professional dance musician . . . and my first interviews were with people I had met in the music business. I asked them to put me in contact with other [marijuana] users who would be willing to discuss their experiences with me . . . Although in the end half of the fifty interviews were conducted with musicians, the other half covered a wide range of people, including laborers, machinists, and people in the professions.

You might wonder why snowball sampling was a useful technique for this study. In the 1960s, marijuana use was stigmatized and many years away from even being considered decriminalized or legalized. Accessing users through informal networks enabled Becker to include many different types of people in his study, several of whom may have been more willing to participate because they were referred by people they knew or trusted.

Although snowball sampling can be useful for hard-to-reach populations and sensitive topics, Jaime Waters (2015) cautions that using this approach can be difficult if the topic is *too sensitive*. He described a study of people over 40 who used illegal drugs and were not involved in the criminal justice system, in which he found that the threat they felt at being revealed made them hesitant to participate. He argues that, in such cases, it could be helpful if the researchers are part of the population being studied and are as similar as possible to the community in terms of demographic background. If people are not part of a social network around the issue at hand, it can be hard to gain access to them using snowball sampling.

of creating such a sampling frame means that a non-probability approach is the only feasible one. Moreover, even if it were possible to create a sampling frame of marijuana users, it would almost certainly become obsolete soon because this population is constantly changing—people become and cease being marijuana users all the time. The problem with snowball sampling is that it is unlikely to be representative of the population, although, as Becker's experience suggests, the very notion of a population can be a problem.

Snowball sampling is typically used within a qualitative research strategy, where generalizing to the larger population is not the main objective. Francisco-Menchavez's (2018) study used snowball sampling in addition to purposive sampling. The fifty migrant Filipina women she interviewed in New York introduced her to their families and kin networks in the Philippines. Using snowball sampling, she conducted an ethnography with eleven extended family networks in the Philippines, which enabled her "to integrate and study the transnational life and formations of care within constellations of families" (138). Even though many qualitative researchers use snowball sampling, the method is not entirely irrelevant to quantitative research: when the researcher needs to focus on relationships between people, tracing connections through snowball sampling can be a better approach than conventional probability sampling. Statistically small groups—gay men enrolled in Catholic seminaries, for example—are researchable with a snowball approach, as taking a random sample from that population would not be feasible.

Quota Sampling

The aim of **quota sampling** is to produce a sample that reflects a population in terms of the relative proportions of people in different categories

---

quota sampling A non-probability sampling method that matches the proportions of people in different categories in the population.

(gender, ethnicity, age, socioeconomic status, region of residence, etc.) or in combinations of these categories. Unlike a stratified sample (the probability sampling version of this type), a quota sample is not random, given that the final selection of people is left up to the researcher. Researchers can use sources such as the Census and the General Social Survey to compute the quotas they want to use; however, quota sampling does not require a sampling frame. The Census would be used just to get a sense of the numbers of certain characteristics in a population of interest, not as a list of elements from which to gather the sample.

Researchers can find it challenging to gain access to the population of people experiencing homelessness who live in tent encampments. What non-probability sampling techniques could be most useful if you were recruiting members of this group?

Once the categories and the numbers of people to be selected within each category (the quotas) have been decided, researchers merely have to recruit people who fit those categories. As in stratified sampling, the population may be divided into strata covering several characteristics (e.g., gender, employment, and age) all at once. Census data can identify the number of people who should be in each subgroup; thus, the numbers to be interviewed in each reflect the population.

In quota sampling, the researcher ensures their final sample includes their chosen strata, but they actually recruit their sample using an additional non-probability sampling method. For example, Michelle Fine et al. (2003) combined purposive and quota sampling in their mixed-method study of youths' experience with surveillance from authority figures in New York City. Their purposive strategy included recruiting youth participants from a diverse range of places, including parks, street corners, schools, libraries, community colleges, and other public sites. They also used quota sampling to create what they described as an "ideal sampling framework," in which they used US Census data to determine the city's demographics and recruited a sample that reflected that breakdown. When they noted that they were missing a certain type of participant, they actively sought it out to ensure they followed the demographics.

While researchers such as Fine et al. sampled groups proportionately, there can be good reasons to sample disproportionately. Let's look at a hypothetical study of gender and unemployment. The research team may use the Census or unemployment statistics to determine the proper proportion of each gender in their sample. Accordingly, an interviewer may be told to find and interview thirty unemployed people at an assigned location, such as at the city's Human Services Agency. The team may decide to include transgender as a gender category, but it is not possible to precisely estimate the percentage in the population because the category is not included in official statistics. But, because studies have shown that transgender people are more likely than cisgender people to be unemployed, the researchers might decide to use a disproportionate quota sample and

---

---

recruit an equal number of transgender and cisgender people. This is a strength of quota sampling: researchers can recruit people with characteristics that their sample should include.

Sampling Error

When researchers develop and carry out their sampling strategy, they must ensure that the sample accurately represents the population from which it was gathered or is the most ideal group from which to study their topic. To accomplish this, they strive to reduce errors in the sampling process that might introduce bias or non-representativeness. In the following sections, we first explore the general concept of sampling error, followed by some specific considerations for reducing error, such as deciding on an appropriate sample size and lowering non-response. We also touch on how sampling relates to concerns around making sure your study measures what you set out to measure (validity) and whether your study's measurements are consistent (reliability).

Let's consider a hypothetical study of whether people watch televised sports. The population for this study is 200 people and the sample is 50; the former is divided equally between those who watch (100) and those who do not (100). If the sample is representative, it should also be equally split (Figure 4.1). If there is a small amount of sampling error, so that the sample contains one person too many who does not watch sports and one too few who does, it would look like Figure 4.2. Figure 4.3 shows a more serious error, with three too many who do not watch and three too few who do. Finally, Figure 4.4 shows a severe overrepresentation of people who do not watch sports: 35, as opposed to the 25 that would be there if the sample were perfectly representative. These figures illustrate the consequences of sampling error. As the errors increase, the conclusions made about the population relying on the gathered sample will become increasingly less accurate.

Sampling error can never be eliminated. Even with a well-crafted probability sample, a degree of error is likely to creep in. Just do 20 coin flips a few times and you'll see the surprisingly large number of outcomes that are not 10 heads/10 tails. However, probability sampling stands a better chance than non-probability sampling of minimizing sampling error, so it's unlikely that the sample will look like Figure 4.4 when it is used properly. Moreover, probability sampling allows you to employ tests of statistical significance that permit you to make inferences about the population from which the sample was selected, with a known probability of error. Researchers can improve the consistency of their measures—their reliability—through their sampling methods. For instance, comparing data from different samples collected from the same population enables a researcher to assess their measures' reliability (Lameck 2013).

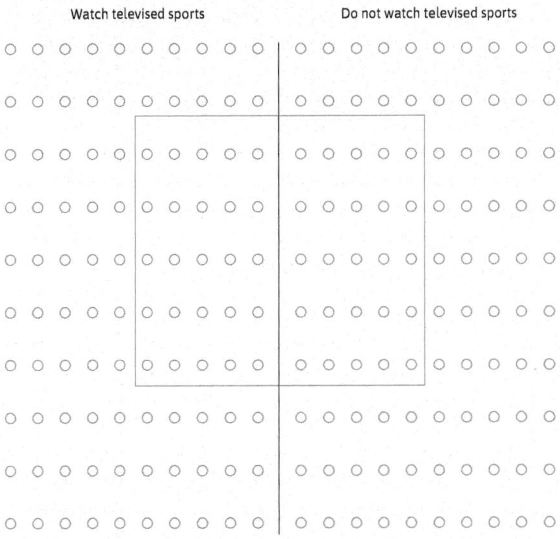

FIGURE 4.1 **A sample with no sampling error**

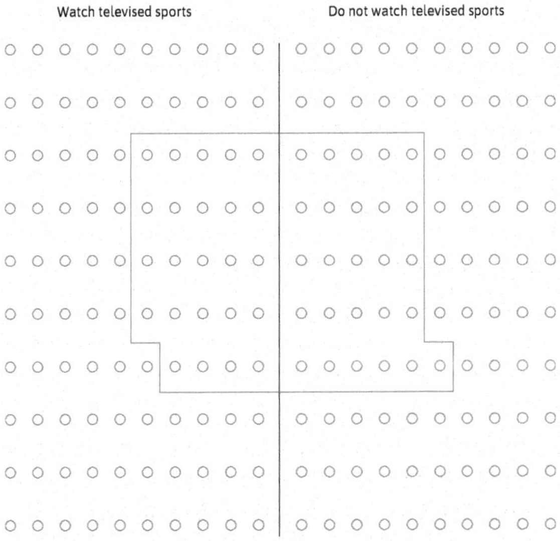

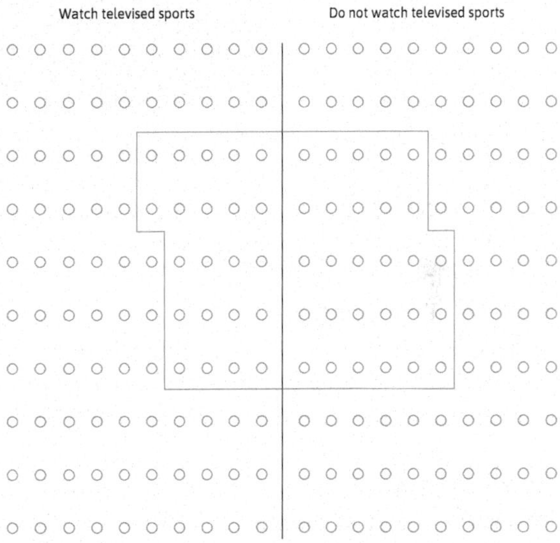

FIGURE 4.3 **A sample with a fair amount of sampling error**

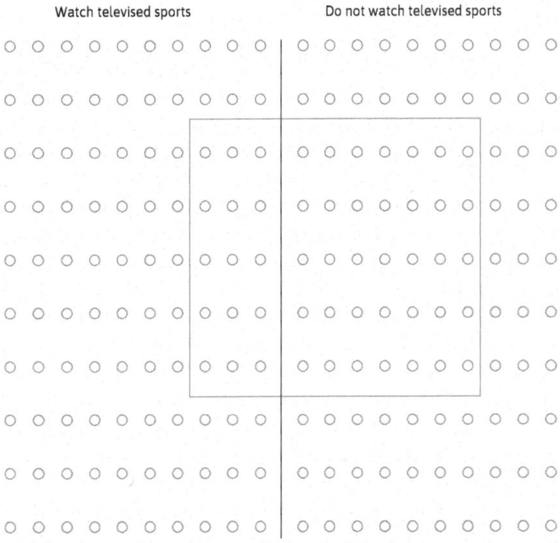

FIGURE 4.2 **A sample with very little sampling error**

FIGURE 4.4 **A sample with a lot of sampling error**

Response Bias and Sampling Error

Researchers have two concerns around sampling error in relation to response: low **response rates** from the sample and biases regarding who does or can respond. Therefore, **non-response bias** is increasingly considered to be a greater concern than the response rate itself (Johnson and Wislar 2012). The response rate can be defined as the percentage of the sample

People's everyday lives and movements changed drastically during the early stages of the Covid-19 outbreak in North America, with many people spending much more time at home and only certain essential workers leaving home for their jobs. How does a situation like this affect sampling bias if you chose to recruit people for a study by approaching them in public or contacting them in their homes?

that actually participates in the study. It is often a good deal less than 100 per cent, partly because there are usually some people in the sample who will either refuse or be unable to participate, who cannot be contacted, or who turn out to be unsuitable for the study. Non-response can be a cause of sampling error. What if the people who do or do not participate share certain characteristics, which makes the sample unrepresentative? Are the people who cannot be contacted richer and on vacation? Are the ones who can be contacted unemployed or home-bound?

The problem with this kind of response is that those who agree to participate may differ from those who refuse or cannot be reached; this difference may be relevant to the subject being investigated and may have to be taken into account in the analysis. For example, Doug Meyer (2010, 2012) found that LGBT people of color are less likely than White LGBT people to report their experiences of hate violence to authorities and

tend to define these experiences as less severe than White people do (even when they experienced a high level of physical violence). Thus, when a researcher recruits a sample of hate violence survivors, the social conditions LGBTQIA2S+ people who are BIPOC experience can prevent them from defining themselves as part of the sample category. Their non-participation has significant consequences on the knowledge produced about hate violence (especially because research shows LGBTQIA2S+ people from BIPOC communities are at higher risk than White people due to intersectional marginalization). Non-response compromises the validity of your findings—your sampling strategy must not be conducted in a way that makes it challenging for members of your sample to participate.

Researchers sometimes take steps to determine the level and effects of non-response bias. In their examination of how socio-economic status might determine people's sense of mastery over their work, Scott Schieman and Atsushi Narisada (2014) analyzed a representative sample of Canadian workers. They noted that people who experienced conflicts between family and work might have chosen to leave the workforce and thus might not have been part of their sample—this absence may have caused the researchers to underestimate the negative effects of role conflict. They proposed to explore this possibility by conducting additional qualitative analyses to develop a deeper

---

response rate The percentage of people contacted to participate in a study, usually survey research, who go on to participate.

---

non-response bias A bias introduced when sample participants differ from non-participants in meaningful ways; can occur due to low response rates.

understanding of how role conflict might affect choice to work and feelings of mastery at work.

Reducing Response Bias and Sampling Error

One way to reduce response bias is to increase participation in the study. Given that perfect response rates are rare, sample size may have to be adjusted. If the goal is a sample of 450 people working in service industry jobs and earlier surveys suggest that the response rate will be approximately 80 percent, it may be advisable to sample 575 individuals, assuming that approximately 115 (20 percent) will not participate and leaving room for some additional refusals. Researchers should also clearly communicate about their research to possible participants, avoid making participation seem onerous, use a communication method that works best for their potential participants (e.g., email, telephone, snail mail, and personal contact) and follow up after first contact, and engage in clear, personable, and respectful interactions.

When a researcher uses probability sampling, they seek to eliminate sources of bias through random selection. If a random method is not used, there is a risk that the selection process will be affected by human judgment, so that some members of the population are more likely to be selected than others. Yet even when random selection occurs, chance and non-response can create errors. It is typical for researchers using probability sampling techniques to test the potential bias of their sample using mathematical means.

Researchers who use non-probability sampling are also concerned about bias. But snowball sampling enables them to gain access to a larger sample of people than they would typically have direct contact with and to gain access to hard-to-reach populations for which no sampling frame exists. In quota sampling, researchers get a sense of the types of people represented in the population and then recruit people fitting those categories, thereby making their sample more representative.

Sample Size and Sampling Error

Sample size affects researchers' ability to estimate population parameters from their sample data. Decisions about sample size are not straightforward, and the quest for the perfect sample is usually constrained by the practical considerations of cost and time.

You may be surprised to learn that the *absolute* size of a sample is more important than the proportion of the population that it comprises. A national probability sample of one thousand residents of Mexico has about as much validity as one of one thousand US residents, even though the US population is almost three times larger. Although not guaranteed, sampling error tends to decrease as sample size increases. Common sample sizes are 100 (minimum), 400, 900, 1,600, and 2,500. The degree to which a larger sample reduces sampling error is computed mathematically in quantitative research; the increases given here cut the sampling error by half, one-third, one-fourth, and one-fifth, respectively. Notice that the increases in precision become less pronounced (going from 100 to 400 reduces sampling error by half, but 400 to 900 reduces it by only one-third). This difference would determine whether a quantitative researcher felt compelled to have a sample of 900 versus feeling comfortable with one of 400. Considerations of time and cost would profoundly affect sample size in this instance. If you decided to recruit 900 people instead of 400, it would not reduce the sampling error by much but would demand more time and other resources.

Yet another consideration is the heterogeneity of the population being sampled. When a population is heterogeneous with regard to characteristics relevant to the study, as a whole country or city normally is, the samples drawn are likely to be highly varied. When it is relatively homogeneous, such as a population of students or members of a particular occupation, the amount of variation is less. Generally, the greater a population's heterogeneity, the larger a sample should be in order to maximize the chances that all groups will be adequately represented. Larger sample sizes increase the representativeness of the sample, so this is another way to improve the validity of a study.

Qualitative data collection is more time-consuming and can be more costly than quantitative research, although the former's sample sizes are often smaller. When selecting their sample, qualitative researchers take their study's aims into account and consider how to adequately capture the population of interest with their sample. They also pay attention to concerns such as the population's level of heterogeneity or elements that would provide detail crucial to furthering their understanding of the topic (as described in Box 4.4).

Considerations during the Sampling Process

As previously mentioned, most probability sampling depends on the sampling frame. Findings can be generalized *only* to the population from which the sample was taken. It is easy to think that results have a broader applicability, but findings from a study based on a random sample of adults from Minneapolis/St. Paul cannot be easily generalized to the whole state of Minnesota, much less to other regions of the United States. The opinions of these residents may be different from those held by people who live in Atlanta, Honolulu, or New York.

Time period is also a concern, no matter what sampling type. Is there a point when findings no longer apply? No one should assume that the findings of a 1970 study of senior citizens' personal finance habits apply to today's seniors. The rising costs of health care, housing, and food—combined with fewer employer-managed pension programs and longer lifespans—have changed many seniors' financial management strategies. But even when there is no definable or recognizable source of relevant change, there is still the possibility (even the likelihood) that the findings are time-specific.

As this chapter demonstrates, researchers must take several factors into account when developing their sampling strategy:

- *Considering ultimate goals*: Do they want to make inferences from the sample to the population or perhaps engage in generalization and theory development in relation to their conceptual understandings? This objective may affect the choice to conduct either probability or non-probability sampling.
- *Gathering a good sample*: A sample must accurately represent the population from which it was gathered or be the most ideal group from which to study the topic of interest. Researchers must decide on an appropriate sample size and determine the best way to encourage members of the sample to participate in the research (reducing non-response).
- *Considering challenges*: Researchers must think about whether their population has attributes that introduce challenges in gathering a representative sample, such as it being an invisible or hard-to-reach population. If they cannot find a sampling frame for their population, they must engage in non-probability sampling.

No matter which sampling technique researchers use, they need to be thoughtful about how they select the sample, reflexive of how their research questions and goals suggest a particular sampling strategy to adopt, and transparent about their method of sample selection and possible biases that could result from their choice.

Key Points

Introduction: Why Do Researchers Rely on Sampling?

- A sample is a subset of a population, and sampling is a process in which a researcher determines what people or entities to include in a study.

Sampling in the Research Process

- A researcher must first determine what elements they are studying, which can be people, cities, regions, schools, media sources, and many other things.

- It is vital to gather a sample systematically and in a manner that reduces bias.

Generalizability and Representativeness

- When determining sampling strategy, researchers must choose a sampling strategy that best helps them reach their research goals.
- Representative samples are reflective of the population as a whole and are often achieved through probability sampling.

Probability Sampling

- Probability sampling uses random selection, which gives each member of the population an equal and known chance of being included in the sample.
- A sampling frame, used in probability sampling, details an accurate list of all members within a population, which is used to gather the sample.

Types of Probability Sampling

- Types of probability sampling include simple random, systematic, stratified random, and multistage cluster.
- Simple random sampling, systematic, and stratified sampling require a sampling frame, while multistage cluster sampling can be conducted without a sampling frame.

Non-Probability Sampling

- Non-probability sampling uses non-random selection, meaning that members of the population have an unequal chance of inclusion in the sample.
- Non-probability sampling is used either when adequate sampling frames are unavailable or when research goals do not require data collected through strictly random methods.

Types of Non-Probability Sampling

- Types of non-probability sampling include convenience, purposive, snowball, and quota; qualitative researchers often use these sampling strategies.
- Convenience sampling can be helpful in pilot studies and snowball sampling can help a researcher recruit hard-to-reach people or invisible populations.

Sampling Error

- Researchers want to reduce the possibility of making sampling errors due to low response rates or gathering a biased sample.
- Deciding upon an appropriate sample size can help reduce sampling error, and larger sample sizes tend to decrease the likelihood of sampling error.

Considerations during the Sampling Process

- Findings using probability sampling can only be generalized to the population from which the sample was taken.
- Findings from a sample are time-specific, and conclusions drawn from a sample may not be relevant at a later time period.
- When determining sampling method, a researcher must assess their ultimate goals and ensure the sample they recruit is the most ideal to study their topic.
- Researchers should consider what factors might make it difficult to attain a representative sample and then plan to effectively respond to those challenges.

Questions for Review

1. What does each of the following terms mean: population; sampling; sample?
2. What are two main aspects of developing a sampling plan?
3. Why do researchers engage in sampling?
4. What are the goals of sampling and what type of knowledge does it allow researchers to produce?
5. What is probability sampling and what type of analysis can a researcher conduct using this sampling method?
6. Why would a researcher choose probability sampling?
7. What are the main types of probability sampling and why would a researcher choose one type over another?
8. What type of probability sampling could you use to conduct a study of social-emotional development of children enrolled in US preschools? Explain your choice and how you would gather this sample.
9. Define non-probability sampling. Why would a researcher use this form of sampling instead of probability sampling?
10. Why might qualitative researchers, in particular, prefer to use non-probability sampling?
11. Describe when each type of non-probability sampling might be most useful or appropriate.
12. A researcher wants to learn about services provided to people who have been victimized by violent crime and recruits people from a local

support group for families impacted by gun violence. What kind of sampling strategy is the researcher using?

13. What are the main areas of potential bias in sampling?
14. How does sampling error affect the representativeness of a sample?
15. What factors should be taken into account in deciding sample size?

16. How does sampling strategy relate to research goals?
17. Why are sampling frames so important in probability sampling?
18. What must researchers keep in mind when they seek to generalize from one location or time period to another?

Portfolio Exercise

Draft a detailed, 2- to 3-page sampling plan for the research interests you have written about in previous portfolio exercises. Address the following questions:

a. How would you describe your intended population?
b. What elements will your sample include?
c. Is there a sampling frame to refer to? How might you access it?
d. Will you use probability sampling or non-probability sampling? What specific sampling method

will you use and how will you carry it out? Why are you choosing this sampling method?
e. What is your estimated sample size? What are its potential strengths and weaknesses?
f. What steps will you take to reduce sampling errors?
g. How will you ensure that the sample collected will be representative of your population? If your sample is not representative, explain your reasoning.

Interactive Activities

1. Imagine your class is conducting a study of your fellow students' commuting experiences, using probability sampling. As a class, discuss the population, elements, and sampling frame for this study.
2. Divide into breakout groups that meet (1) synchronously in person or online or (2) asynchronously to consider which type of probability sample should be used for the study. With your group, discuss the four options before deciding on one and determining how you would carry it out. Later, present

your group's choice to the class for a discussion of the pros and cons of each method. In an asynchronous environment, this can take place in a new discussion forum including all class members.
3. Now imagine the commuting study will focus on first-generation students at your university. Repeat the steps of the previous exercise, but this time discuss the options for a non-probability sample.
4. For an interactive exercise on using probability samples to make inferences about populations, consult

Online Resources

General Introductions to Sampling

- Sampling: *National Information Center on Health Services Research* & Health Care Technology (NICHSR)
  www.nlm.nih.gov/nichsr/stats_tutorial/section2/ mod1_sampling.html

- Sampling: Social Research Methods Knowledge Based
  https://socialresearchmethods.net/kb/sampling. php

- Sampling: US Bureau of Labor Statistics
  www.bls.gov/opub/hom/topic/sampling.htm
- Why Probability Sampling: Pew Research Center
  www.people-press.org/methodology/sampling/
  why-probability-sampling/7/

Selecting a Simple Random, Stratified, and Cluster Sample

- Video: Simple Random Sampling
  www.youtube.com/watch?v=yx5KZi5QArQ&NR=1
- Video: Cluster Sampling
  www.youtube.com/
  watch?v=QOxXy-l6ogs&feature=related

For more resources please visit
www.oup.com/he/bryman-reck-fields1e

PART III
Modes and Practices of Inquiry

A fundamental distinction in social research is between qualitative and quantitative research—between ways of exploring experience, meaning, and meaning-making in social life (qualitative research) and of identifying and understanding broad patterns of social life, opportunities, and outcomes (quantitative research). Both modes are recognized as distinct methodologies and perspectives, and we treat them as such in this book. We also recognize that many researchers "mix" methods, drawing on both qualitative and quantitative approaches to understanding the social world. Researchers use various study designs to collect and analyze their data, including experimental, cross-sectional, longitudinal, and case study designs. These designs—and their theoretical, ethical, and feasibility considerations—span research modes and practices.

5

How Can Researchers Understand Meaning, Process, and Experience in the Social World?
Qualitative Research

Qualitative analysis focuses on the meanings conveyed in words and images, and examines social processes and contexts influencing people's experiences. Instead of using numbers to quantify patterns the way quantitative research does, qualitative methods take an interpretive approach to analysis.

Reading this chapter will help you to

- define qualitative research and describe the main approaches and unique attributes of this form of research;

- explain how qualitative research emerged as a recognized methodology;

- understand the main goals of qualitative researchers: seeing through the eyes of research participants, providing rich description of the context, exploring social processes, and employing an open-ended, flexible structure;

- outline the main steps in qualitative research;

- recognize the distinct perspective of qualitative research; and

- identify the main differences between qualitative research and quantitative research.

Think about arriving for the first day of a new class with a new professor. How do you figure out whether you will like the class or how well it fits with your interests and learning style? When you first enter the room, you look around, observing who is there and assessing who you'll be learning with in the class. What does it mean if you see some friends? If you're a person of color, how important is it to you if there are other BIPOC in the room? If you're an LGBTQIA2S+ student, how does it make you feel if you recognize fellow students who are also LGBTQIA2S+? If you are a person with a mobility disability, how do you assess the room's arrangement and the degree to which it's accessible for you? After you choose your seat and start to talk to other students, what do you ask them? "Have you had this professor before?" or "Does this professor lecture the whole time, encourage class discussion, grade fairly?" As the first class session proceeds, what can you learn by observing how the professor acts, talks, interacts with students, and answers questions? What does the syllabus tell you about what will happen this semester and what your experience might be?

Social research has a lot in common with the work you might do to assess how you will feel about a professor's class. When you observe the classroom setting and students, take note of how the professor acts, ask your classmates about their unique knowledge and personal experiences with the professor, and analyze the content of the syllabus, you are already engaging in fundamental practices of qualitative research.

Introduction: How Qualitative Research Favors Depth over Breadth

When they use qualitative methods, researchers seek to understand the world in a manner that emphasizes social process, context, and meaning. As Whittemore, Chase, and Mandle (2001) describe, "Qualitative research seeks depth over breadth and attempts to learn subtle nuances of life experiences as opposed to aggregate evidence" (524, citing Ambert, Adler, Adler, and Detzner 1995). Rather than approach meaning by enumerating patterns and measuring the relationships among variables, as quantitative researchers do, qualitative researchers use more of an open-ended, interpretive approach. They seek to understand life from the perspective of those who live it and to learn about what social experiences mean to them, in their words and through

What aspects of a classroom environment do you observe on the first day of class? What are you looking to understand when you observe these things? How might this be similar to what a researcher does?

their interpretations. Consider some distinguishing features of the qualitative approach:

- It usually involves an **inductive** view of the relationship between theory and research. Qualitative researchers begin their research with open-ended research questions rather than hypotheses. They gather data first and then develop theories and concepts from these data, rather than beginning with a theory that they test through research.

inductive research   An approach to inquiry that begins with collection of data, which are then used to develop theories, hypothesis, and concepts.

interpretivism   A way of understanding social life that emphasizes people's interpretations of the world.

constructionism   A way of understanding social life as the product of interactions and negotiations among people.

naturalism   Research that seeks to minimize the use of artificial methods and other disturbances to social worlds being studied.

ethnography (or ethnographic research)   A method in which researchers immerse themselves in social settings for an extended period of time, observing behavior and interacting with study participants in order to understand people's culture and experiences

participant observation   A data collection technique often used during ethnography, in which researchers interact with, observe, and listen to people in a research setting, taking notes on what occurs.

field notes   Detailed notes that researchers take in the field, describing events, conversations, and behavior and forming the primary source of data from participant observation.

- Qualitative research is normally **interpretivist** in that it seeks to understand social life through the interpretations of those living it.
- Qualitative researchers are often **constructionist** in that they understand social life to be created by interactions and negotiations among people, rather than being a fixed structure to which individuals must conform and adapt. They take particular interest in the ongoing construction of social reality and how this occurs through the interactions between individuals and groups within a broader social context that influences their actions.
- The approach is **naturalistic** in that qualitative researchers try to minimize the disturbance they cause to the social worlds they study, yet they also recognize that they are involved in the study and consider their positionality. Often, qualitative researchers reflect on and write extensively about their methodological approach. Doing so ensures they are transparent about their choices, which can be useful to the community of researchers who can learn from their experiences. Through this reflection, researchers also consider how their own perspectives and identities may have affected their research and influenced their choices and findings.

These are overarching characteristics that much qualitative research has in common; nevertheless, qualitative researchers can differ significantly in both approach and subject matter. No qualitative research approaches these aspects the same way.

In addition to sharing particular approaches to the research endeavor, qualitative researchers also go about gathering their data in a variety of ways, using the following qualitative data-collection techniques:

- **Ethnography/participant observation.** These terms are sometimes used interchangeably, but understanding the distinctions is important. When we use the term *ethnography*, we refer to the general practice of researchers immersing themselves in a social setting for some time, seeking to understand people's culture and experiences. So, ethnography is an overall approach to research and a mode of analysis. Participant observation is a method of data collection often used during ethnography. Researchers engaging in participant observation interact with, observe, and listen to people in their setting. They take notes about what happens, which become data called **field notes**. Along with participant observation, ethnographers often use further methods of data collection, including some of the types described next. Chapter 10 examines participant observation and ethnographic methods.
- **Qualitative interviewing.** Qualitative researchers engaged in ethnographic research or participant observation also typically conduct a substantial amount of qualitative interviewing. This is in-depth, semi-structured or unstructured interviewing. When qualitative researchers choose to interview people, they seek to learn from them about what their experiences are and how they understand those experiences. Their questions tend to be open-ended, and the structure of the interview is flexible. Qualitative interviewing is not used only within ethnographic studies; in fact, many researchers use it as their sole data collection method. Chapter 9 discusses qualitative interviewing in greater detail.
- **Focus groups.** This form of research brings several people together to be interviewed at once, often using a semi-structured format. Through focus groups, researchers can learn not only about people's experiences and perceptions, but also about group dynamics and how people in social groups make sense of their lives. Chapter 9 also covers focus groups.

Some data collection techniques are used by both quantitative and qualitative researchers, but each research orientation encourages a particular approach to the data collection and analysis:

- **Content analysis.** This is the analysis of the messages communicated in written and illustrated texts and documents. In their analysis, qualitative researchers assess common themes in communication and analyze them as narratives conveying particular meanings. A qualitative approach to content analysis would examine how ideas are communicated, what messages the narrative conveys, and how the communication themes are situated within an overall context. Chapter 11 discusses content analysis as practiced in qualitative and quantitative research.
- **Available** (or **existing**) **data.** Some researchers make their qualitative data available for other researchers to examine and analyze using different research questions. Oral histories, interview transcripts, and field notes are collected in repositories made available to other researchers. Chapter 12 provides more information on the use of available,

---

qualitative interviewing In-depth, semi-structured, or unstructured interviewing that usually aims to capture the subjective experience of social processes and conditions.

---

focus groups A semi-structured interview format in which several people are interviewed together in order to learn about people's experiences and perceptions, group dynamics, and processes through which social groups make meaning.

---

content analysis The examination of texts, including both written and visual materials, with interest in how the material contributes to and reflects meaning and representation.

---

available (or existing) data Data collected by a researcher or institution and made available to others to analyze.

In July 1919, a Black teenager swimming in Lake Michigan drowned after White youths threw rocks at him for drifting across an unofficial barrier between areas considered "White" and "Black." Riots broke out after the police refused to arrest the White men eyewitnesses identified as causing the youth's death, and Chicago mayor "Big Bill" Thompson called in the National Guard to restore order.

In July 2020, police were called to prevent demonstrators from gathering outside of the private residence of Illinois Governor J. B. Pritzker. The demonstrators were protesting the use of force by police and calling for the release of wrongfully incarcerated people.

or existing, data in qualitative and quantitative research.

Quite often, qualitative studies will use a multimethod approach. For example, in addition to observing and conducting qualitative interviews, an ethnographer may also analyze texts and documents. In this chapter, we define qualitative research, explore the main goals in qualitative work, describe the common steps taken in qualitative studies, and examine the particular perspective qualitative research offers about the social world.

The Emergence of Qualitative Approaches

Qualitative research developed as a recognized mode of inquiry in the early twentieth century. There is a long history in the social sciences of trying to reconcile quantitative and interpretivist approaches to understanding the social world, with sociologist Max Weber's work (1904) as an early example (Aspers and Corte 2019, 142). The Department of Sociology at the University of Chicago greatly

BOX 5.1 Exploring Racial Attitudes Using Qualitative Interviews Versus the Survey Method

Survey data since the mid-1900s has revealed that fewer and fewer White people in the United States subscribe to the overtly racist and stereotypical views that were common in the Jim Crow era—an era when most White people openly supported racist practices like segregation. Howard Schuman, et al. (1997) studied how racial attitudes in the United States changed over time by examining survey data from opinion polls. The team found that White people hold a contradictory set of opinions. In just one of their findings, 90% of White people claimed they'd have no objection to Black people moving into their neighborhood, yet the data also showed that White people's racial concerns greatly influence their housing choices (Schuman et. al, 1997). Survey data revealed an important trend in which it seems that racist attitudes have decreased, but contradictions such as these remain and are important to understand.

Schuman and his colleagues noted that measuring beliefs about race is a complicated methodological endeavor, and surveys may not be the best way to measure people's attitudes. This is where qualitative research can come in: to ask and answer questions that quantitative research may not be able to explore as effectively. In his book *Racism without Racists: Color-Blind Racism and the Persistence of Racial Inequality in America*, Eduardo Bonilla-Silva (2018) explores the operations of contemporary racism. He argues that White racial ideology since the 1960s has taken the form of "color-blindness," an ideology that espouses that race is no longer a central organizing feature of society. This viewpoint enables Whites to claim they are not racist because they "don't see color." Bonilla-Silva analyzes the contradiction between the enduring and extensive examples of racial inequality in society and the fact that many White people claim that race is no longer a significant social category.

To better understand this situation, Bonilla-Silva examines the ways that White people explain their views and make sense of the experiences of people of color. He describes these explanations as justifications Whites make to place the responsibility for contemporary racial inequality in the laps of people of color; people who believe racial inequality no longer exists tend to conclude that negative outcomes stem from personal failures. Such justifications enable White people to deny they have any responsibility or role in this system.

Bonilla-Silva argues that surveys are most useful in gathering information that provides a snapshot of the dynamics of race in the United States, and they are less useful in delving deeply into racial perspectives such as these. He explains,

> [A]lthough surveys are useful instruments for gathering general information on actors' views, they are severely limited tools for examining how people explain, justify, rationalize, and articulate racial viewpoints. People are less likely to express their positions and emotions about racial issues by answering "yes" and "no" or "strongly agree" and "strongly disagree" to questions. Despite the gallant effort of some survey researchers to produce methodologically correct questionnaires, survey questions still restrict the free flow of ideas and unnecessarily constrain the range of possible answers for respondents (2018, 11).

Bonilla-Silva points out that in the post–Civil Rights Movement era, it is generally less acceptable for people to openly express viewpoints that may be considered racist, and he feels this could affect the ways in which people fill out surveys: they may select answers they believe to be more socially acceptable, even if they do not accurately reflect their views. Bonilla-Silva concludes that surveys can reveal broad patterns to racial attitudes, while interviews provide an in-depth understanding of how these beliefs work.

influenced the development of qualitative research methodology as an institutionalized type of social science research in in the 1920s and 1930s. Known as "the Chicago School," the program's researchers were particularly interested in urban inequalities and community development. During this time, it was common to apply evolutionary theories to humans, meaning that people were viewed as being individually responsible for their own plights owing either to genetic or to personal flaws (Farber 2008). Chicago School researchers believed social structures and contexts shaped people's lives, and they viewed the city as the laboratory in which they could explore these dynamics; in their studies they sought to paint an in-depth picture of people's everyday lives in the city. For example, Paul Cressey (1932) studied the dance halls and commercial recreation spaces where people spent time, E. Franklin Frazier (1932) studied Black families' experiences in Chicago, and Samuel Kincheloe (1938) examined how churches responded to the transforming life in the city.

Another hallmark of the Chicago School was its emphasis on fieldwork—research conducted in the places where people live their lives—as the best way to understand fully the experiences of individuals and communities. Many Chicago School researchers conducted extensive field ethnography in the neighborhoods, homes, clubs, and public places inhabited by residents of Chicago and other cities. They immersed themselves in these places for long periods of time, observing people's lives and interviewing them about it. They collected transcripts of in-depth interviews and informal conversations and took copious field notes describing events and people's actions and expressions.

In qualitative work like this, researchers entered the field with open-ended questions rather than preformed hypotheses. Their questions guided the exploration, and the areas of focus often shifted during the research period as they noted what dynamics were most important, common, or even particularly surprising. This method was different from a quantitative model of inquiry, in which a researcher had to specifically define their focal variables ahead of time and then explore the relationships between these variables by numerically mapping trends, relationships, and patterns among them (see Chapter 6). This approach is still the foundation of much qualitative research.

The Chicago School's qualitative model of study fell out of favor after World War II, when non-quantitative research methods were criticized for being non-scientific, and quantitative survey methods became the dominant paradigm in sociology (Aspers and Corte 2019, 142; Rawls 2018, cited in Aspers and Corte 2019). There is often a strong distinction made between qualitative and quantitative work, and these two research orientations are definitely different; however, there is a tendency to frame these differences in an evaluative manner that attempts to determine which is "better" or more trustworthy. In this book, we do not position any research method or orientation as better or worse than the other; instead, we consider how each mode of research enables us to ask and answer questions. A certain research orientation might be better suited to a particular interest or research inquiry, but this does not make it superior on the whole.

Defining Qualitative Research

What is qualitative research? Patrik Aspers and Ugo Corte (2019) extensively reviewed articles discussing qualitative research methods, empirical studies, and textbooks to assess how qualitative researchers define the methodology. They concluded that qualitative research is defined by four attributes (2019, 150–154).

1. *Process.* Rather than beginning with a set of variables, analyzing their attributes, and developing conclusions, qualitative researchers conduct their studies using what is described as an *iterative* process. They begin with categories or concepts they are interested in, gather data about them, reflect on what these data reveal about the concepts, and then gather more data to further understand the ideas they are developing. Another way to phrase this is that the qualitative research process often shifts between evidence and theory-building.

2. *Distinctions.* The process qualitative researchers use in their studies enables them to develop in-depth analysis of cases to observe the key characteristics of those cases and their unique qualities. Researchers seek to understand the complex and multilayered aspects of cases to develop new understandings about their distinctions.

3. *Closeness.* Through the methods qualitative researchers use to gather data, they develop what could be understood as *closeness* to the topic and

situations they're studying. They get close to the texts and documents they analyze and close to the participants they interview or observe. For example, ethnographic researchers often spend extensive time in the field. When researchers do qualitative interviews, they explore questions in an in-depth manner, encouraging elaboration. In both instances, the extended closeness to the field and participants provides opportunities to explore unexpected or emerging situations. This allows researchers to continually challenge their assumptions, explore their hunches, and develop their ideas in relation to the evidence.

4. *Improved understanding.* While all research enlarges understanding of the topics at hand, qualitative work has a particular approach to improved understanding. All research involves *pre-understanding,* the set of knowledge and assumptions a researcher begins with. The iterative process in qualitative research encourages constant questioning and exploration, as researchers analyze the data during the research process and question the pre-existing assumptions guiding the research. The process of interpretation in qualitative work builds greater understandings as pre-understandings are challenged and the data guide the researchers' deepened understanding of the concepts.

The Main Goals of Qualitative Researchers

Seeing through the Eyes of the People Being Studied

Many qualitative researchers try to view the social world through the eyes of the people they study. For example, Matías Fernández (2018) conducted an 8-month ethnography with day laborers—or *jornaleros,* as they call themselves—in Los Angeles, seeking to understand the combined dynamics of solidarity and competition characterizing the community. Focusing on *jornaleros'* experiences and interpretations, Fernández was able understand their interactions with one another and their relationship to the labor market from their points of view.

Qualitative researchers maintain that they can best develop knowledge by directly interacting with participants to get a sense of who they are. By imagining themselves in others' situations, they can "take the role of the other," to use a phrase coined by John Lofland and Lyn Lofland (1995, 16). This practice reveals itself in frequent references to *empathy.* Here are some examples:

- C. J. Pascoe (2012) spent a year-and-a-half conducting field research and interviews in a Northern California high school to study how teenagers construct and enforce masculinity in school. She found that the young men she studied created their masculine identities by repeatedly sexualizing young women, boasting about their sexual exploits, and directing homophobic insults at each other. She noted racialized distinctions in this process and outlined differences in how Black and White boys' expressions were perceived differently by peers and school authorities. While Pascoe noted that these practices contributed to a hostile climate in school for girls and gay, lesbian, and queer students, she also observed that the boys suffered as a result of the constant pressure they experience to embody normative masculinity.

- Marie "Keta" Miranda (2003) researched Chicana girls in gangs in Oakland, California, exploring how constraining public narratives typically depict them as threatening and criminal, ignoring realities of their lives such as their intimate friendships and culture of solidarity. Miranda collaborated with her participants when determining her research directions and also supported their construction of counter-narratives about their lives through a documentary the girls produced, called *It's a Homie Thang!*

The goal of seeing through the eyes of the people under study is often accompanied by the closely related goal of probing beneath surface appearances. After all, by taking the position of those under study, researchers may be able to see things in a way that an outsider with little direct contact would not. This insight is revealed in a number of studies, such as the following:

- Karrie Shogren, et al. (2015) explored how full inclusion of students with disabilities in general education classrooms affects schools. The study revealed that most students with and without disabilities appreciated the value of inclusive

Methods in Motion | **Applications to Society**

The attacks of September 11th, 2001, were of a kind never seen before in the United States. They caused an unprecedented loss of life, terror, and national grief. In the aftermath of the attacks, US politicians and citizens sought to make sense of the calamity and restore a feeling of security and unity.

What was the experience of Muslim Americans during this process, when the society was attempting to make sense of an attack perpetrated by people with ties to the extremist group al-Qaeda, which claimed allegiance to the Islamic faith? Lori Peek (2010) used qualitative methods to study how Muslim Americans were victimized, encountered discrimination, and adapted to life after the attacks.

Peek wondered why Muslim Americans faced such a significant backlash from so many people in the United States when, for instance, no similarly unified public outrage against White American men occurred after Timothy McVeigh and Terry Nichols killed and injured scores of people by detonating a bomb in Oklahoma City in 1995. She notes that the scale of the 9/11 attacks made them unique and contributed to mass feelings of extreme anger, anxiety, and helplessness, which in turn contributed to a search for someone to blame. That Muslim Americans faced blame and hostility, though, came largely from the fact that anti-Muslim sentiment already pervaded the US cultural atmosphere, and that Muslims were already seen as outsiders in the United States, before 9/11. In addition, Muslims were a visible and identifiable minority who held little formal political power in the United States.

As anti-Muslim hate crimes and violence spiked after 9/11, so did discrimination. Muslims (and people assumed to be Muslim) became subject to frequent searches and interrogations at airports (Peek 2010, 31), and the USA PATRIOT Act enabled law enforcement to profile, question, and detain anyone suspected of supporting terrorism. Peek interviewed 140 Muslim Americans to understand their experiences of this post-9/11 backlash. Her interviewees reported that they had grown up as Muslim Americans with a clear knowledge of their religious minority status, experiencing pressure to assimilate, prejudice, and regular harassment from non-Muslims. However, after 9/11 they increasingly experienced physical assault, verbal harassment, suspicious or hostile stares, and discrimination in employment and housing, at school, and on public transit. While many in the United States experienced fear after 9/11, Peek found that Muslim Americans experienced "compounded fear" (2010, 113), described as backlash-related anxieties that made them scared for themselves and their loved ones' safety and survival.

While some Muslims engaged in strategies to protect themselves from threats, such as by staying at home or hiding their faith, many realized they could not live this way in the long term. Thus, many of Peek's interviewees reported that they developed stronger ties to their religion and their Muslim community, choosing to openly display their faith and learn more about Islam as they sought spiritual solace. They also worked to challenge public misconceptions about Muslims. As one interviewee, Bakir, stated, "I think one of the positive outcomes from [9/11], the only positive thing I've seen so far, is that we have this opening, this chance to educate people and remove ignorance. But it is only going to work if Muslims keep working together" (2010, 145).

As Peek point out, "The wave of hostility that was unleashed after the 9/11 attacks may have victimized Muslims, but they did not become passive victims. Instead, they actively struggled to reclaim their faith and to assert their positions in the American social landscape" (2010, 163). Peek expresses hope that her research can increase understanding of the context of anti-Muslim hostility and consequences for the Muslim American community; this information, she argues, might help prevent such backlashes after other major crises. Whether this anti-Muslim backlash has lessened or changed over time in the post 9/11-era can be tested only through further research and the passage of time.

programs. Emphasizing students' perspectives offered insights from the group of people who are most affected by school policy reform decisions.

- Scott Vrecko (2015) studied illicit use of prescription stimulants at a US university, uncovering the varied ways students access the drugs and their reasons for using them. The student users acquired the drugs from multiple sources (including family, friends, drug dealers, and clinicians), and they used stimulants not only to improve their academic performance but also to cope with their everyday stresses.

What assumptions might you have about these street musicians' motivations and experiences? That they're panhandling or down on their luck? That they're hoping to be discovered or just trying to share their music with a public audience? Qualitative research can enable you to probe underneath surface appearances or assumptions and see the musicians' world through their own eyes.

- Baker A. Rogers (2019) interviewed 51 transgender men about their experiences living in the Southeast United States. The interviews offered insights into how gender norms demanding people subscribe to a binary gender performance might affect the self-presentation of transmasculine people. The majority of participants in the study presented themselves in a gender normative way and attempted to be perceived as cisgender men (sometimes referred to as "passing"). The men in the study shared that their desire to pass related to the positive self-confidence and psychological boost they felt when being seen as men, privileges they received when perceived as cisgender men, and safety they experienced in situations where they might experience anti-trans violence.

The empathetic effort to understand the world through the eyes of their participants can present researchers with practical dilemmas. For example: how far should one go to develop empathy? What if participants' experience includes illegal or dangerous activities? There is also the risk that the researcher will be able to understand some of the people's perspectives in a particular social scene but not those of others, such as people of a gender or race different from their own. These and other practical challenges will be addressed in later chapters. Though some may view these challenges as problems, many qualitative researchers consider them instead to be core questions. Qualitative researchers' commitment to asking these questions—consistently reflecting on and wrestling with their implications—is a strength of the method.

Providing Rich Description of the Context

Qualitative researchers are much more inclined than their quantitative colleagues to include descriptive detail when reporting their research. These details are important because we can better understand the behavior of social group members when we have knowledge of the specific environment in which they operate. Behavior that initially appears ridiculous or irrational may make more sense when understood in the context in which it takes place.

The emphasis on context in qualitative research goes back to classic studies in social anthropology. Many anthropological studies demonstrated how practices that seemed illogical when viewed through White, Western eyes (e.g., a magical ritual that accompanies the sowing of seeds) make sense when they are understood as part of the society's belief system. For example, during his 18 months of ethnographic research in a men's prison, Michael Gibson-Light (2018) noticed that cigarettes, the longstanding source of currency in informal prison exchange, had been replaced by seemingly unlikely items: ramen noodle packets and honey buns. He was curious about how "ramen money" had become so valuable in prison, wondering: "after generations of the dominance of cigarettes as prison money, what explains the emergence of items of sustenance as central units of exchange?" (200).

To answer a question such as this one, a researcher must develop a contextual understanding of social behavior, and descriptive information helps flesh out the complexities of the social context. It was during the early months of his fieldwork at "Sunbelt State Penitentiary" (or "SSP"—a pseudonym) that Gibson-Light first heard about "soups" being used as payments and observed people incarcerated in the prison exchanging ramen noodles to pay debts. Over several months, he talked to both staff and incarcerated people about what he saw as a surprising and somewhat strange practice, gathering scores of accounts describing the value of soup in the prison economy:

> "One way or another, everything in prison is about money," stated one soft spoken prisoner. "Soup is money in here. It's sad but true," said another. As one man asserted, "you can get a *lot* with soups." Another went further to state that "a soup is *everything*" and many will trade anything they own to get one" (211).

These details enabled Gibson-Light to understand more about how "soups" were situated within overall practices of resource exchange within the prison.

To further analyze these resource exchange systems, Gibson-Light needed to understand them within the overall prison context. He noticed that ramen and other types of food were a valuable commodity, and that the people incarcerated in the prison also often stole food items. He understood this to stem from the current context in which prisons are sites of increasing deprivation, where imprisoned people are expected to purchase their own amenities (such as hygiene items) and where the meals provided are smaller and less nutritious than in previous eras. As one person at SSP shared, "They pay us 20 cents an hour, don't feed us enough at meals, and jack up the prices of everything in commissary. Big surprise that people are stealing fresh vegetables" (214). Gibson-Light explains, "To be sure, selling vegetables was a profitable hustle. 'Fresh veggies are like lobster in here,' said one man, biting into what he called a 'black market zucchini' on his lunch break" (214). As Gibson-Light shares details about people in prison grappling with and expressing frustration over prison deprivation, the importance of ramen money became clearer.

Including details like these helps Gibson-Light to convey important information about the context, and analyzing data such as this is how qualitative researchers develop their conclusions. Qualitative researchers must be thoughtful about the details they include in their accounts of what goes on in the setting under investigation. Lofland and Lofland (1995, 164–65), for example, warned against what they called "descriptive excess" in qualitative research, whereby the amount of detail overwhelms or inhibits the analysis of the data. Qualitative researchers must strike a balance: to paint a dynamic and complex picture of their settings and the context without becoming lost in descriptive detail.

Exploring Social Processes

Qualitative researchers tend to view social life in terms of processes. This tendency reveals itself in a number of ways, but the main one is the concern with showing how events and patterns unfold over time. Qualitative evidence often conveys a strong sense of change and flux and thus captures how individual and group actions unfold in a series of steps that are related to one another and that influence particular outcomes.

Qualitative research using participant observation is particularly well suited to the study of process. Ethnographers are typically immersed in a social setting for a long time—in many cases, for years. Consequently, they are able to observe how events develop over time and how the different elements of a social system (such as values, beliefs, and behavior) interconnect. Tracing interdependent streams of actions and events allows the researcher to present social life as a process (see Box 5.2).

A sense of process can also be developed through in-depth interviewing, in which participants are asked to reflect on the activities leading up to, during, or following an event. Robert Weiss (2005), for example, interviewed 89 middle-class workers in the Boston area about their retirement

What processes might unfold in anti-fracking activism versus anti-death penalty activism or other social movements? How would qualitative research provide information about the process involved in various social movements?

experiences. His interviews illustrated how retirement is not a discrete moment in time, but a process in which retirees' status and self-conception shift in multiple ways as they conclude their careers.

BOX 5.2 Process in Anti-Fracking Activism

Amanda Buday (2017) conducted over 200 hours of participant observation and 43 in-depth interviews during the development of the Illinois Hydraulic Fracturing Regulatory Act. She examined the advocacy process pursued by a variety of political and community stakeholders concerned about the environmental consequences of using the hydraulic fracturing technique ("fracking") to harvest gas and oil from shale rock. She discovered that local grassroots activists were marginalized within state politics and that they found it necessary to form allegiances with a professionalized environmental advocacy organization to pursue their goal to ban fracking in rural communities. This arrangement offered the activists

more political recognition, but it also forced them to narrow the range of tactics they could use to oppose local fracking operations.

Ultimately, Buday's work uncovered hidden insights into the dynamics of activists' processes in at least two ways. First, observing the movement over time made it possible to highlight developments and interconnections between events as the movement evolved in its allegiances and strategies. Second, connecting these events with the political context demonstrated how grassroots activists' choices can be limited as they seek influence within the powerful levels of government while also trying to maintain their group cohesion and strategic autonomy.

The **life history** approach is another form of qualitative research that can be used to show process. In his classic study of a poor Mexican family, Oscar Lewis (1961) conducted extended interviews with the family members to reconstruct their life histories. Through the hundreds of questions Lewis asked members of the Sánchez family, he was able to explore their memories of various life stages and develop understandings of their experiences, goals, and viewpoints as they developed and changed over the course of their lives.

Employing an Open-Ended, Flexible Approach

Most qualitative researchers try not to impose a predetermined set of assumptions on the social worlds they study; they resist tendencies to prioritize the researcher's perspective at the expense of the perspective of the research participants. When the structure of data collection is predetermined, the steps are often planned ahead of time on the basis of *researchers'* prior ruminations and expectations about a social reality that they may have never encountered before. Such structure limits the degree to which the researcher can genuinely adopt the worldview of those being studied and can lead to serious misunderstandings. A less rigid approach enhances the likelihood that the research will reveal aspects of people's social world that are particularly important to them—aspects that might never even cross the mind of a researcher using a more rigidly structured method. Thus, qualitative researchers avoid limiting areas of inquiry, and the research questions they ask tend be open-ended.

For example, Nicole Dezrea Jenkins (2019) conducted an ethnography in a West African-owned braiding salon in Las Vegas, Nevada, because she was interested in Black women's experiences in beauty salons. She did 24 months of participant observation, interviewed people, and analyzed the content of online reviews. When she began the study, her main goal was to describe the setting and interactions within it from an intersectional perspective. Jenkins noted that previous salon ethnographies had not analyzed the gendered and racialized aspects of beauty work, so she wanted to explore this in a space catering to Black women. She conducted her research in a salon she called "Mimi's African Braiding and Weaving Salon."

Jenkins approached her ethnographic research in an open-ended manner, spending her time there in a variety of ways (answering phones, sweeping up, or just hanging out) and allowing her focus to narrow and develop as she became better acquainted with the dynamics in the setting. Her flexibility as a researcher enabled her to remain open to seeing the realities of what occurred at the salon and led her down avenues of research she had not anticipated.

When Jenkins began the study, she did not expect that nationality and citizenship differences, rather than a shared sense of Black womanhood, would arise as primary to the interactional dynamics in the salon. Most of the braiders were born outside of the United States: 9 in Senegal (the owner's country of origin), 3 in Nigeria, and 1 in Haiti. Braiders distinguished themselves from the customers by emphasizing that Africans' manners were different from Americans'—characteristics they used to distance themselves from Black American women. They also distanced themselves from other Africans, and Jenkins observed braiders engaging in microaggressions towards Ethiopian customers and treating them with exasperation and rudeness. Black American women emphasized braiders' immigrant status, distancing themselves from them by criticizing their accents or their continued use of their first language. They also distinguished themselves from the braiders by expressing admiration for them in a way that homogenized African culture.

Jenkins's research enabled her to conclude, "The women developed their sense of selves centered on their ideal black woman-ness yet created distance in tandem. In the process, they often deployed stereotypical ideologies in culturally insensitive ways that stigmatized black women collectively" (832).

---

life history method A qualitative method that emphasizes people's experiences and connections with larger societal events across lifetime, usually through analysis of interviews and personal documents.

The open-ended approach Jenkins used in her ethnography allowed her to learn about factors that divide Black women; consider the complex intersection of race, gender, and nationality in the salon space; and consider the implications of these factors on Black women's continued experiences of marginalization.

Ethnography, with its emphasis on participant observation as a main form of data collection, is particularly well suited to this open structure. It allows researchers to immerse themselves in a social setting with a general research idea in mind and then gradually, through observation, narrow it down to a more specific topic as they see what is most prevalent in the setting, as Jenkins did.

The Main Steps in Qualitative Research

Figure 5.1 outlines the main steps in the qualitative research process. We explore these steps in greater detail using Annette Lareau's (2011) study comparing family life in middle-class, working-class, and poor Black and White households.

Lareau began with a focus on two broad class categories, which she defined by occupation:

- middle-class (parents with jobs requiring educational credentials and who were supervisors or managers); and
- working-class (parents with jobs requiring no higher education and who did not hold managerial power).

In her research, she examined connections between class, race, and parenting strategies.

Step 1. Asking general research question(s). Lareau was interested in the factors that most influence family life, parenting styles, and children's experiences. A common assumption in the United States is that the class system is open, and anyone can move up the class ladder through hard work. When thinking about factors that differentiate people, many first think of race, rather than class, as the primary characteristic contributing to people's different ways of being and opportunities. In her study, Lareau sought to explore

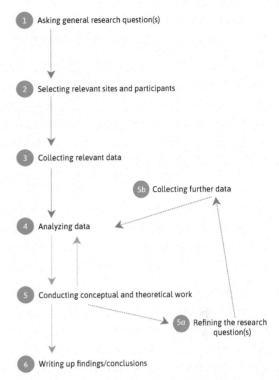

FIGURE 5.1 The main steps in qualitative research

how social class affects the organization of parenting practices, children's lives, and their future opportunities: this became her guiding research question.

Step 2. Selecting site(s) and participants. Lareau conducted her research in a school in a Midwestern town and two schools in the Northeast. Lareau had ideally wanted to conduct research in schools that were integrated along race and class, but she found it difficult to find schools in her regions of choice that were integrated by both social class and race. Lareau chose to prioritize schools that were racially integrated and contacted administrators in school districts that met her criteria. They helped her select the final list of schools to approach and facilitated her reaching out to school principals. She identified relevant research participants by approaching parents of children enrolled in these schools. She created lists of students grouped by race and class and used systematic sampling (selecting every "nth" name) to select which families to approach about participating in the research. She also recruited teachers and professionals working with the children at the schools.

Step 3. Collecting data. Over the span of 8 years, Lareau and a team of research assistants conducted the study in four phases. First, Lareau observed two third-grade classrooms in the Midwestern town she called "Lawrenceville," conducting in-depth interviews with parents, guardians, and professionals working with 31 children. Next, Lareau and the team observed classrooms in the two Northeastern schools, which she called "Swan" and "Lower Richmond," conducting in-depth interviews with 40 families of children enrolled in the schools. Third, the team chose 12 families with whom to conduct intensive ethnographic research, and over a two-year period they spent time with the families at home, on outings, and in their daily activities. Finally, they conducted in-depth interviews with parents, guardians, siblings, and children in those families. The participants in the study were equally distributed in terms of race and class level. Lareau primarily used two types of data: (1) field notes based on the team's participant observation of family life and (2) detailed transcripts of interviews.

Step 4. Analyzing data. Lareau and her team used common methods to analyze the data. In all, the team had conducted interviews with parents of 88 children, and Lareau manually coded these interview transcripts. Coding is a process in which the researcher reads the transcripts line-by-line and describes each line of data with a word or phrase (code) that captures the meaning of what is conveyed in the data (this process is discussed in depth in Chapter 13). Coding allowed Lareau to note key themes and topics in the interviews, which she then input into a qualitative analysis software program.

For the field note data collected from observing the 12 families in depth, Lareau states she analyzed it "the old-fashioned way"—manually and without computer software. She repeatedly read and re-read the field notes, which were arranged for each family chronologically. She developed an analysis by noting themes in the data, discussing her ideas with others, reading academic literature to help her develop an argument, and then linking her argument to examples from the data. As Lareau fleshed out these ideas,

she also looked to her data for examples that might contradict her argument.

Step 5. Conducting conceptual and theoretical work. A key finding in Lareau's study related to how class influences family life. All the families shared the characteristic of being loving and supportive, with parents wanting the best for their children. Distinct differences in family life were present when comparing middle-class families to working-class/poor families, and Lareau observed they had different "cultural logic[s] of child rearing" (2011, 3). These different approaches influenced parents' interactions with their children, how they organized the children's time, and how they taught the children to behave towards major institutional authorities like teachers or doctors. Lareau found that parents' social class influenced children's experiences in a way that could transmit advantages to middle-class children and disadvantages to working-class/poor children.

Lareau noted that middle-class parents raise their children using a process she called "concerted cultivation," in which children participated in many organized activities, were encouraged to actively question adults, and developed tangible skills. These experiences encouraged them to develop a sense of entitlement when operating within major institutions and to behave in a manner leading to success within these institutions.

In contrast, working-class and poor parents employed a process she called "accomplishment of natural growth," where children were allowed to "be kids," enjoyed leisure time and strong extended kin relationships, were not involved in many organized activities, and were not encouraged to question authority. These experiences encouraged them to act reserved around authority figures, not asserting themselves within major institutions and mistrusting those institutions. As a result, they engaged in institutional settings in a manner that disadvantaged them.

Step 5. (a) Refining the research question(s), and (b) Collecting further data. Usually the initial collection and interpretation of data lead to a sharpening of the research question(s), which is followed by additional data gathering to address the more specific concerns contained in the revised research questions. This occurred between phase one and phase two of Lareau's study. Her original observation and interviews in Lawrenceville enabled her to crystallize the focus of her research and plan for the next phases at Lower Richmond and Swan. Her early data collection and interpretation of the data enabled her to see how to proceed in the next phases.

Qualitative researchers typically view the data collection, analysis, and theorizing stages as a cycle. For instance, they often analyze their data as they collect them, and then pursue new directions as the data present them. This analysis of early data then affects what data researchers collect later on as they proceed in the study. As mentioned earlier in the chapter, this strategy is frequently described as *iterative*. Lareau interviewed some parents and professionals two or even three times in the course of her research, each time adapting her focus in the light of her developing ideas.

Step 6. Writing up findings/conclusions. In any type of research, an audience has to be convinced of both the credibility and the significance of the interpretations offered. Lareau's work includes lessons for those interested in social inequality and even those interested in parenting practices. Lareau made clear to her readers that her study was not intended to evaluate or define "good" or "bad" parenting choices. Instead, she concludes that her findings have implications for our understandings of social inequality. She explains that "social class also gives parents a different set of economic resources and, crucially, a different set of cultural repertoires for managing the experiences of their children as they interact with institutions such as schools, courts, hospitals, and government agencies" (2011, 265). Lareau points out that the economic and material resources of middle-class families put them in a privileged position from which to cultivate their children through activities such as sports, drama, or music. Such cultivation becomes a cumulative force of material privileges and cultural resources that provide opportunities and advantages within major institutions.

The Distinct Perspective of Qualitative Research

Qualitative and quantitative approaches offer unique perspectives on a variety of methodological issues—for example, the importance of **objectivity** and how researchers' **subjectivities** can and should shape research. Qualitative and quantitative researchers also have different ideas about **generalizability**: whether research findings should apply to as large a population of people as possible or yield in-depth understandings of small groups and individuals. Another point of difference lies in the concern with **replicability**—that is, whether another researcher could repeat the research and come to the same conclusions. In the sections that follow we explore qualitative researchers' ideas about objectivity, generalization, and replicability in greater depth (further discussion of these in relation to quantitative research will occur in Chapter 6).

The Question of Objectivity

While researchers embracing **positivism** emphasize objectivity as a key goal, qualitative researchers think about objectivity by considering the relationships

---

objectivity A position that approaches social phenomena as if they have an existence independent of social actors or their perceptions; it calls on researchers to draw conclusions based on facts that are not influenced by values, bias, or preconceptions.

---

subjectivity An approach to research that allows researchers' values, identities, and biographies into the research process; it calls on researchers to consider how the conclusions they draw reflect and are shaped by those commitments, feelings, and experiences.

---

generalizability The extent to which a research finding can be applied to people, groups, and social conditions the researcher did not directly observe.

---

replicability The property of a study that would allow another researcher to repeat the research and achieve the same findings.

---

positivism An epistemological position that advocates using empirical methods and logic to study of social reality.

Mixed Methods in Action | Using Mixed Methods to Confirm Findings

After the first edition of Annette Lareau's book *Unequal Childhoods* was published in 2003, she received questions about how typical the families in her ethnography were. To explore this question, she and some collaborators conducted a quantitative secondary analysis of the Panel Study of Income Dynamics (PSID) dataset, a longitudinal study of a representative sample of families (Lareau, Weininger, Conley, and Velez 2011), examining the data to explore links between social class and children's use of time.

The researchers examined a specific module in the PSID, the Child Development Survey (CDS), which provided detailed data on children in the PSID a few years after Lareau conducted her ethnography. Using proxy measures of social class—mother's education and family income—they found that social class was also strongly related to children's use of time in these data. There were no major differences between Black and White children's participation in organized activities, but they did find differences across class. For example, children whose mothers had higher levels of education were involved in more organized activities, and children whose mothers had lower levels of education had more unstructured leisure time.

The researchers also noted similarities around how much time children spent with extended family, in that middle-class children in the PSID-CDS data spent less time with relatives than did working class children. However, these data also showed that Black children were more likely than White children to spend time with extended family, which was a departure from the ethnographic findings. Language use and conversation were significant elements of the parenting models that Lareau observed in her ethnography, but this type of language use and interaction was not able to be examined using the PSID-CDS data (which only measured language in the form of test scores and reading ability).

Thus, the quantitative analysis was able to confirm some findings, raise questions suggesting avenues for more exploration, and demonstrate how ethnographic methods might be better suited than survey data to uncover certain key interactional dynamics within families.

between *power, authority,* and *knowledge production.* Some research uses quantitative methods to test hypotheses and presents finding in terms of formulas, numbers, and statistics. Since the Enlightenment, this language—the language of quantitative research—has held great authority.

However, feminist and other scholars emphasizing the importance of anti-oppression research have long pointed out that the knowledge produced using methods assumed to be objective and trustworthy is still knowledge produced by *people*—people with perspectives, power, biases, and inevitable gaps in their understandings. Women and transgender people (Collins 1986; Harding 1987; Currah and Stryker 2015; Stryker 2008), BIPOC (Cooper 1892; DuBois 1903; Gutiérrez y Muhs, Niemann, González, and Harris 2012; Moraga and Anzaldua 1983; Zia 2000), post-colonial scholars (Spivak 1994; Tuhiwai Smith 1999), working-class people (Dews and Law 1995; Fazio, Launius, and Strangleman 2020), people with disabilities (McRuer 2006; Price 2012), LGBTQIA2S+ people (Ferguson 2004; Ghaziani and Brim 2019; Nash and Browne 2010), and other marginalized groups have noted that their perspectives are often omitted from widely accepted knowledge produced by people in positions of power and asserted to be complete, objective, and trustworthy.

Qualitative analysis frequently highlights people's engaging and intimate stories about their experiences. Unlike findings expressed using statistics and numbers, findings presented through people's stories may appear impressionistic and subjective. As readers have their own reactions to the stories they read, they may wonder what role the researcher's reactions, values, and opinions play in the analysis. It is a mistake to assume that quantitative work is, by its nature, objective and that qualitative work, by its nature, is not. No matter whether a researcher conducts extensive statistical tests or in-depth participant observation, *all* researchers must be aware of and think about power, perspectives, and choices as they move through the steps of research.

Just like quantitative researchers, qualitative researchers follow a set of systematic procedures when gathering and analyzing data (we will discuss qualitative data analysis further in Chapter 13). In their presentations of research findings, qualitative researchers place an emphasis on sharing their participants' stories, because these are needed to explore in depth and meaningful information about people's lives. The researcher includes those stories that represent dynamics and themes that emerge in a systematic analysis of their data. These dynamics and themes constitute a pattern that spans the people and settings studied.

Qualitative researchers' commitment to thinking about power and their use of systematic procedures makes their work more objective than some assume. However, qualitative researchers also ask whether objectivity *should* be the goal of research. In fact, many consider subjectivity a strength of qualitative research. Ethnographic researchers often spend long periods of time in the field and form relationships with the people there. They conduct in-depth interviews with people, often about deeply personal experiences. In the process, qualitative researchers may risk the perception of bias as they form close personal relationships with the people they study. But conventional demands for distance and objectivity can replicate a troubling power hierarchy in which researchers' goal is to obtain information from people they treat as depersonalized research subjects (Esterberg 2001; Oakley 1981). Qualitative researchers find that relying on their interpersonal skills, engaging honestly with their research participants, and developing trust with them leads to more accurate and meaningful findings. Participants are more willing to open up to someone who makes

them feel comfortable, and researchers can learn from the contours of the relationships they form with participants—what's required to establish and maintain trust, and what gets in the way of trust. This is often described as developing **rapport** with participants—a cornerstone of qualitative data collection. Rapport is discussed more in Chapter 9.

The Demand for Generalizability

If a team of researchers studied how a particular group of youth experiencing homelessness dealt with the stigma of homelessness, as Anne R. Roschelle and Peter Kaufman (2004) did in the San Francisco Bay Area, people might ask whether their findings apply to any, most, or even all youth experiencing homelessness—that is, people might ask if the findings are representative of some larger population (generalizable) and thus trustworthy. But Roschelle and Kaufman's qualitative research orientation was formulated with a goal of sharing in-depth and distinctive information about the specific people they studied. Because of this, Roschelle and Kaufman studied a smaller sample than a quantitative researcher studying homelessness might. They focused specifically on young people who received residential, educational, and social support in one Bay Area organization called "A Home Away from Homelessness." Does this mean that the insights Roschelle and Kaufman offer apply only to the specific people and place they studied?

Roschelle and Kaufmann did not gather a random sample that represents the population of all homeless youth. They, like many qualitative researchers, used non-probability sampling. In fact, with some social groups, such as youth experiencing homelessness, undocumented people, or sex workers, it may be impossible to enumerate the population in a precise manner. Under these conditions, the selection of a representative sample is impracticable. In most cases, qualitative researchers do not strive to use their sample to produce knowledge generalizable

---

rapport A relationship developed between the researcher and an individual or group of people, allowing both to understand, trust, and communicate with each other.

to a large population, as discussed in Chapter 4. Such research normally stands on its own, providing in-depth analysis of a person or a small group of people—a goal different from that of quantitative research.

This is not to say that findings from a qualitative study like the one conducted by Roschelle and Kaufmann have no application to other populations or other settings. Qualitative researchers approach generalization about the people or events they study by identifying elements that are shared among those people or common in those situations (Williams 2000). In other words, they seek to build broader conceptual understandings of the people's characteristics, their experiences, and the context surrounding them. Roschelle and Kaufmann's focus on youth experiencing homelessness in the San Francisco Bay Area provided information about those youths' lives, but it also yielded generalizations about what it *means* to be a homeless kid in a world that stigmatizes homeless people. For these youth, "This social reality epitomizes the violence of poverty and ultimately results in a lack of consistency, stability, and safety in their lives. Furthermore, these kids exist in a constrained public domain and are forced to carve out their own space in a limited urban environment that is generally hostile to them" (Roschelle and Kauffman 2004, 41). The researchers identified how youth experiencing homelessness exist within a dramatically inequitable social context that causes them to face particular hardships and stigmas.

Roschelle and Kaufmann's goal was not to identify experiences common to all youth experiencing homelessness. Instead, their goal—and accomplishment—was to contribute to people's conceptual understanding of significant social processes and experiences related to stigma and homelessness. Their research expanded understandings of how unhoused youth engage in practices to reduce their stigma and make themselves appear socially acceptable and more like housed people using what are called "stigma management" techniques. They furthered understanding of stigmatization as a social process, noting that unhoused youths' stigma management techniques were constrained by their vulnerable social structural position. Lack of money and housing made it difficult for the youth to hide their homeless status due to their hand-me-down clothing and inability to invite friends home to hang out. Further, when they tried to manage their stigma by acting out in ways typical of their middle-class peers, like showing off physically or acting sexually precocious, their homeless status led outsiders to interpret their behaviors as problematic or even sinister. As such, this research expands our understanding of stigmatization as a social process by revealing how "the parameters of acceptable and unacceptable behavior are mediated by one's social location" (Roschelle and Kauffman 2004, 41). Qualitative research thus builds social theory, allowing researchers to explore and compare experiences of stigmatized groups.

The Goal of Replicability

Another way people evaluate a study is to see if its results can be replicated: if another researcher can repeat a study and get the same results (a process often referred to as a **restudy**), the consistency of results suggests the study is thought to be trustworthy. Even though replicability is one characteristic of valid research, replication is uncommon in qualitative research.

Nicole Dezrea Jenkins (2019), whose research involving an African-owned hair-braiding salon we considered earlier in the chapter, spent two years observing, interviewing, and hanging out with the people in the salon. The exact process she went through to collect and analyze data over the course of the study could probably not be replicated, as it relied a great deal on her personal ingenuity. One strength of observational research is

---

restudy The process of reproducing a study previously completed by researching a topic, population, or situation again at a different time.

its open-ended nature. Different researchers choose to observe different things, and as a result they may come up with different findings. Further, ethnographers follow the lead of those in their field sites—so the people Jenkins researched led her in directions important to them, and those directions enabled her to understand their behaviors and experiences. These differences and variations are valued sources of insight.

For these reasons, qualitative researchers face difficulties when revisiting ground previously covered by another researcher. This may not inspire confidence in the replicability of qualitative research, but most qualitative researchers would suggest thinking about replicability in a different way. Jenkins would probably suggest that other researchers take her findings and choose certain *concepts* to study further, such as beauty industry labor or distinctions enforced within marginalized populations (rather than attempting to replicate her exact study). Qualitative researchers hope other researchers will engage in research that deepens our understanding of the social categories and theories they develop in their studies.

Barber and long-time civil rights leader James Armstrong gives a patron a trim in the same shop where Armstrong once cut Dr. Martin Luther King Jr.'s hair. How might an observational study in this barbershop be different from Nicole Dezrea Jenkins's study of the African-owned hair-braiding salon in Las Vegas? What kinds of gender dynamics, community building, and political organizing might occur among the men in this shop compared to the clientele of the Las Vegas salon? What would be the strengths of using an open-ended approach or conducting this research with a goal of further exploring the concepts of connection and division that Jenkins found in her study?

Considering Qualitative Approaches

As we have discussed in this chapter, qualitative researchers use various data collection techniques to explore their topics in an in-depth manner, gathering detailed and specific information about their areas of interest and the communities they study. They follow a series of organized steps and systematic procedures through which they examine their topics, procedures characterized by a combination of both structure and flexibility. Qualitative researchers study a wide range of subjects and approach their studies in a variety of ways, yet also share certain approaches towards research. Common features of qualitative studies include their open-ended nature, their goal of gathering deep and detailed information to understand life in context, an allegiance to flexibility, and the aim of understanding life from their participants' perspectives. Quantitative research, the methodology to which we turn in the next chapter, offers a different and equally valuable approach to studying social life.

Key Points

Introduction: How Qualitative Research Favors Depth over Breadth

- Qualitative researchers tend to produce inductive, constructionist, and interpretivist studies, focusing on meanings rather than numbers.
- Qualitative research is naturalistic in that it typically minimizes the disturbances caused to the social worlds being studied.
- Ethnography, participant observation, qualitative interviewing, and focus groups are all types of qualitative research. Content analysis and analysis of available data can be approached with either quantitative of qualitative research, yet these methods are conducted differently depending on the methodology.

The Emergence of Qualitative Approaches

- Qualitative research became a recognized method during the early twentieth century, when sociologists at the University of Chicago used ethnography to explore urban inequalities.
- While there are many distinctions between qualitative and quantitative approaches, neither is superior to the other; they each enable researchers to explore questions in a particular way.

Defining Qualitative Research

- Four main attributes define qualitative research: process, distinctions, closeness, and improved understanding.
- Together, the main attributes of qualitative research involve a cycle of gathering evidence and building theory, understanding the distinctiveness of the cases under study, closely observing the topics, and challenging pre-assumptions to deepen understandings.

The Main Goals of Qualitative Researchers

- Qualitative research is particularly well suited to study topics in an in-depth way that examines social context and emphasizes what social dynamics mean to those who experience them.

- Main goals of qualitative research include seeing through the eyes of research participants, providing rich description of the context, exploring social processes, and employing an open-ended, flexible approach.
- To avoid limiting areas of inquiry, qualitative research questions are usually open-ended.

The Main Steps in Qualitative Research

- Qualitative research can be broken down into six steps:
  1. Asking general research questions
  2. Selecting relevant site(s) and subjects
  3. Collecting relevant data
  4. Analyzing data
  5. Conducting conceptual and theoretical work
     a. Refining the research question(s)
     b. Collecting further data
  6. Writing up findings/making conclusions
- Qualitative researchers typically view the data collection, analysis, and theorizing stages as iterative or cyclical processes.

The Distinct Perspective of Qualitative Research

- Qualitative researchers approach the question of objectivity by considering the relationships between power, authority, and knowledge production.
- In most cases, qualitative research is not intended to produce knowledge generalizable to a large population. Instead, qualitative researchers strive to contribute to the development of more nuanced theoretical and conceptual understandings of social life.
- While replicability is a goal of some researchers and is one characteristic of valid research, replication is uncommon with qualitative research because of the unique and specific nature of qualitative research studies. A qualitative approach to replicability would consist of restudying concepts examined in previous work.

Questions for Review

1. What do the terms inductive, constructionist, and interpretivist mean in relation to qualitative research? How do these influence qualitative research studies?

2. When did qualitative research emerge as a recognized methodology, why was the methodology favored at that time, and what sorts of studies did early qualitative researchers engage in?

3. Describe the four attributes that define qualitative research and discuss how these enable qualitative researchers to develop particular understandings about their topics.

4. What topics or situations might be particularly useful to study using qualitative methods? Why?

5. What are the main goals of qualitative researchers and how are they unique to this methodology?

6. Why is it important to establish context in qualitative research?

7. Which qualitative data collection methods can be used to explore social processes?

8. What are the benefits of using an open-ended and flexible structure in qualitative research?

9. What are the six steps of the qualitative research process, and how do these steps relate to one another?

10. What steps of qualitative research are considered iterative? How do these iterative processes benefit the researcher?

11. What considerations might you make when thinking about whether you are approaching your research objectively or not?

12. Discuss this statement: Relying on interpersonal skills, engaging honestly with research participants, and developing trust with them often leads to researcher bias and thus less accurate and meaningful information.

13. What does it mean for a qualitative researcher to emphasize generalizing about concepts?

14. Rather than replicating a qualitative research study, what might researchers do to further understanding of a topic from a qualitative study?

Portfolio Exercise

1. Consider how you might use qualitative research to advance an understanding of the research topic you have been working on in previous Portfolio Exercises. For this Portfolio Exercise you will prepare a short visual presentation pitching your research as a qualitative study. Use the software of your choice (i.e., PowerPoint, Google Slides, Prezi, etc.) to present the following information:

   a. A description of what and whom you are researching. Include a brief overview of your population and sample as addressed in previous Portfolio Exercises.

   b. The context. Outline the details of your research (who, what, when, where, why, and how).

   c. Your research objective: what are you trying to understand or interpret through this study?

   d. The question(s) that is central to your research.

   e. The qualitative data collection method(s) you are considering. (Generate ideas and don't worry too much about the details; we will explore this concept further in Chapters 8–12).

   f. A brief explanation (in one or two slides) of how steps 1–3 of the qualitative research process relate to your topic.

   g. A discussion of 2–3 of the following aspects in relation to your topic:

      i. Why would it be important to try to "see through the eyes of your participants" in your study?

      ii. What aspects of the context do you feel it might be important to explore?

      iii. What social processes might be necessary to examine, and what type of data collection method could reveal those processes?

      iv. What benefits might come from approaching your topic with an open-ended approach and flexibility about the process? What might be challenging about this?

      v. How would you approach the topic of objectivity? Think about approaching the topic using systematic steps, your identity in relation to the setting and participants, and how you see yourself engaging in your setting.

Interactive Activities

1. As a class, divide into small groups meeting in person or online. With your group, complete the following steps:

   a. Come up with a topic that could be researched using qualitative methods.

   b. Produce research question(s) that could be used to investigate the topic.

   c. Select a hypothetical group or setting to be studied.

   d. Describe some qualitative methods that could be used to study the topic.

   e. Create a summary of your discussion to present to the rest of the class for comment and critique.

2. As a class, divide into three groups meeting in person or online and participate in what's called a "jigsaw" activity. Your professor should assign three empirical articles using qualitative methods that focus on a similar topic (e.g., the school-to-prison pipeline, media representations, or health care experiences with Covid-19) or the same population (e.g., activists, pre-school students, domestic workers). Participate in a class discussion exercise in three phases:

   a. In step 1, each group becomes responsible for reading one of the three assigned articles: they should read it and discuss together what they learned from it and reflect on the methods, findings, and conclusions.

   b. In step 2, each person is now an "expert" on the article they read. The groups should redistribute and become groups of three—with an "expert" on each of the three assigned articles making up each group. Each person should take a turn to teach their new group what they learned from the article they read and share information about the methods, findings, and conclusions.

   c. In step 3, the groups should reflect on the three approaches to the similar topic/setting/population and what is similar and different in the researchers' approach, methods, and findings. As a large group, reflect on what the groups observed about the comparisons and what these tell you about qualitative research approaches.

3. As a class, divide into groups meeting in person or online. Each group will be provided with excerpts from two to three qualitative studies in which the researchers outline their methods and reflect on their approach to the research. Read the excerpts and, with your group, discuss the following questions:

   a. What were the research questions in the study?

   b. What methods of data collection did the researcher use?

   c. What was their chosen setting and study sample?

   d. How did those data collection methods, setting, and sample enable them to explore their research questions?

   e. How does the researcher discuss issues such as their research process, their personal relation to the setting and population, methodological challenges they faced?

   f. What does the researcher discuss in relation to questions of objectivity and generalizability?

   g. What would be different if this researcher approached this topic using quantitative methods instead of qualitative methods?

Online Resources

- The International Institute for Qualitative Methodology, based at the University of Alberta in Edmonton, sponsors conferences and research training programs involving qualitative research methods. Their International Journal of Qualitative Methods is available free online.
  www.iiqm.ualberta.ca

- QualPage is a resource center with information for qualitative researchers, especially those interested in data analysis software.
  https://qualpage.com

- Syracuse University's Center for Qualitative and Multi-Method Inquiry hosts the open-access publication *Qualitative & Multi-Method Research*.
  www.maxwell.syr.edu/moynihan/cqrm/qmmr/

- The Center for Qualitative and Multi-Method Inquiry also hosts a useful Qualitative Data Repository.
  https://qdr.syr.edu/

- You can find examples of qualitative studies in the journals *Qualitative Research* and *Qualitative Sociology Review*; you may have to access these journals through your institution's library server.
  https://journals.sagepub.com/home/qrj
  www.qualitativesociologyreview.org/ENG/index_eng.php

For more resources please visit
www.oup.com/he/bryman-reck-fields1e

6

How Can Researchers Enumerate and Examine Broad Patterns to Social Life?
Quantitative Research

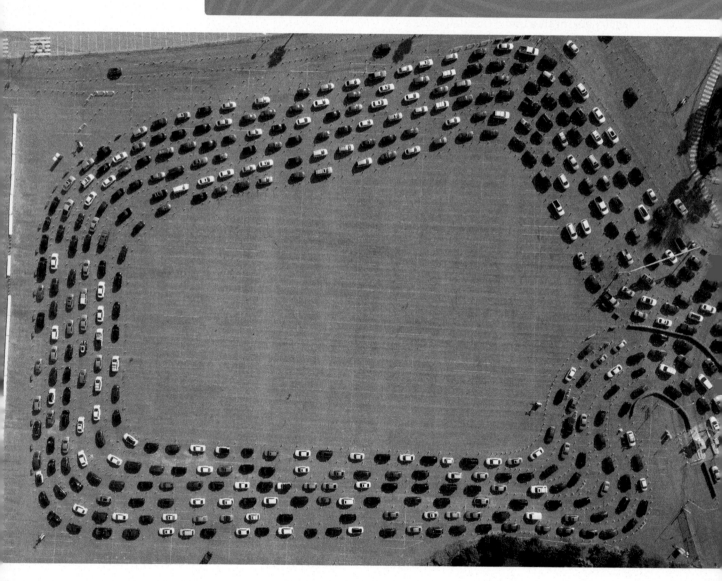

▲ AP Photo/Ringo H.W. Chiu

Quantitative analysis focuses on using numerical data to explore patterns in social life. This approach emphasizes using statistical methods to assess trends in people's experiences, attitudes, and opinions. Quantitative studies understand the meaning of social life by quantifying patterns and frequencies.

Over the course of this chapter, you will learn how to

- define quantitative research and understand the how quantitative researchers approach their work;

- recount the history of quantitative thinking in social science and how statistical studies became a recognized and valued part of the discipline;

- outline the main goals of quantitative researchers, including establishing causality, generalization, and replication;

- identify the sequence of steps used in quantitative research;

- describe the distinctive perspective of quantitative researchers; and

- recognize how quantitative research differs from qualitative research.

For his class project, Mario wants to ask other students about their recreational use of prescription drugs and its effects on school performance and social behaviors. How will he get the information he needs? He soon realizes that writing effective questions is more difficult than he imagined. His first question—"Do you take prescription drugs?"—is too vague because people might take medicine their doctor prescribed to treat an illness or take drugs recreationally that were not prescribed to them. What about the type of drug? People might take Xanax that they purchased from a friend to cope with anxiety during exams or keep the inhaler their doctor prescribed for a bad cold in case they catch another one.

Mario considers other potential problems: What if some people refuse to discuss their illicit use of prescription drugs? Will some of his classmates be offended by the question? He needs to ask the questions in a way that encourages people to answer while approaching such sensitive topics ethically. Maybe people will be more likely to answer honestly if they can complete the survey anonymously. But how will he know they're answering honestly? Is there a second method he could use to verify his results? For instance, could Mario observe people at a party where drugs are being taken and count how often people use different substances? This might clarify whether people's behavior is consistent with what they report in the survey.

Once he has asked the basic questions about prescription drug consumption, how will Mario approach the parts of his research question related to school performance and social behavior? What aspects of school performance interest him? Which social behaviors? How should the information be recorded in numeric form? When he has finished analyzing the data, will his findings apply to some larger population, such as all university students?

The questions that Mario is wrestling with are common in social research. In this chapter, we will explore how social scientists deal with these and related issues in quantitative research.

Introduction: How Quantitative Research Examines Broad Trends and Patterns

Researchers who specialize in **quantitative research** methods use numbers to analyze the social world. They seek to understand social life by enumerating patterns and assessing the frequencies of particular experiences, opinions, or behaviors. Quantitative researchers gather numerical information to understand aggregate trends and patterns in social

---

quantitative research Inquiry using numerical data-gathering techniques and statistical analysis.

life. They attempt to grasp the implications of those patterns by measuring the relationships between and among different **variables**. They also assess how accurately their numbers might capture reality and consider places where their measurements may be in error.

As we read in the previous chapter, qualitative researchers approach their studies in an open-ended, iterative way. By contrast, quantitative researchers determine their research variables ahead of time and then study those variables using a consistent technique that does not deviate throughout the research process. When they use quantitative methods, researchers seek to understand the world broadly, numerically examining a large number of cases; this is different from qualitative research, which seeks to understand a smaller number of cases in more detail.

---

variables Attributes or characteristics that may change over time, across different conditions, or from case to case.

---

deductive research An approach to inquiry that begins with a statement of theory from which hypotheses may be derived and tested.

---

objectivism An approach or position that views social phenomena as though they have an existence independent of social actors or their perceptions and that calls on researchers to draw conclusions based on fact without the influence of values, bias, or preconceptions.

---

concepts General or abstract ideas that serve to organize observations about some aspect of the social world.

---

positivism An epistemological position that advocates using empirical methods and logic to study of social reality.

---

survey research A research design in which researchers collect data through questionnaires or structured interviews, often to detect relationships among variables.

---

questionnaire A collection of standardized questions and response items that respondents complete without aid of an interviewer.

---

content analysis The examination of texts, including both written and visual materials, with interest in how the material contributes to and reflects meaning and representation.

Consider some distinguishing features of the quantitative approach:

- It often takes the form of **deductive research**, beginning with a hypothesis or theory that quantitative researchers then test by gathering data.
- Quantitative research reflects **objectivism**—that is, the idea that social reality exists as an object independent of people's actions or perceptions, reflecting the view that social reality can be systematically measured and understood.
- Quantitative researchers strive to understand *patterned relationships in the social world* and how particular factors influence, or cause changes in, other factors (this is referred to as *causality*). This means that quantitative researchers must pay particular attention to precisely defining and measuring social **concepts** to assess the relationship among variables.
- The approach is traditionally associated with the ideal of objective, error-free research. While many quantitative researchers diverge from traditional modes of **positivism** , some quantitative research is still guided by this ideal. It means that quantitative researchers have to be transparent and careful about how they define the concepts under study and collect data about them. They must also identify and disclose any amount of error they have introduced into their study.

Like qualitative researchers, people who practice quantitative research go about gathering their data in a variety of ways. **Survey research**, one of the most common social science data collection methods, involves structured interviews and **questionnaires** (reviewed in Chapter 8). This technique enables quantitative researchers to explore a variety of questions using a standardized format. It also lends itself well to categorizing and comparing responses.

Quantitative and qualitative researchers share some data collection techniques but use them in different ways. One example is **content analysis**, which involves analyzing communication patterns in texts and documents. Quantitative researchers conducting content analysis examine texts to assess the frequency that particular phrases or ideas occur, and how different ideas expressed might relate to one another. They assess how meanings are conveyed in visual media or written texts by examining the patterned nature of that communication and frequencies of certain expressions and themes. Their studies often focus on print or visual media and online or social media content. (We explore content analysis in Chapter 11.)

Another method used by quantitative and qualitative researchers is the **analysis of existing data** (or **available data**). Secondary analysis of existing data (described in detail in Chapter 12) entails examining data that other researchers have gathered. This method is common in quantitative research because of the availability of large data set such as census data, the General Social Survey (GSS), government statistics, and others. Researchers can use these data to analyze a wide range of research questions and hypotheses.

In this chapter, we define quantitative research, explore the emergence of this type of research in social science, discuss the key goals in quantitative work, outline the typical steps used in quantitative studies, and reflect on the unique contributions quantitative research makes to social scientific research.

The Emergence of Quantitative Approaches

Among the many people instrumental in helping to establish sociology as an area of study, August Comte (1798–1857) was particularly significant. Comte coined the term sociology and outlined four main principles that still form the basis of a great deal of sociological work (Weinstein 2010). These principles inform sociological research of all methodologies and have had particular influence on the emergence of quantitative approaches.

The first principle that Comte emphasized was *positivism*, a practice in which researchers develop conclusions based on careful observation of the elements under study. Empiricism—a way to develop understandings by looking to the "real world" for evidence—is the bedrock of positivism. Comte believed sociology must be a *scientific* study of people's worlds; in order to improve society, sociologists'

conclusions must come from careful study and not from what they wish or assume to be true (Weinstein 2010, 2). Scientific disciplines may take different approaches to producing knowledge, but this point remains the basis of all scientific study: that inquiry begins with observations of phenomena in the real world (Field 2016).

Comte's next principle was that sociology should focus not on the individual but instead on groups, institutions, and societies—what he described as *aggregates*. Thus, the basis of sociology lies in understanding how individuals exist within and are influenced by broader levels of society.

Comte's third principle was that the study of human experience is more complex than studies of other scientific arenas because so many variables affect human behavior. Humans act with complex intentions while also being affected by biological, environmental, physical, and emotional factors. This recognition of the complexity of social life influenced Comte's allegiance to quantitative sociology.

Comte's fourth principle was that those who study the complex human world require a shared and precise language through which to understand it. For Comte, this language was mathematics (Weinstein 2010, 2–3).

Much of Comte's approach applies to any kind of research, not just quantitative work. All sociological research emphasizes the complexity of the social world and the relationship between individual experience and broader systems like groups, institutions, and societies. Both quantitative and qualitative approaches are empirical, designed to observe phenomena in the "real world" in a systematic way in order to develop conclusions. As described above, this is a basis of positivism. It was in Comte's opinions about *how* people should study social life and understand these things that we see the development of a specific approach to positivism and empiricism—an approach embracing quantitative analysis.

These foundational ideas about sociology as a discipline emerged in western Europe, where society was

---

analysis of existing (or **available**) **data**   Research using data that have been collected by a researcher or institution and made available for others to analyze.

undergoing intense change. During the Enlightenment period, from the seventeenth to the nineteenth centuries, the authority of European monarchies and religious institutions was undermined and political and social revolutions introduced new forms of knowledge. First came a commitment to developing knowledge through the senses and observation (empiricism), using reason, and following the scientific method (Foucault 1994 [1970]). Then came an allegiance to positivism that included not just an embrace of empiricism but additional commitments to objectivity, seeking universal truths about the world, and using the scientific method.

In Comte's time, mathematics—especially statistics and probability theory—was gaining traction as a mode of thought. Science and mathematics were still quite radical at a time when spiritual explanations and royal decrees had recently been the only accepted truths. Yet Comte believed that statistical analysis was the most appropriate mode of thinking for scientific sociological work. Belgian statistician Adolphe Quetelet (1796–1874) was another highly influential figure in the development of quantitative social science. Like Comte, he felt that scientific sociology was best practiced and advanced through statistical analysis (Weinstein 2010, 3).

The development of computing technology affected the possibilities of statistical research. In your view, how might quantitative research have become more accurate and complex as computers have become more accessible and sophisticated over time?

The language of science and math still holds a great deal of authority. In more recent times, technological advances in computing have given quantitative social science researchers more options to achieve the types of analyses that early sociologists desired. The emergence of digital computers after World War II allowed statisticians to analyze larger samples and more variables quicker and with less error than had been possible with manual calculations. With this expansion of computing power came the ability to test and explore hypotheses more rigorously than ever before (Weinstein 2010, 4).

As computer hardware improved in the late 1950s, so did computer programming language that became useful to statisticians. In 1959, FORTRAN ("formula translator") was invented, enabling statistical computation of data in large databases. This was the precursor to more recent statistical software packages based on the FORTRAN language but offering many more options for inputting data and running tests. The most often used software package is PASW Statistics (previously known as SPSS—Statistical Package for the Social Sciences). Programs like PASW have enabled people of varied skill levels to conduct statistical analysis and quantitative research (Weinstein 2010, 4).

The Main Goals of Quantitative Researchers

Testing Hypotheses to Establish Causality

Much quantitative research involves a search for causal explanations. Quantitative researchers are rarely satisfied with merely describing *how* things are: they are keen to find out *why* things happen—what causes things to be how they are. Figuring out cause and effect is an important aspect of research. For instance, data collected early in the Covid-19 pandemic indicated that Indigenous, Black, and Latinx people in the United States were at higher risk than other groups of experiencing severe Covid illness. No matter their age, people in these groups were more likely to need hospitalization and to die from Covid-related illness (Centers for Disease Control

and Prevention 2020). In order to understand and prevent such occurrences, people working in public health needed to know what causes this greater risk.

Rather than simply describing the existence of a phenomenon, causality enables us to understand much more about why that phenomenon occurs. Researchers examining hate violence, for instance, may want not only to describe its characteristics but also to identify its causes. They may seek to explain how committing hate violence reflects personal characteristics (such as individual prejudice) or social characteristics (such as low social mobility). To establish causality, researchers try to determine what factors (variables) bring about particular results. When studying hate violence, they might test whether individual prejudice or low social mobility (the independent variables) contribute to a person committing hate violence (the dependent variable).

Study design (discussed more in Chapter 7) helps determine the strength of a causal argument. In an experimental design, researchers manipulate the independent variable, leading to little ambiguity about the direction of causal influence; it is clear in an experimental design whether the independent variable causes a change in the dependent variable. However, most social survey research relies on a cross-sectional design in which data on all variables are collected simultaneously. Even if a researcher can identify a relationship among variables, the direction of causal influence can be unclear because it can be hard to assess whether a particular independent variable preceded the dependent variable in time. For example, increased drug use might precede a change in a person's friendship network, or changes in a person's friendship network might precede an increase in a person's drug use. That ambiguity makes it difficult to ascertain a causal relationship (for an example of this, see the Mixed Methods in Action box below). Researchers rely on statistical tests to determine the likelihood that they have misjudged the causal relationships they find between their variables.

For example, Francis A. Pearman II and Walker A. Swain (2017) sought to assess what factors made neighborhoods more likely to become gentrified. Lower-income neighborhoods often have higher populations of BIPOC residents and also fewer

This billboard is a public service announcement to the Navajo community suggesting that Covid-19 is caused through airborne transmission of a virus passed when people close together are unmasked. In public health, it's important to know what factors cause disease. Why might it also be important to research the social factors that cause Indigenous communities to be at greater risk of contacting and dying from Covid?

BOX 6.1 Determining Causal Variables

Geoffrey T. Wodtke (2018) provides an example of a quantitative researcher trying to understand causality. Wodtke set out to explore the hypothesis that White people with more education have a stronger understanding of racism as a structural (not individual) issue. Specifically, he wanted to see whether an assumed relationship between education level and views about racism might be caused by other variables.

Analyzing data from the General Social Survey (GSS) and Study of American Families (SAF), Wodtke created statistical models that took into account what are described as *confounding variables*—that is, variables that might not be included in an analysis but that account for a perceived causal relationship. Once Wodtke conducted more robust statistical analyses, he concluded that certain demographic and family characteristics influence people's educational attainment and attitudes (such as their siblings' views and family environment), meaning that the assumed causal relationship between education and racial attitudes is more complicated than originally thought. Wodtke noted that he was unable to assess the extent to which factors unobserved in his data may affect racial attitudes and concluded with suggestions for further research using a quasi-experimental design (discussed in Chapter 7).

resources due to a long history of governmental disinvestment in low-income communities. Generally, upper-income neighborhoods have higher resources and lower-income neighborhoods lower resources, resulting in higher- and lower-resourced schools, respectively. The typical model of schooling is that students attend schools in their neighborhoods, so a school's demographics often reflect the neighborhood where it is located. Pearman and Swain became interested in "school choice initiatives," which allow families to send children to schools outside their neighborhoods. If parents elect to participate in a school choice program, their local school may not "look like" the neighborhood in which it is located. Pearman and Swain wondered if wealthy families might be more likely to move into low-income neighborhoods and begin gentrifying them if they had the option to send their children to higher-resourced schools in other neighborhoods. They considered how school choice programs might contribute to racial segregation and gentrification—specifically, does greater school choice increase gentrification of neighborhoods inhabited by lower-income communities of color? They point out that the existing literature does not consider school choice programs as one cause of gentrification.

Analyzing data collected between 2000 and 2012 from the American Community Survey, the Census, the National Center for Educational Statistics (NCES), and the Schools and Staffing Survey (SASS), Pearman and Swain found that expansion of school choice programs increased the possibility of gentrification in racially isolated neighborhoods by 22%—double the baseline likelihood of gentrification (Pearman and Swain 2017, 214). They found that neighborhoods with higher proportions of residents of color and a neighborhood school policy were less likely to experience gentrification. Pearman and Swain considered alternative explanations for the causal relationship between school choice and gentrification, though. First, other variables might explain the relationship. To assess whether this was the case in their study, the researchers tested and controlled for a large number of alternative variables in their analysis. (As we discuss in Chapter 14, when a researcher *controls* for a variable, it means they hold the variable constant in order reduce the

possibility that the controlled variable causes the observed relationship). Second, the relationship could be explained by "reverse causality": in other words, affluent White families moving into lower-income BIPOC communities motivated school choice policies to be implemented rather than the other way around. Pearman and Swain conducted a test to confirm that this was not likely to be the case, and thus felt confident in their analysis.

Well-constructed quantitative research inspires confidence in the researcher's causal inferences. As mentioned above, quantitative researchers who employ cross-sectional designs often use techniques such as statistical controls that allow them to make causal inferences. Even if quantitative researchers cannot make causal arguments, they can establish important **correlations** among variables—noticing social attitudes, behaviors, and characteristics that vary and have effects on one another.

Precise Measurement and Reducing Errors

Quantitative researchers take great pains to minimize, if not eliminate, routine errors while conducting their research. Careful and precise measurement of the concepts they study helps them ensure they are measuring what they think they're measuring. They also analyze the degree to which they can be confident in their conclusions and how much error may have been introduced into their studies. The following are some examples of researchers describing their measurement strategies:

- Melissa Brown et al. (2017) analyzed tweets from #SayHerName, a campaign motivated by Sandra Bland's death to highlight violence against Black women. Bland was arrested after a minor traffic stop in 2015 and died mysteriously by hanging in her cell three days later after police failed to follow safety and wellness checks. Brown et al. explored how the campaign employed a social

---

correlation The relationship between two or more variables; a strong *positive correlation* means that an increase (or decrease) in an independent variable is associated with an increase (or decrease) in a dependent variable, while a *negative correlation* means that as the independent variable rises, the dependent variable falls (and vice versa).

A concern about gentrification is that it changes the neighborhood in ways that appeal to people with more social and economic resources, which then makes it harder for the original community to remain in the neighborhood. How might a concern like school choice drive gentrification and give some people more options and other people fewer options? What other variables might a researcher need to test before they concluded that school choice policies influence gentrification?

movement mobilization agenda embracing intersectionality. They conducted a content analysis of more than 400,000 tweets connected to #SayHerName. To do so, they had to determine what tweets would be included, and how the research team would define which tweets related to the campaign under analysis. Tweets are useful as data since an organizational scheme already exists in the platform: the hashtag, which enables users (and researchers) to find, read, and share tweets using the same phrase. These researchers analyzed all tweets and retweets using the hashtag #SayHerName between January 19 and October 14, 2016. They found that people used this hashtag to spotlight the issue of violence against Black women, demand justice, honor survivors, and increase exposure about the disproportionate violence faced by Black transgender women.

- Seunghye Hong, Wei Zhang, and Emily Walton (2014) examined determinants of mental health among Asian American and Latino people, hypothesizing that strong social cohesion positively affects mental health. They used secondary analysis of data from the National Latino and Asian American Study (NLAAS), which is the first study using a national sample of US

Mixed Methods in Action | The Case of Displayed Emotions in Convenience Stores

Many people assume that the friendlier retail workers are with their customers, the better their sales will be. After conducting a literature review, Robert I. Sutton and Anat Rafaeli (1992) hypothesized a *positive relationship—that is, both variables either increase or decrease simultaneously*—between the display of positive emotions (smiling, friendly greeting, eye contact) by staff to shoppers and the level of retail sales; in other words, they hypothesized that when retail staff are friendly and give time to shoppers, higher sales follow. Sutton and Rafaeli had collected data from 576 convenience stores in a US retail chain. They conducted structured observation of the retail workers to gather numerical data on the display of positive emotions and examined quantitative sales data for the other variable (retail commerce).

Contrary to the researchers' expectation, the data did not support their hypothesis: stores in which retail workers were less inclined to smile, be friendly, and so on, had better sales. To understand this finding, Sutton and Rafaeli conducted a qualitative investigation of four stores. They used several methods: unstructured observation of interactions between staff and customers; semi-structured interviews with store managers; informal conversations with store managers, supervisors, executives, and others; and data gathered by posing as customers. The qualitative investigation confirmed that the display of positive emotions was linked to lower sales (a *negative* relationship). However, they found that sales were not caused by the display of workers' emotions: instead, the workers' emotional displays were caused by the amount of sales. In stores with high levels of sales, staff was under greater pressure and encountered longer checkout lines. Therefore, they had less time and inclination for the pleasantries associated with the display of positive emotions, which was more common during times of slow customer traffic. Thus, the causal sequence was not:

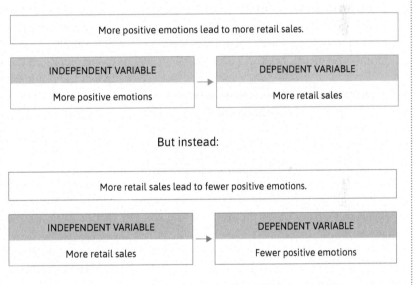

Sutton and Rafaeli's research illustrates how difficult it can be to infer the causal direction when using a cross-sectional research design. The researchers gathered qualitative data to help them make sense of their quantitative findings; their mixed methods research design enabled them to better understand their hypotheses and assess the causal relationship between their variables.

Latinxs and Asian Americans exploring mental health. In one example, the researchers measured neighborhood cohesion using a 4-item scale. In this scale, respondents answered questions about whether they get along with neighbors, if neighbors support each other, whether neighbors can be trusted, and if they thought neighbors would help in an emergency. A set of questions like this (instead of just one question) makes a measure more robust and trustworthy. Hong, Zhang, and Walton also used a statistical test (called Cronbach's alpha) to assess how reliable this set of questions was in measuring social cohesion. They found that people living in highly dense neighborhoods had poorer mental health, but experiences of neighborhood social cohesion improved mental health. These outcomes were more positive for Latinos than they were for Asian Americans, which suggested the need to understand more about race, social cohesion, and mental health.

To guard against measurement problems and error, and to protect the credibility of their research, quantitative researchers take care to spell out the procedures and practices they undertook on the way to their study findings. This habit of transparency allows others to identify possible errors or gaps in the research. It also provides other researchers with the opportunity to replicate their work and thus confirm findings.

Generalization

Let's say you wanted to study workplace sexual harassment in the banking industry by sending a questionnaire to 50 employees at 10 banks in your city. Would you results apply to all employees of the 10 banks? Would they apply to employees of all the banks in your city? What about all banks in your state?

Quantitative researchers often want to assess the extent to which their findings can offer information about situations, settings, or people that they did not directly study. This is generalization. Since it is rarely feasible to send questionnaires to a whole population

(all retail workers, all residents of a town, all citizens of a country, or even everyone in an organization), the people surveyed are typically a sample of the larger population. It's important to determine how reliable it is to use information from a sample to make inferences about a larger group; thus quantitative researchers take steps to reflect upon how much they can generalize from their sample to a broader population.

When generalizing, statistical researchers do not claim they know for certain that what they've found in their sample absolutely reflects the population. The foundation of statistics is the branch of mathematics called probability theory, which deals with chance, or how likely it is that something might happen. A researcher must determine the chance, or probability, that they are correct if they use their findings to make inferences about something they have not studied directly (Weinstein 2010, 146).

To be able to effectively generalize from a sample to a population, the sample must be as representative of the population as possible. This demands a large (at least 100) and well-selected sample. Probability sampling (discussed in Chapter 4) is a procedure that largely eliminates systemic bias by using a random selection process. This does not guarantee a representative sample, but it does improve the chances of getting one. Probability sampling helps with generalization because you can use mathematics to figure out the likelihood that you have made errors.

Sarah A. Font, et al. (2018) studied 8,452 youth in Wisconsin's foster care system, comparing outcomes of those who experienced permanent placement (reunified with their birth parents, adopted, or united with legal guardians) and those who aged out (separated from the foster system at age 18 rather than ever entering a permanent placement). The researchers studied state social welfare system data for 2005–2015 from the Wisconsin Multi-Sample Person File (MSPF) and Wisconsin Department of Public Instruction (DPI). Their sample included children who were younger than 16 in 2005 and at least 19 in 2015. They found that earnings were similar across all of the groups, but aged-out youth and those who were adopted had similar (and higher) likelihood of attending college than those who were reunified or placed with a guardian. Within the group of aged-out youth, those who had spent more time in the foster system before age 18 had higher earnings than the other aged-out youth and were more likely to graduate high school.

This study includes sample data representing the population of foster youth in the state of Wisconsin. So, can this sample data possibly be generalized to the entire population of foster youth in the United States? These researchers state that although they would like to use their data to generalize their findings beyond Wisconsin, they cannot because they gathered the data from this specific state's population at a particular point in time. Font, et al. suggest that their findings might still be practically useful to reformers and practitioners in the child welfare system (2018, 725). Indeed, their findings counter widely accepted beliefs that youth who are reunified with family or gain permanent placement have better outcomes than youth who age out. Given that reunification with birth parents is a priority in child welfare policy, these findings raise important points: there are probably many disparities families face that could disadvantage children who are reunified and the child welfare system has much to consider when assessing how to provide resources to best support children's well-being and success.

As this example shows, gathering a representative sample is required for the researcher to have confidence that the outcomes might apply to people beyond their respondents. But researchers must only apply the findings to the population at hand; this is why Font, et al. did not claim their findings applied to foster youth outside of Wisconsin. Nevertheless, they were able to demonstrate that the concepts they examine merit deep consideration by people concerned with child welfare system outcomes. The goal of arriving at generalizable findings, and the ways in which researchers reflect upon their limitations and opportunities, can be seen as one of the key ways quantitative researchers consider the implications of their studies.

The Main Steps in Quantitative Research

Figure 6.1 outlines the main steps in quantitative research. This list is an ideal account of the process: research is rarely as linear or straightforward as the figure implies. However, it represents a useful starting point for learning about the main facets of quantitative methods.

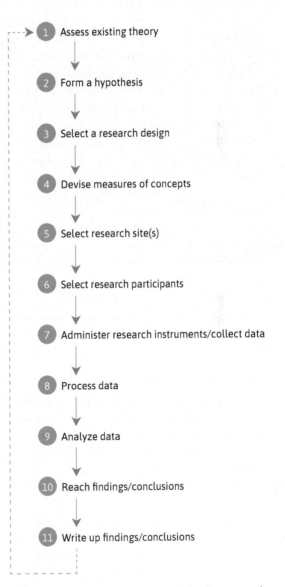

FIGURE 6.1 **The main steps in quantitative research**

How can quantitative research help to reveal important information about situations such as police stops? Think about how a researcher following the steps of quantitative research could describe the racial breakdown of who is stopped most frequently and explore the possible consequences of these police practices.

To illustrate these steps, let's consider Joscha Legewie and Jeffrey Fagan's (2019) research examining the relationship between aggressive police tactics in low-income BIPOC communities and the educational outcomes of youth in those neighborhoods. Legewie and Fagan focused on the New York City Police Department's (NYPD) program "Operation Impact," which increased police presence in high-crime neighborhoods under the auspices of reducing crime. Launched in 2004, this program increased police stops in areas labeled "impact zones," neighborhoods deemed to be crime hot spots (Legewie and Fagan 2019, citing Golden and Almo 2004). The program permitted the police in these areas, which were in mostly Black and Latinx neighborhoods, to routinely stop, question, and search people, even when they had broken no laws.

In their research, Legewie and Fagan examined how living in environments subject to aggressive police presence could have negative ramifications on young people's school performance. Here are the steps they followed in their quantitative research.

Step 1. Assess existing theory. Theories about policing strategies and stratification formed the basis for

Legewie and Fagan's study. A theory that greatly influenced their work is James Q. Wilson and George L. Kelling's (1982) "broken windows" theory, which suggests that neighborhoods with signs of "social disorder" such as visible graffiti, people hanging out, and dilapidated buildings encourage lawbreaking behavior. This theory has had a profound influence on policing strategies, inspiring a shift in which behaviors such as loitering, vandalism, and jaywalking have been blamed for social disorder and are now highly criminalized. In their literature review, Legewie and Fagan found conflicting theories about the effects of such policing practices on education: some scholars suggest aggressive policing reduces the negative effects crime can have on children, thus improving their educational outcomes; others posit that aggressive policing can adversely affect children's educational outcomes by causing increased stress and routine trauma, encouraging youth to distrust authorities and institutional actors. Legewie and Fagan's study explored the accuracy of these theories.

Step 2. Form a hypothesis. Noting these differing theories about policing's positive or negative effects on educational performance, Legewie and Fagan hypothesized that living in an Operation Impact zone would affect students' academic performance.

Step 3. Select a research design. To explore this hypothesis, Legewie and Fagan designed a study in which they would collect information about New York students' academic performance, their neighborhood of residence, and local police practices. These data exist in school and police records, so the researchers designed a study in which they conducted an analysis of existing data.

Step 4. Devise measures of concepts. Quantitative researchers must devise careful and precise ways to measure the concepts under investigation. This study explored the relationships among many complex concepts, but three main ones were educational performance, neighborhood, and exposure to Operation Impact. Legewie and Fagan

used test scores from the New York State English Language Arts (ELA) and Mathematics Test as one measure of several they combined to assess academic outcome. This test is taken annually by students in third grade to eighth grade. The researchers defined neighborhood by designating 1,257 geographic areas using the impact zone boundaries, and then used student addresses to determine the neighborhood they lived in. They also examined the concept "degree of exposure to Operation Impact" by counting the number of days each area was part of Operation Impact during a school year.

Step 5. Select research site(s). The researchers began with an overall interest in the relationship between aggressive policing and educational outcomes, and early in the process chose New York City as their research site. This choice made sense, since Operation Impact was one of the first and most expansive programs of its kind.

Step 6. Select research participants. This step entails choosing the elements to study (also referred to as units of analysis). "Elements" here can be people, institutions, or events. This study compared a few elements. One was individual students enrolled in New York City schools from kindergarten to eighth grade. Another was neighborhoods designated as impact zones during the 10-year period in which Operation Impact existed.

Step 7. Administer research instruments/collect data. Legewie and Fagan analyzed two data sources. New York City Department of Education (NYCDOE) records provided information from 2003–2012 about K–8 students' demographics, test scores, neighborhood of residence, language status, and socioeconomic indicators. The second source was NYPD data from 2004-2012 recording pedestrian stops (when, where, and why an officer stopped and questioned someone, and details of the events); arrests (date, time, charge, and demographics of arrested person); and crime complaints (crime reported, date, time, location, suspect's demographics). They also analyzed maps provided by NYPD demarcating the boundaries of impact zones.

Step 8. Process data. Before any data collected can be analyzed, the information must be systematically recorded. When Legewie and Fagan developed their plan to measure their concepts (as described in step 4), they needed to translate them into numerical values that could be plugged into statistical analysis programs. A good example of this is the way they processed their measures of students' level of Operation Impact exposure during a school year. They created a scale to measure the amount of exposure to Operation Impact with values ranging from 0 to 1. This ranged from "not exposed to Operation Impact" (0) to "exposed for the whole school year" (1). They counted the number of days each neighborhood was part of Operation Impact during a school year, and this number of days became "amount of exposure." They then assigned each student a value in that range based on their address.

Step 9. Analyze data. Researchers choose among various statistical techniques to analyze their data. They also try to determine whether the measures are reliable and assess possible errors. Legewie and Fagan's analysis involved multiple considerations. For instance, they had to consider that impact zones are not defined as such randomly: the NYPD designated certain areas impact zones owing to their crime rates and factors deemed important to police officials. Because impact zones could have different characteristics than other areas, such as higher crime or poverty, the researchers had to control for certain variables. In other words, they had to analyze the data in such a way that they could confidently identify the effects of policing on educational outcomes and be sure those outcomes were not caused by some other variable, such as poverty. Legewie and Fagan conducted their next phases of analysis using regression, a statistical method that allows them to measure how their variable of interest—educational performance—was affected by a multitude of other variables. In one analysis, they examined how race, age, and exposure to Operation Impact affected ELA test scores; in another, they examined race, age, and test scores for students, noting test score changes over time (from two years before to two years after Operation Impact was instituted in the neighborhood).

Step 10. Reach findings/conclusions. After completing their study and analyzing the data, Legewie and Fagan needed to determine whether their findings supported their hypothesis, consider how their conclusions supported or refuted existing theory, and assess the implications of their work. They found that their hypothesis was supported—that living in an Operation Impact zone did affect students' academic performance. Of course, *how* living in an impact zone affected academic performance was the crux of their analysis: they found a difference in effects depending on children's race, gender, and age. The results of this study provided evidence that this policing strategy has the greatest negative effects on the academic performance of African American boys aged 13–15.

Step 11. Write up findings/conclusions. This study, presented in the American Sociological Association journal *American Sociological Review*, reached a wide audience of people concerned about criminal justice, race, and inequality. The article sheds light on ways that aggressive policing can contribute to social inequality, noting that the criminal justice system not only affects people arrested or incarcerated but also infiltrates everyday life and affects people at the community level. Further, the researchers suggest that this can result in long-standing consequences for Black teenage boys, as their decreased educational performance can cause barriers to future success. Once published, these researchers' findings become part of the field's stock of knowledge and theories, supporting future researchers as they take step 1 in quantitative research (and qualitative researchers as they pursue their studies).

Methods in Motion | **Using Quantitative Methods in Exploratory Studies**

Zaynah Rahman and Matthew Witenstein (2014) studied the bicultural conflicts young South Asian Americans from immigrant families face as they navigate between school, which emphasizes and demands individuality, and home, which values collectivity. The researchers used cultural values conflict theory, developed by Inman, et al. (2001), to frame the study and applied it to cultural conflict experienced by both young women and young men (earlier studies had typically applied it to female participants only).

The study's sample included 95 South Asian American college students (38 men and 57 women) recruited from California and Georgia. They were either second-generation immigrants (born in the United States to immigrant parents) or 1.5-generation (having immigrated to the United States before age 13). The researchers developed a questionnaire that asked about the students' backgrounds, demographics, school and career choices, and a range of social outcomes. They measured family conflict using a scale with 18 items, examining the dynamics of family cultural conflict about academic and sociocultural decisions.

The researchers found that all of the study participants, no matter their gender or economic background, had high academic performance and lofty goals; they also experienced a great deal of stress and family conflict. The results showed that the highest levels of cultural conflict students experienced related to disagreements around balancing study and recreation time and to parents comparing them to others. Young men experienced greater conflict with family over academic decisions, while women and lower-income participants had more conflict with their families over social decision making.

The researchers concluded that these findings were consistent with other research that suggests men are expected to be family leaders and are given more social freedom and independence.

Parents tended to want their daughters to stay closer to home; they have been found to overprotect their daughters to prevent them from being too connected to the dominant culture. Even though there were no differences in academic goals or performance by class, families from higher economic backgrounds have been found to be more liberal about cultural traditions, which can lead to less family conflict over social decision-making.

This study of South Asian American students examines bicultural conflict within a community that has not been extensively studied. It offers both gender and class comparisons. The results were consistent with other research on South Asian American parents and children, but the addition of the analysis on men offered insights not seen in other research. As is common for many 1.5- and second-generation children from collectivist cultures, the students sought to balance the expectations of their South Asian culture and community and the individualistic norms of the United States, exploring their hyphenated identities. The findings suggest that academic institutions hoping to better support this group should be more aware of how bicultural conflict can affect South Asian American students' experiences and the stresses they might encounter.

The study authors point out that their small sample size limited their ability to do more in-depth statistical analyses. Most of the students were of Indian and Hindu background, which also limited the researchers' ability to generalize their findings to a broader population of South Asian American students. Thus, this exploratory study is an important launching point to other studies that pursue more inter-group comparisons with larger samples, as it revealed aspects of the topic that merit further investigation. This study demonstrates that quantitative research can be effectively used in exploratory studies on populations or settings that have yet to be extensively researched.

The Distinct Perspective of Quantitative Research

The methodological perspective embraced by quantitative researchers foregrounds goals of objectivity and the importance of pursuing consistent and reliable measures of the social world. To understand the multidimensional nature of social life, quantitative researchers analyze multiple variables to explore the validity of existing theories and test intriguing hypotheses. To do so, they formulate their studies in a manner emphasizing precise measurement and develop findings that can be generalized to large populations of people. These aspects all form the basis of the particular perspective of quantitative research.

Systematic Study and the Question of Objectivity

All social research is influenced by the **scientific method**. This is not because sociologists view social research studies as though they were natural science studies, but because the scientific method is a model for how to conduct careful research.

For instance, the scientific method embraces the importance of systematic observations of the empirical world. It reminds us to be skeptical about where knowledge comes from and reflect upon the research process and to share our results in a community of professionals who offer feedback and keep us accountable to professional standards. It is not that quantitative social science researchers view themselves as, say, biological researchers; instead, they turn to the strengths of the scientific method to understand social reality. This includes formulating research questions, researching existing sources about the questions, developing hypotheses from this inquiry, empirically testing the hypotheses, and statistically analyzing the evidence to determine whether to accept the hypothesis. That process supports quantitative researchers' goal of systematic and consistent research practices that analyze the world

using prescribed steps and strive for critical, logical, and consistent empirical observation.

While contemporary quantitative researchers do not, on the whole, model their studies on the work of natural scientists, the early origins of this field were grounded in attempts to develop social science in the mold of natural science. As described earlier, the positivist paradigm has guided a great deal of academic research and had considerable influence on early quantitative work. An investment in objective research has traditionally been a mainstay of the positivist perspective. Objective research has often been defined as research that is value-free, where the person doing the study has little to no impact on the research setting they are studying. Quantitative social science researchers increasingly reject this notion of objectivity and acknowledge that they, as people studying social worlds they inhabit, have perspectives and positions.

Naturally, quantitative researchers hold a range of opinions on the question of objectivity. Some still believe that it is possible to approach their studies relying on statistical principles and scientific approaches that largely remove them from influencing their studies. Others find claims to objectivity deeply suspect. Tukufu Zuberi and Eduardo Bonilla-Silva (2008), researchers who study race using statistics, unsettle the idea that researchers' identities can be separated from the ideas they produce. Zuberi and Bonilla-Silva argue that ideas about race produced through research are influenced by the social context in which they are produced and the positionality of those who produce them. They critique a cornerstone of objectivity: the idea that there is a universal reality that exists separate from our perceptions of it, and that we can apprehend that reality and reveal it without inserting our perspectives.

Tukufu Zuberi states, "I believe social science is at its best when it is self-critical and relentlessly self-correcting. In order to be self-correcting we must be open to a critical evaluation of the methods we use and the conclusions that we have come to" (2008, 10–11). Jay Weinstein (2010) would suggest this critical evaluation must include a recognition that statistics are a *tool* used to do good social science research, and that how researchers use this

---

scientific method   An approach to research that consists of observation, measurement, and experiment and the formulation, testing, and revising of hypotheses.

tool determines the quality of the work. This point emphasizes the need for self-reflection and consideration of the ways we approach our studies. As he explains, "Statistics clearly plays a central role in sociology, especially in applied sociology. Yet it cannot substitute for well-developed theory, careful data collection, and old-fashioned hard work" (7). What this careful approach entails relates to another cornerstone of quantitative work: precise measurement.

Precise and Accurate Measurement

Most quantitative researchers seek results that can be viewed as trustworthy and consistent. To these ends (and as we suggested in Chapter 3), quantitative researchers are thoughtful about the way they measure concepts and gather data. For example, quantitative researchers carefully study current research and theory and use this work to develop their research designs and strategy of measuring their concepts and variables.

In developing useful measurement strategies, quantitative researchers face several challenges. One comes when researchers confront the fact that people responding to a question on a survey might interpret its key terms in a way others might not. Consider the question "What is your social class?" Here, "class" might refer to current wealth, educational status, or ancestry going back generations. Many methodologists find significant variations in respondents' interpretations of such terms. Hence, quantitative social researchers test for shared meanings and, as discussed earlier, often use multiple indicators to measure concepts.

Another issue that can affect the trustworthiness of results is whether the people completing a questionnaire are the appropriate people to shed light on the subject at hand. As Aaron Cicourel (1982) points out, some researchers assume that survey respondents have (1) the knowledge they need to answer the questions and (2) a belief that the topic matters in their everyday lives. But is this the case? How can researchers who pose a set of questions designed to measure attitudes toward government–community relations, for example, be sure that respondents have sufficient interest in the topic to provide meaningful responses? Quantitative researchers often approach

this concern by paying particular attention to their sampling procedures. Ensuring that the sample they gather is representative of the overall population of concern and that it is appropriate to the study can help to ensure that the responses they receive will provide data relevant to their research questions. Probability sampling techniques enable quantitative researchers to determine the representativeness of a sample mathematically and thus know the trustworthiness of their measures.

Quantitative researchers must also pay attention to how well something like a questionnaire measures people's actual behavior. One strategy is to adopt robust measurement schemes that include multiple questions and indicators on each concept and variable the researchers seek to understand. Mixed methods studies are also useful, by enabling a researcher to explore the accuracy and meaning of survey results by considering them in light of insights gleaned from observations, or interviews. Because much of our social world is affected by long-term, ongoing social processes, using multiple research instruments can help researchers develop richer understandings about the operations of everyday life.

Finally, quantitative researchers consider the origins and applicability of their measurement schemes. On this point, Zuberi (2008) emphasizes the distinction between mathematics and statistics. Mathematics uses numbers to develop logical calculations based on a set of proofs. Statistics is a form of applied mathematics that is "a system of estimation based on uncertainty" (13). Zuberi points out that the use of statistical methods is determined by practitioners in the field, based on a long process of professional consensus-building among social scientists. He points to the historical development of statistical social science and argues that this history impacts current statistical measures, citing in particular the way researchers today measure race. Statistics gained great currency as a mode of thought in the early 20th century, when scholars were preoccupied with understanding the contours of racial difference. This "racial science" was part of the eugenics movement, which focused on scientifically categorizing humans to "improve" the population through selective breeding. Ultimately, some people used eugenics as a scientific foundation for their argument that White people were superior to people of other races, an argument that inspired the atrocities in Nazi Germany. Zuberi argues that even though most social scientists currently use statistics in an attempt to counter racist hierarchies, many studies employ a limited understanding of race that can be traced back to this early origin of racial science.

Zuberi asserts that much statistical work treats race as if it is an unalterable and stable characteristic, even though definitions of race have changed over time. As he explains, "Racial identity is about shared social status, not shared individual characteristics. Race is not about an individual's skin color. Race is about an individual's relationship to other people within the society" (2008, 12). Zuberi calls attention to issues quantitative researchers must consider, namely, how do we develop sound measurement strategies, what might the consequences be if we do not precisely and accurately measure our concepts, and why is it important for our agreed-upon and even time-tested measurement strategies to be interrogated for ways they might be limited or even oppressive?

Multidimensional Interpretations of Everyday Life

Quantitative researchers often aim to measure complicated, dynamic social processes. As Charles Ragin (2014 [1992]) points out, documenting social change and transformation is not as simple as developing a formula of A + B = C. Instead, Ragin notes that "it is usually combinations of conditions that produce change" (24). Social life isn't static; it is produced through the interaction of multiple overlapping dynamics. Understanding this complexity is quantitative researchers' core goal, but understanding social life as a series of quantifiable patterns is a complicated endeavor.

Quantitative researchers use many strategies to understand how people interpret their everyday existence. They might ask respondents what they think about social inequality and then explore the links between those responses and variables such as age, gender, class, and ethnicity. When trying to understand marriage choice, a researcher might ask how often people choose to get married, what marriage means to a person, and why they may or may not choose to get married. Hayward Derrick

---

BOX 6.2 **The Gap between Stated and Actual Behavior**

A study of racial prejudice conducted many years ago by Richard LaPiere (1934) illustrates that there may be a difference between what people say and what they do. LaPiere travelled the United States from 1930 to 1932 with a young Chinese couple. From a distance, he would observe whether the man and his wife were refused entry at hotels and restaurants. Of 66 hotels approached, only one turned the couple away; of 184 restaurants and diners, none refused them entry. Six months later, LaPiere sent questionnaires to the hotels and restaurants visited. One question asked: "Will you accept members of the Chinese race as guests in your establishment?" Of those that replied, 92 per cent of restaurants and 91 per cent of hotels said no.

LaPiere's simple yet striking study clearly illustrated a gap between reports of behavior and actual behavior. The fact that the question asked was somewhat vague is not usually noted in connection with this widely cited study. "Will you . . . ?" can be interpreted in two ways: as a question about the future or as a question about current policy. Why the more obvious formulation "Do you . . . ?" was not used is unclear, though it is unlikely that this point had a significant bearing on the findings and their implications for survey research. On the other hand, the results might have been just another example of the widespread difference between holding a prejudiced attitude and engaging in a discriminatory act.

Horton and Lori Latrice Sykes (2001) discuss the importance of measuring variables in different ways. When it comes to measuring race, for instance, they note that racism exists on micro and macro levels, varies across contexts, and changes over time. Thus, "to properly measure racism, models must be used that capture the multilevel and multidimensional aspects of the concept while simultaneously accommodating the element of change" (241). Any interpretation researchers offer, whether in a qualitative or quantitative study, will be shaped by the dynamic, multidimensional conditions that make all analysis difficult—and vital. Each of these research methodologies approach understanding the complex social world in different ways.

Quantitative researchers commonly study multiple concepts by analyzing them together and separately in a variety of ways. This is where control variables become useful. As we have seen throughout this chapter, statisticians determine whether the relationship between variables they've measured actually exists by controlling for the effects of other possible "confounding" variables. Recall, for instance, how Legewie and Fagin (2019) made sure that it was the exposure to the Operation Impact program, not poverty or other factors, that affected students' outcomes. Along the same lines, Wodtke (2018) controlled for various other variables in his effort to understand how education affects beliefs about racial inequality; by taking this approach, he found evidence that family factors might account for the previously observed relationship.

Some Contrasts between Qualitative and Quantitative Research

In this chapter and in Chapter 5, we have explored the particular perspectives, methods, and approaches that characterize qualitative and quantitative research. Each interprets the goal of knowledge production in a somewhat different way, and still both types of research make valuable contributions to social scientific knowledge—not only through findings from specific research projects, but also through the questions researchers raise about the research process and knowledge production itself.

Table 6.1 highlights some main differences between qualitative and quantitative research. These differences will come into sharper focus over the course of the chapters that follow. As with any summary of a large body of material, the table outlines general tendencies. The full picture is more nuanced: there are always exceptions to these general points.

Words versus Numbers

- Qualitative researchers use mainly words and descriptions in their analyses of society.

TABLE 6.1 | Common Contrasts between Qualitative and Quantitative Research

Qualitative	Quantitative
Words	Numbers
Participants' points of view	Researcher's point of view
Researcher close	Researcher distant
Theory development	Theory testing
Flexible structure	Rigid structure
Contextual understanding	Generalizable knowledge
Rich, deep data	"Hard," reliable data
Micro	Macro
Meaning	Behavior
Natural settings	Contrived settings

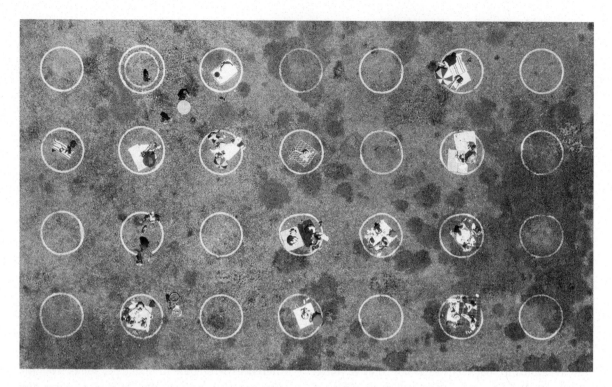

The Covid-19 pandemic has affected people's everyday life across the globe in significant ways. Social distancing recommendations have altered public spaces and how we navigate them. In what different ways might qualitative and quantitative researchers study the experience of spending time at a public park that is now organized into social distancing circles?

- Quantitative researchers typically use precise, numerical measurements to calculate statistics to understand social life.

Participants' Point of View versus Researcher's Point of View

- In qualitative research, the investigation is structured by the people being investigated: their perspective—what they see as important—provides the point of orientation.
- In quantitative research, investigators are in the driver's seat; their concerns structure the investigation.

Researcher Is Close vs. Researcher Is Distant

- In qualitative studies, researchers seek involvement with the people they study, so that they can see the world through their eyes. They view this closeness as vital to deep understanding of people's lives.
- In quantitative research, researchers tend to be less involved with their participants and in some cases, as in research based on self-completed questionnaires, they may have no direct contact at all with participants. Quantitative researchers often consider this distance desirable, because they feel it makes their research objective.

Theory and Concepts Developed from Data versus Theory and Concepts Tested in Research

- In qualitative research, concepts and theories develop as the data are collected, reflecting an inductive approach.
- Before data collection begins, quantitative researchers typically have a theory in mind that they want to test, reflecting a deductive approach.

Flexible Structure versus Rigid Structure

- In qualitative research, the approach is open-ended, in order to allow the researcher to get a sense of the meanings people derive from their everyday lives and to permit the development and elaboration of concepts and theories as the data are collected.
- Quantitative research is typically highly structured to maximize validity and reliability.

Contextual Understanding versus Generalizable Knowledge

- Qualitative researchers focus on understanding the behavior, values, and beliefs of the people in their study. Their findings usually develop out of the context these people find themselves in; hence the insights gained help researchers develop understandings of social concepts but may or may not apply to other people.
- In contrast, quantitative researchers strive to reach findings they hope will be applicable to some larger population.

Rich, Deep Data versus "Hard," Reliable Data

- Qualitative researchers note that their contextual approach and often-prolonged involvement in a setting means that the information they collect is rich, nuanced, and detailed.

- Quantitative researchers often describe their data as "hard"—robust and unambiguous—because their measurement techniques are so precise.

Micro versus Macro

- Qualitative researchers are usually concerned with in-depth analysis of small-scale aspects of social reality, such as personal interaction—which they then analyze as indicative of wider social dynamics.
- Quantitative researchers often seek to uncover large-scale social trends and connections between variables; as we noted above, their research is generally designed to be applicable to large populations.

Meaning versus Behavior

- Qualitative researchers, it is sometimes said, focus primarily on the meaning of behavior for the actor.
- Quantitative researchers focus more on specific patterns in people's behavior.

Natural Settings versus Contrived Settings

- Qualitative researchers investigate people in their natural environments, such as a social gathering or the workplace.
- Quantitative research is conducted in a contrived context, such as an experiment or a formal interview setting.

Key Points

Introduction: How Quantitative Research Examines Broad Trends and Patters

- Quantitative researchers typically begin their study with a hypothesis or theory that they test by gathering data.
- Quantitative researchers adopt an approach to research and largely reflects an objectivist conception of social life.
- Quantitative researchers seek out the why, or the causation behind how things are.

- If quantitative researchers cannot make causal arguments, they can still establish important correlations among variables.
- Quantitative researchers most often use the survey method and analysis of existing data, but also conduct content analysis.

The Emergence of Quantitative Approaches

- August Comte was an early influence on the field of quantitative social science and influenced the status of statistics as a tool to analyze society.

- The development of better computing technology and computer software expanded the use of statistical research methods.

The Main Goals of Quantitative Researchers

- The main goals of quantitative research include testing hypotheses to establish causality, using precise measures and reducing errors, and generalizing findings from a sample to a broader population.
- Probability sampling is typically the first choice among researchers seeking a representative sample.

The Main Steps in Quantitative Research

- Typically, there are 11 sequential steps in quantitative research:

1. Assess existing theory
2. Form a hypothesis
3. Select a research design
4. Devise measures of concepts
5. Select research site(s)
6. Select research participants/respondents
7. Administer research instruments/collect data
8. Process data
9. Analyze the data
10. Reach findings/conclusions
11. Write up findings/conclusions

The Distinct Perspective of Quantitative Research

- The distinct perspective of quantitative research emphasizes systematic, objective study; precise and accurate measurement; and understanding the multidimensional dimensions of social life.

Questions for Review

1. What are some distinguishing features of quantitative research?
2. What are some main data collection methods quantitative researchers use, and what understandings does each of them offer?
3. What role did quantitative research play in the early development of social science?
4. Outline the main goals of quantitative researchers. What is to be gained by achieving them?
5. How do quantitative researchers approach challenges in finding causality?
6. Why is careful measurement such a mainstay of quantitative research?

7. What steps do researchers take in order to assess whether they can use their results for generalization?
8. What are the main steps in quantitative research?
9. To what extent do these steps follow a strict sequence?
10. What are some of the distinct offerings of quantitative research?
11. Discuss this statement: "Quantitative research is trustworthy because it is objective and unbiased."
12. How do quantitative researchers develop studies and gather information to help them understand the complex and multidimensional nature of the social world?

Portfolio Exercise

1. Consider how you might conduct quantitative research for your research topic. For this Portfolio Exercise you will prepare a short visual presentation pitching your research. Use the program of your choice (i.e., PowerPoint, Google Slides, Prezi, etc.) to present the following information:

   a. Your research objective: what are you trying to understand or interpret through this study?
   b. Your hypothesis and how you have developed it.
   c. The quantitative data collection method(s) you are considering using. (Generate ideas and

   don't worry too much about the details; we will explore this concept further in Chapters 8–12.)
   d. An overview, in 2–3 slides, of how steps 1–6 of Figure 6.1 relate to your topic.
   e. A discussion of 2–3 of the following aspects in relation to your topic:
      i. How did you develop your theory/hypothesis? Are there other variables you might consider?
      ii. What data collection technique do you propose, and why would this help you explore your hypothesis most effectively?

iii. How would you approach the topic of objectivity? Think about approaching the topic using systematic steps and what you would need to do to develop precise measures.

iv. What benefits might come from approaching your topic using a deductive model of thinking? What might be challenging about this?

Interactive Activities

1. Referencing Table 6.1 in the text, select a general research topic by which to evaluate the perspective of quantitative research. Using the quantitative column to guide your notes, generate bullet lists and questions about your topic relative to each of the general attributes of quantitative research. Each word or phrase in the column should be addressed as its own categorization or subtopic (i.e., numerical data, macro focus, interest in behavior, etc.). Be sure to identify the *"what"* as well as the *"why."* Once completed, pair up with a classmate in person or online and partake in a peer review, considering the strengths and weaknesses of choosing quantitative research in relation to their selected topic.

2. As a class, decide on a topic (tobacco products and youth, alcohol and college students, adults and depression, online versus in-person learning, etc.) to consider causal relationships. On your own, generate at least one casual sequence that you think could relate to the topic, labeling your variables. Explain why you hypothesize this causal relationship. How might your variables interact in that sequence? Then, write all potential relationships on the board. Select 3 new sequences to analyze and discuss each, addressing the following:

   a. Do you believe these variables are causally related? Why or why not?

   b. How can this relationship be tested in quantitative research?

   c. What potential causes or unidentified variables might provide an alternative explanation for this causal relationship?

3. As a class, divide into groups meeting in person or online. Each group will be provided with excerpts from 2–3 quantitative studies in which the researchers outline their methods and reflect on their approach to the research. Read the excerpts and, with your group, discuss the following questions:

   a. What were the hypotheses in the study?

   b. What theories or other empirical studies inspired them to develop those hypotheses?

   c. What methods of data collection did the researcher use?

   d. What was their focal population and study sample?

   e. How did those data collection methods and sample enable them to explore their hypotheses?

   f. How does the researcher discuss issues such as their research process, their variables under consideration, how they measured the variables, and methodological challenges they faced?

   g. What does the researcher discuss in relation to questions of objectivity and generalizability?

   h. What would be different if this researcher approached this topic using qualitative methods instead of quantitative methods?

Online Resources

- Utah State University's YouTube channel features an instructive video on the differences between quantitative and qualitative research studies.

www.youtube.com/watch?v=RZcfmA1l6cE

For more resources please visit
www.oup.com/he/bryman-reck-fields1e

7

Where Do Principles and Practice Meet in Research?
Study Design

A study design (or research design) is a framework for collecting and analyzing the data needed to answer the questions a researcher poses. The researcher's choice of design reflects not only the empirical questions the researcher is asking, but also the researcher's theoretical orientation. In choosing a study design, the researcher will also be mindful of the kind of design that is most convincing in the academic and policy conversations the researcher hopes to enter and influence. Finally, the researcher will, understandably, lean toward designs that are compatible with the research methods and approaches with which they are comfortable.

Reading this chapter will help you to

- discuss how theory and previously published studies affect the choice of study design;

- consider ethical and feasibility questions when settling on a study design;

- explain the strength and logic of experimental designs;

- discuss why a researcher might turn to a quasi-experimental design;

- identify the relative advantages of cross-sectional designs, longitudinal designs, and case study designs; and

- provide examples of each study design introduced in the chapter.

Imagine a map of your hometown. The official town version might include highways and streets, government buildings, and major landmarks. If you and your friends charted how you get around town, you might include bus routes, shortcuts through yards and alleyways, and a wholly different set of landmarks. A long-term resident might focus on buildings that have been razed to make room for new developments, places they once lived, businesses that have closed, and the ones that have replaced them. A politician might want a map that indicates voting districts, party affiliations by neighborhood, and voter turnout in previous elections. Each map would tell a true story about the town, but each story would vary significantly.

Study designs are like maps: they are different ways to make sense of the social worlds that interest us. We might wonder how frequently something happens in that world and for whom it happens. We might be curious about how a phenomenon changes over time in that world. We might want a snapshot of that world so we can consider the moment in detail. Or maybe we want to better understand an injustice in order to rectify it. Each design offers insight. The question is, what insight do we seek?

Introduction: Choosing a Study Design for Your Research

A **study design** is a broad structure that guides the gathering and analysis of the data that will help answer a research question, test a hypothesis, or explore an emerging idea or area of interest. It reflects the aims of the particular study, as well as broader commitments to ideas, communities, and methods. As we discussed in Chapter 1, research questions emerge from a similar variety of influences. Do you hope to describe how one set of social conditions affects another? If so, you might consider an experimental or quasi-experimental design. Is your goal to explore how a social phenomenon changes over time? Think about a longitudinal design then. Maybe your aim is to examine a phenomenon's links to other events and situations. In that case, a longitudinal,

---

study design (or **research design**) A framework for collecting and analyzing data and for presenting results.

There can be many maps to help visitors navigate and understand a particular place. What are the different maps you could create for your campus, neighborhood, or hometown?

cross-sectional, or case study design might be appropriate. Are you interested in the meanings that people attach to behaviors, events, and identities? Then a case study design may provide the in-depth look you will require.

As with other methodological issues we explore, the choice of study design is fundamentally a decision the researcher makes based on a number of factors. Your answers to the following questions will begin to shape the research design you ultimately choose.

- *What have other researchers done?* As you become familiar with previously published research on your topic, notice the study designs others have used. Is there a standard or tradition in your field that you want to follow? Or perhaps you want to challenge that standard by introducing a design

that others have not yet implemented. You might be able to gain new insight into a social problem by studying it over time or by studying a single case in greater depth.

- *How does theory fit into your study?* If you plan to test a theory, you are doing deductive research and will need to carefully conceptualize and operationalize your terms. If, on the other hand, you hope to generate theory, you are doing inductive research. Your design should allow you to collect data and then move toward broad statements about social life.
- *How many times do you need to observe the phenomenon that interests you?* To track change over time, you'll need to analyze data collected at more than one point in time. If you're interested in a single moment—even an extended event or process—once may be enough.

How many people or instances do you need to observe? If you hope to discover a broad social pattern, you will want to speak to many people or observe many occasions of the behavior that interests you. If you are studying a process, you may want to observe it multiple times, in a natural setting. If you want to study an attitude, behavior, or event in greater depth, it may be enough to examine fewer instances—perhaps even one—in a case study.

What ethical considerations does your study raise? Think about what it will mean to gather and analyze the information you need to answer your research question. Perhaps you want to hear directly from people about their experiences. If the topic is intimate or sensitive, you might benefit from establishing and maintaining relationships with the people you study; in this case, you may wish to speak with them multiple times or hang out with them for an extended period. Perhaps the information is already available—documents or images produced as an ordinary part of social life or because other researchers collected the data as part of their studies. If so, you might be able to design a study that draws on existing data and doesn't require direct interaction with participants.

What resources do you have to support your work? Study design is a practical decision, and resources—including time, funding, colleagues and team members, and inside connections—are a concern. Collecting data more than once and over an extended period necessarily requires more resources. Settle on a study design that allows you to take advantage of the resources you have at your disposal.

What modes of inquiry appeal to you? Perhaps you are inclined to conduct a survey or spend time in a community. Before deciding, you should always think your impulses through and make sure they represent sound choices for the study at hand. But you also do not want to ignore those inclinations altogether: following your hunch may be the best or easiest route to completing the study.

Your answers to these questions may not lead you straight to an obvious choice of study design. In fact, some of your answers may lead you to rethink other questions. Perhaps the ethical issues cause you to reconsider your initial leaning toward qualitative interviews; you might also discover that your commitment to studying social change over time leads you to seek the funding necessary to complete a longitudinal study with a larger sample. These concerns—sampling, ethics, data collection methods, and more—span the research process and multiple chapters of this book. Allow yourself to consider and reconsider a range of questions so you arrive at a balanced and well-considered study design.

Four designs are common in social research:

1. experimental
2. cross-sectional
3. longitudinal
4. case study.

In the following sections, we will consider each of these in detail.

Experimental Design

Imagine you are interested in cause and effect relationships, like what causes some people to get higher grades after participating in a tutoring program while others' grades to stay the same, or why some people get promoted quickly in their jobs while others advance more slowly. An experimental design could be a good choice to help you answer these types of questions. An experiment's greatest strength lies in isolating the effects of a small number of factors and uncovering why cases vary from one another and why things happen the way they do. Correlation, time order, and non-spuriousness (discussed in Chapters 6 and 14) are easier to establish with an **experimental design**, when researchers can be

---

experimental design A research design that rules out alternative explanations of findings by randomly assigning participants to one of two groups: an experimental group that is exposed to the influence and a control group that is not exposed to the same influence.

BOX 7.1 Participatory Action Research: Collaborative Study Design

How do you think that participating in a PAR study might, like education, have a positive impact on women in prison?

Participatory action research (PAR) takes a different approach to decisions about study design. People who are usually the focus of research instead work with researchers to design and implement a study in order to produce knowledge that is mutually beneficial. Researchers from the Graduate Center at the City University of New York (CUNY) collaborated with women in prison at the Bedford Hills (NY) Correctional Facility in participatory action research on the impact of educational programs like the "College Bound" program created by incarcerated people and advocates at Bedford Hills in the mid-1990s.

When studying a group, such a prison population, researchers usually design the study themselves and then seek the involvement of research participants to complete a survey or interviews. In this case, the CUNY research team adopted a PAR strategy. They recruited fifteen of the women incarcerated at the prison to participate in a seminar on research methods. This group became a PAR team that developed and implemented a mixed-methods study focused

confident that they have generated a nomothetic explanation by controlling the influence of factors that complicate everyday social life.

Experimental designs span sociological research. For example, some sociologists interested in social power study social networks and exchange in order to understand how people accrue and maintain status. They are often interested in the relationship among power, resources, and the networks that connect people. They wonder, for example, if a negotiation's outcomes are shaped by the perceived (rather than actual) value of a person's resources. Social network researchers can use experimental methods to create situations in a controlled setting—such as a laboratory, a computer lab, or computers located in private and connected through a protected online network—and then observe how people handle themselves in that environment.

Manipulation

When conducting a true experiment, researchers do something—for example, introduce a factor or isolate an influence—and observe the effects. Put more formally, an experiment manipulates an independent variable to determine its influence on a dependent variable. Typically, the researcher on the different ways that having access to a college education in the prison affected the women. The team of faculty, graduate students, and incarcerated women interviewed currently and formerly incarcerated women about their experiences; conducted focus groups with students, dropouts, and incarcerated women's adolescent children; interviewed correctional officers; surveyed university administrators; analyzed archival college records and documents; and encouraged the Department of Corrections to do a 36-month study comparing recidivism rates among formerly incarcerated women who had and had not taken college classes while inside.

The team of university and imprisoned researchers attempted to co-facilitate all the planning, data collection, and analysis as much as possible, with the "outside" and "inside" researchers sharing power in the process. The goal was to make the incarcerated members equal partners in the research and to emphasize their issues, perspectives, and analysis. The realities of prison life made this goal difficult to achieve: for example, "inside" researchers wanted to conduct data

analysis but had no access to locked cabinets in which they could store the interview transcripts (to maintain confidentiality), and they were not allowed recording devices (to ensure accuracy of details). Many felt uncomfortable co-authoring published articles that critiqued the prison system for fear of incurring retribution while still incarcerated.

Despite the challenges, the PAR study provided "strong confirmation of the impact of college in prison on women, their children, 'peace' in the prison, post-release outcomes, the leadership women provided in communities post-release and the tax benefits saved by society *not* having to subsidize those who return to incarceration" (Fine and Torre 2006, 260). The team produced a report that they sent to all US governors and all New York State senators and assembly members. They also published academic papers, produced advocacy brochures for community organizations in English and Spanish, and created and managed an informational website. Together, the team succeeded in answering a research question about college in prison from the perspective of incarcerated individuals.

assigns some participants to an experimental group, in which the independent variable is changed or manipulated, and others to a control group, where no manipulation takes place. The researcher then observes and measures the dependent variable to understand the impact of the manipulation: are the outcomes for the experimental and control groups different? If so—and provided the difference can be attributed to the manipulation—the researcher can reasonably conclude that the factor they introduced is the cause of the experimental outcome (Figure 7.1). Because study participants may vary in unknowable ways—differences in outcome may be a result

of something other than their having encountered the influence being examined—the researcher has to (1) statistically "control" for other potential differences between the control and experimental groups and (2) rule out alternative explanations for any observed differences.

Devah Pager's 2003 study of incarceration, racism, and employment discrimination in US cities is an experiment conducted with manipulation of the independent variable. Pager sent Black and White men to apply for real-life entry-level positions in Milwaukee and, later, New York City. The applicants were paired on relevant characteristics, including race,

BOX 7.2   Nomothetic and Idiographic Explanations

How might you design a study to assess the impact of Black Lives Matter activism on voting behaviors?

When selecting a study design, researchers must consider the aims of their study and what understandings they hope to develop. Quantitative researchers lean toward research designs that generate *nomothetic explanations*, which can be applied to the general population represented by the sample of people who actually participated in the study. When pursuing this kind of generalizable finding, researchers usually adopt a deductive approach and adhere to structured methods of data collection and analysis that other researchers can replicate. Nomothetic explanations are often causal explanations and thus satisfy three criteria (as discussed in Chapters 6 and 14): correlation, time order, and non-spuriousness. A nomothetic explanation that meets these criteria is powerfully generalizable.

Qualitative researchers, on the other hand, are usually less interested in discovering general laws and principles than in obtaining rich descriptions of individuals or groups based on the perceptions and feelings of the people studied. The descriptions usually involve or imply proximate, specific causes that are not meant to explain other situations or the behavior of people who were not part of the research. Such *idiographic explanations* usually involve a detailed "story" or description of the people studied that is based on empathetic understanding.

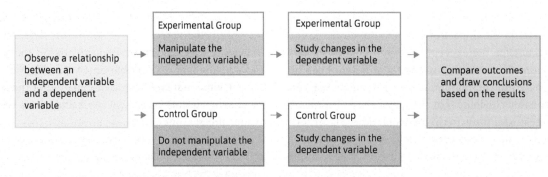

FIGURE 7.1   **Steps in an experiment: Experimental group versus control group**

For example, qualitative analysis of voting behaviors among Black voters in 2020 may find that Black Lives Matter and anti-racism protesting generated a sense of urgency among those who had not voted in previous elections. That finding is not meant to apply to other Black people or other elections and social movements; it is simply an idiographic explanation that helps to explain why these particular voters behaved as they did. A quantitative analysis might examine a nomothetic explanation of differences in voting behaviors between those Black voters who participated in anti-racism protests in 2020 and those who did not. Controlling for other conditions (including, but not limited to, the Covid-19 pandemic and previous political participation and voting behavior), the researcher may be able to isolate the impact of anti-racist protest on voting.

As we note in Table 7.1, nomothetic and idiographic aims help determine researchers' choice of study design and their data collection methods. We discuss each of these methods in later chapters of this book.

TABLE 7.1 | Study Designs Used for Nomothetic and Idiographic Research

Research Type	Aims	Compatible Study Designs	Compatible Data Collection Methods
Nomothetic	To obtain, through quantitative data, findings that can be generalized to the broader population.	Experimental Cross-sectional Longitudinal	Questionnaires and structured interviewsContent analysisExisting data
Idiographic	To obtain, through qualitative data, a rich description of individuals or small groups.	Cross-sectional Longitudinal Case Study	Qualitative interviews Ethnography and participant observation Content analysis Existing data

Note: Researchers choose research designs and data collection methods that reflect their pursuit of idiographic or nomothetic explanations.

job history, education, and physical appearance. On a rotating basis, participants were given the task of indicating on the job application that they had a criminal record. Pager found that a criminal record serves as a significant barrier to employment, particularly for Black men. Race was also a barrier: in fact, White men who reported criminal records were treated more favorably than were Black men who reported no record. As Pager writes, "The persistent effect of race on employment opportunities is painfully clear in these results. Blacks are less than half as likely to receive consideration by employers, relative to their White counterparts, and Black non-offenders fall behind even whites with prior felony convictions" (2003, 960). Experiments like Pager's offer a way to isolate and study racism and other persistent inequalities in our world.

One challenge is that many of the independent variables of interest to social researchers cannot be manipulated. Some sociologists (see e.g., Lipset 1990)

Consider Pager's study of incarceration, racism, and employment discrimination. Beyond the experimental design she used, what other study designs could shed light on her findings?

maintain that a country's national character is affected by whether the country came into existence through revolution. To test this idea experimentally, revolution would have to be induced in some randomly selected areas to produce new countries, while in others no revolution would be fomented. The researcher would then compare the national characters of the revolutionary countries with the non-revolutionary ones. Needless to say, such experimental manipulations would be difficult—if not impossible—to carry out.

This example raises another challenge, namely that ethical concerns often preclude experiments. Suppose you are interested in the effect of nutrition on children's academic performance. A researcher could select a pool of six-year-old participants at random and place them in two groups: one group is fed unhealthy food for a month and the other is fed nutritious food. Then, you would test both groups to see if they differed in academic ability. Although sound from a methodological standpoint, such a study would introduce serious ethical problems

around denying some children nutritious food for an extended period of time. The ethical problem surrounding this example is obvious, but in other experiments it can be much subtler. For instance, could we conduct an experiment that involves withholding medical treatment, job opportunities, or valuable information?

Another reason experiments are challenging in sociology is that many areas of interest—gender roles, political preferences, the formation of social movements, and so on—have complex, long-term causes that cannot be easily simulated in experiments. People's lives are composed of entangled identities, biographies, opportunities, and constraints. Researchers committed to intersectional theories approach social categories, differences, and inequalities as simultaneously occurring and shaping one another. They reject the idea that we could—or even should—consider race, gender, class, and other social difference independent of one another.

Even with these caveats in mind, sociologists do rely on experimental designs. The increasing availability of "big data" online makes experimental manipulation more feasible (see Chapter 12). Online and offline, the field experiment model allows researchers to manipulate variables in a real-world setting (the field) rather than a laboratory or simulated environment. The strength of field experiments is that they allow social processes to unfold in natural situations. The researcher can thus understand how things would look in "real life." Devah Pager's 2003 study described earlier is an example of such a field experiment.

Mixed Methods in Action | Using Experiments to Study Class, Gender, and Employment Discrimination

A mixed-method study conducted by Lauren A. Rivera and András Tilcsik (2016) indicates that employment discrimination extends beyond entry-level positions into elite professional arenas. Their research involved three methods of data collection and analysis: a résumé audit experiment (like Pager's), a survey experiment, and qualitative interviews. In the résumé audit, Rivera and Tilcsik sent résumés of fictitious "higher-class" and "lower-class" law-school students to elite US law firms. All "applicants" were graduating from non-elite but selective law schools; they were also randomly assigned markers of social class and gender, such as last name, history of receiving financial aid, and hobbies.

Higher-class men applicants were most likely to be invited for an interview in the audit. Higher-class women did not experience the same advantage.

A later survey and qualitative interviews with law firm employers suggested that, while law firms anticipated that higher-class men would "fit in" with the firm's culture, they expected that higher-class women would eventually feel the pull of motherhood and be less committed to the firm's work. This expectation influenced employers' interest in interviewing women, regardless of whether their résumés indicated that the applicants were currently parents or planned to become parents. The experimental design effectively demonstrated a causal relationship between gender and likelihood of being invited to an interview at elite law firms, a cause-effect relationship that would be difficult to prove using other research designs. Combining the résumé audit experiment with surveys and interviews allowed the researchers to further analyze the reasons contributing to these trends.

Quasi-Experiments

The conditions required in an experimental design are often difficult to achieve; researchers cannot always isolate and manipulate the independent variable that interests them or assign study participants to experimental and control groups. In these cases, researchers may turn to **quasi-experimental designs**. As in experiments, participants in quasi-experiments are subject to some condition, and the focus is on whether study outcomes are the result of that condition.

A common type of quasi-experiment compares data collected before and after a government or industry policy shift. For example, researchers might compare the number of car accidents before and after a speed limit is lowered. If the number of accidents decreases after the speed limit has been lowered, the policy would appear to be a success, but the researcher cannot be certain because there is no control group not experiencing the change. Perhaps

the change was caused by something other than the reduction in the speed limit. The researcher would need to control for other factors that contribute to vehicle speed and to traffic collisions, including police enforcement, road conditions, installation of speed cameras, and the relative safety of road infrastructure.

Quasi-experimental designs have been particularly prominent in **evaluation research** studies, which examine the effects of organizational innovations such as a longer school day or greater worker autonomy in a plant. Quasi-experiments are also used

---

quasi-experimental design A research design whose logic and process resemble an experiment but does not involve the same manipulation and control of influences.

---

evaluation research Research undertaken to assess the impact of real-life interventions, including policy changes and social programs.

to evaluate the effectiveness of institutional policies. The essential question asked by evaluation studies is whether a policy initiative or organizational change has achieved its goals. Ideally, the design would have a treatment group and a control group. Since it is often unfeasible or unethical to assign research participants randomly to the two groups, such studies are usually quasi-experimental. For instance, data gathered from people before a change may be compared with data acquired after; the "before" people become the control group, the "after" people the experimental group. This approach has the added advantage that the two groups are basically the same, making random assignment unnecessary.

Karen Suyemoto, Stephanie C. Day, and Sarah Schwartz (2015) conducted a quasi-experimental study using this technique. Their study examined how Asian American youths' participation in a social justice-oriented program affected their racial/ethnic identities and perspectives on social justice. They studied eight high school students of Chinese, Vietnamese, and Chinese-Vietnamese background who participated in a year-long program sponsored by a community-based youth empowerment organization working with Asian Pacific American youth in Boston. They conducted interviews before and after program participation and observed the program activities. Comparing the interviews before and after the program, the researchers were found that the participants had a much more complex understanding of race and racism, they had developed stronger racial identities, and they expressed a greater sense of empowerment and more investment in social justice action.

Though experimental designs, organized around nomothetic thinking, are fairly entrenched in evaluation research, in recent years evaluations based on qualitative research and idiographic thinking have emerged. The strongest qualitative evaluation builds on an understanding of the context in which an intervention occurs and the diverse viewpoints of the stakeholders (Greene 2000). Seunghyun Yoo, Carolyn C. Johnson, Janet Rice, and Powlin Manuel (2004) evaluated an abstinence-only teen pregnancy prevention program. In interviews and focus groups with principals, teachers, peer mentors, and students, they asked about people's experience of the program, challenges in its implementation, and overall value of the instruction. Assessments of the last item were mixed, but there was general consensus that peer mentoring was especially valuable. This qualitative evaluation provided important insight into the impact of an intervention schools and communities offer in response to a vexing social problem.

BOX 7.3 Characteristics of Compelling Evaluation Research

Experimental and quasi-experimental research has been pivotal in studies of sex education. As communities and policymakers debate how to promote young people's sexual health and prevent disease, infection, and unwanted pregnancies, the content and delivery of sexuality education in schools and community-based organizations feels important.

Douglas Kirby (2007) devoted his career to evaluating the effectiveness of these programs. In one study, Kirby et al. reviewed research that met their criteria for compelling evaluation studies, including experimental or quasi-experimental design (intervention and comparison groups and data collected before and after the intervention), a sample size of at least 100, and measures of program impact on sexual behaviors. The included studies were conducted in 10 developed countries and 18 developing countries. The researchers found that sex education programs generally have a positive impact on young people's sexual behavior, but specifically how and why they have this impact is not clear. Researchers have to turn to another study design to figure out the how and why. Case studies are one option, as we discuss later in the chapter.

Collecting Data at Different Points in Time: Cross-Sectional and Longitudinal Design

Cross-Sectional Design

Researchers using a **cross-sectional design** collect data to represent a single point in time. The single point may be extended—a summer, a month-long policy debate, a school semester, or a basketball season—but it represents one unit of time for the research; there are no before-and-after comparisons. In addition, cross-sectional studies do not involve any manipulation of the independent variable: they are like snapshots of a group or phenomenon.

A cross-sectional design entails the collection of data on more than one case, whether these are people, families, neighborhoods, cities, nations, artists, or musical styles. Researchers conducting such studies are interested in variation between and among instances of a phenomenon, which can be established only when more than one example is examined. As we discussed in Chapter 4, a larger number makes it more likely that researchers will encounter variation in the behaviors, attitudes, or conditions that interest them, and for those researchers conducting statistical analysis, a larger number of cases will satisfy the requirements of statistical techniques possible only with large sample sizes.

In cross-sectional studies, data are collected on two or more variables, which are then examined to detect patterns of association. This approach sometimes makes it difficult to show cause and effect because the independent and dependent variables are measured simultaneously, making any demonstration of time order (showing that the cause actually precedes the effect in time) hard to demonstrate. For instance, there is a well-supported negative relationship between social class and serious forms of mental illness: more poor people are diagnosed with mental illness than are wealthy people. But there is also a debate about the nature of that relationship. Does poverty lead to stress and therefore to mental illness? Or does mental illness lead to difficulties in holding down a job and thus poverty? Or is it a bit of both? The direction of the influence is unclear:

research suggests an association between the two variables, but no clear causal link. A cross-sectional design will help show the relationship between social class and mental illness, but it will not provide sufficient evidence to establish whether one of these variables precedes (and thus possibly causes) the other. In Chapter 14, we will address this challenge further when we discuss quantitative analysis strategies for drawing cautious inferences about causality using cross-sectional designs.

As noted in our discussion of experimental design earlier in this chapter, manipulating the variables of interest is difficult in much social research. This is a key reason most quantitative social research employs a cross-sectional design rather than an experimental one. Ethnicity, age, gender, and social backgrounds are more or less "givens" and not really amenable to the kind of manipulation necessary for a true experimental design. Fictitious manipulations are possible—such as when an experimenter digitally alters résumés to represent different races or social classes to see the effects on job offers—but the manipulation is limited to the external signs of race and class, missing more subjective and experiential aspects.

Yet, the fact that certain variables are givens provides a clue as to how to make causal inferences in cross-sectional research. Many variables of interest can be assumed to exist prior to other variables. In a relationship between ethnic status and voting behavior, the latter cannot be the independent variable because it occurs after ethnicity. Still, ethnicity cannot be said with certainty to be the cause of the decision to participate in an election or to vote for a particular candidate: it is just one of many prior conditions. Causal inferences can only be drawn cautiously from cross-sectional data.

Cross-sectional design is well suited for qualitative research and its pursuit of insight into meanings and experiences of social life. Paige Sweet (2015) conducted interviews with medical advocates and health care providers whose work focuses on domestic violence. She found that advocates and providers

---

cross-sectional design A study design in which data are collected at (and thus represent) a single point in time.

use discourses of "risk" to explain women's vulnerability to violence; they no longer describe it as a product of patriarchal conditions. According to Sweet, notions of risk "degender" domestic violence and cast women as passive victims of their partners' abuse. In quantitative studies, a cross-sectional design allows researchers to explore the interplay between and among variables to develop understandings about key patterns in the social world. Eric Anthony Grollman (2017) explored the meaning and experience of risk in a cross-sectional quantitative study of the relationship between, on the one hand, young people's experiences with race and gender discrimination and, on the other, their participation in risky sexual behaviors. Analyzing data from the Black Youth Culture Survey, a nationally representative survey of Black, Latinx, and White heterosexual youth, Grollman found that experiences of discrimination are associated with risky sexual behaviors but not with negative outcomes of those behaviors. In addition, Grollman did not find a relationship between experiences of discrimination and young people's use of condoms or contraceptives. Grollman urges readers not to presume that risk extends uniformly across the whole of young people's sexual lives. Both cross-sectional studies cited here provide insight into meaning—the language used to explain women's vulnerability to violence and the meaning of risk and experience across young people's lives.

Longitudinal Design

Are you curious about people's experiences over time, like how a child with divorced or separated parents fares throughout their life? Or maybe you wonder about how the characteristics of various time periods affect people's lives? Do you wonder how the emergence of smart phones affected people's technology use and social interaction? Are you curious about how this is going to shift over time as communication technology keeps advancing? These studies would be well suited to a longitudinal design—a

study design in which researchers study changes over time. With a **longitudinal design**, cases are examined at a particular time (T1) and again at a later time or times (T2, T3, and so on)—much like a series of cross-sectional studies. Thus, like experimental designs, longitudinal designs allow insight into the time order of variables and are better able than cross-sectional designs to establish the direction of causal relationships.

Let's say that we wanted to study the relationship between total household income and academic success. Specifically, we want to see if any gaps in grades between children from low-income and high-income households change over time. We might begin by examining the final-term grades and household incomes of a random sample of first-grade students. We would then track the academic performance of the same sample of students at regular intervals—say, every three years—to see if differences in academic performance correlating with household income narrow or widen over time.

Because potential independent variables can be identified at T1, the researcher is better positioned to infer that the effects identified at T2 occurred after changes in the independent variables—for example, aging, shifts in employment, political movements, and life transitions like marriage or parenting. In all other respects, the points made about cross-sectional designs are the same as those for longitudinal designs (because ultimately researchers use a cross-sectional design at each of the time periods they examine in their longitudinal study). Yet in spite of its heightened ability to show cause and effect, longitudinal designs are sometimes not an option in social research because of the additional time and cost involved.

There are three basic types of longitudinal design:

1. the trend study
2. the panel study
3. the cohort study.

As summarized in Table 7.2 and illustrated in Figures 7.2, 7.3, and 7.4, each type looks at change over time in a single population; what varies is the sample.

---

longitudinal design A research design in which data are collected on at least two separate occasions in order to capture social process and/or change over time.

TABLE 7.2 | Trend, Panel, and Cohort Studies

	Trend	**Panel**	**Cohort**
Population	Same each time	Same each time	Same each time
Sample	Different each time	Same each time	Same each time, and all participants share a characteristic of interest to the researcher

In a **trend study**, the sample is different each time (Figure 7.2). The researcher is tracking changes broadly, across a population, and selects a different sample to represent that population at each time of data collection. For example, a researcher might look at changing political attitudes and voting behaviors among first-year college students in the United States during the 2020, 2024, and 2028 presidential election years.

In a **panel study**, the same people, households, or other groups are studied on at least two different occasions (Figure 7.3). For example, the Panel Study of Income Dynamics (PSID) was established in 1968 as part of the US War on Poverty. Administered by the University of Michigan, PSID is the world's longest-running longitudinal household survey.

Another example of a panel study is the National Longitudinal Survey of Youth 1997 (NLSY97), a longitudinal project that follows a sample of children and youth born in the United States between 1980 and 1984. Nearly 9,000 respondents were surveyed annually until 2009 and are now interviewed every other year. Data are collected by the US Bureau of Labor Statistics and are publicly available from

trend study A longitudinal design in which researchers collect data at least two times about a single, constant population of people.

panel study A longitudinal design in which researchers collect data on two or more occasions about a single, constant sample of people.

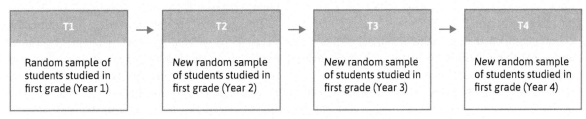

FIGURE 7.2 **Four-year trend study of elementary student achievement**

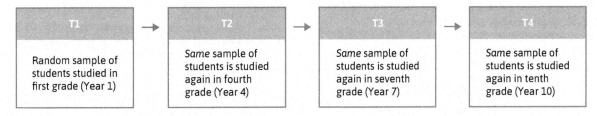

FIGURE 7.3 **Ten-year panel study of the effects of family household income on academic success**

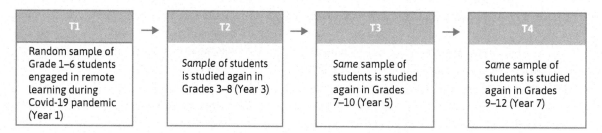

FIGURE 7.4 **Seven-year cohort study of lasting implications of remote learning during Covid-19 pandemic for academic success**

Round 1 (1997–1998) to Round 17 (2015–2016). Questions address issues including education and training; parents and families; sexual activity and pregnancies; and attitudes and expectations. Researchers have used NLSY97 data to explore topics such as the long-term consequences of bullying (Quinn and Stewart 2018) and parental influence over their children's financial decision making (Tang, Baker, and Peter 2015).

A *cohort* is a group of people who share an experience, such as being born in the same year or graduating from a particular school at the same time. A **cohort study**, then, involves studying members of a cohort over time, but the same people may not be studied each time (Figure 7.4). The US National Longitudinal Survey of Mature Women and of Young Women first surveyed women aged 30–44 and 14–24 in 1967; the study continued to survey these two cohorts annually until 2003. Researchers used these data to explore, for instance, how members of these cohorts contended with multiple marriages (Jacobs and Furstenberg 1986) and volunteered in their communities (Rotolo and Wilson 2004).

Panel and cohort studies face some shared challenges. One is sample attrition: some participants may drop out, move away, or die at later stages of the research. Replacement of lost participants is expensive and often impossible. In a panel study, replacement would mean the researcher is no longer

studying a stable panel. In a study of the educational attainment of immigrant youth, Ronit Dinovitzer et al. (2003) were able to talk to only 65 percent of those originally surveyed 19 years earlier. Comparing the demographic characteristics of those who participated in the second round with those who exited the study, the authors found no significant differences. This sort of comparison is a common practice: when no difference is found, the losses are treated as random and thus acceptable to ignore. The main problem with attrition is that it may be a source of bias: those who leave the study may differ in some important respects from those who remain, and those who remain may not constitute a representative sample. However, there is some evidence from panel studies that attrition declines with time: after the first or second wave of data collection, attrition slows and those still on the panel tend to remain.

Both cohort and panel studies are vulnerable to *panel conditioning effect*, whereby continued participation in a longitudinal study affects respondents' behavior or reports of those behaviors. Florencia Torche, John Robert Warren, Andrew Halpern-Manners, and Eduardo Valenzuela (2012) conducted a methodological experiment in order to examine panel conditioning effect on high school students participating in a longitudinal study of substance abuse. The team analyzed data from the Longitudinal Survey of Drug Use, conducted in Santiago, Chile, in 2008 and 2009. In the first wave of data collection, 4670 students completed questionnaires that included a drug module, and a

---

cohort study A longitudinal design in which the researcher collects data at least two times about a sample of people who share a significant life event.

small group (329 students) completed surveys with no drug module (because this methodological experiment was part of a larger study of adolescent substance use, the researchers limited the number of students who did not provide this baseline data). In the second wave of data collection, one year later, all respondents answered questions about alcohol, drug, and cigarette use. This time the research team found lower rates of reported substance use among those who answered questions about substance use in the first wave. That is, controlling for other differences among students (for example, school, socioeconomic status, family, and academic performance), those students who had already answered a question about substance use were less likely to report using alcohol, cigarettes, and drugs when asked a second time. Torche et al. suggest the questions themselves may have caused this change in reported substance use by sparking "reflection and learning prompted by emotions of anxiety, guilt, or embarrassment after acknowledging a non-normative behavior" (913). The research team encourages researchers to correct for bias that results from panel conditioning affect, and to conduct methodological experiments like this within their own longitudinal studies in order to better understand how panel conditioning may have impacted their results and findings.

Case Study Design

The basic **case study design** entails a detailed and intensive analysis of a single case or, sometimes, a few cases. A case may be

- *a community*, as in Carol Stack's study (1983) of "The Flats," a low-income urban Black community; Susan Krieger's study (1983) of identity in a lesbian community; or Randol Contreras's study (2013) of the drug trade in the South Bronx;
- *an organization*, such as the holistic health center studied by Sherryl Kleinman (1996), or *members of a single organization*, such as Katrinell Davis's study (2017) of African American

women workers in a San Francisco Bay Area public transit system;
- *a person*, as in Joshua Gamson's (2006) study of Sylvester, a disco singer, songwriter, and dancer in 1970s and 1980s San Francisco or Aldon Morris's study (2017) of the role W.E.B. Du Bois played in the founding of American sociology;
- *an event*, like Eric Klinenberg's study (2002) of fatalities during the Chicago heat wave of 1995 or Arlene Stein's study (2001) of a battle over gay rights in an Oregon community; or
- *a neighborhood, city, or state*, as in Mary Pattillo's study (2008) of race and class in Chicago's North Kenwood–Oakland neighborhood, Lynd and Lynd's study (1929) of "Middletown" (see Box 7.5), or Theda Skocpol's comparative analysis (1979) of social revolutions in China, France, and Russia.

When the predominant research orientation is qualitative, a case study tends to take an inductive approach to the relationship between theory and research. If the researcher adopts a quantitative strategy, the research is often deductive, guided by specific research questions or hypotheses derived from social theories.

Robert K. Yin (2018) distinguishes three types of case studies:

- In the *critical case*, the researcher has a clearly specified hypothesis, and a case is chosen on the grounds that it will allow a better understanding of the circumstances under which the hypothesis does or does not hold. Consider the classic study by Festinger et al. (1956; reprint 2008) of a doomsday/UFO cult. The fact that the world did not end allowed the researchers to test propositions about how people respond to thwarted expectations. What did cult members

---

case study design A research design that entails detailed and intensive analysis of either a single case or, for comparative purposes, a small number of cases.

Methods in Motion | Gang Involvement, Recovery, and the Masculine Body

Edward Orozco Flores (2016) studied two cases of faith-based programs in Los Angeles that aimed to help men end their gang involvement and build new lives. Flores conducted 18 months of ethnographic fieldwork with the two programs, exploring, among other things, how the programs taught men to embody their exit from gang life. Narratives of addiction and recovery were central to the men's exits, and a rejection of an "embodied gang masculinity" was central to their displays and performance of gang recovery. Men were encouraged to renounce masculinities associated with gang involvement (tattoos, haircuts, particular styles of dress) and to adopt new models (remove tattoos, grow their hair out, and wear polo shirts, collared shirts, or suits). Flores's rich description of the recovery and embodiment in his two chosen cases offers a nuanced explanation of how this embodied masculinity helped the men to construct new moral universes in which they not only distanced themselves from gang life but also rose above it.

What is so meaningful about a polo shirt? What picture of masculinity does it offer?

Case studies are often associated with qualitative research. Exponents of this design tend to favor methods like participant observation and unstructured interviewing, and studies of individual people often use the life history or biographical approach. Such qualitative methods can be particularly helpful in generating an intensive, detailed examination of a case. However, case studies can also use some combination of quantitative and qualitative methods or rely exclusively on quantitative data collection and analysis.

Case studies are sometimes difficult to distinguish from other research designs because almost any kind of research can function as a case study. The research emerging on the 2016 presidential election illustrates the fine lines between study designs. Both studies featured in Box 7.4 might function as case studies or as cross-sectional studies; 2016 voting behaviors might also become part of a longitudinal study. Even research based on a national, random sample of Californians could be considered a case study of California. What distinguishes a case study is the idiographic goal of finding and providing a rich description of features of the case that may be unique to time and place.

BOX 7.4 **The Case of the 2016 Presidential Election**

The 2016 presidential campaign and election of Donald J. Trump prompted a number of quantitative case studies. Researchers are interested in the particular case of the election because of what it might tell us more broadly about, among other things, electoral politics, social divisions and inequalities, and shifting allegiances. Jacob Bor (2017) looked at county-level voting data and data on life expectancy. He found that counties with declining or stagnant life expectancy rates saw an increase in Republican vote shares from 2008 to 2016. He suggests that, since the Trump administration made significant cuts to public health funding, this voting behavior may have broad implications: "Health gaps are likely to continue to widen without public investment in the conditions that support population health" (2017, 1562).

White voters supported Trump more than any other racial group, and Eric D. Knowles and Linda R. Tropp (2018) looked at the relationship between Whites' everyday experiences of diversity and their support (or lack of support) for Trump. They found that White people who experience economic struggle were more likely to report feelings of threat in the face of racial and ethnic diversity. Whites who were not struggling experienced racial and ethnic diversity as an opportunity for contact with people unlike themselves; these White voters reported a lower sense of threat and less support for Trump. Insights from studies of the case of the 2016 election may shed light on future presidential contests.

---

do when, after quitting their jobs, leaving their homes, and waiting on a mountaintop, nothing happened? Did they sneak down and move to another town? No: they decided that their faith had saved humankind and that their new role was to tell others of that miracle so more people could be converted to their religion.

- The *extreme*, even *unique*, *case* is a common focus in clinical studies. The well-known (albeit controversial) study by Margaret Mead and Franz Boas (1928 [1973]) of growing up in Samoa seems to have been motivated by her belief that it represented a unique case and thus could challenge the then popular nature-over-nurture hypothesis. She reported that, unlike adolescents in most other societies, Samoan youth did not suffer a period of anxiety and stress in their teenage years. She explained this finding by their culture's strong, consistently enforced standards of conduct and morality. These factors were of interest because they challenge many commonplace assumptions about teenagers and the inevitability of adolescent angst.

- The basis for the *revelatory case* exists when the researcher considers a phenomenon not previously studied. This can happen when previously unavailable evidence becomes accessible, a new technology emerges, or an unprecedented event occurs. For example, as we write this textbook, teams across the world are studying the impact of the Covid-19 pandemic. This unprecedented health crisis presents researchers with the opportunity and responsibility to study this revelatory case.

As we have mentioned, one of the standard criticisms of the case study is that its findings cannot be generalized across populations. Case study researchers argue that this sort of generalizing is not the purpose of their craft. A valid and deeply understood picture of one case is more valuable than a potentially less valid picture of many. Qualitative researchers aim to generate an intensive examination of a single case, and this depth of idiographic understandings offers an alternative to the generalizability of a nomothetic approach.

BOX 7.5 Longitudinal Research and the Case Study

Case study research frequently includes a longitudinal element. The researcher is often a participant observer in an organization or a member of a community for many months or years, or may conduct interviews with individuals over a lengthy period. Moreover, the researcher may be able to inject an additional longitudinal element by analyzing archival information and asking respondents to recall events that occurred before the study began, thus discovering some history.

A longitudinal element also occurs when a case that has been studied is returned to at a later time.

A particularly interesting study is "Middletown," the pseudonym for an American Midwest town first studied by Robert Staughton Lynd and Helen Merrell Lynd (1929) in 1924–1925 and then restudied in 1935, during the Depression, to see what changes had occurred (Lynd and Lynd 1937). In 1977, the community was again restudied, this time in a post–Vietnam War setting (Bahr et al. 1983), using the same research instruments but with minor alterations to the design. Interestingly, this study of a single case over time found that little had changed in Middletown's attitudes and culture.

TABLE 7.3 | Research Strategy and Research Design

Research Design	General Research Orientation	
	Quantitative	**Qualitative**
Experimental: Explore causal relationships	Most experiments involve quantitative comparisons between experimental and control groups on the dependent variable. Example: Pager (2003).	Experiments are not used in qualitative research, though they may inspire or be inspired by qualitative findings. Pager (2003) included qualitative interviews in her study to flesh out the findings of her field experiment.
Cross-sectional: Explore a single moment	Survey research and structured observation on a sample at one point in time; content analysis of a sample of documents. Sometimes there is a comparison, as in cross-cultural research. Example: Grollman (2017).	Qualitative interviews or focus groups at one point in time are two forms; qualitative content analysis of a set of documents relating to a single period is another. Example: Sweet (2015).
Longitudinal: Map change over time	Survey administered with a sample on more than one occasion, as in panel and cohort studies; content analysis of documents relating to different time periods. Example: Dinovitzer et al. (2003).	Ethnographic research conducted over a long period, qualitative interviewing on more than one occasion, or qualitative content analysis of documents relating to different time periods. Example: Lynd and Lynd (1929).
Case study: In-depth consideration of one or more instances of something	Survey research conducted on a single case with a view to revealing important features about its nature. Examples: Bor (2017) and Knowles and Tropp (2018).	Ethnographic study of, for example, an organization, person, family, or community; qualitative interviewing focused on a single case. Example: Flores (2016).

Modes of Inquiry and Study Design

By now, you should appreciate that the qualitative and quantitative modes of inquiry—discussed in Chapters 5 and 6, respectively—are differently associated with the research designs described in this chapter. Table 7.3 shows the typical form associated with each combination of research orientation and research design. The examples are all discussed earlier in this chapter. The table refers to data collection methods we introduce in Part IV of this textbook. As always, the glossary provides a quick reference for unfamiliar terms.

The distinctions among study designs are not always clear cut. For example, life history studies, research that concentrates on a specific issue over time, and ethnography—in which the researcher examines change in a single case—contain elements of both longitudinal and case study design. We will discuss life history, ethnography, and other specific methods of data collection and analysis in later chapters. For now, note that some studies span categories—for example, longitudinal case studies—and do not belong to one category or another. Like the maps we might draw of our hometown, study designs offer overlapping pictures of a social world. The researcher's task is to keep their focus on the insights they seek in their study. A study design that reflects the insights of previous research, current theoretical understandings, a sound sampling and measurement plan, ethical concerns and commitments, and available resources, along with the researcher's inclinations and interests, will help maintain that focus.

Key Points

Introduction: Choosing a Study Design for Your Project

- When designing a study, researchers make a series of decisions about data collection and analysis that allow them to make generalizable arguments, establish causal relationships, or produce an empathetic understanding of social life.
- A sound study design reflects insights from previous research, a commitment to test or generate theory, a consideration of the amount and kind of data needed to answer a research question, ethical concerns, available resources, and the researchers' strengths and inclinations.
- Four key research designs are experimental, cross-sectional, longitudinal, and case study.

Experimental Design

- Experimental designs involve isolating the effects of a small number of factors in order to control the influence of other elements, rule out alternative explanations, and produce an understanding of a causal relationship that can be generalized to a broader population.
- Quasi-experimental designs—for example, natural experiments and evaluation research—adopt the experimental logic of comparison, often considering a *before* and *after*, but do not involve the same manipulation and control of influences that experimental designs do.

Collecting Data at Different Points in Time: Cross-Sectional and Longitudinal Design

- By collecting and analyzing data from a single point in time, cross-sectional design offers a "snapshot" of social life.
- In a longitudinal design, data are collected at multiple points in time, allowing researchers to trace and understand change over time.

Case Study Design

- Case studies involve an in-depth examination of single or limited cases, often using qualitative methods of data collection and analysis.

Questions for Review

1. How does previous research figure in the choice of study design?
2. What is the relationship between theory and study design?
3. How do ethical considerations figure in the choice of study design?
4. What are some practical concerns when designing a study?
5. What makes an experimental design especially effective when trying to establish a causal relationship?
6. What do researchers manipulate and what do they control in an experiment?
7. What is the difference between an experimental and a quasi-experimental design?
8. What makes experimental and quasi-experimental design good choices for evaluation research?
9. What is a cross-sectional research design?
10. What challenges does a researcher face when trying to establish a causal relationship in a cross-sectional study?
11. What makes a cross-sectional design easier to implement than many experimental designs?
12. What distinguishes a longitudinal design from a cross-sectional design?
13. What are the distinguishing characteristics of trend, panel, and cohort studies?
14. What is a case study?
15. What are the distinguishing characteristics of critical cases, extreme or unique cases, and revelatory cases?

Portfolio Exercise

1. After reflecting on your previous portfolio exercises and your research topic, answer the following questions.
   a. What have other researchers done that relates to your study? Name the study and describe the research briefly but specifically.
   b. What theory (or theories) are relevant for your study? Will your research be deductive or inductive? Explain why.
   c. How many times will you need to observe the phenomenon that interests you?
   d. How many people or instances do you anticipate you will need to observe?
   e. What ethical considerations does your study raise? How will you navigate these ethical considerations while conducting your research?
   f. What mode(s) of inquiry appeal to you? Why?

Review your answers and decide what study design you will adopt in your proposed research. You may want to keep it simple and avoid a mixed methods study while you're still learning about research methods. If you propose mixed methods, explain what you'll learn from each method you adopt.

Interactive Activities

1. In small groups meeting online or in person, generate a list of as many correlations as you can (e.g., the correlation between the number of fire trucks at a fire and the amount of fire damage, the amount of fire damage and the home insurance coverage, the home insurance coverage and the love people have for their home). After 15 minutes, a spokesperson from each group presents their correlations to the rest of the class, who decide which ones are spurious correlations and what additional factors might account for the otherwise spurious correlation.

2. Working in groups meeting online or in person, sketch a study of the following topics using each the four study designs discussed in this chapter: experimental, cross-sectional, longitudinal, and case study.
   a. Unemployment in the wake of public health responses to the Covid pandemic
   b. Access to Covid testing
   c. Mental health and physical distancing
   d. Presidential campaigning during physical distancing

What does each design offer? What are the designs' limitations? What design seems, on the whole, to be most promising?

Online Resources

- The libraries of the University of Southern California offer a descriptive list of research designs. **https://libguides.usc.edu/writingguide/ researchdesigns**

- The Black Youth Project Survey provides information on "the ideas and attitudes of young people in the realms of sex, intimacy and health, political participation, race, ethnicity, gender and sexual orientation, rap music and videos, religion as well as current public policy impacting, in particular, young African Americans." **http://blackyouthproject.com/project/ black-youth-project-survey-methodology/**

- The National Longitudinal Study of Adolescent to Adult Life (Add Health) began in 1994-95 with a representative sample of US adolescents in grades 7–12. Researchers have followed the Add Health cohort into young adulthood with four in-home interviews. The most recent round of data collection was in 2008, when the sample was aged 24–32. **www.cpc.unc.edu/projects/addhealth**

- The National Longitudinal Survey of Youth (NLSY97) is one of a number of longitudinal surveys the US government conducts. (Others are the National Longitudinal Surveys of Mature Women and of Young Women, also mentioned in this chapter.) NLSY97 collects data on a nationally representative sample of approximately 9,000 people who were 12 to 16 years old in December 1996. **www.bls.gov/nls/nlsy97.htm**

- Begun in 1968, the Panel Study of Income Dynamics (PSID) is the world's longest-running longitudinal household survey. **https://psidonline.isr.umich.edu**

For more resources please visit
www.oup.com/he/bryman-reck-fields1e

PART IV
Gathering Information

After researchers determine their research questions, they must decide the best information to gather—in other words, what data to collect—in order to answer those questions. Some data collection methods, such as structured interviewing and questionnaires, are used most often in quantitative studies that seek to assess broad patterns of experience and measure relationships among many variables. Methods such as qualitative interviewing and ethnography, which explore experiences and behaviors in depth and emphasize meaning, are qualitative data collection strategies. Other methods, such as content analysis of textual material and secondary analysis of existing data, might be approached through either quantitative or qualitative approaches. Many researchers combine data collection methods and data sources in order to fully flesh out their research questions, and their choice of data collection method is motivated by the questions they seek to answer.

8

How Do Researchers Study Patterns that Span Populations and Categories of Experience?
Questionnaires and Structured Interviews

▲ Jeffrey Isaac Greenberg 20+/Alamy Stock Photo

CHAPTER OVERVIEW

Asking questions about people's behavior, attitudes, norms, beliefs, and values is one of the most popular strategies for gathering data in the social sciences, and survey research is among the most frequently used methods of collecting this kind of data. Survey research allows sociologists to identify patterns that extend across large populations and categories of people. The strength of this approach is that it allows for standardization in the way questions are asked and answered. Because study participants respond to identical (or nearly identical) cues and often choose from a fixed range of answers, researchers can record the replies efficiently and confidently. Data gathered in well-designed surveys promises to be generalizable—a gold standard in social research.

Reading this chapter will help you to

- describe the types of questions included in surveys;
- distinguish between questionnaires and structured interviews;
- recognize survey research as a sort of social interaction;
- discuss the advantages and disadvantages of closed- and open-ended questions;
- explain the principles for writing questions and determining question order;
- apply strategies for designing questionnaires and conducting structured interviews; and
- identify the benefits of conducting pilot studies and pre-testing questions.

We encounter surveys throughout our everyday lives. We complete them when we interview for a job, seek medical care, and post an online review. At the end of this course, you will likely complete an evaluation asking you to rate the course and the instructor. The survey's results offer instructors a picture of student experiences and help them identify teaching strengths and weaknesses. Across multiple students in a single class, multiple classes in a single semester, and multiple semesters in a single career, this information can reveal patterns in instructors'

in-class performance, including ways their teaching has improved over time. Academic departments can learn about students' experience of required and elective courses, and universities can gain a sense of instructors' relative performance in different fields and degree programs. Because of the high stakes for students, instructors, and campuses, researchers and university administrators usually take great care to elicit valid and reliable information. At their best, course evaluations reflect the principles that guide strong survey research.

Introduction: Why Surveys Are Efficient

Survey researchers strive to give all participants the same experience. When the questions and research encounter are held constant, researchers can be confident that differences in responses reflect differences between people and their lives, not differences that their studies introduced. This sort of control is essential to understanding broad patterns in people's behaviors and attitudes—across campuses,

age cohorts, faith communities, health experiences, political and social conflicts, voting publics, cities, countries, and more.

The format's efficiency similarly helps researchers gather information relatively quickly and easily across these large groups, capturing snapshots of people's lives that, together, offer a compelling portrait of social life. For example, the US Census and American Community Survey (ACS) gather vast amounts of information about housing, employment, education, and other topics vital to understanding the makeup of the US population. The government uses these data when making decisions about such things as budget distribution and voting districts.

This chapter focuses on constructing and administering a survey; we will discuss different methods of **survey research** and principles for designing questions. As you read, keep in mind previous discussions of research ethics (Chapter 2) and quantitative research in general (Chapter 6). You will learn more about survey research conducted with preexisting surveys and big data in Chapter 12.

Different Kinds of Surveys

Surveys generally include questions addressing several areas.

- *Personal, factual questions* ask participants to provide personal information (e.g., age, occupation, marital status, and income) or to report behavior. Respondents often must rely on their memories to answer these questions—for example, when they report how often they attend religious services or go to a movie.
- *Questions about others* help highlight respondents' perceptions of how other people and groups act or feel. These questions assess people's opinions about others; they do not help researchers gather factual truths.
- *Factual questions about an entity or event* allow respondents to act as informants. For example, a researcher might ask people about a protest

they attended or witnessed—how many people were there, the reason for the demonstration, the wording of protestors' chants and signs, how the police responded, etc. Because this information may not be readily or reliably available from other sources, these questions can offer important details. However, researchers must account for the fact that most people are not systematic observers in everyday life, and preconceptions affect their perceptions and recollections.

- *Questions about attitudes and beliefs* appear routinely on surveys. The General Social Survey (GSS) has been conducted for nearly fifty years in the United States and includes questions about social characteristics and attitudes. Questions explore respondents' feelings about such issues as affirmative action, climate change, gun control and ownership, and LGBTQIA2S+ rights. Many countries have similar ongoing surveys.
- *Questions about knowledge* can assess respondents' grasp of information about specific content areas. For example, researchers studying compliance with Covid-related public health measures may want to know how much community members know about disease transmission. Researchers interested in the impact of particular public health interventions might ask questions that assess risk behaviors in a community before and after the launch of a health education campaign.

Survey research takes two basic forms (Figure 8.1): **questionnaires** and **structured interviews**. We will consider each of these forms in the sections that follow.

---

survey research The study design and method in which researchers collect data through questionnaires or structured interviews, often to detect relationships among variables.

---

questionnaire A data collection method in which respondents complete questions and response items without the aid of an interviewer.

---

structured interview A data collection method in which an interviewer asks all respondents the same questions, in the same order, and with aid of a formal interview schedule; sometimes called a standardized interview.

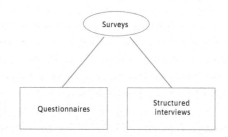

FIGURE 8.1 Questionnaires and structured interviews

Mixed Methods in Action | Gender and Gaming in Online Worlds

Dmitri Williams et al. (2009) conducted a mixed-methods study of over 7000 players in a massively multiplayer online game (MMOG). Players completed an online survey that included demographic questions (age, gender, and education) and questions about relationship status, health, reasons for playing the game, and time spent playing. The researchers also used unobtrusive methods to analyze records of player interactions and, again, how much time people

How would you go about using questionnaires or structured interviews to determine whether girls and women underreport the time they spend gaming because of gender norms that suggest this behavior is more suitable for boys and men?

spent playing. They found that girls and women are among the most "hardcore" players, dispelling expectations that an overall lack of strong female characters and roles makes MMOGs unappealing to female players.

This finding highlights the value of mixed methods in ensuring accurate measures. As indicated, the authors measured hours playing in two ways: self-report questionnaires (respondents indicated hours of play) and actual (once

respondents agreed to participate in the study, the game recorded their hours of play). All players underreported their hours, and the discrepancy for girls and women was three times that for boys and men. This mixed-method approach produced a more accurate picture, revealed an intriguing gender disparity, and raises an important question: Do girls and women underreport time spent gaming because of gender norms that suggest this behavior is more suitable for boys and men?

Questionnaires

When completing questionnaires, participants must read the questions and record their own answers. There is no one to ensure that they do not skip or miss a question or abandon the survey. Therefore, researchers must rely on different strategies to make sure participants can understand and effectively respond to the questions. Such strategies include relying on closed-ended rather than open-ended questions, friendly designs, and brevity, which we will discuss in this chapter.

Questionnaires are a popular data collection method because of their many advantages. Here are two significant ones:

- *Cheap, quick, and convenient to administer.* Questionnaires provide an invaluable alternative to the expense of hiring and training interviewers to conduct structured interviews. A thousand questionnaires can be mailed or emailed to a geographically dispersed sample in one batch.

- *Minimal influence of researcher and interviewer.* Questionnaires offer particular control over potential influence and bias. As previously stated, there is no one to read the questions to the respondent in the wrong order, to present them in different ways to different participants, or to state the items with varying emphases from person to person. No interviewer means no **interviewer effects**.

But, just as with any method of data collection, questionnaires also have some disadvantages:

- *Cannot explain questions or instructions.* With no one to help participants with questions they do not understand, the researcher needs to ensure that questions and instructions are clear and the questionnaire easy to complete.
- *No opportunity to probe.* A mark placed between "agree" and "strongly agree" in the provided answer categories could indicate several things, such as the respondent falling between the two possibilities. A survey researcher will not have a chance to ask for clarification.
- *Questionnaire can be read as a whole.* When respondents are able to read the whole questionnaire before providing an answer, the researcher cannot be sure that questions have been answered in the desired order.
- *Not appropriate for some participants.* Participants whose literacy and facility with the language is limited may not be able to complete a questionnaire. Even if the survey meets the needs of some participants, a diverse sample that includes people from different age cohorts, socioeconomic groups, or subcultures may require more flexible data collection.
- *Greater risk of missing data.* Incomplete questionnaires are more common than incomplete interviews. Long questionnaires introduce the risk of **respondent fatigue** risks and may discourage people from participating at all.
- *Cannot verify who filled out the questionnaire.* Once the questionnaire is out of their hands, researchers cannot be sure who actually completes it. Classmates, members of a household, or coworkers might have helped the designated respondent.

Structured Interviews

In a structured interview (sometimes called a standardized interview), the interviewer asks questions listed on an **interview schedule**, a formalized script that indicates the wording and order of the questions, which interviewers should follow exactly. The consistency should ensure that all interviewees experience the same form of questioning and receive the same interview stimulus. In survey research, the goal is aggregation (adding together to indicate group rates), which is reliable in a structured interview only if respondents reply to identical cues. The questions usually offer a fixed range of answers to choose from.

---

interviewer effects   Data variations introduced by an interviewer's presence, including impact of perceived identities, style and personality, and question wording.

---

respondent fatigue   Diminishing interest in or energy to participate in research and to provide meaningful quality responses to a researcher's questions or presence in the field.

---

interview schedule   A collection of questions asked during structured interviews in a specified order and with consistent wording.

What are some advantages to using a standardized interview schedule over a questionnaire with less structure?

Survey researchers rely on structured interviews instead of more open-ended forms (see Chapter 9) to promote standardization in both the asking of questions and the recording of answers. Standardization has two closely related virtues: it reduces **response bias**, and it ensures greater accuracy and ease in processing respondents' answers. However, structured interviews provide no guaranteed protection against interviewer error. Some interviewers may embellish or otherwise change a question or be reluctant to ask certain questions, perhaps because of embarrassment. Therefore, training interviewers and monitoring their performance for variation is crucial.

Online Opportunities

To ensure a high response rate, researchers use various ways to circulate their surveys. Some researchers rely on the mail to distribute their questionnaires, while others deliver and collect them in a single location, as is done for course evaluations. However, the internet and social media have changed the landscape of survey research. Increasingly, questionnaires are administered by email (sent directly to participants either in the body of an email or as an attachment) or the web (participants are directed to a website containing the survey). Both online formats are low-cost—even less expensive than mailed questionnaires.

Widely available software packages like SurveyMonkey and Qualtrics can be programmed to ensure that each respondent completes the questionnaire only once. These packages can also improve participants' experience by showing only one question at a time (or, if the researcher prefers, allowing participants to scroll down and look at all the questions in advance), prompting them to answer questions they skipped or missed, permitting them to save their responses and return to the survey later, and giving them the time required to provide detailed responses to open-ended questions. Analysis is facilitated as researchers can download the results into a database.

Online surveys give researchers access to unique populations, such as people who share a particular interest (for example, online dating or gaming) or stigmatized populations who are difficult to reach

offline (for example, people who have eating problems or hold extreme political views). For people who spend significant amounts of meaningful time online (social media influencers or students enrolled in online courses), online surveys may be an especially important method of data collection.

Like any method, electronic questionnaires also have drawbacks. For an email or web survey to work, researchers must be able to format appealing surveys that are easy to navigate, and respondents must be able to navigate websites or manage attachments. Some people continue to be suspicious about sharing personal information online and may worry that their identity cannot be protected. Participants may find it easy to dismiss a request to complete an online survey, thus affecting response rates. This format typically has response rates similar to mailed surveys, but lower than telephone and in-person interviews. Online formats can also make it difficult to know that the respondent was an intended member of the sample.

Computers can also facilitate data collection in structured interviews. For example, with computer-assisted interviewing (CAI), a question appears on the screen, the interviewer keys in the reply, and the computer shows the next question. This approach is especially helpful when using **filter questions** to determine whether questions should be posed to each respondent. CAI may also make it easier to randomize the order of certain questions because the responses given may depend on the sequence of items. In a study of bias against a range of political ideologies, Jarret T. Crawford et al. (2015) shuffled the order in which scenarios were presented to participants. Doing so minimized the difference it might make if a liberal or conservative ideology consistently appeared first in the survey's series of ideologies.

---

response bias Errors and inaccuracies in data collection resulting from question and survey design or concerns with social desirability.

---

filter questions Survey or interview questions that determine whether participants have the experience or other qualifications required to answer additional questions.

The American Community Survey is an ongoing national survey project that reports annually on social and demographic trends relating to employment and income, housing, education, race and ethnicity, and other topics. What are the advantages to being able to administer the ACS questionnaire online?

We will look at constructing questionnaires and structured interviews more closely later in the chapter. First we will discuss the social influences on survey responses and survey question design.

Anticipating Response Errors

Because survey research takes place through predetermined questions on paper, on screen, or in conversation with an ostensibly neutral interviewer, we can easily forget that this method involves social interaction. Seymour Sudman and Norman Bradburn (1974) described the survey as a sort of microsocial system with two available roles (researcher and respondent) and a shared task (completing the survey).

---

acquiescence Respondents' tendency to agree with researchers' questions and perspectives, as they understand them.

---

social desirability Respondents' tendency to align themselves with positive social connotations through their responses to survey questions or their presentation of self in the field setting.

Researchers convey their interests to participants; participants share their attitudes, beliefs, and histories with researchers; and both parties likely anticipate a larger audience—the public, policymakers, and others who will read about the research and formulate their own ideas about the study and its participants.

Keeping the social nature of surveys in mind can help researchers remember that people's responses may be motivated by something other than a desire to provide an accurate accounting of their experiences. Instead, they may be motivated by **acquiescence**, **social desirability**, or a lack of interest:

- *Acquiescence* refers to the tendency to agree or disagree with a set of questions or items, regardless of content, just to be cooperative or to please the researcher. A survey might ask students whether they regularly eat meals purchased from campus and whether the cost of such food is prohibitive. If someone answers "yes" to both questions, at least one of the responses is likely inauthentic. To identify respondents likely to acquiesce, researchers may include some items that, like this example, logically call for opposite positions; if participants are consistent in their attitudes, they can neither agree nor disagree with all the items. Those participants whose answers demonstrate this inconsistency may have to be removed from the study.

- *Social desirability* occurs when participants provide replies that are insincere but that make them appear respectable or likable. This phenomenon has been demonstrated in studies of minor anxieties, where many people will deny experiencing such emotional issues. The appeal of social desirability is complicated, as what people consider socially undesirable depends on their social position and context. As we discuss in Box 8.1, particular social desirability concerns may arise in the midst of political conflict.

- *Lack of interest* may lead some respondents to provide answers simply to be done with the interview or questionnaire. When completing a

> ## BOX 8.1 Survey Research and Social Desirability in the Midst of Ethnoracial Conflict
>
> In a study of political attitudes about the future, peace, and conflict among Israelis and Palestinians, Oded Adomi Leshem et al. (2020) realized that social desirability might be a factor. Specifically, Palestinian participants might be unwilling to express ideas contradicting the consensus about the importance of political self-determination and statehood. In response, the researchers decided to have half of the surveys be interviewer-administered and the other half self-administered. They hypothesized that participants would be more likely to conform to the political consensus when a Palestinian interviewer administered the survey than when the survey was self-administered.
>
> Participants' answers to questions directly related to the Palestinian struggle suggested this hypothesis was correct. Participants expressed less willingness to collaborate with Israelis in a movement toward peace and greater commitment to ongoing conflict when the survey was administered by a Palestinian interviewer. In self-administered surveys, participants were no less committed to Palestinian well-being and justice; however, they expressed greater willingness to work with Israelis and less commitment to an ethos of conflict.
>
> Survey research offers important insight into intense political conflict. However, without careful attention to the social desirability implications of how a survey is administered, researchers may not gain a nuanced understanding of seemingly intractable strife.

form about health history, a patient may begin reviewing the long list of conditions carefully but eventually tire of the task and start checking boxes haphazardly. To avoid this problem, researchers may use a strategy similar to one used to get around acquiescence—that is, they may design a set of questions that cannot be answered truthfully or consistently by selecting a single response category from beginning to end.

Researchers describe the problems that arise from these challenges as **response errors**. If undetected and unaddressed, they undermine the integrity of a study. Questions arise: Have the researchers captured an accurate picture of the behaviors and attitudes they want to understand? Are the researchers even measuring the concepts at the core of the study? To prevent these flaws, survey researchers spend a great deal of time structuring and wording the questions, designing the survey and structured interview guide, and administering the survey.

Writing Survey Questions

The individual questions and other items that make up a questionnaire or structured interview are the foundation of survey research. Questions need to focus the respondent's attention in the right direction, keep the respondent engaged and interested, and hold consistent meaning across multiple respondents. The survey instructions should be clear, allowing participants to feel capable and satisfied as they move through the survey.

Choosing Closed-Ended or Open-Ended Questions

The questions we pose help to determine the sorts of interactions participants have with our research interests. Do we want participants to indicate where they fit in a predetermined set of categories? Do we want them to share their ideas with fewer constraints?

---

response errors Distortions in survey results caused by participants providing false or inaccurate information.

Closed-ended questions (or fixed-choice questions) allow researchers to learn where participants fit into a theory, hypothesis, or framework they hope to test, while **open-ended questions** allow researchers to learn from responses they did not anticipate.

Closed-Ended Questions

Closed-ended questions appear more frequently than open-ended questions on surveys because they are so well-suited to this method. Here are some of the benefits:

- *Data collection is straightforward and efficient.* Closed-ended questions can be answered quickly, as respondents or structured interviewers check a box, circle an item, or click a response category to indicate the appropriate answer.
- *Closed-ended questions require minimal "on the spot" interpretation.* Such questions ask respondents to select from the answers provided; the response can be easily assigned to a category.
- *The provided answers may help clarify questions.* Participants may not be sure what a question is getting at; the response categories often shed some light on the researcher's intentions and interests.
- *Preparing for data analysis is straightforward.* Researchers can use spreadsheets and quantitative data analysis programs to record and later analyze responses to closed-ended questions.
- *Closed-ended questions enhance the comparability of answers.* Because these questions do not vary and participants choose their responses from a selection provided, researchers can easily compare information across multiple participants.

---

closed-ended questions Interview or questionnaire items that present respondents with a fixed set of possible answers to choose from; also called fixed-choice questions.

---

open-ended questions Interview or questionnaire items that allow respondents to formulate their own answers rather than presenting respondents with possible answers to choose from.

Of course, even well-written closed-ended questions present some challenges. Understanding these limitations—including those given here—will help researchers understand what claims they can make after analyzing the data.

- *Questions and answers may lack spontaneity and authenticity.* Questions about, for example, gender, age, or income may be asked and answered with a sense of habit—selecting and providing answers without thinking through the complexities of each element. Questions that feel obligatory may make responses feel less spontaneous and more impersonal.
- *Fixed-choice categories may be limited.* Closed-ended questions require researchers to anticipate possible responses to their questions. Participants might struggle to find an answer category that they feel applies to them and thus grow irritated with the survey. Others may find themselves in the answers but differ in their interpretation of the possibilities. For example, what does it mean to "strongly agree" with a political sentiment? Have the participants been moved to action and protest or might they be moved someday? Do they talk openly about their political conviction or feel especially drawn to the sentiment? Such limitations can reduce the validity of the survey research.

As discussed in Chapter 3, fixed-choice categories should also be as exhaustive as possible and mutually exclusive (see Box 8.2).

Open-Ended Questions

Open-ended questions may address some of the limitations of closed-ended questions:

- *Participants can answer in their own terms.* They are not limited to possibilities chosen by the researchers and may appreciate the opportunity to correct ideas about their community.
- *Open-ended questions allow unusual and unexpected responses.* Such questions offer participants a chance to fill in any gaps in the closed-ended options.

BOX 8.2 **Exhaustive and Mutually Exclusive Categories**

To be exhaustive, answer categories for closed-ended questions should anticipate every possible response. For instance, if a researcher wanted to know a US voter's preferred political party, both the major (Democratic and Republican) and minor (Libertarian, Green, and Constitution) parties must be included for the list to be exhaustive. Anticipating every possible response to some questions, however, may be difficult and unwieldy. A common compromise—which also avoids long lists—is to include the most likely answers and "other." Participants who choose the latter can then be invited to elaborate. Should a particular "other" response appear frequently when pre-testing questions in a pilot study, it can be added to the final survey.

For survey questions to be mutually exclusive, researchers must ensure that response categories do not overlap. When the age categories offered are "20–30," "30–40," and "40–50,"

thirty- and forty-year-old participants fit into two categories. Because the answers are not mutually exclusive, these respondents will not know which category to select.

Exhaustive and mutually exclusive categories ensure reliable and valid results; they can also help participants feel that the researcher recognizes and respects their experiences and histories. The United States has a long history of insisting that categories of race and ethnicity are mutually exclusive: a person is White, not Indigenous; Black, not Asian; Middle Eastern, not Latinx. Lived experiences of race and ethnicity undermine this perspective, with many people holding multiple and overlapping identities. Recognition of this fact has led to changes in addressing people's racial identities (Snipp, 2003). In the US Census, for example, respondents can now select multiple categories.

- *Participants' knowledge and experience comes to the foreground.* Because open questions do not suggest answers, researchers can tap into participants' understanding of issues and clarify the salience of the topics and questions guiding the study.
- *Open-ended questions facilitate exploration of new or changing areas.* Researchers sometimes include a few open-ended questions to

A Montana census worker enters information into her phone on behalf of a member of the Crow Indian Tribe in Lodge Grass, Montana. The Census is one of the most important social surveys conducted in the United States. Why might it be important for census questions to be written so that people's backgrounds and experiences are captured accurately?

Methods in Motion | **Foregrounding Experiences of Asian American Men: Open-Ended Questions about Stressful Experiences of Masculinity**

In their study of Asian American men, masculinity, and stress, Alexander Lu and Y. Joel Wong (2013) used open-ended questions to elicit "candid disclosures that participants might hesitate to discuss but might willingly write" and to allow "participants to reveal as much or as little as they want" (353). Their open-ended query stated the following:

> The following questions are about gender issues. Please describe your personal experience of what it means to be a man by completing the following sentence: "As a man . . ." 10 times. Just give 10 different responses. Respond as if you were giving the answers to yourself, not to somebody else. There are no right or wrong responses. Don't worry about logic or importance, and don't over-analyze your

responses. Simply write down the first thoughts that come to your mind. (353)

Lu and Wong achieved breadth and depth: their use of the survey method allowed them to reach immigrant and US-born Asian men across the country, and their open-ended questions allowed the participants to share their experiences in their own words. The researchers' analysis suggests that racialized stereotypes about Asian American men make it difficult for them to succeed in some arenas (for example, dating and sports). The men's accounts in the open-ended questions pointed to the profound stress of having to overcome racial discrimination while also conforming to dominant ideas about manhood.

---

address issues they are just beginning to explore. These responses can help researchers to generate better worded, truly exhaustive, and otherwise stronger categories for closed-ended questions in later surveys.

Here are the disadvantages:

- *Participants may not want to take the time required to respond.* People generally expect surveys to be quick and easy to complete, and they may feel discouraged by the greater time and effort required to compose responses to open-ended questions.
- *Accurate recording of the answers is time-consuming.* Respondents are likely to have longer answers to open-ended questions than to comparable closed-ended questions, and the respondent or interviewer will have to record the response in full.

---

coding The process of labeling, categorizing, and organizing data collected in order to facilitate qualitative or quantitative analysis.

- *Analysis takes time.* If the researcher wants to use quantitative methods of analysis with open-ended questions, the answers will need **coding**, which requires significant time and effort. See Chapters 13 and 14 for more on data analysis.

These drawbacks tend to limit the use of open-ended questions in survey research. Closed-ended questions align with most researchers' goal of collecting information from many people efficiently and easily. A mixture of both question types often allows a researcher to achieve breadth and depth.

Linking Questions and Overall Aims

Through the wording of questions and response categories, each survey or structured interview question should promise insight into the research topic.

Keep the Research Objective in Mind

Survey questions should be designed to answer researchers' queries. A study of housing discrimination in the United States probably requires asking participants to identify their race/ethnicity, but not every study calls for this information. Focusing on the overall research question (or questions) ensures that the researcher covers all relevant topics and reduces the risk of pursuing irrelevant issues and wasting participants' time.

Make Sure Each Question Elicits a Specific and Useful Bit of Information

Decisions about the wording of survey questions should be driven by what the researcher wants to know. Consider this question:

> Do you have a car?

What is the question trying to determine? Car ownership? Access to a household car? Use of a company car? The ambiguity of the word "have" means that a "yes" answer could signify any of the three. To find out whether a respondent *owns* a car, the question should specifically address ownership.

Similarly, consider the question

> How many children do you have?

This question may seem straightforward, but does "children" include stepchildren and adopted, foster, and grown children? If the researcher wants to document the composition of the participants' households, the crucial question might be

> How many people under eighteen years of age live with you at home?

If the aim is to understand caretaking responsibilities, the question might read,

> How many people under eighteen years of age do you care for?

Be specific in order to help participants answer confidently and to ensure the question elicits the information needed.

Are Questions and Response Categories Clear and Precise?

Word choices and phrasing are key to gathering data that will answer researchers' questions and represent participants' experiences accurately in the study findings. Following are some principles to guide question writing (see also "Methods in Motion: Asking Better Questions about Crime, Violence, and Victimization" later in the chapter).

Avoid Overly General Questions

A question such as "How satisfied are you with your job?" lacks specificity. Does it refer to satisfaction with pay, working conditions, the nature of the work, or all of these? Unless the question specifies the object of the satisfaction, respondents' interpretations are

---

Methods in Motion | Question Wording: Discrimination or Unfair Treatment?

As Eric Anthony Grollman and Nao Hagiwara (2017) demonstrate, our capacity to document and examine experiences of discrimination may be changing as the wording of surveys shifts.

They reviewed 221 publicly available surveys and found a slight increase in questions featuring the language of "unfair treatment" where once they might have featured "discrimination." Notions of fairness (and unfairness) apparently strike some researchers as more neutral—and less provocative and charged—than the language of discrimination. According to Grollman and Hagiwara, the change

in language reflects more of a quiet drift than a collective and informed decision on the part of survey researchers. Whether the terms are interchangeable is unclear; so too is the question of whether studies of unfair treatment also capture experiences of systemic discrimination. Grollman and Hagiwara "recommend that researchers use measures that correspond with the phenomena they set out to study. Short of conclusive evidence that individuals understand unfair treatment and discrimination as the same experience, researchers err in using the former to study the latter, and vice versa" (2017, 294).

Timing is important in conducting a survey. How do you think the Covid-19 pandemic has affected people's "typical" cellphone use?

likely to vary, creating a source of error. Try asking questions that address the specific aspects of employment at the heart of your research question.

Avoid Ambiguous Terms

Survey participants will also likely assign diverse meanings to ambiguous measures of frequency, such as "often" and "regularly." Consider a question a researcher might ask people who report owning a cellphone:

How often do you use your cellphone?

☐ Very often
☐ Quite often
☐ Not very often
☐ Not at all

With the exception of "not at all," the provided response categories are vague. Ask instead about actual frequency:

How often do you use your cellphone?

(Please check whichever category comes closest to the number of times you use our cellphone.)

☐ More than 10 times a day
☐ 5–9 times a day
☐ 1–4 times a day
☐ A few times a week
☐ A few times a month
☐ Almost never

Though a precise description may be difficult to achieve, specificity should remain the goal. In addition, a question about cell phone "use" may not be specific enough. Common words may mean different things to different people. The researcher may want to know whether participants use the phone for calls, music, games, or texting. Be sure to define your terms as clearly as necessary.

Minimize Technical Terms

Simple, plain language is best in survey questions. Avoid questions like

Do you sometimes feel alienated from your work?

Many people will not be familiar with the term "alienated," even if they feel things that a researcher would define as alienation. One or more of the following questions will likely be more successful:

Do you sometimes feel isolated at work?

How important is the mission of your workplace to you personally?

How much say do you have about the organization of your workday?

The strongest surveys use language that is consistent with respondents' understandings and knowledge, including terms appropriate to their experience, socio-economic status, age, or literacy level.

Spell Out Abbreviations and Acronyms

Survey questions should be free of abbreviations and acronyms whenever possible. If abbreviations are necessary, they should be spelled out at their first use.

Did you submit a FAFSA (Free Application for Federal Student Aid) for the current academic year?

Have you ever made a financial donation to the National Rifle Association (NRA)?

Use your judgment to decide whether the spelled-out version should come first or appear inside the parentheses.

Methods in Motion | **Asking Better Questions about Crime, Violence, and Victimization**

In 1992, the US Bureau of Justice Statistics (BJS) redesigned its National Crime Victimization Survey to better capture (1) incidences of sexual assault and rape and (2) experiences of crime and violence committed in the home, by family members, and/or by friends and intimates. As evident in Table 8.1, new questions acknowledged that not all crime is easily or readily defined as such and that crime occurs at the hand of people we know well, acquaintances, and strangers.

The BJS published a special report on these changes in 1995 and reported an immediate shift in reported rates of violent victimization (Table 8.2). Though the degree of change varied by genders and perpetrators, every category saw some increase. Clearly, question wording mattered.

TABLE 8.1 | Screener Questions for Violent Crimes

New (beginning January 1992)	Old (1972–1992*)
1. Has anyone attacked or threatened you in any of these ways a. With any weapon, for instance, a gun or knife b. With anything like a baseball bat, frying pan, scissors, or stick c. By something thrown, such as a rock or bottle d. Include any grabbing, punching, or choking e. Any rape, attempted rape or other type of sexual assault f. Any face to face threats OR g. Any attack or threat or use of force by anyone at all? Please mention even if you were not certain it was a crime. 2. Incidents involving forced or unwanted sexual acts are often difficult to talk about. Have you been forced or coerced to engage in unwanted sexual activity by a. Someone you didn't know before b. A casual acquaintance OR c. Someone you know well?	1. Did anyone take something directly from you by using force, such as by a stickup, mugging, or threat? 2. Did anyone TRY to rob you by using force or threatening to harm you? 3. Did anyone beat you up, attack you, or hit you with something, such as a rock or bottle? 4. Were you knifed, shot at, or attacked with some other weapon by anyone at all? 5. Did anyone THREATEN to beat you up or THREATEN you with a knife, gun, or some other weapon, NOT including telephone threats? 6. Did anyone TRY to attack you in some other way?

* In 1992, half of the sampled household responded to the old questionnaire, and half to the redesigned survey.

Source: R. Bachman and L. E. Saltzman (1995). *Violence Against Women: Estimates from the Redesigned Survey.* US Department of Justice, Office of Justice Programs, Bureau of Justice Statistics.

TABLE 8.2 | Changes in Reported Rates of Violent Victimization, 1987–1991 and 1992–1993

	Average Annual Rate of Violent Victimizations per 1,000 Persons	
Old survey methodology, 1987–1991	Female	Male
Intimate	5.4	0.5
Other relative	1.1	0.7
Acquaintance/friend	7.6	13.0
Stranger	5.4	12.2
New NCVS methodology, 1992–1993	Female	Male
Intimate	9.3	1.4
Other relative	2.8	1.2
Acquaintance/friend	12.9	17.2
Stranger	7.4	19.0

Source: R. Bachman and L. E. Saltzman (1995). *Violence against Women: Estimates from the Redesigned Survey*. US Department of Justice, Office of Justice Programs, Bureau of Justice Statistics.

Avoid Questions that Include Negatives

Questions that include negative terms such as "not" pose some risks. Respondents may miss the negative and give answers opposite to what they intended.

Researchers can often eliminate negative terms and avoid questions like the following:

> Do you agree with the view that university students should not have to take out loans to finance their education?

Instead, ask the question in its positive form. For example,

> Some university students have to take out loans to finance their education. Is that fair?

Questions with double negatives are never appropriate; respondents may not interpret them correctly. Instead of,

> Would you rather not drink non-alcoholic beer?

try,

In a survey on shared domestic responsibilities, how would you write survey questions that get at the nuances visible in this image?

Have you ever chosen non-alcoholic beer over alcoholic beer?

Straightforward Question Structures

The structure of your questions should be easy to understand and answer. The following guidelines can help.

Avoid Double-Barreled Questions

A double-barreled question addresses more than one topic, as in the following:

How frequently do you and your partner work together on cooking and cleaning?

Partners may collaborate extensively and frequently on cooking but never with cleaning or vice versa. Because this question will likely elicit an ambiguous description of partners' approach to both tasks, pose two distinct questions.

Avoid Leading Questions

Leading, or loaded, questions push respondents in a particular direction. For example,

Would you agree to cutting taxes, even though welfare payments for the neediest sections of the population might be reduced?

This phrasing will likely make it difficult for some people to agree, even if they feel that taxes are too high. Try breaking this question into multiple items addressing tax cuts, social welfare programs, and governments' responsibilities to the poor.

BOX 8.3 Double-Barreled Questions

Double-barreled questions take many forms. Here are some subtle versions of the problem—and some solutions.

Which party did you vote for in the 2020 federal election?

What if the respondent did not vote in that election? Participants who did vote would have chosen multiple candidates, sometimes from different parties, for multiple offices. This one question is really multiple questions. If the researcher's focus is the presidential election, the survey could pose the following, which is more specific:

Did you vote in the 2020 presidential election?

☐ Yes
☐ No

If YES, which presidential candidate did you vote for?

☐ Joe Biden (Democrat)

☐ Donald Trump (Republican)
☐ Howie Hawkins (Green)
☐ Jo Jorgensen (Libertarian)
☐ Other

The following is another type of double-barreled question:

How effective has your job search strategy been?

☐ Very effective
☐ Fairly effective
☐ Not very effective
☐ Not at all effective

A respondent may have used multiple job search strategies—for example, responding to job ads, conducting informational interviews, making cold calls, and attending job fairs—with varying success. A question or series of questions that evaluate each strategy's success would allow respondents to avoid averaging their assessments.

Ensure Symmetry between a Closed-Ended Question and Its Answers

A common mistake is to pose a question with answers that are not aligned with it. Here's an example of a question that uses a Likert scale:

Do you believe in God?
☐ Strongly agree
☐ Agree
☐ Neither agree nor disagree
☐ Disagree
☐ Strongly disagree

These categories are not logical responses to the question. In this case, one or the other has to change. For example, we can edit the answer categories to

☐ Yes
☐ No
☐ I am unsure.

Ensure That the Answers Provided for a Closed-Ended Question Are Balanced

In the previous example, the revised categories regarding belief in God offer balanced fixed-choice options—a good idea when offering positive and negative options. This set of responses is weighted toward a favorable response:

☐ Excellent
☐ Good
☐ Borderline
☐ Poor

"Excellent" and "Good" are both positive; "Borderline" is a neutral or middle position; and "Poor" is a negative response. This set would be improved by adding a second negative response choice, such as "Very poor."

Are Participants Prepared to Answer Your Questions?

Requisite Knowledge

There is little use in asking about matters unfamiliar to respondents. For example, asking the general public questions about student aid would be pointless; few people outside higher education—and

even some students, faculty, and administrators—have firsthand experience with the topic. Similarly, people who do not follow international politics are unlikely to provide meaningful responses regarding foreign affairs.

Memory Problems

Don't overstretch people's memories. While some people may be able to report how often they used their cellphones in the last twenty-four hours, that will be a stretch for many and few will be able to offer an accurate answer for any longer period of time.

Question Order

Remembering that research is a social interaction can help researchers make sound decisions about question order. Good survey research is like a good conversation: it has a clear topical thread, holds our interest, and doesn't ask us to reach too far beyond our expertise and experience. With the conversation model in mind, here are some guidelines for making decisions about question order.

- *Early questions should be important or meaningful to participants.* Though usually a focus of qualitative interviewing (see "Methods in Motion," Chapter 9), interest and rapport also motivate participants to complete surveys and structured interviews. This might mean asking questions directly related to the announced research topic or posing questions that tap into a sense of self or priorities—such as identities or positions on contentious political issues.
- *Questions that may cause embarrassment or anxiety are generally better later in the survey.* This placement allows the respondent to become comfortable and get over any initial nervousness. However, don't leave difficult questions for the end of a survey. Respondents should not leave the interview or complete the questionnaire with significant self-doubt, misgivings, or negative feelings.
- *Group questions logically in related sections.* Do not jump back and forth from one topic to another.

BOX 8.4 **Don't Know**

Though "don't know," "unsure," or "no opinion" regularly appears as an option in closed-ended questions concerning attitudes, researchers differ over whether it should be used. The main argument for including these answer categories is to ensure participants are not forced to claim views they do not actually hold. Some researchers offer the option as a filter question: "Do you have an opinion on this issue?" Only those respondents who answer "yes" get the second question about their specific viewpoint. A filter question such as this, or a "neutral" option in a question, can identify *fence-sitters*: people who don't have strong feelings on an issue but will choose a side if that is their only option. Including a "neutral" category that helps researchers identify fence-sitters can increase the reliability of their measures (Schaeffer and Presser, 2003).

However, some researchers worry that a "neutral" option offers an easy way out for *floaters*: respondents who do not take the time to think about the issue or are hesitant to express their opinions and will usually choose "don't know" if it is offered as an option. A series of experiments by Jon A. Krosnick et al. (2002) found that many survey participants who claim to have no opinion on a topic actually hold one. Those with lower education levels are especially likely to select the "don't know" answer; questions that appear later in a questionnaire are also more likely to elicit the response. The latter finding implies a question order effect (addressed later in this chapter): respondents may become increasingly tired or bored as the questioning proceeds and therefore lazier in their answers. The researchers concluded that the option does not enhance data quality and may prevent some participants from expressing their opinion; therefore, they would *not* offer a "don't know" option unless absolutely necessary.

Methods in Motion | **Getting Help in Designing Questions**

Sometimes the best thing researchers can do is to put themselves in the position of the respondent. Trying to work out a response might reveal the ambiguities inherent to a question like "Do you have a car?" or "How many children do you have?" Putting oneself in the respondent's position can reveal the difficulty of answering poorly constructed questions.

Perhaps the survey questions do not apply to the researcher. For example, a twenty-two-year-old student conducting a survey of retired people in their sixties will not have the required experience to answer the questions. The researcher might try the questions out on some friends, classmates, or family members, as in a pilot study (discussed later in this chapter). Pre-testing the questionnaire with people who are part of the group being studied can help ensure that the questions read well on their own and connect with one another and that all of the key issues have been included.

Another strategy is to learn from others' example. Check out surveys—regardless of the topic—designed by experienced researchers to see models of what to do and what to avoid.

When reviewing a survey instrument as a whole, researchers should keep in mind two general principles about question order:

- All survey respondents should receive questions in the same order.
- Researchers should be sensitive to the effects one question could have on subsequent questions.

For example, if some participants have been asked a question on unemployment and others have not, the latter's responses to other questions may reflect this omission. If a later question asks about the causes of increasing crime, those who were previously asked about unemployment may mention it as a cause more often than those who were not asked about it. Overall, question order can have two main unintended consequences:

- *Contrast effects*, in which question order causes a *larger difference* between responses than there would be otherwise. A way to avoid contrast effects is to have general questions precede specific ones. For example, asking how happy someone is in their relationship before asking how happy or unhappy they are in general may alter the response to a later question about general happiness. If a specific question comes first, participants also might feel they have already covered the topic and thus discount the general question.
- *Assimilation effects*, in which the order causes responses to be *more similar* than they would have been. Pew Research Center researchers Kennedy and Hartig (2019) found an assimilation effect in its 2008 poll about how Senate leaders should work with each other and President Obama. If a question about whether Democratic leaders should work with or challenge Republican leaders came first, respondents more often said Republicans should work collaboratively with Obama (81 percent vs. 66 percent). When the question asking whether Republican leaders should work with Obama came first, fewer people answered that Democratic leaders should work collaboratively with Republican leaders (71 percent vs. 82 percent).

Thinking about the questionnaire or interview as a social interaction can help a researcher make sound decisions about question order. Survey questions represent an unfolding conversation and thus should be logical and sensitive.

Questionnaire Design

The layout of the questionnaire on paper or screen should be easy on the eye and thus facilitate the respondents' answering all applicable questions. A variety of text styles (fonts and print sizes, boldface, italics, or capitals) can enhance the questionnaire's appearance so long as they are used consistently; too much variety can become a distraction. Thus, all general instructions should appear in one style, all headings in a second, all specific instructions in a third (for example, "Go to question 7"), and so on.

Vertical and Horizontal Fixed Answers

Bearing in mind that most questions in a questionnaire are likely to be closed-ended, a researcher must decide whether to arrange the fixed answers vertically or horizontally. A vertical arrangement is usually used with Likert scales (Figure 8.2). Many researchers prefer this style because it reduces confusion and clearly distinguishes questions from answers. The horizontal format (Figure 8.3) carries the significant risk that respondents, especially if they are in a hurry, will mark the wrong space.

Clear Instructions for Responding

Should participants place a checkmark by the appropriate answer? Should they underline it? Circle it? Can they choose more than one answer? If instructions are unclear and some respondents make mistakes, their responses will have to be excluded from analysis. They become **missing data**.

---

missing data Data that are not available because, for example, a respondent in social survey research has not answered a question.

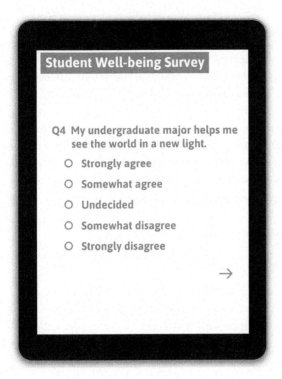

FIGURE 8.2 **Vertical question format**

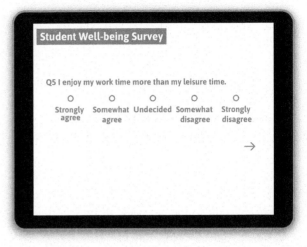

FIGURE 8.3 **Horizontal question format**

Here's one possibility for instructing participants to select a single answer:

Please choose the ONE answer that best represents your views by placing a checkmark in the appropriate box.

Here's one inviting respondents to select as many categories as apply to them:

Please choose ALL answers that represent your views by placing a checkmark in the appropriate boxes. You may check more than one box for each question—choose as many as apply to you.

Open-ended questions require different instructions. It is a good idea to let the participant know how long their answer can or should be with a clearly delineated box. For example,

Using the space below, describe the highlights of your experience.

Regardless of the question type, clear instructions ensure that participants know how to respond and that researchers are confident that the information elicited will be useful.

Questions and Answers Bundled Together

A question, or the question and the answers that accompany it, should not be split between pages. If a question appears at the bottom of a page and the responses on the next page, participants may fail to answer the question or pay insufficient attention to it and give a superficial answer.

Conducting Structured Interviews

The interaction between interviewer and respondent serves much the same function as the questionnaire. Here, the interviewer takes responsibility for ensuring that the exchange is easy for the respondent, facilitating participation. Interviewers must be properly trained and supervised to ensure that they administer the structured interview correctly. The following strategies are key to successful structured interviews.

Know the Interview Schedule

Before interviewing anyone, an interviewer should have a thorough knowledge of the interview schedule. That knowledge helps interviewers feel at ease and reduces interviewer variability in asking questions.

Introduce the Research

Prospective respondents have to be offered a credible rationale for participating in the research, in particular for giving up their valuable time. The interviewer might offer this introductory text aloud, as part of a spoken welcome to the interview, or present the respondent with a printed card to read (as discussed in Box 8.5). The more compelling the rationale, the higher the response rate is likely to be.

Stick to the Interview Schedule

A primary aim and strength of survey research is to ensure that each respondent is asked exactly the same questions. The researcher wants to be sure, as much as possible, that differences in people's responses reflect meaningful differences between participants—not variations in how they received the questions. While the impact of disparity in wording differs from context to context and is difficult to quantify, even small variations can affect replies. Some interviewers may embellish or otherwise change a question once an interview is underway. Adhering to the interview schedule is crucial for a structured interview, however. Even if a respondent provides an answer to a question scheduled to be asked later, the interviewer should still ask the question at the scheduled point.

Record Answers

Interviewers should record respondents' replies as precisely and verbatim as possible. This task is pretty straightforward with fixed-choice categories, as in a closed-ended question. It is more challenging if they have to record answers to open-ended questions.

BOX 8.5 Topics and Issues to Include in an Introductory Statement

Both questionnaires and structured interviews require an introductory statement that orients the respondent to the research topic, describes the role of the survey in the overall study, and explains how the respondent was chosen to participate.

An introductory statement to a prospective respondent should accomplish the following.

- Identify the auspices under which the research is being conducted (for example, a university or agency).
- Indicate the researcher's institutional affiliation, including whether the researcher is a student collecting data for a thesis.
- Describe the research topic and its significance.
- Indicate the kind of information being collected.
- Explain how the respondent was selected (for example, by a random process, by convenience, or because of special characteristics).

- Reassure the respondent that all information collected will be confidential and that the person will not be identifiable in data analysis and reports.
- Explain that participation is voluntary.
- Give the respondent the opportunity to ask questions.
- Provide a contact telephone number and/or email address.

Questionnaires can open with a brief paragraph providing these details. Interviewers will likely deliver much of this information verbally at the beginning of a structured interview, or in a consent form or other document that participants can take with them at the interview's conclusion. Interviewers who are conducting a structured interview on behalf of another researcher should also introduce themselves to the respondent and explain their role in the study.

BOX 8.6 Telephone Surveys in the Age of Cell Phones and Robo Calls

The Pew Research Center reports a significant decline in telephone survey response rates, from 36 percent in 1997 to 6 percent in 2018 (Kennedy and Hartig 2019). According to Pew, nonresponse is an ongoing and widespread concern among survey researchers as it compromises their ability to draw reliable and valid conclusions from survey data and increases the cost of survey research.

Survey researchers have long contended with potential participants' concerns about privacy, a general sense of busy-ness, and a lack of interest. The Pew researchers, Caroline Kennedy and Hanna Hartig, suggest that another obstacle to participation may be the increase in telemarketing and other robo calls. Public opinion polls often appear as unknown numbers on people's phones, leading potential participants to mistake them for telemarketing efforts and even scams.

Kennedy and Hartig urge their readers not to give up on survey research:

> While low response rates don't render polls inaccurate on their own, they shouldn't be completely ignored, either. A low response rate does signal that the risk of error is higher than it would be with higher participation. The key issue is whether the attitudes and other outcomes measured in the poll are related to people's decisions about taking the survey.

As is so often the case, the debate returns to how well the researcher understands the data: the sample, potential biases, and more.

Probe

If participants in a structured interview do not understand the question and struggle to provide an adequate answer, or if they do not provide a complete answer, interviewers may need to probe for more information. Some general probing tactics are as follows.

- If further information is required, usually in the context of an open-ended question, standardized probes should be employed, such as "Can you say a little more about that?" or "Are there any other reasons why you think that?"
- If, with a closed-ended question, the respondent's answer does not match any of the pre-designed options, the interviewer should repeat the fixed-choice alternatives and make it clear that the respondent must choose one.
- When the interviewer needs to know about something that requires quantification, such as the number of visits made to a doctor in the last month or the number of banks in which the respondent has accounts, but the respondent answers in general terms ("a few") the interviewer needs to press for a more precise answer. For example, the interviewer might ask, "Fewer than three?" or "Can you be more specific?"

While probes can clarify a response, they can introduce problems that come with variation. Interviewers may approach probing differently: on a team, some interviewers may be more inclined to probe than others, and some may introduce their own probes. Even a single interviewer might vary interview to interview. Pilot studies and interviewer training should help prevent these problems.

Prompts

Prompting occurs when the interviewer suggests a specific answer to an open-ended question. It should be used only as a last resort—if ever. Interviewers should always give respondents the time and freedom to come up with their own replies. Otherwise the data gathered will likely not only be inauthentic but also reveal more about the interviewer than the interviewee.

Telephone Interviews

In a traditional structured interview, an interviewer stands or sits with the respondent, asks a series of questions, and records the answers. Computer-assisted interviewing (CAI) and webcams offer online options, while telephone interviews are another inexpensive alternative to in-person interviews. Phone interviews do not require travel and are easy to supervise, particularly when several interviewers are calling from the same location at the same time. Finally, these interviews can reduce the influence of interviewer characteristics on participants' answers.

On the other hand, telephone interviewing suffers from certain limitations. They can be inaccessible for deaf or hard of hearing participants. Since poorer households may not have phones, more affluent people pay to have unlisted telephone numbers, and younger people often use cell phones only, telephone interviewing raises the issue of sampling bias. One sovution is *random digit dialing*, in which a computer randomly selects telephone numbers within a predefined geographical area. However, given that people are often inundated with telemarketing and spam calls, they will often not answer a call from an unfamiliar number. This could introduce a response bias in terms of who is willing and unwilling to answer a call from an unfamiliar number.

Pilot Studies and Pre-Testing Questions

Researchers conduct pilot studies before collecting data to ensure the quality of not only individual questions but also the research instrument as a whole. As the following list shows, pilot studies may be particularly crucial in research using questionnaires, since there will be no interviewer present to clear up any confusion:

- If the study uses mainly closed-ended questions, a researcher can pose open-ended questions in pilot qualitative interviews and then use them to generate the fixed answers to closed-ended questions.
- If everyone (or virtually everyone) who answers a question gives the same answer, the resulting data are not likely to be useful. A pilot study gives researchers an opportunity to identify such questions and modify them as necessary to elicit more varied answers.
- If multiple participants skip the same questions, researchers can edit them to eliminate unclear or threatening phrasing or poorly worded instructions.

When conducting structured interviews, pilot studies have particular uses:

- Working in advance with a structured interview schedule can help interviewers gain some experience and develop confidence.
- Pilot interviews can identify questions that make participants uncomfortable, are difficult to understand, or that do not hold participants' interest.
- Researchers can observe the interviewers' performance during the pilot interviews and identify additional training needs to address before launching the formal study.

The sample for a pilot study should not include people who may become members of the full study's sample, since participation in the pilot could affect their later responses. If the population being investigated is small (e.g., sociology majors at a single university), do a pilot study on respondents from a different but similar population (anthropology majors at the same university or sociology majors at a nearby school). Otherwise, you may be forced to exclude people from the sample in the actual study, making recruitment more difficult, affecting the representativeness of the sample, and limiting the generalizability of the results.

Key Points

Introduction: Why Surveys Are Efficient

- The strength of survey research lies in all participants encountering the same questions and research stimuli. This consistency allows researchers to be confident that differences in responses reflect differences between people and not differences that the study introduced.

Different Kinds of Surveys

- Survey questions can elicit information about the respondents and their understanding of other people; respondents' attitudes and beliefs; and respondents' knowledge about specific subjects.
- Survey research takes two forms: questionnaires and structured interviews.
- In survey research, the standardization of survey item wording, question order, and methods of recording responses minimize interviewer-related error.
- Participants complete questionnaires by reading and responding to items—primarily closed-ended questions—on paper or online.
- Structured interviews are like questionnaires in that they involve formally scripted questions and response categories but are administered in person, over the phone, or online. All formats involve an interviewer who asks the questions and records responses.
- Surveys, whether questionnaires or structured interviews, are social interactions and responses may be shaped by participants' wish to please the researcher or appear socially desirable.

Writing Survey Questions

- While open-ended questions have some advantages in survey research, closed-ended ones are typically preferable. They facilitate the asking of the questions, the recording of answers, and the coding of data.
- Open-ended questions can play a useful role in eliciting unanticipated responses and in formulating fixed-choice answers.
- All survey questions should elicit specific and useful information relevant to the overall research objective.
- Survey researchers should attend to the impact question order and wording can have on participants' responses to survey items.

Questionnaire Design

- The visual presentation of closed-ended questions and their general layout are important considerations in designing questionnaires.

Conducting Structured Interviews

- Knowing and sticking to the interview schedule are crucial to the strength of this data collection method.
- Questions that probe and prompt participants are an option in structured interviews, but they should be used judiciously so as not to unduly introduce variation into data collection.
- Phone interviews are often a convenient and inexpensive alternative to in-person interviews.
- However, because not all potential participants will be reachable by phone, telephone interviews may introduce concerns about response bias.

Pilot Studies and Pre-Testing Questions

- A pilot study involving the pre-testing of questions can identify problems in question formulation and survey design.

Questions for Review

1. What role do consistency and control play in survey research?
2. What sorts of information can be elicited with questionnaires or structured interviews?
3. What are the relative advantages and disadvantages of questionnaires?
4. What are the relative advantages and disadvantages of structured interviews?
5. What are interviewer effects and how do they affect data collection?
6. How do email and web surveys differ? How do embedded email questionnaires and attached

questionnaires differ? What is the significance of these differences?

7. What are the relative advantages and disadvantages of online surveys over traditional survey research?

8. How does social desirability and acquiescence contribute to response error in survey research?

9. How can a researcher guard against the possibility of participants losing interest in their survey?

10. What are the advantages of closed-ended questions (vs. open-ended questions) in survey research?

11. What are the limitations of closed-ended questions? How can the impact of those limitations be minimized?

12. What principles should guide question order in survey research?

13. What makes a vertical format preferable to a horizontal format when presenting answers to closed-ended questions?

14. What is the difference between probing and prompting? What risks does each pose?

15. How successful is the structured interview in reducing interviewer variability? Explain your answer.

16. What strategies can interviewers use to reduce response bias?

17. How can a researcher try to prevent response errors?

18. Under what conditions are telephone interviews preferable to in-person interviews?

19. What do researchers gain by piloting surveys and pre-testing questions?

Portfolio Exercise

To what extent would survey research be an appropriate method to gather data for your research? Review your research topic/question, revising as necessary to reflect your current thinking. Will survey research provide insight into this question? Why or why not? If not, explain why. If yes, write a questionnaire or structured interview guide to add to your portfolio. Refer to the chapter materials, including the online resources provided, as you draft the survey. As applicable, include questions that will gather demographic information as well as follow-up clarifying questions.

Interactive Activities

1. Working with a classmate, design an introductory statement for a survey on university student shoplifting. Include all relevant details—for example, how the potential respondent was selected and how confidentiality will be maintained. Share your statement with the rest of your classmates online or in class and ask for comments on its strengths and weaknesses.

2. In small groups, compose one 10-item structured interview schedule that addresses the question, "How much time do students on this campus spend in paid employment?" When finished, have one of your group members administer the survey in person, online, or via video call to members of another group. After the interviews, ask the participants to comment on the experience of completing the survey—for example, the clarity of questions, whether they felt tempted to edit their responses to make a favorable impression, and whether the fixed responses adequately accounted for their responses. Return to your group and revise the interview schedule based on the feedback.

3. In small groups, draft 10 survey questions designed to measure attitudes toward a controversial topic (for example, assisted suicide, gay marriage, or animal rights) and to gather relevant sociodemographic data. Share the questions with the rest of the class online or in class and invite critique. Once all groups have shared their work, return to your group to revise the questions in response to your classmates' feedback. Present your amended questions, with commentary on how you have addressed weaknesses in the original draft.

4. Listen to the podcast *Give Methods a Chance* (https://thesocietypages.org/methods/) episode featuring Naomi Sugie's discussion of using smartphones to collect data. In small groups online or in class, discuss this technology's part in a long history of innovation in survey research, answering the following questions:

a. What advantages do this technology and its functions offer researchers?
b. What sorts of information are smartphones especially well-equipped to gather?
c. How do smartphones facilitate access to and participation of hard-to-reach populations?
d. How did the use of smartphones contribute to Sugie's insights into the reentry experiences of men recently released from prison?

Online Resources

- Jenna Ann Lamphere's article "Best Practices: From Research Problem to Survey Administration" offers suggestions and tips for students developing a survey.
  http://trails.asanet.org/Pages/Resource. aspx?ResourceID=13579

- The University of Washington Office of Educational Assessment offers Tips for Writing Questionnaire Items.
  https://s3-us-west-2.amazonaws.com/uw-s3-cdn/ wp-content/uploads/sites/123/2016/03/ 24185543/OEA_QuestionnaireTips.pdf

For more resources please visit
www.oup.com/he/bryman-reck-fields1e

9

How Do Researchers Learn about People's Perspectives and Lives?
Qualitative Interviewing

CHAPTER OVERVIEW

Qualitative researchers, as we saw in Chapter 5, seek to gather detailed information about people's experiences in order to understand their perspectives and how they make meaning in their lives. This chapter is concerned with qualitative interviewing, which is the method qualitative researchers use most frequently to collect this sort of information.

Qualitative interviews, unlike the structured interviews used in the survey method, typically involve open-ended questions and a flexible structure. The open-ended nature of these interviews allows researchers to explore their research questions deeply because they can ask questions about their main topics of interest, ask follow-up and probing questions, and also explore unexpected areas their interviewees introduce. The combination of structure and flexibility in qualitative interviews allows researchers to collect in-depth and nuanced information about their participants' lives. In this chapter, we will discuss two types of one-on-one interviews—unstructured and semi-structured—and examine the focus group method, used to interview groups rather than individuals.

Reading this chapter will help you to

- describe the main characteristics of and differences between unstructured and semi-structured interviewing;
- understand how to prepare for a qualitative interview, including devising an interview guide;
- grasp the principles of how to interview someone successfully;
- identify the importance of recording and transcribing qualitative interviews;
- understand how to conduct focus groups, including selecting participants and moderating the discussion;
- examine interactions between participants in focus groups; and
- recognize the potential contributions and challenges of online interviewing and focus groups.

Can you remember a time when you met someone at a party and had a really interesting conversation where you felt like the two of you really got to know each other? How about the opposite, where you got stuck in a conversation that consisted of nothing but superficial small talk and was, as a result, so boring that it was uncomfortable?

What was it that made one conversation seem boring and shallow and the other fun and connected? For one thing, the level of rapport you have with someone really affects how good the conversation feels. In good conversations, there's often a comfortable and considerate energy between the people. Bad conversations tend to feel stilted, a bit tense, and possibly even disrespectful. And what makes it so one conversation is superficial and the other feels like you've known someone for years?

When someone asks you about yourself, listens, and shows interest in what you say, and then wants to know more about the things you're sharing, they learn a lot more about you. This is different from a person cornering you at a party and just peppering you with general questions, moving from topic to topic without actually inquiring more about anything you've said.

When we have conversations with people, we're honing our interview skills, just like researchers do. If we interact in an engaging way and ask questions that make us feel like we really get to know the person, we're approaching that conversation in ways similar to how qualitative researchers approach their interviews. While effective interviewing techniques take practice and time to develop, interview skills are part of a habit many of us engage regularly in everyday conversation.

Introduction: Why the Interview Is the Most Widely Used Qualitative Research Method

The interview is probably the most widely used method in qualitative research. Its flexibility and relatively low cost make it an attractive option for many researchers. Qualitative interviews typically employ an open-ended structure that the researcher can modify both in individual interviews and across the research study as new questions emerge. Qualitative interviewers are free to vary both the order and the wording of questions, and they may even ask unplanned questions to follow up on interviewees' replies. Many researchers also interview the same person more than once.

Qualitative interviews are quite different from structured interviews (discussed in Chapter 8). The former are designed to reveal how interviewees interpret and make sense of issues and events, which makes them differ from structured interviews. In qualitative interviews, interviewees can introduce topics important to them, and the interviewer can probe for more detail on the person's experiences. In this way, a qualitative interview involves exploring topics that were not pre-determined by the researcher.

Here are a few examples. Lisa M. Martinez (2014) interviewed undocumented young Latinxs to understand how federal immigration law reforms such as DACA (Deferred Action for Childhood Arrivals) and local policies such as Colorado's ASSET (Advancing Students for a Stronger Economy Tomorrow) affected their lives. Bic Ngo and Melissa Kwon (2015) interviewed queer Hmong American youth in an attempt to explore how they negotiate both their LGBTQIA2S+ identities and their family and kin relationships, and Kristin Lavelle (2015) interviewed White Southerners about how they remembered segregation and civil rights movements in North Carolina. Projects like these are usually not designed to test pre-determined hypotheses or theories, but to gain deeper insight into people's experiences and perspectives.

Types of Qualitative Interviews: Unstructured and Semi-structured

There are two main types of qualitative interviews:

1. unstructured interviews
2. semi-structured interviews

An **unstructured interview** tends to be similar in character to a "real" conversation. The interviewer may ask just a single question on a topic of interest; then the interviewee is allowed to respond freely, with the interviewer pursuing points that seem worthy of follow-up. To prepare for an interview with so little structure, the researcher often uses at most a memory aid: a small set of self-prompts to investigate certain topics. Unstructured interviews often occur spontaneously in field settings while a researcher is engaging in participant observation (see Box 9.1).

A **semi-structured interview** is also meant to be conversational, but the researcher typically enters the interview with an interview guide: a list of questions or fairly specific topics to be covered. The interviewee still has a great deal of leeway in deciding how to reply (see Box 9.2 for an illustration). The interviewer may not ask questions in the exact order they appear in the guide, and the interviewers and might ask some additional questions in response to what the interviewee says (these are called follow-up questions, or probes). Nonetheless, the interviewer usually ensures the interviewee addresses all of the questions on the list and uses similar wording when asking questions from the guide.

---

unstructured interview   A free-form and conversational qualitative interview in which the researcher is free to pursue a set of topics as they arise.

---

semi-structured interview   A qualitative interview in which the researcher uses a detailed interview guide for all respondents to explore certain topics in depth, though the interviewer may add unique probes or change the order of questions.

BOX 9.1 Unstructured Interviewing

In their study of how Black men experience denial of access to nightclubs in Athens, Georgia, via dress code enforcement, Reuben A. Buford May and Kenneth Sean Chaplin (2008) complemented their semi-structured interviews with observation in the downtown club scene. This excerpt from an informal conversation between May and a man who'd just been denied entry shows their use of unstructured interviews "on the street":

The security outside this club manages the doors and decides who is allowed in. How might unstructured interviews with security and patrons shed light on the process people go through to gain entry into the club?

When Joe looked up and saw me, I said, "What's up man?" He looked frustrated,

"Nothing man." We shook hands as he continued. "They're tripping over at Figaro's."

"What do you mean?" I asked.

"They wouldn't let me in with blue jean shorts," Joe said. "You know a lot of places have their guideline, you know, the dress code. But to me it just seems like it's to exclude blacks from coming in," he said.

"Why does it seem like that?" I asked.

"The dress code policy or whatever is basically, no jean shorts, no athletic wear, no jewelry, no excessive jewelry. Anything that's like, in reference to the hip-hop culture is excluded. You know what I'm saying, it's excluded from downtown but at the same time they wanna play all the hip hop music, you know what I'm saying. But they don't want black people in the club. It's like a contradiction. They can play the music, but we can't dress the part. You know" (2008, 65).

Through an unstructured conversation conducted on the street, May and Chaplin gained insight into participants' understanding and experience of dress codes and exclusion.

Researchers often refer to semi-structured and unstructured interviews collectively as *in-depth interviews* or *qualitative interviews*, although the types can produce markedly different results. The choice of one type over the other is affected by a variety of factors:

- Researchers who feel that using even the most rudimentary interview guide hinders access to the worldviews of members of a social setting are likely to favor an unstructured approach.
- If the researchers are beginning the investigation with a fairly clear focus or intentions, a

The red handprint is a symbol meant to build awareness about missing and murdered Indigenous women and girls (MMIWG). While many seek to amplify the issue using this symbol, others are concerned it has become appropriated and reduced to simply a social media hashtag. How might in-depth interviews help a researcher learn about the meaning of this symbol to those who use it? Could oral histories with Indigenous elders shed important light on the historical violence against Indigenous women that led to the adoption of such a symbol of resistance?

(which we discuss later in this chapter), **life history interviews**, and **oral history interviews**. Life history and oral history interviews may be combined with personal documents such as diaries, photographs, and letters, and it may be used to study one or more lives in a single project. Participants are invited to look across their entire life course in detail and to report their experiences and how they understood their world. Kathleen Blee (1998) describes her decision to use unstructured life history interview techniques in her study of women involved in racist and anti-Semitic social movements in the United States:

> As respondents narrate stories of their lives, they reveal what events and processes they view as central and pivotal to their lives and to what they attribute changes in their lives over time. I used this format for two reasons. First, I wanted to avoid the pronounced tendency of racist activists to substitute organizational doctrine for personal belief in standard interview settings, such as in media interviews in which members of organized racist groups simply utter propagandistic slogans in response to any question. Second, I wanted to elicit narrative accounts of the causal ordering of events in the respondent's personal and political history for a larger study of the connection between identity transformation and racist activism among women. (Blee 1998, 387)

As this example suggests, life history interviews have the advantage of illustrating *process*: how events unfold and interrelate in people's lives over long periods of time.

Robert Atkinson (1998) observed that the duration of life history interviews varies considerably from study

semi-structured interview allows them to address more specific issues.

- If there will be multiple interviewers, semi-structured interviewing will help ensure that interviewing styles are comparable.
- Multiple-case study interview research generally needs some structure to ensure cross-case comparability.

A variety of specialized interview forms fall under those two main headings, including focus groups

---

life history interviews A qualitative interview method in which the interviewee is asked to report their experiences and their understanding of events across their entire life course.

---

oral history interviews A variant of the life history interview in which the interviewee is asked to reflect on certain historical events or eras they have lived through.

BOX 9.2 Semi-structured Interviewing

In her research on Filipina migrants' care work, Valerie Francisco-Menchavez (2018) used qualitative interviewing to understand her participants' migration experience and how they maintained family connections across long distances. Here are some sample interview questions and probes:

Interview questions	Probe questions
How did you make your decision to migrate?	What are the reasons for your migration?
How did you tell your children and family?	Were they okay with your decision?
Tell me about your migration story.	When you arrived, tell me about a happy and difficult experience you had here.

---

to study, but that it usually takes two or three sessions lasting 60 to 90 minutes each. He also provided a catalogue of questions that can be asked, and divided them into the following groups (Atkinson 1998, 43–53):

- *Birth and family of origin* (e.g., "How would you describe your parents?")
- *Cultural traditions* (e.g., "Was your family different from others in town?")
- *Social factors* (e.g., "What were some of your struggles as a child?")
- *Education* (e.g., "What are your best memories of school?")
- *Love and work* (e.g., "How did you end up in the work you do or did?")
- *Inner and spiritual life* (e.g., "What are the stresses of being an adult?")
- *Major life themes* (e.g., "What were the crucial decisions in your life?")
- *Vision of the future* (e.g., "Is your life fulfilled yet?")
- *Closure questions* (e.g., "Have you given a fair picture of yourself?")

A variant of the life history interview is the oral history interview. Historians use this technique to ask participants to reflect on certain historical events or eras they have lived through, often emphasizing how those events affected their life. Researchers sometimes combine the information gathered in oral history interviews with other sources of data, such as archival documents, family photographs, or newspaper clippings.

The chief challenge with the oral history interview (which it shares with the life history interview) is the possibility of bias caused by memory lapses and distortions. On the other hand, oral history testimonies and life history interviews can give a voice to groups typically marginalized in historical research. As Nan Alamilla Boyd and Horacio Roque Ramírez (2012) assert in the introduction to their edited volume on LGBTQIA2S+ oral history, "Recognizing that queer histories often go unmentioned in mainstream historical texts … this book recognizes that an injustice has occurred and that those seeking justice sometimes have to create new methods. As such, queer oral histories have an overtly political function and a liberating quality" (2012, 1).

Preparing for a Qualitative Interview

When preparing to conduct a qualitative interview, no matter the type, researchers have significant questions to consider: What are the interview goals? What topics should the interview cover? What questions should be asked to explore those topics effectively?

Determining Interview Goals and Topics

John Lofland and Lyn Lofland (1995, 78) encourage researchers to prepare for qualitative interviews by asking themselves, "Just what about this thing is puzzling me?" Early research questions should be broad and wide-ranging—that is, not so specific as to close off the alternative avenues of inquiry that may arise during interviews. As researchers develop an interview plan, they must outline what Robert Weiss describes as the "substantive frame" of their study, which is "the set of topics the study explores" (1994, 15).

Imagine doing a study of neighborhood activism. You'd have to decide what broad information and specific details you would like to explore in interviews. Weiss (1994) describes two approaches you might use to gather information, and each focuses on a particular type of information:

- A *diachronic report* (199, 42-43) explores experiences along a timeline. Using this model, you would ask questions exploring how a person first became involved in activism and how their involvement developed over time, seeking to explore what factors affected the types of involvement at different moments.
- A *synchronic report* involves dividing topics "into its significant sectors and moving in logical sequence from sector to sector" (1994, 44). Thus, you would not examine participants' activism in terms of a timeline, but instead might ask questions focused on what specific factors and experiences influenced activists' goals, relationships, and decisions, and how these relate to one another.

Some interviews follow one or the other of these models; many others explore both types of information. The key is to remain aware that the lines of inquiry in an interview stem from your research questions and aims.

---

interview guide A specific plan for conducting a qualitative interview; can be a brief or an elaborate list of areas to be covered or questions to be asked.

Writing an Interview Guide

After researchers determine their study aims and substantive frame, they develop a plan for conducting the interview. A first step is to write an **interview guide**. A qualitative interview guide can consist of a brief list of memory prompts for areas to be covered in unstructured interviewing or a more elaborate interview guide that includes a list of issues to be addressed or questions to be asked in semi-structured interviewing. Most crucial is that the guide allows for flexibility so interviewers can pursue leads research participants offer as they open up and share their perspectives. Figure 9.1 presents the steps required to prepare an interview guide.

When writing an interview guide, the researcher should make sure the questions focus on topics that interviewees can effectively report on. Interview questions typically cover topics such as people's values, beliefs, behaviors, roles, relationships, settings, feelings, and experiences. The researcher should also make sure that the guide

- explores the research questions in enough depth;
- has a logical, flexible order that flows smoothly but still allows for changes in the question order and the questions asked;
- uses language that is comprehensible and familiar to interviewees;
- avoids judgments and leading questions; and
- includes prompts for the researcher to record contextual information, such as the interviewee's name, age, gender, occupation, or length of involvement with a group.

An effective ordering of the questions in an interview guide might include "warm up" questions at the beginning to make interviewees feel at ease and to gain their trust, more controversial or emotional questions in the middle, and "cool down" questions at the end to ensure interviewees aren't left in a vulnerable state. The principles guiding question order in a qualitative interview are similar to those we outlined in our discussion of structured interviews and questionnaires.

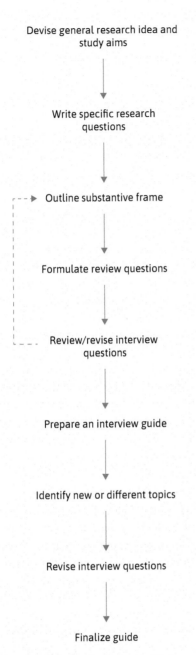

FIGURE 9.1 Preparing an interview guide for a semi-structured interview

Addressing Practical Concerns

Before the interview begins, researchers have practical details to attend to.

- *Become familiar with the interviewee's situation and environment.* Having a sense of interviewees' general circumstances—the roles they play, the responsibilities they hold, the difficulties they may face, even the language they use—will make it easier to put their comments in context.

- *Prepare any necessary technology.* Qualitative researchers nearly always record and then transcribe their interviews, since simply taking notes risks losing specific word choices and phrases.

- *Choose an appropriate location.* Researchers seek a setting that is quiet enough to allow for recording and private enough to ease any concerns the interviewee might have about being overheard. At the same time, researchers make sure that the setting is not so secluded that it could make the interviewee feel uncomfortable.

- *Communicate important details.* The interviewee must know the time and location of the interview, how to find the meeting location, and how to reach the interviewer if they need to reschedule.

- *Prepare the paperwork.* All consent forms should be printed and ready for the interviewees to sign. Researchers should bring a pen and a second copy of the consent form for the interviewee's records. Finally, have a clean copy of the interview guide on hand to consult.

- *Develop good interview habits.* Researchers prepare for the interview by cultivating the skills of a quality interviewer (see Box 9.3).

Be thoughtful as you prepare. If you are a novice interviewer, conduct some practice interviews with a friend or colleague who can represent the experience of your interviewees. Or you might have someone interview you using your prepared interview guide. This strategy allows you to get a sense of how it feels to hear and respond to the questions; you'll get a fresh perspective on the wording and order of your questions, and you might identify questions or topics you have inadvertently omitted.

BOX 9.3 Developing Effective Interviewing Skills

Steinar Kvale (1996) proposed that a successful interviewer should develop these ten characteristics:

- **Knowledgeable:** understands the topic of the interview.
- **Structuring:** tells the interviewee the purpose of the interview; asks if the interviewee has questions.
- **Clear:** asks simple, easy, and short questions; does not use jargon.
- **Gentle:** lets people finish; gives them time to think; tolerates pauses.
- **Sensitive:** listens attentively both to what is said and to how it is said; is empathetic.
- **Open:** responds to what the interviewee considers important; is flexible.
- **Steering:** knows what paths and threads to pursue in the conversation.
- **Critical:** is prepared to challenge interviewees when, for example, their replies are inconsistent or troubling.

- **Remembering:** relates what is said to what has previously been said.
- **Interpreting:** clarifies and extends the meaning of interviewees' statements without imposing meaning on them.

We add the following three to Kvale's list:

- **Balanced:** does not talk too much, which can make interviewees passive, or too little, which can cause interviewees to feel that their responses are not satisfactory.
- **Non-judgmental:** communicates neither negative nor positive judgment about what an interviewee recounts.
- **Ethically sensitive:** has a clear sense of professional and interpersonal ethics; treats all answers confidentially and recognizes and respects the personal risk many interviewees take when they share details of their lives.

Conducting Qualitative Interviews

When conducting qualitative interviews, researchers have many issues to think about. They must form a relationship with the interviewee that helps the person feel respected and comfortable. They also need to ask questions and respond to the interviewee in ways that lead to detailed and clear information.

Building a Relationship with the Interviewee

A positive relationship between interviewer and interviewee will encourage the latter to feel comfortable sharing, lead to better information for the research, and make the experience a good one for both parties. Some researchers describe this as developing "rapport"; Weiss (1994) calls it creating a "research partnership."

Interviewers must consider various dynamics that could affect their relationships with participants. For example, when reflecting upon the interview partnership, researchers should consider their own identity and social position. Do we need to be similar to the people we interview for them to trust us and for us to understand them? Is it possible to interview people different from us and still get good information? Discussing her research with Filipinx Americans in San Diego, Yen Le Espiritu (2001) reflects upon how her background as a Vietnamese immigrant woman may have affected her research. She emphasizes that the relationships she forged with her participants came not just from her status as a fellow Asian American, but also from her choice to share her own experiences:

> I did not remain detached but actively shared my own experiences of being an Asian immigrant woman... I do not claim these shared struggles grant me 'insider

status' into the Filipino American community; the differences in our histories, cultures, languages, and, at times, class backgrounds, remain important. But I do claim that these shared experiences enable me to bring to the work a comparative perspective that is implicit, intuitive, and informed by my own identities and positionalities—and with it a commitment to approach these subjects with both sensitivity and rigor (2001, 419).

Both the experiences she had in common with her interviewees and the ways her status diverged from theirs were integral to the research partnership forged during her study.

Espiritu's decision to share her experiences with her interviewees reflects a feminist critique of the idea that the most effective studies are those where researchers share nothing about themselves with their participants. Feminists have noted that this practice introduces or exacerbates a power imbalance when researchers expect interviewees to share intimate details of their lives but share nothing personal in return. Feminists point out that some mutual sharing may lead to *more information* as interviewees come to trust the researcher.

Power differences can affect an interview in multiple ways. While Espiritu sought to lessen the distance between herself and her interviewees by sharing her experience as an immigrant, she notes class and other differences influenced the interviews. Some interviewees may have heightened power in comparison to an interviewer (say, an elite, business owner, or community leader) and feel comfortable sharing their opinions and exerting control over the interview process. On the other hand, they could be less forthcoming to maintain their perceived reputation.

The issue of power in an interview often involves a researcher occupying a higher social position than that of the participant, as in Espiritu's case. However, there can also be an imbalance of power when a researcher holds less power than the research participant, as when the participant is a powerful elite.

Sarah Mayorga-Gallo and Elizabeth Hordge-Freeman (2016) approach the question of researcher subjectivity and power from an intersectional perspective rather than a binary insider–outsider perspective that assumes these power relationships are always stable. Doing research in the United States and Brazil (in Durham, North Carolina, and Salvador, Bahia), the researchers recognized that their power depended on where they were and who they interacted with in the field. Many White people in Durham perceived Mayorga-Gallo, a light-skinned Latina raised in the US since age 2, as White. This placed her into a position of power, although it did not align with her identity or lived experience. This perception afforded her the ability to more easily study White people, an uncommon experience for BIPOC researchers. At the same time, it took longer for her to gain the trust of her Black and Latinx interviewees, because they viewed her as different from them due to her light skin, non-immigrant status, and university affiliation.

The hierarchical nature of Mayorga-Gallo's relationship with participants was apparent when she had to deal with the painful experience of having White interviewees openly express racist views to her. In this case, a researcher who appeared to be on an equal footing with her participants was actually in a disempowered position.

Hordge-Freeman, a dark-skinned Black woman raised her whole life in the United States, also experienced insider and outsider status during her research on Black families in Salvador, Brazil. Afro-Brazilians experience structural and interpersonal marginalization in Brazil, and Black Brazilians identified with her and also highly respected her as an American. White Brazilians also viewed her highly, with her Americanness making her "not like" Black Brazilians, whom they disparaged. White Brazilians' heightened power in comparison to Hordge-Freeman made them trust her, "compliment" her for being so different from Black Brazilians, and freely express anti-Black racism in front of her.

When a researcher studies someone with less social power or who faces marginalization, the person may feel it risky to share their experiences or be uncomfortable in a one-on-one interview with someone holding a high degree from a university. Some propose researchers should share power

What do you feel are the factors that lead to an interview being comfortable, with strong rapport between interviewer and participant? How might social markers like race, gender, ability, class, or sexual orientation affect rapport? What are ways a researcher might approach an interview to make it a positive and open experience where they get good detail about their topic?

race, and class characteristics. In some cases, social privilege—Whiteness, masculinity, a stereotypically middle-class bearing, and a lack of visible disabilities—may lend interviewers authority; in some cases, that authority will bring trust, and in other cases suspicion. Too much rapport, however, can bring additional risks. For example, if an interviewer is overly friendly, participants might wish the interview was more focused and efficient; they might also tailor their answers to please the interviewer.

through such means as including some reciprocal sharing during the interview, asking for feedback and allowing the participants to read transcripts and write-ups, and working to develop an interactional style that is comfortable and empathetic (Råheim et al. 2016). Researchers' choices about how to navigate power differences are part of their ethical considerations and opportunities for reflection during the research process (Karnieli-Miller, Strier and Pessach 2009).

Interviewers must forge relationships with participants fairly quickly in order to encourage them to participate in and persist with the interview. Rapport is not simply a matter of being friendly and putting participants at ease—contact matters. Rapport is probably easier to achieve in a face-to-face interview than over the telephone, where the interviewer is unable to offer the visual cues of friendliness (such as smiling or maintaining good eye contact) that help to create and sustain a positive relationship.

Some interviewer characteristics can have an impact: participants may be more likely to trust people who share life experiences or their gender,

Asking Good Questions and Following Up Effectively

In addition to considering the interviewing relationship, interviewers must think about how to ask questions so that the interview is generative. This requires asking the right types of questions, asking them in a meaningful order, and responding appropriately to what is said in the course of the interview.

The types of questions asked in qualitative interviews are highly variable. Kvale (1996) suggested nine types, and most interviews contain virtually all of them:

- *Introducing questions* get an interview started: "Please tell me about when your interest in X first began"; "Have you ever … ?"; "Why did you go to … ?"
- *Follow-up questions* ask the interviewee to elaborate an answer: "What do you mean by that?" Kvale suggested repeating significant words in an answer to stimulate further explanation.
- *Probing questions* get the interviewee to further develop an idea they've offered: "You said earlier that you prefer not to do X. Can you say what kinds

BOX 9.4 Asking Questions to Elicit Detail and Specificity

Megan Comfort et al. (2005) interviewed women with incarcerated male partners about their experiences in prison visiting rooms. The researchers found that correctional officers treated these women as out-of-control sexual beings who enticed their partners into misbehavior. In the following excerpt from a transcript, the interviewee (indicated by "P"; the interviewer is "I") shares how officers in the visiting room constantly assumed her actions were sexual in nature and sought to control her behavior (2005, 8):

P: Say for instance like one day I was eatin' a popsicle. I guess I must have been eating it seductive and maybe I was. I don't—what you want me to do just bite it? It's cold. ... So the guard said you know walked over to him [my husband] and did like this [crooked his finger to call the prisoner to him]. ... And he just basically told him, 'Your wife can't be eating that popsicle like that.' 'How the hell I'm eating my popsicle?' So he said, 'You can't eat the

popsicle like that. If you're going to eat it eat it.' I said, 'Okay.'

I: He said that directly to you?

P: No. My husband came back and said it to me. The guard didn't say nothin' to me.

I: And what'd you say?

P: I said, 'Well how in the hell am I supposed to eat my popsicle?' He said the guard said if you're gonna eat it eat it. [laughs] So I kinda laughed about that cause it didn't make no sense. And I kinda copped an attitude. 'I'll just throw the goddamn thing away.'

I: And you didn't eat it?

P: And I got an attitude about it. I gave it to my baby. ... Yeah. I seriously caught a attitude about it and said, 'You can't do nothing in this damn place.'

In this excerpt, the interviewer created space for the participant to share her story, responding at certain moments with questions that encouraged clarification and further detail.

---

of things have put you off it?"; "In what ways do you find X disturbing?" (Box 9.2 provides more examples.)

- *Specifying questions* ask for clarifying information: "What did you do then?"; "How did (name) react to what you said?"; "What effect did (event) have on you?"

- *Direct questions* are often yes/no questions, requiring the interviewee to take a stand: "Do you find it easy to keep smiling when serving customers?"; "Are you happy with the way you and your partner decide how money should be spent?"

- *Indirect questions* can supplement questions about the interviewee's own view by asking them about others' perspective and experience: "What do most people around here think of the ways that management treats its staff?"

- *Structuring questions or statements* facilitate the unfolding of the interview: "Now I would like to move on to a different topic."

- *Silence*, or a pause, will give the interviewee an opportunity to reflect and amplify an answer.

- *Interpreting questions* check whether the interviewer understands what the interviewee has said: "Do you mean that your leadership role had to change from one of encouraging others to a more directive one?"

As this list suggests, a primary job of the interviewer is listening—being attentive to what the interviewee is saying or not saying. Interviewers must listen actively without being intrusive—a difficult balance. They must remain attuned and responsive not just to what is said or omitted, but also to what the interviewee is doing. For example, body language can indicate that the interviewee is becoming uneasy with a line of questioning. An ethically sensitive interviewer does not place undue pressure on an interviewee and is prepared to cut short any line of questioning that is a source of anxiety.

During an interview, how the researcher responds to the interviewee's statements will affect the strength of the research partnership and the value of the information shared. Box 9.4 provides an example of interview techniques encouraging more detail and specificity. Ultimately, flexibility in interviewing means a researcher responds to what interviewees say and follows up on the intriguing points they make. A flexible interviewer varies the order of questions, follows the interviewee's lead, and works to clarify inconsistencies or vague responses.

Making Notes on the Interview

Immediately after the interview, record your initial thoughts about it and any contextualizing information that may prove useful when you are assessing the transcript. In particular, note how the interview went, the interviewee's reactions and expressions, your own feelings about the interview, and new avenues of interest the interview raised. These notes are much like the field notes ethnographers write (see Chapter 10) and the analytical and procedural notes qualitative researchers write as part of data analysis (see Chapter 13).

Recording and Transcribing Interviews

Qualitative researchers are frequently interested both in *what* people say and *how* they say it—for example, the words they choose and emphasize, and pauses or hesitations in their speech. If these details are to be woven into an analysis, the interview should likely audio record interviews in order to have access to the complete series of exchanges in an interview. Because interviewers are supposed to be highly alert to what is being said—following up on interesting points, prompting and probing where necessary—they shouldn't also have to concentrate on writing down what interviewees say. In addition, recording interviews allows scrutiny of the transcripts by other researchers, who can evaluate the original analysis or even conduct a secondary analysis.

Despite its many values, recording comes with certain costs. A recorder can upset respondents, who may become self-conscious or alarmed at the prospect that their words will be preserved. Most people will allow their interviews to be recorded, though a small number may refuse. (When that happens, the interview can still proceed with the interviewer taking notes). If an interviewer is relaxed about the recording device, it will usually put the interviewee at ease.

Another consideration is the time required to transcribe a recorded interview. Transcription can take a lot of time. The usual estimate is five to six hours of typing per hour of speech, although transcription software along with computer keyboard shortcuts for stops and starts makes the task much easier. Speech-to-text software, a technology that transcribes spoken words directly into a text file, is also available. However, the software is not yet perfectly accurate, especially for focus groups.

Who should do the transcribing—the interviewer (more familiar with what was actually said) or someone more skilled in and with more time for transcribing (saving the interviewer time)—is the subject of some debate. Furthermore, the vast amounts of text produced must then be read. Alan Beardsworth and Teresa Keil (1992) reported that their 73 interviews on vegetarianism generated "several hundred thousand words of transcript material" (262). Clearly, even though transcription has the advantage of keeping the interviewee's (and interviewer's) words intact, it generates piles of text to analyze. It's no wonder that writers like Lofland and Lofland (1995) advise researchers not to leave the analysis of qualitative data until all the interviews have been completed and transcribed: waiting may make this task seem overwhelming. In addition, insights may be gained by examining the content of early interviews and pursuing those emerging themes in later interviews.

Focus Groups

Most people think of an interview as an exchange between one interviewer and one interviewee. Another technique—the **focus group**—involves speaking with more than one (usually at least four) interviewees at the same time; the participants typically share relevant characteristics, such as age, gender, race, or experiences. Focus groups are essentially group interviews in which the interviewees can speak to and interact with one another.

A focus group offers the opportunity to study how people collectively make sense of a phenomenon and construct meanings of it. A focus group can explore research questions like those addressed in a one-on-one interview. Yet focus groups allow researchers to explore questions geared around how groups of people collectively make sense of their lives and shared experiences.

Focus group researchers typically try to provide a fairly unstructured setting in which the person who runs the focus group, usually called the **moderator** or **facilitator**, guides the session but interjects only minimally. The main person leading the research study might choose to be the moderator, or someone else involved in the study may be a better choice. A moderator should be someone who will make the participants feel comfortable, perhaps sharing an identity or set of experiences with them. For instance, focus groups with youth may benefit from a younger moderator.

Conducting Focus Groups

A number of practical aspects guide the conducting of focus groups.

Number of Groups

The number of focus groups required for a particular study varies, but it generally ranges from 10 to 15. Fewer groups are unlikely to capture the experiences of the whole set of people you're interested in. On the other hand, involving too many groups can waste time and resources. Once the moderator can anticipate fairly accurately what the next group is going to say, enough groups have participated. This notion is similar to **theoretical saturation** in grounded theory, discussed in Chapters 4 and 13.

Many focus group researchers like to ensure that different demographic groups are included (and thus a range of views captured). This likely requires a large number of groups. David Miller et al. (1998) included 52 groups, with 351 total participants, in their research on the representation of AIDS in the mass media. Their groups were made up of people in a variety of situations. Some were what they described as "general population groups" (for example, a team of civil engineers working on the same site), but others were made up of people likely to have a special interest in AIDS, such as male sex workers and intravenous drug users. The multiple perspectives offered insights about how media affects audiences' understandings of AIDS.

Some research involves fewer groups, such as Murray et al.'s (2015) research on views about safety planning interventions for those at risk of intimate partner violence in central North Carolina. To gather insights into the service providers' experiences in this region, the researchers recruited participants from 9 agencies offering a diverse range of services and conducted 9 focus groups with 62 service providers.

Size and Makeup of Groups

David Morgan (1998a) suggested that a single focus group should contain 6 to 10 members. He recommended group size should be on the smaller end of that spectrum when the participants will likely have a lot to say, as often occurs when they are emotionally involved with the topic, when the topic is

---

focus group A semi-structured interview in which several people are interviewed together in order to learn about people's experiences and perceptions, group dynamics, and processes through which social groups make meaning.

---

moderator (or **facilitator**) A person (usually the researcher) who runs a focus group session, guiding discussions with minimal intervention.

---

theoretical saturation In grounded theory, the point where emerging concepts have been fully explored and no new insights are being generated.

In what situations would it be good to recruit people to participate in a focus group who are unknown to each other or to recruit people who are from natural groups? If you wanted to recruit hockey fans like those pictured here to study attitudes about sports, is this a natural or unknown group? What if you recruited fans participating in their office fantasy sports league?

controversial or complex, or when exploring personal interpretations. A larger group is appropriate when the researcher wants to gather lots of ideas from fewer people.

Researchers may put participants into separate groups on the basis of age, gender, education, experiences, and so on. Aasim Padela, Liese Pruitt, and Saleha Mallick (2017) held 13 focus groups (102 total participants) in their study of how American Muslims' religious faith and feelings of trust in the health care system influenced their health care decision-making process. They held separate groups for men and women and the groups were mostly homogenous in terms of ethnicity: three South Asian groups, two African American, four Arab, and two with diverse ethnicities. The aim was to look for any variation in how the different groups discuss the matter at hand, as well as shared or distinct views in the homogenous groupings.

A further issue in designing a focus group is whether to select people who are unknown to each other or to use natural groups (for example, friends, co-workers, or students in the same class). Some researchers prefer to exclude people who know each other, fearing that known status differences or pre-existing patterns of interaction would contaminate the session. Ferrera et al. (2016) conducted 49 focus groups with participants recruited from 15 of Chicago's predominantly Black neighborhoods forming the patient base of the University of Chicago Medicine system. Because Black women are 41 percent more likely to die of breast cancer than White women, the researchers sought to understand Black Chicago residents' beliefs and feelings about the disease and its treatment. The focus groups were heterogeneous: each was arranged to match the demographics of the neighborhood from which it was recruited, but the participants did not know one another.

Others prefer to select natural groups whenever possible. In her research on second-generation Arab American youth identity, Kristine Ajrouch (2004) recruited her participants from a Dearborn, Michigan, school's social studies classes. She was interested in community influences on youth identity formation and noted that "School settings often represent a microcosm of society reflecting social patterns that shape daily experiences for those coming of age" (376). Her selection of youth who knew each other was a highly appropriate choice because it enabled her to specifically explore both their shared and unique understandings.

Recruiting people from natural groups is not always feasible, however, because of the difficulty of getting everyone in the group to participate. It also may not be desirable: Morgan (1998a) argues that people who know one another may share certain assumptions that they feel no need to justify. He suggested that when the researcher wants to make such assumptions explicit, a group of strangers is a better choice.

Asking Questions and Level of Moderator Involvement

How involved should the moderator or facilitator be? As with other questioning strategies, the most common approach is middle-of-the-road. Researchers routinely prepare a fairly small number of general questions to guide a focus group session. If the discussion goes completely off topic, it may be necessary to refocus the participants' attention. Even then, the moderator must be careful, because apparent digressions can reveal something of significance. More direction is probably needed if the participants do not address the research questions or do not follow up on another person's particularly meaningful point.

Phil Macnaghten and Michael Jacobs's (1997) middle-of-the-road approach to question structuring can be seen in the following passage, in which a group of working women express cynicism about government and experts regarding the reality of environmental problems ("F" is "female" and "Mod" is "moderator"):

F: They only tell us what they want us to know. And that's just the end of that, so we are left with a fog in your brain, so you just think—what have I to worry about? I don't know what they're on about.

Mod: So why do Government only tell us what they want us to hear?

F: To keep your confidence going. (All together)

Mod: So if someone provides an indicator which says the economy is improving you won't believe it?

F: They've been saying it for about 10 years, but where? I can't see anything!

F: Every time there's an election they say the economy is improving. (1997, 18)

In this exchange, the moderator focuses on the topic to be addressed but is also able to pick up on what the group says.

Group Interaction in Focus Group Sessions

Symbolic interactionists hold that meanings and understandings are not derived by people in isolation but develop out of interactions and discussions with others. The opportunity to observe such interaction is a significant strength of focus groups and also a reason why a moderator might lean towards minimal intervention into a focus group discussion.

In the context of their research on AIDS coverage in the mass media, Miller et al. (1998) drew attention to two types of interaction in focus groups: complementary and argumentative. *Complementary interaction* allows collective interpretations and understandings to develop, with each participant building on the preceding remark. The following passage taken from Ajrouch's (2004, 383) research on second-generation Arab-American teenagers' identity formation exemplifies this approach (all speakers were group participants):

Hanan: You know the girls that wear scarves? No offense, but girls that wear scarves get talked about more than girls that don't wear scarves.

Lynn: Yeah, because they expect the girl not to do anything wrong, whatsoever. One little mistake she makes, even if she swears once. She shouldn't be wearing a scarf if she swore once. I don't know, something like that.

Miriam: Respect the thing that's on your head. Respect this, respect that.

This sequence brings out an emerging consensus about how and why girls who wear the hijab are held to a higher standard and subject to social control.

However, as Miller et al. (1998) suggested, *argumentative interaction* in focus groups can be equally revealing. Participants might question other participants' accounts, challenge one another, or ask each other questions about their statements. The following exchange between participants, from a focus group that Esther Madriz (2000, 841) held as part of her research on fear of crime, illustrates these sorts of interactions:

Mixed Methods in Action | Understanding Indigenous Masculinity, Culture, and Health

In their mixed methods study of how Indigenous men's identities and the structural conditions they encounter affect their health and lifestyle choices, Ka'imi Sinclair et al. (2020) conducted 15 focus groups and a survey with a total of 151 American Indian men in Minneapolis, Minnesota, Oregon, and Arizona. Of particular concern to these researchers was the ways Indigenous men's current health is affected by generational trauma and oppression stemming from colonization, contemporary settler colonialism (an ongoing process in which colonial institutions displace Indigenous communities in favor of settler populations), racism, and other forms of oppression. This mixed methods study demonstrates in particular how focus groups can flesh out quantitative data while bringing valuable insight into a group's understandings about their lives.

The researchers collected and analyzed their quantitative data and qualitative data separately. First, they asked their participants to complete a survey. The questionnaire used for the survey had questions about demographics, values, views of masculinity and men's roles, health choices, psychological well-being, physical activity levels, and eating habits. After completing the survey, the men took part in focus groups that explored their experiences as men, their health and lifestyle, and supports and barriers to healthy behaviors.

From the survey, the researchers learned that the men all shared the values of mental and emotional strength, good parenting, responsibility, and spirituality. Caring for family and community and knowing their culture and traditions were also important. Differences came about in views on the importance of managing their temper (fewer in Portland rated this important) and maintaining healthy body weight (Phoenix participants rated this less important). There were no major differences in mental distress across the sample, but 63–70 percent were rated as being moderately mentally distressed, and 8–15 percent severely distressed. Almost 50 percent of the men were unemployed, and half of those unemployed were not college graduates. A majority of the sample reported an interest in learning to prepare healthier food, and about 50 percent ate fast food 12 times per week, reporting that healthy food is too expensive. Fewer than 50 percent found it hard to

---

Maria: No, I tell you, *de verdad*, I am not afraid of crime.

Juana: Well, you are saying now that you are not afraid of crime. So, then, why did you say before that you don't like to go out alone at night?

Rosa: Yes, that's true. You did say that before.

Maria: Okay, I am talking more in general. I try not to be afraid.

Disagreement can give participants a chance to revise their opinions, clarify them, or to think about why they hold them.

In a focus group, participants are able to take control of the discussion and even subvert the goals the researcher had for the session. Madriz (2000, 840) describes this as "horizontal interaction" (communication between and among participants), which may occur more even than the "vertical interaction" between moderator and group. As a result, participants' points of view can sometimes be more likely revealed in a focus group than in a traditional interview, and a facilitator can help create space for participants to share their understandings.

find time to exercise, and many reported engaging in a variety of physical activities.

In their qualitative analysis, three research team members coded the focus group transcripts line-by-line, using analysis software to identify key themes in the data. They then paired the results and integrated their analysis to determine places where the quantitative and qualitative findings differed, converged, or complemented one another. The findings converged around masculinity, community, culture, and physical activity. The data demonstrated that the men found it important to engage in activities that helped themselves as well as the community, and that this was integral to their self-concept as men. The participants emphasized the importance of culture and linked this to their desire to engage in physical activity such as pow wow dancing or foraging for traditional food or medicine. The interview data also confirmed the survey findings about diet; the focus groups provided more detail on the men's agreement about healthy food being expensive, that they regularly ate fast food, and that they wanted to eat more Native foods. The qualitative and quantitative data diverged around spirituality, as many reported it important in the survey but discussed a lack of understanding about spirituality

and how to live a more spiritual life in the focus groups. Also, a large number of men reported in the survey that they would exercise more if family supported them, but this sentiment was not expressed in the focus groups.

The researchers noted that the qualitative data expanded their understandings about the quantitative findings. Focus group discussion helped clarify that the men's lack of peer support, adherence to masculine norms, and views of healthy food and weight loss could prevent them from prioritizing a healthy body—even though they reported this as important in the survey. The focus group also helped expand the findings about structural conditions surrounding the men, as they displayed a nuanced understanding of settler colonialism and hegemonic masculinity's effects on their perspectives on health, health-related behavior, and adherence to tradition.

In this mixed methods study, the researchers were able to explore the core trends and patterns from the survey in a meaningful way using a focus group. This enabled them to confirm and expand on the quantitative findings, as well as creating space through which the participants could articulate important details about their experiences in a community setting.

Recording and Transcribing Focus Groups

Recording may be even more necessary with focus groups than with other forms of qualitative interviews. Writing down exactly what is said but also who says it is too difficult when several people are speaking simultaneously and rapidly. Transcribing focus group sessions is also more complicated and hence more time-consuming than with other interview forms. Focus group transcripts may have more missing data than other transcripts, mainly because of audibility problems. Sometimes voices are hard to distinguish, making it difficult to determine who is speaking. Also, people sometimes talk over one another, making transcription even more difficult. A high-quality recording device, capable

of picking up even faint voices from many directions, is a necessity.

Challenges and Limitations of Focus Groups

Despite their various advantages, focus groups pose several challenges:

- *Balancing control*: Researchers must determine the extent to which they should allow the participants to "take over" the discussion and strike a delicate balance in deciding how involved moderators should be.
- *Amount of data*: Michael Bloor (2001) suggested that one focus group session can take up to eight hours to transcribe—somewhat longer than an

BOX 9.5   On-on-One Interviews vs Focus Groups

When should a researcher choose a one-on-one interview, and when is a focus group a better choice? This decision involves a combination of research aims and interview dynamics. Individual interviews are more appropriate than focus groups when

- the researcher wants to understand and probe into people's specific and in-depth experiences around a topic,
- participants are likely to disagree profoundly with each other,

Focus group interviews allow for more flexibility and participant involvement than one-on-one interviews do. What insights might a focus group interview provide that are different from a one-on-one interview, and vice versa?

- participants are not comfortable in one another's presence (for example, people in hierarchical relationships), or
- the researcher wants to explore controversial topics, embarrassing issues, or intimate details of private lives that might cause discomfort when discussed in a group setting (Madriz 2000).

A focus group can be the better choice when

- the researcher is interested in group perspectives and commonalities or differences of opinion on a topic,

- a researcher is more interested in multiple opinions on a topic than in-depth individual perspectives,
- the researcher wants to focus time and effort, gathering information from more people quickly rather than from fewer people more slowly in individual interviews, or
- there is particular concern that the interviewer's status might affect responses one-on-one (interviewer bias), since focus groups encourage less emphasis on the facilitator.

equivalent personal interview—because of variations in voice pitch and the need to identify who says what.
- *Data analysis*: Developing an analysis strategy that incorporates both the themes of the discussion and the patterns of interaction is not easy.
- *Planning and arranging the group*: It may be hard to get people to agree to participate, and harder still to get them to show up to the focus

group. Researchers may offer small incentives, such as gift cards, to encourage participation and still find that some people will not turn up.
- *Dynamics within the group*: Researchers must deal with participants who are either too reticent to speak up or who hog the stage. Richard Krueger (2002) suggests facilitators can respond to people dominating the group by saying something like

"That's one point of view. Does anyone have another point of view?" (59). As for those who are reluctant to speak, Krueger recommended that they be actively encouraged to say something.

These challenges can be reframed as opportunities. Sensitivity to group dynamics can spark an interest in whether agreement among focus group participants is more common than disagreement. If so, one reason might be group pressure to conform. Participants may also be more likely to express socially acceptable views in a group setting than in individual interviews. David Morgan (2002) describes a study in which group interviews with boys on the topic of relationships with girls were compared with individual interviews on the same subject. Alone, the boys expressed a degree of sensitivity that was not evident in the group context, where they tended to express more macho views. This difference suggests that in the group setting the boys were trying to impress each other or avoid embarrassment and were influenced by peer pressure. But this does not mean that such data are tainted: in fact, it may be the gulf between privately and publicly held views that is of interest.

Online Interviews and Focus Groups

Conducting qualitative interviews and focus groups online has become increasingly common as technology has improved and people increasingly communicate online. They are also seen as a way to reach more people, as populations have become increasingly geographically dispersed and the importance of accessibility has received more recognition (Deakin and Wakefield 2014, Janghorban, Roudsari, and Taghipou 2014). However, while online interviews can increase accessibility for some people, they can reduce access for those without technical skills or access to the necessary hardware and software. Particular considerations arise when doing online interviews or focus groups.

Online Qualitative Interviews

Conducting qualitative interviews through videoconferencing technologies is still relatively new, but the Covid-19 pandemic has made them increasingly a feature of everyday life. Some researchers argue that online interviews offer many advantages over in-person interviews (Deakin and Wakefield 2014, Hanna 2012, Iacono, Symonds, and Brown 2016). These interviews require no travel, they can easily be postponed and re-scheduled, and interviewees are likely to feel safe and secure in the setting they choose. Moreover, both audio and visual aspects of the interview are easily recorded, and some programs offer captioning, which eases transcription.

Challenges remain, however. Body language and cues can be more difficult to read over videoconference, since often the screen shows only the face and upper body. Researchers must be conscious of "looking at" the person, which typically means looking at the camera and not the screen. Technical glitches can also create difficulties, so verifying the reliability of the connection and participants' ability to use the software is crucial to pre-planning (Seitz 2016, 230–232).

Online Focus Groups

Researchers must decide whether the online interaction will be synchronous (conducted in real time) or asynchronous (conducted with time gaps between questions and responses). Often online focus groups are asynchronous, occurring through listservs or email distribution lists. Because people can respond and post at any time, they do not have to schedule times to chat, and moderators need not actively facilitate the discussion (Madge and O'Connor 2002, 94). In synchronous online focus groups, participants type their responses more or less immediately to whatever has just been "said," whether by the moderator or by other participants. All are simultaneously online, so contributions can be responded to as soon as they appear on the screen. Mann and Stewart (2000) suggested that an online focus group should have between six and eight people. Larger groups make it difficult for some people to participate, especially those with limited keyboard skills. Also, moderating the session can be more difficult with larger numbers.

It remains to be seen whether online interviews and focus groups will remain popular and even replace in-person qualitative data collection. The former are certainly likely to be used for certain kinds of research topics and samples. Research focusing on use of technology or experiences in online environments are particularly fitting for online focus groups. People who are geographically dispersed or inaccessible are especially suitable for online focus group research; slow typists are not well-positioned for asynchronous focus groups. In-person focus groups take a great deal of time and administrative effort to plan and schedule, so some researchers prefer the convenience of an online medium.

Our discussion of the different dynamics that can be explored using a focus group compared to a one-on-one interview suggests that researchers must reflect on their research aims when selecting a data collection method. These considerations should always guide researchers as they decide what type of data will best allow them to explore their questions of interest.

Key Points

Introduction: Why the Interview is the Most Widely Used Qualitative Research Method

- Interviewing is the data collection used most often in qualitative research.
- Qualitative interviews offer an open-ended and flexible structure through which researchers can explore people's lives in a detailed way.

Types of Qualitative Interviews: Unstructured and Semi-structured

- There are two main types of qualitative interviews: unstructured and semi-structured.
- Unstructured interviews are more conversational and have the least amount of structure to them. Semi-structured interviews follow a guide and a specific set of topics, yet also have a flexible structure.
- Within the two main categories are life history interviews (which ask participants to report their experiences and how they understood their world) and oral history interviews (which ask participants to reflect on historical events or eras they have lived through, often emphasizing how these events affected their lives).

Preparing for a Qualitative Interview

- To prepare for a qualitative interview, a researcher should determine their goals and the topics they'll explore, write an interview guide, and address practical concerns such as location, consent forms, and recording strategy.
- An interview guide should explore the research questions in depth without being judgmental, leading, or using unfamiliar terminology.
- The question order should be logical, but flexible, ensuring the establishment of rapport and exploring the overall research question.

Conducting Qualitative Interviews

- Researchers must build a relationship with the interviewee, reflecting on positionality and power dynamics to establish comfort and a strong rapport.
- Follow-up, probing, and asking specific questions can help solicit further information from interviewees.
- Interviews should be recorded and transcribed for accuracy, and interviewers should make notes about body language and reactions during the interview.

Focus Groups

- Focus groups are group interviews in which a moderator or facilitator (usually the researcher) guides the session.
- Focus groups reflect the processes through which meaning is constructed in everyday life and within group interaction.
- Moderators lean toward minimal intervention and ask open-ended questions which the group

explores together. Observing group discussion and interactions is a significant strength of the focus group method.

- Transcribing focus groups is time-consuming yet important, to get details on what occurred during the group interview.

Online Interviews and Focus Groups

- Online interviews and focus groups can increase accessibility across distances and reduce access for those without technological skill or internet access.

Questions for Review

1. Why are qualitative interviews such a popular data collection method? What type of information do they provide to researchers?
2. What are the differences between unstructured and semi-structured interviewing?
3. How might researchers approach semi-structured interviewing with both structure as well as flexibility? Why would they want to use this model?
4. What are the differences between life history and oral history interviews?
5. How should researchers choose the questions in their interview guide, and how does this relate to their research question, study aims, and substantive frame?
6. What considerations need to be kept in mind when preparing an interview guide?
7. What kinds of questions can be included in an interview guide?
8. What skills does the interviewer need to develop for qualitative interviewing?
9. What does a researcher gain through developing a positive relationship with their interviewee?
10. How might power differences or similarities affect the relationship between interviewer and interviewee?
11. How would you define "good interview questions"?
12. What methods can be used to ensure the interviewee provides specific and in-depth information?
13. What are some reasons to record and transcribe qualitative interviews?
14. What advantages can a focus group offer compared to an individual qualitative interview?
15. In what circumstances would selecting a natural group to participate in a focus group be an advantage?
16. What can a researcher learn from examining group interaction in focus groups?
17. Can online, text-based interviews really be personal interviews? Explain.

Portfolio Exercise

Write a paragraph describing how a qualitative interview (any type) would help you explore your research question. Then, develop an interview guide related to your primary research question. Begin by writing your research question and then do the following, referencing chapter materials to help you:

a. develop a substantive frame for the research question (the set of main topics you want to explore in the interview),

b. list a set of sub-topics, or areas you would need to explore within each of these main topics,

c. turn each sub-topic into a question (considering what you learned in this and previous chapters about how to write open-ended, non-judgmental, non-leading questions),

d. for each question in your guide, write additional follow-up and probing questions to aid you in soliciting clear and detailed responses, and

e. arrange the questions in a logical order, ensuring that introductory questions (to help engage the interviewee and develop rapport) are at the beginning, more controversial or emotionally intense in the middle, and "cool down" questions at the end.

Interactive Activities

1. In groups of 4 or 5, students select a research question provided by the instructor (topics could include opinions on physician-assisted suicide, effects of social media on friendship, consequences of gentrification, etc.) and create a substantive frame, including one topic area for each group member. Dividing the list among the group, each member writes a broad interview question on their subtopic. Underneath their question, they then place a vertical line down the center of the paper, labeling the left side *main questions* and the right *follow-up/probing questions*, and pass the paper to another group member. Every group member is given 2-3 minutes to add at least one main and one follow up/probing question on the subtopic. Repeat until the entire group has added to each paper. This can be done by hand in an in-person synchronous class or in a google doc in an online meeting.

    Then, as a group, review and discuss all the questions, taking 10–15 minutes to address the following:

    a. How would the suggested questions help gather both general and specific information about the research question?

    b. Why are probing questions necessary? How do they differ from main questions?

    c. Are there any other questions that could be beneficial in eliciting information about the research question, or are any topics missing?

    d. Discuss how to turn these questions into an interview guide, considering logical question order and warm-up and cool down questions.

    In an asynchronous class, students could be grouped by topic they've chosen and each one could write 4-5 main questions with probing questions. In an online forum discussion, they could share their questions and the group can reflect on the discussion questions mentioned previously and the similarities and differences in their questions.

2. Divide the class into small breakout groups of 6-10 that meet either (1) synchronously in person or online or (2) asynchronously. The groups decide on a general topic relative to their city, school, or institution (e.g., perceptions of public transportation, opinion of campus services, reactions to local homelessness, etc.) and develop a set of 3-5 questions for a short focus group discussion based on the topic.

    Next, randomly assign the roles of group facilitator, note-taker, and participants in the mock focus group. Conduct either a synchronous online or in-person focus group, or an asynchronous online focus group. The facilitator will state the purpose of the focus group and ask the questions on the interview guide, allowing participants time to respond and utilizing probing and follow-up questions when necessary. The note-taker will observe the focus group and assess the following:

    a. How effectively do the questions explore the topic? How do they flow?

    b. Did the respondents raise any topics that could have been further explored?

    c. How did the facilitator approach the group moderation and how did this affect the discussion?

    d. What individual and shared meanings emerged from the focus group discussion?

    e. What are your thoughts about the advantages or disadvantages of the type of focus group conducted (synchronous, asynchronous, online, in-person)?

    At the conclusion of the focus groups, all note-takers share their findings with the class, which discusses the following:

    a. What are the advantages and/or disadvantages of the focus group method compared to one-on-one qualitative interviews for researching the topics chosen?

    b. How did it feel to facilitate, participate in, or observe the focus groups? What did you notice about the experience and what does it teach you about this method?

c. Why might it be important to develop group understandings and explore group experiences about these topics using a focus group?

3. Students choose a topic from a list provided by the instructor (items could include, for example, college students' alcohol and marijuana use, perceptions of high school dress code policies, or political affiliation and community engagement). They then write independently about their selection, addressing how they would approach it using each of the following methods:

a. one-on-one interviews (semi-structured and unstructured),

b. focus groups,

c. an online interview or focus group.

After everyone finishes writing, form a group with the students who wrote on the same topic and discuss the strengths and challenges these methods might pose.

Online Resources

- For additional information on focus group interviews, see Richard Krueger's Designing and Conducting Focus Group Interviews.

www.eiu.edu/ihec/Krueger-FocusGroupInterviews.pdf

For more resources please visit
www.oup.com/he/bryman-reck-fields1e

10

How Can Researchers Study the Patterns of People's Lives?
Participant Observation and Ethnography

▲ Mira/Alamy Stock Photo

The term "participant observation" describes a two-part method of data collection: researchers both *participate in* and *observe* the groups or settings that interest them. By carefully and systematically watching, listening to, and experiencing the aspects of social life that interest them, participant observers gain insight into social conditions and processes.

Though the terms "participant observation" and "ethnography" are often used interchangeably, they are not one and the same. Ethnography is a qualitative approach to studying social life that involves extended engagement with the lives of the people and settings under study; participant observation is the primary method of collecting data in ethnographic research. Ethnographers' aim is to learn from prolonged participant observation—but in many cases also interviews and collects data (all discussed in other chapters)—about what it means to live as a member of a group, in a setting or culture, or in the midst of social conditions and inequalities.

Reading this chapter will help you to

- identify reasons for adopting participant observation as a method of data collection;

- follow the guidelines for choosing a research site;

- apply strategies for gaining and maintaining access to participants;

- describe ways to identify and learn from informants;

- explain the different roles that participant observers can assume in fieldwork;

- use suggestions for writing field notes;

- discuss innovations in ethnographic research;

- employ tactics for ending an ethnographic study; and

- distinguish the advantages and disadvantages of ethnography relative to qualitative interviewing.

Since Louise Fitzhugh's *Harriet the Spy* was first published in 1964, many have felt drawn to its title character. Harriet follows a "spy route" each afternoon through her neighborhood, carefully observing friends, family members, peers, and strangers, and recording her observations in a notebook. She is perceptive and witty, and her "spying" reflects the appeal of observation and the thrill of becoming an expert on everyday life. Her descriptions are perceptive and insightful, but also a little hurtful in their honesty. Fitzhugh's novel thus demonstrates the risks and ethics of recording our thoughts about others—that is, the importance of striking a balance between observing people's lives and respecting them. Though tricky, this balance is possible, especially if we keep in mind the ethical concerns discussed in Chapter 2.

If the idea of inserting yourself into a social setting and getting to know the people there over an extended period appeals to you, you might consider participant observation and ethnography. What kinds of groups or social settings intrigue you? Sports teams? Political activists? Classroom teachers? Polyamorists? Hospital emergency rooms? Women's shelters? All of these groups can be subjects of participant observation and ethnographic research.

Introduction: Why Participant Observation and Ethnography Are Not the Same

Different terms are used to describe the process of directly observing people in a social setting for extended periods of time. In practice, people often use "participant observation" and "ethnography" interchangeably. We will use **participant observation** to describe the method of sustained observation of people and participation in social settings in everyday conditions. Participant observation is a component of **ethnography**, the general practice of trying to understand people and

Imagine you volunteered to work at your campus food pantry. How do you think you might learn about food insecurity by spending time with people experiencing it?

settings by (1) living (working, playing, agitating, learning) alongside them and (2) making sense of that engagement.

In participant observation, researchers interact with the people they are studying, listening to what these people say in impromptu conversations with them and with other members of the setting, and asking additional questions. The aim is typically described as **immersion**: participant observers think,

---

participant observation A data collection technique often used during ethnography, in which researchers interact with, observe, and listen to people in a research setting, taking notes on what occurs.

---

ethnography A method in which researchers immerse themselves in social settings for an extended period of time, observing behavior and interacting with study participants in order to understand people's culture and experiences.

---

immersion An ideal of ethnographic research, in which researchers seek an in-depth understanding of settings or people by engaging fully in the experiences and practices of the group.

---

talk, move, and feel alongside the people they study in order to think, talk, move, and feel like them (Desmond 2016). Typically, participant observers and ethnographers gather additional supporting data through documents and interviews, especially on matters about which they are unclear about or that are not directly observable.

Ethnographers face a wide range of challenges and opportunities in the course of research, and they have innumerable strategies for dealing with those experiences. Matthew Desmond (2016) suggests these strategies reflect ethnographers' general approach to the world:

> I tend to think of ethnography as a sensibility, ... a fundamental way of being in the world.... If we approach ethnography as a sensibility, then we can begin cultivating a set of skills or disciplines long before we actually enter the field. It is possible to transform yourself into an ethnographer—day in, day out—so that when the time comes to set foot in the field, you already are one. (404)

This chapter will focus on the skills and disciplines associated with ethnography as a sensibility and way of being. Our focus will be the data ethnographers gather through participant observation; we will discuss other methods ethnographers use, including interviews and document analysis, in other chapters.

Why Participant Observation?

Participant observation and ethnography often represent an opportunity to study a researcher's immediate world. Course instructors often counsel students to "begin where they are." Perhaps they and their siblings migrated to the United States; they may want to study migration as a family experience. Maybe they are part of an often misunderstood music scene; an ethnography could clarify its cultural significance and interpersonal dynamics. Or maybe a researcher is a devoted podcast listener and wonders how podcasters find an audience in the vast world of podcasting; attending some podcast festivals in order to hang out with production teams and avid podcast listeners might offer some insight. Researchers also reach beyond their immediate worlds, to encounter new problems and perspectives.

Participant observation allows researchers to enter a world and gain a sense of what it means to make a life there. Ethnographic analysis promises to shed light on new areas of interest and generate novel understandings that researchers long thought settled. Through careful analysis of participant observation and other qualitative data, ethnographers locate people's decisions, relationships, opportunities, and circumstances in broader social contexts. Ethnography is interpretive work—an opportunity to tell a compelling story about social life.

However, like every method of data collection, participant observation brings with it challenges and limitations. Ethical challenges can feel especially acute since relationships with participants are more immediate and intimate than in most other data collection methods. Researchers may not be able to avoid disrupting study participants' lives, simply through their presence in the field. The method also requires significant time from the researcher—regular visits to the research setting over an extended period of time. The demands of occupying the research settings as a participant and an observer can be awkward and frustrating. And, as compelling as ethnographers' stories may be, small sample sizes mean they will not be easily generalized to larger populations.

Selecting and Navigating a Setting

Choosing a Site

Choosing a site for ethnographic research often begins with issues of interest: what people, setting, or question matters to researchers, will hold their attention, or will be of interest to their audiences? Choosing a site involves considerations about sampling, discussed in Chapter 4. Ethnographers may face opposition, or at least indifference, to their research interests: the people they want to study may not want to be studied. Therefore, before committing to a site, ethnographers must be confident that they can connect with enough **informants** to reach their targeted sample size, so they will be able to analyze a variety of perspectives and ranges of activities. In addition, they should develop a preliminary plan for sampling in the field before they select a site.

Ethnographers—especially those who are more participants than observers—may find that they can make more formal requests for the names of people who may have relevant information and who can be contacted. These requests help constitute the participant observer's efforts to construct their study sample and determine the generalizability of their findings. (Note that probability sampling is almost never used in ethnographic research. This approach is often unfeasible because it is difficult, if not impossible, to map "the population" from which a random sample would be taken.)

Entering and Navigating the Setting

One of the most important and challenging steps in participant observation is entering the setting and launching a set of relationships with the people one wants to study—what researchers often describe as "gaining access." This process depends on several things, including researchers' personal histories with the people, settings, and issues they plan to study; the implications of their identities for the people and settings that interest them; and their comfort in new social settings.

Personal histories can make access to some settings and groups seem easily within reach. If a researcher played rugby, gaining access to a team might feel straightforward. If a researcher was a teen mother, a support group for young parenting women might feel like familiar and welcoming ground. If a researcher lives in a gentrifying neighborhood,

---

informant A study participant with specialized knowledge or insight to offer a researcher.

Mixed Methods in Action | Triangulation and Multi-Method Research

As Norman Denzin (2015) argues, qualitative research is an inherently and historically *multi-method* approach to social research. Ethnographers routinely engage in participant observation, conduct informal and formal interviews with participants, and collect documents and other material from the settings they observe. These are all distinct methods, promising their own insights and making their own demands on the researcher and the study participants.

Qualitative researchers have done this mixing in the name of "triangulation," or what Denzin defines as "the combination of multiple methodological practices, empirical materials, perspectives, and observers in a single study [and] a strategy that adds rigor, breadth complexity, richness, and depth to any inquiry" (2015, 82). He explains that the aim in triangulation is not to secure an objective understanding of reality but to pursue an in-depth understanding. This distinction is an important one, pointing as it does to different ideas about the goals of research and the nature of knowledge. These ideas, inherent to all research methods, may prove difficult to comfortably reconcile in multi-method and mixed method research.

it might be easy to talk with people about their sense of recent changes on their streets. Without these personal experiences and histories, gaining access can feel more challenging. Yet ethnographers often study sports they don't play, identities they don't share, and experiences that are not their own. The question is not *whether* our biographies matter but *how* they matter.

Open versus Closed Settings

As ethnographers work to gain access, an early consideration is whether the setting is relatively open (public) or closed (private or restricted) (see Lofland and Lofland 1995). Open settings include libraries, bars, parks, and sidewalks; closed settings include formally restricted organizations such as companies and firms, schools, support groups, summer camps, and cults. Researchers also try to gain access to informally closed settings, such as a lounge for LGBTQIA2S+ students. The line between open and closed settings can be murky. Officially, anyone can enter open settings; however, it can be quite difficult

to gain the meaningful access necessary to make observations and talk to people. "Open" does not necessarily mean easy access to the people and interactions of interest.

Sometimes the process of gaining access in ostensibly open settings can take on an almost formal quality: for instance, when talking to a gang leader in the street, researchers may have to answer some pointed questions about their goals. Formally closed organizations and social movements sometimes create contexts that have a public character, such as meetings arranged for members or prospective recruits. In his study of western Canadian separatists—people who believe that their region should form its own country—Edward Bell (2007) attended separatists' meetings and rallies that were open to the public. Through those settings, he was able to gather a lot of information about the movement and its leaders without securing formal access to them.

Overt versus Covert Participant Observation

Gaining access can be challenging and intimidating. Even as **overt participant observation** is preferred, adopting a covert role—not disclosing one's status as a researcher—may seem like the quickest way to remove some of those difficulties. However, the

overt participant observation Field research in which participants know they are being studied and understand the aims and status of the researcher.

TABLE 10.1 | Advantages and Disadvantages of the Covert Role

Advantages	Disadvantages
Easier access. Adopting a covert role can help with access problems; the researcher probably needs no special permission to gain entry to a social setting or organization.	*Challenges when note taking.* Taking notes is difficult and sometimes impossible without raising suspicion and perhaps revealing that the notetaker is conducting research.
Greater access to illicit behavior. Because the researcher does not disclose their intentions, participants are less likely to shift illegal, stigmatized, or secret behaviors to protect against the presence of an outsider or observer.	*Limited data-collection options.* The covert researcher cannot conduct interviews formally and overtly; steering informal conversations in particular directions can increase the risk of detection.
Less reactivity. Because study participants do not know they are being observed, their behavior will not reflect the presence of a researcher.	*Anxiety.* Immersion and close relationships with study participants create a stressful environment; worries about detection only add to the anxiety. If the participant observer is found out, the whole research project may be jeopardized. In extreme cases, such as covert research on illicit behavior, being found out could even compromise the researcher's safety.
	Ethical problems. Covert observation violates two important tenets of ethical research: a responsibility not to deceive participants and to obtain informed consent (see Chapter 2). The decision to veer from these ethical standards is significant, and researchers should do so only when truly necessary to gain valuable insights.

decision to conduct **covert participant observation** should rest on several factors. Table 10.1 features the few advantages and the greater disadvantages of adopting a covert role.

In her study of relationships between domestic workers and their employers, Judith Rollins (1985) was a covert observer: she fabricated letters of reference and an employment history in order to secure a position. **Deception** seemed necessary to gaining meaningful insights into power, social inequality, and justice. Rollins offers a compelling argument for covert observation, deception, and other ethical compromises.

Miriam Glucksmann (1994) provides another interesting case. In the 1970s, she left her academic post for a job on a factory assembly line in an effort to explore feminism's relevance to working-class women. In a sense, she was a covert observer, but her motives were primarily political, not academic.

When she began the research, she had no intention of writing about her experiences. Nevertheless, she did eventually publish a book under a pseudonym. Was she an overt or a covert observer? Was she neither? Both? Whichever description applies, her experience might be termed "retrospective ethnography": an ethnography that relies on observations gathered before the researcher decided to conduct a study. In a retrospective ethnography, covert observation may be inevitable.

covert participant observation Field research in which researchers conceal their researcher status and study aims from the people being studied.

deception The practice of concealing or misrepresenting an aspect or entirety of one's research aims to study participants.

BOX 10.1 The Lies of Ethnography

In 1993, Gary Fine published a now classic article on what he described as "Ten Lies of Ethnography." Fine aimed to describe "compromises [an ethnographer] frequently makes with idealized ethical standards" (Fine 1993, 267). Researchers make such compromises not because they are casually dishonest or cynical but rather because, once in the field, they "must make choices which impel them to behave in ways that differ from how they would like 'the general public' to assume that they behave" (1993, 268). For example, though ethnographers may want to subscribe to the ideal of the "kindly" or "friendly" ethnographer, they do not always like the people they study and, when writing about and presenting their research finding, ethnographers regularly criticize the behavior and beliefs of people toward whom they were only friendly while in the field. Similarly, while an ethnographer may aim to be "precise" and "observant" when writing field note accounts of their participant observation, ordinary human failings (forgetfulness, limited vision or hearing) mean that field notes are inevitably incomplete.

Fine concludes that these compromises are necessary to a method that strives to identify patterns to people's experiences of the social world. Ethnographers learn through immersion and share through description. He writes,

> Perfection is professionally unobtainable. These lies are not lies that we can choose, for the most part, not to tell . . . We ethnographers cannot help but lie, but in lying, we reveal truths that escape those who are not so bold. (Fine 1993, 290)

While compromises—that is, lies—may be inevitable, Fine encourages ethnographers to be more transparent with one another and with readers about the ways the ideals are unattainable and even undesirable. Aim for precision, for example, but be franker about the limits to the friendship you seem to offer those you study. Precision is key to trustworthy findings, while the guise of friendliness may do more to protect the researcher from difficult feelings than it protects study participants or advances sociological understanding.

Practical difficulties also arise in covert observation. How will researchers explain their presence in the setting? How can they move through it and explore the questions that interest them? How will they take notes without revealing their research aims? Even as the overt role is preferred, the "overt versus covert" distinction varies from context to context—often within the same research project. Although ethnographers may seek access through an overt route, many of the people with whom they come into contact may be unaware of their status as researchers.

Tactics and Resources when Gaining Access

Gaining access to settings—whether open or closed—requires strategic planning, hard work, and sometimes luck. Researchers have developed a range of tactics for gaining access to sites that will allow them to explore their interests and questions:

- *Use friends, contacts, and colleagues to facilitate access.* Eventually researchers may need to speak with an organization or group leader, and that person is likely to be a stranger. An introduction from someone who knows the researcher well can help the leader—and the researcher—feel more comfortable.
- *If possible, someone in the setting can vouch for the researcher and the value of the research.* Such people are considered "**sponsors**." If a sponsor at a lower level of the hierarchy

---

sponsor A person in the research site with power and authority who supports and helps makes a study possible.

grants permission, the researcher may still need clearance from leaders, managers, or executives. People who must grant a researcher access to a setting or group are sometimes called "**gatekeepers**."

- *Offer something in return.* The offerings can be mundane, even if they're also helpful. In a school-based ethnography, a researcher might offer to lead an after-school tutoring hour for students. If observing a sports team, the researcher could offer to help carry equipment to and from practice. Offerings can also be more formal, like a written report or presentation on the research findings to a gathering of interested group members. No matter what is offered, researchers should consider how that commitment might shift their relationship to the group or organization. Will students think of them as a teacher and be less likely to speak frankly? Will carrying equipment make it difficult to hang out with team members before and after practice?

- *Provide a clear explanation of the study aims and methods.* Participant observers should prepare and practice this explanation—in written and spoken form—before seeking access. Explanations should feature language that people who are not familiar with social research can understand. A meeting can provide an opportunity to address people's concerns and explain what will happen in the course of the ethnography.

- *Be prepared to negotiate.* Participants may want something in return for their participation, and they may want to set limits to the researcher's access. Participant observers may need to make some compromises even as they gain access.

- *Be frank about the amount of people's time and other resources the study will likely require.* Resources include insights, space, and time. Time is an especially important issue for organizations, non-profit groups, and individuals. Frankness from the beginning will prevent participants from resenting the researcher's presence and the study as the participant observation unfolds.

Ultimately, relationships are key to access. Sometimes introductions facilitate those relationships.

Other times, hanging out is the path to building the necessary connections. Anthropologist Clifford Geertz coined the term "deep hanging out" in 1998 to describe the ethnographic practice of immersing oneself in a setting, spending extended time with members of the group being studied, and participating in the formal and informal life of the setting. According to Geertz, deep hanging out promises to yield a deeper understanding of a setting as the researcher becomes familiar to others, gains their trust, and has access to what might otherwise be guarded information.

It may be tempting to abandon a setting if access—let alone deep hanging out—seems unlikely. However, perseverance often pays off. Robin Leidner (1993) was determined to study McDonald's as part of her ethnographic research on the routinization of service work. She explains,

> The company was a pioneer and exemplar of routinized interaction, and since it was locally based, it seemed like the perfect place to start. McDonald's had other ideas, however, and only after tenacious pestering and persuasion did I overcome corporate employees' polite demurrals, couched in terms of protecting proprietary information and the company's image. (1993, 234–235)

This kind of determination is necessary whenever the target is a specific organization or group (for example, a particular religious sect or social movement). Rejection can mean having to shift one's focus or even finding a completely different research topic.

But blocked access does not have to mean the end of a study. For many settings and groups, there are multiple paths to access. Similarly, for many research questions, several potential cases will be suitable.

Maintaining Access

Continued access is not guaranteed after a researcher makes initial contact and gains entrée to the group. Maintaining access is an ongoing activity

---

gatekeeper A person with the authority, power, and status to grant researchers access to participants and settings.

any time the goal is immersion in a social setting and experience.

In her ethnographic study of class identity among Mexican-American and White girls in California's Central Valley, Julie Bettie (2014) dressed in ways that distanced her from schoolteachers and administrators—an important distance for a thirty-one-year-old woman trying to gain the trust of high-school girls. Though Bettie had official access to the school, she also had to maintain everyday access to multiple groups of girls—preps, working-class students, Mexican-American girls, White girls—who had conflicting senses of style and self-presentation. Bettie "didn't try to adjust to each group [she] spent time with, but rather wore a generic 'costume' that was virtually the same every day" (2014, 20). This generic costume allowed her to move between groups, forging relationships with girls across the racial and economic spectrums that interested her.

The mundane details of self-presentation can help deflect questions about the researcher's presence and intentions in the setting. If the people being studied have concerns about the researcher, they may appear to go along with the research but in fact sabotage it, engage in deception, provide misinformation,

or not allow access to "back regions" of the setting (Goffman 1959). Ethnographers have identified several ways to maintain ongoing access to settings, whether open or closed:

- *Play up credentials.* Participant observers can talk about past work, personal experience, and knowledge of the group. By sharing empathetic understanding of group members' problems, ethnographers can signal their trustworthiness.
- *Don't give people reasons to dislike you.* Be overtly non-judgmental when witnessing or listening to accounts of informal activities or the organization's workings. Participant observers should also ensure that any information they receive doesn't get back to others, whether bosses or peers.
- *Play a meaningful role in the setting.* This may involve adopting a particular demeanor and style of dress (what researchers sometimes call "constructing a front"), helping out occasionally, or offering advice and input.
- *Be prepared for tests of competence and credibility.* When doing research on gang members in a poor community, Ruth Horowitz was frequently told "confidential" stories. Many of the stories turned out to be fictional; they were actually tests to see if she could keep a secret (Gerson and Horowitz 2002). These tests may arise without warning and without intention—school-based researchers may find their loyalties tested when teachers decide mid-year to go on strike.

In her ethnographic research among girls at a California high school, Julie Bettie, then in her early 30s, had to dress in a way that would distance her from teachers and administrators. As a researcher, how would you present yourself in order to gain the trust of high school students?

Members of hierarchical organizations commonly believe that researchers have been put in place to check up on them. Group members may also worry that

BOX 10.2 Building Relationships with Informants

Ethnographers rely heavily on their interactions, conversations, and relationships with study participants. This is especially true of those who develop an understanding of the research and are able to identify situations, events, or people likely to be helpful to the investigation (commonly referred to as **"key informants"**). William Foote Whyte's (1955) *Street Corner Society* provides a classic example. Whyte lived for three years among Italian immigrants on Boston's North End in an attempt to learn about social class and social structure, including the differences between what Whyte called "corner boys," whose lives revolved around street culture on the North End, and "college boys," who pursued higher education and upward mobility beyond their neighborhood.

Though Whyte's book did not receive much attention at the time of its original publication, *Street Corner Society* has gone on to be a classic in ethnographic research and, in particular, as an example of the relationship building at the center of much successful participant observation. Here Whyte quotes Doc, his key informant:

> You tell me what you want to see, and we'll arrange it. When you want some information, I'll ask for it, and you listen. When you want to find out their philosophy of life, I'll start an argument and get it for you. If there's something else you want to get, I'll stage an act for you. (Whyte 1955, 292)

Doc was also helpful in warning Whyte that he was asking too many questions, telling him to "go easy on that 'who,' 'what,' 'why,' 'when,' 'where' stuff" (1955, 303).

Key informants can provide support that eases the challenges of fieldwork. However, undue reliance on them can lead researchers to see social reality through their eyes only. Remember that the ethnographer's aim is usually to understand the setting or group *as a whole*.

In addition, participant observers usually encounter other people who will act as informants even if their accounts or perspectives have not been solicited and their contribution doesn't rise to that of a key informant. Some researchers prefer unsolicited information because of its spontaneity and naturalism. Often, study participants develop a sense of the events or encounters that the ethnographer will want to see. During his research on soccer hooligans, Gary Armstrong (1993) sometimes got tips from a group of Sheffield United fans who called themselves "Blades":

> I often travelled on the same coach as Ray [an informant]; he would then sit with me at matches and in pubs ...giving me background information. Sometimes he would start conversations with Blades about incidents which he knew I wanted to know about and afterwards would ask "Did you get all that down then?" ...There was never one particular informant; rather, there were many Blades. (Armstrong 1993, 24–25)

Unsolicited offers of information are attractive to ethnographers because of their apparent spontaneity. In their classic study of medical school culture, Howard Becker et al. (1961) felt they learned more about everyday experiences of medical school from comments students offered without prompting. However, as Martyn Hammersley and Paul Atkinson (1995, 130–131) observed, it's important to recognize that such offers may occasionally be staged for the participant observer's benefit.

Solicited accounts can be obtained in two ways: by interviewing (see Chapter 9) or by casual questioning during conversations (though in ethnographic research the boundary between an interview and a conversation is by no means clear). When the researcher needs specific information on an issue that does not lend itself to direct observation or that is not cropping up during "natural" conversations, solicited accounts are likely the only way forward.

---

key informant A person who shares expertise, knowledge, and authority with an ethnographer and, in doing so, is integral to the study's success; often the only one of their kind in the study.

what they say or do may get back to colleagues or to administrative agencies. For example, when Karen Sharpe 1998, 366) began research in a red-light area, she was thought to be "anything from a social worker to a newspaper reporter with hidden cameras and microphones." John Van Maanen (1991a) noted that when conducting ethnographic research among police officers, it's not unusual to observe activities that reflect badly on the police and may even be illegal. In such situations, the researcher may struggle with multiple responses: Should I establish credibility with the people I'm studying, practice discretion, and maintain access to this setting? Or am I becoming complicit with police behaviors that I find objectionable and that hurt others? A clear understanding of one's research aims and social convictions—and the relationship between the two—will help researchers decide the lengths to which they will go to secure and maintain access.

Time in the Field

As stated earlier, an ideal in ethnographic research is immersion—becoming integrated into the setting and people's lives. For three years, Ranita Ray (2018) spent five to seven days a week with socioeconomically disadvantaged Black and Latina young women in the Northeastern United States. She met their families and traveled with them to visit family members out of town; she drove them to and from work; and hung out with them, their friends, and their romantic/sexual partners after school, in the evenings, during holidays, and on weekends. As Ray explains, "I aimed to situate myself in their lives as intensely as possible. Although the youth initially identified me as a researcher, over time I became more of a friend" (2018, 5).

Such intensive data collection has significant benefits. Ray was able to "gather unanticipated insights, discoveries, and complexities" (2018, 5) about the lives of young women whom researchers and policy makers often think they already understand. Her immersive experience meant that the women's lives—not the existing research on young women, poverty, gender, sexuality, and race—filled her thinking. However, the data collection required a great deal of time and emotional energy from Ray and the participants. When imagining the scale of an ethnographic project, researchers must consider the time, energy, and other resources that, first, are available to them and, second, are required to do their topic justice.

Balancing Participation and Observation

Ongoing access to a field setting is related to the roles participant observers adopt in that setting. Often the various roles in fieldwork are arrayed along a continuum from complete involvement to complete detachment (see Figure 10.1).

Let's take a closer look at each role:

- *Complete participant*: A functioning member of a social setting whose research aims are unknown to members—in other words, a covert observer. Complete participants engage in regular interaction with people and take part in the daily life of a setting; while in the setting, they never reveal their aims or practices as researchers. In private, after they leave the field setting, they assume the researcher's role and take notes.
- *Participant-as-observer*: Like the complete participant, participants-as-observers are members of the settings they study, but they have revealed their researcher status. In her study of youth social movement organizations in Oakland, California, Andreana Clay (2012) adopted this role, working with young people and staff as they led workshops and challenged racism and other injustices in their communities. Their

FIGURE 10.1 Classification of participant observer roles

relationships were often casual, verging on friendship and mentorship. The members of the activist organizations worked, talked, and hung out with Clay, even as they also understood that she was studying them.

- *Observer-as-participant*: The researcher is mainly an interviewer and observer and participates only marginally in the group's activities. Minimal participation may be appropriate when studying potentially dangerous or politically charged settings or issues. For example, legal and safety restrictions may mean researchers have few opportunities for genuine participation in police operations.

- *Complete observer*: A complete observer remains at a distance and does not participate in the social setting under study. As a result, there may be less risk of people behaving unnaturally because they know they are being observed. However, most writers do not include this role as a form of ethnography because it does not involve immersion. The potential for understanding is greatly reduced because the researcher does not ask questions or try to empathize with the people being studied. This possibility is also difficult to achieve, since even the researcher's presence could be considered a form of participation. Because in-person observation can alter participants' behavior, Hospodsky et al. (2014) relied on video surveillance to record hand hygiene among students in a Kenyan primary school. Researchers can also take on the role of complete observer through a fully observational study of online life—for example, reading blogs, following Instagram accounts, or tracking engagement with Twitter and TikTok feeds.

Participant observers may strive to adopt a single role along this spectrum. However, in the course of a single ethnographic project, it's more likely that they will assume the full gamut at different times and for different purposes. For example, ethnographers may aim to approach the setting as observers-as-participants but find that members of the setting want more from them and require them to act more like participants-as-observers. Even if it were possible, it is probably undesirable to adhere to a single role over the entire course of a project (Gans 1968), as such an approach would limit the ethnographer's flexibility in handling situations and people.

Each approach has advantages and disadvantages. Recall Table 10.1 on the complete participant, or covert observer, role. The participant-as-observer role offers an opportunity to get close to people and to gain insight into their lives; however, researchers may over-identify with setting members. A strong sense of allegiance with setting members may make it difficult for ethnographers to think critically about the issues they study. The observer-as-participant role carries the risk of creating or maintaining distance between the ethnographer and people in the settings they study. Distance can get in the way of understanding the social setting and its people sufficiently and thus encourage incorrect or insensitive inferences. The risks brought by distance are even greater for the complete observer.

Active or Passive?

How active or passive should the ethnographer be? In most studies—even when the researcher is mainly an observer—involvement in the group's activities will be unavoidable from time to time. For example, Gary Fine (1996) carried out his research on the work of restaurant chefs largely through semi-structured qualitative interviews. Even in the midst of this more passive participation, Fine sometimes found himself in the kitchen washing dishes to help out during busy periods.

Sometimes participant observers feel great pressure to become actively involved in the groups they study. A failure to participate might suggest a lack of commitment and lead to a loss of credibility in the eyes of the people studied. This risk may be especially acute when studying a group that requires loyalty—activist groups, groups engaged in illegal or dangerous activity, or groups that understand themselves to be at odds with mainstream norms and institutions. Victor Rios found this to be the case while he conducted fieldwork for his study of crime and policing in the lives of Black and Latino boys and young men (2011). Rios grew up in the

BOX 10.3 Online Ethnography

Social media and other online spaces are primary locations for participating in social networks, asserting and exploring identities, and acquiring information about the world. Ronald Hallett and Kristen Barber (2014) argue that if research is going to explore the full complexity of people's lives, ethnographers must study online spaces.

Hallett and Barber ventured into cyberspace after in-person methods proved unworkable in their study of an organization for undocumented college students in California. Hallett began by researching the life history of a particular student but found it difficult to keep in touch with him. The student didn't have a phone, and email messages often went unanswered. Hallett soon learned that the most dependable means of communication was Facebook, which the student checked many times a day. Facebook posts and comments were also an invaluable source of ethnographic information about the organization—for example, how it established a sense of community and how its

How do you think you might go about conducting an online ethnography of skater culture?

members viewed the plight of undocumented students. Hallett notes: "I had considered asking participants to journal about how they spent time and perceived the educational process. I soon realized that students were already 'journaling' on their Facebook pages, and these posts were more natural than I may have received if they had used paper and pencil to write at my request" (2014, 316). Online ethnography, like ethnography in "real life," emphasizes how people interact with each other, express themselves, and live their lives.

same community and shared many experiences with the people he studied, but when he spent time in the setting as a researcher—with a researcher's priorities and questions—some of the boys suspected he was a snitch (Fenstermaker and Jones 2011). Participating as a researcher meant he was less actively involved in many activities than members were, which made the boys unsure about his allegiances.

Under such circumstances, researchers may feel that their only choice is to actively participate, even in illegal or dangerous behavior. However, many writers counsel against active participation in such activities. Both Armstrong (1993) and Giulianotti (1995) refused to fight while doing their research into soccer hooliganism. Giulianotti wrote: "My own rules are that I will not get involved in fighting or become a go-between for the two gangs in organizing fights" (1995, 10). Such personal rules would be difficult to follow if conducting covert research on people involved in crime or dangerous actions: if the people being studied do not know the researcher is a researcher, how would they understand and react to the decision not to actively participate in group activities?

Field Notes

Because of the frailties of human memory, ethnographers must record their observations. Written **field notes** are usually the primary source of data from participant observation: they provide a sustained and reflective account of the researcher's time in the setting, and they form the basis of the analysis. Field notes include detailed summaries of events and behavior, as well as the researcher's experiences of and initial analytical reflections on them. In particular, notes should include descriptions of

- *the setting*—how it looks, sounds, smells, and feels;
- *people in the setting*—central figures and those on the periphery;
- *interactions*—those between people in the setting and those involving the researcher; and
- *methodological problems and decisions*—for example, efforts to maintain access, responses from study participants to the researcher's presence, and answers to questions about the research process.

Some general principles guide any efforts to record the key dimensions of whatever is observed or heard:

- Record notes, however brief, as soon as possible after seeing or hearing something interesting.
- Write up full field notes at the end of the day or, at the latest, within twenty-four hours.
- Include details such as location, date, time of day, people present or notably absent, people involved in a particular exchange or event, what prompted the exchange or event, and immediate implications of the exchange or event.

- Ensure notes are vivid, clear, and complete. If in doubt, write it down.

It's best to take notes as soon as something significant happens and before other observations, ideas, and distractions fill your memory. However, in many settings, wandering around with a notebook and continually scribbling in it can make the people being observed feel self-conscious. While it wouldn't be conspicuous to jot notes while observing university classrooms, that same behavior would set a researcher apart at a school concert or during an after-school support group meeting. In order to respect the setting and maintain access, researchers often take small amounts of time away from the group to write down their observations. They might, for example, duck into a restroom, turn down a hallway, or stand off to the corner of a room after a key incident or exchange unfolds in order to jot notes on a slip of paper or into their smartphone. These jotted notes will likely contain only key words that will help them remember and recount the event later when they write field notes.

Strategies for taking field notes will depend in part on, first, the stage of the research process and, second, the guiding research questions. During the earliest days in a setting, participant observers record as much as possible, getting to know the people, norms, and patterns. With more time in the field, research questions usually become more focused and, accordingly, observations and field notes become oriented to those questions. However, it's important to maintain an open mind throughout in order to maintain a strength of qualitative research—its flexibility with respect to the themes explored.

Armstrong (1993, 12) wrote that his research on soccer hooliganism "began without a focus" and he thus "decided to record everything." A typical Saturday would mean 30 pages of handwritten notes. Such open-endedness usually cannot last long, because trying to record the details of absolutely everything

---

field notes Detailed notes that researchers take in the field, describing events, conversations, and behavior and forming the primary source of data from participant observation.

is so tiring. Eventually the ethnographer begins to narrow the focus of the research.

For most researchers, the equipment needed for recording observations consists mainly of a notepad and pen. Some prefer to type notes into their smartphones, a practice that can be particularly unobtrusive in settings where texting is common. A digital recorder may be useful, but its presence could make study participants feel uneasy, and transcription will take time. Photography can be an additional source of data, and pictures help to stir the ethnographer's memory. However, in some kinds of research (especially involving crime and deviance) photography may not be feasible. The researchers' aims should always be to write field notes that are as detailed as possible for later analysis, and to record observations in a manner that allows researchers to interact with others while ensuring people in their settings feel comfortable and respected.

Types of Field Notes

Researchers collect different types of field notes when conducting participant observation. The following classification of field notes is based on categories suggested by John Lofland and Lyn Lofland (1995) and Roger Sanjek (1990):

- *Mental notes*: particularly useful when it is inappropriate to be seen taking written notes; however, they should be put into writing at the earliest opportunity.
- *Jotted notes*: brief notes to jog the memory about events. Lofland and Lofland (1995, 90) described them as "little phrases, quotes, key words, and the like." Such notes need to be taken inconspicuously, preferably out of sight, then written up more fully later.
- *Full field notes*: the main data source in ethnographic research. Full notes should be written as soon as possible, usually at the end of the day. Provide as much detail as possible about events, people, and conversations. A particular comment from a subject or an account of an event may not seem important at the time, but its significance may become apparent later on, once the researcher has developed an interpretive structure. Without good notes, valuable data may be lost. Write down, in brackets, initial ideas about your interpretations, impressions, and feelings.

The Ethnographer's Place in Field Notes

Field notes are at their liveliest when written in the first person and in the present tense, as though the scene and interactions were unfolding across the pages. Customarily, the ethnographer's presence is evident in field notes, as researchers record their experiences as participants and observers—what they experienced as well as what they witnessed in the setting.

Field notes are written primarily for the researcher's own use—unlike the written paper, article, or book that will eventually be produced for others' consumption. These essentially private documents are an opportunity to

Ethnographic research relies on detailed accounts of events and conversations witnessed in the field. What are the challenges of taking notes in the field?

BOX 10.4 Emotions in the Field and in Field Notes

Conventional understandings of research suggest that ethnographers' reflections, opinions, and feelings should be kept separate from their observations in order to prevent distorting data and biasing study results. Kleinman and Copp (1993) challenge this view when they argue that participant observers cannot immerse themselves in a setting without also bringing their perspectives, histories, and feelings to the setting. The researcher's experience of the setting is a source of insight into the setting. As such, even as it seems to violate an expectation that researchers remain objective, ethnographers do

well to allow themselves to document and explore their own feelings in their field notes and then to subject those feelings to analysis: What assumptions underlie those reactions? What do those feelings tell researchers about themselves? About their role in the setting? About other people's roles and feelings in the setting? About fieldwork?

Researchers' feelings about the settings and people they study reflect, in part, the social conditions they are studying. Taking those feelings seriously—that is, recording and analyzing them—is another route to ethnographic insight.

record not only a faithful account of what the researcher observed in the setting but also initial thoughts about what the observations might mean, analytical questions to pursue in later visits to the setting, and methodological decisions and challenges that emerge during participant observation (see Box 10.4).

These analytical threads within field notes do not take the place of concerted qualitative data analysis. This analysis begins immediately; as Sherryl Kleinman and Martha Copp assert, it is "one of the central 'oughts' of qualitative research: to simultaneously collect data and analyze it" (1993, 18). In practice, this means that, while still conducting participant observation, researchers write sustained analytic memos or notes in which they record initial thoughts on the data and begin to develop the concepts, interpretations, and theories that make sense of what they are observing. (We will address memos, notes, and other analytic strategies in further detail in Chapter 13.)

Innovations in Ethnographic Research

Within the broader school of participant observation and ethnography, researchers have proposed a number of innovative methods that build on the strengths of ethnography and identify new sources

of data, reposition the researcher in the field, and address troubling ethnical concerns. We outline some of these innovations in the following sections.

Visual Ethnography

Visual media offer particular insight into people's lives. Some researchers analyze the visual texts that ordinarily fill those lives—for example, music videos, advertisements, and clothing. We will address these qualitative studies of visual texts in Chapter 11. Here we explore visual ethnography: studies in which researchers ask participants to produce visual texts that document their experiences. These visual texts become qualitative data much like interview transcripts or field notes.

Visual ethnographers identify and "read" images; their focus is not the words, interactions, and physical spaces that ethnographers usually work with. At the same time, however, visual ethnographers remain sensitive to concerns that are important to all ethnographic studies. These include contexts in which the images were generated; the potential for multiple meanings among researchers, study participants, and others; and the possibility that the researcher has influenced the image and its presentation. Such ethical issues may not be as pronounced when working with other kinds of data. Visual ethnographers

Methods in Motion | **Visual Media in Ethnography**

Throughout her career, Wendy Luttrell has worked with young people to create visual media that explore their experiences of social inequality, difference, and education. In one study (Luttrell 2003), girls in a school for pregnant teens created collages illustrating their experiences of their bodies, youth, and parenting. In another study (Luttrell 2010), immigrant students took photographs documenting their understanding of diversity in their schools and the relationship between their experience of family and schooling. Luttrell found that the immigrants living in the greatest relative safety and stability were most likely to participate in the photo project. Those who participated went to great lengths to ensure adults read their photos respectfully and accurately, suggesting they could not trust adults to do so without their intervention. The same social inequalities that interested Luttrell as subjects to study went on to shape her experience of gathering data to analyze.

must take special care to protect privacy, anonymity, and confidentiality if images depict the faces, bodies, or homes of participants or other people.

Institutional Ethnography

Sociologist Dorothy Smith has developed an approach called institutional ethnography (2005) that explores how institutional discourses (typically texts found in the workplace) relate to people's everyday experiences with institutions, and how examining institutional relationships may reveal larger systems of social control and power in a society (Devault 2006). Institutional relationships are analyzed in detail, with the aim of discovering how they affect the personal experiences of the individuals involved.

The approach can be explicitly change-oriented in that previously unrecognized opportunities to transform institutions may come to light as the research runs its course, and the researcher may even collaborate with the people studied in an effort to create institutional relationships that serve them better.

Autoethnography

The principle and practice of reflexivity is at the core of autoethnography. Carolyn Ellis, a leader in articulating and practicing this method, describes it as "research, writing, story, and method that connect the autobiographical and personal to the cultural, social, and political" (2004: xix). The method challenges the distinction between the researcher and the researched and instead insists that the ethnographer's experience of the world is a window into the organization and implications of that world. Autoethnographic data focus on the researcher's feelings, thoughts, interactions, and observations in an effort to understand broader social conditions and concerns.

Just as autoethnographers reject an ideal of research as neutral and objective, so too do they pursue unconventional modes of disseminating their findings. They produce plays, write novels and poetry, and publish academic articles that center their own experiences. Tony E. Adams, Stacy Holman Jones, and Carolyn Ellis (2015) suggest criteria for assessing autoethnographic work across these genres: authors should place high value on the insights to be gained from personal experience, offer a responsible and compelling narrative, enact responsible relationships when conducting research and sharing results, and make a meaningful contribution to knowledge.

Feminist Ethnography

For many researchers, ethnography is integral to feminist social research and social change because it documents people's lives and activities, understands women from their perspective, and understands study participants in context. Beverley Skeggs (2001, 430) observed that many feminist researchers have considered ethnography's "emphasis on experiences and the words, voice and lives of the participants" well suited to the goals of feminism.

However, in the widely cited article "Can There Be a Feminist Ethnography?" Judith Stacey (1988) challenged the widespread view that ethnography represents a particularly feminist research method. With its emphasis on empathetic understandings and subjective experience, *all* ethnography grounds research in people's daily lives: ethnographers build relationships with their study participants in hopes of learning intimate details about their lives. Ultimately, according to Stacey, these details become data for the ethnographer.

In an effort not to exploit participants, feminist ethnographers may strive to treat the researcher–researched relationship as a reciprocal process in which the researcher can provide something in return for information. However, Stacey also notes that the connection between the researcher and the researched may be real, but it can also feel exploitative:

> No matter how welcome—even enjoyable—the fieldworker's presence may appear to "natives," fieldwork represents an intrusion and intervention into a system of relationships, a system of relationships that the researcher is far freer to leave. (1988, 23)

Skeggs's (1994, 1997) ethnographic research on young women represents an attempt to create a non-exploitative relationship with the people being studied. Over the course of 12 years, Skeggs (1997) conducted an ethnographic study of 83 working-class White women, beginning with their enrollment in a college "caring" course and continuing as they navigated the labor market, further education, and family life. The elements of a distinctively feminist ethnography are evident in her commitment to documenting women's lives and allowing their experiences to come through, while also pointing to the significance of context. Skeggs notes the following:

- "This ethnography was politically motivated to provide space for the articulations and experiences of the marginalized" (1997, 23).
- The "study was concerned to show how young women's experience of structure (their class and gender positioning) and institutions (education and the media) frame and inform their responses and how this process informs constructions of their own subjectivity" (1994, 74).

Skeggs felt that her relationship with the women was not exploitative. For example, she wrote that the research enhanced the women's "sense of self-worth," giving them "the opportunity to be valued,

knowledgeable, and interesting." She also claimed she was able to "provide a mouthpiece against injustices" and listen "to disclosures of violence, child abuse, and sexual harassment" (1994, 81). She maintained,

> The young women were not prepared to be exploited; just as they were able to resist most things which did not promise economic or cultural reward, they were able to resist me.... They enjoyed the research. It provided resources for developing their sense of self-worth. More importantly, the feminism of the research ... provided a framework which they use to explain that their individual problems are part of a wider structure and not their personal fault. (1994, 88)

According to Skeggs, the feminist researcher offers help or advice to her study participants and may give a public airing to normally marginalized voices. In some cases, the feminist ethnographer may even work directly with study participants in an effort to help them improve their lives.

Exiting the Field Well

As Desmond writes, "The hardest feat for any fieldworker is not getting in; it's leaving" (2016, 336). Knowing when to stop participant observation is not an easy or straightforward matter. Many researchers build close relationships with the people they study, and ending a study may feel like walking away from friends. Even those who have not formed friendships with participants may wonder if it's time to leave the setting: Have they gathered enough data? Are they taking more than they should from the setting? Do they know enough? How can they repay the group members for what they have contributed to the study?

Often, the decision to end data collection reflects personal considerations. Inexperienced researchers may need more time in the field to achieve their research goals than experienced researchers do. The rhythms of ethnographers' career or personal life—the end of a sabbatical leave or the need to submit a manuscript by a certain date—may necessitate withdrawal from the field. In addition, ethnographic research can be highly stressful. Ethnographers may feel that they have had enough of participant observation that places them in tense situations (as in research on interpersonal conflict, social inequalities, or systemic violence). The emotional demands of maintaining the researcher's marginal and observant position in social settings and the need to maintain a front may also wear thin.

Ultimately, the decision to end participant observation is one of sampling, which we discussed in Chapter 4. Ideally, fieldwork will come to a close when the researcher has reasonable answers to the formulated research questions. The participant observer may even feel a strong sense of déjà vu towards the end of data collection as new observations reiterate what has already been discovered. In the language of grounded theory, all the researcher's categories may become thoroughly saturated.

Whatever the reason for bringing ethnographic research to a close, disengagement has to be managed—promises must be kept. For example, was a report promised as a condition of entry? Ending participant observation also means that ethnographers must provide honest and satisfying explanations for their departure. Participants may know that the researcher is not a permanent presence in their social setting, but over a long period of time they can forget; therefore, farewells may have to be arranged. It's essential to remember the ethnographer's ethical commitments—for example, to ensuring that persons and settings are kept anonymous and to providing a fair, even if critical, account of the setting and people observed. Some ethnographers find that their ethical obligations and their newly forged relationships with participants mean that they have long-term commitments to the people and settings they study. They may finish collecting data but not truly exit the setting.

Comparing Ethnography and Qualitative Interviewing

Qualitative interviewing without immersion in a social setting (discussed in Chapter 9) and ethnography are probably the two most prominent methods of data collection in qualitative research, and each offers different understandings about the social worlds they study.

Ethnography
Insight into Social Reality

As we noted in Chapter 5, seeing through others' eyes is one of the main purposes of qualitative research. Ethnographers are especially well placed to gain insight into social reality in this way, because of their prolonged immersion in particular social settings. They are not only in much closer contact with people for a longer period of time than interviewers are, but they also participate in many of the same kinds of activity as the people they are studying. Research that relies on interviewing alone entails more fleeting contacts, although qualitative interviews can last many hours and re-interviewing is not unusual.

Knowledge of the Local Language

Ethnographers are in a unique position to understand group culture by becoming familiar with the community's "argot": its informal slang and special uses of words. Learning that informal language takes prolonged observation.

Things Taken for Granted

Because interviews rely primarily on the interviewees' accounts of their world, elements that the interviewees take for granted may not be mentioned. For example, sex workers may never mention their relationship with neighborhood business owners because they are so commonplace, and an interviewer may never think to ask about it. By contrast, an ethnographer immersed in the street scene will probably observe that sex workers have to deal with hostile business owners on a regular basis—so much so that it helps to define their daily lives.

Deviant and Hidden Activities

Many people are reluctant to talk about certain activities in one-on-one interviews: drug-taking, violence, shoplifting, illegal commerce, self-harm, and so on. For that reason, much of what is known about subcultures that engage in deviance or commit crime has been gleaned from ethnography. Ethnographers have also uncovered information about workplace resistance practices (such as industrial sabotage) and groups that support deviant ideologies (such as White supremacists). Ethnographers are better positioned than interviewers to infiltrate the social worlds of people who are wary of talking to outsiders.

Sensitivity to Context and Flexibility

Extensive contact with a social setting allows the ethnographer to map the context of people's behavior. Interacting with people in a variety of different situations makes it possible to connect behavior and context. In an interview, researchers typically learn about how people understand and explain their behavior, but less about what they actually do.

Naturalistic Emphasis

Ethnography can be more naturalistic because the researcher confronts members of a social setting in their natural environments. Even at its most informal, interviewing is less naturalistic and tends to interrupt the normal flow of events.

Qualitative Interviewing

Issues Resistant to Observation

Many issues are simply not open to observation, so asking people about them may be the only way to get information. Consider intimate partner violence. It would not be feasible for a researcher to be in other people's homes, waiting for violence to unfold.

Reconstruction of Events and Future Plans

In-depth reconstruction of past events and plans for future behavior is not possible through observation alone. Qualitative research entails reconstruction of events when interviewees are asked to think about how a series of previous activities might have created a current situation. Most qualitative studies ask about events that occurred before the study began; some call this "retrospective interviewing."

Less Intrusive in People's Lives

Interviews in qualitative research can last a long time—many hours, even—and re-interviewing is common. Nevertheless, the impact of undergoing an interview is typically less than the impact of having to deal with an ethnographer on a regular basis. Ethnography can be especially intrusive, for example, in

Imagine you wanted to research homelessness in your community. Weigh the advantages of ethnography versus qualitative interviewing. What different aspects of homelessness would you be able to learn about using each of these methods?

organizational settings where the researchers may disrupt the rhythms of the workday.

Longitudinal Research

In most cases, interviewing can be carried out within a longitudinal research design somewhat more easily than ethnography can because repeat interviews are typically easier to organize than repeat visits to the research settings. Ethnography can be used for longitudinal studies, but ethnographers usually can't spend weeks, months, and years away from their normal lives, which limits the extent to which an ethnographic study can be longitudinal. When this research is conducted on an episodic basis or in a setting to which researchers have access as part of their normal lives, however, a longer time period may be feasible. In Patricia and Peter Adler's (1998) study on children's friendships, the researchers engaged in 8 years of participant observation but observed mostly after-school activities in their children's community.

Breadth of Coverage

Interviewing may allow access to a wider variety of people and situations. In ethnographic work, the researcher is invariably limited to a fairly restricted range of people, places, and incidents. An ethnographer observing a large organization, for example, is unlikely to have extensive knowledge of operations outside the area under study.

Choosing between Ethnography and Interviews

When Howard Becker and Blanche Geer (1957, 28) proclaimed more than half a century ago that the "most complete form of the sociological datum . . . is the form in which the participant observer gathers it," Martin Trow (1957, 33) reprimanded them for making such a universal claim. He argued that "the problem under investigation properly dictates the methods of investigation." We share Trow's position. All research methods are appropriate for some issues and not for others.

Our discussion of ethnography versus qualitative interviews draws attention to some of the factors that researchers should consider when choosing a method. The points raised can also be used to evaluate existing research.

Key Points

Introduction: Why Participant Observation and Ethnography Are Not the Same

- Participant observation is a data collection method in which researchers observe and participate in the social settings, lives, and phenomena of interest to them.
- Ethnography is a social science approach in which, through participant observation and other data collection methods, researchers immerse themselves in the everyday lives of the people they are studying and observing.

Why Participant Observation?

- Participant observation is often a feasible method for gaining insight into the relationships, conditions, and institutions that constitute people's everyday lives.
- While the immediacy of participant observation may afford special insight, it also raises ethical questions and places special demands on the researcher.

Selecting and Navigating a Setting

- When choosing a site, researchers should consider what will be of interest to them and their audiences, as well as the feasibility of the study.
- Gaining and maintaining access depends on the researcher's personal histories with the groups and settings that interest them, their comfort in new social settings, and their capacity to play a meaningful and respectful role in the setting
- Gaining access often requires that researchers' entries be smoothed by "sponsors" and a "gatekeeper."

- Key informants develop an understanding of the research and are able to identify situations, events, or people likely to be helpful to the investigation.

Balancing Participation and Observation

- Roles in fieldwork are arrayed along a continuum from complete involvement to complete detachment.
- Ethnographers will likely adopt a variety of roles at different times and for different purposes in the course of a single project.

Field Notes

- Field notes include detailed summaries of events and behavior, the researcher's experiences of those events and behaviors, and the researcher's initial analytical reflections on them.

Innovations in Ethnographic Research

- Innovations in ethnographic research include visual ethnography, institutional ethnography, autoethnography, and feminist ethnography.

Exiting the Field Well

- Knowing when to end ethnographic research is often difficult, but it should be considered once sampling has been exhausted and when all of the researcher's categories are thoroughly saturated.
- When exiting the field, researchers should be sure to remember to keep promises, provide honest and satisfying explanations for their departure, and adhere to the ethical commitments of the study.

Comparing Ethnography and Qualitative Interviewing

- Both ethnography and qualitative interviewing allow researchers to understand different aspects of social life. The choice of method depends on the researcher's questions and aims.

Questions for Review

1. What are some distinguishing characteristics of an "ethnographer's sensibility"?
2. What are the promises and challenges of participant observation as a data collection method?
3. What are some primary considerations when choosing a setting for participant observation and ethnographic research?
4. What resources and personal assets can a researcher use to smooth the process of gaining access to a research site?
5. What are the relative advantages and disadvantages of open and closed research settings?
6. What are the relative advantages and disadvantages to overt and covert participant observation?
7. What is the role of key informants in ethnographic research?
8. What conditions influence participant observers' decisions to be active or passive in their research settings?
9. What information should field notes contain?
10. What are some principles and practices for writing detailed and useful field notes?
11. Where and how should the researcher appear in field notes?
12. How do visual ethnographers read images?
13. What are the research and social change aims of institutional ethnography?
14. What is the relationship between autoethnography and conventional methods of conducting and disseminating research?
15. What tensions characterize the debate over feminist ethnography?
16. When is it time to end participant observation?
17. What ethical, practical, and methodological concerns should a researcher consider when exiting the field?
18. What type of information can a researcher gather using qualitative interviewing compared to ethnography?
19. What types of topics are more appropriate to study using qualitative interviewing vs. ethnography?

Portfolio Exercise

Imagine that you are competing for a grant to conduct participant observation that will address your research question or topic. The field work might be the primary mode of data collection or a component of a study that relies primarily on other data collection methods. Write a 2- to 3-page proposal outlining how you will use participant observation in your study. Address the following questions:

a. What research question(s) will you explore through participant observation?

b. Will participant observation be a primary mode of data collection in your study? Why or why not?
c. Where or with what group will you conduct participant observation?
d. How do you plan to gain access?
e. What balance do you expect to strike between participation and observation?
f. At what point do you expect you will be able to conclude your research?

Interactive Activities

1. As a class, visit a safe, public, and highly trafficked space on campus (for example, a residence hall lobby, café, bookstore, gym, or library space) or online (for example, a message board, chat room,

or other virtual community). Conduct participant observation for twenty minutes, leaning toward the observer-as-participant model. If conducting participant observation on campus, half of the students jot notes on what they see; the other half jots notes on what they hear. If conducting participant observation online, half of the students jot notes on text; the other half jots notes on images and other non-textual information. Back in class, pair students into groups consisting of one person who relied on sound and one person who relied on sight and have them compare jottings. Their discussions should address the following, relying on their assigned senses or focuses.

a. What did you note about the physical setting?
b. What interactions between other people and between yourself and people in the setting did you note?
c. What people, interactions, sensations, or characteristics stood out in your jottings?
d. What difference do you see between the two jotted notes? To what extent do you attribute those differences to the senses or focuses you were assigned? How else might you explain those differences? For example, might you be perceived differently by others? Did you observe from different vantage points?

2. Select an online space where there is a flow of community interaction (for example, an Instagram hashtag, Facebook feed, dating app, or interactive message boards) and actively participate in or observe the group for twenty minutes. Through a combination of field notes and screenshots, record data that reveals common-sense assumptions of the group, or local meanings important to the conversation. In jottings, reflect on your experiences of conducting the research and participating and observing in the online setting. Then, in small groups, answer the following questions:

a. What community and online source of interaction did you observe? How did you gain access to this group?
b. What role did you take in the research? Were you covert or overt? Active or passive?
c. What were common topics on the thread?
d. What impression did you gain of the people who participate in this online setting? What questions do you have after observing/participating?
e. How does your positionality to the research topic and/or population affect your observations, credibility, and access?

Online Resources

- Teaching Online Participant Observation is an exercise that will give you practice conducting online participant observation.
  http://trails.asanet.org/Pages/Resource.aspx?Resourceid=13666

- You can find many examples of ethnographic studies in the academic journals Ethnography

and Journal of Contemporary Ethnography. You will probably have to log on to your institution's library server to gain access.
http://eth.sagepub.com
http://jce.sagepub.com

For more resources please visit
www.oup.com/he/bryman-reck-fields1e

11

How Do Researchers Study the Ways Meanings Are Communicated in Everyday Life?
Content Analysis

CHAPTER OVERVIEW

Content analysis involves examining printed, visual, aural, or virtual material—documents, images, and more. Content analysis examines what different forms of communication reveal about a society, a culture, or people's relationships. By formally categorizing the content of different kinds of communication, researchers can look for meaning in the patterns and trends content analysis reveals. Both qualitative and quantitative methods can be used in content analysis, and researchers will sometimes use both approaches together.

Reading this chapter will allow you to

- understand the kinds of information that researchers use content analysis to explore;

- identify the features of materials typically studied with content analysis;

- describe how researchers choose materials for content analysis;

- explain how quantitative and qualitative approaches are used in content analysis;

- outline the elements of coding and analyzing communication content; and

- recognize unique issues content analysis researchers must consider.

During their study group meeting, Martín tells his friends about the class lecture on media representation he just attended. He says, "My professor showed Gina Rodriguez's Golden Globes acceptance speech from a few years ago. She talked about what I've always felt—how hard it was growing up to not see any Latinxs on TV."

He shows them the clip, and Anthony asks, "What does she mean when she says that the award represents 'a culture that wants to see themselves as heroes'?"

"Well," Martín explains, "We're rarely the lead character. And she's speaking for all Latinxs because she has a platform to represent us."

Asha says, "I can relate. It would be nice if we Muslims were the heroes sometimes—and not just in the terrorist roles."

"It isn't fun always being the villain," Minh adds. "I wish the lesbian characters on TV wouldn't either be evil or get killed off!"

Julia agrees: "Visibility and positive representation is really important. My grandma is seriously still obsessed with *I Love Lucy* because it was the first time she'd seen an interracial relationship on TV! She always says she feels like people treated her and Grandpa with more respect because of it."

"I wonder how much this has all changed," Martín says. "Maybe we could figure out how a researcher would study all this."

Issues about media representation and its effects aren't only of interest to people like Martín and his friends, social researchers are also intrigued by this subject. How mainstream media represents people and social life, what story we tell in our social media posts, or how official documents communicate about major social issues and institutional processes are common topics researchers explore. This type of research is described as unobtrusive methods, and in these studies researchers analyze communication content to explore questions similar to the ones these friends had: what information is being conveyed, what does it tell us about social relations, and how might it affect people's ideas about themselves and others?

Introduction: Why Content Analysis Is an Unobtrusive Method of Research

In previous chapters, we've explored how social researchers use surveys, questionnaires, interviews, and observation to collect their data and learn about people's experiences. These sources of information are by no means the only ones available to a researcher. Sometimes researchers gather data using **unobtrusive measures** (Lee 2000). Researchers using unobtrusive methods conduct their social investigations without directly engaging with people in a research setting.

Eugene Webb et al. (1966 [2000]) coined the term "unobtrusive measures" to describe data collected without directly interacting with research participants. Webb and his colleagues believed important insights could be gleaned from observing people while not engaging with them (non-participant observation) and by examining such data as physical traces (how people and groups leave evidence about their lives in their environments—for instance, trash or graffiti) and documentary sources (like archival documents and information; Lee 2000).

There are two main types of unobtrusive research we discuss in this book:

1. analysis of existing data that others have already collected, such as government statistics (discussed in Chapter 12); and
2. content analysis, which examines communication in various documentary sources.

This chapter explores the last of these unobtrusive research methods: **content analysis.**

When conducting content analysis, researchers study forms of communication to see how they express information about fundamental social experiences and relationships and how communication content works to produce meanings about the world. The communication studied—the "content"—can come from any data source that can be "read" (including both written documents and visual materials such as photographs).

A key feature of content analysis is that the people who produced and were featured in the communication materials being studied did not know they were being or would be studied. This presents an advantage in that it removes **reactive effects**, a common threat to the **validity** of the data. A risk also arises: researchers must weigh the ethics of their data choices (following guidelines such as those outlined in Chapter 2), considering the possibility they might reveal someone's identity or otherwise subject them to harm when they use sources that were never intended for research. The sources of content analysis we examine in this chapter include personal and official documents, online communication, and print media sources.

Documents for Study

When selecting documents to study using content analysis, researchers must consider whether the documents are appropriate to choose as their data. John Scott (1990) asserted four criteria for assessing the quality of documents in unobtrusive research:

1. *Authenticity.* Is it a genuine, authentic, and original document?
2. *Credibility.* Are the contents of the document free from error and distortion?

---

unobtrusive measures Research methods that do not require interactions with participants and thus do not introduce reactivity.

---

content analysis The examination of texts, including both written and visual materials, with interest in how the material contributes to and reflects meaning and representation.

---

reactive effects (or **reactivity**) The impact on research when participants know that they are being studied, which may result in atypical or inauthentic behavior.

---

validity A research criterion concerned with the integrity of a study's conclusions.

Researchers must also be aware of the types of documents they are choosing and what information might be contained in them. For example, they should recognize the different forms of communication contained within personal documents, official texts, and mass media sources.

Personal Documents

Personal documents include items people gather across their lives, which make up the formal and informal, intentional and accidental record of their experiences, relationships, struggles, accomplishments, and more. They can be written materials, like diaries, letters, and autobiographies; they also include visual objects, such as photographs.

Diaries, Letters, and Autobiographies

Sometimes studied as part of a **life history** (or **biographical**) **method**, diaries and letters can be either primary sources of data or adjuncts to other sources, such as life story interviews.

What type of document is this? What form of communication might you hope to understand if you chose an advertisement like this as data? How would you go about assessing the quality and appropriateness of this document for a study about the tobacco industry or gender?

3. *Representativeness.* Is the document typical of what it is supposed to represent?
4. *Meaning.* Is the meaning of the document comprehensible?

Authenticity and accuracy are concerns with these personal documents. Is the purported author of the letter or diary the real author? How do we assess the document's accuracy? How can a researcher determine if existing documents produced by members of oppressed groups accurately represent a life or time period if those groups were

life history (or **biographical**) **method** A qualitative method that emphasizes people's inner experiences and their connections to larger societal events throughout the life course; the main sources of data are usually life history interviews and personal documents.

largely unable or unwilling to document their lives? Since literacy rates were low in the past, letters and diaries were largely the preserve of a small class of wealthy, literate people. Moreover, because boys were more likely to receive an education than girls were, women's voices tended to be underrepresented in these documents. Some researchers also argue that women were less likely than men to have had the self-confidence to write diaries. Therefore, such historical documents are likely to be biased in terms of their applicability to the society as a whole. A further problem is the selective survival of documents like letters: what proportion are damaged, lost, or thrown away? Are the personal documents of certain classes, races, or genders more likely to be preserved?

Finally, understanding the meaning of a document is often challenging. Some pages in a letter or diary may be missing or damaged, or the writer may have used abbreviations or codes that are difficult to decipher. As Scott (1990) observed, letter writers tend to leave much unsaid when they take it for granted that the addressees share the same values, assumptions, and information. He advised that researchers studying a document will craft *literal* understandings (based what the document technically says) and *interpretive* understandings (reflecting what it conveys based on the unique time and place in which it was produced). Estelle Freedman (1998), in her study of the relationship between Miriam Van Waters and Geraldine Thompson (Box 11.1), suggests that a definitive, factually accurate meaning is challenging to ascertain. Her work began with the question: Was Van Waters a lesbian? Over time, Freedman sought to understand the expressions and meanings of sexual identity circulating in Van Waters' historical context and had to caution herself against applying contemporary definitions of lesbian identity expression onto the documents.

Scott recommended a healthy skepticism regarding the sincerity with which writers report their feelings. Famous people who are aware that their letters or diaries will be of interest to others may be careful about how much of themselves they reveal in their writings. Similarly, adolescent diary-keepers are often aware that their parents could "accidentally" read what they write. What is *not* said can be of great importance. A particularly poignant illustration is Pamela H. Sugiman's (2004) suggestion that many Japanese-Canadian women interned during World War II decided not to write about their experiences in order to shield their children from such a painful episode in their family histories. Researchers must be conscious of possible differences between social reality and the *representation* of reality in documents. This distinction is of interest in content analysis studies, where researchers are curious to see how people craft stories about their lives.

Visual Objects

Photographs have the potential to reveal important information about social life and relationships, and Scott (1990) emphasizes the multiple ways photographs depict life. He explains that many family photos are records of ceremonial occasions such as graduations, bar mitzvahs, or quinceañeras or of recurring events such as reunions and holidays. He distinguishes three forms of the home photograph:

1. *idealization:* a formal portrait of a wedding party or a family in its finery;
2. *natural portrayal:* an informal snapshot capturing action as it happens (though there may be a staged component);
3. *demystification:* depicting the subject in an atypical—often embarrassing—situation.

Distinguishing among these types of representation will help researchers probe beneath the superficial appearance of images. As Scott explains:

> There is a great deal that photographs do not tell us about their world. Hirsch [1981, 42] argued, for example, that "The prim poses and solemn faces which we associate with Victorian photography conceal the reality of child labor, women factory workers, whose long hours often brought about the neglect of their infants, nannies sedating their charges with rum, and mistresses diverting middle class fathers" (Scott 1990, 195).

Photographs, then, must not be taken at face value when used as data, and the viewer must have

BOX 11.1 Using Historical Personal Documents: The Case of Miriam Van Waters

Estelle B. Freedman studied the historical personal documents of Miriam Van Waters (1887–1974), a prison superintendent and penal reformer of the early twentieth century. Van Waters favored education and community building over punishment, and her prison reform work garnered much support from like-minded philanthropists. One supporter was Geraldine Morgan Thompson, Van Waters' patron and romantic partner for many years. During the conservative backlash after World War

What dilemmas do researchers face when using historical personal documents as primary sources? How might these affect researchers' ability to uncover truths of marginalized people's lives through historical research?

II, Van Waters' methods and personal life came under fire. Conservative corrections officials depicted her as a subversive threat; accusations of lesbianism were one of their core charges. To protect herself, Van Waters burned most of the daily letters she had received from Thompson over the previous two decades. She wrote in her journal, "The burning of letters continues . . . One can have no personal life in this battle, so I have destroyed many letters over 22 years" (Freedman 1998, 181).

This diary entry both saddened and inspired Freedman, who wanted to understand the contours of Van Waters' sexual identity. Van Waters' private writing explained why Freedman could find so little evidence of the women's relationship. The entry suggested a lack of personal documents depicting LGBTQIA2S+ lives might itself have something to teach us, indicating that some people protected themselves from exposure by ensuring no evidence of their sexuality existed.

considerable knowledge of the social context in order to get its full meaning. Box 11.2 addresses context and underlying meanings in research using personal photographs. Further, a researcher's interpretations should not be accepted uncritically. The "prim poses and solemn faces" of Victorian portraits might well "conceal" a bleak and miserable reality, but could

they not also hide moments of human warmth, compassion, and fun?

Rasul A. Mowatt (2012) examined late nineteenth- and early twentieth-century photos and textual accounts depicting lynching of Black Americans to analyze the ways many White people treated these acts of racist violence as a recreational activity and

BOX 11.2 Photographs of the Magic Kingdom

Robert I. Sutton (1992) noted a paradox about visitors to Disney theme parks. The Magic Kingdom is supposed to be "the happiest place on Earth," yet it is clear that some people do not enjoy themselves. Time spent waiting in lines is a particularly common gripe (Bryman 1995). Nonetheless, because people expect their visit to be momentous, they take photos that support their assumption that the parks are happy places. When they return home, they "discard photographs that remind them of unpleasant experiences and

This family seems to be enjoying their vacation, but should we conclude that it was fun in every respect? Or that they were all having fun at the moment this picture was taken? How do researchers best approach the use of photographs as data, taking into account that they may not provide a complete record of an event or experience?

keep those that remind them of pleasant experiences" (Sutton 1992, 283). Positive feelings about the experience are a post-visit reconstruction, substantially aided by the saved photos. Thus, the photographs provide an incomplete, somewhat distorted record.

This situation has transformed with new technology, as people now take many more photographs of their lives and share them with more people. How common is it to see Instagram or Facebook photos of people having unpleasant experiences on their holidays? Do people delete

or discard digital photos as they did when photos were developed? In a study of web-based family photography, Luc Pauwels (2008) concluded that digital technology has made it easier for families to "construct fictions and fantasies" and to project their values and norms than was the case when paper-based family albums were more common. With social media, the purpose of photo-assisted reconstruction seems to be expanding: photos may be used not only to create happy memories but also to present a public image of oneself as a fun-loving, interesting person.

public spectacle. Mowatt explored the content of the images, the contexts in which they were produced, and the perspectives of those creating and sharing the images. He considered how the material depicted specific instances of racial violence yet represent the operations of the pervasive racism of the time; he wondered how this mentality and set of structural conditions still affects social life and racial violence.

Representativeness is a particular problem in photo analysis, according to Scott. Photos that survive the passage of time—in archives, for example—are unlikely to be representative for the simple reason that somebody once decided they should be preserved. The discussion in Box 11.2 suggests that retained photos may reflect the needs and biases of the people who make those decisions. Another problem relates to the issue of what is *not* photographed; unhappy events or conflictual moments may not become photos. The question of representativeness relates both to what survives and to what people choose to keep; the selective survival of photographs may be part of a constructed reality that family members (or others) set out to produce.

Official Documents

Companies (and organizations generally) produce many documents in print and/or electronic form; some of these—annual reports, press releases, advertisements, and public relations materials—are in the public domain. Other documents, such as company newsletters, organizational charts, meeting minutes, memos, correspondence (internal and external), and manuals for new joiners, may not be accessible to the public. As with the materials considered in the previous section, documents from institutional sources require scrutiny around issues of credibility and representativeness. People who write documents generally want to convey a particular point of view. This point of view often represents the official story an institution seeks to convey about its activities. Researchers are particularly interested in these official stories and the ways institutions frame them through official documents.

Mass Media Outputs

Newspapers, magazines, and other print media are potential sources for social scientific analysis. For example, to learn about the health information Native Americans receive, Sherice Gearheart and Teresa Trumbly-Lamsam (2017) examined 644 stories in

---

Mixed Methods in Action | Educational Policies and Access for Children with Disabilities

In her educational policy research, Sarah Jessen (2012) analyzed official documents from New York City's small schools and school choice policies. After New York's school principals were allowed to delay acceptance of some special education students and English language learners, a civil rights violation complaint was filed against the city's Department of Education. Office of Civil Rights (OCR) documents outlined their ruling that there was no violation. The OCR cited school district data showing that students were receiving their chosen placement more often than they had previously, and that most small schools were immediately accepting them.

Jessen's analysis revealed that these official documents excluded different levels of special education services. Students with higher accessibility needs were most often placed at large schools; thus, the new policy did not equally include them. To more fully understand the disjuncture between the official explanation of inclusion and the realities, Jessen interviewed school administrators and talked with families who faced barriers in finding schools appropriate for their children with intellectual disabilities or learning differences. She compared the latter with the official narratives of school choice disseminated by the education department.

Because she was able to analyze the claims made in the OCR's document in relation to existing school data, Jessen could assess the former's credibility and note that the OCR did not accurately present the data. While this document may have been representative of the school's perspective on the issue, it did not tell the entire story. Consequently, the contents could not be regarded as "free from error and distortion" (Scott 1990). As Jessen's study suggests, additional exploration of claims made in official documents can be used to develop insights into the factors that lie behind their representation of reality.

20 tribal newspapers over a 1-year period; they found that the articles lacked coverage of the main health issues affecting the Indigenous population and had little information that would motivate readers to take action to improve their health.

Visual media such as television programs, commercials, and films are also good reflections of communication trends. Sejin Park, Zienab Shoieb, and Ronald E. Taylor (2017) examined messages in 125 US Army commercials airing between 2001 and 2014 to understand the organization's recruiting messages. They found that reserve recruiting focused on the economic benefits of service, such as college money. Active-duty recruiting commercials also described service as personally transformational or emphasized that the military was in need of more soldiers (the latter occurred in periods with more active wars).

Other studies explore the social and political implications of the materials they examine. Michelle D. Byng (2010) conducted a content analysis of stories published in *The New York Times* and *The Washington Post* between 2004 and 2006 to analyze how these newspapers framed debates over Muslim women's veiling in France, Britain, and the United States. She found that, while these papers were critical of European laws banning the hijab or niqab, they also constructed an image of an ideal Muslim American woman as one who chooses not to veil.

Media are pervasive in our everyday lives, and they are among the forces shaping people's perceptions of reality. Content analysis can help us explore this influence. A researcher might gather a sample of local television news episodes to see how they represent topics like crime, homelessness, immigration, or the local economy. The researcher could analyze what types of crimes local news shows report on the most and compare this to local crime statistics and data from a survey asking viewers what crimes they believe are most common. This would enable comparison of the actual crimes reported, the "story" local news crafts about crime, and people's perceptions of crime.

Determining the authenticity of mass media outputs is sometimes challenging. The authors are not always identified, as in the case of a TV news report,

---

BOX 11.3 Questions to Ask When Examining Communication Content

Suppose you were interested in how newspapers covered crime during the "war on drugs" in the 1990s. You might come up with the following questions:

- Did certain newspapers report more crimes than others, and how did they discuss the incidents?
- How much crime was reported? Where did these stories appear—on the front or inside pages?
- Did both columnists and reporters write about crime? How did each frame their stories?
- Were some crimes given more attention than others? How were different crimes depicted?
- Did more crime stories appear during the week or on weekends?
- What sorts of crime predominated in newspaper articles (crimes against person or property)? How were victims and perpetrators described?
- How has the coverage of drug crime changed over time?

Most content analysis focusing on media is likely to entail several research questions, generally revolving around the same five W's that are the basis of any news report: *who* (does the reporting); *what* (gets reported); *where* (does the issue get reported); *why* (does the issue get reported); and *when* (does it get reported). But researchers are also interested in what media coverage omits. For example, interviews with the accused's family are rare; such inattention is notable, suggesting priorities among writers and publishers.

so it is sometimes difficult to know whether a given account was prepared by someone in a position to understand the facts. Credibility is frequently an issue, and distortion, partial information, or biased perspective is often reflected in the sources. Representativeness may not be a problem with newspaper or magazine articles, since many publications make a point of maintaining a consistent tone or representing a particular ideology.

Other Texts: Real-Life and Online Communication

While content analysis often examines printed **texts** and documents, researchers also analyze other types of communication materials. For instance, if you were interested in gender roles or representations, you could look at tweets using the hashtags #timesup or #MeToo, art gallery exhibits, profiles on heterosexual and LGBTQIA2S+ dating sites, hip hop lyrics, or celebrities' Instagram posts.

In a qualitative study, A. Golinkoff, Willie Baronet, Carolyn Cannuscio, and Rosemary Frasso (2016) viewed the messages that people experiencing homelessness write on signs as texts that signify something important about both the people and, more broadly, poverty and homelessness. A researcher interested in activist messages might document signs held by participants at a reproductive rights protest and analyze the key communication themes.

Websites, despite the speed with which they may be refreshed (weekly, daily, hourly), have become fruitful ground for content analysis. In an early study, Sean P. Hier (2000) studied the messages on a Toronto-based White supremacy website and remarked on how it allowed visitors to access and contribute to the site's racist content with an anonymity that would be impossible to maintain while, say, attending an anti-immigration rally or subscribing to a hard-copy neo-Nazi newsletter. For that reason, he speculated that it might be more successful in reaching ordinary people than non-Internet sources would be. Websites' use of images can also be quite

revealing. Chelsea Heuer, Kimberly J. McClure, and Rebecca M. Puhl's (2011) investigation of images accompanying online news stories focused on obesity found that 72 percent of the images depicted people with fat bodies in a stigmatizing manner.

Other forms of online communication that have been used as objects of analysis include internet forums, chatrooms, and social media feeds. Social researchers have analyzed social media such as Facebook, Twitter, and YouTube. In 2007, the sportswear company Nike began N7, an initiative focused on funding health promotion programs targeted to Native Americans by selling products with Indigenous-inspired designs and cultural references. W. Scott Sanders, Selene G. Phillips, and Cecelia Alexander (2017) analyzed Twitter to explore the campaign's effectiveness and whether its social media advertising reached Native Americans. Their analysis showed that states with higher populations of Indigenous people had more campaign followers than other states, yet this audience tended to be centered in urban areas even though more Indigenous people live in rural areas. The researchers' statistical analysis confirmed their hypothesis that Tweets incorporating meaningful cues of Indigenous ethnic identity (race of model, hairstyle, body art, fashion, language, and others) elicit more identification. Tweets in the campaign employing visual ethnic identity cues were favored and retweeted more often than text-based ethnic identity cues.

Websites have enormous potential as sites for unobtrusive research, but it's important to keep Scott's criteria in mind. Anyone can set up a website, so you have no guarantee that a person offering information is an authority. Is the information on the site credible, or might it be distorted for some reason? For example, a site that encourages you to buy a product might exaggerate its value. Given the internet's constant flux, it's doubtful that one can ever know how representative websites on a certain topic are. In a related vein, any one search engine can provide access to only a portion of the web; there is evidence that even the combined use of several search engines may reveal fewer than half of the existing sites, and there is no way of knowing if they are a biased sample.

---

texts Documents, images, and other recorded material that may be analyzed for symbolic value.

Researchers analyzing websites need to recognize these limitations as well as the opportunities available. Scott's suggestions invite consideration of why a website was constructed. For commercial reasons? Political reasons? You should be no less skeptical about websites than about any other kind of document. Using both traditional print materials and online materials will allow you to cross-validate sources.

The Range of Text Sources

Many content analysis studies examine documents to see how meanings are conveyed, but meanings are not conveyed only in words. Buildings, graffiti, clothing, technologies, and theme parks are all phenomena through which meanings are communicated. For this reason, they are considered "texts" in the same way that written documents are texts. As texts, these phenomena are materials that signify ideas and social dynamics and that can be interpreted through "reading" to produce understandings of what they symbolize and express.

Let's consider, for a moment, the built environment as a text. A curb cut in a sidewalk can be read as evidence that people who use mobility devices are included in the planners' vision of who should freely move about in public space. The lack, inconsistent presence, or intermittent positioning of curb cuts demonstrates that people with disabilities have a "lack of meaningful participation in the public arena" (Rogers and Swadener 2001, 109). Thus, sidewalks can be seen as texts useful to read through content analysis; someone trying to understand the dynamics of accessibility in built environments shouldn't only look at written textual evidence to understand it.

The message on this protest sign critiques the criminalization of people experiencing homelessness. What different understandings about homelessness could you develop by analyzing texts such as these protests signs, policy briefs, news stories, police reports, or signs people experiencing homelessness hold while panhandling?

> ## BOX 11.4 Checklist for Evaluating Documents
>
> Keep the following questions in mind as you determine the value of documents you are considering using in a content analysis study.
>
> - Who produced the document?
> - For what purposes was the document produced?
> - Was the author in a position to write authoritatively about the subject?
> - Is the material genuine?
>
> - Did the author have a particular slant to promote?
> - Is the document typical of its kind? If not, is it possible to establish how atypical it is and in what ways?
> - Is the meaning of the document clear?
> - Can the events or accounts presented in the document be corroborated?
> - Are there different interpretations of the document from the one you offer? If so, what are they?

Choosing Documents to Examine: Sampling

To make a content analysis study compelling, researchers must carefully select the materials they intend to treat as data. They do so by following sampling procedures like those we outlined in Chapter 4. Just like researchers studying people and settings, researchers using unobtrusive methods must define the parameters of the population of documents they're studying, based on their research question. The population could be all tweets from major political candidates during an election cycle, all newspapers published in the United States, or all yearbooks from a particular college. The researcher then gathers a representative sample of documents from that population.

Researchers can take different approaches to sampling in content analysis. Here are a few examples:

- To examine media sexualization of women, Erin Hatton and Mary Nell Trautner (2013) engaged in purposive sampling to choose a magazine through which to study pop culture representation: they selected magazine covers from *Rolling Stone*, which has featured a range of cultural icons since it was first published in 1967. From their population of all covers issued between 1967 and 2009, they collected a sample of 1006 items. For the final sample, Hatton and Trautner chose covers that portrayed individual people or multiple people with a central figure (i.e., no crowd shots, text or cartoons, or collages).

- Josh Grimm and Julie L. Andsager (2011) studied California newspaper coverage of H.R. 4437, a proposed law to bar undocumented immigrants from public service access and penalize anyone aiding undocumented people. The researchers chose newspapers with high circulation in geographically and racially diverse areas, and then clustered them based on these characteristics. They found articles using search terms "H.R. 4437, immigration, illegal immigrant, and immigration protest" (775). To choose individual articles for analysis, they used systematic random sampling.

- To study e-cigarette marketing strategies, Rachel A. Grana and Pamela M. Ling (2014) entered the terms "e-cigarette," "electronic cigarette," "e-cig," and "personal vaporizer" into four search engines. After noting that all four offered similar results, they searched again, using two of the search engines, and gathered the first 50 hits for each term. They found 233 retail sites, 62 of which met their inclusion criteria: (1) the site's purpose was to sell e-cigarettes and accessories; (2) e-cigarettes could be purchased through the site; and (3) the website had a primary brand

Methods in Motion | **Donald Trump's Rhetoric and the Creation of Moral Boundaries**

Using content analysis, researchers can examine how political rhetoric might become a vehicle of social change. Michèle Lamont, Bo Yun Park, and Elena Ayala-Hurtado (2017) explored this question by examining the techniques Donald Trump used to galvanize voter support in his 2016 presidential campaign speeches. While middle-class voters formed the majority of Trump's supporters (Henley 2016), almost 70 percent of White people without college degrees voted for the real estate magnate and reality TV star turned politician (Fidel 2016)—a margin not seen since the 1980s. Lamont, Park, and Ayala-Hurtado did a qualitative content analysis of 73 of Trump's campaign speeches to explore how he reached out to different constituencies. In particular, they found that Trump used rhetoric that encouraged White working-class people to construct moral boundaries between themselves and other groups.

The research team found that workers were the most frequently referenced group in the speeches they sampled. Lamont, Park, and Ayala-Hurtado examined the frequency of particular statements, as well as the meanings conveyed by them, to understand the rhetorical trends in Trump's speeches. They found that Trump repeatedly positioned himself as the candidate who cared for workers and, with his now famous pledge to "make America great again," could restore their status by granting them the dignity and respect he avowed they deserved. He emphasized that the problems of working-class people were not of their own making but a result of global policies, structural trends, and overregulation.

Lamont, Park, and Ayala-Hurtado also found that Trump used rhetoric to establish boundaries between White working-class people and other groups. Trump overarchingly described immigrants in negative terms—depicting Latinx immigrants as criminals and rapists who exploit "the system," Muslim immigrants as Islamic terrorists, and Syrian refugees as a drain to resources—and he positioned them all as risks to public safety, American values, and access to jobs. When Trump discussed Latinx people,

he used discourses connecting them to "illegal" immigration much more often than depicting them as workers. He often described African Americans as hard workers, though he constructed boundaries between Black and White workers by describing the former as "they" rather than including them in the "we" of all workers. He also regularly posited a connection between Black communities and violence.

While Trump's most frequent references to gender were in relation to his opponent, Hillary Clinton, he also portrayed women as vulnerable to the perils of Islamic terrorism and emphasized men's responsibility to provide for them and protect them. He mentioned LGBTQIA2S+ people the least of all groups and did so in mostly positive terms, yet he also positioned LGBTQIA2S+ people and Muslims as two distinctly different groups and claimed that protection of LGBTQIA2S+ people demands disavowal of Islam and strict immigration policies curtailing Muslim immigration.

These findings led the researchers to conclude that Trump used rhetoric that encouraged White, heterosexual working-class voters—heterosexual males in particular—to construct symbolic moral boundaries between themselves and elites, Black and Latinx communities, immigrants, Muslims, women, and LGBTQIA2S+ people. He encouraged White workers to "assert what they believe is their rightful place in the national pecking order in relation to these groups" (2017, S155), using language designed to persuade them that he was on their side. This content analysis allowed the researchers to develop a theory of boundary-making to understand the ways politicians use powerful rhetoric to craft voters' senses of themselves. They argue that this research provides a nuanced understanding of how candidates use language to encourage political participation through the creation of moral boundaries. Such an analysis would be useful to apply to other candidates to assess the various ways they construct moral boundaries between voters whose support they seek and other groups.

identity, did not sell other tobacco or non-tobacco products, and was in English. These 62 sites became their sample.

Analyzing Communication Trends and Meanings Using Quantitative and Qualitative Approaches

Researchers can use content analysis to study communication using either qualitative or quantitative methods, or a blend of the two. Because content analysis examines what different forms of communication reveal about a society, a culture, or people's relationships, meanings and interpretations are important considerations. While both qualitative and quantitative content analysis analyze meanings conveyed through communication, they approach analysis in different ways.

Quantitative content analysis collects numerical data on specific elements found in images, text, or verbal content in order to study the frequency and patterns of these elements statistically. This kind of analysis may emphasize how frequently certain images, words, or ideas are used, particularly in relation to other images, words, or ideas (Oleinik 2011, 860). Quantitative content analysts typically define the categories of interest ahead of time and then cull through data to see when and in what contexts these categories show up and how they relate to other categories.

---

quantitative content analysis An analytic approach using a pre-specified coding scheme to identify patterns and frequencies of communication in documents and texts.

---

qualitative content analysis An inductive approach to analysis that focuses on how meaning is produced and communicated in texts by allowing categories of interest to emerge from data during the course of study.

---

coding The process of labeling, categorizing, and organizing data collected in order to facilitate qualitative or quantitative analysis.

Qualitative content analysis examines both the content and the contextual meaning of communication, using a more inductive strategy to identify themes and patterns. Rather than being predetermined, the categories of interest typically develop from the data itself. Through examining the data, researchers discover and revise the categories of interest to understanding the way meanings are produced and conveyed.

Like in all social research, content analysis is systematic: researchers clearly specify rules for the categorization of material and thoughtfully choose data examples from their sample. This process is defined as **coding**. In data analysis, both qualitative and quantitative researchers often begin with a specific set of concepts they "look for" when coding documents. The coding will inevitably reflect the researcher's interests and concerns and therefore be a product of a researcher's subjective interest and theoretical framing of the topic as well as the ideas or hypotheses they seek to better understand. However, once the rules have been formulated, the goal is to apply them systematically and without bias. In the sections below, we describe the quantitative and qualitative coding approaches used in two different content analysis studies.

Analyzing Communication Using Qualitative Measurement and Coding

Joy Leopold and Myrtle P. Bell (2017) used a multi-step coding technique in their study of media representation on the Black Lives Matter (BLM) movement. They used a common practice in content analysis: combining quantitative measures to determine the frequency of certain communication elements with qualitative analysis to interpret the meanings and implications of the communication. Leopold and Bell used a "protest paradigm" framework to guide their strategy of coding media stories, which they describe "as a pattern of news coverage that expresses disapproval toward protests and dissent" (721, quoting Lee 2014). This model focuses on five key aspects of coverage:

1. framing the stories in negative ways;
2. relying on statements by people in power;

3. including superficial responses from bystanders to make claims about how the general public feel;

4. omitting the social impetus inspiring protest; and

5. relying on negative or demonizing images of protesters.

The researchers wondered how much journalistic coverage of BLM followed these trends and to what degree the coverage employed particularly racialized depictions. They began by operationalizing each aspect of the protest paradigm—for instance, defining what kinds of language and images would count as "demonization." They looked to other researchers' work and found that they operationalized demonization by assessing the tone of statements. So, Leopold and Bell operationalized demonization as including three elements: (1) the degree to which the overall tone was positive, negative, or neutral; (2) the amount of detail describing violent protester-police clashes; and (3) whether the articles portrayed the protests as illegal or disorderly.

Next, Leopold and Bell performed what they described as textual analysis on 15 of the 79 articles in their sample, which allowed them to "identify the presence and significance of any paradigm characteristics and reveal (if any) other elements that further contribute to the marginalization of the BLM protests and protesters" (2017, 724). After finding that the articles strongly represented both the protest paradigm elements and additional negative depictions, the researchers developed a codebook including all the elements. More detail on some of their coding categories and examples can be seen in Table 11.1, which shows that Leopold and Bell used percentages to assess the degree to which a certain theme was present, but they did not do a statistical analysis on the trends.

Leopold and Bell thus followed a coding technique often used in quantitative content analysis: operationalizing elements ahead of time and then measuring the frequency of the elements in the sample. Yet as they found evidence of these elements in their data, they also found depictions of interest that didn't fit any of their coding categories; thus,

they revised their coding scheme and, in this way, expanded their understanding of the protest paradigm. This model is similar to the ethnographic content analysis described by David L. Altheide (1996). Altheide explained that his method differed from quantitative content analysis in that the researcher constantly revises the themes or categories distilled from the examination of documents. He describes ethnographic content analysis this way:

> The aim is to be systematic and analytic but not rigid. Categories and variables initially guide the study, but others are allowed and expected to emerge during the study, including an orientation to *constant discovery* and *constant comparison* of relevant situations, settings, styles, images, meanings, and nuances (1996, 16; emphases in original).

Leopold and Bell engaged in a similar process of discovery, and the researchers refined their original coding themes and concepts, generated new ones, and sought to understand the context within which the representations were generated. After refining their codebook to include the protest paradigm and the other negative depictions they noted, they analyzed all 79 articles in their sample. Their ensuing analysis demonstrated that journalistic coverage of BLM protests included strong messages demonizing the protests and depicting them as illegitimate, akin to riots, and disruptive to normal city life; opinions of bystanders and officials were the main voices in the stories, while depictions of protesters focused on their clothing, accessories, and theatrical actions.

Analyzing Communication Using Quantitative Measurement and Coding

A good example of a quantitative coding scheme can be seen in Samantha Goodin, Alyssa Van Denburg, Sarah K. Murnen, and Linda Smolak's (2011) analysis of the sexualized characteristics of clothing marketed towards 6- to 14-year-old girls. Examining all the clothing marketed to "tweens" on the websites of 15 national stores, the authors measured the degree to which clothing had childlike, sexualized, or adultlike characteristics. Creating models inspired by previous research measuring sexualizing clothing

TABLE 11.1 | Samples from Leopold and Bell's (2017) Codebook

The Protest Paradigm and Additional Characteristics: News Frames[a]

Operationalization: Riot

Percent present: 22

Example:

> *WSJ.* Police, armed with 5.56 mm assault-style rifles and shotguns loaded with non-lethal rounds faced off with protestors, staring at them through gas masks. Several buildings nearby had windows shattered including the front door to the fire department. A Little Caesars restaurant, a self-storage facility, and local meat market were looted and burned as a chaotic scene broke out along a main commercial strip . . . roving groups focused on looting and vandalizing businesses (November 26, 2014).

The Protest Paradigm and Additional Characteristics: Invocation of Public Opinion[a]

Operationalization: Quotes from bystanders

Percent present: 32

Example:

> *St Louis Post-Dispatch.* Winter said he was sure there were some racial disparities in Missouri that needed to be addressed but didn't think standing behind a "made-up charge about a white police officer" was the right way to go about it. Additionally, he didn't approve of the way the marchers were conducting themselves. "These people are on a road trip," Winter said. "It's like a high school graduation party driving around, honking their horns and having a good time" (December 6, 2014). "At least they aren't looting anything," said Craig Valentine, 44, sitting in stalled traffic" (November 30, 2014).

The Protest Paradigm and Additional Characteristics: Reliance on Official Sources and Definitions[a]

Operationalization: Quotes from official sources

Percent present: 46

Example:

> *WSJ.* "I am deeply saddened for the people of Ferguson who woke up to see parts of their community in ruins," the governor said. "No one should have to live like this. No one deserves this. We must do better and we will" (November 26, 2014). *St Louis-Post-Dispatch.* "These senseless acts of violence have been devastating to the city of Ferguson," said Dan Isom, director of the Department of Public Safety. "These criminals must and will be held to account for their actions" (November 27, 2014).

The Protest Paradigm and Additional Characteristics: Demonization[a]

Operationalization: Social and economic disruption

Percent present: 54

Example:

> *WSJ.* Protestors in Oakland, Calif., wearing T-shirts reading "black lives matter" shut down train service on the Bay Area Rapid Transit system between San Francisco and the East Bay for more than an hour Friday morning. The protestors chained themselves to each other and to trains, blocking service in both directions at the system's West Oakland station . . . carries as many as 400,000 passengers daily (November 28, 2014). *NY Times.* In New York, thousands of people have tried to close major roads, bridges and tunnels, disrupting the rhythms of the city. In Berkeley, Calif., an Amtrak train was forced to stop, a central freeway was closed for hours and regional commuter trains were halted (December 14, 2014).

The Protest Paradigm and Additional Characteristics: Delegitimization[a]

Operationalization: Appearance and performance

Percent present: 56

Example: *NY Post*. The black caskets were placed in Foley Square, with one, marked "Staten Island," embellished with various names, including Garner's and the day he died—July 17, 2014 . . . The Union Square rabble rousers met their cohorts in Foley Square . . . (December 5, 2014).

The Protest Paradigm and Additional Characteristics: Blame Attribution[c]

Operationalization:

Percent present: 19

Example: *St Louis Post-Dispatch*. On Sunday, a man fired shots at two St Louis officers about 6 p.m. as they were responding to a call for "suspicious person" in the 4,500 block of Chouteau Avenue. They returned fire, and he ran. Nobody was hit or arrested. (October 10, 2014) *NY Post*. A cop's personal car was set ablaze near the 77th Precinct station house in Crown Heights, Brooklyn. Some four or five people were spotted running from the scene, and cops suspect the torching may be related to the protests (October 10, 2014).

The Protest Paradigm and Additional Characteristics: Protester Quotes (total)[c] 66%

Operationalization: Relevant

Percent present: 23

Example: *St Louis Post-Dispatch*. "We need people to have discussions with children about what systematic oppression is," she said (August 31, 2014).

Operationalization: Irrelevant

Percent present: 43

Example: *NY Times*. "I didn't like the fact that people were profiting off T-shirts, flags and hats," said Jay Bad Heart Bull, 36, who runs a nonprofit in Minneapolis. "I even saw a dog with a shirt that said, 'I can't breathe.' I respect the hustle, but I want it to be for a purpose. How does that help our community?" (December 14, 2014).

Notes: a) Protest paradigm characteristics; b) [does not appear in excerpt]; c) Additional characteristics identified through textual analysis.

Source: Excerpted from Leopold and Bell (2017, 728–730).

and multiple research team discussions, they coded an item of clothing as "sexualizing if it (a) revealed a sexualized body part, (b) emphasized a sexualized body part, (c) had characteristics associated with sexiness, and/or (d) had writing on it with sexualizing content. Sexualized body parts included the chest, waist, buttocks, and legs" (2011, 5). Goodin and colleagues coded some clothing as "emphasizing" when it drew attention to sexualized body parts, and some as "childlike" when they had light colors or "childlike

prints." The researchers then placed the clothing items into four categories: childlike, definitely sexualizing, ambiguously sexualizing, and adultlike.

To determine this coding system's validity, the researchers performed a study in which 31 college students rated the sexiness level of nine clothing items randomly presented to them on a computer. Statistical analysis found that the participants did not rate the "definitely sexualizing" and "ambiguously sexualizing" items as very different from one another, though

Can you notice patterns in these papers' coverage of BLM protests that echo Leopold and Bell's protest paradigm? Or do you see other themes? How might you analyze these stories by coding the framing and imagery in them?

they did judge the "childlike" consistently as the least sexualized. Using inter-rater coding, the researchers found agreement to range from 95 to 98 percent. They resolved the disagreements around differentiating between the "definitely sexualizing" and "ambiguously sexualizing" categories by choosing the latter, more conservative option. After performing statistical analysis on all of their variables, they found that clothing marketed to tweens had the most sexualizing characteristics: overall, 29.4 percent of the clothing had sexualizing features. Interestingly, 86.4 percent of the clothing with sexualizing characteristics also had childlike features (for example, a low-cut dress with

spaghetti straps and a pastel-colored butterfly). Given how common it was that girls' clothing items would have both sexualizing and childlike characteristics at the same time, the researchers concluded that the sexualized nature of girls' clothing was "covert and complicated" (2011, 8).

Developing Coding Strategies in Content Analysis

As our discussion suggests, coding is a crucial part of content analysis. When developing a coding scheme, researchers often create formal guidelines known as a **coding manual**. It provides a list of all the dimensions; the different categories subsumed under each dimension; the codes (which may be numbers or descriptive words) that correspond to each category;

---

coding manual   The list of codes used in analysis of particular set of data.

and guidance to coders on what should be taken into account in coding a particular dimension. Some of the categories and dimensions in Leopold and Bell's (2017) coding manual are shown in Table 11.1.

The coding manual provides a complete list of all categories for each dimension to be coded, as well as guidance on how to interpret the dimensions. This guidance must be detailed to ensure the reliability of the coding. Researchers enter their data into a form called a **coding schedule**. In their coding schedule, Goodin et al. (2011) would have entered descriptions providing details of each store, each clothing category, each item of clothing (including its range of sizes and the ages it was intended for), and numerous other categories. In statistical studies like this, the codes can be compiled in a data file for analysis with a software package such as IBM SPSS Statistics (SPSS).

When devising a content analysis coding scheme, researchers should consider issues of sampling, measurement, and analysis like the following:

- *Are the categories mutually exclusive?* There should be no overlap in the categories supplied for each dimension. If the groups are not

In what ways might a quantitative coding scheme be useful when analyzing gender differences in clothing for younger children? What are the benefits of analyzing what ideas about gender are common in young kids' clothing by examining the frequency and content of particular messages? How would that compare to a qualitative approach?

mutually exclusive, coders will not know how to code an item that fits into more than one.

---

coding schedule A form listing all possible codes in coding manual; when completed, it includes data examples, details, and frequencies.

- *Is the set of codes exhaustive?* Every possible dimension should have a category.
- *Are the instructions clear?* Coders should be clear about what factors to take into account when assigning codes. In quantitative content analysis, coders generally have little or no discretion in deciding how to code the units of analysis.
- *Are the unit of analysis clear?* For example, in a study of crime reporting in the local press, there is both a media item (for example, one newspaper article) and a topic to be coded (one specific offense). In practice, a researcher is interested in both but needs to keep the distinction in mind.

To enhance the quality of their coding scheme, researchers sometimes conduct a pilot study to identify difficulties, such as finding there is no code to cover a particular case (not exhaustive). A pilot test will also help to reveal if one category of a dimension includes a large percentage of items. When this issue occurs, it may be necessary to break that category down to allow for greater specificity. Pretesting coding scheme involves ensuring consistency between coders (**inter-coder reliability**) and ensuring consistency of individual researchers' codes (**intra-coder reliability**).

What Aspects of Communication Do Researchers Focus on in Analysis?

What content analysis researchers count or look for in their data depends on their research questions. As in any study, the units of analysis reflect the types of issues the researcher is studying. Generally, when developing their coding strategy, researchers might concentrate on words, subjects and themes, and value positions.

Words

Determining the frequency with which certain words are used is often the first step in content analysis. Elizabeth Jagger (1998) counted words such as "slim" and "non-smoker" in dating profiles to compare women and men with respect to what each deemed desirable in a date (see Box 11.5). Counting particular words can reveal what ideas are common or emphasized.

A variation on this process is the search for pairings of keywords. This sort of research became much easier with improvements to search engine technology and the growth of online news sources, both around the turn of the twenty-first century. Sean Hier (2002) found that in coverage of raves, the stories frequently linked the terms "rave" and "drug use." He argued that this combination might encourage readers' view that raves are dangerous and in need of control.

Subjects and Themes

A more interpretative approach is required to code text in terms of subjects and themes. The analyst searches not just for the obvious, or manifest, content but also for some of the underlying, or latent content. In reports on crime, such questions might include the following: Is the victim blamed along with the accused? Is the occupation of the accused or the victim stated? If not, is it implied in an address or a picture?

Another example is Bradley Bond's study (2013) in which he noted how frequently children's television programs included characters with a physical disability. He wanted to understand the portrayal's context and therefore determined how to measure personality traits of characters with disabilities and attitudes of non-disabled characters towards them.

Value Positions

A further level of interpretation is likely when the researcher seeks to demonstrate that a particular text's author has taken a certain *value position*, conveying their principles or describing their standards for what is right or wrong. For example, is a journalist who writes about crime sympathetic or hostile to the accused? Is all the blame put on the accused, with the implication that punishment is appropriate? Or is the focus on social conditions, with the assumption that less blame should be placed on the accused? Researchers must consider whether there is manifest indication of the writer's value positions or if inferences can be made from the latent content.

Content analysis can reveal value positions by pointing to ideologies, beliefs, and principles. For

---

inter-coder reliability   The degree to which two or more people agree on the coding of an item.

---

intra-coder reliability   The degree to which an individual coder is consistent over time in the coding of an item.

BOX 11.5 Finding Love: Then and Now

For decades before the advent of dating apps, the most common way for singles to advertise their availability was by posting an ad in the classified section of a print newspaper. Jagger (1998) analyzed a sample of 1094 heterosexual dating advertisements gathered in 1996 from four newspapers with a general readership. She noted the common tendency for men and women to market themselves in terms of their lifestyle choices (film preferences, clubs frequented, sports activities, etc.). Jagger also found that women were far more likely than men to stress the importance of economic and other resources in a preferred partner. Women were somewhat more likely to promote themselves in terms of physical appearance, yet men were just as likely to describe themselves as "slim." More generally, her results pointed to the significance of the body in identity construction for both sexes (classified ads were text-heavy and would seldom have featured photos).

Of course, much has changed since Jagger did her research. Online dating is now the medium of choice, with apps and websites that cater to a range of subgroups and desires. The cost to place a classified ad in a newspaper was based on the number of words in the ad; this encouraged people to be economical in the details they shared. Dating sites today allow participants to give far more information about themselves, accompanied by photos that enable people to present themselves as they wish to be seen.

There is much interest around how users of these sites choose people to contact. One study examined the profile views and emails of almost 6,000 people in Boston and San Diego using online dating services to find long-term heterosexual relationships. Their choices suggested a sorting process in which they sought partners whose profile features matched their own attributes (Hitsch, Hortaçsu, and Ariel 2010). This result is particularly interesting in relation to the concern about the distortion of personal characteristics in online profiles. For example, Jeffrey A. Hall, Namkee Park, Hayeon Song, and Michael Cody (2010) used self-reports of probable misrepresentation on dating sites and found that men were more likely than women to be deceptive about their personal assets (for example, income), but that there was no gender difference in misrepresentation of relationship goals (for example, interest in pursuing a serious relationship). Women were found to be more likely to misrepresent their weight, while men were more likely to mislead about their age.

In addition to dishonesty and misrepresentation, interactions on dating sites might reflect some problematic aspects of social inequality. For example, Tinder has a reputation for providing male users a medium to engage with women in crude ways. Aaron Hess and Carlos Flores conducted a content analysis of the "Tinder Nightmares" Instagram page, where posters "document the lewd and perverted courtship attempts and the humorous and witty efforts women offer in response" (2018, 1086). The researchers argue that these posts demonstrate that many men express a toxic and hypersexual masculinity on the app. Hess and Flores analyze the Tinder Nightmares Instagram page as a site in which women create space for themselves and bond with each other by posting the men's problematic Tinder messages and their responses to them.

In a study of the app Jack'd, which is geared to men who have sex with men, Brandon Miller (2015) found that men emphasized their own masculinity in their profiles. Thus, expressions of hypermasculinity occur among men who have sex with men as well as among heterosexual men, yet the former describe this as a desirable trait on the app. Miller did not see many expressions of racial preferences, which he notes could have to do with the fact that 74 percent of the sample profiles were from BIPOC men. Other studies of gay male dating and hookup sites note a significant proportion of racialized language as users describe who they are and are not interested in (Callander, Holt, and Newman 2012) and claim their interest in partners of certain races are personal desires and have nothing to do with racism or a preference for Whiteness (Riggs 2013).

instance, Patricia Bromley, John W. Meyer, and Francisco O. Ramirez (2011) studied social science textbooks from around the world published between 1970 and 2008 to explore their hypothesis that education has become more "student-centered," reflecting a transition to a more rights-oriented global society. They created a coding scheme meant to capture values of student-centrism, international orientation, and human rights. They also developed particular student-centered themes to assess, including whether books included children and their rights as topics, used pictures and engaging images, and designed content so children could actively engage with the text. Overall, they found a large increase in student-centrism since 1970, with the biggest leap occurring after 2000.

Key Considerations in Content Analysis

Content analysis can be approached in a precise, quantitative form, which can make it a quite transparent research method. Because this transparency can make replication relatively easy, many feel this can be a particularly "objective" method of analysis. Even in quantitative content analysis, though, it's almost impossible to devise coding manuals that do not require some interpretation by the coder. Interpretations may be particularly challenging when the aim is to identify latent meanings (as opposed to the more readily apparent manifest meanings). Further, a more mechanical analysis (like counting certain words) differs from one that emphasizes themes in the text, which entails a higher level of abstraction and a correspondingly greater risk of measurement invalidity. Thus, coders must approach the process thoughtfully and develop coding schemes that reflect useful theories and operationalizations and that different coders can apply consistently.

Content analysis is a highly flexible method, applicable to several different kinds of communication content. Although it is often applied to mass media outputs, it has a much broader applicability and is useful as an unobtrusive, non-reactive method. Newspaper articles and television scripts are generally not written with the expectation that a systematic analysis might one day be carried out on them.

Content analysis has been used to facilitate studies of social groups that are difficult to access. For example, much of what social scientists know about the social backgrounds of elite groups, such as company directors and top military personnel, comes from content analyses of publications such as *Who's Who* and the business pages of newspapers. Now imagine what the internet has done to open up a world of groups and subgroups whose writings would never have been available for study. For example, countless subcultures' interactions would be available to study using the platform 4chan; if you were interested in studying groups associated with white supremacy, like QAnon, this could be a platform in which you'd access their discussion boards. Regardless of the medium, researchers should always remember that content analysis can only be as good as the documents it explores. Recall that Scott (1990) recommended assessing documents in terms of authenticity, credibility, representativeness, and meaning.

Despite the insights content analysis offers into patterns and meanings in communication, this method may not be helpful in answering why a trend in communication occurs. For example, Jagger's analysis of dating advertisements (Box 11.5) clearly showed that both men and women put less emphasis on the "attractiveness, shape and size" they desired in a partner than they did on their own appearance (1998, 807). Further research, drawing on the wealth of data available from online dating sites, is needed to determine why this was the case. Similarly, Natalie Fenton, Alan Bryman, and David Deacon (1997) found that sociology was only the fourth most common discipline explicitly referred to (after psychology, economics, and social policy) when mass media reported about social science research, but it was by far the most frequently inferred discipline (not directly mentioned but apparently under discussion). Again, however, the reasons behind this phenomenon could only be a matter for speculation. Researchers should always consider which "why" questions can and cannot be answered by examining texts and think about how they might understand more about the reasons for particular communication trends.

Theory can help researchers explore answers to their "why" questions. Content analysts can better understand communication trends by applying theory to their findings and can also use their data to further develop theoretical ideas. Jagger (1998) placed her findings on dating ads in the context of then current ideas about consumerism and the body. And Mowatt's (2012) content analysis of lynching photography was underpinned by theoretical ideas pertaining to racism, recreation, and Whiteness. Some content analysis is accused of being atheoretical because an emphasis on quantitative measurement can easily lead researchers to focus on what is measurable rather than what is theoretically significant or important. Such studies do rely on theory in order to develop their measurement strategies, however, and these researchers might then consider how their findings circle back to inform the original theory.

A researcher could also understand the meaning of communication trends by complementing a content analysis with other data that offer deeper understanding of the messages. For instance, in a study of the 2014 chemical spill in the West Virginia Elk River, Tracey Thomas et al. (2016) tried to get a sense of how the media framed the disaster. They examined print, online, and television media coverage over a 24-day period from the time the spill occurred until the end of the official state of emergency. To further assess the meaning and effects of this media framing, the researchers interviewed stakeholders who had been involved in disaster response to assess their interpretations and responses to the media coverage.

As the examples in this chapter show, content analysis is a highly versatile research method. It can be used on all sorts of "texts," from archival documents and photographs to online materials, advertising, clothing, and even architecture. It lends itself well to both quantitative and qualitative approaches and can be used to supplement other approaches—like ethnography or survey research—just as easily as it can be used as a primary method of research.

Key Points

Introduction: Why Content Analysis Is an Unobtrusive Method of Research

- Content analysis is an unobtrusive data collection method that allows researchers to examine how various forms of communication express information about social experiences and produce meanings about the world.
- Content analysis can be quantitative and/or qualitative.

Documents for Study

- The four criteria for assessing the quality of documents are authenticity, credibility, representativeness, and meaning.
- Content analysts might analyze personal documents, official documents, mass media outputs, websites, visual media, and other "texts" like buildings or clothing.

Choosing Documents to Examine: Sampling

- Researchers approach sampling in content analysis as they would in any other study.

Analyzing Communication Trends and Meanings Using Quantitative and Qualitative Approaches

- Qualitative content analysis focuses on the meaning of documents and texts, allowing for categories to inductively emerge from the data.
- Quantitative content analysis is often deductive, examining the variable features of communication and statistically analyzing the communication trends.
- Coding is the process of systematically categorizing data. Codes can be words that are repetitively used, subjects and thematic concepts, or value positions.

Key Considerations in Content Analysis

- Researchers can encounter difficulties when attempting to determine the meaning of communication, because there is much interpretation involved.

- Applying existing theory and combining content analysis with other forms of data can help researchers understand the meaning of communications they've analyzed.

Questions for Review

1. What is content analysis, and what information about the social world can it provide? How does this compare to other data collection techniques?
2. What can researchers understand using each type of data source, and what considerations must they take into account for each type?
3. Apply Scott's four criteria to the various documents and texts studied in content analysis and think about steps necessary to determine the quality of each type of document.
4. What is the importance of investigating the five W's of each document?
5. What sampling techniques are utilized in content analysis studies?
6. What are similarities and differences between how qualitative and quantitative content analysis researchers approach analysis?

7. What potential pitfalls need to be guarded against when devising coding schedules and manuals?
8. When developing a coding scheme, what different considerations would researchers take if they focus on words, subjects and themes, or value positions?
9. What challenges might a researcher encounter when trying to interpret meanings using content analysis?
10. Discuss the following statement: "One of the most significant virtues of content analysis is its flexibility—that is, that it can be applied to a wide variety of documents."
11. What is the relationship between content analysis data and theory?

Portfolio Exercise

1. How can your research question/topic be examined using content analysis? What types of documents could you analyze for communication trends about the population or topic you're researching? Reflecting on the chapter, write a 2- to 3-page proposal that addresses the following:
   a. What research question would you use to do a content analysis study?
   b. What types of documents would you analyze and what might they reveal about your question?

   c. How would you gather a sample of the documents?
   d. How could you assure that your documents are authentic, credible, representative, and meaningful to your work?
   e. Would you approach analysis using quantitative and/or qualitative techniques?
   f. How would you approach analyzing the documents?

Interactive Activities

1. The class divides into small groups meeting online or in person. Each group selects a topic of interest that has been reported in the news—a protest, a political event, a human-interest story, etc. With your group:

   a. Select three online accounts of the event for analysis.
   b. Decide on at least three themes in the accounts that are noteworthy, as well as other aspects of the stories that seem relevant—e.g.,

the people featured, the way "facts" are conveyed, the details included, the tone of the presentation.

c. Produce both a coding schedule and a coding manual to do a content analysis of the three accounts.

d. Create a numerical summary of the three accounts based on the data gathered in the coding schedule.

e. Discuss salient interpretations of the meanings conveyed through the accounts, and if possible, relate them to hypotheses or theories (either original or established in the literature) that may follow from the content analysis.

With your group, present the results of your analysis to the class, either in person or online. Be prepared to answer questions and respond to critical commentary!

2. Use the Checklist for Evaluating Documents (Box 11.4) to evaluate two types of data: one official document produced by an organization or governmental body and one video source from a news agency (your instructor may supply the examples or let you find them on your own). For each source, work through the checklist, writing your responses to each of the questions below.

a. Who produced the document and why was it produced?

b. Was the author in a position to write/speak authoritatively about the subject?

c. Did the author/creator have an ax to grind or a particular slant to promote?

d. Is the document typical of its kind? If not, is it possible to establish how atypical it is and in what ways?

e. Is the document's meaning clear?

f. Can the events or accounts presented in the document be corroborated?

g. Are there different interpretations of the document from the one you offer? If so, what are they? Have you discounted them? If so, why?

3. As a class, divide into small groups either online or in person. Your instructor will provide each group with 3–5 photographs depicting personal or public life, including at least one of each type

discussed in the text (idealized, natural portrayal, and demystified). Using these images, identify each type of photograph. Then, as a class, discuss the following for each photograph:

a. The five W's of the photograph.

b. What the photograph can tell us about the subjects.

c. The limitations in our ability to understand each of these photos.

d. How interviews or oral histories could pair with these photographs to provide more understandings about the subjects and their interactions.

4. Divide into small groups that will act as "research teams," either online or in person. Your instructor will assign you to study a particular children's picture book. The book will depict stories about a particular topic, such as divorce, bullying, friendship, or gender non-conforming children (the example questions below focus on this last topic as an example). Nominate a person in your group to read the assigned book aloud to the group. As this is happening, other members of the group should take notes on key themes in the book including these questions:

- *Identity & Expression:* How does the book depict gender non-conforming children's identity and expression?

- *Social Context:* What does the book say about the social context surrounding gender non-conforming children? Who is the audience?

- *Narrative Devices:* How does the book tell the story in order to accomplish a certain goal?

With your group, report back to the class and describe your story as well as the key themes you have noted. Your instructor will record the details from each book in relation to the three themes (Identity and Expression; Social Context; Narrative Devices) so that you can see how the themes are expressed in the sample of books the class read. At the end, with your group discuss the data you have collected and reflect on themes you have noticed across the sample of books. (Examples of books useful for this exercise can include: *They, She, He, Me: Free to Be!* by Maya Christina

Gonzalez; *I am Jazz* by Jessica Herthel; *Julian is a Mermaid* by Jessica Love; *One of a Kind Like Me (Único Como Yo)* by Laurin Mayeno; *The Boy & the Bindi* by Vivek Shraya; Jack (Not Jackie) by Erica Silverman)

Online Resources

- Chris Flipp presents an excellent video providing an overview of content analysis.
  www.youtube.com/watch?v=Y0__d1QsR04

- Dennis List offers a helpful overview of software available for content analysis.
  www.audiencedialogue.net/soft-cont.html

- To access an exercise focused on adult Halloween costumes and gender markers, go to Jennifer Lynn Keys's Gender Markers in Adult Halloween Costumes at the Teaching Resources and Innovations Library for Sociology.
  http://trails.asanet.org/Pages/Resource. aspx?ResourceID=12785

For more resources please visit
www.oup.com/he/bryman-reck-fields1e

12

What Can Researchers Learn from Information Others Collected?
Existing Data

CHAPTER OVERVIEW

This chapter examines sources of data that researchers use but that they did not collect themselves. These existing data, as they are called, include government and state records and data collected by other researchers. This type of data is different from the data considered in previous chapters, which have been obtained using processes devised by the researchers themselves (surveys, interviews, observation, and so on).

When researchers study existing data made available by public agencies or other researchers, they use an unobtrusive method called secondary data analysis, which lets them examine the data through the lens of their own research questions.

Reading this chapter will help you to

- understand what the term existing data means and what type of information researchers can obtain from existing data;

- distinguish between different forms of existing data, including large surveys, official statistics, official government documents, oral histories, and big data;

- explain the criteria for evaluating each of the above sources and the considerations researchers must take when analyzing these data;

- appreciate secondary analysis as a form of unobtrusive research and understand how it is performed on existing data;

- outline the advantages and disadvantages of secondary analysis.

What's your opinion on the role school should play in a society? Specifically, what is K–12 education *for*? Is school supposed to educate young people, encourage their imaginations, and build their knowledge? Should it prepare students for college and university? Should it offer them training and skills so that they can enter the workforce as soon as they reach adulthood? Maybe you believe that education is about providing shared experiences that help young people socialize and make friends, develop hobbies, and explore their interests?

Even though many people agree on some of the outcomes that schooling should provide in a society, many researchers and community advocates have suggested that school directs only some students toward higher education, work, and opportunity. Indeed, some sociologists have argued that schools operate in a way that leads some students not toward a good job or college but toward the criminal justice system—a dynamic described as the *school-to-prison pipeline*.

Researchers studying school discipline have found evidence that school policies and practices have become highly punitive in recent years, leading many students to become criminalized and involved in the criminal justice system in ways that reflect their treatment in in their schools (Alexander 2010; Barnes and Motz 2018; Mallett 2016; Snapp et al. 2015). But how would a researcher document a connection between two systems that seem, on the surface, to be completely unrelated: K–12 education and prison?

Researchers have explored this relationship by investigating schools' discipline records, noting the numbers of students being sent to the principal's office, suspended, or expelled. These records enable researchers to note if particular students receive harsher discipline than others—if, for instance, some students receive warnings and others receive office referrals or suspensions for similar infractions. Researchers could also see if these responses have changed over time or are specific to schools located in certain neighborhoods. As we will see later in the chapter, when researchers have studied this phenomenon by examining disciplinary records, they've found stark evidence that BIPOC students, LGBTQIA2S+ students, and students with disabilities face harsher discipline and more often drop out or get "pushed out" of school—and into the juvenile justice system.

Studying school records and assessing trends such as these is one example of the type of research this chapter focuses on, research relying on data that is available to study because it has already been collected by other people or institutions. Researchers call these *existing data*.

Introduction: Research Using Shared Data

As we have seen in previous chapters, researchers gather data in a variety of ways, whether it be directly from participants through questionnaires and interviews or unobtrusively from sources such as newspapers or social media. **Secondary data analysis**, an unobtrusive method, uses **existing data** (also sometimes called *available data*). Agencies or researchers collect and make data available for others to view and analyze. The information often comes from survey data collected by researchers and made accessible for others' use; other sources of existing data include oral history archives and one's surrounding environment.

Another common source of secondary data is statistics gathered by large organizations or government agencies. Such **official statistics** (sometimes referred to as **existing statistics**) include police logs, medical records, school reports, and census data. When they conduct secondary data analysis, researchers analyze the data others have collected according to their own research questions or hypotheses. In other words, they examine the material in a different light.

Secondary analysis can involve topics never anticipated by those originally responsible for collecting the data. When data are made available to other researchers, the original data collectors formally support the exploration of additional research questions. The researcher conducting secondary analysis should fully investigate the existing data, assessing how the data were collected, what sampling techniques were used, what questions were asked, how the variables were measured, what variables were included, and so on. In other words, they must assess the quality of the data and what the data consist of. Once researchers have assessed these attributes, they can confidently develop new research questions, hypotheses, or plans for analyzing variables in the data.

Large Surveys as Existing Data

Conducting **survey research** can be time-consuming and expensive, usually well beyond the means of most students; even professional researchers lack the resources and access to conduct extensive surveys. This is where secondary data analysis comes in. Social scientists as well as organizations including government departments and university-affiliated research centers have conducted large surveys and amassed a great deal of data about the population. Many of these data sets are now available to other researchers for their own use. In addition, some organizations maintain extensive archives of data sets for researchers to access. This section considers the different kinds of survey data available to social researchers, touching on ways these are used.

---

secondary data analysis Analysis conducted by researchers other than those who originally collected the data, often for purposes not anticipated in the original data collection.

---

existing (or available) data Data collected by a researcher or institution and made available to others to analyze.

---

official (or existing) statistics Data compiled by or on behalf of state agencies in course of conducting their business.

---

survey research The study design and method in which researchers collect data through questionnaires or structured interviews, often to detect relationships among variables.

Secondary Data Analysis of Existing Data Sets

Many large US surveys produce high-quality data sets that researchers can use. These surveys are particularly useful for secondary analysis because their methodology is publicly available for review and their data come from large samples gathered using probability sampling techniques. (These and additional data sets are listed under Online Resources at the end of the chapter.)

General Social Survey

Since 1972, the GSS (General Social Survey) has provided data on US residents' opinions on such issues as national budget priorities, crime and punishment, intergroup relations, and confidence in institutions (see Box 12.1 for more detail on the GSS).

Landon Schnabel (2016) used GSS data to examine how differences in religiosity between men and women relates to their income levels. He found that the most religious in each gender group were low-earning women and high-earning men, but that the religiosity differences within each gender (comparing wage levels) were just as large as the differences across gender, and varied by race.

In another study using GSS data, Sarah Nelson Glick and Matthew Golden (2010) compared Black and White people's attitudes toward homosexuality and the rates of men in these populations reporting that they had sex with men. They combined this examination with an assessment of how sexual stigma might affect HIV transmission among men who have sex with men (MSM). The researchers found that the proportion of White people stating that homosexuality is "always wrong" decreased by almost 20 percent after the 1970s but remained unchanged among Black people. People who knew a gay person were less likely to hold negative views. MSM who held negative attitudes towards homosexuality were less likely to report ever having been tested for HIV, and Black MSM were about twice as likely to report that homosexuality is "always wrong" compared to White MSM. These researchers concluded that there are racial differences in attitudes towards

homosexuality, and these relate to experiences of internalized stigma that might place Black MSM at higher risk of contracting HIV.

Because of the extensive information gathered by the GSS about people's opinions and behaviors, this data set affords researchers the opportunity to explore many different research questions and variables of interest about social life.

Social Justice Sexuality Project

The Social Justice Sexuality Project (SJS) contains data from over 5,000 Black, Latinx, Asian and Pacific Islander, and multiracial people who identify as LGBTQIA2S+. One of the largest national surveys of its type, the study explores racial and sexual identity, religion, health, family, and community engagement.

Megan C. Stanton, Lisa Werkmeister Rozas, and Marysol Asencio (2019) used SJS data to explore the relationship between citizenship status and LGBT people's ability to be "out" and live openly. They found that people who were born as US citizens were more likely to be out compared to people who were not citizens or naturalized citizens. They also noted that White people were more likely to be out than were people of color, no matter their citizenship status. The researchers used the SJS data because the dataset includes so many responses and data specifically about LGBT people of color's experiences. These researchers noted some limitations in the data that suggest a need for further research on their questions. For instance, the SJS data distinguishes between sexual orientation and gender identity, but survey questions around being out did not specify whether people were responding about being open about their gender identity and/or sexual orientation. Although Stanton, Rozas, and Acensio used the acronym "LGBT" to describe the sample and people's degree of openness, the researchers conclude that further research should explore differences between transgender people and gay, lesbian, bi, and other sexual identities.

The SJS data set offers information about a population whose experience may not be the focus in other surveys and who can be hard to reach when sampling. Because interconnections between race and sexuality are meaningfully included in the survey instrument, this data provides researchers important details about the lives of BIPOC people identifying as LGBTQIA2S+.

American National Election Studies

The American National Election Studies (ANES) consists of data from national surveys of American voters conducted before and after every presidential election. The data include studies going back to 1948 and cover voting, public opinion, and political participation. Because ANES data provide information about a whole range of voting and political behaviors, researchers can use them when exploring various aspects of people's political participation.

Jody Baumgartner and Brad Lockerbie (2018) analyzed ANES data in their exploration of the relationship between political satire viewership and political mobilization. They found that people watching late-night shows including the most political satire (*The Colbert Report* and *The Daily Show*) had higher levels of voting than did those who watched less satirical shows (such as *Late Night with David Letterman*).

Salil Benegal (2018) used ANES data combined with public opinion survey data from the Pew Research Center to examine the relationship between racial attitudes and opinions about climate change during the presidency of Barack Obama, finding that those who expressed the most racial resentment also believed the scientific findings about climate change the least.

United States Census

The US Census Bureau collects general data on the nation's people and the economy. It conducts the Population and Housing Census—which counts every resident in the United States—every 10 years; the agency also gathers data through more than a hundred other surveys of households and businesses every 1–5 years.

The in-depth nature of census data enables a robust analysis of social trends. Nada Wasi, Bernard van der Berg, and Thomas Buchmueller (2011) used information from the 2000 US Census to find that mothers of children with disabilities were only slightly less likely to work outside the home than mothers of children without disabilities. This finding was unlike prior studies that showed that mothers of children with disabilities were much less likely to work outside the home. The authors considered these findings in relation to more recent public policy changes creating greater support systems for parents of children with disabilities, noting these may affect their ability to be employed (150).

Collaborative Psychiatric Epidemiology Surveys

The Collaborative Psychiatric Epidemiology Surveys (CPES) includes three nationally representative surveys exploring cultural and ethnic differences in mental illnesses, psychological distress, and informal and formal service use among the US population.

Goosby et al. (2012) used information from this data set to compare stress experiences of African American and Black Caribbean parents and their children. They found that both African American and Black Caribbean youth had strong self-esteem, but that Black Caribbean youth were better able to cope with their parents' expressions of stress. They considered how Black ethnic groups are positioned differently in the social structure and have unique family socialization experiences that could affect such outcomes.

Similar to the SJS data set, the CPES data offer specific information about BIPOC communities who might find themselves treated as a homogenous group (or not specifically measured) in other data. For researchers who wish to look deeper into ethnic differences within the topic of mental health, this source of data could be useful.

Accessing Data Sets for Secondary Analysis

Researchers have many ways to access existing data from large surveys for their research. Going directly to the websites of the GSS and the US Census Bureau is one option, but other academic resources support researchers seeking access to various data sets. The Inter-University Consortium for Political and Social

---

BOX 12.1 **The US General Social Survey**

Features

In 1972, the National Opinion Research Center (NORC) introduced the United States General Social Survey (GSS), which canvasses opinions on such major topics as health, social support, crime, community relations, government budgets, work, and social institutions. The GSS has two principal objectives: (1) to gather data regularly on US social trends and (2) to provide information on policy issues of current interest. The survey is a continuing research project that operated on an annual cycle between 1974 and 1994 (except for 1979, 1981, and 1992), and now occurs biennially. Each survey classifies subjects by age, sex, education, and income. The GSS is the second-most frequently analyzed source of data in the social sciences (the US Census is the first).

Collection Methods

NORC researchers based at the University of Chicago conduct face-to-face interviews with respondents. The target population is adults (18 and over) living in American households; the sample size for each cycle is approximately 60,000 households, generally one person per household.

Availability

GSS findings form the basis of a series of publications that present national and regional summary data, primarily as tables and charts, along with initial analyses and findings. Public-use microdata files, together with supporting documentation, are available for secondary analyses. These files contain individual records, screened to ensure confidentiality.

Research (ICPSR) at the University of Michigan is a coalition of over 750 academic institutions offering access to over 65,000 data sets for social science research. Through ICPSR, researchers can gain access to survey data sets, search for publications related to certain data, and search for particular variables of interest. The majority of ICPSR's more than 250,000 research files are freely available for public use, and protections have been implemented to ensure participants' confidentiality. The consortium also offers restricted-use data, which contain more sensitive information or which could not be altered to remove identifying features of participants (doing so can sometimes compromise the data quality). Researchers must apply for access to restricted-use data and adhere to guidelines for maintaining confidentiality; student researchers seeking access must have a faculty sponsor. ICPSR also offers training and education programs in research, data management, and analysis. The CPES data set mentioned above is curated by ICPSR.

The University of California at Berkeley manages the Survey Documentation and Analysis (SDA) archive—a set of programs that enables users to do web-based analysis of survey data. The SDA archive also allows access to many data sets from national surveys such as the GSS and ANES, as well as data focused on various topics including health and economics. A researcher can use the SDA archive to access the data set in which they are interested and also run analyses of variables using the SDA's web-based system.

The Institute for Social Research and Data Innovation (ISRDI) at the University of Minnesota is an interdisciplinary research institute that encourages research and collaboration among University of Minnesota faculty and students. The ISRDI runs two research centers: the Minnesota Population Center (MPC) focuses on demographic research, and the Life Course Center (LCC) focuses on life course research. Despite its dedication to interdisciplinary collaboration among University of Minnesota researchers, ISRDI also develops and disseminates data to researchers worldwide. One of ISRDI's data dissemination programs, IPUMS (which originally stood for Integrated Public Use Microdata Series), provides the most extensive database of census and survey data from around the world, organized by topic. IPUMS data from the US censuses alone date from 1790 to the present. ISRDI's other data archive, the Minnesota Research Data Center (MNRDC) affords researchers access to federal data that are not public. Access to MNRDC data requires a proposal, while IPUMS is public-access.

Many universities have resources to help students and faculty navigate data sets such as the GSS and the census. They also often have subscriptions to platforms providing access to social science data and tools for data visualization and management, such as Social Explorer. Contacting the research support at your university library is a good first step to finding out how to embark on secondary analysis of available survey data.

Considerations in Secondary Analysis of Large Survey Data

There are many benefits to engaging in secondary analysis of large survey data. First, most large survey data employed for secondary analysis are of high quality. The sampling procedures have been rigorous, in many cases producing samples that are as close to representative as is reasonably possible. Although those responsible for these studies face the same problems of **non-response** as anyone else, well-established procedures are usually in place for following up with non-respondents, thus keeping this problem to a minimum. Second, the samples are often national in scope, or at least cover a wide variety of regions, which is a highly desirable—and costly—feature. Third, many large surveys have been generated by highly experienced researchers and social research organizations with strong control procedures to check on data quality.

In addition, large samples (such as those in the GSS) offer an opportunity to study subgroups. A sample of 100 people, for example, might include

only three people over age 85. No researcher wants to talk about those three seniors, as in "only 33 per cent of those in the oldest age category are in good health": that amounts to one person. With a national sample of 1,500, the number increases to 45. This number is still small, but it allows a more meaningful estimate of seniors' health (especially because the sampling procedures are well carried out in the GSS). Raoul Liévanos (2015) was able to study a large sample using data from the 2000 US Census to study how economic deprivation, immigration status, and race affect people's vulnerability to cumulative health risks from air toxicity. As his units of analysis, he used census tracts, geographic boundaries the Census creates to categorize the people within geographically organized residential areas. Each tract includes between 1,500 and 8,000 people, and Liévanos included all 64,738 tracts in the study. This spatial analysis found that economically deprived Black residents and low income, non–English-speaking Asian American and Latinx immigrants were most exposed to clusters of air toxicity that led to health risks. These findings enabled him to reveal the geographic organization of toxic environments and argue for the need for multi-racial and multi-lingual environmental justice interventions.

Another valuable feature of secondary analysis of large surveys is that it can provide an opportunity for longitudinal research. Sometimes, as with the GSS (see Box 12.1), a panel format (in which the same participants are examined at different times) is used to chart trends over time. Similarly, because certain interview questions are recycled and asked of different samples each year, shifting opinions or changes in behavior can be identified.

Challenges can arise when conducting secondary analysis of large survey data. For one, the data can be complex. Some of the best-known data sets employed for secondary analysis, such as the GSS,

---

non-response A situation that occurs if someone in a sample refuses to participate in the study, cannot be contacted, or for some other reason does not supply the required data.

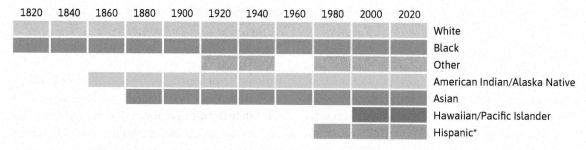

* The US Census recognizes Hispanic as an ethnicity rather than a race. The 2020 Census questionnaire asked respondents to identify race and whether they are of Hispanic origin in two separate questions.

FIGURE 12.1 **Race categories on the US Census questionnaire, 1820-2020**

The first US Census, conducted in 1790, divided the population into free White males, free White females, slaves, and "all other persons." Researchers who use secondary analysis of survey data are restricted by the ways the original researchers measured and coded the data. Since race has been measured in different ways through the history of the census, how could that affect what a researcher can understand about the population's racial demographics over time?

are large both in the numbers of cases and in the numbers of variables they contain. Sometimes the sheer volume of data can present problems, and a period of acclimatization may be required. A researcher analyzing survey data is also confined to the ways the original researchers measured and coded the data, which might limit their analysis. For example, there has been extensive discussion of how the US Census Bureau has measured race and ethnicity over time and the ways this has changed to acknowledge the racial diversity in the United States as well as people's preferred language. An example is the 1980 Census, where the only designated racial/ethnic categories were White, Negro, Aleut, Eskimo, American Indian, Chinese, Japanese, Filipino, Hawaiian, and Part Hawaiian; it was not until the 2000 Census that people could only select more than one race (See Figure 12.1).

Another challenge is that some of the most prominent data sets used for secondary analysis are *hierarchical*, meaning that the data are collected and presented at the level both of the household and of the individual (and sometimes at other levels as well). Different data may apply to each level. For instance, household-level variables such as the number of cars may be included, while individual-level data on income and occupation are found. The secondary analyst must decide which one to use; if the decision is to analyze individual-level data, they must be extracted from the data set.

Mixed Methods in Action | Wealth Inequalities: Bringing Existing Data to Life using Interviews

Existing data have the potential to tell important stories about the world around us and document key social phenomena. When researchers combine analysis of existing data with exploration of additional types of data, that story becomes even more nuanced.

For example, Thomas M. Shapiro has done a great deal of research on the relationship between wealth inequality and racial inequality in the United States. In one of his papers (Shapiro 2006), he argues that the best way to reduce the racial wealth gap is to devise social policy that makes home ownership more possible for a mass number of people in the United States. Shapiro argues that the wealth gap is particularly dramatic when comparing White families with Black and Latinx families. He focuses on wealth (assets that can be accumulated) rather than income (amount of money people earn from salaries), because wealth is the key to families having a safety net as well as passing on advantage (or disadvantage) to their children and generations that follow.

In his book focused on this research, *The Hidden Cost of Being African American: How Wealth Perpetuates Inequality* (Shapiro 2004), Shapiro studied wealth differences between Black and White families. For this research, he examined existing data such as mortgage industry lending data, economic data from the Pew Hispanic Research Center, policy data from the Joint Center for Housing Studies of Harvard University (JCHS), data from the Census and the Bureau of Labor Statistics, transcripts of congressional hearings about housing, and others, to outline the stark differences in wealth privilege between Black and White families and the historical reasons underlying such differences. He complemented this analysis of existing data by interviewing 183 families on their experiences with wealth and how their wealth affected their lives. He noted that families with greater wealth had more freedom, choices, and a heightened ability to transform their circumstances even when working lower wage jobs. A powerful aspect of his work combining economic data with interviews is that he tells stories that shed light on people's family histories and everyday lives related to their economic status, offering a dynamic personal complement to dramatic economic data.

Analysis of Official Statistics

Official statistics are another common example of existing data available for secondary analysis. Organizations' data about their activities are often made available to the public. An example is the bipartisan National Conference of State Legislatures (NCSL), an organization that collects information and develops programs to increase the effectiveness and collaboration of state legislatures.

William Hicks et al. (2015) used official statistics gathered from the NCSL to examine how US political parties attempt to gain influence by enacting laws that require voters to show government-issued identification. This requirement reduces turnout because some voters—especially BIPOC people, people with disabilities, low-income voters, and the elderly—have difficulty securing such documents. These researchers examined an NCSL data set including statistics about more than 26,000 bills focused on voter ID to explore why some state legislatures are more apt to introduce and adopt restrictive voter ID laws. They found that Republican lawmakers were more likely to influence the passage of such laws in "battleground" states (states with closer election margins) where they held enough power to control the state's legislative agenda. Hicks, McKee, Sellers, and Smith argue that Republicans' pursuit of restrictive voter ID laws

Which voters are likely to experience this ID requirement as an obstacle? What official documents might a researcher study to understand voter ID requirements?

reflects an electoral reform strategy focused on securing more votes in elections with close voting margins (2015, 29).

Researchers often analyze official statistics such as these along with other data. For example, Liam Downey, Kyle Crowder, and Robert Kemp (2016) accessed official statistics from the Environmental Protection Agency's (EPA) Risk-Screening Environmental Indicators (RSEI) project. The RSEI data provide estimates of the concentration of industrial air pollution and thus enabled them to assess the level of environmental hazards in neighborhoods. The researchers combined this information with US Census information on neighborhood demographics as well as household and individual data from the nationally representative Panel Study of Income Dynamics (PSID), on families with children. Trends they found include that single-parent families lived in neighborhoods with pollution more than 30 percent higher than two-parent family households (543). Black families lived in neighborhoods with 74.5 percent and Latinx with 56.9 percent higher pollution levels than White families, and they found that race was more significant than family structure in its effect on the level of pollution experienced (545).

BOX 12.2 **Federal Statistics**

City, state, and federal agencies are often required to keep running records of their activities. Federal agencies that collect these kinds of statistics include the following:

- The Department of Housing and Urban Development (HUD) collects information on housing issues in the United States, such how many people live in government-subsidized public housing units.

- The Federal Bureau of Investigation (FBI) is responsible for compiling crime statistics by collecting data from local law enforcement agencies around the country.
- The US Department of Labor collects data that are used to estimate unemployment levels.

These are just a few examples of institutions and organizations collecting statistics that can be subsumed under the general category of "official statistics."

Considerations in Secondary Analysis of Official Statistics

Official statistics have many advantages over some other forms of data, such as those based on surveys. Because the data are often based on whole populations rather than samples, researchers obtain a comprehensive picture of the people in question. They offer an overview of social life and an opportunity to compare between people, groups, geographic locations, and time periods. In addition, because many institutions make their data freely available to the public, an abundance of information is available to researchers. Official statistics also offer important insight into the major institutions that collect them. They can be analyzed to examine how government budgets are spent, how policies are implemented, and how schools, hospitals, the police, and other publicly funded agencies perform their responsibilities.

The problem of **reactivity** is less pronounced with official statistics than when data are collected by interview or questionnaire because the people being described are not being asked questions as part of a research project. In addition, there is a greater prospect of analyzing the data both longitudinally and cross-culturally. Because government organizations compile data on the same measures over many years, researchers can chart trends over time and perhaps relate them to broader social changes. As well, official statistics from different nations can be compared for a specific area of activity. Émile Durkheim's ([1897] 1952) study of suicide, for example, was the result of a comparative analysis of official statistics from several countries.

As with any type of data, a researcher must also consider the disadvantages and limitations of official statistics. Official statistics are collected by major institutional bodies for administrative reasons, which are different from the aims of a researcher pursuing a specific research question. Official statistics can be misleading because the people included in the data have been chosen by the agencies compiling the statistics. For example, Bruce Western (2014) analyzed official data on unemployment and poverty and found government surveys do not count people in institutional settings. He argued that this exclusion enables the incarcerated poor to be hidden from view: the large racial disparity in incarceration allows standard labor force data to significantly understate racial inequality in employment and overstate economic growth.

There are also many ways people and phenomena are inadvertently undercounted in official statistics. Crime statistics are often deceiving because many crimes go unnoticed or unreported so are not captured in statistics. Sexual violence, intimate partner violence, and hate crimes are notably underreported. For these reasons, a substantial amount of crime—often referred to as "the dark figure"—is not included in crime statistics. Official unemployment statistics may similarly misrepresent the "real" level of unemployment. People who have given up trying to find work are often missed, while those who work in the "underground or informal economy" (and are not actually unemployed) may be included.

Official statistics may also be limited by the ways people in official agencies define the issues. One contemporary example has to do with data collected on police use of deadly force, discussed in Box 12.3, and how some police institutions define a "justifiable" shooting. Official statistics may not reflect how community members or a researcher would define the issues.

Issues of **reliability** and validity loom large in official statistics. Reliability is jeopardized when the definitions and policies regarding the phenomenon to be counted vary over time. For example, if a local government decides to devote more police resources to monitoring an activity such as camping out on the sidewalk, sex work, or driving while intoxicated, those rates will almost certainly "increase." Moreover, police officers may be less likely than usual

---

reactive effects (or reactivity) The impact on research when particiknow that they are being studied, which may result in atypical or inauthentic behavior.

---

reliability The research criterion concerned with the degree to which the measure of a concept is stable or consistent.

to let perpetrators off with a warning during such crackdowns. Zero-tolerance programs foster the same results. This situation illustrates how variations over time in official counts of certain activities may not be the result of actual changes but instead changes in the willingness to expend resources on surveillance or to proceed with prosecutions.

Official agencies also must respond to the prevailing social conditions and their effects on organizations' priorities. For example, the Center for Medicare and Medicaid Services (CMS) suspended non-emergency survey activity in March of 2020 in response to the emergent demands of the Covid-19 epidemic. They prioritized data collection about emergency issues related to Covid-19 in order to assess the most pressing threats to safety and public health at that time. The Covid-19 pandemic thus has not only affected routine data collection practices in official agencies, but also created new areas of focus for data collection about the situation.

BOX 12.3 Social Justice Movements and Official Statistics

The use of official statistics for social research is sometimes controversial. In particular, activists and researchers have expressed concerns about the way statistics on crime and other forms of deviance are collected.

This cause has been taken up by activists opposed to police violence against BIPOC communities. For example, when George Zimmerman was acquitted after shooting and killing Trayvon Martin in 2013, Alicia Garza, Patrisse Cullors, and Opal Tometi created the Black Lives Matter (BLM) movement to challenge anti-Black racism. The movement grew in its early years after police officer Darren Wilson shot and killed Michael Brown in Ferguson, Missouri, and Eric Garner died after New York police officer Daniel Pantaleo subdued him using a choke hold prohibited by NYPD regulations. The protests arising in Summer of 2020 after police killed Breonna Taylor in Louisville and George Floyd in Minneapolis have been described as the largest public protests in US history.

One of the goals in BLM's platform is to document the extent of deadly force against BIPOC people. This goal may seem straightforward, especially since the FBI has been collecting data on police practices since 1930. However, while the FBI has a database of how many law enforcement officers are killed in the line of duty each year, there is no comprehensive or reliable national data set on how many civilians police shoot and kill each year. This discrepancy exists because the Justice Department allows law enforcement organizations to self-report on officer-involved shootings as "justifiable homicides."

In 2015, BLM's exposure of the lack of reliable data on officer-involved shootings inspired researchers working with *The Washington Post* to compile such statistics from multiple data sources. That same year, the *Post* recorded twice as many officer-involved killings as what the FBI reported. The data revealed not only more police killings than what was recorded in the official statistics but also a racial disparity in who was most at risk of deadly force. In the majority of cases where White suspects were shot and killed by police, the suspect had attacked someone with a weapon or had a gun. In comparison, in the cases where police killed people exhibiting less threatening behavior, 3 in 5 of those killed were Black or Latinx. Further, Black men were 40 percent of the unarmed men police shot to death in 2015, although they make up only 6 percent of the overall US population (Kindy, Fisher, Tate, and Jenkins 2015). As a result of pressure from the BLM movement and evidence gathered by organizations like *The Post*, the FBI stated that it would improve its data collection of fatal police shootings and launched the National Use-of-Force Data Collection project in 2019. However, participation was voluntary and only 40 percent of police agencies submitted data for 2019 (Jackman 2020).

The collection of statistics can be limited by the complicated nature of social life. Statistics of people who have died from suicide almost certainly fail to include many cases. Determining whether a death was intentional can be difficult in the absence of a note. Moreover, those responsible for concluding whether a death resulted from suicide may come under considerable pressure not to record it as such, perhaps because of religious taboos or potential social stigma.

Finally, not all of the data that official agencies make public is complete or coded consistently. In

---

Methods in Motion | Racial Disparities in School Discipline

What factors help, or hinder, children's success in school? This question has long fascinated both educational researchers and the general public. Although legislation brought about through the *Brown v. Board of Education* ruling (1954), the Civil Rights Act (1964), and the Individuals with Disabilities Education Improvement Act (2004) expanded protections for students and demonstrated promises of educational opportunity for BIPOC students and students with disabilities, inequities continue to exist.

The dynamics around student discipline represent a persistent issue of educational opportunity and equity. Some scholars and education advocates have noted the disparities that exist around the widespread use of out-of-school suspension and expulsion as a disciplinary practice, which begins as early as elementary school. Using a data subset of 436 schools (collected by the School-wide Information System), Russell Skiba, Robert Horner, Choong-Geun Chung, and their research team (2011) explored the degree to which racial disparities exist in nationwide school discipline practices. They examined the demographic details of students receiving a discipline referral, the behavior leading to the referral, the details of the situation and people involved, the infraction cited, and the consequence imposed by the school.

Skiba et al. found that "across an extensive national sample, significant disparities exist for African American and Latino students in school discipline" (95–101). African American students were significantly more likely than White students to receive an office discipline referral (ODR) in elementary school, and both Latino and African American middle-school students were significantly more likely to receive ODRs than their White peers were. Additionally, both African American and Latino students were more likely than White students to receive suspension or expulsion for minor and moderate infractions such as disruptions or tardiness/truancy, beginning at the elementary school level and continuing into middle school. The authors conclude,

> Opportunity to remain engaged in academic instruction is arguably the single most important predictor of academic success. In the absence of an evidence-based rationale that could explain widespread disparities in disciplinary treatment, it must be concluded that the ubiquitous differential removal from the opportunity to learn for African American and Latino students represents a violation of the civil rights protections that have developed in this country since *Brown v. Board of Education*. We propose here that the existing empirical evidence for disproportional school discipline by race, and the severe effect of exclusionary discipline on educational success, make disproportional application of exclusionary discipline an issue in need of immediate and substantive response (104).

These researchers' analysis of over 400 schools' official documents enabled them to examine major trends in school discipline across American educational institutions. Their analysis of the variables race, type of infraction, and referral/suspension allowed them to come to important conclusions about the dynamics of racial inequity in school discipline practices.

their research on neighborhood pollution and family structure, Downey, Crowder, and Kemp (2016) had to rely on RSEI data from the 1990s because the publicly available data after 1999 did not include details of pollution level by census tract (540–541). Thus, they had to consider the limitations of their analyses because of this—especially because this is still the data providing the best estimates of industrial air pollution. Researchers sometimes invoke the Freedom of Information Act to access information from government agencies. This 1967 law allows people to request records from federal agencies, who are required to provide the information unless the information is exempted from the Act due to privacy or national security or because it is legally privileged communication.

Analysis of Government Documents

As described above, governmental agencies compile vast quantities of statistical information. The state is also the source of a large amount of potentially interesting textual material, such as official reports or transcripts of procedures. Imagine you were interested in how your local city council approaches the question of affordable housing. You could look to the meeting transcripts from their Land Use Committee and assess how they discuss the issues and come to decisions. Researchers often analyze such information using content analysis techniques (discussed in Chapter 11) and can use qualitative methods examining the meanings produced in the documents or quantitative methods to assess the frequency of statements or the relationships between different variables within the text; they may also combine methods.

Susan Webb Yackee (2012) was interested in how government agencies make decisions, so she examined documents from US Department of Transportation agencies outlining the rules they must follow when making changes in federal regulations. These documents allowed her to understand the processes through which the agencies developed, discussed, and resolved policy change proposals. Through this, Yackee outlined the ways in which proposals

and decisions were made as well as lobbyists' involvement throughout the process (their comments advocating for particular changes were included in the documents). These documents, along with interviews with involved parties, enabled Yackee to study interest groups' far-reaching influence on government officials' policy decisions during ex parte (off the public record) conversations. She found that lobbyists exert influence not only during active policymaking periods but also during the pre-policy and agenda-setting stage; they persuade politicians to remove unwanted items from the policy agenda and to include desired items in the considered policy proposals.

Another example of research involving government documents is Robert Lee Maril's (2012) book examining the construction of walls at the US–Mexico border as a political solution to unsanctioned immigration. Maril analyzed multiple forms of data, including government documents and official statistics. The construction of a physical wall at the border was a significant focus of Donald Trump's platform and presidential agenda in 2016, but policies seeking to create barriers to entry at the border preceded his term. Maril's work focuses on the earlier policies during the Clinton, Bush, and Obama presidencies, which sought to create a "virtual" border wall between the United States and Mexico.

In his research, Maril examined the negotiations between the government and private contractors to develop a militarized zone at the border and a "wall" consisting of high-tech surveillance reinforced through regular Customs and Border Protection patrols. Maril analyzed the political decision-making process through examining the debates among lawmakers during Congressional immigration hearings, text of immigration legislation supporting the construction of border fencing, and defense contractors' Congressional testimony. He also examined US government budget documents addressing funding for immigration enforcement and border fencing. His analysis revealed evidence of gross fiscal mismanagement and lack of oversight of the tax dollars spent on hiring contractors to construct border fencing: he found that the government gave funds to companies without any competitive bidding process, and that much of the federal money was spent by contractors that did not fulfill the objectives they promised in their fence construction projects.

His analysis (supported by interview and observation data) helped Maril argue that new border fencing construction should be halted pending an assessment of existing policies around border control and immigration. He also called for a review of the need for militarized border zones generally and of the ways in which multinational corporations benefit from American border security policies.

Considerations in Secondary Analysis of Government Documents

Secondary analysis of government documents has many benefits for a social researcher. Many documents have been collected by the government over time, so analysis of existing government documents allows for longitudinal analysis. Examining the documents across different administrations, time periods, or countries can yield important comparative information and insight into how government policy-making, decision-making, and approaches to governance shift over time or vary depending on location. Additionally, these are data that a researcher

Analyses of government documents by nonpartisan watchdog organizations came to conclusions similar to Maril's about the Trump administration's plans to build a physical wall. US government spending data suggest that the Trump administration granted contracts for border wall construction exceeding the amount Congress appropriated in a limited bidding process in which they waived federal contracting laws (Summers 2020). Both community and academic research organizations analyze government data; when studying such recent public policies, it can take some time for peer-reviewed academic researchers to publish their findings. If you were to compare recent administrations' approaches to immigration and policies on border security, what sorts of government documents would be important to analyze?

typically cannot gather on their own; they are unique to the agencies and organizations involved, because they document their work processes. Because of this, government documents offer vital insight into official processes as they are documented.

Scholars studying government documents must always remember that these are the "official story" that the government captures. Many times that is an in-depth story, as conveyed through precise transcripts of meetings and hearings. However, there are many government processes that are not captured in such transcripts. In addition, the documents produced by governments vary over time as policies dictating required documentation shift, and as a result some processes may not even be documented. Many documents are not readily available, which may lead a researcher to invoke the Freedom of Information Act.

Analysis of Oral History Collections

Oral histories and life history interviews housed in archives can be valuable secondary data for qualitative researchers exploring a variety of research interests. Many libraries and archives include holdings of oral histories that can be accessed in person or online if the sources have been digitized. Some examples of oral history collections include the following:

1. The ACT UP Oral History Project is geared toward providing both individual stories and collective views of the activist group ACT UP (AIDS Coalition to Unleash Power), which was a direct-action organization founded in 1987. The project includes interviews with 187 surviving members of the organization, which are available for free download. Many include video clips available for streaming.
2. The Crossing Borders, Bridging Generations (CBBG) oral history project at the Brooklyn Historical Society is a collection of 107 stories of mixed-heritage people and families in Brooklyn, New York. This project is part of the Historical Society's larger collection of more than 1,200 oral histories. The collection has interviews in hard-copy transcripts and audio formats accessible through their site.
3. Densho: the Japanese American Legacy Project is an archive of primary sources pertaining to the experience of Japanese Americans between the early 1900s and the 1980s. They offer over 900 oral history interviews for researchers, which are transcribed and in video format. A primary focus of the archive is the mass incarceration of Japanese Americans during World War II.
4. The Northern Arizona University collection includes materials about life in the Colorado plateau area and northern Arizona. Many of the oral histories are in video format and include interviews with a wide range of people and communities. These are particularly valuable for researchers studying groups indigenous to the region, including oral histories of Paiute, Hopi, and Navajo people in the Grand Canyon and Arizona Strip region.
5. The United States Holocaust Memorial Museum has the world's largest collection of Holocaust testimonies and offers access to many video oral histories online. The testimonies in the archive include those from Holocaust survivors from a range of targeted groups (such as Jewish, gay, Roma, and others) as well as from Nazi collaborators, concentration camp liberators, and witnesses to the atrocities.

These examples are but a few of the archives providing useful oral history data. Researchers using this kind of data can often unearth previously unheard stories in them, as Karma R. Chávez (2012) did in her work using the ACT UP Oral History Archive. Chávez examined protests in 1992–1993 against the two-year detainment of almost 300 HIV-positive Haitian refugees in Guantánamo Bay, Cuba, resulting from the 1987 ban against HIV-positive people immigrating to the United States. Chávez analyzed ACT UP actions against this incarceration, arguing that they disrupt the notion that ACT UP was an organization focused solely on health policy affecting White gay men and challenging the tendency to

How might oral histories about the early years of the AIDS/HIV pandemic be instructive when thinking about government responses to public health crises? How would you combine secondary analysis from the ACT UP Oral History Project with data from the current Covid-19 pandemic to explore this issue?

focus on White, privileged people's struggles with HIV over poor BIPOC people's experiences. She explains, "[R]emembering ACT UP's work on Haiti has profound implications for the memory of past AIDS and queer activism and the possibilities for AIDS and queer coalition building in the present and future" (Chávez 2012, 64).

Considerations in Secondary Analysis of Oral Histories

Available oral histories have a great deal to offer researchers, in that they provide in-depth and comprehensive stories about people's lives. When a researcher has a particular topic or community in which they're interested, oral history collections can be useful. For example, the Densho project could be a vital resource for a researcher interested in how elders in the Japanese American community contended with incarceration during World War II. The oral history collection is a way to preserve the voices for future generations of researchers.

Oral histories are different from other types of interviews. They are meant to capture a detailed picture of someone's life and experiences within their historical moment. An in-depth interview, in comparison, often focuses on a topic that stems from research questions. This makes oral histories useful for secondary analysis, in that the information captures more subjects and is of a broader focus than information curated through the lens of a specific research topic. For example, although the Densho project has a primary focus on the wartime experience of incarcerated Japanese Americans, the oral histories in the collection likely touch on other aspects of the Japanese American experience during the mid-twentieth century.

BOX 12.4 Physical Traces as Existing Data

American cities and towns occasionally crack down on fliers illegally posted to utility poles, fences, trees, and construction sites. What can a social researcher learn from this form of public communication? What do we lose when these measures of accretion are stripped away?

The world in which we live can be a site of existing data. When we look around at the environment, we see much evidence of people's lives and the activities in which they engage.

We use the term *physical traces* to describe the evidence people leave of their lives within the natural and built environment. For instance, when you next go for a walk in the park, note the combination of "official" and "unofficial" paths and walkways. What paths do park authorities maintain, and how do these reveal the ways they would like people to navigate the environment? What areas have been worn down by people using them and creating additional paths? How might this reveal the preferred routes of dog walkers, mountain bikers, or people experiencing homelessness who camp in the park? Eugene Webb, Donald Campbell, Richard Schwartz, and Lee Sechrest (2000) describe the ways people "wear down" the environment through their use of it as *measures of erosion*. What might you be able to learn about social life by analyzing such measures of erosion in the park?

In another project, you could note which seats in a movie theatre are more worn down than others to see where people prefer to sit or examine what parts of an outdoor play structure are most well used to get a sense of what children prefer to do in their play. You can also learn about social life by examining what are known as *measures of accretion*, which are the layers that accumulate

A limiting factor to secondary analysis of oral histories relates to the question of whose stories have been captured within oral history collections. Especially in the past, stories of marginalized people were captured less frequently than were those of more privileged people. Privileged people's stories have often been considered more valid or important, and it can be risky for marginalized people to share their stories. Imagine, for example, a Japanese American grappling with the invitation to share their life history after they had just been liberated from internment camps and were trying to re-enter life in a society that still denied them citizenship and the right to own land. In addition, some topics have only recently been deemed important enough to explore or were previously viewed only through the lens of shame and stigma, such as sexuality or disability. This can introduce challenges for and convey information about life in that current moment or past times. For instance, a research study by William Rathje and Cullen Murphy (1993) called "The Garbage Project" examined household garbage since 1973 to understand people's recycling practices, food waste, dietary habits, and items they accumulate and throw away.

Hostile architecture is an important physical trace to consider when studying the lives of people experiencing homelessness. The term describes a common urban design practice in

"Hostile architecture" refers to urban design practices that target certain people and behaviors in public spaces. What people and practices are the measures shown here targeting? How likely would you be to notice them if you weren't a member of a targeted group?

which public spaces are built in a manner that discourages people from using them in manners property owners dislike. These measures include metal grommets on rails and walls to prevent skateboarders from grinding on them, spikes on surfaces and protruding metal bars on bus stop benches preventing people from lying down on them, or sprinklers or speakers playing loud music placed in areas someone might try to sleep at night. James Petty's (2016) work on controversy over "anti-homeless spikes" in London explores how public resistance to such measures may not signify true discomfort with punitive and exclusionary structures negatively affecting people experiencing homelessness but instead an overall distaste for both visible reminders of homeless people as well as of the measures taken to remove them.

a researcher hoping to conduct a secondary analysis of oral histories.

Analysis of Big Data

Big data refers not only to the information retailers or healthcare institutions collect about us, but also the massive repository of digital information collected through search engines and social media platforms. The rapid expansion of technology has made it possible to gather vast amounts of data from the digital traces we leave behind whenever we use a cellphone or the internet. This information is not only massive but rapidly changing.

---

big data Large quantities of data, collected in traditional ways by companies or institutions and through digital means.

The data collected by government, technology companies, retailers, and others capture millions of people's activities, preferences, and communication networks. "First-party" data holders are organizations that collect data from their users, such as Google, Amazon, or Facebook. "Third-party" data firms are those that purchase the data that other organizations have collected from their users and then market it. Using this data, the government can track people's activities, companies can determine how to market products, and a potential employer can gather information about applicants. The information is collected into data sets that can be analyzed to understand market trends and online behaviors. For example, retailers use the data to understand purchasing trends and what items internet shoppers click on, which helps them develop their marketing strategies, sometimes tailoring them to users fitting a particular customer profile. Governments use such data to assess national security concerns, such as behavior of people who could be planning violence or developing a network to engage in acts of terrorism. Controversy often surrounds the accumulation of big data, such as when for-profit colleges were found to target students and leave them in extreme debt and when the company Cambridge Analytica harvested data from multiple sources (including Politico and Facebook) to target voters, which some critics believe influenced the outcome of the 2016 presidential election.

Social science researchers initially used the internet as a recruitment tool for their studies. Today, researchers often study life on the internet—and the digital data available enables them to do so. David Lazer and Jason Radford (2017) outline three main categories of big data sources, which they describe as *digital life, digital trace data,* and *digitalized life data.*

Digital life refers to people's actions and behaviors in online platforms such as Instagram, Snapchat, or Facebook. Scholars and retailers can access these data to analyze people's behaviors. Some people who study these platforms see them as representations of the wider society, examining such things as how

social inequality operates, how people network with others, share news, or mobilize politically. Others look at these platforms as social realms in and of themselves, considering what human life and interaction looks like in these online settings.

Those examining *digital traces* examine what people "do" using their devices; this focuses on the records of actions people engage in digitally. This examination of big data forms a chronicle of actions, like how long people spend on the phone, whether they're texting or talking or streaming videos, what they click on, or where their navigation app sends them as they travel from point A to point B.

When studying *digitized life,* someone would consider the degree to which people's lives are digitized, exploring how potentially non-digital aspects of life have become encapsulated in digital form. For instance, how does the constant video recording of public places serve as a record of human activity? What information can be gleaned through scouring digitally scanned documents like newspapers and books—sources that have become digitally available only relatively recently?

Considerations in Secondary Analysis of Big Data

There are many benefits to conducting secondary analysis of big data. Big data can encourage researchers to use new methodologies. Paolo Parigi, Jessica Santana, and Karen Cook (2017) argue that researchers have a unique opportunity to study human interaction using big data. They explore how to take advantage of large, available online data archives using a method called *online field experiments* to assess the underlying influences of and dynamics within social interactions. Because people's social interactions now often take place in digital arenas, these authors argue this is an important setting in which to observe people's behaviors. Their study sought to explore what factors led people to trust others on online sharing economy platforms. They explored how experience with the sharing economy might affect people's interpretation of information and development of trust. They did an online experiment with users of Airbnb in which they invited users to engage in a game with others and used this to test which factors led to greater trust. They were also able to assess participants' demographics and behavior on the Airbnb platform in relation to their behavior during the experiment. This background information enabled the researchers to understand more about the group of people involved in the experiment and their choices.

Because of the quantity of information that big data represents, researchers must think about what methods they want to use to sift through the data and how this relates to their research aims. The massive scale of big data means that these existing data naturally align with quantitative analysis and statistical methods. The large number of people that can be captured combined with the extent of the information available means a quantitative researcher could explore the relationships between a vast array of variables to develop a quite complex analysis of social life.

Big data is useful not only to quantitative researchers, though. Arielle Hesse et al. (2019) point out that qualitative software can be also used to analyze the vast amount of textual data that exist (for instance in social media); they suggest that big data has enabled "the emergence of large-sample qualitative research" (556), and, although big data repositories consist of a great deal of statistical information, the textual information also lends itself to qualitative discourse analysis studies.

While big data has great potential to offer important information to researchers, it also presents many challenges. Researchers must consider the type and the quality of big data—how it is gathered and how rapidly it changes. A great deal of the available data are gathered by governments and corporations for their own ends, whether for national security or for commercial motives. Because of this, these organizations may not make the data available for research or make it available at a cost. The question of who has access to all of this data is an important one with consequences for academic research. Because

corporations mostly are the ones with access to the data—not researchers unaffiliated with corporations—some argue there is a digital divide between those who do and don't have access to big data (Boyd and Crawford 2012). Katie Metzler et al. (2016) surveyed over 9,000 social scientists doing research with big data and found that 32 percent of them found it difficult to access the data sets in which they were interested (12). Also, a majority of them encountered challenges teaching about big data because students do not typically have high-level quantitative analysis and computer programming skills at the undergraduate level (16).

Lazer and Radford (2017) point out that the digital archives of big data do not typically include information that has been scientifically collected in the way a researcher would collect data. Big data tends to capture technology-related behavior, ranging from web browsing to credit card use, and so the information it represents largely captures those people with access to and knowledge of available technology. Those who do not use technology are not included.

Also, the collected information is characterized by constant and quick changes due to the nature of information technology. The complexity of the data could be a bit overwhelming, and a researcher would need to really study and become familiar with a significant volume of the data before tackling their analysis. The sheer amount of information, as well as the changing nature of the information that's gathered, can make it difficult to truly define the parameters of big data and make it difficult to know how to handle the information. A new field of data science has gained ground in recent years in order to determine how to best manage and analyze this information, and many of the people involved in this industry come from a computer science background.

Considerations When Conducting Secondary Analysis

There are several reasons for considering secondary analysis as a serious alternative to collecting new data. As described above, large surveys, government documents, oral histories, and big data all have specific advantages and disadvantages as a source of secondary analysis. There are also advantages and disadvantages shared by all of these types of data, which researchers must take account of when choosing to conduct secondary analysis.

Advantages of Secondary Analysis

Resources: Cost and Time

As we've noted, secondary analysis offers good-quality data for a fraction of the cost involved in collecting new data. Collecting data takes a great deal of time and resources, and engaging in secondary analysis means conducting research that demands much less time and cost compared to collecting new data.

More Time for Data Analysis

Precisely because data collection is time-consuming, the analysis of the data is often rushed. Working out what to make of the data requires considerable thought and, often, willingness to learn unfamiliar analysis techniques. While secondary analysis invariably entails a lot of data management—partly to get to know the data and partly to put it into an appropriate form—the analysis phase should not be underestimated. Freedom from the task of collecting fresh data means that data analysis can be better planned and executed.

New Interpretations from Reanalysis

Data can be analyzed in so many different ways that there is almost always additional insight to be gained from them. For example, a researcher conducting a secondary analysis may look at relationships between concepts or variables that have not been previously considered, prompting a reconsideration of the data's relevance. Also, new methods of data analysis, with the potential of allowing different interpretations of the data, are continuously emerging. As awareness of such techniques spreads, and their potential relevance is recognized, researchers can apply them to existing data sets.

Opportunity for Cross-cultural (International) Analysis

It's easy to forget that many findings may not apply to countries other than the ones in which the research was conducted. Cross-cultural research can address that issue. There would be many ways to do secondary analysis to explore cross-cultural dynamics. A researcher could analyze oral histories from people in different countries to examine experiences in similar time periods (e.g., the Cold War era, or the period when the expansion of technology affected global communication trends) or of people in similar communities worldwide (e.g., anti-imperialist activists in the Global North and South, or people with disabilities in eastern and western Europe).

Opportunities for such cross-cultural analysis appear to be increasing. For example, common core questions may be used in national surveys conducted in several countries. Britain, Canada, and the United States all have an equivalent of the GSS. Many researchers do cross-cultural analysis using large survey data. One example is Jolynn Haney's (2016) research on negative attitudes toward LGBTQIA2S+ people in the United States and the Netherlands (2016). Haney used data from the World Values Survey (WVS) to examine individual level (micro-level) influences on "homonegativity," a focus different from studies that often analyze cross-cultural attitudes about LGBTQIA2S+ people on a macro-level. She explains, "The WVS was initiated in 1981 as a standardized method of collecting and comparing cross-national data on cultural values," employing identical survey questions and sampling techniques in over 100 different countries (2016, 1362). Using these data, Haney was able to conclude that homonegative responses were higher in the United States compared to the Netherlands (25.1 percent vs. 4.1 percent). In both countries, two strong predictors of homonegativity were resistance to living near a person with HIV/AIDS and resistance to living close to a foreign worker or immigrant; this finding shows an interesting interconnection between xenophobia, ableism, and homophobia. Haney points out that these findings demonstrate a dual issue that could be addressed through public education and policy focused to lessen "negative public health perceptions linked to the LGBT community" (1369) and challenge assumptions about recent immigrants' cultural differences and competition for jobs.

Wider Obligations of the Social Researcher

For all types of social research, participants give up some of their time, usually for little or no reward. Using secondary data spares an already over-surveyed public yet another round of questions. Indeed, much social research is chronically under-analyzed because primary researchers tend to focus on only their own research questions or to lose interest in the existing data when they think of a new set of research questions. Making data available for secondary analysis enhances the chances that the data will be put to additional use and explored to its fullest potential.

Opportunity for Longitudinal Analysis

Another valuable feature of secondary analysis is that it can provide an opportunity for longitudinal research. Sometimes, as with the GSS (see Box 12.1), a panel format (in which the same subjects are examined at different times) is used to chart trends over time. Similarly, because certain interview questions are recycled and asked of different samples each year, shifting opinions or changes in behavior can be identified.

For these reasons, secondary analysis should be considered not just by students but by all researchers. In fact, some granting agencies require applicants proposing to collect new data to demonstrate that relevant data are not already available.

Limitations of Secondary Analysis

There are some drawbacks to analyzing data gathered by others.

Lack of Familiarity with the Data

With data collected by others, a period of familiarization is necessary to become acquainted with a wide array of variables, the ways they were coded, and various aspects of their organization. This period can be quite prolonged with large data sets.

No Control over Data Quality

While secondary analysis offers researchers the opportunity to examine data of far higher quality than they could collect themselves, this point applies mainly to reputable data sets such as the GSS and others. With lesser-known data sets, more caution may be necessary with regard to data quality, although the archives holding the data usually perform certain fundamental checks.

Absence of Key Variables

Because secondary analysis entails the analysis of data collected by others for their own purposes, one or more of the secondary analysts' key variables may not be present or may be measured differently in different years. David Walters (2004) had this problem in a study of incomes earned by graduates of various kinds of post-secondary programs; therefore, he had to modify the original data. Similarly, an analyst might want to see if a known relationship between two variables holds even when other variables that are not part of the data set are taken into account. Considering more than one independent variable at a time is a form of *multivariate analysis*, a topic we touch on in Chapters 6 and 14.

Secondary analysis is a common research method for the many reasons outlined in this chapter. Whether used alone or in combination with other data collection methods, secondary analysis can provide important insights into major social trends and organizational activities and allow researchers to explore new and interesting hypothesis in existing data.

Key Points

Introduction: Research Using Shared Data

- Researchers using secondary data analysis analyze data collected and made available by other researchers.
- Types of existing data include large surveys, official statistics, government documents, oral histories, and big data.

Large Surveys as Existing Data

- Examples of large surveys include the GSS and the Census.

Analysis of Official Statistics

- Some organizations and university consortiums maintain achieves of data sets for researcher use.

Analysis of Government Documents

- Organizations and state and federal agencies like the FBI and the US Department of Labor collect data that are referred to as "official statistics."
- Local, state, and federal government agencies produces a great deal of information in documents (called government documents) that can be used in secondary data analysis.

Analysis of Oral History Collections

- Oral histories and life history interviews housed in archives can be valuable secondary data sources for qualitative researchers.

Analysis of Big Data

- *Big data* refers to the massive sources of data which are collected through traditional methods by companies and institutions, often through digital sources.

Considerations When Conduction Secondary Analysis

- Secondary analysis offers quality data for a tiny fraction of the cost and time involved in collecting new data allotting more time for analyzation.
- Secondary analysis can provide an opportunity for longitudinal research, cross-cultural (international) analysis, or the studying of subgroups from a larger sample.
- New interpretations can be drawn from secondary sources during reanalysis of data.
- Considering that secondary analysis entails the analysis of data collected by others for their own purposes, one or more of the secondary analysts' key variables may not be present or may be measured differently with the passing of time.

Questions for Review

1. What types of material do researchers examine using secondary analysis? What sort of information do each of these different types of material offer to a researcher?
2. What unique strengths and limitations must researchers consider when analyzing large surveys, official statistics, government documents, oral histories, and big data?
3. What are the most common large surveys used in secondary analysis?
4. How do researchers access data from large surveys?

5. What are the benefits of using official statistics in research?
6. How might official statistics be biased?
7. Why would a researcher want to analyze government documents versus (or in combination with) official statistics?
8. What types of information might be available to a researcher studying oral history archives?
9. What are "physical traces" and how can they be used as existing data?
10. What is big data, how is it gathered, and for what purposes?

11. What dynamics might big data enable a researcher to understand, and what are its limitations?

12. What are the advantages of secondary analysis in research?

13. What are the potential limitations of secondary analysis?

Portfolio Exercise

1. How can you examine your research question/ topic through secondary analysis? What types of official statistics, government documents, oral history archives, physical traces or big data sources can you use in your research? Reflecting on Chapter 12, write a proposal which outlines and addresses the following:
   a. What is your research question?
   b. What type of existing data might be useful to analyze to help explore your research question? Discuss how official statistics, government documents, oral history archives, physical traces or big data sources may or may not be useful to your study.
   c. If you imagine analyzing existing data in your study, what data sources would you use?
   d. How do you feel these sources would illuminate aspects important to your research questions?

Interactive Activities

1. Divide into small groups either in person or online. Each group focuses on one of the following data archives of official statistics and government documents:
   a. The National Archives Catalog: The National Archives and Records Administration is an independent agency of the United States government charged with the preservation and documentation of government and historical records (https://catalog.archives.gov/)
   b. The United States Census Bureau (https://data.census.gov/cedsci/)
   c. Catalog of US Government Publications (https://catalog.gpo.gov/F?RN=291998357)
   d. USA.gov—the official web portal of the United States federal government (www.usa.gov/statistics)

First browse the sites to assess and understand the information available on them. Then as a group:
   • identify three research questions or objectives that could be addressed using your secondary data sources, and
   • discuss how do these questions use the data in a way different from the aims of the original data collector

Once you have finished, the groups will take turns proposing their research questions and describing their sources to the class, opening up the class for discussion about the merits of using the source to explore the proposed questions.

2. Select one of the following oral history archives from the text and pull a few audio samples for the class to access.
   a. The ACT UP Oral History Project (http://actuporalhistory.org/)
   b. The Crossing Borders, Bridging Generations (CBBG) oral history project at the Brooklyn Historical Society (http://dlib.nyu.edu/findingaids/html/bhs/arms_2011_019/)
   c. Densho: the Japanese American Legacy Project (http://densho.org)
   d. The Northern Arizona University collection (https://nau.edu/special-collections/)

e. The United States Holocaust Memorial Museum (www.ushmm.org/collections/the-museums-collections/about/oral-history)

As your instructor plays the audio (or a selected clip from the interview) for the class, take notes, coding fo.r reoccurring key concepts and themes. After listening to the oral history, write for 15 minutes, considering the following questions:

a. Who is the subject of this interview? Whose stories does it tell?

b. What was the original intent of the oral history interview?

c. What key themes did you notice in the oral history?

d. How could you use this data in secondary analysis?

Finally, write a sample research question that investigates the possibilities of this oral history as a secondary analysis data source.

Online Resources

Existing Data Sets: Large Surveys

- General Social Survey (GSS)
  https://gss.norc.org/

- The Social Justice Sexuality Project (SJS)
  https://socialjusticesexuality.com/

- American National Election Studies (ANES)
  https://electionstudies.org/

- The United States Census Bureau
  www.census.gov/

- US Census Bureau Data
  https://data.census.gov/cedsci/

- Collaborative Psychiatric Epidemiology Surveys (CPES), 2001–2003
  www.icpsr.umich.edu/icpsrweb/ICPSR/studies/20240/version/8

- PEW Research Center
  www.pewresearch.org/

Accessing Existing Data Sets

- The Inter-University Consortium for Political and Social Research (ICPSR) at the University of Michigan
  www.icpsr.umich.edu/icpsrweb/index.jsp

- The University of California at Berkeley Survey Documentation and Analysis Archive (SDA)
  http://sda.berkeley.edu/index.html

- The Institute for Social Research and Data Innovation at the University of Minnesota
  https://isrdi.umn.edu

- The ISRDI's data dissemination program, IPUMS, and other data archive the Minnesota Research Data Center (MNRDC)
  www.ipums.org/
  www.mnrdc.umn.edu

- Social Explorer
  www.socialexplorer.com

Official Statistics

- The National Conference of State Legislatures (NCSL)
  www.ncsl.org/

- Freedom of Information Act
  www.foia.gov/

- The Washington Post database of police shooting data
  www.washingtonpost.com/graphics/investigations/police-shootings-database/

- The Guardian (British News source) also has a database of officer-involved shootings in the US during 2015 and 2016:
  www.theguardian.com/us-news/ng-interactive/2015/jun/01/the-counted-police-killings-us-database

Oral History Archives

- The ACT UP Oral History Project
  http://actuporalhistory.org/

- The Crossing Borders, Bridging Generations (CBBG) oral history project at the Brooklyn Historical Society
  http://dlib.nyu.edu/findingaids/html/bhs/arms_2011_019/

- Densho: the Japanese American Legacy Project
  http://densho.org

- The Northern Arizona University collection
  https://nau.edu/special-collections/

- The United States Holocaust Memorial Museum has the world's largest collection of Holocaust testimonies
  www.ushmm.org/collections/the-museums-collections/about/oral-history

For more resources please visit
www.oup.com/he/bryman-reck-fields1e

PART V

Making Sense and Sharing What We've Learned

While data analysis seems like the final step in the research process, researchers plan their analysis strategies in a project's early stages, and different methodological orientations suggest particular directions for analysis. This could mean carefully measuring concepts and deciding early on what statistical tests to use after data collection. Or it could involve inductive approaches in which qualitative data are analyzed as they're collected to help the researcher refine the study and determine which avenues to further explore. No matter what methodology they use, data analysis is an iterative process that allows researchers to derive meaning from their data. Writing is another element that spans the research process. Approaching writing as both a process and a skill allows us to develop ourselves as thinkers who can use writing as a path to build our understandings and share the knowledge we've gained through research.

13

How Do Researchers Develop Inductive Findings?
Qualitative Data Analysis

▲ *Legacy Project @ PS250*, by Ellie Balk, www.elliebalk.com. In June 2012, students, faculty, and staff of PS 250 middle school in Brooklyn, NY, created self-portraits on glass for this mosaic. The tiles are organized by grade and color-coded by class number. Used with permission of the artist.

Analyzing qualitative data collected through interviews, participant observation, or unobtrusive measures like content analysis is creative, systematic, and never straightforward. For one thing, such data typically form a large body of initially unstructured textual material. Moreover, qualitative research emphasizes interpretive processes that are not easily codified. This chapter will examine some general systems for qualitative data management and analysis.

Reading this chapter will help you to understand

- strategies for managing and organizing qualitative data;

- coding as a key process in qualitative data analysis;

- grounded theory as a general approach to qualitative data analysis, including its processes, outcomes, promises and limitations;

- narrative analysis, an approach that strives to reduce fragmentation;

- intersectional analysis, an approach to data analysis that emphasizes intersecting experiences of social difference and inequality;

- strategies for avoiding the fragmentation of data; and

- the possibilities and limitations of using computer-assisted qualitative data analysis software (CAQDAS).

The US folklorist, novelist, and anthropologist Zora Neale Hurston (1942) once wrote, "Research is formalized curiosity. It is poking and prying with a purpose" (143). Her curiosity focused on Black life and racial struggle: she conducted interviews and fieldwork in lumber camps, documented the sexual exploitation of Black women, and explored the spiritual and religious lives of people in the American South and the Caribbean. She deposited her interviews in public archives, wrote plays and novels, and published news articles. Across all these genres, she sustained her curiosity. She listened carefully to the world that interested her and then identified patterns to the experiences of being Black, a woman, or poor. Hurston's findings are now fundamental to how we understand these lives.

Social research is all about poking and prying with a purpose—that is, finding and explaining patterns. Qualitative social research may seem far removed from novels and plays, but Hurston's career points to how much they share. The **concepts** and **categories** that qualitative researchers look for as they navigate vast seas of data represent meaningful patterns to social life. This world of meanings, perceptions, and feelings has a coherence to it—narratives that can be told. Qualitative researchers strive to understand and tell those stories.

Introduction: Why Managing Qualitative Information Can Be Challenging

Making sense of the texts—words, images, and experiences—contained in field notes, interview transcripts, or other documents allows us to pursue lines of thought and interpretation that are rarely pursued in quantitative studies.

One challenge of qualitative research is that it rapidly generates a large, cumbersome database.

---

concepts General or abstract ideas that describes observations and ideas about some aspect of the social world.

---

categories Cluster or collection of instances that share characteristics or features.

Seated left, Zora Neale Hurston listens to blues singer and guitarist Gabriel Brown in Eatonville, Florida. The photo was taken by Alan Lomax, an ethnomusicologist whom Hurston enlisted to record Brown's music, preserving it for generations of folk music students and enthusiasts. As a social researcher studying contemporary musical culture, what questions would you ask about the blues, US South, and race?

Managing all of that information is not easy, especially for the researcher confronting it for the first time. *What do I do with it now?* is a common refrain. Procedures for analyzing qualitative data are not nearly as codified as they are for quantitative data, largely because many researchers feel codification is undesirable in this largely interpretive method. Nevertheless, there are some broad guidelines and strategies that we will explore in this chapter.

Managing and Organizing Qualitative Data

As Kristin Esterberg notes, qualitative researchers can feel as if they are "swimming in a pool of paper" when they begin to analyze their data in earnest

(2001, 151). They may find themselves sifting through a seemingly endless list of computer files containing field notes and interview transcripts. A researcher might be surrounded by stacks of documents—meeting agendas, DJ playlists, course syllabi—that they gathered while working in the field.

The first step is to make sure all interviews have been transcribed and all field notes written up. Every digital file should have a consistent and easily searchable file name that includes relevant information. For example, names for interviews conducted in a school-based ethnography might include the interview number and participant's role: 001—Student, 002—VicePrincipal, 0030—HealthTeacher, and so on. File names for field notes could include the date and site of the observation, with 170926—DramaClass referring to a drama class observed on September 26, 2017, and 170927—ParkingLot to refer to time spent the next day in the school parking lot before and/or after school. (Using two digits to indicate the year, then month, then day will allow file names to appear in chronological order.)

Once everything has been named and labeled, it's time to organize the data. Files can be organized by data collection method: place field notes in one folder, notebook, or binder and interview transcripts in another. Data might also be organized chronologically (field notes, transcripts, and documents all filed in order of completion) or by type of participant (student interviews together, then teachers, then administrators). Or use

Even in the digital age, qualitative research can produce a dizzying amount of paper documents, jotted notes, newspaper clippings, and transcripts. What system of organization would you adopt to organize qualitative data?

some combination of these different systems. Let's return to the school-based ethnography example. Chronological order makes sense if the data will be considered in the order it happened over the semester. Arranging the data first by type and then

---

BOX 13.1 Organizing Data

In a participatory action research (PAR) study of HIV education with incarcerated women of color, Jessica Fields, Isela González, and co-authors (2008) conducted a series of workshops in San Francisco County Jail. Preparing each workshop meant creating supporting materials: an outline of the workshop prepared in advance (what the university researchers called "preps"); "legacy wall" material, in which the combined research team documented each workshop and in this way created a "legacy" to help orient newcomers; and other teaching materials, including handouts, field notes, and interview transcripts.

The university researchers also wrote a series of documents after each workshop:

- *progress notes*, which are one- or two-page documents in which they noted any challenges or achievements, items they needed to bring to the next workshop, and other logistical concerns;
- *field notes*, which were usually about five to seven pages long and documented the workshops as completely as possible; and
- *notes-on-notes*—another term for what we will call "analytic memos"—in which they identified themes, questions, and ideas they wanted to explore further.

TABLE 13.1 | Data Inventory of Workshops from a PAR Study

Workshop	Progress Notes	Field Notes	Notes-on-Notes	Materials°
11		JF KH	KH	prep; legacy
12	EF	MR	MR	prep
13	KH	JF EF	EF	prep; legacy
14*		JF KH	KH	
14	MR EF	JF MR EF	MR	prep; legacy; roles handout
21	KH	JF KH EF	EF KH	prep; legacy
22	MR	JF KH	MR KH	prep
23	EF	MR		prep; transcript (from 23); legacy
24	KH	JF	KH	prep; research statements
31	EF	JF EF	JF EF	prep; role play handout; legacy
32	MR	JF KH	KH†	prep; interview themes handout; legacy
33	EF	JF MR	MR	prep; legacy
34	KH	JF KH EF	KH EF	prep; legacy
41	MR	JF KH	KH†	prep; legacy
42	EF	JF MR	MR	prep; legacy
43	KH	KH EF	EF KH†	sample field notes; legacy
44		JF KH	KH	miscellaneous; program

*Black History Month workshop

†Single N-on-N addresses multiple workshops

°Also includes Roles, Coding Themes, Property Note Letter, and Resources handouts, used throughout workshops

by participant category would enable the researcher to read through all the student interviews first, to see what patterns emerge across their accounts. See Box 13.1 for another example.

Other practical considerations remain. Are hard copies or digital copies best? Regardless of which format(s) you choose, backup copies are essential. Esterberg issues an important reminder: "You can't analyze data that you can't find" (2001, 157). It will be easier to find things with a complete list of all the collected data.

As the stream of documents threatened to become overwhelming, the university researchers Described in Box 13.1 created an inventory document (Table 13.1) that recorded workshop numbers, associated notes (progress, field, and notes-on-notes), the initials of the researcher(s) who authored the document, and related materials. The table is filled with abbreviations that, while not intended to be understood by others, allowed the researchers to keep things organized.

Approaches to Qualitative Analysis

As we discussed in Chapter 10, qualitative researchers generally aim for immersion during data collection: they think, talk, move, and feel alongside the people they study in order to think, talk, move, and feel like them. Ideally, immersion continues after they've left the field, during the period of concerted data analysis, when information is organized and catalogued. Here, researchers read through all the data multiple times and fill their minds with the voices, interactions, conflicts,

---

BOX 13.2 Iterative Analysis: Repeated, Systematic, and Varied

Iterative processes are a mainstay of qualitative analysis. Researchers visit their data and emerging analysis multiple times, repeating steps, looking for new insights, and checking unfolding revelations against the existing data. For some qualitative researchers, iteration is quite rigid: they repeat the same steps in precisely the same order multiple times. For others, it is more reflexive, with researchers analyzing data throughout the collection process, committing to writing analytic memos as they also write field notes and transcribe interviews. By doing so, they aim to have the emerging analysis shape the path of their data collection.

No matter what the iterative process looks like, it should reflect the researcher's study design. When Fields et al. (2008) worked with public health educators and incarcerated women of color in San Francisco County Jail, their participatory action design meant involving the women in the data analysis. Every few workshops, the team of university and incarcerated researchers spent time analyzing transcripts together inside the jail. Halfway through the series, the university researchers organized the insights emerging from these analysis sessions into a series of statements, as follows.

- There are limited quality resources for women in jail and even fewer resources for monolingual Spanish-speaking women.

- Many women of color want to learn about HIV so they can help their children make healthy choices about preventing the virus.
- For some women of color, incarceration is the only time they have access to health care and safe spaces for women.
- Women often choose food, money, love, and/or drugs over safer sex.
- Women put themselves at risk in relationships with men who do not respect their bodies and sexual health.

The university researchers brought the statements to their collaborators inside the jail for their feedback. The incarcerated women then fine-tuned, contested, and affirmed the statements. Some disagreed that monolingual Spanish-speaking women did not have adequate resources. Others expressed interest in the last statement and asked that upcoming workshops have a new focus: what keeps women in relationships that even they recognize are bad for them? That interest helped shape the later data collection as, for example, subsequent interviews explored reasons women stay in these relationships, and theories emerged regarding the value of intimacy in women's lives.

---

questions, and ideas running through field notes and transcripts. Immersion requires that researchers allow themselves to be overwhelmed and trust themselves to find patterns, explanations, and theories.

Qualitative data analysis is inductive. For example, an analysis of gender—as an identity, set of meanings, or organizing and stratifying idea—emerges from a close reading and careful **coding** of field notes, transcripts, and other qualitative data. Qualitative analysis is also *iterative*, occurring in multiple steps that are completed repeatedly and

systematically, with each one informing the next (see Box 13.2 and Chapter 5).

Coding

Coding is the starting point for most forms of qualitative data analysis. Reading a portion of data and describing it with a code allows the researcher to reflect upon and keep track of what is happening or

---

coding The process of labeling, categorizing, and organizing data collected in order to facilitate qualitative or quantitative analysis..

being conveyed in the data. These codes emerge after data collection, when they are used to label events, utterances, and interactions; to distinguish between and compile themes that emerge in that labeling; and to organize the researcher's thinking. In their classic guide to qualitative research, *Analyzing Social Settings,* John and Lyn Lofland (1995) identified a series of questions to ask when developing codes; they include the following:

- What is happening in this interaction/utterance/behavior?
- What are people doing?
- What do people say they are doing?
- What kind of event is going on?
- What does this interaction/utterance/behavior represent?
- What is this interaction/utterance/behavior about?
- What question does this interaction/utterance/behavior suggest?
- What sort of answer to that question does this interaction/utterance/behavior imply?

The aim of these questions ranges from description to categorization, from speculation to theory building. Whatever the questions' focus, they are designed to generate ideas by approaching the data from multiple directions.

These questions can help shape an iterative analytic process guided by the following principles and practices:

- *Begin coding as soon as possible, ideally while data collection is still underway.* Simultaneous and iterative data collection will sharpen the emerging understanding of the data and help to ease the feeling of being swamped when data collection ends.
- *After data collection is complete, read through the data without taking any notes or assigning any interpretations.* Just take the data in; become reacquainted with the feeling of being in the setting from beginning to end, conducting all of the interviews, or encountering the range of material in the setting. You're likely to encounter some data that have become unfamiliar with

time. After completing this initial read, it's time to jot down a few notes about what seems especially interesting, important, or significant.

- *Read them again.* Read through the data again, but this time make marginal notes about any significant remarks or observations. Initially, the notes will be straightforward: notes regarding key terms that participants repeat, words they seem reluctant to use, points of conflict or agreement, or assumptions that carry across the data. With this jotting, coding begins: the researcher is generating terms that will help in interpreting the data.
- *Don't worry about generating too many codes in early stages of analysis.* Some codes will be fruitful, others not. The important thing is to be as inventive and imaginative as possible; coding can be trimmed and streamlined later.
- *Remember that any one interaction/utterance/behavior can, and often should, be coded in more than one way.* An outburst of anger, for example, can be seen as an emotion, a cause of stress, or the beginning of a new level of integration. The outburst might also be coded to indicate who got angry, who was the object of the anger, or what was the substantive source of frustration. Researchers should notice—and note—many possible and relevant interpretations of a single instance.
- *Review the codes across the data.* Look at codes across multiple sets of field notes or multiple transcripts. Consider field notes and transcripts in relation to one another. Are multiple words or phrases currently describing the same phenomenon? If so, decide which one offers the most incisive description and remove the other(s). Are there connections among codes? Do participants seem to believe one thing tends to be associated with or caused by something else?
- *Review codes in light of the existing literature.* Do some of the codes relate to concepts and categories other researchers have identified and named? If so, would it make sense to use the existing terms? Doing so might place the study's findings in a broader conversation about issues of interest to the researcher and the field. Or do the codes suggest a revision or rethinking of ideas other researchers have advanced? Perhaps this is where the study's contribution to the literature lies.

- *Consider more general theoretical ideas.* Begin creating some general theoretical ideas about the data. Try to outline connections between concepts and any developing categories. Consider in more detail how they relate to the existing literature. Develop theories and questions about perceived links and check the data for confirmation.
- *Finally, keep coding in perspective.* It's only one part of the analysis, an important mechanism for thinking about the meaning of the data and for reducing the data to a manageable size. The larger task of interpretation awaits, including making connections between codes, reflecting on the overall importance of the findings for the research literature, and pondering the significance of the coded material for the lives of the people who are the subjects of the research.

There is no one correct approach to coding data. In their classic discussion of qualitative data analysis, Amanda Coffey and Paul Atkinson (1996) point to three levels of coding. The first level involves basic coding. Let's return to the case of the interview Megan Comfort et al. (2005) conducted with the woman partner to an incarcerated man, featured in Box 9.4. In this excerpt, a basic code could be "conflicts with guards" or "family visits." Such a coding scheme might be a good place to start, but it is unlikely to provide more than a superficial analysis.

A second level involves a deeper awareness of the content of what study participants say and the organization of the social setting or conditions the researcher is studying. In the Comfort interview, an example of this second-level coding might be "perceived sexual behaviors" or "surveillance from guard." A third level moves away from the literal—what participants say or do, for example—to explore broad and implicit themes. Again, the Comfort interview provides some examples of this level of coding: a researcher might assign the code "strategies of resistance" or "modes of enforcement."

Examining the interconnections between codes may reveal that some are dimensions of a broader phenomenon. For example, "surveillance from guard" may come to be seen as part of general "interruptions of intimate relationships," and "perceived sexual behaviors" may come to be seen as one of

several "strategies of resistance." In this way, a map of the more general or formal properties of the concepts begins to emerge. The researcher will develop this preliminary map in later qualitative analysis.

Grounded Theory

The most frequently used approach to qualitative analysis is **grounded theory**, which is "derived from data, systematically gathered and analyzed through the research process" (Strauss and Corbin 1998, 12). Grounded theory's two central features are a commitment to developing theory out of (that is, "grounded in") data and an iterative approach in which data collection and analysis proceed in tandem, repeatedly referring to and changing in response to each other.

Coding is a basic feature of grounded theory, beginning soon after the initial collection of data. Kathy Charmaz, a leading voice in grounded theory, asserts that in grounded theory analysis, "the researcher's interpretations of data shape his or her emergent codes" (2000, 515). The process of interpretation in grounded theory is marked by *constant comparison* of new and existing data within a particular concept or category. This comparison requires sensitivity to differences between emerging concepts/categories. Researchers can write analytic memos about concepts and categories as coding unfolds.

Grounded theory analysis continues until researchers reach **theoretical saturation**, which happens when there are no new insights to be gained from reviewing old data or collecting new information. Theoretical saturation is a guiding principle in **theoretical sampling**, which we discuss below. The aim of theoretical sampling is not to get to a sample

---

grounded theory An approach to qualitative data analysis in which data collection and analysis proceed iteratively, producing a theoretical understanding.

---

theoretical saturation In grounded theory analysis, the point at which emerging concepts have been fully explored and no new insights are generated.

---

theoretical sampling Data collection and/or selection of cases guided by emerging theoretical considerations and repeated until theoretical saturation is reached.

size statistically large enough to allow for generaliz-able results but rather to sample until the researcher has achieved conceptual breadth. As few as a dozen interviews may be enough to make a claim about a homogenous group; comparisons among groups or variables will require more.

Coding in Grounded Theory

In grounded theory, coding involves reviewing qual-itative data and assigning labels or names to items that share a similar theme, hold potential theoretical significance, or seem particularly salient to the social worlds the researcher is studying. Because grounded theories emerge from the data, coding is usually ten-tative and fluid, particularly in the earliest stages. Researchers label observations, utterances, interac-tions, and other passages in the data that seem to be potential indicators of concepts and categories.

Note the tentativeness of this description: "that seem to be potential indicators." Qualitative re-searchers learn to live with and value caution and contingency while analyzing data. As they assign codes, the aim is first to describe what is happening in their data, and then to look back on the multiple codes that were assigned to identify and describe patterns and recurring situations in the data. Thus, qualitative researchers repeatedly review, group, compare, and regroup indicators to see which concepts/categories they fit with best. Codes are

---

open coding An early stage of qualitative analysis in which the researcher stays close to the data and gener-ates concepts that may later be grouped together to form categories.

---

line-by-line coding An in-depth method of analysis in which the researcher applies a code to every line of field notes or transcripts.

---

axial coding A process in qualitative data analysis of re-lating codes to one another with the aim of making con-nections between concepts and categories.

---

focused coding The formal and systematic application of most frequently occurring or compelling codes to qual-itative data.

---

renamed and reassembled throughout the process. If more than one researcher is doing the coding, com-promises are likely. Ultimately, such an extended and iterative coding process requires flexibility, pa-tience, and creativity.

Researchers practice different types of coding as they generate grounded theory.

- **Open coding** is undertaken with the objective of not imposing researchers' own or others' predetermined ideas. Researchers stay close to the data and generate the concepts that are later grouped together to form categories. Thus, concepts such as trust, surveillance, or affection could emerge during open coding. Depending on the researcher's aims and the insights gleaned from initial open coding, these concepts might remain separate categories or later be combined into a broader category called "emotion."

- **Line-by-line coding** helps researchers dig even deeper into the data by focusing on small units—literally individual lines on the page. One strength of line-by-line coding is its attention to detail: a researcher may produce as much as one code per line of text. Another strength lies in the process of making the data seem unfamiliar. The researcher codes each line on the page, not each sentence, paragraph, or idea. The process may seem strange at times, and that strangeness—the act of making the data unfamiliar—is this method's asset. Line-by-line coding might reveal that an interview passage that seems to be about anger might also be about insecure employment or rivalry.

- **Axial coding** is "a set of procedures whereby data are put back together in new ways after open coding, by making connections between categories" (Strauss and Corbin 1998, 96). Codes are linked to contexts, consequences, patterns of interaction, and apparent causes. For example, the categories of "anger" or "emotion" could be linked to the contexts in which they are expe-rienced or expressed, for example, contexts of hardship or loss.

- **Focused coding** is "the procedure of selecting the core category, systematically relating it to

BOX 13.3 Line-by-Line Coding

As a first stage of coding, Charmaz (2004) recommends line-by-line coding, in which virtually every line in the transcript or other data source has a code attached to it (Figure 13.1). This way, the qualitative researcher does not lose contact with the data and the perspectives and interpretations of those being studied. The line breaks in field notes and interview transcripts are likely random—a function of the margins set in the formatted document and not a reflection of some organic meaning in the text.

91. SAM	
92 No, err but I've always moved around... since leaving school. I've	*peripatetic lifestyle*
93 always been in a partnership, err, I've alwasys seemed to. It's been a	*partnership/relationship*
94 long-term partnership so l've never been sort of out of parterships	*Long term relationships*
95 so it's not been too bad. For years and years i've lived with people.	*partnerships acceptable.* *Shared accomm.*
96 But when I've had domestics and things like that, well you see, I	*Domestics*
97 left home at fifteen years old and I've never been back to live with	*Chose independence*
98 my mum and dad. I'm one of them sorts of people who don't like	*Characterises self as* *independent*
99 going and lying about on friend's couches or putting on people. So	*Not reliant on others*
100 really, yes, if I've had domestics and that, I've gone and slept in	*Domestics*
101 'car-for days on end sometimes. But really this is my first time	*Slept in car*
102 that I've actually come away from everybody and lived by meself.	*Hostel seen as live alone*
103 I have been homeless but I've never had a place by meself. I'm just,	*Never lived on own*

FIGURE 13.1 **Example of line-by-line coding**

This arbitrariness becomes helpful for line-by-line coding because the spacing/spatial reorganization can make the data slightly unfamiliar and its meaning less stable in the researcher's mind.

---

other categories, validating those relationships, and filling in categories that need further refinement and development" (1990, 116). A core category is the focus around which other categories are integrated—what Anselm Strauss and Juliet Corbin called the storyline that frames the account. In the case of hardship and loss, the core category might be "adaptation."

These four types of coding are really different moments in the same process, each relating to a different point in elaborating concepts and categories. Open and line-by-line coding happen in initial stages of a project, when it's important to be open-minded and to generate as many new ideas—that is, codes—as necessary to organize the data. Axial and focused coding happen later, when researchers understand what codes appear most frequently and seem most revealing. Combining the initial codes generates new codes. The data are then re-explored and re-evaluated in terms of the selected codes.

Outcomes of Grounded Theory

Coding in grounded theory yields a series of different products, all of which move the analysis toward the formulation of theory:

- *Concepts.* The "building blocks of theory" (Strauss and Corbin 1998, 101), concepts are the discrete phenomena produced through open coding.
- *Categories.* At a higher level of abstraction, a category subsumes two or more concepts. An especially crucial concept may become a core category (see Box 13.4).

- *Properties.* Categories have properties—attributes or aspects that differentiate them from other categories. As qualitative researchers identify categories, they also ascertain those defining properties and begin to distinguish between categories.
- *Working hypotheses.* Theories often begin as "working hypotheses," or initial hunches about patterns, comparisons, and relationships between concepts.

Theories emerge as researchers define concepts, develop categories, articulate working hypotheses, and begin to build a theoretical framework that explains social conditions, phenomena, or injustices. The steps leading to these theories are somewhat nebulous; as we noted in the opening pages of this chapter, qualitative analysis is difficult to codify. Nevertheless, we can describe the grounded theory process as it generally unfolds:

- The researcher begins with a general research question, then initially samples relevant people and/or incidents and collects relevant data.
- The researcher codes data and may generate concepts at the level of open coding.
- There is a constant and repeated movement among these steps—posing a question, constructing a sample, collecting data, and coding those data. Early coding regularly suggests a need for new data, which leads to *theoretical sampling*—data collection and coding that is guided by and intended to test emerging understandings in grounded theory analysis.
- Through repeated comparison of indicators and concepts, the researcher generates categories, striving to ensure a fit between indicators and concepts.
- Categories become saturated in the course of the coding process.
- The researcher explores relationships among categories and allows working hypotheses about connections between categories to emerge.
- Theoretical sampling calls for further data collection.

- The collection of data is likely to be governed by the theoretical saturation principle and the testing of working hypotheses, which leads to specification of theory.
- Researchers sometimes take insights generated in the grounded theory process to additional, different settings. By applying the insights to different social conditions (e.g., another school, racialized interaction, or stigmatized group),

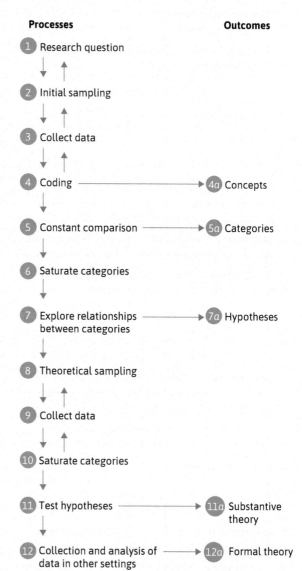

FIGURE 13.2 **Processes and Outcomes in Grounded Theory**

BOX 13.4 **Categories in Grounded Theory**

Jason Whiting et al. (2014) used grounded theory to explore how male perpetrators of intimate partner violence perceived their actions. The researchers suggest that examining offenders' points of view is important to fully understand intimate partner violence and to develop effective therapies and interventions.

Qualitative interviews with 13 men were conducted, with the following three research questions guiding the analysis:

- How do men who have been violent describe their relationship in terms of abuse?
- What do men believe contributes to the violence?
- How do they feel about the violence in their relationship?

Prior to open coding, the data were examined to identify "significant statements." Open coding was then performed by labeling the selected statements with descriptors. Next, a process of axial coding grouped the data into "identifiable categories that tied together" (279).

Although perpetrators routinely tried in interviews to justify or rationalize their violent behavior, another category—remorse—emerged during axial coding. One interviewee stated, "I have always been upset by the abusive behaviors," while another said, "I was in the wrong forever [sic] putting my hands on her" (282). As the researchers considered these and other remarks the interviewees made about rebuilding relationships with abused partners and about their relationships with their children, the category of remorse came up more and more often.

The authors mention that a finding of perpetrator remorse is rare in studies of intimate partner violence. Whiting et al. take the position that violence is inexcusable and acknowledge that the offenders' remorse may be an attempt at manipulation. However, they also argue that counselors and other professionals should consider the remorse expressed by perpetrators as a starting point to help them develop empathy for their victims and to reflect on how intimate partner violence offends their values.

---

a researcher might strengthen their grounded theory, extending its reach and developing more abstract categories. In doing so, the researcher generates what Strauss and Corbin call "formal theory."

These steps are summarized in Figure 13.2. Any diagram is only an approximation, and this is particularly true here, partly because of the multiple approaches to grounded theory and partly because of the challenges in conveying its iterative nature. In this diagram, arrows pointing in both directions indicate the *recursive* (back-and-forth) relationship between data collection and analysis.

Analytic Memos

An important tool in grounded theory research is the **analytic memo**, consisting of notes that researchers write for themselves during ongoing inductive analysis. Memos can provide a reminder of what a particular concept or category refers to. They can also be an opportunity to note conceptual links among interviews or to record analytic questions that the researcher wants to return to later in the analysis

---

analytic memo A brief written exploration of concepts, questions, and emerging analysis that a researcher produces during iterative inductive analysis.

Trust

Person's expectation that the word, promise, oral, or written statement of another individual or group can be relied on (Rotter 1980). Word, promise, or statement may be explicit or implied, imagined, or actual.

Sociological social psychology reminds us that promises, trust, and intimacy occur in dyads and in romantic relationships, but also, for example, in groups, institutions, and among strangers.

Thus, promises could range from

- a promise to keep workshop conversations confidential
- a promise to protect one's partner from HIV and STI infection
- a promise from a criminal justice system to be fair and impartial

Sociological social psychological research also points to social conditions that foster and undermine trust—whether generalized, particularized, or personalized. (See review article: Sandra Susan Smith, "Race and trust." *Annual Review of Sociology* 36 (2010): 453–475).

Trust is diminished by

- historical and contemporary experience of discrimination
- socialization
- neighborhood disorder
- unstable relationships

Trust is enhanced by

- shared group membership
- embeddedness in closed social networks
- reputation for trustworthiness

These social conditions help to explain why race makes such a difference to trust in the United States. Blacks overwhelming distrust of Whites.

- ongoing discrimination
- disordered neighborhoods (immediate circumstances)
- lessons from adults (as youth) and then from peers
- histories of betrayal at hands of White people
- absence from networks

Questions and ideas to consider further: Data suggest trust is not only a matter of calculating the trustworthiness of the trustee or determining the best strategies for self-protection. Indeed, trust is a story about the truster as well as the trusted. Trusters may want to claim the experience of trust for themselves. Is that the case? Trust is an affective stance—a position one assumes in relation to others. Think about trust as a sort of oppositional claim, helping to bring one's sense of oneself, community, and intimate possibilities into line with one's hopes and desires.

FIGURE 13.3 **An analytic memo**

process. Overall, analytic memos can be useful in helping researchers to crystallize their ideas and keep track of their thoughts on various topics; they also help to shape the researchers' reflections on broader issues.

Figure 13.3 presents an example of an analytic memo, taken from the Fields et al. (2008) study of HIV education for incarcerated women (discussed in Boxes 13.1 and 13.2). The researchers coded for implicit and explicit expressions of trust in their analysis of their

---

Concepts, categories, coding, theoretical sampling, and theoretical saturation are all key features of the grounded theory approach, and all were in play when Charmaz (1997) used grounded theory to examine the identity dilemmas of men with chronic but not terminal illnesses. The chief steps in her analysis were

- interviewing men and a small number of women;
- exploring the interview transcripts for gender differences;
- searching for themes in the men's interviews and published personal accounts such as autobiographies (e.g., "accommodation to uncertainty," as the men found ways of dealing with the unpredictable paths of their illnesses);
- building "analytic categories from men's definitions of and taken-for-granted assumptions about their situations" (1997, 39);
- conducting further interviews to refine the categories;
- rereading personal accounts of chronic illness with a particular focus on gender;
- reading a new group of personal accounts; and
- making "comparisons with women on selected key points" (1997, 39).

How do you think Covid-19 challenged notions of vulnerability and masculinity among North American men? Which groups of men in particular may have faced greater "identity dilemmas," to use Charmaz's term?

Based on this analytical procedure, Charmaz helped to explain the importance of notions of masculinity in maintaining an identity for chronically ill men. Of particular significance in this work is the idea of "identity dilemmas": the ways that men approach and possibly resolve the assault on their traditionally masculine self-images. Through this iterative grounded theory process, she showed that men often use strategies to re-establish earlier selves in order to preserve their identities, at least in their own eyes. The idea of identity dilemmas is now broadly applicable to other groups and people contending with challenges to their self-images and -definitions.

field notes and interviews. The memo specifies a definition that will guide later data analysis, helping them to code for instances of trust with care and precision. The memo includes references to previous research to be cited in publications resulting from this coding. It also includes questions and ideas that the researchers will explore further as coding and analysis continue.

Promises and Limitations of Grounded Theory

The influence of grounded theory and its core elements, from coding and analytic memos to the very idea of allowing theory to emerge from data, extends beyond grounded theory practitioners. It is evident across not only published research articles but also recently developed computer software. In many cases, software programs have been written with grounded theory processes in mind.

Nevertheless, like any approach to data analysis and theory building, grounded theory presents some challenges. Most social researchers are sensitive to ongoing debates and prevailing concepts in their disciplines, and it can be challenging to suspend this awareness until the late stages of analysis, when theories are supposed to emerge. However, even for grounded theorists, the aim is not to achieve theory-neutral observation; few people today even believe that this is possible. Most researchers agree that insights and analyses are conditioned by what they already know about the social world. Grounded theorists recognize that those perceptions will shape data analysis and data collection. The task is to make

---

BOX 13.6 **Emotion in Analysis**

A goal of the study by Fields et al. (2008) was to write (with the help of a team of student research assistants) field notes and analytic memos documenting the workshops and their emerging analysis. The notes included the university researchers' accounts of being surprised and indignant at the persistent surveillance to which the incarcerated women and university researchers were subject. The university researchers also described their resistance to the idea that their incarcerated collaborators were untrustworthy. These team members bristled at calls from jail deputies to count pens and pen caps at the end of each session. When the incarcerated researchers asked how to punish those who broke confidentiality, their university colleagues urged them to practice trusting one another.

The issues here are practical and analytical. Trust is central to the PAR approach, and the university researchers needed to establish a different sort of relationship with the incarcerated women if they were to work together. Those relationships were also integral to the understanding of race and racism, incarceration, and vulnerability that would

emerge from the study. Discussions of trust shifted across the course of the field notes. Initially, the university researchers wanted to trust their incarcerated colleagues, to distance themselves from the deputies, and to establish the trusting relationships that PAR, anti-racist feminism, and their personal ethics seem to call for. In these early field notes, the university researchers seemed to rush past any obstacles to trust. Later, they recorded moments of trust that felt more like products of the collaborators' time together—the interactions, accountability, history, and promises kept.

Attention to their own emotional experience of the field allowed the entire team to understand that meaningful trust emerges over time, and that it is the product of something even as it also anticipates a future of interactions. Trust has a particular temporal quality: people often want to build on trust—have it exist before we act—but it is the product of past conditions and something we achieve. This idea became apparent through analytic attention to emotions across the field notes.

room for new insights and not to let preconceptions crowd out new understandings.

Often, researchers contend with tight deadlines and cannot enact grounded theory analysis in its ideal form. For example, perhaps they cannot transcribe an interview and write a memo about it before conducting another interview. They might decide to listen to the interview and jot some notes before conducting the next one, or they might write an analytic memo about their experience of the interview—almost like field notes—instead of writing about the specific interview exchanges they would notice if reading a complete transcription. The aim is not to achieve the ideal but instead to strive for and to get as close to the ideal as possible.

Another challenge lies in fragmentation. Grounded theory tends to invite researchers to code their data into discrete chunks, and some believe that this kind of fragmentation results in a loss of context and narrative flow (Coffey and Atkinson 1996). To avoid this loss, researchers can use computer software to retain a sense of the coded exchange or behavior's conditions. Regardless of whether they are working with digital or paper copies, researchers can return to the complete field notes or transcript regularly to ensure that their analysis maintains that context.

Other Methods of Qualitative Analysis

Though grounded theory is the most widely practiced and cited method of qualitative data analysis, there are other qualitative methods for researchers to choose from. Often researchers use these methods in conjunction with those of grounded theory. We outline some of these analytic alternatives below.

Narrative Analysis

The term **narrative analysis** covers a wide variety of approaches based on the search for and analysis of stories that people tell to understand their lives and the world around them. As Brian Roberts (2002) observed, the term is often used to refer both to the research approach and to the accounts that it examines—the stories that people tell about their lives and

other events. In general, narrative analysis entails sensitivity to the connections among people's accounts of past, present, and future events and states of affairs; to people's sense of their place in those situations; to the stories they generate about them; and to the significance of context for the unfolding of events and people's sense of their roles in them.

How can researchers use narratives to analyze a social trend such as the increasing number of women getting tattoos, a phenomenon that challenges the standard "masculinity" of male tattooing? As part of a three-year participant observation study, Michael Atkinson (2002, 2004) elicited tattoo narratives from the women he interviewed. Drawing on feminist theories about bodies, he found that these women did not consider themselves misfits, though they use tattoos to signify their "established" or "outsider" constructions of femininity. Ideas about femininity, including conformity and resistance to cultural norms, are crucial in explaining women's tattooing.

Catherine Kohler Riessman (2004) distinguished four models of narrative analysis:

1. *Thematic analysis* examines what is said rather than how it is said.
2. *Structural analysis* emphasizes how a story is told. Issues of content do not disappear, but attention is focused on the use of narrative mechanisms to increase the persuasiveness of a story.
3. *Interactional analysis* looks at the dialogue between the storyteller and the listener. The co-construction of meaning by the two parties is especially prominent, though content and form are also taken into account.
4. *Performative analysis* analyzes narrative as a performance and explores the use of words and gestures to get a story across. This model of narrative analysis also examines audience responses to the narrative.

All four of these models can be applied to data acquired through a variety of research methods (notably semi-structured and unstructured interviews and participant observation), but narrative analysis has also become an interviewing approach in its own right.

Michael Atkinson found (2002) that ideas about conformity and resistance to cultural norms are crucial in explaining women's tattooing. What kinds of questions do you think he asked to arrive at this finding? How would you study whether his findings hold true today, 20 years later?

Coffey and Atkinson (1996) stated that a narrative should be examined in terms of the functions that it serves for the teller. The aim of narrative interviews is to elicit participants' reconstructed accounts of connections between individual events and between events and contexts. Robert Miller (2000) proposed that narrative interviews in life story or biographical research are far less concerned with eliciting facts than with drawing out interviewees' reflections and interpretations, as revealed in their accounts of their lives or families.

---

intersectionality A theoretical framework committed to understanding social categories, identities, and hierarchies as interrelated systems and experiences.

Intersectional Analysis

The term **intersectionality** was originally coined by legal scholar and critical race theorist Kimberlé Crenshaw, though intersectional thinking has a long history in Black feminist thought. Intersectionality describes an approach to thinking about social differences and inequalities. While people are often inclined to think about race, gender, sexuality, ability, class status, and other social categories one at a time, intersectionality asks us to think about them in relation to one another—that is, as intersecting experiences. Crenshaw developed this idea in response to legal systems routinely asking women of color who were victims of violence, harassment, or discrimination whether they were victims of either sexism or racism. She argued

---

Mixed Methods in Action | Analyzing Girls' Thinking About Femininity and Sexuality

In a study of US girls' gendered and sexual behavior and desires, Deborah Tolman surveyed 148 English- and Spanish-speaking eighth-grade girls in a Northeastern US high school (1999). The survey included questions about the girls' sexual behavior and health and their beliefs about femininity. Tolman and her research team identified 46 girls whose responses fell on the low or high ends of a measure of beliefs; they then conducted qualitative interviews with those girls. In the published paper, Tolman presents quantitative analysis of the survey data, a brief qualitative analysis of interview data, and then an in-depth analysis of a single case from the interviewed sample: a 13-year-old girl who calls herself "Will Smith" and is critical of conventional gender norms. As Tolman explains, "Will Smith exemplifies a pattern identified in these interviews. Girls who articulated a critical perspective on unequal gender arrangements and

norms of femininity were better able to answer questions about how being a girl affected the choices they made in their relationships."

Quantitative analysis of the survey data helped Tolman identify a range of relationships to femininity and sexual health. With a shift to qualitative analysis, Tolman was able to identify patterns in the girls' critical thinking about gender, sexuality, and agency. In a qualitative analysis of a single interview, Tolman offers a nuanced picture of a girl with a particularly critical and healthy take on femininity. The reader comes to understand how Will Smith's "ability to see, know, and understand how girls are positioned as sexually vulnerable by cultural norms of femininity constitutes a strength that needs to be recognized and built upon" (1999, 137). Quantitative analysis helped Tolman recognize a broad pattern, while qualitative analysis helped her understand the extremes of and exceptions to that pattern.

---

that this question is impossible to answer. A Black woman is never simply a woman or a person of color; she is always both, and more. Similarly, any study participant is never simply a person living in poverty, a person with disabilities, or a member of the LGBTQIA2S+ community. People hold such identities simultaneously, and each identity shapes our experiences of the others.

The idea of intersectionality has been influential in many contemporary social movements. In areas like feminism, LGBTQIA2S+ rights, and Black Lives Matter, intersectionality has changed the way people think and act. The same is true in social research. Hae Yeon Choo and Myra Marx Ferree (2010) identified three practices of intersectional analysis:

- *group-centered*, in which researchers focus their questions and findings on the experiences of marginalized people and communities;
- *process-centered*, in which researchers consider how one site of oppression and inequality—gender,

for example—shifts across different axes of power like race or sexuality; and
- *system-centered*, in which researchers analyze sites of oppression and inequality as always intersecting and relating to one another, with no one site ever being primary.

With these frameworks in mind, Choo and Ferree revisited some classics of sociological research to see how intersectionality would change and strengthen their analyses. They found that some of these ethnographies held up White and middle-class people as the norm, even as they told important stories about people of color and poor people.

Choo and Ferree urge researchers to move beyond supposedly giving voice to marginalized people and communities. They hope researchers will instead analyze social inequalities and differences as relational and dynamic—the product of social processes and interactions between individual and institutional factors. They also encourage recognizing that an intersectional analysis requires seeing that race, gender, class, and other social differences span all groups. That is, race shapes White people's lives as much as it shapes the lives of people of color.

Data Fragments and Contexts

Sensitivity to the issue of data fragmentation has been heightened by a growing interest in narrative analysis since the 1980s. For example, Riessman became concerned about fragmentation when coding themes in her structured interview study on divorce and gender. She described these concerns in the first of her many book-length discussions of narrative analysis:

> Some [interviewees] developed long accounts of what had happened in their marriages to justify their divorces. I did not realize these were narratives until I struggled to code them. Applying traditional qualitative methods, I searched the texts for common thematic elements. But some individuals knotted together several themes into long accounts that had coherence and sequence, defying easy categorization. I found myself not wanting to fragment the long accounts into distinct thematic categories. (1993, vi)

Riessman's account suggests several possibilities: that the coding method can fragment the data; that some forms of data may be unsuitable for coding; and that researchers can produce narrative analysis, since what she provided in this passage is precisely a narrative.

Interest in narrative analysis certainly shows signs of growing, and in large part this trend parallels the rebirth of interest in the life history approach.

Methods in Motion | The Promise of Unexpected Findings

One of the key insights of qualitative research is that people often interpret their situations in ways that an outsider might not expect. Take the example of women with eating disorders. You might imagine that they would wish to alter their eating habits, but Krista Whitehead (2010) found that some women with anorexia nervosa and bulimia do not want to change; in fact, they may seek to develop a collective identity with women in similar situations by interacting with them on pro-eating disorder (Pro-ED) websites. These sites are controversial in that they do not present eating disorders in a negative light or recommend that people living with eating disorders pursue treatment; instead, they seek to promote solidarity and companionship among people who have the condition and do not want to recover. Some of the people who visit Pro-Ed websites revel in their situation, such as one woman who wrote that "Ana [anorexia] loves me, She may use me, But she won't forget me. I am not her victim, I am one of her lovers. Every day I pray to be loved above the rest" (Whitehead 2010, 617).

The research involved "virtual ethnography," in which Whitehead regularly and closely monitored postings made on Pro-ED websites. Taking a grounded theory approach to the issue, she identified five practices that contributed to the development of a collective identity:

1. encouraging surreptitious eating behaviors by sharing stories about how they hid their bulimia from their partners or family members;
2. focusing on domestic tasks such as cooking (e.g., sharing recipes for dishes that are delicious but not calorific and are easily purged);
3. encouraging the idea that beauty, particularly thinness, is essential to self-worth;
4. promoting friendships among people with eating disorders and even casting the disorder as a friend; and
5. drawing inspiration from celebrity women who have battled eating disorders or are simply thin and considered beautiful.

The author concludes that these practices are "gendered" in the sense that they reinforce and reproduce dominant norms and stereotypes about what it means to be a woman.

Nonetheless, coding is likely to remain prominent, for several reasons: it is widely accepted in the research community; not all analysts are interested in research questions that lend themselves to narratives; grounded theory and the techniques associated with it are influential; and the growing use of computer software for qualitative data analysis frequently invites a coding approach.

Regardless of analytical strategy, qualitative research strives to move beyond description. It is not enough to simply say, This is what my subjects said and did; isn't that interesting? Interpretation and theorizing are necessary. Some may worry that focusing interpretation requires researchers to impose their voice and thereby contaminate participants' words and behaviors. However, researchers' commitment to doing justice to what they have seen and heard must be balanced against the fact that findings acquire significance in an intellectual community only when they have been subject to reflection. The researcher has to do more than simply take notes or record answers.

The Technology of Analysis

The tools of analysis range from low-tech to high-tech. For example, some qualitative researchers still prefer to print hard copies of their field notes and interview transcripts and then write early codes in the margins; they may use sticky notes, colored pens, and highlighters to mark significant passages. Others, having recorded all of their field notes on laptop, tablet, or smartphone, use the comment function of their word-processing software to insert remarks. After refining their notes into codes, researchers sort passages into categories by cutting and pasting—either

Although many quantitative researchers rely heavily on computer-assisted data analysis, some qualitative researchers remain hesitant to adopt CAQDAS. What are some objections are to using software to analyze qualitative data? How valid do you think those concerns are?

literally, with scissors and paste, or electronically, by moving text from one document to another. Regardless of whether they're cutting and pasting electronic or paper text, researchers need to carefully label the origins of each chunk with, for example, participant name, date of observation, and other relevant identifying material. These labels will make it easier to locate these portions of the document and the contexts in which they initially occurred.

Computer-assisted qualitative data analysis software (CAQDAS) is an increasingly popular option for working with qualitative data (see Box 13.7). Most of the best-known programs allow researchers to code text and retrieve it later, tasks that were once done manually. Researchers using the software can search for all chunks of text relating to a code and then cut and paste them together. CAQDAS cannot replace a human being making choices about the codes, coding

---

BOX 13.7 To CAQDAS or Not to CAQDAS?

While the use of computer software is almost universal in quantitative data analysis, qualitative researchers often avoid CAQDAS. With a small data set, such programs may not be worth the time and trouble required to become familiar with new software. On the other hand, learning new software will give you skills that you may need in the future, for several reasons.

While CAQDAS may boost the legitimacy of qualitative research, simply by appealing to a cultural fondness for technology, there are arguments for not using it:

- Most of the coding and retrieval features needed for qualitative data analysis, such as search, cut, and paste, already exist in word-processing software. Using Microsoft Word may be enough for smaller qualitative projects—a decision that would save not only money but also the time required to learn new software.
- Some researchers worry that CAQDAS coding represents the quantification of qualitative text and diminishes the value of qualitative research by subjecting it to reliability and validity criteria appropriate to quantitative research.
- Others feel that the software reinforces and even exaggerates the tendency towards a fragmentation of the textual materials, interrupting the natural flow of interview transcripts and field notes. Context is crucial to qualitative

research; as CAQDAS pulls data excerpts from original data sources, it may push context to the sidelines.
- Coffey et al. (1996) argue that the style of coding and retrieving qualitative data analysis in most CAQDAS presumes a grounded theory methodology. In their view, the emergence of grounded theory as a new standard is inconsistent with a key strength of qualitative research: its flexibility.

On the other hand, CAQDAS packages have their virtues:

- CAQDAS programs like NVivo and Dedoose invite thought about "trees" of interrelated ideas—a useful feature that encourages researchers to consider possible connections between variables.
- The software makes it possible to count the frequency with which a particular form of behavior occurs or a particular viewpoint is expressed in interviews. This feature can help quantitative researchers understand how representative quotations from interview transcripts or field notes may be.
- CAQDAS enhances the transparency of qualitative data analysis. Published reports are often unclear about how qualitative data were analyzed (Bryman and Burgess 1994). The software may force researchers to be more explicit, reflective, and instructive about the process of analysis.

textual materials, or interpreting findings. As with quantitative data analysis software, the researcher must still decide which variables to analyze, select analytic techniques, and then make sense of the results.

CAQDAS is likely too expensive for personal purchase, though there are student and educational discounts, and some universities subscribe to these software packages in order to make them available to students, staff, and faculty. Demonstration copies of some of the main packages can be downloaded from the distributors' websites.

Key Points

Introduction: Why Managing Qualitative Information Can Be Challenging

- Analyzing qualitative data is never straightforward; the process is inductive, iterative, and exploratory as it seeks to find and explain patterns.

Managing and Organizing Qualitative Data

- Qualitative analysis begins with the organizing of data.

Approaches to Qualitative Analysis

- Grounded theory is an approach to qualitative data analysis that uses the data analyzed in iterative processes to generate theory.
- Coding begins when researchers read through their data with fresh eyes without taking any notes or making interpretations; they may then repeat this process, allowing for new ideas and recurring themes to emerge.
- When researchers have fully explored emerging concepts and qualitative data analysis yields no new insights, theoretical saturation has been achieved.

- Researchers pursue multiples types of coding when generating grounded theory: line-by-line, open, axial, and focused coding. Line-by-line coding, typically done in the first stage of the coding process, helps researchers keep focus on the data in relation to the perspectives and interpretations of those being studied.
- The perceptions and social positions of researchers and interviewees have the potential to shape data analysis and data collection.
- Researchers write analytic memos throughout the inductive process of qualitative data analysis. These memos include explorations of concepts, questions, and emerging analysis for researchers to explore further in the coding process.

Other Methods of Qualitative Analysis

- Innovations in qualitative research include narrative and intersectional analysis.

The Technology of Analysis

- Computer-assisted qualitative data analysis software (CAQDAS) supports the qualitative data analysis by offering systems for cataloguing data and themes to facilitate data access.

Questions for Review

1. What are the first steps when analyzing qualitative data?
2. Describe the iterative nature of qualitative analysis. How does this iterative nature shape the findings achieved in qualitative data analysis?
3. Describe the different types of coding and how they interact with one another.

4. What are the risks of data fragmentation when coding?
5. What are the main features of grounded theory?
6. What role does coding play in grounded theory analysis?
7. What is theoretical saturation? How does this concept relate to grounded theory?

8. What are the products of grounded theory? How do they emerge from the grounded theory process?

9. How can researchers generalize findings achieved in the grounded theory process?

10. What are the roles of memos in grounded theory?

11. In what ways does narrative analysis provide a solution to data fragmentation?

12. How does the emphasis on stories in narrative analysis represent a distinctive approach to the production and analysis of qualitative data?

13. How do the practices of intersectional analysis shape coding processes and subsequent data analysis?

14. How does intersectional analysis challenge the effort to "give voice" to marginalized communities and people?

15. What are the applications, possibilities, and limitations of using CAQDAS programs?

Portfolio Exercise

If you haven't already, use the interview guide you wrote in your Chapter 9 portfolio exercise to carry out a brief qualitative interview, or conduct a session of participant observation. Make sure to record and transcribe this interview or write complete field notes; then, line-by-line code and open-code the transcript or field notes. In 2–3 pages, write an analytic memo in which you (1) name emerging concepts and ideas and (2) note questions that you would like to keep in mind as you conduct further observations or interviews and perform further coding.

Interactive Activities

1. Working with a collection of birthday greetings—cards, memes, GIFs—provided by the instructor, review the images and text that constitute the birthday messages. Focus on open coding, noting what strikes you about the cards—for example, the sentiments expressed; gendered, racialized, class, and sexual imagery; and colors and figures featured in the illustrations. Join a group with two other students, online or in person, and compare your notes. Discuss the results of the open coding, generating a thorough list of ideas and insights.

2. Review the list of codes generated in the initial open coding of the greeting cards. Write the codes on sticky notes—one code per sheet. Working with partners, students move the sheets around, clustering those that seem to belong to the same category. Do not think too much about what makes them belong together; focus instead on brainstorming and following your hunches. Once the partners are satisfied with the grouping, begin naming and defining the categories. Partners should come to some agreement on the terms and definitions, but also keep in mind that these will likely be revised in later iterations of the analytic process.

3. Again working with your partner, review the codes—terms and definitions—and begin to map relationships among the ideas. Which terms are related to others? For example, are some sentiments likely to be associated with particular images? Are some sentiments more likely to be expressed in cards that seem to be intended for younger or older recipients? Identify and then describe those relationships, identified through a process of axial coding, once again noting that these descriptions are likely preliminary.

4. In an exercise of focused coding, partners now apply the codes to a second set of greeting cards. Note while coding how well they apply to these new data, what new codes may be needed, what other relationships emerged, and what existing codes require renaming or redefinition.

Online Resources

- You can learn more about grounded theory online through the Grounded Theory Institute. **www.groundedtheory.com**

- Graham R. Gibbs presents a series of helpful videos on grounded theory. In Grounded Theory: Core Elements he introduces the idea of developing grounded theory. In Part 1 of his series on open coding, he explains what open coding is and introduces key elements. In Part 2, he outlines the various stages of open coding.

www.youtube.com/watch?v=4SZDTp3_New
www.youtube.com/watch?NR=1&v= gn7Pr8M_Gu8

www.youtube.com/watch?v=vi5B7Zo0_OE&NR=1

- If you'd like to experiment with CAQDAS, you can download a trial a version of NVivo software. **www.qsrinternational.com/products_free-trial-software.aspx**

For more resources please visit
www.oup.com/he/bryman-reck-fields1e

14

How Do Researchers Develop Deductive Findings?
Quantitative Data Analysis

▲ From Ablynx (Infographics XXXXL Part 2), courtesy of ONTWERPBUREAU SOON

This chapter examines basic and regularly used methods for analyzing quantitative data. Our focus is not to examine the mathematical formulas used to develop quantitative findings but to think about quantitative analysis as a tool researchers use to understand and present their findings in particular ways. We will revisit the logic of quantitative research to gain insight into how researchers explore sociological questions using statistical data analysis.

Reading this chapter will help you to

- recognize the importance of anticipating questions about analysis early in the research process, before all the data have been collected;

- define the different kinds of variables generated in quantitative research;

- comprehend the difference between descriptive and inferential statistics;

- outline methods for analyzing a single variable (univariate analysis);

- understand measures of central tendency in univariate analysis, including the mean, median, mode, range, and standard deviation;

- identify ways of visually presenting data;

- distinguish methods for analyzing relationships between two variables (bivariate analysis); and

- describe techniques for analyzing relationships among three or more variables (multivariate analysis).

Statistics show that taller people have larger vocabularies than shorter people. Did you know that? The relationship between height and vocabulary is an interesting correlation to consider, but the claim that greater height *causes* people to know more words is quite misleading. Think about it: What happens as babies grow? They get taller; so, height increases as age increases. Furthermore, they become physically able to talk, go to school, and engage in interactions with people who teach them more words. To really understand why certain people know more words than others, we would have to take all these influences into account.

When we attempt to make conclusions about the world, we analyze the multiple factors that might cause certain outcomes. In the language of statistics, we analyze the relationships between variables. And we must do so in a way that avoids being misled into false conclusions or assumptions. This chapter discusses how researchers use numerical data to explain complex social phenomena; they examine interactions among variables in order to better understand many topics, including how people attain language.

Introduction: Why Data Analysis Is the Starting Point for Quantitative Research

As we have seen in previous chapters, quantitative researchers gather their data in multiple ways. They might analyze existing data sets, code media content, or conduct a questionnaire. These **raw data** are in numerical form; researchers need to process, or analyze, them to answer research questions or assess hypotheses. Quantitative researchers use statistical tools to perform this **data analysis**. To keep the focus on methodological

---

raw data Data that have been collected but not processed for use or analysis.

---

data analysis The process of examining, processing, and organizing data to gather information and develop conclusions from it.

approaches, we'll avoid the formulas that underpin those techniques. One chapter could not do justice to the topic of numerical data analysis, and we recommend that you consult books that provide more detailed and advanced treatments (for example, Field, Miles, and Field 2014 or Field 2016) and websites listed at the end of this chapter.

Before we begin, a warning is in order: the biggest mistake in quantitative research is thinking that data analysis decisions can wait until after the data have been collected. Researchers' approach to their quantitative data collection determines the type of analysis that is possible. Therefore, although data analysis *is* carried out after collection, it's essential to know beforehand what techniques will be used. Researchers should design their studies with the data analysis in mind for three main reasons:

1. The statistical techniques that researchers can use depend on how they measured their **variables**. More sophisticated statistical tests can be used with variables that are measured more precisely.
2. The size and nature of the sample can impose limitations on the techniques that are suitable for analyzing the data set.
3. Quantitative analysis is often an iterative process: researchers move between their hypotheses and existing theory and their data, testing their hypotheses and looking for additional possible explanations of the relationships they see.

We will return to these three points throughout the chapter.

---

variable   An attribute or characteristic that may vary over time or from case to case.

What factors might influence the vocabulary of each child in this family? What variables might you take into account when assessing their literacy and vocabulary?

Types of Variables

How researchers classify their variables determines how they can analyze them. Researchers use different levels of measurement as they define their variables. This concept was also explained in Chapter 3; for a refresher, see Table 14.1, which is a copy of a table provided in Chapter 3. In this chapter, we focus on how level of measurement relates to analysis.

Nominal variables capture important information about categories, but they are not a complex measurement. For example, religion is a common nominal variable and someone might be able to select from the categories Muslim, Protestant, Hindu, Jewish, Roman Catholic, Other, and None. People might select "Muslim" because they are culturally Muslim but not observant or because they engage in daily Muslim spiritual practices.

Ordinal variables can be ranked, so more complex statistical tests can be used to analyze them. While these ranked variables can be analyzed with a greater level of complexity than nominal variables, the distinction between each rank isn't precise. Ordinal variables are often measured using a Likert scale: a question "How frequently do you pray?" could include the categories

TABLE 14.1 | Levels of Measurement

Level	Description
Nominal	Names only, with no rank order or other value (e.g., gender or sexual identity)
Ordinal	Rank-ordered named categories (e.g., level of education)
Interval	Named categories with meaningful and consistent distances, arbitrary zero categories, and possibly negative values (e.g., temperature)
Ratio	Named categories with meaningful and consistent distance and true zero category but no negative values (e.g., height)

Very Frequently, Frequently, Occasionally, Rarely, Very Rarely, or Never. "Very" indicates greater frequency than "occasionally," which indicates greater frequency than "rarely." Yet the difference between "frequently" and "occasionally" is probably not the same as that between "occasionally" and "rarely," and so on.

Interval/ratio variables have a specific unit of measurement that can be used for the categories, and so the distances or amount of difference between them can be made identical across the range. The values take the form of actual numbers (such as 1, 4, 7.5, etc.), so this enables more complex numerical analysis. For example, a person who spends 30 minutes praying every day is spending ten minutes less than someone who spends 40, and the same difference exists between someone who spends 10 minutes and another who spends 20 minutes.

At the interval/ratio level of measurement, it is possible to say that two scores are equal or not equal, to know when they have greater or lesser values, and to specify the distance or amount of difference between them. This is the highest level of measurement—that is, it allows the widest range of analysis techniques.

In this chapter, we use the inclusive term "interval/ratio," but researchers sometimes distinguish between interval and ratio variables. Ratio variables are interval variables with a fixed and non-arbitrary zero point (as in a wind speed of 0 miles per hour). Take, for example, two annual incomes: $30,000 and $45,000. They are nominally unequal, and the first is $15,000 less than the second. But with that real 0, one can also say that the first is 2/3 of the second (or the second is 1.5 times the first) or in a 2:3 *ratio* to the second. Many social science variables exhibit this quality, including income, age, and years of school

completed. An interval variable is different from this. Sometimes we measure variables like racism with a series of questions, which are then added up as a score on a scale. Scoring a zero doesn't mean a respondent has zero racism the way that zero dollars means they have no dollars. As a result, we can't take ratios with interval level data and we can't say things like respondent A has two thirds the level of racism compared to respondent B.

Because statistical tests align with particular types of variables, the way you measure your variables determines how you can statistically analyze them. Let's look at average income within racial groups. It would make sense to compute an average income: as a ratio variable, it is a number with a zero point and all the distances between the values are even. But race is a nominal variable. As such, there is no order to the categories, and we cannot calculate an average. Similarly, it would be impossible to compute the average of the ordinal variable measuring educational experience as elementary school graduate, high school graduate, some college, and college graduate because there is no even spacing between the four levels. However, if we asked, "How many years of schooling have you had?" we would have a ratio variable and could determine average years of schooling. So, a variable must be interval or ratio in order for a researcher to take an average of it. Computing averages is possibly the simplest example of statistical analysis, but this concept applies to all the more complex statistical tests as well. What we want to convey here is that each statistical analysis method we use requires certain numbers or values.

Although we described Likert-scale variables as ordinal, statisticians actually consider them "in between" ordinal and interval. Strictly speaking, items with Likert-style response categories produce ordinal variables. However, many writers argue that they can be treated as though they produce interval/ratio variables because of the relatively large number of categories they generate. For a brief discussion of this issue, see Bryman and Cramer (2001, 58–59).

To perform certain statistical analyses, researchers often assume Likert-scale intervals are evenly spaced and treat the variables as interval. Is this faulty logic and mathematics? Statisticians create a set of checks and balances by ensuring they do not measure their concepts using only one variable—they often create scales, measure their concepts using multiple questions, and then use statistical measures to test the validity of their measurement strategy. In this way, they can assess how well a set of Likert-scale questions, for instance, measured a concept.

What is important to understand about all of this is that when researchers develop their measurement strategies in the early stages of their research, the type of analysis they hope to do later guides their construction of variables. The levels of measurement they use determine what statistical methods they can later use to understand their data and thus influences the complexity of their analyses.

Descriptive and Inferential Statistics

Statistics can be used for many different types of analysis, so it is important to consider your goals when gathering and analyzing your data. Is your purpose solely to describe trends in your sample, or would you like to use data from your sample to make generalizations about a larger population? **Descriptive statistics** are tools you can use to detail and interpret the key features of a data set, summarizing the main trends in data collected from a

---

descriptive statistics Tools used to describe and interpret the key features of a data set, summarizing the main trends in data collected from a sample.

---

inferential statistics Tools used to analyze the characteristics of the sample to make inferences about the population from which it was drawn.

---

sample. A frequent goal with descriptive statistics is to describe the distribution of the variables and relationships among the variables in a sample.

Inferential statistics, on the other hand, analyze the characteristics of the sample to make inferences about the population from which it was drawn. The goal is to use information about a sample to make generalizations about the population it represents. Researchers need to assess how much they can trust that the sample accurately represents that population. Researchers use inferential statistics to measure how *confident* they can be in making inferences about the population being studied. If your sample was not gathered randomly or does not accurately reflect the group you want to learn about, it may not be representative, leading to error in your results.

Thus, descriptive and inferential statistics offer different options and serve different purposes. Descriptive statistics can help you paint a picture of your sample. You may want to explore the degree to which these characteristics exist throughout a population, using inferential statistics. Quantitative researchers generally engage in both description and inference. They describe what their data reveal and then assess the robustness of those findings using inferential statistics. Box 14.1 and the Mixed Methods in Action feature discuss different ways that researchers can use descriptive statistics to develop information about samples and populations.

Quantitative Analysis as a Tool for Understanding

Quantitative analysis can be used to describe patterns in numerical data and to make generalizations from a sample to a population. But *how* can it accomplish these goals? Quantitative researchers pursue their analysis by using statistical thinking to ask and answer questions in a particular kind of way.

In quantitative studies, researchers seek to understand something about the variables in which they are interested. You might want to know the frequency of a certain occurrence and could ask,

BOX 14.1 Using Descriptive Statistics to Examine Race and Social Mobility in a Population

Researchers can form a robust understanding of a population by using descriptive statistics to analyze population data. Raj Chetty et al. (2018) used sophisticated forms of descriptive statistics to analyze the factors that affect intergenerational mobility, or how children's economic status compares to that of their parents.

The researchers' target population was children born between 1978 and 1983 who were either US-born or authorized immigrants in childhood, with parents also born in the country or authorized immigrants. To study this cohort, the researchers used large data sets that were representative of the US population, including the 2000 and 2010 US Census, the 2005–2015 American Community Surveys, and federal tax return data from 1989, 1994, 1995, and 1998–2015. They found that their sample included approximately 94 percent of their sample frame and thus was representative of their target population (2018, 13). Because they had close to population data (that is, since the sample included such a high percentage of their sample frame), they could feel confident that their analysis reflected experiences in that entire population.

In their research, Chetty et al. explored two main research questions: how does parental income affect the income levels of Black and White children, and what methods might be needed to reduce race-based intergenerational income gaps? In their analysis, the team outlined racial disparities in income and examined how and why those inequalities vary across racial groups through generations. They found that Hispanic and Asian children have steady rates of upward mobility compared to White children, while American Indian and Black children have

lower rates. As they analyzed variables to attempt to understand these differences, the researchers demonstrated the significance of environmental factors and debunked theories that upward mobility is a result of individual aptitude or effort. They found that, for Black boys, exposure to particular neighborhood factors in childhood affects mobility. For example, lower poverty rates, lower levels of anti-Black bias, and more stable families lead to more upward mobility for Black boys (41–42). Thus, the researchers suggest that specific neighborhood–level elements can create barriers to mobility, such as the fact that 62.5% of America's White children grow up in areas with low poverty, while only 4.2 percent of Black children grow up in areas with a poverty rate lower than 10 percent (42).

Chetty et al. conclude that focusing on these factors can improve social mobility and racial and economic equality. They write,

> Our results suggest that efforts that cut within neighborhoods and schools and improve environments for specific racial subgroups, such as black boys, may be more effective in reducing the black-white gap. Examples include mentoring programs for black boys, efforts to reduce racial bias among whites, or efforts to facilitate social interaction across racial groups within a given area (43).

In this example, the researchers were able to make conclusions about the broader population because they analyzed population data. This is different from what usually occurs when a researcher gathers data from a subset of a population and draws conclusions that are based on making inferences from a sample to a population.

"How many death row inmates in the United States have been executed?" Digging into the data, you'd find that the answer is 1,494 people since 1976 (Death Penalty Information Center 2019c).

The question is an important one, but the data tell us little and don't lead to an understanding of any sociological factors or context. Let's say you take your question to a deeper analytical level: "What

Mixed Methods in Action | Using Descriptive Statistics and Focus Groups to Understand Health Barriers in a Sample

Laura D'Anna, et. al (2018) conducted a mixed-methods community health needs assessment study of Cambodian and Latinx residents of Santa Ana, California. The researchers first selected neighborhoods with large Cambodian and Latinx populations using multistage cluster sampling. The survey was administered to a sample of 36 Cambodians and 29 Latinos, who were recruited through systematic random sampling by researchers who went door-to-door in a primarily low-income neighborhood made up almost exclusively of Cambodian refugees and Latino (mostly Mexican) immigrants. The researchers also conducted four 90-minute focus groups with residents of the neighborhood, including some residents who

had accessed services at an organization called The Cambodian Family (TCF) and other residents who had not. The researchers used purposive and snowball sampling to recruit the 20 Cambodian and 18 Latino participants for the focus groups, putting up fliers at TCF and using word of mouth.

The goal of the study was to identify factors that served as barriers to or facilitators of good health among members of the Latinx and Cambodian communities, and ways the programs could be enhanced to increase these groups' access to and use of health and social service resources. The researchers' analysis of the rate of responses to survey questions among the two ethnic groups is summarized in Table 14.2.

TABLE 14.2 | **Self-Reported Barriers to Health among Cambodian and Latino Residents of Santa Ana, California**

	Cambodians	Latinos
Rated their health as poor or fair	69.4%	58.6%
Diagnosed with depression	22.2%	13.8%
Report regular feelings of stress and worry	60.0%	27.6%
Have health insurance	86.1%	72.4%

Source: D'Anna et al. 2018, 1246–1247.

is the relationship between race and executions?" Examining these two variables would lead to this information: 34.2 percent of defendants executed between 1976 and 2018 were Black, 8.5 percent were Latinx, and 55.7 percent were White (Death Penalty Information Center 2019b). These data indicate that the death penalty affects White people more than it does the other two racial groups.

Ending analysis with this data can be misleading because it doesn't give us all the answers. If you were to think more about these percentages, you might wonder how these numbers compare to the groups' demographics in the population. 2019 Census data indicates that White people make up 60.7 percent of

the US population, Blacks/African Americans make up 13.4 percent, and Latinx make up 18.1 percent (US Census 2019). Asking about the relationship between these two variables gives you something to explore: an association that starts to reveal important social issues around the fact that White and Latinx people have been executed at rates of 5 percent and almost 10 percent *lower* than their overall population numbers, respectively, while Black defendants are executed at rates that *exceed* their numbers in the overall population by almost 21 percent.

This process is definitely a start, and it gives you some important social issues to explore. But to really understand them, you have to ask a question that

The researchers found that 47.2 percent of the Cambodian participants identified crime and gang-related activities as the most significant threats to physical and mental health, while 33.3 percent pointed to lack of access to healthy and affordable food, compared to 69.0 percent and 37.9 percent of Latino respondents, respectively. Both groups (77.8 percent Cambodians and 66.5 percent Latino) described their families and friends as strong support networks and their cultures as supportive of their health. In proposing their recommendations for services and programs to help improve their health, 20.7 percent of the Latino participants suggested increasing police presence to reduce violence, 27.6 percent wanted affordable community-based health care to be more accessible, and 27.6 percent wanted more access to areas for recreation and exercise. Among the Cambodian participants, 41.7 percent suggested increasing police presence and 27.8 percent wanted more access to healthy and affordable food (1246–1250).

Overall, the focus groups provided an effective way to explore the participants' views of factors influencing their mental and physical health, community barriers and supports to health, and gaps in resources for health maintenance. The focus group data offered insights to flesh out the statistical trends, and the participants' stories provided more details about experiences and opinions.

The authors suggest the data represent a snapshot of the health challenges low-income urban Latino immigrant and Cambodian refugee communities face. The researchers' analysis of the data on health outcomes, community connections, and perceived health needs allowed them to understand these individual communities and to note important trends in both their shared and distinct experiences. The respondents reported poor physical and mental health even though many of them had health insurance coverage. Thus, the researchers propose that access to health care for disadvantaged communities could be improved through "Systems solutions [that] should include broad representation from multiple community sectors that support a patient-centered integrated model of care that goes beyond the traditional medical model" (1258).

While the authors do generalize from their findings to consider the larger population of low-income urban Latinx immigrant and Cambodian refugee communities, they do not use inferential statistics to assess how good this generalization might be. Because of the way their sample was drawn and the fact it is relatively small, using inferential statistics would be misleading.

enables a more complex sociological question: What accounts for these racial differences in executions? To explore the execution of Black defendants, you could add the crime victims' race as a variable to the equation. Although only 50 percent of murder victims nationally are White, over 75 percent of the victims in cases resulting in executions were White. Since 1976, just 21 White defendants have been executed for killing Black victims, but 290 Black defendants have been executed after being convicted of killing White victims (Death Penalty Information Center 2019a).

To think further about executions of Latinx inmates, adding a variable of population change offers more information. The number of Latinx people executed per year has fluctuated since 1976 but reached an all-time high in the 1990s and remained high until 2016 (Death Penalty Information Center DPIC 2019c). During the same period, the Latinx population grew significantly (Brown 2014). It is quite likely that this population's growth adds more information about the executions of Latinx people compared to other groups. Thus, combining analysis of the variables

- population change,
- race of defendant,
- race of victim, and
- execution

offers a much more nuanced and sociological analysis of these trends.

This discussion above shows that, as we add variables to the analysis, the examination becomes more complex and we can understand more through the process. Looking at one variable offers a snapshot of a trend but little understanding of it; adding another gives us something to explore but little comprehension of the context. Adding a third variable helps us to comprehend more of the social factors surrounding the trends that interest us. Using statistics as a tool of analysis affords researchers the ability to ask and answer such questions at different levels of complexity; these types of examination are known as *univariate*, *bivariate*, and *multivariate analysis*.

Univariate Analysis

This section outlines two common approaches to **univariate analysis**, which examines one variable at a time. The first is the use of visuals, such as tables and charts, to present a single variable. The second is the calculation of average values in a variable.

Visual Presentation of Univariate Data

When presenting data, researchers often use tables and charts. In our example of death row executions, it might be useful to provide a **frequency table** that

---

univariate analysis The simplest form of quantitative analysis, consisting of data analysis conducted on one variable.

---

frequency table A table that displays the number and/or percentage of units (e.g., people) in different categories of a variable.

---

measure of central tendency A measure designed to represent the central value in a set of scores; examples include the mean, median, and mode.

---

includes the number and percentage of people (or whatever else constitutes a case in the study) belonging to each category of the variable in question (see Table 14.3). Frequency tables are typically created using software such as PASW Statistics (previously known as SPSS)

In addition to tables, researchers often use diagrams to display quantitative data. With nominal or ordinal variables, the *bar chart* and *pie chart* are two of the easiest to use to compare variables. A bar chart of the data in Table 14.3 is presented in Figure 14.1. The height of each bar represents the number of people in each category. A pie chart such as the one presented in Figure 14.2 displays the same data as a table or bar chart, but because the entire circle represents the sample, it more clearly shows the size of each category relative to the sample. The percentage of the whole sample that each slice represents is also represented in this diagram.

These tables and diagrams have the potential to present information at a low level of analytical complexity. Note that these are simple representations and offer only a snapshot of one variable's distribution. Given our discussion about how we might understand the dynamics of race and execution differently by adding additional variables to the analysis, we must think about what these visuals do, and don't, tell us.

Measures of Central Tendency

Measures of central tendency provide, in one number, a typical or "average" score for a distribution or group of scores captured from a single variable. Three measures of central tendency are commonly used: the *mode*, *mean*, and *median*. The ability to use a particular one depends on the level of measurement. For example, as previously mentioned,

TABLE 14.3 | Example of a Frequency Table: Race and Executions, 1976–2018

Race	Number of Executions	Percentage of Sample
Black	512	34.5
Latinx	127	8.3
White	832	55.6
Other	24	1.6

Source: Death Penalty Information Center 2019b.

Total Number of People Executed in the United States, 1976–2018, by Race

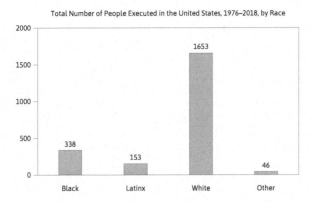

FIGURE 14.1 **Race and executions presented in a bar chart**

Distribution of People Executed in the United States, 1976–2018, by Race

FIGURE 14.2 **Race and executions presented in a pie chart**

we can't average a nominal variable such as race. How, then, can we assess the distribution of a variable's attributes, and how does this relate to level of measurement?

One way that researchers analyze how variables are distributed is to compute the **mode**, the value that occurs most frequently in a set of scores. Returning to our example, "White" is the mode of race of people executed because it is the most frequent category. The mode can be used with all types of variables, but it is most applicable to nominal data.

Say you were interested in learning how long people are on death row before being executed. To obtain such information, you could compute what is called the mean score. The **mean** is the average as it is understood in everyday use; that is, the sum of all numbers in a distribution divided by the number of scores. Teachers use the mean when they want to figure out the average score students earned on an assignment: they add all the scores in the class and then divide by the number of students to arrive at the mean score. In the case of the

How can quantitative research be used as a tool for understanding the degree to which the death penalty is just and fair?

time on death row, you would examine the details of each person executed in a given year, noting how many months passed between their sentencing and execution. You would then add all those values together and divide the sum by the number of people who had been executed that year. Figure 14.3 shows

---

mode The value that occurs most frequently in a set of scores.

---

mean The "average," or the sum of all the scores divided by the number of scores.

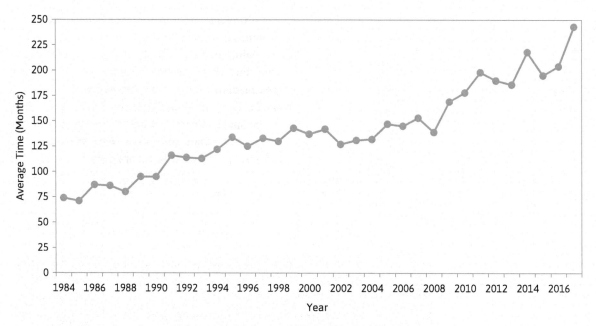

FIGURE 14.3 **Mean time (in months) between sentencing and execution, 1984-2017, presented as a line chart**

the mean value of number of months between sentencing and execution for each of the years between 1984 and 2017. These means are depicted as a line chart, another way to represent univariate data visually. As Figure 14.3 indicates, the mean number of months between sentencing and execution rose from 74 months (6.2 years) in 1984 to 243 months (20.3 years) in 2017.

The usefulness of the mean as a representative score can be limited if there are **outliers** (extreme values at either end of the distribution) that exert considerable upward or downward pressure. For example, if because of exceptional circumstances one person executed in 2017 had spent 400 months on death row, and the next highest total was 290 months, the outlier would dramatically affect the overall mean score for that year. So, a researcher must always consider how

---

outlier   An extreme value (either very high or very low) in a distribution of scores with the potential to distort both the mean and the range.

---

median   The midpoint in a set of scores arranged in numerical order.

the values at the lower and higher ends alter the mean: Taking outliers into account, does the mean still offer a reasonable measure of the values?

When outliers might affect the computation, researchers may choose to examine the **median**, which is not affected by outliers. The median is the midpoint in a distribution of scores, derived by arraying all the results in order (typically from the lowest to the highest) and then finding the middle one. If there is an even number of values, the median is calculated by averaging the two middle numbers in the distribution.

Say you want to understand more about overall trends in executions. Looking at data describing number of executions each year between 2000 and 2016 (Snell 2019), you can compute that the mean number of people executed each year as 49.6. Looking closer, you notice that the greatest number of executions (85) took place in 2000 and the lowest number (20) in 2016. How do these outliers affect the mean? Calculating the median can give you a more precise measure. Listing the numbers, you can see that the middle value is 46. You can see this value bolded in the list of all the numbers from the data below.

20
28
35
37
39
42
43
43
46
52
53
59
60
65
66
71
85

With a median of 46, half the values in the distribution are below 46 and half of them are above. So, while the mean could lead you to the conclusion that about 50 people were executed each year, the median shows a more detailed picture: in half of the years between 2000 and 2016, fewer than 46 people were executed and the other half of the years, more than 46 people were executed. The median can be used with both interval/ratio and ordinal variables, but it cannot be used with nominal data (such as race or ethnicity) because those scores cannot be ranked.

When the mean and median are similar or equal numbers, the distribution is symmetrical. Figure 14.4 provides an example of this through a data visualization called a *histogram*. Imagine a teacher gave an exam and computed the mean and median of the test to see how the students did, on average. Figure 14.4

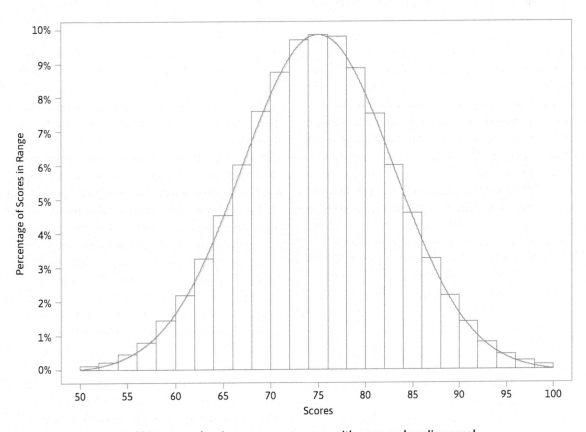

FIGURE 14.4 Symmetrical histogram showing scores on an exam with mean and median equal

Source: (Reck, 2020)

shows a symmetrical set of scores where the median and mean are equal: 75.

In this example, both the mean and the median provide useful measures of the typical student performance on the test because outliers did not skew the number. However, when a set of values has outliers, the median can better reveal differences in the data than the mean can. Imagine if you were computing home values in an area where some houses are worth millions of dollars, but most are valued around $200,000. The high-priced homes might dramatically affect your computation of the mean.

When the mean and median are not equal to one another, the distribution is asymmetrical, or **skewed**. Income is a good example of commonly skewed data: it's more common for people to earn between low and medium level salaries than it is for people to earn high salaries. High salaries increase the mean value and make the mean a less accurate measure of typical salary. Analyzing US Census data, the Congressional Research Service found the mean household income in 2015 was $79,263. The high incomes earned by the small minority of households inflated that mean dramatically, though. This is apparent when we consider the median income value, which was much smaller: $56,516 (Donovan, Labonte, and Dalaker 2016). In this case, the mean presents a picture of typical household economic status that suggests incomes are generally higher than they are. For

this reason, the median is the measure that offers more accurate information about typical household income.

Measures of Dispersion

The amount of variation in a sample—that is, its **dispersion**—can be just as important as its typical or most frequent value. Using the example of test scores, a midterm and final exam could have the same mean of 60 percent, but what if most people scored between 50 and 70 on the midterm, while the grades on the final exam ranged evenly from the low 20s to 100? In the language of testing, the first test would be described as one that does not discriminate, because all the students got fairly close marks. The second test—the final exam—would be of concern because the grades were so widely dispersed. Was there something unfair or inequitable about the exam that made the scores so inconsistent? So, in addition to calculating a measure of central tendency to assess the typical or central value, it is important also to determine how the values are dispersed in relation to that central measure.

The simplest way of measuring dispersion is to calculate the **range**, which is the difference between the highest value and the lowest value in a distribution of interval/ratio scores. We can calculate range with interval/ratio variables because they are variables with numerical values. Range can be applied to an ordinal variable, but it is more definitional than numerically descriptive—for example, a range from working class to upper class. When looking at months spent on death row from 1984 to 2017, we can see that the range is 172 (Death Penalty Information Center 2019d), which is wide, suggesting important differences in how long people are living on death row over the span of those decades. Like the mean, the range is influenced by outliers, and so it is not a particularly detailed **measure of dispersion**.

The range offers a way of considering a set of scores in terms of the highest and lowest values. More often, though, researchers will consider scores in terms of how they differ from a representative value—typically the median or the mean. This sort of analysis relies on a measure of dispersion called

---

skewed distribution A distribution of scores in which values do not cluster around the center of the set but are instead extreme in one direction or the other.

---

dispersion The degree of variability of values in a sample.

---

range The difference between the maximum and the minimum score in a set of scores associated with an interval or ratio variable.

---

measure of dispersion A measure (such as the range or standard deviation) that summarizes the degree of variability in a set of scores.

the **standard deviation**, or how scores vary in relation to the mean, using interval/ratio level variables. The standard deviation allows researchers to understand whether most values are similar to or different from the mean. A standard deviation of 0 would indicate that there was no difference between the individual scores in the distribution and the mean; in other words, it would indicate that all of the scores were the same. That would be an unusual outcome: in any study, sociological or biological, individual scores will typically vary in relation to the mean.

Researchers use statistical tools to calculate the mean and standard deviation in order to explain what the distribution of scores looks like. If a set of scores has a standard deviation close to zero, most of the values are near the average. As the standard deviation increases from zero, the numbers spread out. Thus, the finding the standard deviation helps researchers describe their data and how spread out the values are.

Understanding the extent of variability in your data will help you evaluate how confident you can be making conclusions about the population you're studying. If you continue learning about statistics, standard deviation will be a key concept you'll learn much more about.

Bivariate Analysis

Researchers increase their understanding about a variable by exploring how it might relate to others. This process involves **bivariate analysis**, which examines whether there is a relationship between two variables. Dozens of techniques are available, but their use depends on the measurement level of the two variables being analyzed.

As we outlined in Chapter 3, quantitative researchers study the relationships between variables to see how one variable might cause another to change. In other words, they examine how an **independent variable (IV)** might influence a **dependent variable (DV)**. Consider the following research question: How does including students with disabilities in general education classrooms affect their academic performance? This relationship could be broken down into variables:

INDEPENDENT VARIABLE (IV)	DEPENDENT VARIABLE (DV)
Including students with disabilities in general education classrooms	Academic performance of students with disabilities

The research question could also be translated into a hypothesis: *As students with disabilities are integrated into general education classrooms, their academic performance will improve.* This hypothesis assumes that a relationship exists between the variables, in that an increase in inclusion leads to an increase in academic performance.

When researchers use statistics to measure the relationships between two variables, they are looking for two main things. They want to know *how strong the relationship is.* For instance, *how much* does inclusion affect the academic performance of students with disabilities? Greatly, slightly, or not at all? If inclusion has a great effect on performance, this would be a meaningful finding. Then, when they are using ordinal, interval, and ratio variables, the researcher also has to figure out *whether the relationship is negative or positive.* This doesn't refer to the value of the relationship—whether it's good or bad—but to the direction of the relationship: whether inclusion increases academic performance (positive) or decreases it (negative).

Researchers can use a variety of statistical methods to determine the strength and direction of a variable relationship, including the following (see also Table 14.4):

- A *contingency table*, like a frequency table, allows two variables to be analyzed simultaneously so that relationships between them can be

---

standard deviation   A measure of how scores are dispersed around the mean.

---

bivariate analysis   An examination of the relationship or differences between two variables.

---

independent variable (IV)   A variable that has (or is assumed to have) an influence on a dependent variable.

---

dependent variable (DV)   A variable that is influenced (or assumed to be influenced) by an independent variable.

TABLE 14.4 | Methods of Bivariate Analysis Using Various Variable Types

	Nominal	Ordinal	Interval/Ratio
Nominal	Contingency table + chi-square ($\chi2$) + Cramér's V	Contingency table + chi-square ($\chi2$) + Cramér's V	Contingency table +chi-square ($\chi2$) + Cramér's V
Ordinal	Contingency table + chi-square ($\chi2$) + Cramér's V	Kendall's tau-b	Kendall's tau-b
Interval/Ratio	Contingency table + chi-square ($\chi2$) + Cramér's V	Kendall's tau-b	Pearson's r

examined. It uses percentages to show the relationship between independent and dependent variables and shows patterns of association (see Table 14.5 for an example).

- A *chi-square* ($\chi2$) tests how likely it is that an apparent relationship between two variables is due to chance. It also examines whether there is some pattern in a contingency table.
- *Cramér's V* is a measure that examines the strength of the relationship between nominal variables.
- *Kendall's tau-b* is a measure that assumes there is an order to the data and examines the strength and direction of any pattern between variables.
- *Pearson's r* is used with ratio/interval level data to measure a linear trend between variables that reveals direction and strength. It can be modified (using what's called *regression*) to assess how much a change in one variable affects change in the other variable.

If you move beyond this chapter's brief introduction to statistics, you'll learn more about how these tests work and how to use them to analyze your data. For the remainder of this section, we will use two studies to focus on how researchers approach bivariate analysis and what it can explain about relationships between variables.

Gender and Opinions on Marijuana Legalization

Laurel Elder and Steven Greene (2019) were interested in why in the United States women are less likely than men to support marijuana legalization, given that women are typically more liberal on many issues. To explore this gender difference, the researchers examined data from a 2013 Pew study that included several questions about opinions on the drug. In this bivariate comparison, men were more liberal than women on 4 of the 6 attitude measures that made up a marijuana support

TABLE 14.5 | Contingency Table Showing Gender and Marijuana Support (Percentage Responding "Yes")

	Men	Women
Marijuana should be legal	59	49
Marijuana is a gateway drug	63	58
Enforcement costs exceed benefit	78	73
Comfortable being around marijuana	55	42
Marijuana should be legal for medical use	83	82
Federal government should enforce marijuana laws in all states	64	63
Have ever used marijuana	55	42
Have used marijuana in past year	13	10
Sample size (*n*) = 1,501		

Source: Elder and Greene 2019, 114.

scale (Table 14.5). Women were much less likely to report having used marijuana, and they reported feeling much less comfortable being around marijuana than men did. Men were only less liberal than women around legal enforcement, which aligns with the fact that men have been found to be more conservative about criminal justice overall.

While Elder and Greene's bivariate analysis answered a question about how gender correlates to opinions about marijuana, it raised another: why do these differences in opinion exist? The bivariate comparison starts us on a path toward understanding how gender affects opinion but doesn't get us very far. To explore this dynamic with greater layers of complexity, the researchers needed to consider how additional variables might interact with gender to affect differences in opinion—in other words, to determine what other social factors might combine with gender to account for men's and women's contrasting views on marijuana policy. To explore these social factors, Elder and Greene analyzed multiple variables, which we will discuss in the next section. But first, we'll introduce another example study that began with bivariate analysis.

Religious Service Attendance and Interracial Dating

Research suggests that people who attend religious services more regularly than others are also more resistant to becoming involved in interracial relationships. To examine this connection, Samuel Perry (2014) used data from the Baylor Religion Study (BRS), a 2007 Gallup Organization poll. This randomly selected sample included 1,648 US adults who completed a questionnaire about their religious beliefs and perspectives. Through a bivariate analysis, Perry found clear evidence that as the frequency of religious service attendance increased, the degree of engagement in interracial dating decreased. Specifically, 50 percent of people who never attend had interracially dated, 32.4 percent who attend services two to three times per month had interracially dated, and 26.8 percent who attend services several times per week had interracially dated (451). This strong bivariate relationship confirmed other researchers' previous findings.

Nevertheless, Perry put forth two related concerns about this finding, arguing it does not fully explain the situation. First, he pointed out that most researchers use religious service attendance as a proxy variable to measure "religiosity," even though the terms are not conceptually identical. For this reason, he claimed that the examination of factors that might cause those who attend services more frequently to date within their race is not completely accurate. He says this topic is particularly important to examine further "considering the apparent contradiction that while virtually all religious traditions formally condemn racial or ethnic prejudice and promote love for others, those who more frequently participate in formal religious services seem relatively more discriminating in their romantic relationships" (2014, 443).

Second, Perry believes that we can more deeply understand the connection if we examine the contours of religious participation as involving multiple variables rather than just viewing it as whether someone attends religious services regularly. In his view, analyzing factors influencing people's religious participation, their connection to religious communities, and how their religious involvement affects the type of partner they want would produce a more robust understanding of this situation. Hence, he began his study focusing on a meaningful bivariate relationship and then enlarged his understanding by considering the interaction between more variables.

Multivariate Analysis

Multivariate analysis entails the simultaneous analysis of three or more variables. It is sometimes called *elaboration* because it is more complicated and creates a more valuable picture than bivariate analysis. (For more information on the techniques, consult a textbook on quantitative data analysis, for example, Field, Miles, and Field 2014 or Field 2016.) Multivariate analysis is used in three main contexts, which are explained in Box 14.3.

Multivariate analysis is commonly used by quantitative researchers, who tend to have larger samples than qualitative researchers do. Multivariate analysis provides an effective way to turn these large

---

multivariate analysis   The examination of relationships among three or more variables.

BOX 14.2 Relationships Not Causality

Analyzing associations between variables reveals *relationships*, not *causes* (although finding associations helps in the search for causes). Similarly, the *direction* of causation cannot be determined by merely establishing that a relationship exists between two variables. In some cases, what appears to be a causal influence working in one direction may actually work the other way around. An example of the problem of causal direction was presented in Chapter 6, where Robert I. Sutton and Anat Rafaeli

The old adage "practice makes perfect" suggests causality. Even if an artist regularly practices their painting technique, what variables other than practice might influence their success as a painter?

(1992) expected to find that a display of positive emotions (for example, smiling or friendliness) by retail checkout staff caused increased sales, but the relationship appeared to flow in the opposite direction: levels of retail sales seemed to exert a causal influence on the display of employees' emotions.

There are times when one may feel confident in inferring a causal direction. People's voting habits cannot influence their age; if the two variables are related, age is the independent variable. It is not uncommon for researchers to draw inferences about causal direction based on common sense assumptions of this kind. However, some relationships may be non-causal; that is, the relationship between two variables may be caused by a third variable. For example, Jackson Bunch, Jody Clay-Warner, and Jennifer McMahon-Howard (2013) analyzed how being victimized by violent

crime might affect people's lifestyle choices. They tested the hypothesis that victimization leads to either subsequent high-risk or constrained behaviors. They found that people who had been victimized did engage in higher-risk behaviors later than did non-victims. However, they were able to use regression to more closely analyze the relationship between multiple variables and note that other underlying demographic, lifestyle, or environmental differences pre-victimization had more of an impact on their activities than a victimization event alone. For example, people who had experienced victimization were more likely to be younger, live in urban areas, have higher levels of previous victimization, ride public transport, and rent their homes compared to non-victims. Thus, the relationship between victimization and lifestyle choice was found to be spurious, or non-causal.

What's your hypothesis about why some people are more likely to support marijuana legalization? What variables would you study to test this hypothesis using bivariate analysis? What additional variables would you add to conduct multivariate analysis on this issue?

samples into models that then can be generalized to the broader population using inferential statistics.

Elder and Greene's Multivariate Analysis

Elder and Greene (2018) engaged in multivariate analysis to test four main hypotheses about the reason for the gender gap in opinions about marijuana policy:

1. Parents will be more conservative about marijuana than non-parents, and parenthood will affect women's opinions about marijuana policy more than men's.
2. Highly religious people and born-again Christians will have more conservative attitudes about marijuana; women's higher religious commitment will affect their attitudes about marijuana.
3. White men are more liberal about marijuana, so they are the reason for the gender gap in attitudes about marijuana policy.
4. Men are more likely than women to use marijuana, and this accounts for the gender gap in opinion about marijuana policies (110–12).

An analysis of each hypothesis revealed some interesting findings. The researchers found that being a parent did not predict either men's or women's opinions about marijuana policy. Attending church or identifying as a born-again Christian strongly predicted conservative views, and this was much more the case for women. In order to explain this difference, the researchers needed to continue analyzing additional variables. Starting with a bivariate analysis, they found that White males were much more liberal about marijuana, followed by BIPOC men and White women; BIPOC women were the least liberal. To tease out if they could conclude that Whiteness strongly affected opinions, they analyzed the interplay between gender, race, opinion, and other variables like religiosity. In this analysis, the researchers *controlled* for the variable Whiteness; that is, they did a statistical test where they could specifically measure how much that variable affected the change in the other variables to assess its effect.

When controlling for Whiteness, gender was still a significant predictor of opinion. Those findings show that, although White males are more liberal about marijuana, just being White and male does not cause someone's opinion. Exploring further, they found a strongly significant statistical relationship between those reporting having used marijuana and holding more liberal views. Adding this variable into their statistical analyses made the influence of gender on marijuana opinion shrink considerably, to the extent that it was no longer statistically significant. Thus, from analyzing the interplay between all these different variables, the

BOX 14.3 Three Considerations in Multivariate Analysis

One use of multivariate analysis is to establish a relationship between two variables. To do so, not only must there be logical and temporal evidence of a relationship, but the relationship must also be shown to be *non-spurious* (i.e., genuine and authentic). A **spurious relationship** exists when there appears to be a relationship between two variables, but the relationship is not real: it is being produced because each variable is related to a third variable. For example, there is a positive relationship between income and voting behavior such that the more income people have, the more likely they are to vote for a conservative party. Does this mean that having more money *causes* people to move to the ideological right? Or could this relationship be explained by a third variable: age? The older one is, the more likely one is to have a higher salary; and the older one is, the more conservative one tends to be. If the apparent relationship between income and voting behavior is in fact a function of age, that relationship is spurious.

Another aspect to consider is the existence of an **intervening variable** causing the relationships. An intervening variable suggests that the relationship between the two original variables is not a direct one. Assume that there is a positive relationship between income and self-esteem—the higher one's income, the more positive one feels about oneself. But maybe there is more to it than that. Maybe income affects overall levels of physical vibrancy (richer people tend to be more physically fit and to smoke less than poorer people), which in turn affects self-esteem:

---

spurious relationship A non-causal relationship between variables that can be attributed either to coincidence or to the impact of a third variable that the analysis has not accounted for.

---

intervening variable An unobserved variable that can explain the relationship between independent and dependent variables and may itself be a cause of dependent variable.

income → physical vibrancy → level of self-esteem.

If this is true, what should happen to the relationship between income and self-esteem if physical vibrancy is controlled? (Remember: to control a variable is to hold it constant. Controlling in this instance might involve taking only people with high levels of physical vibrancy and seeing whether there is still a positive relationship between income and self-esteem among them.) If physical vibrancy were an intervening variable, that would weaken or eliminate the association between income and self-esteem. Also, notice the word "control." The purpose of controls is to make cross-sectional research more like an experiment in which random assignment makes all other things equal or controlled.

The third consideration is to look for what statisticians call an interaction. If the relationship between two variables holds for only some groups or situations, an interaction exists. The term is used in a statistical sense here, one that is different from its everyday meaning. In statistical terms, if the effect of one independent variable varies at different levels of a second independent variable, there is an interaction. Returning to the earlier hypothesis about inclusion of students with disabilities in general education classrooms improving their academic performance, might the relationship between level of inclusion and academic performance differ depending on the type of disability the student has? You may want to break down the relationship between inclusion and performance for students who are autistic, have intellectual disabilities, are blind, and have other disabilities. Perhaps academic performance of autistic students increases a great deal while that of students with intellectual disabilities does not. Or, academic performance of students with a moderate hearing disability improves less than students who are completely deaf. If this happens, we can say that the relationship between inclusion and academic performance is moderated by type or degree of disability. In other words, there is an interaction between inclusion and type or degree of disability.

researchers were able to conclude: "To a large extent, the reason there is a gender gap on attitudes about marijuana is because there is a gender gap in the use of marijuana" (2019, 118).

Perry's Multivariate Analysis

In his study, Perry (2014) also examined the interplay of multiple variables to understand the original bivariate relationship more deeply. To do so, he relied on existing research to develop hypotheses he then tested. He theorized that people who attend religious services more frequently are more embedded in their religious community, with deep ties to the people and influenced by the community's values and viewpoints. He proposed that when people attend religious services regularly, it indicates something about how religious they are, but also demonstrates their connection to a religious subculture and is "an indicator of social embeddedness within a specific religio-cultural community that inevitably defines cultural boundaries ("us" and "them")" (2014, 443, citing Durkheim [1912] 2008 and Stark and Glock 1968). This connection narrows their views of who might be potential dating partners to those within their religious communities. Analysis of US religious congregations has found that the majority of them are racially homogenous, which Perry asserts lowers the possibility of cross-race intimate relationships because of the tendency towards religio-cultural *endogamy* (desire to marry within their religio-cultural group).

To analyze the interaction between these factors, Perry proposed the following hypotheses:

H1: Persons who attend religious services more frequently will be less likely to have engaged in interracial dating or romance.

H2: Persons who attend religious services more frequently will express a stronger desire for religio-cultural endogamy.

H3: Persons who express a stronger desire for religio-cultural endogamy will be less likely to have engaged in interracial dating or romance.

H4: Including desire for religio-cultural endogamy in multivariate models will mediate the effect of religious service attendance on interracial romantic engagement, as indicated by a large reduction in the size and significance of the effect of religious service attendance (2014, 447).

These hypotheses outline a dynamic in which Perry believed that the original relationship between religious service attendance and interracial dating is "actually mediated through a preference for religio-cultural endogamy" (447). Thus, frequent religious service attendance is posited to have both direct and indirect influence on preference for same-race romantic partners. Figure 14.5 represents his hypothesized interaction between these variables.

Before pursuing his multivariate analysis, Perry ran another bivariate test comparing people who have dated interracially with the view of the importance of their partner holding the same religious views. This showed a significant relationship in that the more people wanted their partner to share their religious views, the less likely they were to have dated interracially: 33 percent who stated it was either "somewhat" or "very" important that their partner share their religious views, 43 percent who said it was "not very important," and 55 percent who stated it was "not important at all" had dated interracially (450).

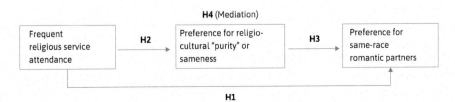

FIGURE 14.5 Perry's hypothesized mediation of variables
Source: Perry, 2014 (447).

To explore the second hypothesis, Perry examined religious service attendance in relation to a preference for religious "sameness" in a partner. He controlled for multiple different variables such as political conservatism, biblical literalism, education, US region, gender, and type of religious affiliation. He found that being politically conservative and a bible literalist had the strongest relationship with desire for religio-cultural "purity" or sameness. From this, he concluded that those with more traditional practices were more apt to desire religio-cultural endogamy.

If you were conducting a multivariate analysis of religiosity and interracial dating, how would you consider the addition of the variable sexual orientation? Would you analyze sexual orientation as a control variable? Do you think sexual orientation might be an intervening variable?

Perry then tested the third hypothesis and analyzed the relationship between several variables to see the degree to which people who express more desire for religio-cultural endogamy had engaged in interracial romance. He controlled for various demographic variables, such as race/ethnicity, age, region, gender, and religious affiliation and ideological variables such as religiosity and political views. With these controls, the original bivariate association between biblical literalism was shown to not be a primary predictor of interracial dating. He explains that this reveals holding traditional religious views does not result in lack of involvement in interracial relationships: "The fact that neither biblical literalism nor religious tradition is significantly related to interracial romantic engagement in the multivariate models suggests, at the very least, that the relationship between religious participation and interracial romance is not likely due to theological conservatism or traditionalist denominational teachings on interracial relationships" (453).

In his final tests, of hypothesis four, Perry combined analysis of all these variables, combining level of desire for religio-cultural endogamy with frequency of religious service attendance. He found that the relationship between attending religious services and interracial dating was no longer significant, though the desire for endogamy was still strongly related to people's potential to interracially date. Thus, he concluded that the effect of religious service attendance on interracial dating was *completely mediated* by people's desire to marry within their religio-cultural group (religious endogamy). It was by engaging in this multivariate analysis that Perry was able to deeply understand the perceived relationship between people's religious service attendance and their involvement in interracial romance. This analysis enabled him to conclude that "The findings from this study suggest that the frequency of religious service attendance—viewed as an indicator of social embeddedness within a specific religio-cultural community—influences Americans' propensities to engage in interracial romance by engendering a preference for religio-cultural purity or sameness in romantic partners that limits respondents' likelihood to date across racial–ethnic boundaries" (456).

These two examples have hopefully made clear that multivariate analysis can be used to determine how the variation in the dependent variable is explained or predicted by the independent variables. In addition, it provides a test to find out which, if any, of the independent variables are significant predictors after controlling for the others. If you pursue further education in statistics, you will learn about the use of *multiple linear regression* as a way for statisticians to examine the amounts of variation independent variables cause in dependent variables in multivariate analysis. As quantitative researchers analyze their data, they perform such tasks to closely examine the links between individual variables and query how the interplay of multiple variables might offer a deeper understanding of bivariate relationships.

Quantitative analysts use mathematics to explore patterns and trends in the social world. But statistical methods are much more than a way to crunch numbers to produce numerical results. As this chapter has explored, statistical analysis is a mode of thought and particular orientation towards understanding social life. Quantitative analysis is not only a mathematical process; it is an intellectual one where researchers ask and answer increasingly complex questions of their data.

Key Points

Introduction: Why Data Analysis Is the Starting Point for Quantitative Research

- The statistical techniques researchers can use depend on how they measure their variables and their sample size.
- Quantitative analysis is an iterative process, circuitously moving between hypotheses, existing theory, and collected data to generate possibilities and identify relationships across the data.

Types of Variables

- The three main types of variables are nominal, ordinal, and interval/ratio.
- Different statistical tests align with particular variable type, so the way researchers decide to measure their variables determines the statistical analyses they can do.

Descriptive and Inferential Statistics

- Descriptive statistics are used to describe the distribution of the variables and relationships among the variables in a sample.
- Inferential statistics analyze the characteristics of the sample to make inferences about the populations from which they are drawn.

Quantitative Analysis as a Tool for Understanding

- Statistics are a mathematical tool used to analyze data and also an approach to analysis—quantitative researchers can use statistics to ask and answer questions with a varying degree of complexity.
- Researchers increase their understanding about variables by exploring how they might relate to others, examining relationships between two variables (bivariate analysis) and multiple variables (multivariate analysis); as researchers introduce more variables into their analysis, their understanding becomes more complex.

Univariate Analysis

- In univariate analysis, a researcher examines one variable at a time.
- Frequency tables, diagrams, and graphs such as bar and pie charts are used to visually present univariate data. Measures of central tendency are ways to summarize univariate data, expressed as mean, median, and mode.

Bivariate Analysis

- Bivariate analysis examines the relationship between two variables.
- When analyzing the relationship between an independent and dependent variable, a researcher considers how strong the relationship is and whether the relationship is positive or negative.

Multivariate Analysis

- In multivariate analysis, a researcher examines the relationship between three or more variables; this is sometimes referred to as elaboration.
- Multivariate analysis, such as linear regression, is a tool that enables a researcher to determine the amount of variation independent variables cause in dependent variables, analyze whether an intervening variable can account for the observed variation, and assess whether the relationship is spurious.

Questions for Review

1. What main factors determine what statistical tools a researcher can use?
2. What does it mean that statistical analysis is an "iterative" process?
3. Why is it important to be able to distinguish between the three types of variables outlined in this chapter: nominal, ordinal, and interval/ratio?
4. How does level of measurement relate to statistical analysis?
5. How are descriptive and inferential statistics different from one another?
6. What can a researcher understand using descriptive statistics compared to when they use inferential statistics?
7. Why would we describe statistics as an analytical tool rather than just a set of mathematical equations?
8. The questions a researcher can explore get more complex as they add more variables into their analysis. Why is that?
9. What do different ways of visually presenting data offer a researcher in terms of describing their data?
10. What are the benefits and disadvantages of understanding data using the range, mode, median, and mean?
11. Why would a researcher analyze the standard deviation in their data?
12. Can one infer causality from bivariate analysis?
13. What are the limitations in using bivariate analysis to test a hypothesis?
14. How do multivariate analyses offer more information than bivariate analyses?
15. What is the difference between a spurious relationship and an intervening variable?

Portfolio Exercise

1. Looking back to your portfolio exercise from Chapter 8, make the edits proposed in the peer review process and finalize your survey. Write a 3- to 4-page report addressing the following questions:

   a. What types of variables does your survey consists of?
   b. What are 2 to 3 working hypotheses about relationships you suspect could exist between variables in your data?
   c. Thinking about univariate analysis, what single variables would be important to analyze in your survey to start exploring your hypotheses?
   d. Consider bivariate analysis, what are some relationships between pairs of variables that might of interest to help you explore your hypotheses?
   e. Now move from bivariate to multivariate analysis. What additional variables might you add to your pairs in question d that would offer you more information to explore your hypotheses?
   f. Thinking back to the sampling strategy outlined in your portfolio exercise in Chapter 4, would you be able to generate descriptive or inferential statistics from your data? Both?

Interactive Activities

In small groups with other students meeting in person or online, randomly select 5 cases from the Washington Post's Fatal Force database (https://github.com/washingtonpost/data-police-shootings).

1. Each group creates a google sheet to present collected data on your assigned subjects, addressing the following categories:

   a. Name
   b. Gender
   c. Race/Ethnicity
   d. Age
   e. City
   f. Armed/Unarmed
   g. Manner of Death
   h. Signs of Mental Illness
   i. Body Camera / No Body Camera
   j. Threat Level
   k. Fleeing / Not Fleeing
   l. Date

After having combed through the information provided in the database, import census information/variables based on the census tract in which the incident occurred: these data can be accessed via the US Census Bureau (https://data.census.gov/cedsci/), which also offers a tutorial on how to access neighborhood-level data (https://www.census.gov/data/academy/data-gems/2020/how-to-access-data-for-your-neighborhood.html). Add the following categories for each case into your spreadsheet:

a. Population size
b. Race/ethnicity percentiles
c. Percentage of occupied housing units

Finally, search for online newspaper articles covering the incident, importing the following information:

a. Number of responding officers
b. Sex of officer
c. Race of officer
d. Incident time

Once all the data have been gathered and organized, review the data as a group. Discuss—what statistical tools introduced in this chapter might be useful to present and analyze this data? How might you visually represent trends in this data? Are there variables that you might understand better by measuring the mean, mode, median, and/or range? What are some hypotheses you might explore about different independent and dependent variables? Consider how a researcher might approach understanding more about this topic using univariate, bivariate, and multivariate analysis. How might the analysis get more complex as you analyze the relationships between and among more variables?

This exercise is inspired by Reginald A. Byron: see Teaching About Police Violence with Open Source Police Shootings Data and Census Data (http://trails.asanet.org/Pages/Resource.aspx?ResourceID=13468), through the Teaching Resources and Innovations Library for Sociology (TRAILS).

2. Read an article employing quantitative analysis assigned by your instructor. In small groups meeting online or in class, discuss the article, focusing on these questions:

   a. What are the hypotheses guiding this study and how did the authors develop them?
   b. What are some variables the researchers explore in this research? What are these variables' levels of measurement?
   c. What relationships between variables do the researchers explore? (Think about independent and dependent variables, strength and direction of relationships.)
   d. Do the researchers use univariate, bivariate, and/or multivariate analysis? How do you know?
   e. Do you notice the researchers discussing measures of central tendency or measures of dispersion in their study?
   f. Do the researchers use descriptive statistics, inferential statistics, or both?

Online Resources

- The United States General Accounting Office (GAO) offers a useful introduction to quantitative data gathering and analysis.
  www.gao.gov/special.pubs/pe10111.pdf

- Online Stat Book presents a video explaining levels of measurement:
  www.youtube.com/watch?v=B0ABvLa_u88

- Veritas Tutors presents a video illustrating the notion of correlation:
  www.youtube.com/watch?v=SaSpZdf1oHU

- IBM SPSS offers a free trial download of their software.
  www.ibm.com/analytics/spss-statistics-soft-ware?lnk=STW_US_STESCH&lnk2=trial_SPSS&pex-p=def&psrc=none&mhsrc=ibmsearch_a&mhq=spss

For more resources please visit
www.oup.com/he/bryman-reck-fields1e

15

How Do Researchers Record and Share Their Work?
Writing and Dissemination

CHAPTER OVERVIEW

Writing is a practice that extends across the research process. Through writing, researchers craft survey questions, record observations in an ethnographic study, develop their ideas, and communicate them to others. Dissemination—the act of sharing research findings with others—begins once researchers have material to work with and findings to communicate. Through papers, presentations, posters, podcasts, and other modes of communication, researchers share insights gained through their study. In this chapter we will explore these various means of disseminating research findings.

Reading this chapter will help you to

- describe different steps in the writing process, including setting goals, freewriting, and sharing writing with others;

- engage in the revision processes;

- complete such important research writing tasks as preparing literature reviews, presenting quantitative and qualitative data, and compiling reference lists;

- discuss the place of reflexivity and creativity in writing;

- identify questions to ask when beginning to write;

- employ strategies to support effective dissemination; and

- describe sections of a written, verbal, and audio presentation.

Most of the time, to be a student is to be a writer. Students write class notes, exams, essays, papers, emails, and text messages—all as part of their schoolwork. And yet, many students would only reluctantly call themselves writers because, too often, the identity feels presumptuous: it suggests that they're claiming to be a *good* writer or that others should *want* to read their writing. Most people struggle with writing and produce mediocre—if not horrible—first drafts. They share their writing with others only when necessary: the deadline has arrived, their grade rests on having someone read the essay, or they will fail the class if they don't complete the exam.

But what if people decided to try on this label of "writer" and take writing seriously as a challenge and opportunity? After all, a writer is simply someone who writes and perhaps wants to be better at writing. Everyone pursuing a university or college degree or studying research methods also has to write, and everyone likely wants to improve, even if that goal seems ambitious. In this chapter, we assume that to be a researcher or a student of research is also to be a writer.

Introduction: How to Get Started

The trick with writing is that there's really no trick. Writers have to show up regularly, take chances, ask others for help, and learn from successes and failures. At the core is a basic tenet of writing: "You need to start somewhere" (Lamott 1994, 25).

Getting started means loosening the grip of perfectionism. The goal is not to write a perfect sentence, paragraph, or draft on the first try. Instead, the goal is to get something on paper that you can work with, improve, and ultimately share with others. After all, research is about gaining insight into the world and sharing that insight with others. Until study results enter the public domain—presented to a room full of peers in a paper read at a conference, shared online as a podcast, or published in a book or journal for other researchers or students—those results have little impact beyond satisfying the researcher's

---

BOX 15.1 How, When, and Where to Write

How you write can be as important as *what* you write. Do you prefer to use pen and paper or a computer? Those who write in longhand might favor particular pens or types of paper and notebooks. Those who write on a tablet or laptop might like a particular font.

The time of day can matter as well. Generally, mornings are a good time to write: you're rested and less distracted by the events of the day. However, some writers believe they're "night people" and prefer to write in the evening. Pay attention to your rhythm throughout the day. When are you better

Do you prefer to write with pen and paper or on a computer? Are you more productive when working at a desk or sitting comfortably on a couch? What's your most productive time: early morning or late at night? Writing is a skill that takes practice, so it's good to learn the most favorable writing conditions for you.

able to focus? When are you at your most creative? While many writers imagine that they need big blocks of time to write well—and thus cannot write unless they have a big block of time ahead of them—this is an often unrealistic expectation. Knowing when you write best can help you get a lot done in a short period of time; a well-timed hour in front of the computer might yield more pages than four hours during a time when you're more inclined to nap, read, or hang out with friends.

Finally, notice *where* you write. Quiet places with few potential interruptions are usually best, but you may not always have access to such spaces. If your home is crowded or noisy, check out the library or a quiet corner of a study hall on campus. A coffee shop might be a good place, with access to WIFI and caffeine, but at certain times of day, cafés can be noisy. Move around and experiment. Get to know yourself as a writer, particularly the places, times, and tools that best support your writing.

---

curiosity. Disseminating new findings ensures that they enter the research literature and contribute to the growing understanding of social issues.

Start Early and Write Every Day

Don't wait for the perfect time to start writing. Try to write something—*anything*—related to your project every day. Many people imagine that writers should

know what they will write before they begin writing, but an early start on writing is an early start on discovery, the central task of research. The writing process forces researchers to think about issues such as how best to present and justify the research questions and how to structure the discussion of the literature cited. Peter Elbow describes writing as an "inductive process" that "will lead you to new insights and new points of view you couldn't reach by reasoning alone" (1998). Natalie Goldberg, another author of books on writing, echoes this sentiment: "Writing," she says, "is the act of discovery" (2016). As we write, we articulate our ideas. We recognize the potential of those ideas, notice where we get stuck in our thinking, and understand what thinking, reading, and research we still need to do.

Starting early also helps writers resist procrastination—a habit that often results in rushed, last-minute work that is usually messy and disorganized. The presentation of findings and conclusions is a crucial aspect of the research process; failing to produce a convincing account because of time pressures means a researcher has done their work—and themselves—an injustice.

Freewriting

One popular strategy for getting started is **freewriting**: writing without interruption for a designated period of time—often fifteen to thirty minutes. The aim is to write without editing, to suspend the internal critic that encourages writers to edit sentences while crafting them or to anticipate the negative feedback their ideas might spark.

Those who recommend freewriting argue that the *creative* work of generating words is too often hampered by the *critical* work of applying criteria to the writing. Are the words smart enough? Are the sentences long enough? Do the words demonstrate sufficient understanding and insight? Will readers be interested? These are all reasonable questions, but they're not questions to ask at every stage of the writing process. You can deal with those issues later, when editing begins. When you are starting out, don't worry about finding the perfect word or crafting the perfect sentence; in other words, don't get in the way of your ideas; just let them flow, and evaluate later. Eventually, inspiration will come. In the meantime, simply write, knowing that the time for editing is later.

---

freewriting Writing without interruption and without editing.

Effective Writing

Effective writing means many things, including clear organization that reflects an articulated and sustained purpose or argument, sentences that are easy to read and understand, and deliberate and precise word choices. Attention to these details can support revision and the development of a writing voice.

Effective Grammar, Usage, and Punctuation

Grammar, usage, and punctuation are building blocks of good writing. Grammar involves rules for the construction of sentences and functions of words (for example, subject–verb agreement and the use of adverbs and adjectives). Usage refers to rules for the normal and correct use of words. For example, most people may understand the grammatically correct placement of "ain't" in a sentence, but they may differ on whether they should use the word in a sentence. Usage questions are often context specific. For example, the term "data" is formally a plural noun ("datum" is the singular) requiring a plural verb:

The *data are* conclusive: this candidate is likely to win.

However, it's usually fine to use a singular verb in everyday usage:

The *data shows* that this candidate is likely to win the election.

Punctuation—for example, periods, colons, and commas—helps organize writing by indicating the beginnings and ends of ideas and points of emphasis. Learning the rules of punctuation can help researchers communicate their ideas more effectively. At the end of this chapter, you will find suggestions for style guides that offer advice on grammar, usage, and punctuation.

Avoiding Prejudicial Language

Writing should be free of language that suggests prejudicial thinking, including sexist, racist, heterosexist, ableist, and transphobic words. Such language ranges from pronouns used to refer to others, terms adopted to denote racialized categories, and assumptions made about what constitutes "normal" behavior, identities, and lives.

There has been a similar shift in language used to describe gender and sexual identity. While some people embrace the term "queer" to point to a broad community, others prefer "lesbian, gay, bisexual, transgender, queer (LGBTQ)" because this term recognizes the different identity groups that constitute diverse sexual and gender communities. Still others prefer to name a more detailed and accurate list of the groups: for example, lesbian, gay, bisexual, transgender, queer, intersex, asexual, Two-Spirit (LGBTQIA2S+). This is the term that we use throughout this text.

Professional **style guides** increasingly take a stand on these issues. The American Psychological Association (APA) advises writers to "put people first, not their disability." According to this principle, for example, the term "Person with a disability" is preferable to "disabled person." Similarly, "people with a mental illness" is preferred over "the mentally ill." This nonprejudicial language insists on the personhood of people with disabilities and refuses to recognize their disability before their humanity. We've included links to these APA discussions at the end of this chapter.

The task for writers is to understand the prevailing conventions in the communities they are speaking to or about. What are the formal style guidelines in the academic discipline or profession? What language will the audience—academic and non-academic—expect to hear? How do the people studied describe themselves? Personal and political commitments matter as well: With what priorities does the researcher want to align?

Style Guides

As we've noted, you'll find a list of online and printed resources on grammar, usage, and punctuation at the end of this chapter. Consider purchasing at least one of the suggested books and bookmarking at least one website. Get used to referring to these resources while writing in order to learn the rules and apply them effectively.

Instructors commonly require students to submit bibliographies in a particular format. For example,

an instructor might want students to use the American Sociological Association's style. The *ASA Style Guide*, currently in its sixth edition, covers references (including online and social media sources), grammar, and formatting, among other topics. This guide is largely based on the *Chicago Manual of Style*, another popular and influential resource. Some instructors may require students to use the style of the American Psychological Association, commonly referred to as "APA style." These styles outlined in these guides vary in subtle but definite ways, as illustrated below.

The method students use will depend on the academic discipline and an instructor's preferences. The best bet is to get familiar with the styles popular in the discipline. Purchase print copies of style guides online or through local bookstores; locate quick guides through an online search. See the end of the chapter for some links to these guides.

Feedback and Revision

The best writers edit and revise their work many times before they consider it finished. Feedback from instructors, peers, and others with expertise in or familiarity with a topic can help writers improve what they've written for a particular assignment and their writing overall. Readers with little background can ensure the writing is clear, engaging, and free of jargon.

Feedback will likely include some focus on structural and technical requirements. For example, a writer may need to format margins in a specific way, demonstrate an understanding of particular concepts, or use a certain style for citations and reference lists. Be sure also to check for proper grammar, ensure that information and sources are properly cited, and confirm that arguments are clear and strong.

When writing a course paper—and before submitting the final version—classmates could review one another's work according to the assignment instructions. For example, do the papers include all of

---

style guide A reference book or manual that outlines standards for grammar, usage, formatting, and citation.

Chicago Manual of Style, 17th Edition (author-date)	
Book (in text)	(Du Bois 1990)
Journal Article (in text)	(West and Zimmerman 1987)
Book (bibliography)	Du Bois, W.E.B. 1990. *The Souls of Black Folk*. New York: Vintage Books.
Journal Article (bibliography)	West, Candace, and Don Zimmerman. 1987. "Doing Gender." *Gender & Society* 1 (2): 125–51.
American Psychological Association, 7th Edition (APA)	
Book (in text)	(Du Bois, 1990)
Journal Article (in text)	(West & Zimmerman, 1987)
Book (bibliography)	Du Bois, W. E. B. (1990). *The Souls of Black Folk*. New York, NY: Vintage Books.
Journal Article (bibliography)	West, C., & Zimmerman, D. (1987). Doing Gender. *Gender & Society*, 1(2), 125–151.
American Sociological Association, 6th Edition (ASA)	
Book (in text)	(Du Bois 1990)
Journal Article (in text)	(West and Zimmerman 1987)
Book (bibliography)	Du Bois, W. E. B. 1990. *The Souls of Black Folk*. New York, NY: Vintage Books.
Journal Article (bibliography)	West, Candace, and Don Zimmerman. 1987. "Doing Gender." *Gender & Society* 1(2):125–51.

the required information? Do they answer the specific questions the instructor posed?

When receiving feedback and revising, think beyond these technical concerns and keep overall writing practice and strengths in mind. Seek out feedback on the quality of the writing as *writing*. Think of the process as an opportunity to cultivate skills and artistry as a writer—the grammar, usage, punctuation, style, and writing voice. Sharing early and unpolished drafts is scary, but remember: it's a sign of a strong writer.

As with writing, it's a good idea to learn the best proofreading methods for you: Do you proofread better on paper or onscreen? Right away while ideas are still fresh in your mind, or 24 hours later, when you can take a clear look at your writing? Either way, don't let proofreading be just a quick final read-through done in haste: taking time with this step can help you avoid critical or embarrassing errors.

Developing a Writing Voice

Another aim for student writers is to discover and maintain a writing voice. Just as you would in speech or song, as a writer, you should sound like yourself, connect with an audience, and get your point across.

Learning to write in an academic setting and as a researcher can sometimes feel like it requires you to stop sounding like yourself: you begin using terms and sentence

BOX 15.2 **Writing Groups**

Writing groups provide an opportunity to share writing, get feedback, and learn from other writers. Groups might range from three to six people who meet weekly or monthly. Group members can agree to share and comment on course papers, freewriting, graduate school applications, or resumes. If one goal is to support regular and frequent writing, all members might share brief excerpts of their work at each meeting. If the goal is to ensure members receive feedback on nearly complete pieces, the group might focus on a single person each time—perhaps reading and commenting on a complete paper. No matter the group's focus and practice, members should support one another through writing slumps, celebrate one another's successes, and always recognize one another as writers.

Sharing your work with classmates or colleagues is a good way to get valuable feedback. What ground rules would you need to set for a writing group to promote a comfortable, productive exchange of feedback and constructive criticism?

structures that feel unfamiliar or alienating, and the idea of your own voice seems more and more remote. However, you still can and should develop your own writing voice. Being from a particular part of the world and belonging to different communities is important to your thinking about the social issues you study. Why shouldn't it also matter to your writing? Developing your writing voice allows you to adopt language and a tone in course papers, ethnographic notes, interview guides, surveys, and literature reviews that help build a meaningful relationship with the people you study and the people who read your work.

To discover and develop your writing voice, try the following:

- *Be clear about your aims.* Decide what you hope to accomplish in your writing. Keeping these goals in mind will help you trim unnecessary and distracting text and allow your aims and voice to shine.

- *Understand your audience.* Determine what your readers need to trust your arguments and remain engaged with your writing. What ideas and assumptions need clarification? Understanding these needs can help you focus your efforts and build a relationship through words on a page.

- *Avoid jargon.* Specialized language can confuse readers, even those with experience in your fields. A straightforward explanation of a complicated idea will go a long way toward establishing the authority and accessibility of your insights. When jargon seems unavoidable, take the time to define terms in your own words so readers know how you understand them.

- *Strive for clear and simple structures.* Long sentences and paragraphs require readers to hold several ideas in their heads for an extended and uninterrupted time. Each period or paragraph break represents a pause, signaling to the readers that they can take a figurative breath as they move through your insights and arguments. Those breaths help the reader feel supported and comfortable, setting the foundation for a good relationship between writer and reader.
- *Identify and learn from writing models.* While reading the work of others, take note of which writers hold their readers' attention and which ones leave readers cold. Read their writing as writing. How do they achieve their success? Think about their word choices; the structure of sentences, paragraph, and arguments; and the overall relationship they build with readers.

Models can help us feel as if we belong. Histories of exclusion and ongoing discrimination may make BIPOC people, first-generation students, students from working-class families, and others vulnerable to feeling that they are not welcome in universities or colleges. This outlook can pose several challenges, in writing and other areas. The language, style, and audience of academic writing can alienate those who already suspect they don't belong in the conversation.

People sometimes refer to these feelings as "impostor syndrome," a term coined by Pauline R. Clance and Suzanne A. Imes in their 1978 study of high-achieving women. The researchers found that, despite significant accomplishments and recognition from their peers, participants in their study feared being exposed as intellectual and professional frauds. The women worried that they hadn't really earned their success and that their achievements were simply the result of luck.

People now use Clance and Imes's term to describe concerns that one's success is a fluke, undeserved, and not the result of one's efforts or skills. How can writers and researchers cope with these feelings? First, recognize that many groups and people struggle with impostor syndrome. Though the feelings may be psychologically isolating, they are sociologically shared. Second, seek out people—"writing role models"—who have confronted and overcome impostor syndrome, even temporarily. These people might be peers, more advanced students, professors, or other mentors. Role models are also available in books and articles. Many accomplished writers have published works about writing despite feeling like a fraud. We have included a list of books on writing at the end of this chapter. Third, if you want to *feel* like a writer, *act* like a writer. Write regularly, share your work with others, and revise your writing. Doing the real work can help defuse feelings of not belonging.

BOX 15.3 **Feeling Stuck**

Writers and researchers regularly get stuck. Some call this frustration "writer's block"; others think about it as procrastination or describe it in terms of perfectionism. Whatever term we use, it means that we're having a hard time getting things done.

There are many paths through this difficulty: taking a break from the computer or desk, getting some rest, or finding a distraction. Reviewing and revising SMART goals might help you move more efficiently through your tasks (see Box 15.4). A freewrite might loosen your writing muscles and help you generate some text. Whatever strategy you adopt, notice whether it helps you find your way back to work refreshed and renewed. Even writer's block is an opportunity to learn more about your writing habits—the habits that help you get good work done and the ones that get in your way.

Disseminating Your Work

Though writing extends across the research process, it is of special importance toward the end of a project, when researchers prepare to describe and share their findings with others. Students' writing often takes the form of a term paper, presentation, or culminating assignment at the end of the semester, and this work may feel like a burden: a major task to complete at the end of the course, when students are already tired, ready for a break, and facing a deadline. But these projects are important opportunities to demonstrate what students have learned and to begin thinking about next steps. Perhaps the final assignment is a research proposal for an empirical study. A student might someday complete that study or use the proposal as a writing sample when applying to graduate or professional school or for a job. Even if the final assignment is unlikely to have a life beyond the course, it is an opportunity to share ideas with an instructor and classmates and to teach them about a group or issue they are unfamiliar with.

Determining Format and Audience

A first step in completing any writing is to get a sense of the project's parameters. Try answering some questions about the audience, potential formats, and institutional expectations.

- *Who is the audience?* The immediate audience may be quite small and specific—an instructor or classmates. Perhaps the paper will be submitted to an academic journal, or the presentation will be featured in a research competition. The audience of the work should inform the shape it takes. If writing a paper for an instructor who wants students to demonstrate their understanding of a set of ideas, focus on meeting that expectation. If speaking to a group of experts, feel free to use more technical language and assume that the listeners will be familiar with some of the basic ideas in the field. If addressing a group of lay people, define terms carefully and connect the ideas to concerns that matter to them.

BOX 15.4 **Setting SMART Goals**

Completing a research project, writing a paper, and designing a presentation are all significant and time-consuming tasks. You may find them easier to complete if the work is divided into smaller, manageable pieces. One strategy is to identify SMART goals. "SMART" is an acronym that represents different things in various models, but we use it to mean the following:

- Specific: The goal names a clearly defined task.
- Measurable: The goal can be quantified in some way, so you will know when you've completed it.
- Attractive: It's a goal you'd like to achieve and that you'll enjoy pursuing.
- Realistic: The goal is achievable given the time, data, background knowledge, and other resources you have on hand.

- Time-bound: The goal names a particular time frame for working on it and a deadline for reaching it.

Here are some examples of SMART goals:

- By December 1, read five articles on vegetarianism collected from *Sociological Abstracts*.
- Before spring break, write a first draft of the 200-word abstract and get feedback from writing group.
- Conduct one open-ended interview each week with a home health care worker (a bigger SMART goal could be to conduct six open-ended interviews by the end of the spring semester).

- *What format will the dissemination take?* Is the aim to produce a paper or a presentation? Will you be using instructional technologies like a PowerPoint presentation, video, or podcast? Whether the format is dictated by course and institutional requirements or students have some freedom in choosing a format, think about how to use the format to make a compelling argument.
- *What are the formal guidelines?* Usually, a course instructor will have specific requirements for final assignments. Look them over carefully and follow them. Students may have to work within specific time limits, present a particular number of slides, or cite a specific number of sources. Instructors may require a certain number of pages or a specific citation style. Students completing undergraduate or graduate theses may have to adhere to institutional or department requirements concerning such things as binding, page margins, line spacing, references, and submission deadlines.

What to Include When Sharing Research Findings

An empirical research paper or presentation typically includes the following sections. Expectations and conventions vary, so make sure the work meets the specific requirements of the institution, instructor, or course.

---

footnotes Notes appearing at bottom of page or slide in sequential order of appearance and offering brief explanation of material in main text.

---

endnotes Notes appearing at end of paper or presentation in sequential order of appearance and offering brief explanation of material in main text.

---

abstract A brief summary of a paper or presentation, touching on relevant literature, study design, data, findings, and significance.

Title

Usually, a title page or slide includes the author's (that is, the student's) name, instructor's name, the course title and number, the date, and the project title. Some instructors will not require a title page for papers, but they will most likely still want students to indicate their name, the course number or title, and the project title, usually in the upper left corner of the first page.

Acknowledgments

Writers often want to recognize the people who helped with the project, such as those who granted access to an organization, read drafts, and/or provided feedback or advice. If the research involved direct contact with the people studied—through interviews or participant observation, for example—the writer may want to thank them as well, provided they have permission to do so and that they will not be violating any requirements for confidentiality or anonymity. Acknowledgments are often offered as a **footnote** or **endnote** attached to the paper title or as part of the spoken script in a presentation.

Abstract

An **abstract** is a summary of the work discussed in the paper or presentation; it is less than one page (often no more than 200 words) and usually appears at the beginning of a written document. Not all institutions or instructors require an abstract, but most journals do. Conference presentations typically require one as part of the initial submission process, and the conference organizers may include them in the conference program.

Karen Kelsky (2011) argues it's possible to write a successful abstract before the research is complete. She suggests the following formula:

1. State a big-picture problem or topic widely debated in the field that the paper or presentation will address.
2. Describe a gap in the literature on this topic.
3. Explain how the project fills the gap.
4. Outline the specific material examined in the paper.
5. State the original argument.

BOX 15.5 **Meeting Deadlines**

Research, writing, and school are filled with deadlines for submitting assignments and papers, university paperwork, abstracts to conferences, and so on. Successful students and researchers learn how to manage deadlines and to generally meet them.

When taking on a task—completing a course, conducting a study, or submitting a conference abstract—first note any and all firm deadlines for accomplishing it. Think about the feasibility of that deadline. What other commitments will need to shift in order to meet it? If the deadline can't shift, work schedules or social plans may have to change to accommodate it.

Next, think about a timeline for meeting the deadline. If a paper is due at the end of the semester, what are some SMART goals you can set—and meet—along the way? Assign those goals specific dates in a calendar. Use the alert function to send yourself reminders on the way toward a larger deadline. If these initial SMART goals are difficult to meet, reconsider the overall plan.

---

6. Provide a strong concluding sentence that affirms that importance and contribution of the research.

Kelsky encourages writing abstracts that address each of these six points. Once drafted, edit the statements to meet required word limits.

Introduction

This section should explain your research topic or your research questions and their importance. In addition,

- describe in general terms the theoretical perspective taken in the paper;
- outline the hypotheses addressed; and
- anticipate the contribution and significance of the research.

Howard Becker (1986) strongly advised against "vacuous" opening sentences, such as "This study deals with the problem of careers." This kind of sentence, he explained, "is evasive, pointing to something without saying anything, or anything much, about it. *What* about careers?" (Becker 1986, 51). To those concerned that too much detail might give away the plot, Becker countered that it is much better to give readers a quick and clear indication of what will be presented. This indication will help readers appreciate the value they'll take from reading the paper. They will understand whether and how it will be worth their time to spend time with the analysis.

The opening is often the most difficult section to write. Consider writing it after drafting the rest of the paper or presentation. It'll be easier to introduce the work once it's written and the topic and its significance are clear.

Literature Review

The **literature review** outlines the main ideas and research already done in the area of interest. Essentially, it helps you situate your work within a tradition of related research. Start this section by identifying relevant social science research and then reading. Here are some strategies to get started.

- *Identify the online catalog of the library's holdings.* University, college, or public library websites features databases itemizing their holdings. Your campus will provide the required permissions to gain access to many items online;

---

literature review An overview of research on a chosen topic that synthesizes and critically assesses previous work and contextualizes current study.

if the items are available in print, your campus library will likely either own them as part of their local collection or participate in a system for interlibrary loan. Make an appointment with a campus librarian who can orient you to your library system's online and print collections.

- *Check databases that compile the larger universe of published research.* The library's home page may also feature databases of books and articles that the library doesn't own or can immediately access. These additional sources are usually attainable through interlibrary loan. Relevant databases include Academic Search Complete, Google Scholar, JSTOR, and Sociological Abstracts. Ask instructors, librarians, and classmates what databases they find helpful.

- *Keep a diary of search terms.* Record the different search terms and keywords used when searching databases and other online resources. Note also the databases searched and which offered the most success. You will likely have to conduct multiple searches on multiple days, and a diary will help you track the work done and identify fruitful paths to keep pursuing.

- *Scan bibliographies for relevant citations.* A bibliography is a record of the readings and authors consulted in the process of conducting research and developing an argument. Review the bibliographies of articles you discover in the literature search and find useful. Imagine being a detective following a thread of clues as one article leads to others.

- *Keep an eye out for review articles.* Some publications publish articles that review the existing research on a topic. For example, the *Annual Review of Sociology*, Volume 45 (2019) includes review articles on Islam; online and offline social networks; social stratification in China; sexual relationships in young adulthood; poverty, race and policing; and morality, reputation, and scandal. These review articles provide a critical review of the existing literature and the state of the field. They usually also suggest directions for future research.

Once you begin collecting articles, begin reading. It's a good idea to start with review articles, as they'll provide an overview of the field. Prioritize widely cited articles over those that have received less attention, and more recent articles over older publications; more recent work will better reflect the current state of the field. There will not always be time to read every article and book in full, so try some time-saving strategies: read abstracts (the summary at the beginning of most research articles), introductions, and conclusions to get a sense of whether you want to read more. While reading, note additional readings you want to check out.

Most important, reflect on the strengths and weaknesses of the research you're reading: notice exciting insights, note omissions and oversights, and identify emerging and lingering questions. Ultimately, the review should do more than simply summarize the relevant literature; it should also establish the importance of the research questions. For example, the basis for the project may be that, although a lot of research has been done on a certain topic or area, little has been done on a particular aspect of it. Explain this state of the field in the literature review. Alternatively, there may be competing positions regarding your topic. After describing those viewpoints in the literature review, explain to your audience that the research that follows will indicate which position provides a better understanding.

The theories, methods, and questions discussed in the literature review should anticipate those that will come up as the paper progresses. Ideally, return to points made in the review when presenting findings and conclusions. And, though the review may be written before collecting or analyzing data, continue reading the relevant literature throughout the research and writing process. Consider the early review provisional and revise it as your thinking evolves. Finally, remember that a literature review is often more extensive in paper than in presentations, posters, or other dissemination modes, where there won't be as much time or space to delve deeply into previous research.

Study Design

Next, authors usually describe the material they analyzed to explore their questions. All empirical researchers, no matter what their methods, need

BOX 15.6 Joining the Conversation

In their book *They Say, I Say: The Moves That Matter in Academic Writing*, Cathy Birkenstein and Gerald Graff (2018) argue that "to give writing the most important thing of all—namely, a point—a writer needs to indicate clearly not only what his or her thesis is, but also what larger conversation that thesis is responding to" (20). In reviewing the previous research—that is, constructing a literature review—writers are identifying the relevant threads of the existing conversation. The study that the literature review introduces is the researcher's contribution to that conversation.

Birkenstein and Graff offer a series of templates in *They Say, I Say* to help writers organize their ideas. Here are just a few of the most useful. Try using them in the literature review and across papers and presentations when clarifying for readers what others say and how you respond.

- X argues _____, and I agree because _____.

- X's argument that _____ is supported by new research showing that _____.
- In recent discussions of _____, a controversial issue has been whether _____. On the one hand, _____ argues _____. On the other hand, however, _____ contends _____. My own view is _____.
- I disagree with X's view that _____ because, as recent research has shown, _____.
- X overlooks what I consider an important point about _____.
- My discussion of X is in fact addressing the larger matter of _____.

These templates should help you do the difficult work of synthesizing the literature and locating your ideas in a bigger conversation.

---

to explain the basis of their claims—who or what they studied, how they selected and gained access to those items, and what they believe those items represent.

Researchers using quantitative methods (for example, surveys) outline sampling procedures, sample sizes, and response rates; they also describe how they measured concepts and summarize their approach to data analysis. In addition, they describe and defend the choices made, such as the decision to use a mailed questionnaire rather than a structured interview or why they chose a particular population for sampling. Researchers who rely on qualitative methods explain who or what they studied, how they recruited participants and/or gained access to the social setting, how many people they spoke to, what items they reviewed, or how many hours they spent in the field. Ethnographers also discuss any difficulties they encountered during recruitment,

while researchers who conducted an interview study will describe their approach to interviewing.

Despite the increasing digitization of many library holdings, it's worth meeting your campus library staff to learn more about resources available through the library, both online and in the stacks.

Like quantitative researchers, qualitative researchers detail their approach to analyzing the data.

As with the literature review, the discussion of study design is likely to be longer in a paper than in a presentation. For the latter, provide the essentials in slides and speech and move quickly to sharing results. If the audience has questions about the study design, they can raise them during the question-and-answer period that usually follows a presentation.

Results and Discussion

Next present the gist of the study findings, including some reflections on the significance of the findings for the research questions and the literature.

Quantitative researchers often separate this into two sections—Results and Discussion. In this model, results are generally presented with little or no commentary on how they relate to the claims made in the literature; the Discussion section addresses the findings' implications for the research questions posed. If you have specified hypotheses, your Discussion should revolve around whether or not they were confirmed. If the hypotheses were not confirmed, your Discussion might include some speculation about the reason. For example, did the sample size represent a limitation, or was a key variable omitted?

Qualitative researchers often present and analyze data simultaneously. This reflects the simultaneous and iterative process of analyzing qualitative data that we discussed in Chapter 13. Similarly, the presentation and discussion of results in a qualitative paper can carry the reader through the inductive process of building theoretical understandings grounded in the empirical data. Each field note excerpt, quotation from an interview, or image should carry the reader toward the larger insight the study offers.

BOX 15.7 Avoiding Plagiarism

Plagiarism is the representation of someone else's ideas, words, or work as one's own. Writers plagiarize when they copy a phrase, sentence, entire paragraph, or more without attributing it to the original author.

Often, plagiarism is the result of an oversight or misunderstanding. A writer may not know how to paraphrase someone's work effectively or fail to note the source of a direct quotation. Even when inadvertent, plagiarism is a significant breach of academic codes of conduct. Many universities and colleges have strict policies forbidding plagiarism and significant penalties for those found to have plagiarized. Penalties for violating codes of academic integrity include loss of credit for an assignment, course grade reductions, academic suspension, and notations on a student's academic record.

The following tips should help protect against plagiarism:

- Take careful reading notes, especially when copying and pasting information you find online. Be sure to always note where direct quotations begin and end and record the full citation information for all sources consulted.
- Learn to paraphrase sources accurately and concisely.
- In general, avoid using more than two consecutive words from sources without enclosing them in quotation marks.

To conduct research is to enter a community of scholars. Plagiarism is a sign of disrespect to the other members of this community. Take care to acknowledge the work of those who came before and make clear which ideas are new contributions.

---

plagiarism representation of someone else's ideas, words, or work as one's own, without adequate attribution, intentionally or unintentionally.

No matter what the mode of data collection and analysis, it will likely be crucial to present some data when sharing and discussing results. Keep the following suggestions in mind:

- When presenting tables, graphs, quotations, and other data, comment on each one to explain why they were included. Offer more than a summary: direct the reader to those parts that are especially striking in light of the research questions. Ask what story the table or data excerpt should convey, and then relay that story to readers.
- Do not include *all* results. This is especially important to remember when preparing a presentation and working with limited time. Share and discuss only those findings that relate directly to the research questions posed. Omitting some findings can be painful, but a focused dissemination will ensure that findings retain an analytical edge and readers do not lose the argument's thread.

The Results and Discussion are often among the most interesting parts of any dissemination efforts. Whether preparing a paper, presentation, or podcast, this is where to develop and share your unique contributions and insights.

Conclusion

In this final section, authors return to the issues that drove their investigation and were presented in the introduction. Linking the study's findings to the hypotheses and theories introduced earlier allows the authors to discuss whether these ideas are supported and what the implications are for further research.

Conclusions often begin with a strong, brief restatement of the study findings, then shift to reflect on what those findings suggest about the research literature, existing theories, or policy debates. Once that is done, discuss the significance of the research. The discussion will likely begin to move away from an analysis grounded exclusively in empirical findings in order to explore the broadest possible empirical and theoretical implications of the study

and inspire further research. It's a delicate balance: generalize findings, while still being careful not to engage in speculations that are not supported by empirical analysis.

Finally, be sure to acknowledge any limitations of the study that cannot be rectified without expanding the scope of the research. Perhaps also suggest avenues for further investigation.

Appendices

Researchers often have material that would help readers assess their work but is too detailed or technical to include in the main text. Such items— questionnaires, coding frames, observation schedules, letters sent to those sampled, letters to and from gatekeepers, and so on—can be included in **appendices** to a paper if the page limit allows.

References

The final pages or slides are usually devoted to a list of publications cited in the manuscript or presentation. The list will include full publication information for online, digital, and print sources—books, articles, chapters, news articles, webpages, videos, social media exchanges, musical recordings, and more—and adhere to guidelines of the chosen style guide. It's easier to write this list if these details have been carefully noted along the way, while reading.

This list of references (sometimes referred to as "works cited") can feel like a purely administrative task. Writers often wait until the end of the writing process, when they're tired and rushing to meet a deadline, to create this section. But if you remember that it offers a history of your thinking about a topic, it can be more than a chore. Writing a reference list is like constructing a picture of a community of thinkers. This step is also an opportunity to give credit to those whose ideas sparked your own.

---

appendix A section included at the end of a manuscript in order to provide readers with supplementary material: additional, but not critical, information about the research.

Methods in Motion | **The Politics of Citation**

Feminist and critical race scholars increasingly draw attention to what many have described as "the politics of citation." If bibliographies represent a history of thinking about a topic, the absence of women, BIPOC thinkers, and LGBTQIA2S+ people contributes to the continued erasure of these scholars from our discipline's past. It turns out that the task of writing a bibliography has political consequences.

Academic social movements have emerged to fight this issue. As described on its website,

Cite Black Women Collective members often wear t-shirts at academic gatherings to remind students and colleagues of citation politics.

Feminist Educators Against Sexism (#FEAS) is "an Australian-based, international feminist collective committed to developing interventions into sexism in the academy and other educational spaces." One of their projects is the Cite Club, in which members share their most recent works with each other and cite others' work whenever possible. The guiding principles of another organization, the Cite Black Women Collective, include "read[ing] Black women's work and acknowledg[ing] Black women's intellectual production" ("Cite Black Women: A Critical Praxis" 2020).

APA and ASA styles call for lists of references, while Chicago Style requires a bibliography. The difference is subtle and important. A bibliography provides a record of all sources consulted in the research and writing processes; a reference list is limited to those sources cited in the paper or presentation.

One quick note: If you are including a website in a bibliography or reference list, your entry should contain the date you last consulted it. Online sources are ever-changing: the website's text may change, or the site might even disappear. The date gives readers a sense of when the bibliographic entry was current.

Presentations

Course instructors sometimes require a presentation rather than, or in addition to, a paper. You may be asked to present in person in front of your classmates or remotely via an online communication and teleconferencing platform. A presentation will likely include much of the same information as a paper: an introduction, a review of the existing literature, a description of the study design, an overview of the study results, and some concluding thoughts. Though the content of both forms may be similar, they each require specific skills and priorities. A presentation is a different situation and medium, and it presents distinct boundaries and opportunities.

Boundaries

Researchers need to work within a series of boundaries when preparing and delivering presentations. For example, they likely have a limited amount of time for delivery. In general, a person can read about 150 words per minute. A twelve-minute presentation, reading from prepared remarks, should be no longer than 1,800 words. If we imagine spending no fewer than two minutes on each slide, there's room in twelve minutes for six slides.

Opportunities

These parameters—12 minutes, 6 slides, 1,800 words—offer not a lot of time, slides, or words. Your challenge is to balance boundaries against opportunities. What expertise or insight can you demonstrate? What idea can you teach the audience in the allotted time?

To achieve clarity about your purpose as a researcher and the audience's interest in and familiarity with your topic, consider the following questions:

- *What do you want people to learn from the work?* Identify an especially surprising insight gleaned from the findings or a result that challenges everyday understandings of a pressing social issue. Think about what most excited you about the research and what you most want people to learn from the project.
- *What do people need to know?* Some members of the audience may be familiar with the topic you're exploring and the language you're using. Regardless, don't assume everyone will understand. Take the time to define terms, detail any necessary histories, and otherwise prepare the audience to take in and understand the information offered.
- *What's your "so what?"* Ensure that the presentation clearly demonstrates that it is worth the audience's time and attention. State the

significance of the research. Have a good answer to the implicit question, "So what?"

Verbal and Visual Content

A research presentation includes meaningful verbal and visual information. Usually, the information presented verbally is primary, with the visual helping speakers make their points more effectively.

Verbal Content

The verbal content of a presentation includes the words used to describe the research and its significance, as well as tone of voice and body language. The audience's attention should focus on the speaker, who should share insights with confidence and clarity.

To this end, make sure to prepare and rehearse the text of the presentation in advance. Practice the timing to ensure you finish delivering the presentation a little before the designated time. On presentation day, you might be nervous, but try to have fun and relax. People especially enjoy presentations from presenters who seem to enjoy presenting. To help you and your audience enjoy the presentation, keep the following in mind.

- Most of us tend to speed up when we speak in front of an audience. Try to speak just a little more slowly than feels comfortable.
- Speak up! Speaking quietly might make it difficult for people who are hard of hearing or who are seated in the back of the room to hear what you are saying.

Whether the presentation is written out in full or organized on note cards, do not simply read the text off the page. The presentation should feel well-prepared, rehearsed, and conversational. Think about the non-verbal cues that accompany the presentation. Be sure to make eye contact with the audience, speak loudly and clearly, and allow yourself to be animated when speaking. Emulate the speaking habits of the presenters who hold your attention.

Visual Content

Visual content includes slides, illustrations, tables, and data. In order to prevent these elements from competing with the verbal parts of the presentation, keep them spare and elegant. Limit bullet points to key ideas. Use images to illustrate a process, behavior, or category. If a slide is cluttered, the audience will become distracted and have difficulty focusing on what's being said. Consider choosing simple solid backgrounds for the slides instead of overly colorful, creative, or expressive slide backgrounds. Remember, the objective is to present the research, not to dazzle the audience aesthetically. Too much visual distraction will likely take away from their ability to focus on the information being provided. Similarly, avoid using fancy transitions or animations between slides of bullet points, since these can be visually distracting.

Ensure that lettering and images are clear and large enough for someone to read and recognize them from the far corner of the room if you are presenting in person. Strive for maximum contrast between the slide background and the font color. Your audience will thank you for choosing a dark slide background, which is much less tiring to stare at than a white or lightly colored screen. Some material works especially well on PowerPoint slides: brightly colored charts with minimal lettering; edited quotations that speak directly to the point being made in your verbal presentation; and images that depict a relationship or process. Even blank slides can be effective: they give the audience a visual rest. Most presentation software allows you to check the accessibility of your slides to ensure they can be viewed and interpreted by readers with low vision. It is a good idea to use this feature before finalizing your slides.

Remember that audience members are likely either listening to the speaker or reading the slides, not both. Verbal and relevant visual information presented together can enhance learning. If they're competing with each other—that is, you're making a point in your spoken delivery that does not address what's on the screen—you'll undermine the audience's learning experience.

Recent Innovations in Presenting and Disseminating Research

Technology, social media, performance, and creative genres offer a host of ways to share research findings. Posters are a well-established dissemination method in social sciences. Increasingly, instructors ask students to create podcasts, post to course blogs, and create YouTube and Vimeo videos. Ethnographers have written poetry and plays that draw on and highlight study participants' accounts of their lives. These innovative approaches to dissemination expand not only the audience of social science research but also common-sense understandings of what constitutes meaningful social science research.

Have you ever recorded a podcast? A podcast can be a great way to share your ongoing work with a community of interested listeners.

Innovation sometimes arises out of necessity. Public health measures during the Covid-19 pandemic forced researchers to find new ways to present their research. Speakers and audiences stopped gathering in classrooms and lecture halls for research presentations, and travel to international academic conferences was put on hold. Presentations had to move online.

Many of principles discussed above apply to online presentations: decide on and maintain a focus, emphasize the significance of the research, and consider both visual and verbal content. Additional considerations when presenting online through a video conference program like Zoom, Microsoft Teams, or Google Meet include the following:

- Check all equipment and rehearse ahead of time to make sure, for example, you are using effective camera angles, have an adequate internet connection, and have tested your audio and video settings.
- Consider whether you can make the presentation interactive through, for example, quizzes, polls, or breaks mid-presentation to take questions and comments.
- Emphasize that, even though you and your audience are online, there is a human presence behind the presentation and research: make sure you are well-lit and properly dressed for the presentation, just as you would be for an in-person presentation, and make eye contact with your audience by looking directly at the camera.

The first few times you present research online, record yourself and then view the presentation later. Learn from your performance—the mistakes as well as the successes.

Issues to Consider when Disseminating Research

The following checklists will help you ensure that your final draft is complete. Consider the content of your work as well as the formatting and organization and be sure to return to earlier chapters of this textbook if you need to review any of the issues named below.

Checklist: Content

- [ ] Does the title of the project correspond well with its contents?
- [ ] Have you clearly specified your research questions?
- [ ] Have you clearly linked the literature reviewed to your research questions?
- [ ] Is your discussion of the literature critical and synthesizing and not just a summary of what you have read?
- [ ] Have you clearly outlined your research design and research methods? Make sure you have explained

  - the reasons you chose and implemented a particular research design or method;
  - how you selected your research participants;
  - what, if any, problems you experienced securing people's cooperation (e.g., response rates);
  - if your research required access to an organization, how and on what basis you achieved access;
  - what, if any, difficulties you encountered in implementing your research;
  - which steps you took to ensure that the research was ethical; and
  - how you analyzed the data.

- [ ] Have you presented your data so they clearly relate to your research questions?
- [ ] Have you used pseudonyms as necessary to preserve the confidentiality of the data and the anonymity of informants and other research participants?
- [ ] Are your interpretations of the data fully supported with tables, figures, or segments from transcripts?
- [ ] Have you commented in the text or in your prepared spoken remarks on every table and/or figure?
- [ ] Does the discussion of the findings clearly relate to the research questions?
- [ ] Does that discussion explain how the findings shed light on the literature presented?

☐ Do the conclusions provide clear answers to your research questions?

☐ Do the conclusions clearly establish what your research contributes to the literature?

☐ Do your conclusions include a discussion of your findings' broader social significance?

☐ Does the writing avoid sexist, racist, and other prejudicial language?

☐ Have you ensured that the text does not make excessive use of jargon?

☐ Does the list of references include all the items referred to in your text?

☐ Does the format of the references follow precisely and consistently the style that your institution or instructor requires or that you've adopted?

☐ Have you acknowledged, preferably in a written or spoken acknowledgments section, the help of others (e.g., your instructor, people who helped with interviews, people who read drafts)?

Checklist: Formatting and Organization

☐ Have you included any necessary appendices (e.g., interview schedule, letters requesting access, communications with research participants)?

☐ Have you consistently labeled every table and/or figure with a title and number?

☐ Have you broken up the text in each chapter or section with appropriate subheadings?

☐ Have you provided transitional phrases and "signposts," so that readers know what to expect next?

☐ Have you met all course requirements, including word count and time limits?

☐ Have you checked that your tenses, margins, pagination, and capitalization are consistent?

And Finally

Remember to fulfill any obligations incurred while conducting the research, such as supplying a copy of the paper, presentation, or other final product to those who have been promised one. Honor and respect whatever relationships were necessary to completing the study.

To share your research with others is to share insights from a sustained, careful, and thoughtful examination of the social world. You have learned something about an issue and can now help others think differently about the conditions in which they live. Through a paper, podcast, poster, or presentation, you point to new possibilities for understanding and even changing our communities. Dissemination means you've considered the many complexities of social research and embraced, even momentarily, the identities of writer and researcher. Congratulations, and welcome to the community of sociological researchers.

Key Points

Introduction: How to Get Started

- Writing habits such as writing regularly, practicing self-discipline, and setting and meeting writing goals can support your success as a writer.
- Freewriting can loosen the grip of perfectionism and support a regular writing practice.

Effective Writing

- Grammar, punctuation, and usage are important building blocks of good writing.
- One task for the beginning writer is developing one's own writing voice.
- Revision is an ordinary and valuable part of the writing process.

Disseminating Your Work

- Dissemination is an opportunity to share what you've learned in a research project and to learn from audience responses to your work.
- Audience and institutional expectations and feedback shape the format and content of papers and presentations.
- Dissemination can take a number of formats, including papers and presentations.
- Research papers include a number of elements, usually including title, acknowledgements, abstract, introduction, literature review, a description of your study design, results, discussion, and conclusions.

Presentations

- Papers and presentations share a number of features, though the formats offer researchers different challenges and opportunities.

- Successful presentations achieve a balance between verbal and visual content.

Issues to Consider When Disseminating Research

- Revision and careful review of near-final products help make dissemination especially effective.

Questions for Review

1. In what specific ways does writing extend across the research process?
2. What is freewriting? What is its value in the overall writing process?
3. What are some of the primary concerns in avoiding prejudicial language in writing?
4. What is a "writing voice"? What are some strategies for developing a writing voice?
5. What are the customary sections of a research paper? What is the usual purpose of each section?
6. In what ways is a literature review like a conversation?
7. In what ways are presentations characterized by both boundaries and opportunities?

Portfolio Exercise

1. Collect all of the writings, presentations, and other documents that you prepared in previous portfolio exercises. Use these completed portfolio exercises to prepare either a written research proposal (probably 8–10 pages; your instructor will confirm) or visual presentation of your work (maybe 10–12 minutes; again, check with your instructor). Your presentation will likely include components outlined in this chapter: Title, Abstract, Introduction, Literature Review, Study Design, Conclusion and a Bibliography. (We have not included a Results and Discussion section here because we assume you have not yet collected and analyzed data systematically; if you have collected and/or analyzed preliminary data, go ahead and share some results.) In some cases, your portfolio exercises will function as first drafts of your proposal; in other cases, your portfolio exercises will have helped to clarify that you will not choose a particular method or strategy in your proposed research.
2. Ensure that your portfolio includes a literature review that places your research questions and hypotheses in the context of previous research, addressing what we already know, or think we

know, about a topic. Make sure to cite your sources and consider the following:

   a. What methods have other researchers used to study this topic?
   b. What theories have been especially influential in this field or subfield?
   c. What publications have been influential on this topic? What do they have to say about this topic?

3. Finally, return to where we started: your research question. Be sure that the final version of your question and the study you've designed accomplishes the following:

   a. describes what you want to know,
   b. is clear and specific,
   c. reflects a sociological imagination,
   d. can be answered through empirical research, and
   e. speaks to the research and broader communities that matter to you.

Your proposed research should now reflect the understanding of research methods that you've gained this semester. Our hope is that this understanding has given shape and direction to your curiosity, commitments, and responses. We trust that you've gained a set of skills and feel better positioned to make sense of the insights other researchers offer and to generate empirical insights of your own. Most of all, we hope you feel prepared to ask and answer crucial questions about the world in which we live.

Interactive Activities

1. Working in small groups, select a topic of interest (for example, university responses to Covid-19 in 2020) and construct a relevant research question or set of research questions based on the topic. In person or online, groups present their questions to the class, which discusses whether the questions are clear, how they could be improved, and what additional questions should be asked.

2. Have your instructor or a campus librarian demonstrate how to use the databases available via the institution's library system.

3. Use your library databases to find five articles that address the research question(s) your group wrote in the first activity. Review the articles you found and those selected by the other members of your group. Construct a series of statements depicting the conversation underway about your topic, using templates from Graff and Birkenstein as models.

4. Set 3 SMART goals; one each for yourself, your classwork, and your potential research. If comfortable, swap your goals with a partner. Do their goals meet the SMART criteria? Suggest revisions to make your partners' goals SMARTer. Revise your own goals based on your partner's feedback.

5. In groups, review the opening pages of 3–4 of the following books. How do the first few pages suggest the authors understand the practice of writing? How might they be useful in supporting your writing practice? What other books have you and your classmates found helpful?

   - Birkenstein, C., and Graff, G. (2018). *They say/I say: The moves that matter in academic writing*. WW Norton & Company.
   - Cook, C. K. (1985). *Line by line: How to edit your own writing*. Houghton Mifflin Harcourt.
   - Elbow, P. (1998). *Writing with power: Techniques for mastering the writing process*. Oxford University Press.
   - Lamott, A. (1995). *Bird by bird: Some instructions on writing and life*. Anchor.
   - Silvia, P. J. (2007). *How to write a lot: A practical guide to productive academic writing*. American Psychological Association.
   - Strunk, W. (2007). *The elements of style*. Penguin.
   - Younging, G. (2018). *Elements of Indigenous style: A guide for writing by and about Indigenous Peoples*. Brush Education.

6. Before or during class, listen to one or both of the following podcast episodes.

   a. *The Allusionist*, Alarm Bells (episode 114; 0:30), in which participants "explain some of the shifts in terminology [used to discuss climate change], the squabbles and the industry interference, and how to communicate about climate in a way that does result in useful action" (www.theallusionist.org/allusionist/alarm-bells).

   b. *Cited*, "I Can't Breathe" (1:01): in which participants "connect police brutality, environmental racism, and Covid-19" (www.citedpodcast.com/podcast/i-cant-breathe/).

   As you listen, consider following questions for discussion afterward.

   - What research is cited in the podcast?
   - What jargon do the participants use? What are their strategies for defining those terms for the audience?
   - How does the presentation of research in the podcast differ from what you've seen in academic papers and presentations?

7. Read an assignment—a recent one, or one you will soon hand in—against the checklists above. Where could you strengthen your work?

Online Resources

You can find ASA, APA, and Chicago style guides online and in print.

- American Sociological Association. 2019. *American Sociological Association Style Guide*. 6th ed. Washington, DC: American Sociological Association.
  www.asanet.org/sites/default/files/savvy/ documents/teaching/pdfs/Quick_Tips_for_ASA_ Style.pdf

- American Psychological Association. 2019. *Concise Guide to APA Style*. 7th ed. Washington, DC: American Psychological Association.
  https://apastyle.apa.org/

- *The Chicago Manual of Style*, 17th ed. Chicago: University of Chicago Press, 2017.
  www.chicagomanualofstyle.org/home.html

- Purdue University's Online Writing Lab (OWL) has a wealth of resources for beginning and experienced academic writers.
  https://owl.purdue.edu/owl/purdue_owl.html

- The APA has guidelines for avoiding prejudicial language.
  https://apastyle.apa.org/ style-grammar-guidelines/bias-free-language/

- The APA also has a discussion of bias-free writing around disability and ableism.
  https://apastyle.apa.org/style-grammar-guidelines/ bias-free-language/disability

- The Manchester University Academic Phrase bank "is a general resource for academic writers [that] aims to provide you with examples of some of the phraseological 'nuts and bolts' of writing."
  www.phrasebank.manchester.ac.uk/ writing-definitions/

- Deborah Lupton's 30 Tips for Successful Academic Research and Writing, available on the LSE Impact Blog, is full of helpful advice for writers.
  http://blogs.lse.ac.uk/impac- tofsocialsciences/2012/11/28/ lupton-30-tips-writing

- The video Writing the Literature Review discusses the fundamentals of this task:
  www.youtube.com/ watch?v=2IUZWZX4OGI&feature=related

- Choosing and Narrowing Research Topics for APA & MLA Essays is a video providing strategies for picking a subject
  www.youtube.com/watch?v=jSHXb83Xtsk

For more resources please visit
www.oup.com/he/bryman-reck-fields1e

Glossary

abstract A brief summary of a paper or presentation, touching on relevant literature, study design, data, findings, and significance.

acquiescence Respondents' tendency to agree with researchers' questions and perspectives, as they understand them.

analysis of existing (or available) data Research using data that have been collected by a researcher or institution and made available for others to analyze.

analytic memo A brief written exploration of concepts, questions, and emerging analysis that a researcher produces during iterative inductive analysis.

anonymity The practice of ensuring that participants' identities are unknown to the researcher, thus ensuring that information provided cannot be linked back to individual participants.

appendix A section included at the end of a manuscript in order to provide readers with supplementary material: additional, but not critical, information about the research.

applied research Research conducted to address practical problems.

available data Data collected by a researcher or institution and made available to others to analyze.

axial coding A process in qualitative data analysis of relating codes to one another with the aim of making connections between concepts and categories.

basic research Research conducted with the goal of advancing knowledge.

Belmont Report A document outlining three main ethical principles—respect for persons, beneficence, and justice—published in 1979 by The National Commission for the Protection of Human Services of Biomedical and Behavioral Research.

big data Large quantities of data, collected in traditional ways by companies or institutions and through digital means.

bivariate analysis An examination of the relationship or differences between two variables.

case study design A research design that entails detailed and intensive analysis of either a single case or, for comparative purposes, a small number of cases.

categories Cluster or collection of instances that share characteristics or features.

closed-ended questions Interview or questionnaire items that present respondents with a fixed set of possible answers to choose from; also called fixed-choice questions.

coding The process of labeling, categorizing, and organizing data collected in order to facilitate qualitative or quantitative analysis.

coding manual The list of codes used in analysis of particular set of data.

coding schedule A form listing all possible codes in coding manual; when completed, it includes data examples, details, and frequencies.

cohort study A longitudinal design in which the researcher collects data at least two times about a sample of people who share a significant life event.

Common Rule The system used currently in the US to protect human participants in research studies; also known as the Federal Policy for the Protection of Human Subjects.

concepts General or abstract ideas that describes observations and ideas about some aspect of the social world.

conceptualization The description or clarification of a concept's meaning, often in the form of a dictionary definition.

concurrent validity The type of validity indicated by relating a measure to existing criterion or a different concept indicator to see if one predicts the other.

confidentiality The protection of the identities of research participants, arising from measures taken by the researcher to ensure that information provided by individual participants cannot be linked back to them.

constructionism A way of understanding social life as the product of interactions and negotiations among people.

construct validity The type of validity established by determining whether concepts being measured relate empirically in the manner that relevant theories predict.

content analysis The examination of texts, including both written and visual materials, with interest in how the material contributes to and reflects meaning and representation.

convenience sampling A non-probability sampling method that is selected because of its availability to the researcher.

convergent validity The type of validity established by comparing two differently developed measures of one concept.

correlation The relationship between two or more variables; a strong *positive correlation* means that an increase (or decrease) in an independent variable is associated with an increase (or decrease) in a dependent variable, while a *negative correlation* means that as the independent variable rises, the dependent variable falls (and vice versa).

covert participant observation Field research in which researchers conceal their researcher status and study aims from the people being studied.

covert research Research conducted without informing the participants that the study is taking place.

critical race theory A theoretical perspective, emerging from legal studies, that focuses on race and power in social life.

cross-sectional design A study design in which data are collected at (and thus represent) a single point in time.

data analysis The process of examining, processing, and organizing data to gather information and develop conclusions from it.

deception The practice of concealing or misrepresenting an aspect or entirety of one's research aims to study participants.

deductive research An approach to inquiry that begins with a statement of theory from which hypotheses may be derived and tested.

dependent variable (DV) A variable that is influenced (or assumed to be influenced) by an independent variable.

descriptive research Research conducted to provide descriptive accounts of people, situations, and settings.

descriptive statistics Tools used to describe and interpret the key features of a data set, summarizing the main trends in data collected from a sample.

dispersion The degree of variability of values in a sample.

disproportionate stratified random sampling A probability sampling method in which units are randomly sampled from strata in numbers not equal (disproportionate) to their representation in the overall population.

element A single case (person, city, etc.) in a population.

empirical research A way of studying and understanding the world through systematic and direct observation.

endnotes Notes appearing at end of paper or presentation in sequential order of appearance and offering brief explanation of material in main text.

epistemology The philosophical field concerned with how we know what we know.

ethnography (or ethnographic research) A method in which researchers immerse themselves in social settings for an extended period of time, observing behavior and interacting with study participants in order to understand people's culture and experiences.

evaluation research Research undertaken to assess the impact of real-life interventions, including policy changes and social programs.

exhaustive The quality of measurement categories that anticipates and meaningfully sorts all possible responses to a survey item and thus all potential units of analysis.

existing data Data collected by a researcher or institution and made available to others to analyze.

experimental design A research design that rules out alternative explanations of findings by randomly assigning participants to one of two groups: an experimental group that is exposed to the influence and a control group that is not exposed to the same influence.

explanatory research Research conducted to explain and predict future conditions for people, situations, and settings.

exploratory research Research conducted to generate questions and hypotheses about emerging or not-yet-defined phenomena.

face validity The type of validity achieved if, on inspection, an indicator appears to measure the concept in question.

facilitator A person (usually the researcher) who runs a focus group session, guiding discussions with minimal intervention.

feminist research A mode of inquiry informed by principles of feminist social movement and committed to addressing power imbalances in the research process and gendered social inequalities.

field notes Detailed notes that researchers take in the field, describing events, conversations, and behavior and forming the primary source of data from participant observation.

filter questions Survey or interview questions that determine whether participants have the experience or other qualifications required to answer additional questions.

focused coding The formal and systematic application of most frequently occurring or compelling codes to qualitative data.

focus group A semi-structured interview in which several people are interviewed together in order to learn about people's experiences and perceptions, group dynamics, and processes through which social groups make meaning.

footnotes Notes appearing at bottom of page or slide in sequential order of appearance and offering brief explanation of material in main text.

freewriting Writing without interruption and without editing.

frequency table A table that displays the number and/or percentage of units (e.g., people) in different categories of a variable.

gatekeeper A person with the authority, power, and status to grant researchers access to participants and settings.

generalizability The ability to make inferences about a population by using sample data.

grounded theory An approach to qualitative data analysis in which data collection and analysis proceed iteratively, producing a theoretical understanding.

hypothesis A tentative assertion that draws on existing research, designed to be tested against empirical findings.

immersion An ideal of ethnographic research, in which researchers seek an in-depth understanding of settings or people by engaging fully in the experiences and practices of the group.

independent variable (IV) A variable that has (or is assumed to have) an influence on a dependent variable.

indicator Something that points to, provides evidence of, or otherwise measures a concept.

inductive research An approach to inquiry that begins with the collection of data, which are used to develop theories, hypothesis, and concepts.

inferential statistics Tools used to analyze the characteristics of the sample to make inferences about the population from which it was drawn.

informant A study participant with specialized knowledge or insight to offer a researcher.

informed consent A core principle of ethical research, stipulating that participants must agree freely and with full understanding to participate in any study.

institutional review board (IRB) A committee that oversees proposed research involving human participants to ensure ethical practices.

inter-coder reliability The degree to which two or more people agree on the coding of an item.

internal reliability The degree to which items that make up a scale or index are consistent or correlated.

interpretivism A way of understanding social life that emphasizes people's interpretations of the world.

intersectionality A theoretical framework committed to understanding social categories, identities, and hierarchies as interrelated systems and experiences.

intersectional theory A theoretical perspective that considers multiple and overlapping systems of discrimination in marginalized and oppressed communities.

interval measurement The measurement level in which distance between named categories is meaningful and consistent, zero categories are arbitrary, and negative values are possible.

intervening variable An unobserved variable that can explain the relationship between independent and dependent variables and may itself be a cause of dependent variable.

interviewer effects Data variations introduced by an interviewer's presence, including impact of perceived identities, style and personality, and question wording.

interview guide A specific plan for conducting a qualitative interview; can be a brief or an elaborate list of areas to be covered or questions to be asked.

interview schedule A collection of questions asked during structured interviews in a specified order and with consistent wording.

intra-coder reliability The degree to which an individual coder is consistent over time in the coding of an item.

key informant A person who shares expertise, knowledge, and authority with an ethnographer and, in doing so, is integral to the study's success; often the only one of their kind in the study.

life history (or biographical) method A qualitative method that emphasizes people's inner experiences and their connections to larger societal events throughout the life course; the main sources of data are usually life history interviews and personal documents.

Likert scale A widely used format in which respondents are typically asked their degree of agreement with a series of attitude statements that together form a multiple-indicator measure. The scale is designed to measure the intensity of respondents' feelings about an issue.

line-by-line coding An in-depth method of analysis in which the researcher applies a code to every line of field notes or transcripts.

literature review An overview of research on a chosen topic that synthesizes and critically assesses previous work and contextualizes current study.

longitudinal design A research design in which data are collected on at least two separate occasions in order to capture social process and/or change over time.

mean The "average," or the sum of all the scores divided by the number of scores.

measurement The process of defining, observing, and recording ideas, experiences, and outcomes of interest.

measure of central tendency A measure designed to represent the central value in a set of scores; examples include the mean, median, and mode.

measure of dispersion A measure (such as the range or standard deviation) that summarizes the degree of variability in a set of scores.

median The midpoint in a set of scores arranged in numerical order.

methodology The theory, justification, and assumptions behind the selection and use of research methods.

missing data Data that are not available because, for example, a respondent in social survey research has not answered a question.

mixed-methods research An approach to inquiry that draws on multiple tools and procedures—often both qualitative and quantitative—to collect and analyze data.

mode The value that occurs most frequently in a set of scores.

moderator A person (usually the researcher) who runs a focus group session, guiding discussions with minimal intervention.

multistage cluster sampling A probability sampling method in which the researcher first samples sets of cases (clusters) and then samples units within them, usually using a probability sampling method.

multivariate analysis The examination of relationships among three or more variables.

mutually exclusive The quality of measurement categories for which each case fits into only one response or variable category.

naturalism Research that seeks to minimize the use of artificial methods and other disturbances to social worlds being studied.

nominal measurement The measurement level in which categories only name phenomena and do not rank order or assign any consistent numerical value.

non-probability sampling The process of using a non-random (but still systematic) sampling method, in which some units in the population are more likely than others to be selected.

non-response A situation that occurs if someone in a sample refuses to participate in the study, cannot be contacted, or for some other reason does not supply the required data.

non-response bias A bias introduced when sample participants differ from non-participants in meaningful ways; can occur due to low response rates.

Nuremberg Code A 10-point ethical code, developed as a result of the Nuremberg trials, that focuses on gaining participant consent, doing no harm, and offering social benefit.

objectivism An approach or position that views social phenomena as though they have an existence independent of social actors or their perceptions and that calls on researchers to draw conclusions based on fact without the influence of values, bias, or preconceptions.

objectivity A position that approaches social phenomena as if they have an existence independent of social actors or their perceptions; it calls on researchers to draw conclusions based on facts that are not influenced by values, bias, or preconceptions.

official (or existing) statistics Data compiled by or on behalf of state agencies in course of conducting their business.

ontology The philosophical field concerned with nature of being and reality.

open coding An early stage of qualitative analysis in which the researcher stays close to the data and generates concepts that may later be grouped together to form categories.

open-ended questions Interview or questionnaire items that allow respondents to formulate their own answers rather than presenting respondents with possible answers to choose from.

operationalization An explanation outlining the process through which a researcher will observe the presence, absence, or degree of a concept's existence.

oral history interviews A variant of the life history interview in which the interviewee is asked to reflect on certain historical events or eras they have lived through.

ordinal measurement The measurement level in which named categories place observed cases and variation into rank order.

outlier An extreme value (either very high or very low) in a distribution of scores with the potential to distort both the mean and the range.

overt participant observation Field research in which participants know they are being studied and understand the aims and status of the researcher.

panel study A longitudinal design in which researchers collect data on two or more occasions about a single, constant sample of people.

participant observation A data collection technique often used during ethnography, in which researchers interact with, observe, and listen to people in a research setting, taking notes on what occurs.

plagiarism   representation of someone else's ideas, words, or work as one's own, without adequate attribution, intentionally or unintentionally.

population   All cases or people covered by a theory or explanation; the universe of units from which a sample is selected.

positionality   The way in which social and structural contexts impact a person's identity, status, and perspectives and affect the amount of power and authority someone holds within interpersonal and institutional interactions.

positivism   An epistemological position that advocates using empirical methods and logic to study of social reality.

probability sampling   The process of using a randomly selected sample in which each unit in the population has a known and equal probability of being selected.

proportionate stratified random sampling   A probability sampling method in which units are randomly sampled from strata in numbers equal (proportionate) to their representation in the overall population.

pseudonym   A made-up name given to a research participant to protect their privacy by concealing their identity in documents and reports related to the research.

purposive sampling   A non-probability sampling method in which researchers choose attributes that are most appropriate to the study; also called judgmental sampling.

qualitative content analysis   An inductive approach to analysis that focuses on how meaning is produced and communicated in texts by allowing categories of interest to emerge from data during the course of study.

qualitative interviewing   In-depth semi-structured or unstructured interviewing that usually aims to capture the subjective experience of social processes and conditions.

qualitative research   Inquiry that uses mainly words, images, and other non-numerical symbols as data and involves little or no quantification.

quantitative content analysis   An analytic approach using a pre-specified coding scheme to identify patterns and frequencies of communication in documents and texts.

quantitative research   Inquiry using numerical data-gathering techniques and statistical analysis.

quasi-experimental design   A research design whose logic and process resemble an experiment but does not involve the same manipulation and control of influences.

questionnaire   A data collection method in which respondents complete questions and response items without the aid of an interviewer.

quota sampling   A non-probability sampling method that matches the proportions of people in different categories in the population.

random sampling   The form of sampling in which the sample is selected randomly and all units of a population have an equal chance of being selected.

range   The difference between the maximum and the minimum score in a set of scores associated with an interval or ratio variable.

rapport   A relationship developed between the researcher and an individual or group of people, allowing both to understand, trust, and communicate with each other.

ratio measurement   The measurement level in which distance between named categories is meaningful and consistent, a true zero category is possible, and negative values are not possible.

raw data   Data that have been collected but not processed for use or analysis.

reactive effects (or **reactivity**)   The impact on research when participants know that they are being studied, which may result in atypical or inauthentic behavior.

reflexivity   The practice of and commitment to considering how one's beliefs, experiences, and presence shapes insights gained through empirical research.

reliability The research criterion concerned with the degree to which the measure of a concept is stable or consistent.

replicability The property of a study that would allow another researcher to repeat the research and achieve the same findings.

representative sample A sample that is a microcosm of the population and similar to the population in all essential respects.

research design A framework for collecting and analyzing data, which outlines a researcher's approach, procedures, and goals.

research ethics The moral and professional standards that guide decisions and actions taken during the research process and define what choices are considered acceptable or unacceptable.

research methods Tools and practices used to gather and analyze information about topics of interest to the researcher and the broader community.

research question An answerable question that organizes data collection and analysis, determines study design, and otherwise provides a foundation for research.

respondent fatigue Diminishing interest in or energy to participate in research and to provide meaningful quality responses to a researcher's questions or presence in the field.

response bias Errors and inaccuracies in data collection resulting from question and survey design or concerns with social desirability.

response errors Distortions in survey results caused by participants providing false or inaccurate information.

response rate The percentage of people contacted to participate in a study, usually survey research, who go on to participate.

restudy The process of reproducing a study previously completed by researching a topic, population, or situation again at a different time.

sampling The process in which a researcher selects a subset of a population to study.

sampling error Differences between the characteristics of a random sample and the population from which it is selected.

sampling frame A list of all the units in a population from which a sample is to be selected.

scientific method An approach to research that consists of observation, measurement, and experiment and the formulation, testing, and revising of hypotheses.

secondary data analysis Analysis conducted by researchers other than those who originally collected the data, often for purposes not anticipated in the original data collection.

semi-structured interview A qualitative interview in which the researcher uses a detailed interview guide for all respondents to explore certain topics in depth, though the interviewer may add unique probes or change the order of questions.

simple random sample A probability sampling method in which each unit selected from the population, and each combination of units, has an equal probability of being included.

skewed distribution A distribution of scores in which values do not cluster around the center of the set but are instead extreme in one direction or the other.

snowball sampling A non-probability sampling method and form of convenience sampling in which the researcher makes initial contact with a small group of people connected to the research topic and then uses them to establish contact with others.

social desirability Respondents' tendency to align themselves with positive social connotations through their responses to survey questions or their presentation of self in the field setting.

sociological imagination The practice of linking people's experiences to social conditions—for example, connecting personal troubles to public issues or individual biography to social history.

sponsor A person in the research site with power and authority who supports and helps makes a study possible.

spurious relationship   A non-causal relationship between variables that can be attributed either to coincidence or to the impact of a third variable that the analysis has not accounted for.

standard deviation   A measure of how scores are dispersed around the mean.

stratified random sampling   A probability sampling method in which units are randomly sampled from a population that has been previously divided into subgroups (strata).

structured interview   A data collection method in which an interviewer asks all respondents the same questions, in the same order, and with aid of a formal interview schedule; sometimes called a standardized interview.

study (or research) design   A framework for collecting and analyzing data and for presenting results.

style guide   A reference book or manual that outlines standards for grammar, usage, formatting, and citation.

subjectivity   An approach to research that allows researchers' values, identities, and biographies into the research process and calls on researchers to consider how the conclusions they draw reflect and are shaped by those commitments, feelings, and experiences.

survey research   The study design and method in which researchers collect data through questionnaires or structured interviews, often to detect relationships among variables.

systematic sampling   A probability sampling method in which units are selected from a sampling frame at fixed intervals (e.g., every fifth unit).

texts   Documents, images, and other recorded material that may be analyzed for symbolic value.

theoretical sampling   Data collection and/or selection of cases guided by emerging theoretical considerations and repeated until theoretical saturation is reached.

theoretical saturation   In grounded theory, the point where emerging concepts have been fully explored and no new insights are being generated.

theory   An idea or system of ideas that provides logical explanations of social phenomena, behavior, and change.

trend study   A longitudinal design in which researchers collect data at least two times about a single, constant population of people.

Tuskegee Syphilis Experiment   An unethical study of untreated syphilis in Black men conducted from the 1930s to 1970s in the United States; the exposure of participant abuses led to the release of the Belmont Report.

univariate analysis   The simplest form of quantitative analysis, consisting of data analysis conducted on one variable.

unobtrusive measures   Research methods that do not require interactions with participants and thus do not introduce reactivity.

unstructured interview   A free-form and conversational qualitative interview in which the researcher is free to pursue a set of topics as they arise.

validity   The research criterion concerned with the integrity of a study's conclusions.

variable   An attribute or characteristic that may vary over time or from case to case.

References

Chapter 1

"*American Sociological Review*: SAGE Journals." 2020. Sage Journals. https://journals.sagepub.com/home/asr

Behar, Ruth. 1996. *The Vulnerable Observer: Anthropology That Breaks Your Heart*. Beacon Press.

Bonilla-Silva, Eduardo. 2006. *Racism without Racists: Color-Blind Racism and the Persistence of Racial Inequality in the United States*. 2nd ed. Lanham: Rowman & Littlefield Publishers.

Clemens, Elisabeth. 2020. "Current Issue." *American Journal of Sociology, 126* (1). www.tandfonline.com/loi/mijs20#.VVtagIVhBc

Durkheim, Émile. (1897) 1952. *Suicide: A Study in Sociology*. London: Routledge.

Gonzalez-Lopez, Gloria. 2004. "Fathering Latina Sexualities: Mexican Men and the Virginity of Their Daughters." *Journal of Marriage and Family 66* (5): 1118–1130. https://doi.org/10.1111/j.0022-2445.2004.00082.x

Martin, Karin A., and Luke, Katherine. 2010. "Gender Differences in the ABC's of the Birds and the Bees: What Mothers Teach Young Children about Sexuality and Reproduction." *Sex Roles 62* (3–4): 278–291. https://doi.org/10.1007/s11199-009-9731-4

Merton, Robert K. 1938. "Social Structure and Anomie." *American Sociological Review, 3* (5): 672–682.

Merton, Robert King. 1967. "II. On Sociological Theories of the Middle Range." In *On Theoretical Sociology: Five Essays, Old and New,* 39–72. New York: Free Press.

Mills, C. Wright. 1959. *The Sociological Imagination*. New York: Oxford.

Oakley, Ann. 2013. "Interviewing Women: A Contradiction in Terms." in *Doing Feminist Research,* 52–83. London: Routledge.

Olsen, Laurie. 1997. *Made in America: Immigrant Students in Our Public Schools*. New York: The New Press.

Smith, Dorothy E. 1987. *The Everyday World as Problematic: A Feminist Sociology*. Toronto: University of Toronto Press.

"Social Forces | Oxford Academic." 2020. *OUP Academic*. http://sf.oxfordjournals.org.

Chapter 2

American Sociological Association. 2018. Code of Ethics. Retrieved April 14, 2019 at: www.asanet.org/code-ethics

American Sociological Association. 2019. A History of the ASA Code of Ethics. Retrieved April 14, 2019 at: www.asanet.org/history-asa-code-ethics

Blass, Thomas. 2002. Stanley Milgram. www.stanley-milgram.com

Cheng, S., and B. Powell. 2015. "Measurement, Methods, and Divergent Patterns: Reassessing the Effects of Same-Sex Parents." *Social Science Research 52*: 615–626. https://doi.org/10.1016/j.ssresearch.2015.04.005

Dinovitzer, R., J. Hagan, and P. Parker. 2003. "Choice and Circumstance: Social Capital and Planful Competence in the Attainments of Immigrant Youth." *Canadian Journal of Sociology 28*: 463–488.

Gates et al. 2012. Letter to the editors and advisory editors of social science research. Retrieved from https://www.impactprogram.org/wp-content/uploads/2012/07/Letter-to-the-editors-and-advisory-editors-of-Social-Science-Research.pdf

Goffman, Alice. 2014. *On the Run: Fugitive Life in an American City*. Chicago; London: University of Chicago Press.

González-López, G. 2011. "Mindful Ethics: Comments on Informant-Centered Practices in Sociological Research." *Qualitative Sociology 34* (3): 447–461.

Hales, J. 2006. "An Anti-Colonial Critique of Research Methodology." In *Anti-Colonialism and Education: The Politics of Resistance*, ed. G. Dei and A. Kempf. Rotterdam: Sense.

hooks, b. 1989. "Feminist Scholarship: Ethical Issues." In *Talking Back: Thinking Feminist, Thinking Black*, 42–48. Boston, MA: Beacon Press.

Humphreys, Laud. (1970) 2017. *Tearoom Trade: Impersonal Sex in Public Places*. New York: Routledge.

Jones, James H. 1993. *Bad Blood: The Tuskegee Syphilis Experiment. New and Expanded ed*. New York, Toronto: Free Press; Maxwell Macmillan.

Kaufmen, P. 2015. The Ethics of Ethnography [Blog Post]. Retrieved from: www.everydaysociology blog.com/2015/08/the-ethics-of-ethnography.html

Khanlou, Nazilla, and Elizabeth Peter. 2005. "Participatory Action Research: Considerations for Ethical Review." *Social Science & Medicine* 60 (10): 2333–2340.

Lewis-Kraus, G. 2016. "The Trials of Alice Goffman." *The New York Times Magazine, January 17, 2016*. Retrieved April 29, 2019 at: www.nytimes. com/2016/01/17/magazine/the-trials-of-alice-goffman.html

Lincoln, Yvonna S., and William G. Tierney. 2004. "Qualitative Research and Institutional Review Boards." *Qualitative Inquiry* 10, no. (2): 219–234.

Manning, W. D., M. N. Fettro, and E. Lamidi. 2014. "Child Well-Being in Same-Sex Parent Families: Review of Research Prepared for American Sociological Association Amicus Brief." *Population Research and Policy Review* 33: 485–502. DOI: 10.1007/s11113-014-9329-6

Milgram, Stanley. 1963. "Behavioral Study of Obedience." *The Journal of Abnormal and Social Psychology* 67(4): 371–378. https://doi.org/10.1037/h0040525

Murphy, Elizabeth, and Robert Dingwall. 2007. "Informed Consent, Anticipatory Regulation and Ethnographic Practice." *Social Science & Medicine* 65(11): 2223–2234.

Newmahr, Staci, and Stacey Hannem. 2016. "Surrogate Ethnography: Fieldwork, the Academy, and Resisting the IRB." *Journal of Contemporary Ethnography* 45(5): 1–25.

Panter, A. T., and Sonya K. Sterba. 2011. *Handbook of Ethics in Quantitative Methodology (Multivariate Applications Book Series)*. London: Routledge.

Parisi, Mimmo. 2018 (Jan. 19). *Mississippi Fact Sheet: Population Growth, Millennials, Brain Drain, and the Economy. A Report to the Governor*. Retrieved June 25, 2019 at: www.nsparc.msstate. edu/wp-content/uploads/2019/04/Mississippi-Population-Fact-Sheet.pdf

Patton, D., P. Leonard, L. Cahill, J. Macbeth, S. Crosby et al. 2016. "'Police Took My Homie I Dedicate My Life 2 His Revenge': Twitter Tensions Between Gang-Involved Youth and Police in Chicago." *Journal of Human Behavior in the Social Environment* 26(3–4): 310–324.

Pawelz, Janina. 2018. "Researching Gangs: How to Reach Hard-to-Reach Populations and Negotiate Tricky Issues in the Field." *Qualitative Social Research* 19 (1). http://jpllnet.sfsu.edu/login?url= https://search-proquest-com.jpllnet.sfsu.edu/ docview/2023750159?accountid=13802

Perrin, A., P. Cohen, and N. Caren. 2013. "Responding to the Regnerus Study: Are Children of Parents Who Had Same-Sex Relationships Disadvantaged? A Scientific Evaluation of the No-Differences Hypothesis." *Journal of Gay & Lesbian Mental Health* 17: 327–336. DOI: 10.1080/19359705.2013.772553

Regnerus, M. 2012. "How Different Are the Adult Children of Parents Who Have Same-Sex Relationships? Findings from the New Family Structures Study." *Social Science Research* 41(4): 752–770. DOI: https://doi.org/10.1016/j. ssresearch.2012.03.009

Rios, V. M. 2015. "On the Run: Fugitive Life in an American City." *The American Journal of Sociology* 121(1): 306–308. Retrieved from: http:// ejournals.ebsco.com.jpllnet.sfsu.edu/direct. asp?ArticleID=48FBB996999AECB302

Robinson, Carol. 2020. "Ethically Important Moments as Data: Reflections from Ethnographic Fieldwork in Prisons." *Research Ethics* 16(1–2): 1–15. https://doi.org/10.1177/1747016119898401

Rosenfeld, M. J. 2015. "Revisiting the Data from the New Family Structure Study: Taking Family

Instability into Account." *Sociological Science 2*: 478–501. DOI: 10.15195/v2.a23

Rosenthal, R., and L. Jacobson. 1968. *Pygmalion in the Classroom: Teacher Expectation and Pupils' Intellectual Development*. New York: Holt, Rinehart & Winston.

Schuler, E. 1969. "Toward a Code of Professional Ethics for Sociologists: A Historical Note." *The American Sociologist 4*(2): 144–146.

Schumm, W. R. 2016. "A Review and Critique of Research on Same-Sex Parenting and Adoption." *Psychological Reports 119*(3): 641–760. DOI: 10.1177/0033294116665594

Small, W., L. Maher, and T. Kerr. 2014. "Institutional Ethical Review and Ethnographic Research Involving Injection Drug Users: A Case Study." *Social Science & Medicine 104*: 157–162.

Tolich, M. 2016. "How Do Emergent Research Questions Confound Mixed Methods Ethics?" *Qualitative Ethics in Practice*. Routledge, 49–58.

Totten, M. 2001. "Legal, Ethical, and Clinical Implications of Doing Fieldwork with Youth Gang Members Who Engage in Serious Violence." *Journal of Gang Research 8*: 35–49.

U.S. Department of Health and Human Services. *Research with Children FAQs*. Retrieved June 23, 2020 from: www.hhs.gov/ohrp/regulations-and-policy/guidance/faq/children-research/index.html

Venkatesh, S. 2008. *Gang Leader for a Day: A Rogue Sociologist Takes to the Streets*. New York: Penguin.

Vidich, A., and J. Bensman. 1968. *Small Town in Mass Society*. Princeton, NJ: Princeton University Press.

Waterston, A. 2012. "Exoticizing the Other and the Author: Commentary on Gang Leader for a Day by Sudhir Venkatesh." *North American Dialogue 15*(1): 13–17.

Wolfe, Anna. 2019. "NSPARC, a Taxpayer-Funded Data Center, Charged $27,750 for Public Records Request." *Mississippi Today*. https://mississippitoday.org/2019/05/24/nsparc-a-taxpayer-funded-data-center-says-public-records-cost-27750-and-take-200-hours-to-complete/

Zussman, R. 2016. "Alice's Adventures in Wonderland: On the Run and Its Critics." *Society*

53(4): 436–443. DOI:http://dx.doi.org.jpllnet.sfsu.edu/10.1007/s12115-016-0039-z

Chapter 3

American Sociological Association. 2003. *The Importance of Collecting Data and Doing Social Scientific Research on Race*. Washington, DC: American Sociological Association.

Becker, Howard S. (1998) 2008. *Tricks of the Trade: How to Think about Your Research While You're Doing It*. Chicago: University of Chicago Press.

Fine, Michelle, Nick Freudenberg, Yasser Payne, Tiffany Perkins, Kersha Smith, and Katya Wanzer. 2003. "'Anything Can Happen with Police Around': Urban Youth Evaluate Strategies of Surveillance in Public Places." *Journal of Social Issues 59*(1): 141–158. https://doi.org/10.1111/1540-4560.t01-1-00009

Gramlich, John. 2018. "U.S. Incarceration Rate Is at Its Lowest in 20 Years." *Pew Research Center*, May 2, 2018. www.pewresearch.org/fact-tank/2018/05/02/americas-incarceration-rate-is-at-a-two-decade-low/

James, S. E., J. L. Herman, S. Rankin, M. Keisling, L. Mottet, and M. Anafi. 2016. *The Report of the 2015 U.S. Transgender Survey*. Washington, DC: National Center for Transgender Equality.

Kanter, Rosabeth Moss. 1977. "Some Effects of Proportions on Group Life: Skewed Sex Ratios and Responses to Token Women." *American Journal of Sociology 82* (5): 965–990.

Martinez, Alexis N, Jennifer Lorvick, and Alex H Kral. 2014. "Activity Spaces among Injection Drug Users in San Francisco." *International Journal of Drug Policy 25* (3): 516–524. https://doi.org/10.1016/j.drugpo.2013.11.008

Ragin, Charles C. (1992) 2014. *The Comparative Method: Moving Beyond Qualitative and Quantitative Strategies*. Berkeley: University of California Press.

Reiner, Robert. 2000. *The Politics of the Police*. 3rd ed. New York: Oxford.

Sumerau, Je, Lain A. B. Mathers, Alexandra Ch. Nowakowski, and Ryan T. Cragun. 2017. "Helping Quantitative Sociology Come Out of the Closet." *Sexualities 20* (5–6): 644–656. https://doi.org/10.1177/1363460716666755

Taylor, Catherine J. 2010. "Occupational Sex Composition and the Gendered Availability of Workplace Support." *Gender & Society 24*(2): 189–212. https://doi.org/10.1177/0891243209359912

Trochim, William M. K. 2020. "Likert Scaling." *Research Methods Knowledge Base.* Conjoint.ly, April 11, 2020. www.socialresearchmethods.net/kb/scallik.php

Williams, Christine L. 1992. "The Glass Escalator: Hidden Advantages for Men in the 'Female' Professions." *Social Problems 39* (3): 253–267. https://doi.org/10.2307/3096961

Williams, Christine L. 1995. *Still a Man's World: Men Who Do "Women's Work."* Berkeley, CA: University of California Press.

Wingfield, Adia Harvey. 2009. "Racializing the Glass Escalator: Reconsidering Men's Experiences with Women's Work." *Gender & Society 23*(1): 5–26. https://doi.org/10.1177/0891243208323054

Zambrana, Ruth Enid, Brianne A. Dávila, Michelle M. Espino, Lisa M. Lapeyrouse, R. Burciaga Valdez, and Denise A. Segura. 2017. "Mexican American Faculty in Research Universities: Can the Next Generation Beat the Odds?" *Sociology of Race and Ethnicity 3*(4): 458–473. https://doi.org/10.1177/2332649217716473

Chapter 4

Abrams, Laura S. 2010. "Sampling 'Hard to Reach' Populations in Qualitative Research: The Case of Incarcerated Youth." *Qualitative Social Work 9* (4): 536–50.

Abrams, Laura, and Theresa Morris. 2010. "Social Work Research Methods: Four Alternative Paradigms." *Qualitative Social Work.* http://search.proquest.com/docview/741611719/

Auster, Carol. 2000. "Probability Sampling and Inferential Statistics: An Interactive Exercise Using M and M's." *Teaching Sociology 28* (4): 379–385. https://doi.org/10.2307/1318587

Becker, Howard S. (1963) 2008. *Outsiders: Studies in the Sociology of Deviance.* New York: Simon & Schuster.

Becker, Howard S. (1998) 2008. *Tricks of the Trade: How to Think about Your Research While You're Doing It.* Chicago: University of Chicago Press.

Bedera, Nicole, and Kristjane Nordmeyer. 2015. "'Never Go Out Alone': An Analysis of College Rape Prevention Tips." *Sexuality & Culture 19* (3): 533–542. https://doi.org/10.1007/s12119-015-9274-5

Benz, Jennifer K., Oscar Espinosa, Valerie Welsh, and Angela Fontes. 2011. "Awareness of Racial and Ethnic Health Disparities Has Improved Only Modestly over a Decade." *Health Affairs (Project Hope) 30* (10): 1860–1867. https://doi.org/10.1377/hlthaff.2010.0702

Breckenridge, Jenna, and Derek Jones. 2009. *"Demystifying Theoretical Sampling* in Grounded Theory Research." *Grounded Theory Review: An International Journal 8* (2). https://doaj.org/article/3d42b7fb11a14f6db675e69673dcdc47

Brown, Anna. 2020. "The Changing Categories the US Has Used to Measure Race." *Pew Research Center, February 25*, 2020. Retrieved from: www.pewresearch.org/fact-tank/2020/02/25/the-changing-categories-the-u-s-has-used-to-measure-race/

Charmaz, K. 2000. "Constructivist and Objectivist Grounded Theory." In *Handbook of Qualitative Research*, ed. N. K. Denzin and Y. Lincoln, 509–535, 2nd edn. Thousand Oaks, CA: Sage.

Chodur, Gwen M, Ye Shen, Stephen Kodish, Vanessa M. Oddo, Daniel A. Antiporta, Brittany Jock, and Jessica C. Jones-Smith. 2016. "Food Environments around American Indian Reservations: A Mixed Methods Study." *PloS One 11* (8): e0161132-e0161132. https://doi.org/10.1371/journal.pone.0161132.

Cruz, José Miguel, Rosario Queirolo, and María Fernanda Boidi. 2016. "Determinants of Public Support for Marijuana Legalization in Uruguay, the United States, and El Salvador." *Journal of Drug Issues 46* (4): 308–325. https://doi.org/10.1177/0022042616649005

Dowling, Julie A. 2014. *Mexican Americans and the Question of Race.* Austin: University of Texas Press.

Francisco-Menchavez, Valerie. 2018. *The Labor of Care: Filipina Migrants and Transnational Families in the Digital Age.* Urbana, IL: University of Illinois Press.

Glaser, Barney G., and Anselm L. Strauss. 1967. *The Discovery of Grounded Theory: Strategies for Qualitative Research.* New York: Adline de Gruyter.

Haack, Lauren, M. Kapke, and Theresa Gerdes. 2016. "Rates, Associations, and Predictors of Psychopathology in a Convenience Sample of School-Aged Latino Youth: Identifying Areas for Mental Health Outreach." *Journal of Child and Family Studies* 25 (7): 2315–2326. https://doi.org/10.1007/s10826-016-0404-y

Johnson, Timothy P., and Joseph S. Wislar. 2012. "Response Rates and Nonresponse Errors in Surveys." *Journal of the American Medical Association* 307 (17): 1805–1806. https://doi.org/10.1001/jama.2012.3532

Lameck, Wilfred Uronu. 2013. "Sampling Design, Validity and Reliability in General Social Survey." *International Journal of Academic Research in Business and Social Sciences 3* (7): 212.

Landivar, Liana. 2013. *Men in Nursing Occupations: American Community Survey Highlight Report.* U.S. Census Bureau, 1–7.

Martinez, Alexis N., Ricky N. Bluthenthal, Torsten Neilands, and Alex H. Kral. 2011. "Assessing Geographic and Individual Level Factors Associated with Arrests Among Injection Drug Users in California." *Health and Place 17* (6): 1258–1265. https://doi.org/10.1016/j.healthplace.2011.06.007

Mathews, Kelly, Jessica Phelan, Nicholas A. Jones, Sarah Konya, Rachel Marks, Beverly M. Pratt, Julia Coombs, and Michael Bentley. 2017. *2015 National Content Test: Race and Ethnicity Analysis Report—A New Design for the 21st Century.* U.S. Census Bureau. https://www2.census.gov/programs-surveys/decennial/2020/program-management/final-analysis-reports/2015nct-race-ethnicity-analysis.pdf

Mays, Steve. "*Cluster Sampling.*" YouTube video, 3:17. [Posted August 2011]. www.youtube.com/watch?v=QOxXy-I6ogs&feature=related

Mays, Steve. "*Simple Random Sampling.*" YouTube video, 4:32. [Posted August 2011]. www.youtube.com/watch?v=yx5KZi5QArQ&NR=1

Meyer, Doug. 2010. "Evaluating the Severity of Hate-Motivated Violence: Intersectional Differences Among LGBT Hate Crime Victims." *Sociology 44* (5): 980–995. https://doi.org/10.1177/0038038510375737

Meyer, Doug. 2012. "An Intersectional Analysis of Lesbian, Gay, Bisexual, and Transgender (LGBT) People's Evaluations of Anti-Queer Violence." *Gender & Society 26* (6): 849–873. https://doi.org/10.1177/0891243212461299

National Institutes of Health. 2002. *Outreach Notebook for the Inclusion, Recruitment, and Retention of Women and Minority Subjects in Clinical Research.* Retrieved at: http://www.chicagoamwa.org/uploads/2/8/7/0/28704181/outreach-notebook-2015.pdf

Schieman, Scott, and Atsushi Narisada. 2014. "In Control or Fatalistically Ruled? The Sense of Mastery Among Working Canadians." *Canadian Review of Sociology 51*(4): 343–374. https://doi.org/10.1111/cars.12051

Strauss, Anselm L., and Juliet M. Corbin. 1998. *Basics of Qualitative Research: Techniques and Procedures for Developing Grounded Theory.* 2nd edn. Thousand Oaks, CA: Sage Publications.

Tongco, Maria Dolores C. 2008. "Purposive Sampling as a Tool for Informant Selection." *Ethnobotany Research and Applications 5*: 147–158. https://doi.org/10.17348/era.5.0.147-158

Waters, Jaime. 2015. "Snowball Sampling: a Cautionary Tale Involving a Study of Older Drug Users." *International Journal of Social Research Methodology 18* (4): 367–380. https://doi.org/10.1080/13645579.2014.953316

Webster, Fiona, Kathleen Rice, and Abhimanyu Sud. 2020. "A Critical Content Analysis of Media Reporting on Opioids: The Social Construction of an Epidemic." *Social Science & Medicine 244*: 1126–1142. https://doi.org/10.1016/j.socscimed.2019.112642

"Why Probability Sampling." *Pew Research Center–U.S. Politics & Policy*, January 28, 2011. www.people-press.org/methodology/sampling/why-probability-sampling/7/

Chapter 5

Ambert, A. M., P. A. Adler, P. Adler, and D. F. Detzner. 1995. Understanding and Evaluating Qualitative Research. *Journal of Marriage and the Family, 57*: 879–893.

Aspers, Patrik, and Ugo Corte. 2019. "What Is Qualitative in Qualitative Research." *Qualitative Sociology 42* (2): 139–160. https://doi.org/10.1007/s11133-019-9413-7

Bonilla-Silva, Eduardo. 2018. *Racism without Racists: Color-Blind Racism and the Persistence of Racial Inequality in America.* 5th ed. Lanham: Rowman & Littlefield.

Buday, Amanda. 2017. "The Home Rule Advantage: Motives and Outcomes of Local Anti-Fracking Mobilization." *Social Currents 4* (6): 575–593.

"Center for Qualitative and Multi-Method Inquiry." *The Maxwell School of Syracuse University.* September 12, 2018. Accessed August 6, 2020. www.maxwell.syr.edu/cqmi/

Collins, Patricia Hill. 1986. "Learning from the Outsider Within: The Sociological Significance of Black Feminist Thought." *Social Problems 33* (6): 14–32.

Cooper, Anna J. 1892. *A Voice from the South.* Xenia, OH: Aldine Printing House.

Cressey, Paul Goalby. (1932) 2008. *The Taxi-Dance Hall: A Sociological Study in Commercialized Recreation and City Life.* Chicago: University of Chicago Press.

Currah, Paisley, and Susan Stryker. 2015. "Introduction: Making Transgender Count." *TSQ: Transgender Quarterly 2*(1): 1–12.

Dews, B., and Law, C. 1995. *This Fine Place So Far from Home: Voices of Academics from the Working Class.* Temple University Press.

Du Bois, W. E. B. 1903. *The Souls of Black Folk.* New York: Bantam Classic.

Esterberg, Kristin G. 2001. *Qualitative Research Methods.* McGraw-Hill.

Farber, SA. 2008. "U.S. Scientists' Role in the Eugenics Movement (1907–1939): A Contemporary Biologist's Perspective." *Zebrafish 5* (4): 243–245. https://doi.org/10.1089/zeb.2008.0576

Fazio, Michele, Christie Launius, and Tim Strangleman. 2020. *Routledge International Handbook of Working-Class Studies.* London: Routledge.

Ferguson, R. 2004. *Aberrations in Black: Toward a Queer of Color Critique.* Minneapolis: University of Minnesota Press.

Fernández, Matías. 2018. "Hanging Out Together, Surviving on Your Own: The Precarious Communities of Day Laborers." *Journal of Contemporary Ethnography 47*(6): 865–887. https://doi.org/10.1177/0891241617716743

Frazier, Edward Franklin. 1932. *The Negro Family in Chicago.* Chicago: University of Chicago Press.

Ghaziani, Amin, and Matt Brim. 2019. *Imagining Queer Methods.* New York: New York University Press.

Gibson-Light, Michael. 2018. "Ramen Politics: Informal Money and Logics of Resistance in the Contemporary American Prison." *Qualitative Sociology 41* (2): 199–220. https://doi.org/10.1007/s11133-018-9376-0

Gutiérrez y Muhs, G., Niemann, Y., González, C., and Harris, A. (eds). 2012. *Presumed Incompetent: The Intersections of Race and Class for Women in Academia.* Boulder, CO: University Press of Colorado.

Harding, S. (ed.). 1987. "Introduction: Is There a Feminist Method?" *From Feminism and Methodology: Social Science Issues,* 1–14. Bloomington: Indiana University Press.

"International Institute for Qualitative Methodology." *International Institute for Qualitative Methodology.* Accessed August 6, 2020. www.iiqm.ualberta.ca/

Jenkins, Nicole. 2019. "Distance in Diaspora: Contested Blackness in Black Women's Identity Making in Contemporary U.S." *Journal of Contemporary Ethnography 48* (6): 806–35 https://doi.org/10.1177/0891241619829210

Kincheloe, Samuel C. 1938. *The American City and Its Church.* Friendship Press

Lareau, Annette. 2011. *Unequal Childhoods: Class, Race, and Family Life,* 2nd ed. Berkeley: University of California Press.

Lareau, Annette, Elliot B. Weininger, Dalton Conley, and Melissa Velez. 2011. "*Unequal Childhoods* in Context: Results from a Quantitative Analysis." In *Unequal Childhoods: Class, Race, and Family Life,* 333–41. Berkeley: University of California Press.

Lewis, Oscar. 1961. *The Children of Sánchez.* New York: Vintage.

Lofland, John and Lyn H. Lofland 1995. *Analyzing Social Settings: A Guide to Qualitative Observation and Analysis.* 3rd ed. Belmont, CA: Wadsworth.

"Managing Data." *Qualitative Data Repository.* April 13, 2018. Accessed August 6, 2020. https://qdr.syr.edu/

McRuer, R. 2006. *Crip Theory: Cultural Signs of Queerness and Disability.* New York: New York University Press.

Miranda, Marie Keta. 2003. *Homegirls in the Public Sphere.* Austin, TX: University of Texas Press.

Moraga and Anzaldua (eds.). 1983. *This Bridge Called My Back: Writings by Radical Women of Color.* New York: Kitchen Table, Women of Color Press.

Nash, Catherine J., and Kath Browne. 2010. *Queer Methods and Methodologies.* 1st ed. London: Routledge.

Oakley, Ann. 1981. "Interviewing Women: A Contradiction in Terms." In *Doing Feminist Research.* ed. Helen Roberts, 52–83. London: Routledge.

Pascoe, C. J. 2012. *Dude, You're a Fag: Masculinity and Sexuality in High School.* Berkeley, CA: University of California Press.

Peek, Lori A. 2010. *Behind the Backlash: Muslim Americans after 9/11.* Philadelphia, PA: Temple University Press.

Price, M. 2012. "Disability Studies Methodology: Explaining Ourselves to Ourselves." In *Practicing Research in Writing Studies: Reflexive and Ethically Responsible Research,* ed. Katrina M. Powell and Pamela Takayoshi, 159–186. New York: Hampton Press.

Rawls, Anne. 2018. "The Wartime Narrative in US Sociology, 1940–7: Stigmatizing Qualitative Sociology in the Name of 'Science.'" *European Journal of Social Theory.*

Rogers, Baker. 2019. "'Contrary to All the Other Shit I've Said': Trans Men Passing in the South." *Qualitative Sociology* 42 (4): 639–662. https://doi.org/10.1007/s11133-019-09436-w

Roschelle, Anne, and Peter Kaufman. 2004. "Fitting In and Fighting Back: Homeless Kids' Stigma Management Strategies." *Symbolic Interaction* 27 (1): 23–46. 10.1525/si.2004.27.1.23

Schuman, Howard, Charlotte Steeh, Lawrence Bobo, and Maria Krysan. 1997. *Racial Attitudes in America: Trends and Interpretations.* Rev. ed. Cambridge, MA: Harvard University Press.

Shogren, Karrie A., Judith M. S. Gross, Anjali J. Forber-Pratt, Grace L. Francis, Allyson L. Satter, Martha Blue-Banning, and Cokethea Hill. 2015. "The Perspectives of Students with and without Disabilities on Inclusive Schools." *Research and Practice for Persons with Severe Disabilities* 40 (4): 243–260.

Smith, Linda Tuhiwai. 1999. *Decolonizing Methodologies: Research and Indigenous Peoples.* New York: Zed Books.

Spivak, Gayatri. 1994. "Can the Subaltern Speak?" In *Colonial Discourse, Postcolonial Theory (Essex Symposia, Literature, Politics, Theory),* ed. F. Barker, P. Hulme, and M. Iversen, 66–111. Manchester, UK: Manchester University Press.

Stryker, S. 2008. *Transgender History.* Berkeley, CA: Seal Press.

Vrecko, Scott. 2015. "Everyday Drug Diversions: A Qualitative Study of the Illicit Exchange and Non-Medical Use of Prescription Stimulants on a University Campus." *Social Science & Medicine* 131: 297–304.

Weber, Max. 1904. 1949. *'Objectivity' in Social Science and Social Policy,* ed. Edward A. Shils and Henry A. Finch. New York: The Free Press.

Weiss, Robert Stuart. 2005. *The Experience of Retirement.* Ithaca, NY: Cornell University Press.

Whittemore, Robin, Susan K. Chase, and Carol Lynn Mandle. 2001. "Validity in Qualitative Research." *Qualitative Health Research* 11 (4): 522–537.

Williams, Macolm. 2000. "Interpretivism and Generalisation." *Sociology* 34 (2): 209–224.

Zia, H. (2000). *Asian American Dreams: The Emergence of an American People.* New York: Farrar, Straus and Giroux.

Chapter 6

Brown, Melissa, Rashawn Ray, Ed Summers, and Neil Fraistat. 2017. "#SayHerName: A Case Study of Intersectional Social Media Activism." *Ethnic and Racial Studies* 40 (11): 1831–1846. https://doi.org/10.1080/01419870.2017.1334934

Cicourel, Aaron. 1982. "Interviews, Surveys, and the Problem of Ecological Validity." *The American*

Sociologist *17*(1). http://search.proquest.com/docview/1294724846/

Hong, Seunghye, Wei Zhang, and Emily Walton. 2014. "Neighborhoods and Mental Health: Exploring Ethnic Density, Poverty, and Social Cohesion Among Asian Americans and Latinos." *Social Science & Medicine 111*: 117–124. https://doi.org/10.1016/j.socscimed.2014.04.014

Horton, Hayward Derrick and Lori Latrice Sykes. 2001. "Reconsidering Wealth, Status, and Power: Critical Demography and the Measurement of Racism." *Race and Society 4* (2): 207–217. https://doi.org/10.1016/S1090-9524(03)00010-X

Inman, A. G., N. Ladany, M. G. Constantine, and C. K. Morano. 2001. "Development and Preliminary Validation of the Cultural Values Conflict Scale for South Asian Women." *Journal of Counseling Psychology 48* (1): 17–27. https://doi.org/10.1037//0022-0167.48.1.17

Lapiere, Richard. 1934. "Attitudes vs. Actions." *Social Forces 13* (1): 230–230. http://search.proquest.com/docview/743053582/

Rahman, Zaynah, and Matthew Witenstein. 2014. "A Quantitative Study of Cultural Conflict and Gender Differences in South Asian American College Students." *Ethnic and Racial Studies 37* (6): 1121–1137. https://doi.org/10.1080/01419870.2012.753152

Sutton, Robert, and Anat Rafaeli. 1988. "Untangling the Relationship Between Displayed Emotions and Organizational Sales: The Case of Convenience Stores." *Academy of Management Journal 31* (3): 461–487. https://doi.org/10.5465/256456

Zuberi, Tukufu., and Eduardo. Bonilla-Silva. 2008. *White Logic, White Methods: Racism and Methodology.* Lanham: Rowman & Littlefield Publishers.

Chapter 7

Bahr, Howard M., Theodore Caplow, and Bruce A. Chadwick. 1983. "Middletown III: Problems of Replication, Longitudinal Measurement, and Triangulation." *Annual Review of Sociology 9*(1): 243–264.

Bor, Jacob. 2017. "Diverging Life Expectancies and Voting Patterns in the 2016 US Presidential Election." *American Journal of Public Health 107* (10): 1560–1562.

Centers for Disease Control and Prevention. 2020. *Health Equity Considerations and Racial and Ethnic Minority Groups.* https://www.cdc.gov/coronavirus/2019-ncov/need-extra-precautions/racial-ethnic-minorities.html

Contreras, Randol. 2013. *The Stickup Kids: Race, Drugs, Violence, and the American Dream.* Berkeley, CA: University of California Press.

Davis, Katrinell M. 2017. *Hard Work Is Not Enough: Gender and Racial Inequality in an Urban Workspace.* Chapel Hill, NC: University of North Carolina Press. https://doi.org/10.5149/9781469630496_davis

Dinovitzer, R., J. Hagan, and P. Parker. 2003. "Choice and Circumstance: Social Capital and Planful Competence in the Attainments of Immigrant Youth." *Canadian Journal of Sociology 28*(4).

Field, Andy P. 2016. *An Adventure in Statistics: The Reality Enigma.* Thousand Oaks, CA: SAGE Publications.

Festinger, Leon, 1956 (2018). *When Prophecy Fails: A Social and Psychological Study of a Modern Group that Predicted the Destruction of the World.* CrossReach Publications via PublishDrive.

Fine, Michelle, and Maria Elena Torre. 2006. "Intimate Details: Participatory Action Research in Prison." *Action Research 4* (3): 253–270.

Flores, Edward Orozco. 2016. "'Grow Your Hair Out': Chicano Gang Masculinity and Embodiment in Recovery." *Social Problems 63* (4): 590–604. https://doi.org/10.1093/socpro/spw017

Font, Sarah A., Lawrence M. Berger, Maria Cancian, and Jennifer L. Noyes. 2018. "Permanency and the Educational and Economic Attainment of Former Foster Children in Early Adulthood. *American Sociological Review 83* (4): 716–43.

Foucault, Michel. (1970) 1994. *The Order of Things: An Archaeology of the Human Sciences.* New York: Vintage.

Gamson, Joshua. 2006. *The Fabulous Sylvester: The Legend, the Music, the Seventies in San Francisco.* New York: Picador.

Golden, Megan, and Cari Almo. 2004. *Reducing Gun Violence: An Overview of New York City's Strategies.* New York: Vera Institute of Justice.

Greene, J. 2000. *Understanding Social Programs Through Evaluation. Handbook of Qualitative Research*. 2nd ed. Thousand Oaks, CA: Sage.

Grollman, Eric Anthony. 2017. "Sexual Health and Multiple Forms of Discrimination among Heterosexual Youth." *Social Problems 64* (1): 156–175. https://doi.org/10.1093/socpro/spw031

Horton, Hayward Derrick, and Lori Latrice Sykes. 2001. "Reconsidering Wealth, Status, and Power: Critical Demography and the Measurement of Racism." *Race and Society 4* (2): 207–17. https://doi.org/10.1016/S1090-9524(03)00010-X.

Jacobs, Jerry A., and Frank F. Furstenberg Jr. 1986. "Changing Places: Conjugal Careers and Women's Marital Mobility." *Social Forces 64* (3): 714–732.

Kirby, Douglas B., B.A. Laris, and Lori A. Rolleri. 2007. "Sex and HIV Education Programs: Their Impact on Sexual Behaviors of Young People Throughout the World." *Journal of Adolescent Health 40* (3): 206–217.

Kleinman, Sherryl. 1996. *Opposing Ambitions: Gender and Identity in an Alternative Organization*. Chicago: University of Chicago Press.

Klinenberg, Eric. 2002. *Heat Wave: A Social Autopsy of Disaster in Chicago*. Chicago: University of Chicago Press.

Knowles, Eric D., and Linda R. Tropp. 2018. "The Racial and Economic Context of Trump Support: Evidence for Threat, Identity, and Contact Effects in the 2016 Presidential Election." *Social Psychological and Personality Science 9* (3): 275–84 1948550618759326.

Krieger, Susan. 1983. *The Mirror Dance: Identity in a Women's Community*. Philadelphia: Temple University Press.

Legewie, Joscha, and Jeffrey Fagan. 2019. "Aggressive Policing and the Educational Performance of Minority Youth." *American Sociological Review 84* (2), 220–47.

Lipset, Seymour Martin. 1990. *Continental Divide: The Values and Institutions of the United States and Canada*. New York, NY: Routledge.

Lynd, Robert S. and Helen Merrell Lynd. 1929. *Middletown: A Study in Modern American Culture*. Orlando, FL: Harcourt Brace.

Lynd, Robert S. and Helen Merrell Lynd. 1937. *Middletown in Transition: A Study in Cultural Conflicts*. Boston: Mariner Books.

Mead, Margaret. (1928) 1973. *Coming of Age in Samoa: A Psychological Study of Primitive Youth for Western Civilization*. New York: Penguin.

Morris, Aldon D. 2017. *The Scholar Denied: W. E. B. Du Bois and the Birth of Modern Sociology*. Berkeley, CA: University of California Press.

"The National Longitudinal Study of Adolescent to Adult Health." 2020. Addhealth.Cpc.Unc.Edu. Accessed August 13. https://addhealth.cpc.unc.edu/

"NLSY97 Data Overview : U.S. Bureau Of Labor Statistics." 2020. Bls.Gov. www.bls.gov/nls/nlsy97.htm

Pager, Devah. 2003. "The Mark of a Criminal Record." *American Journal of Sociology 108* (5): 937–975. doi:10.1086/374403

"Panel Study of Income Dynamics." 2020. Psidonline.Isr.Umich.Edu. https://psidonline.isr.umich.edu/

Patillo, Mary. 2008. *Black on the Block: The Politics of Race and Class in the City*. Chicago: University of Chicago Press.

Pearman, Francis A., II, and Walker A. Swain. 2017. "School Choice, Gentrification, and the Variable Significance of Racial Stratification in Urban Neighborhoods." *Sociology of Education 90* (3): 213–35. https://doi.org/10.1177/0038040717710494.

Quinn, Susan T., and Megan C. Stewart. 2018. "Examining the Long-Term Consequences of Bullying on Adult Substance Use." *American Journal of Criminal Justice 43* (1): 85–101.

Ragin, Charles C. (1992) 2014. *The Comparative Method: Moving Beyond Qualitative and Quantitative Strategies*. Berkeley: University of California Press.

"Research Guides: Organizing Your Social Sciences Research Paper: Types of Research Designs." 2020. Libguides.Usc.Edu. https://libguides.usc.edu/writingguide/researchdesigns

Rivera, Lauren A., and Andras Tilcsik. 2016. "Class Advantage, Commitment Penalty: The Gendered Effect of Social Class Signals in an Elite Labor Market." *American Sociological Revie, 81*: 1097–1131.

Rotolo, Thomas, John Wilson. 2004. "What Happened to the "Long Civic Generation? Explaining Cohort Differences in Volunteerism." *Social Forces 82* (3): 1091–1121. https://doi.org/10.1353/sof.2004.0051

Skocpol, Theda. 1979. *States and Social Revolutions: A Comparative Analysis of France*, Russia and China. Cambridge, UK: Cambridge University Press.

Stack, Carol. 1983. *All Our Kin: Strategies For Survival in a Black Community.* New York: Basic Books.

Stein, Arlene. 2001. *Stranger Next Door.* Boston: Beacon Press.

Sutton, Robert I., and Anat Rafaeli. 1992. "How We Untangled the Relationship Between Displayed Emotion and Organizational Sales: A Tale of Bickering and Optimism." In *Doing exemplary research*, edited by Peter J. Frost and Ralph E. Stablein, 115–28. Newbury Park, CA: SAGE Publications.

Suyemoto, Karen L., Day, Stephanie C., and Schwartz, Sarah. 2015. "Exploring Effects of Social Justice Youth Programming on Racial and Ethnic Identities and Activism for Asian American Youth." *Asian American Journal of Psychology,6* (2): 125–35. https://doi.org/10.1037/a0037789.

Sweet, Paige L. 2015. "Chronic Victims, Risky Women: Domestic Violence Advocacy and the Medicalization of Abuse." *Signs: Journal of Women in Culture and Society 41* (1): 81–106.

Tang, Ning, Andrew Baker, and Paula C. Peter. 2015. "Investigating the Disconnect Between Financial Knowledge and Behavior: The Role of Parental Influence and Psychological Characteristics in Responsible Financial Behaviors among Young Adults." *Journal of Consumer Affairs 49* (2): 376–406.

Weinstein, Jay Alan. 2010. *Applying Social Statistics: An Introduction to Quantitative Reasoning in Sociology.* Lanham, MD: Rowman & Littlefield.

Wilson, James Q., and George L. Kelling. 1982. "Broken Windows: The Police and Neighborhood Safety." *Atlantic Monthly 249* (3): 29–38.

Wodtke, Geoffrey T. 2018. "The Effects of Education on Beliefs About Racial Inequality." *Social Psychology Quarterly 81* (4): 273–94. https://doi.org/10.1177/0190272518804145.

Yin, Robert K. 2018. *Case Study Research and Applications: Design and Methods.* Los Angeles: SAGE Publications.

Yoo, S., Johnson, C. C., Rice, J., and Manuel, P. 2004. "A Qualitative Evaluation of the Students of Service (SOS) Program for Sexual Abstinence in Louisiana." *Journal of School Health 74* (8): 329–334. Retrieved from https://search-proquest-com.jpllnet.sfsu.edu/docview/215674492?accountid=13802

Chapter 8

Bachman, Ronet, and Linda E. Saltzman. 1995. *Violence Against Women: Estimates from the Redesigned Survey.* US Department of Justice, Office of Justice Programs, Bureau of Justice Statistics.

Collins, Brian. 1997. "Sociology." *The Annals of the American Academy of Political and Social Science 549* (1): 207–208. https://doi.org/10.1177/0002716297549001033

Crawford, Jarret T., Sophie A. Kay, and Kristen E. Duke. 2015. "Speaking out of Both Sides of Their Mouths: Biased Political Judgments within (and between) Individuals." *Social Psychological and Personality Science 6* (4): 422–430.

General Social Survey (GSS). 2020. NORC. https://gss.norc.org/

Grollman, Eric Anthony, and Hagiwara, Nao. 2017. "Measuring Self-Reported Discrimination: Trends in Question Wording Used in Publicly Accessible Datasets." *Social Currents 4* (4): 287–305. https://doi.org/10.1177/2329496517704875

Kennedy, Courtney and Hanna Hartig. 2019. "Response Rates in Telephone Surveys Have Resumed their Decline." *Pew Research Center Fact Tank.* February 27. www.pewresearch.org/fact-tank/2019/02/27/response-rates-in-telephone-surveys-have-resumed-their-decline/

Krosnick, Jon A., Allyson L. Holbrook, Matthew K. Berent, Richard T. Carson, W. Michael Hanemann, Raymond J. Kopp, Robert Cameron Mitchell, et al. 2002. "The Impact of 'No Opinion' Response Options on Data Quality: Non-Attitude Reduction or an Invitation to Satisfice?" *Public Opinion Quarterly 66* (3): 371–403.

Lamphere, Jenna Ann. 2018. "Best Practices: From Research Problem to Survey Administration." *TRAILS (Teaching Resources and Innovation Library for Sociology)*. Washington, D.C.: ASA (American Sociological Association). http://trails.asanet.org/Pages/Resource.aspx?ResourceID=13579

Leshem, Oded Adomi, Ismail Nooraddini, and James C. Witte. 2020. "Surveying Societies Mired in Conflict: Evidence of Social Desirability Bias in Palestine." *International Journal of Public Opinion Research 32* (1): 132–142. https://doi.org/10.1093/ijpor/edz002

Lu, Alexander and Joel Y. Wong. 2013. "Stressful Experiences of Masculinity Among U.S.-Born and Immigrant Asian American Men." *Gender & Society 27* (3): 345–371. https://doi.org/10.1177/0891243213479446.

Schaeffer, Nora Cate, and Presser, Stanley. 2003. "The Science of Asking Questions." *Annual Review of Sociology 29* (1): 65–88. https://doi.org/10.1146/annurev.soc.29.110702.110112

Snipp, C. Matthew. 2003. "Racial Measurement in the American Census: Past Practices and Implications for the Future." *Annual Review of Sociology 29* (1): 563–588. https://doi.org/10.1146/annurev.soc.29.010202.100006

Sudman, Seymour, Norman M. Bradburn, and National Opinion Research Center. 1974. *Response Effects in Surveys: A Review and Synthesis*. Chicago: Aldine.

University of Washington, Office of Educational Assessment. 2006. "*Tips for Writing Questionnaire Items*." *University of Washington Survey Resources*. University of Washington. https://s3-us-west-2.amazonaws.com/uw-s3cdn/wpcontent/uploads/sites/123/2016/03/24185543/OEA_QuestionnaireTips.pdf

Williams, Dmitri, Mia Consalvo, Scott Caplan, and Nick Yee. 2009. "Looking for Gender: Gender Roles and Behaviors among Online Gamers." *Journal of Communication 59*(4): 700–725. https://doi.org/10.1111/j.1460-2466.2009.01453.x

Chapter 9

Ajrouch, Kristine J. 2004. "Gender, Race, and Symbolic Boundaries: Contested Spaces of Identity among Arab American Adolescents." *Sociological Perspectives 47* (4): 371–391. https://doi.org/10.1525/sop.2004.47.4.371.

Atkinson, Robert. 1998. *The Life Story Interview*. Thousand Oaks, CA: Sage.

Beardsworth, Alan, and Teresa Keil. 1992. "The Vegetarian Option: Varieties, Conversions, Motives and Careers." *Sociological Review 40* (2) https://doi.org/10.1111/j.1467-954X.1992.tb00889.x

Becker, Howard, and Blanche Geer. 1957. "Participant Observation and Interviewing: A Comparison." *Human Organization 16* (3): 28–32.

Blee, Kathleen. 1998. "White-Knuckle Research: Emotional Dynamics in Fieldwork with Racist Activists." *Qualitative Sociology 21* (4): 381–399. https://doi.org/10.1023/A:1023328309725

Bloor, Michael. 2001. *Focus Groups in Social Research*. Thousand Oaks, CA: Sage.

Boyd, Nan, and Horacio Roque Ramirez. 2012. *Bodies of Evidence: The Practice of Queer Oral History*. http://search.proquest.com/docview/1494000585/

Comfort, Megan, Olga Grinstead, Kathleen McCartney, Philippe Bourgois, and Kelly Knight. 2005. "'You Can't Do Nothing in This Damn Place': Sex and Intimacy Among Couples with an Incarcerated Male Partner." *Journal of Sex Research 42* (1): 3–12. https://doi.org/10.1080/00224490509552251

Deakin, Hannah, and Kelly Wakefield. 2014. "Skype Interviewing: Reflections of Two PhD Researchers." *Qualitative Research 14* (5): 603–616. https://doi.org/10.1177/1468794113488126

Desmond, Matthew. 2016. *Evicted: Poverty and Profit in the American City*. New York: Crown Publishers.

Espiritu, Yen Le. 2001. "'We Don't Sleep Around Like White Girls Do': Family, Culture, and Gender in Filipina American Lives." *Signs 26* (2): 415–440. https://doi.org/10.1086/495599

Ferrera, Maria J., Rebecca T. Feinstein, William J. Walker, and Sarah J. Gehlert. 2016. "Embedded Mistrust Then and Now: Findings of a Focus Group Study on African American Perspectives on Breast Cancer and Its Treatment." *Critical Public Health 26* (4): 455–465. https://doi.org/10.1080/09581596.2015.1117576

Hanna, Paul. 2012. "Using Internet Technologies (such as Skype) as a Research Medium: A

Research Note." *Qualitative Research 12* (2): 239–242. https://doi.org/10.1177/1468794111426607

Iacono, Valeria Lo, Paul Symonds, and David Brown. 2016. "Skype as a Tool for Qualitative Research Interviews." *Sociological Research Online 21* (2): 1–15. https://doi.org/10.5153/sro.3952

Janghorban, Roksana, Robab Latifnejad Roudsari, and Ali Taghipour. 2014. "Skype Interviewing: The New Generation of Online Synchronous Interview in Qualitative Research." *International Journal of Qualitative Studies on Health and Well-Being 9* (1): 24152. https://doi.org/10.3402/qhw.v9.24152

Karnieli-Miller, Orit, Roni Strier, and Liat Pessach. 2009. "Power Relations in Qualitative Research." *Qualitative Health Research 19* (2): 279–289. https://doi.org/10.1177/1049732308329306

Krueger, Richard. 2002. *Designing and Conducting Focus Group Interviews*. St. Paul MN: University of Minnesota. PDF file. www.eiu.edu/ihec/Krueger-FocusGroupInterviews.pdf

Kvale, Steinar. 1996. *Interviews: An Introduction to Qualitative Research Interviewing*. Thousand Oaks, CA: Sage Publications.

Lavelle, Kristen M. 2015. *Whitewashing the South: White Memories of Segregation and Civil Rights*. Lanham: Rowman & Littlefield.

Macnaghten, Phil, and Michael Jacobs. 1997. "Public Identification with Sustainable Development: Investigating Cultural Barriers to Participation." *Global Environmental Change 7* (1): 5–24. https://doi.org/10.1016/S0959-3780(96)00023-4

Madge, Clare, and Henrietta O'Connor. 2002. "On-line with E-Mums: Exploring the Internet as a Medium for Research." *Area 34* (1): 92–102.

Madriz, Esther. 2000. "Feminist Focus Groups." eds, In *Handbook of Qualitative Research*, Norman K. Denzin and Yvonne S. Lincoln, 835–848, 2nd ed. Thousand Oaks, CA: Sage.

Mann, Chris, and Fiona Stewart. 2000. *Internet Communication and Qualitative Research: A Handbook for Researching Online*. Thousand Oaks, CA: Sage.

Martinez, Lisa. 2014. "Dreams Deferred: The Impact of Legal Reforms on Undocumented Latino Youth." *The American Behavioral Scientist 57* (14): 1873. http://search.proquest.com/docview/1622311771/

May, Reuben A. Buford and Kenneth Sean Chaplin. 2008. "Cracking the Code: Race, Class, and Access to Nightclubs in Urban America." *Qualitative Sociology 31* (1): 57–72. https://doi.org/10.1007/s11133-007-9084-7

Mayorga-Gallo, Sarah, and Hordge-Freeman, Elizabeth. 2016. "Between Marginality and Privilege: Gaining Access and Navigating the Field in Multiethnic Settings." *Qualitative Research: QR 17* (4): 377–394. https://doi.org/10.1177/1468794116672915

Miller, David, Jenny Kitzinger, Kevin Williams, and Peter Beharrell. 1998. *The Circuit of Mass Communication: Media Strategies. Representation, and Audience Reception in the AIDS Crisis*. London: SAGE Publications.

Morgan, D. L. 2002. "Focus Group Interviewing." In *Handbook of Interview Research: Context and Method*, ed. J. Gubrium and J. Holstein, 141–159. Thousand Oaks, CA: Sage.

Morgan, David L. 1998. *The Focus Group Guidebook*. London: Sage.

Murray, Christine, E. Horton, G. Johnson, Evette Notestine, Catherine Garr, Higgins Pow, Lori Flasch, and Bethany Doom. 2015. "Domestic Violence Service Providers' Perceptions of Safety Planning: A Focus Group Study." *Journal of Family Violence 30* (3): 381–392. https://doi.org/10.1007/s10896-015-9674-1

Ngo, Bic, and Melissa Kwon. 2015. "A Glimpse of Family Acceptance for Queer Hmong Youth." *Journal of LGBT Youth 12* (2): 212–231. https://doi.org/10.1080/19361653.2015.1022243

Padela, Aasim, I. Pruitt, and Liese Mallick. 2017. "The Types of Trust Involved in American Muslim Healthcare Decisions: An Exploratory Qualitative Study." *Journal of Religion and Health 56* (4): 1478–1488. https://doi.org/10.1007/s10943-017-0387-z

Råheim, Målfrid, Liv Heide Magnussen, Ragnhild Johanne Tveit Sekse, Åshild Lunde, Torild Jacobsen, and Astrid Blystad. 2016. "Researcher-Researched Relationship in Qualitative Research: Shifts in Positions and Researcher Vulnerability." *International Journal of Qualitative Studies on Health and Well-Being 11* (1): 30996. https://doi.org/10.3402/qhw.v11.30996

Seitz, Sally. 2016. "Pixilated Partnerships, Overcoming Obstacles in Qualitative Interviews via Skype: A Research Note." *Qualitative Research 16* (2): 229–235. https://doi.org/10.1177/1468794115577011

Sinclair, Ka`imi, Kelly Gonzales, Claire Woosley, Tish Rivera-Cree, and Dedra Buchwald. 2020. "An Intersectional Mixed Methods Approach to Understand American Indian Men's Health." *International Journal of Men's Social and Community Health, 3* (2): e66–e89. https://doi.org/10.22374/ijmsch.v3i2.35.

Skeggs, Beverley. 2001. "Feminist Ethnography." *Handbook of Ethnography* 426–442. https://doi.org/https://dx.doi.org/10.4135/9781848608337.n29

Trow, Martin. 1957. "Comment on 'Participant Observation and Interviewing: A Comparison.'" *Human Organization 16*(3): 33–35. Accessed April 19, 2020. www.jstor.org/stable/44127709

Weiss, Robert Stuart, and Robert Stewart Weiss. 1994. *Learning from Strangers: The Art and Method of Qualitative Interview Studies.* New York: Free Press.

Chapter 10

Adams, T. E., S. L. H. Jones, and C. Ellis. 2015. *Autoethnography: Understanding Qualitative Research.* New York, NY: Oxford University Press.

Adler, Patricia A., and Peter Adler. 1998. "Transience and the Postmodern Self: The Geographic Mobility of Resort Workers." *The Sociological Quarterly 40* (1): 31–58. https://doi.org/10.1111/j.1533-8525.1999.tb02357.x

Armstrong, Gary. 1993. "Like That Desmond Morris?" In *Interpreting the Field: Accounts of Ethnography,* ed. Dick Hobbs and Tim May, 3–44. New York: Oxford University Press.

Becker, Howard S., Blanche Geer, Everett C. Hughes, and Anselm L. Strauss. 1961. *Boys in White: Student Culture in Medical School.* Chicago: University of Chicago Press.

Bell, Edward. 2007. "Separatism and Quasi-Separatism in Alberta." *Prairie Forum 32 (20)*: 335–355.

Bettie, Julie. 2014. *Women without Class: Girls, Race, and Identity.* Berkeley, CA: University of California Press.

Clay, Andreana. 2012. *The Hip-Hop Generation Fights Back: Youth, Activism, and Post-Civil Rights Politics.* New York: New York University Press.

Denzin, Norman K. 2015. "Triangulation." *The Blackwell Encyclopedia of Sociology.* https://doi.org/10.1002/9781405165518.wbeost050.pub2

Desmond, Matthew. 2016. *Evicted: Poverty and Profit in the American City.* New York: Crown Publishers.

Devault, Marjorie L. 2006. "Introduction: What Is Institutional Ethnography?" *Social Problems 53* (3): 294–298. https://doi.org/10.1525/sp.2006.53.3.294

Ellis, Carolyn. 2004. *The Ethnographic I: A Methodological Novel about Autoethnography.* Walnut Creek, CA: AltaMira.

Fenstermaker, Sarah, and Nikki Jones. 2011. "Victor Rios." In *Sociologists Backstage: Answers to 10 Questions about What They Do,* 111–19. New York: Routledge.

Fine, Gary Alan. 1993. "Ten Lies of Ethnography: Moral Dilemmas of Field Research." *Journal of Contemporary Ethnography 22* (3): 267–94.

Fine, Gary Alan. 1996. "Justifying Work: Occupational Rhetorics as Resources in Restaurant Kitchens." *Administrative Science Quarterly 41* (1): 90–115.

Fitzhugh, Louise. 1964. *Harriet the Spy.* New York: Harper.

Gans, Herbert J. 1968. *People and Plans: Essays on Urban Problems and Solutions.* New York: Basic Books.

Gerson, Kathleen and Ruth Horowitz. 2002. "Observation and Interviewing: Asking, Listening, and Interpreting." In *Qualitative Research in Action,* ed. Tim May, 79–199. London: SAGE Publications.

Giulianotti, Richard. 1995. "Participant Observation and Research into Football Hooliganism: Reflections on the Problems of Entrée and Everyday Risks." *Sociology of Sport Journal 12* (1): 1–20.

Glucksmann, Miriam. 1994. "Working through Gender: The Inter-Weaving of New Technology in Workplace and Home." *Work, Employment & Society 8* (4): 623–628. https://doi.org/10.1177/0950017094008004009

Goffman, Erving. 1959. *The Presentation of Self in Everyday Life*. Edinburgh: University of Edinburgh.

Hallett, Ronald E., and Kristen Barber. 2014. "Ethnographic Research in a Cyber Era." *Journal of Contemporary Ethnography 43* (3): 306–30.

Hammersley, Martyn, and Paul Atkinson. 1995. *Ethnography: Principles in Practice*. 2nd ed. London, New York: Routledge.

Hospodsky, Denina, Amy J. Pickering, Timothy R. Julian, Dana Miller, Sisira Gorthala, Alexandria B. Boehm, and Jordan Peccia. 2014. "Hand Bacterial Communities Vary across Two Different Human Populations." *Microbiology 160* (6): 1144–1152. https://doi.org/10.1099/mic.0.075390-0

Kleinman, Sherryl, and Martha A. Copp. 1993. *Emotions and Fieldwork*. Newbury Park, CA: Sage.

Leidner, Robin. 1993. *Fast Food, Fast Talk: Service Work and the Routinization of Everyday Life*. Berkeley, CA: University of California Press.

Lofland, John and Lyn H. Lofland 1995. *Analyzing Social Settings: A Guide to Qualitative Observation and Analysis*. 3rd ed. Belmont, CA: Wadsworth.

Luttrell, Wendy. 2003. *Pregnant Bodies, Fertile Minds: Gender, Race, and the Schooling of Pregnant Teens*. New York: Routledge.

Luttrell, Wendy. 2010. "'A Camera is a Big Responsibility': A Lens for Analysing Children's Visual Voices." *Visual Studies 25* (3): 224–37.

Ray, Ranita. 2018. *The Making of a Teenage Service Class: Poverty and Mobility in an American City*. Oakland, CA: University of California Press.

Rios, Victor M. 2011. *Punished: Policing the Lives of Black and Latino Boys*. New York: New York University Press.

Rollins, Judith. 1985. *Between Women: Domestics and Their Employers*. Philadelphia: Temple University Press.

Sanjek, Roger. 1990. "Urban Anthropology in the 1980s: A World View." *Annual Review of Anthropology 19*(1): 151–186. https://doi.org/10.1146/annurev.an.19.100190.001055

Sharpe, Karen. 1998. *Red Light, Blue Light: Prostitutes, Punters and the Police*. Aldershot, UK: Ashgate.

Skeggs, Beverley. 1994. "Situating the Production of Feminist Ethnography." In *Researching Women's Lives from a Feminist Perspective*, edited by Mary Maynard and June Purvis, 72–148. London: Routledge.

Skeggs, Beverley. 1997. *Formations of Class and Gender: Becoming Respectable*. London: SAGE Publications.

Stacey, Judith. 1988. "Can There Be a Feminist Ethnography?" *Women's Studies International Forum 11* (1): 21–27. https://doi.org/https://doi.org/10.1016/0277-5395(88)90004-0

Van Maanen, John. 1991. "Playing Back the Tape: Early Days in the Field." In *Experiencing Fieldwork: An Inside View of Qualitative Research*, ed. W. Shaffir and R. Stebbins, 21–42. Newbury Park, CA: Sage.

Whyte, William Foote. 1955. *Street Corner Society: The Social Structure of an Indian Slum*. Chicago: University of Chicago Press.

Chapter 11

Altheide, David. 1996. "Qualitative Media Analysis." *Qualitative Research Methods 38*. doi:10.4135/9781412985536

Bond, Bradley J. 2013. "Physical Disability on Children's Television Programming: A Content Analysis." *Early Education & Development 24* (3): 408–418. https://doi.org/10.1080/10409289.2012.670871

Bromley, Patricia, John W. Meyer, and Francisco O. Ramirez. 2011. "Student-Centeredness in Social Science Textbooks, 1970–2008: A Cross-National Study." *Social Forces 90* (2): 547–570.

Bryman, Alan. 1995. *Back to the Future: Representations of Past and Future*. London: Routledge.

Byng, Michelle D. 2010. "Symbolically Muslim: Media, Hijab, and the West." *Critical Sociology 36* (1): 109–129. https://doi.org/10.1177/0896920509347143

Callander, Denton, Martin Holt, and Christy E. Newman. 2012. "Just a Preference: Racialised Language in the Sex-Seeking Profiles of Gay and Bisexual Men." *Culture, Health & Sexuality 14* (9): 1049–1063. https://doi.org/10.1080/13691058.2012.714799

Fenton, Natalie, Alan Bryman, David Deacon, and Peter Birmingham. 1997. *Mediating Social Science*. London: SAGE Publications.

Fidel, Emma. 2016. "White People Voted to Elect Trump." *Vice News 308*: 125–26.

Freedman, Estelle B. 1998. "'The Burning of Letters Continues': Elusive Identities and the Historical Construction of Sexuality." *Journal of Women's History 9* (4): 181–200. https://doi.org/10.1353/jowh.2010.0237

Gearhart, Sherice, and Teresa Trumbly-Lamsam. 2017. "The Scoop on Health: How Native American Newspapers Frame and Report Health News." *Health Communication 32* (6): 695–702.

Golinkoff, A. et al. 2016. "Cardboard Commentary: A Qualitative Analysis of the Signs from America's Streets." *American Journal of Public Health 106* (11): 1977–1978. doi:10.2105/ajph.2016.303290

Goodin, Samantha, Alyssa Denburg, Sarah Murnen, and Linda Smolak. 2011. "'Putting On' Sexiness: A Content Analysis of the Presence of Sexualizing Characteristics in Girls' Clothing." *Sex Roles: A Journal of Research 65* (1–2): 1–12.

Grana, Rachel A., and Pamela M. Ling. 2014. "Smoking Revolution." *American Journal of Preventive Medicine 46* (4): 395–403.

Grimm, Josh, and Julie L. Andsager. 2011. "Framing Immigration: Geo-Ethnic Context in California Newspapers." *Journalism & Mass Communication Quarterly 88* (4): 771–788.

Hall, Jeffrey A., Namkee Park, Hayeon Song, and Michael J. Cody. 2010. "Strategic Misrepresentation in Online Dating: The Effects of Gender, Self-monitoring, and Personality Traits." *Journal of Social and Personal Relationships 27* (1): 117–135.

Hatton, Erin, and Mary Nell Trautner. 2013. "Images of Powerful Women in the Age of 'Choice Feminism.'" *Journal of Gender Studies 22* (1): 65–78. https://doi.org/10.1080/09589236.2012.681184

Henley, Jon. 2016. "White and Wealthy Voters Give Victory to Donald Trump, Exit Polls Show." *The Guardian*, November 9, https://www.theguardi-ancom/us-news/2016/nov/09/white-voters-victory-donald-trump-exit-polls

Hess, Aaron, and Carlos Flores. 2018. "Simply More than Swiping Left: A Critical Analysis of Toxic Masculine Performances on Tinder Nightmares." *New Media & Society 20* (3): 1085–1102.

Heuer, Chelsea A., Kimberly J. McClure, and Rebecca M. Puhl. 2011. "Obesity Stigma in Online News: A Visual Content Analysis." *Journal of Health Communication 16* (9): 976–987.

Hier, Sean P. 2000. "Contemporary Structure of Canadian Racial Supremacism: Networks, Strategies and New Technologies." *Canadian Journal of Sociology 25* (4): 471–494.

Hier, Sean P. 2002. "Raves, Risks and the Ecstacy Panic: A Case Study in the Subversive Nature of Moral Regulation (1)." *Canadian Journal of Sociology 27* (1): 33–57.

Hirsch, Julia. 1981. *Family Photographs: Content, Meaning, and Effect.* New York: Oxford.

Hitsch, Gunter J., Ali Hortacsu, and Dan Ariely. 2010. "Matching and Sorting in Online Dating. (Report)." *American Economic Review 100* (1): 130–163.

Jagger, Elizabeth. 1998. "Marketing the Self, Buying an Other: Dating in a Post Modern, Consumer Society." *Sociology 32* (4): 795–814. https://doi.org/10.1177/0038038598032004009

Jessen, Sarah Butler. 2012. "Special Education & School Choice." *Educational Policy 27* (3): 427–466. https://doi.org/10.1177/0895904812453997

Lamont, Michèle, Bo Yun Park, and Elena Carina Ayala-Hurtado. 2017. "Trump's Electoral Speeches and His Appeal to the American White Working Class." *The British Journal of Sociology 68*: S153-S180.

Lee, F. L. 2014. "Triggering the Protest Paradigm: Examining Factors Affecting News Coverage of Protests." *International Journal of Communication 8*: 2725–2746.

Lee, Raymond M. 2000. *Unobtrusive Methods in Social Research.* Buckingham, UK: Open University Press.

Leopold, Joy and Myrtle P. Bell. 2017. "News Media and the Racialization of Protest: An Analysis of Black Lives Matter Articles." *Equality, Diversity and Inclusion: An International Journal 36* (8): 720–735.

Miller, Brandon. 2015. "'Dude, Where's Your Face?' Self-Presentation, Self-Description, and Partner Preferences on a Social Networking Application for Men Who Have Sex with Men: A Content Analysis." *Sexuality & Culture 19* (4): 637–658.

Mowatt, Rasul A. "Lynching as Leisure." *The American Behavioral Scientist (Beverly Hills) 56*.10 (2012): 1361–387. Web.

Oleinik, Anton. 2011. "Mixing Quantitative and Qualitative Content Analysis: Triangulation at Work." *Quality & Quantity 45* (4): 859–873.

Park, Sejin, Zienab Shoieb, and Ronald E. Taylor. 2017. "Message Strategies in Military Recruitment Advertising: A Research Note." *Armed Forces & Society 43* (3): 566–573.

Pauwels, Luc. 2008. "A Private Visual Practice Going Public? Social Functions and Sociological Research Opportunities of Web-based Family Photography." *Visual Studies 23* (1): 34–49.

Riggs, Damien. 2013. "Anti-Asian Sentiment Amongst a Sample of White Australian Men on Gaydar." *Sex Roles 68* (11–12): 768–778.

Rogers, Linda J., and Beth Blue Swadener, eds. 2001. *Semiotics and Dis/ability: Interrogating Categories of Difference.* Albany: SUNY Press.

Sanders, W. Scott, Selene G. Phillips, and Cecelia Alexander. 2017. "'Native' Advertising: An Evaluation of Nike's N7 Social Media Campaign." *American Indian Culture and Research Journal 41* (2): 43–63.

Scott, John.1990. *A Matter of Record: Documentary Sources in Social Research.* Cambridge: Polity Press.

Sugiman, Pamela. 2004. "Memories of Internment: Narrating Japanese Canadian Women's Life Stories (1)." *Canadian Journal of Sociology 29* (3): 359–388.

Sutton, Robert I. 1992. "Feelings about a Disneyland Visit." *Journal of Management 1* (4): 278–287. https://doi.org/10.1177/105649269214002

Thomas, Tracey L., Daniela B. Friedman, Heather M. Brandt, S. Melinda Spencer, and Andrea Tanner. 2016. "Uncharted Waters: Communicating Health Risks During the 2014 West Virginia Water Crisis." *Journal of Health Communication 21* (9): 1062–1070.

Webb, Eugene J., Donald T. Campbell, Richard D. Schwartz, and Lee Sechrest. (1966) *2000. Unobtrusive Measures,* 2nd ed. Thousand Oaks, CA: SAGE Publications.

Chapter 12

Alexander, Michelle. 2010. *The New Jim Crow: Mass Incarceration in the Age of Colorblindness.* New York: New Press.

Barnes, J. C., and Ryan T. Motz. 2018. "Reducing Racial Inequalities in Adulthood Arrest by Reducing Inequalities in School Discipline: Evidence from the School-to-Prison Pipeline." *Developmental Psychology 54* (12): 2328–2340.

Baumgartner, Jody C., and Brad Lockerbie. 2018. "Maybe It Is More Than a Joke: Satire, Mobilization, and Political Participation." *Social Science Quarterly 99*(3): 1060–1074. https://doi.org/10.1111/ssqu.12501

Benegal, Salil D. 2018. "The Spillover of Race and Racial Attitudes into Public Opinion about Climate Change." *Environmental Politics 27*(4): 733–756.

Boyd, Danah, and Kate Crawford. 2012. "Critical Questions for Big Data: Provocations for a Cultural, Technological, and Scholarly Phenomenon." *Information, Communication & Society, 15*(5): 662–79. https://doi.org/10.1080/1369118x.2012.678878.

Chávez, Karma R. 2012. "ACT UP, Haitian Migrants, and Alternative Memories of HIV/AIDS." *Quarterly Journal of Speech 98* (1): 63–68. https://doi.org/10.1080/00335630.2011.638659

"Densho: Japanese American Incarceration and Japanese Internment." *Densho.* Accessed March 29, 2020. http://densho.org/

Downey, Liam, Kyle Crowder, and Robert J. Kemp. 2016. "Family Structure, Residential Mobility, and Environmental Inequality." *Journal of Marriage and Family 79* (2): 535–555. https://doi.org/10.1111/jomf.12355

Durkheim, Émile. (1897) 1952. *Suicide: A Study in Sociology.* London: Routledge.

Glick, Sara Nelson, and Matthew R. Golden. 2010. "Persistence of Racial Differences in Attitudes Toward Homosexuality in the United States." *JAIDS Journal of Acquired Immune Deficiency Syndromes 55* (4): 516–523.

Goosby, Bridget J., Cleopatra Howard Caldwell, Anna Bellatorre, and James S. Jackson. 2012. "Ethnic Differences in Family Stress Processes among African-Americans and Black Caribbeans." *Journal of African American Studies 16* (3): 406–422. https://doi.org/10.1007/s12111-011-9203-0

Haney, Jolynn L. 2016. "Predictors of Homonegativity in the United States and the Netherlands Using the

Fifth Wave of the World Values Survey." *Journal of Homosexuality* 63 (10): 1355–1377. https://doi.org/10.1080/00918369.2016.1157997

Hesse, Arielle, Leland Glenna, Clare Hinrichs, Robert Chiles, and Carolyn Sachs. 2019. "Qualitative Research Ethics in the Big Data Era." *American Behavioral Scientist* 63 (5): 560–583.

Hicks, William D., Seth C. Mckee, Mitchell D. Sellers, and Daniel A. Smith. 2015. "A Principle or a Strategy? Voter Identification Laws and Partisan Competition in the American States." *Political Research Quarterly* 68 (1): 18–33.

Jackman, Tom. 2020. "FBI Launched Database on Police Use of Force Last Year, but Only 40 Percent of Police Participated." *The Washington Post.* https://www.washingtonpost.com/crime-law/2020/06/17/fbi-launched-database-police-use-force-last-year-only-40-percent-police-participated/

Kindy, Kimberly, Marc Fisher, Julie Tate, and Jennifer Jenkins. 2015. "A Year of Reckoning: Police Fatally Shoot Nearly 1,000." The Washington Post. www.washingtonpost.com/sf/investigative/2015/12/26/a-year-of-reckoning-police-fatally-shoot-nearly-1000/?utm_term=.4241ff00484f

Lazer, David, and Jason Radford. 2017. "Data Ex Machina: Introduction to Big Data." *Annual Review of Sociology* 43 (1): 19–39. https://doi.org/10.1146/annurev-soc-060116-053457

Liévanos, Raoul S. "Race, Deprivation, and Immigrant Isolation: The Spatial Demography of Air-Toxic Clusters in the Continental United States." *Social Science Research 54:* 50–67.

Mallett, Christopher A. 2016. *The School-to-Prison Pipeline: A Comprehensive Assessment.* New York, NY: Springer.

Maril, Robert Lee. 2012. *The Fence: National Security, Public Safety, and Illegal Immigration along the U.S.-Mexico Border.* Lubbock, TX: Texas Tech University Press.

Metzler, Katie, David A. Kim, Nick Allum, Angella Denman. 2016. *Who is Doing Computational Social Science? Trends in Big Data Research (White paper).* London: SAGE Publishing. https://doi.org/10.4135/wp160926

Parigi, Paolo, Jessica J. Santana, and Karen S. Cook. 2017. "Online Field Experiments." *Social Psychology Quarterly* 80 (1): 1–19. https://doi.org/10.1177/0190272516680842

Petty, James. 2016. "The London Spikes Controversy: Homelessness, Urban Securitisation and the Question of 'Hostile Architecture.'" *International Journal for Crime, Justice and Social Democracy 5* (1): 67. https://doi.org/10.5204/ijcjsd.v5i1.286

Rathje, William L. and Cullen Murphy. 1993. *Rubbish! The Archaeology of Garbage.* New York, NY: Harper Perennial.

Schnabel, Landon. 2016. "The Gender Pray Gap: Wage Labor and the Religiosity of High-Earning Women and Men." *Gender & Society 30* (4): 643–669. https://doi.org/10.31235/osf.io/gmnsj

Shapiro, Thomas M. 2004. *The Hidden Cost of Being African American: How Wealth Perpetuates Inequality.* New York: Oxford.

Shapiro, Thomas. 2006. "Race, Homeownership and Wealth." *Washington University Journal of Law & Policy 20:* 53–74.

Skiba, Russell J., Robert H. Horner, Choong-Geun Chung, M. Karega Rausch, Seth L. May, and Tary Tobin. 2011. "Race Is Not Neutral: A National Investigation of African American and Latino Disproportionality in School Discipline. (Report)." *School Psychology Review, 40* (1): 85–107.

Snapp, Shannon D., Jennifer M. Hoenig, Amanda Fields, and Stephen T Russell. 2015. "Messy, Butch, and Queer: LGBTQ Youth and the School-to-Prison Pipeline." *Journal of Adolescent Research, 30* (1): 57–82.

Stanton, Megan C., Lisa Werkmeister Rozas, and Marysol Asencio. 2019. "Citizenship Status Matters: A Social Factor Influencing Outness among a Diverse National Sample of LGBT Individuals." *The British Journal of Social Work 49* (3): 722–41.

Summers, Ryan. 2020. "'Insecurity': How the Trump Administration is Placing Border Wall Speed Before the Law." *Project on Government Oversight,* June 5. https://www.pogo.org/analysis/2020/06/insecurity-how-the-trump-administration-is-placing-border-wall-speed-before-the-law/

Walters, David. 2004. "A Comparison of the Labour Market Outcomes of Postsecondary Graduates of Various Levels and Fields over a Four-Cohort Period." *Canadian Journal of Sociology/Cahiers Canadiens de Sociologie 29* (1): 1–27.

Wasi, Nada, Bernard Van Den Berg, and Thomas C. Buchmueller. 2011. "Heterogeneous Effects of Child Disability on Maternal Labor Supply: Evidence from the 2000 US Census." *Labour Economics.* https://doi.org/10.1016/j.labeco.2011.09.008

Webb, Eugene, Donald Campbell, Richard Schwartz, and Lee Sechrest. 2000. *Unobtrusive Measures, Revised Edition. Sage Classics 2.* Thousand Oaks, CA: Sage. doi: 10.4135/9781452243443

Western, Bruce. 2014. "Incarceration, Inequality, and Imagining Alternatives." *The Annals of the American Academy of Political and Social Science 651*: 302–306.

Yackee, Susan Webb. 2012. "The Politics of Ex Parte Lobbying: Pre-proposal Agenda Building and Blocking during Agency Rulemaking." *Journal of Public Administration Research and Theory 22*(2): 373.

Chapter 13

Atkinson, Michael. 2002. "Pretty in Ink: Conformity, Resistance, and Negotiation in Women's Tattooing." *Sex Roles 47* (5): 219–235. https://doi.org/10.1023/A:1021330609522

Bryman, Alan and Robert G. Burgess. 1994. *Analyzing Qualitative Data.* London & New York: Routledge.

Charmaz, Kathy. 1997. "Grief and Loss of Self." In *The Unknown Country: Death in Australia, Britain and the USA*, edited by Kathy Charmaz, Glennys Howarth, and Allan Kellehear, 229–41. London: Palgrave Macmillan.

Charmaz, Kathy. 2000. "Constructivist and Objectivist Grounded Theory." in eds, In *Handbook of Qualitative Research*, ed. N. K. Denzin and Y. Lincoln, 509–535, 2nd ed. Thousand Oaks, CA: Sage.

Charmaz, Kathy. 2004. "Grounded Theory." In *Approaches to Qualitative Research: A Reader on Theory and Practice*, ed. Sharlene Nagy Hesse-Biber and Patricia Leavy, 496–508. New York: Oxford University Press.

Choo, Hae Yeon and Myra Marx Ferree. 2010. "Practicing Intersectionality in Sociological Research: A Critical Analysis of Inclusions, Interactions, and Institutions in the Study of Inequalities." *Sociological Theory 28* (2): 129–149.

Coffey, Amanda and Paul Atkinson. 1996. *Making Sense of Qualitative Data: Complementary Research Strategies.* Thousand Oaks, CA: Sage.

Coffey, Amanda, Beverley Holbrook, and Paul Atkinson. 1996. "Qualitative Data Analysis: Technologies and Representations." *Sociological Research Online 1* (1): 80–91. doi:10.5153/sro.1

Comfort, Megan, Olga Grinstead, Kathleen McCartney, Philippe Bourgois, and Kelly Knight. 2005. "'You Can't Do Nothing in This Damn Place': Sex and Intimacy Among Couples With an Incarcerated Male Partner." *Journal of Sex Research 42* (1): 3–12. https://doi.org/10.1080/00224490509552251.

Esterberg, Kristin G. 2001. *Qualitative Research Methods in Social Research.* Columbus, OH: McGraw-Hill.

Fields, Jessica, Isela González, Kathleen Hentz, Margaret Rhee, and Catherine White. 2008. "Learning from and with Incarcerated Women: Emerging Lessons from a Participatory Action Study of Sexuality Education." *Sexuality Research & Social Policy 5* (2): 71–84.

Hurston, Z. N. 1942. *Dust Tracks on a Road.* Philadelphia: J. B. Lippincott & Co.

Lofland, John, and Lyn H. Lofland. 1995. *Analyzing Social Settings: A Guide to Qualitative Observation and Analysis*, 3rd ed. Belmont, CA: Wadsworth.

Miller, Robert. 2000. *Researching Life Stories and Family Histories.* London: SAGE Publications.

Riessman, Catherine Kohler. 2004. "A Thrice-Told Tale: New Readings of an Old Story." In *Narrative Research in Health and Illness*, edited by Brian Hurwitz, Trisha Greenlaigh, and Vieda Skultans, 309–24. Malden, MA: Blackwell Publishing.

Roberts, Brian. 2002. *Biographical Research.* New York: Open University Press.

Strauss, Anselm L., and Juliet M. Corbin. 1998. *Basics of Qualitative Research: Techniques and Procedures for Developing Grounded Theory.* Thousand Oaks, CA: Sage.

Tolman, Deborah L. 1999. "Femininity as a Barrier to Positive Sexual Health for Adolescent Girls." *Journal of the American Medical Women's Association 54* (3): 133–138.

Whitehead, Krista. 2012. "Hunger Hurts but Starving Works: A Case Study of Gendered Practices in the Online Pro-Eating-Disorder Community." *Canadian Journal of Sociology/Cahiers Canadiens de Sociologie 35* (4): 595–626.

Whiting, Jason B., Timothy G. Parker, and Austin W. Houghtaling. 2014. "Explanations of a Violent Relationship: The Male Perpetrator's Perspective." *Journal of Family Violence 29* (3): 277–286. https://doi.org/10.1007/s10896-014-9582-9

Chapter 14

Brown, Anna. 2014. "The U.S. Hispanic Population Has Increased Sixfold Since 1970." *Pew Research Center Fact Tank*, February 26. https://www.pewresearch.org/fact-tank/2014/02/26/the-u-s-hispanic-population-has-increased-sixfold-since-1970/

Bryman, Alan, and Duncan Cramer. 2001. *Quantitative Data Analysis with SPSS Release 10 for Windows: A Guide for Social Scientists.* London: Routledge.

Bunch, Jackson, Jody Clay-Warner, and Jennifer Mcmahon-Howard. 2013. "The Effects of Victimization on Routine Activities." *Criminal Justice and Behavior 41* (5): 574–592. https://doi.org/10.1177/0093854813508286

Chetty, Raj, Nathaniel Hendren, Maggie Jones, and Sonya Porter. 2018. "Race and Economic Opportunity in the United States: An Intergenerational Perspective." *Quarterly Journal of Economics. 135* (2): 711–83. https://doi.org/10.3386/w24441

D'Anna, L. H., V. Peong, P. Sabado, A. Valdez-Dadia, M. C. Hansen, C. Canjura, and M. Hong. 2018. "Barriers to Physical and Mental Health: Understanding the Intersecting Needs of Cambodian and Latino Residents in Urban Communities." *Journal of Immigrant and Minority Health 20* (5): 1243–1260. https://doi.org/10.1007/s10903-017-0677-2

Death Penalty Information Center (DPIC). 2019a. *"Facts about the Death Penalty."* https://deathpenaltyinfo.org/documents/FactSheet.pdf

Death Penalty Information Center (DPIC). 2019b. *"National Statistics on the Death Penalty and Race."* https://deathpenaltyinfo.org/race-death-row-inmates-executed-1976#defend

Death Penalty Information Center (DPIC). 2019c. *"Number of Executions by State and Region since 1976."* https://deathpenaltyinfo.org/number-executions-state-and-region-

Death Penalty Information Center (DPIC). 2019d. *"Time on Death Row."* https://deathpenaltyinfo.org/time-death-row

Donovan, Sarah A., Marc Labonte, and Joseph Dalaker. 2016. *"The US Income Distribution: Trends and Issues."* Congressional Research Service CRS Report Prepared for Members and Committees of Congress. https://fas.org/sgp/crs/misc/R44705.pdf

Durkheim Émile. (1912) 2008. *The Elementary Forms of Religious Life.* New York: Free Press.

Elder, Laurel, and Steven Greene. 2018. "Gender and the Politics of Marijuana." *Social Science Quarterly 100* (1): 109–122. https://doi.org/10.1111/ssqu.12558

Field, Andy P. 2016. *An Adventure in Statistics: The Reality Enigma.* Thousand Oaks, CA: SAGE Publications.

Field, Andy P. and James Iles. 2016. *An Adventure in Statistics: The Reality Enigma.* Los Angeles: Sage.

Field, Andy P., Jeremy Miles, and Zoë Field. 2014. *Discovering Statistics Using R.* London: Sage.

Perry, Samuel L. 2014. "Religious Socialization and Interracial Dating: The Effects of Childhood Religious Salience, Practice, and Parents' Tradition." *Journal of Family Issues 37* (15): 2138–2162. https://doi.org/https://journals.sagepub.com/doi/10.1177/0192513X14555766

Reck, Brian. 2020. *R: A Language and Environment for Statistical Computing.* R Foundation for

Statistical Computing, Vienna, Austria. www.R-project.org/

Snell, Tracy L. July 2019. "Capital Punishment, 2017: Selected Findings." U.S. Department of Justice, Office of Justice Programs. www.bjs.gov/content/pub/pdf/cp17sf.pdf

Stark, Rodney, and Charles Y. Glock. 1968. *American Piety: The Nature of Religious Commitment.* Berkeley: University of California Press.

Sutton, Robert I., and Anat Rafaeli. 1992. "How We Untangled the Relationship Between Displayed Emotion and Organizational Sales: A Tale of Bickering and Optimism." In *Doing exemplary research*, edited by Peter J. Frost and Ralph E. Stablein, 115–28. Newbury Park, CA: SAGE Publications.

U.S. Census Bureau, 2019. "U.S. Census Bureau QuickFacts: United States." *Census Bureau QuickFacts.* Accessed March 19, 2020. www.census.gov/quickfacts/fact/table/US/PST045218

Chapter 15

"*Annual Review of Sociology; Volume 45, 2019.*" ProtoView 2019.45 (2019): ProtoView, 2019-10-01, Vol.2019 (45). Web.

Becker, Howard. 1986. *Writing for Social Scientists: How to Start and Finish Your Thesis, Book, or Article,* 2nd ed. Chicago: University of Chicago Press.

Birkenstein, C. and Gerald Graff. 2018. *They Say/I Say: The Moves That Matter in Academic Writing,* 4th ed. New York, NY: WW Norton & Company.

"*Cite Black Women: A Critical Praxis.*" 2020. Cite Black Women. https://www.citeblackwomencollective.org/our-praxis.html.

Clance, Pauline Rose and Suzanne Ament Imes. 1978. "The Imposter Phenomenon in High Achieving Women: Dynamics and Therapeutic Intervention." *Psychotherapy* 15 (3): 241–247. https://doi.org/10.1037/h0086006

Elbow, Peter. 1998. *Writing with Power: Techniques for Mastering the Writing Process,* 2nd ed. New York: Oxford.

Goldberg, Natalie. 2016. *The Great Spring: Writing, Zen, and This Zigzag Life.* Boston: Shambhala.

Kelsky, Karen. 2011. "How-To(sday): How to Write a Paper or Conference Proposal Abstract." *The Professor Is In.* http://theprofessorisin.com/2011/07/12/how-tosday-how-to-write-a-paper-abstract/

Lamott, Anne. 1994. *Bird by Bird: Some Instructions on Writing and Life.* New York: Pantheon Books.

Credits

Chapter 1

[1.0] Photo by JORGE GUERRERO, SEBASTIEN BOZON, JOSE SANCHEZ, KIRILL KUDRYAVTSEV, SAJJAD HUSSAIN, CHANDAN KHANNA, JOSEPH EID, VLADIMIR ZIVOJINOVIC, MONEY SHARMA, MIGUEL MEDINA, ARUN SANKAR, PEDRO PARDO, ANDY BUCHANAN, ADEK BERRY, BULENT KILIC, CHARLY TRIBALLEAU, JEAN-CHRISTOPHE VERHAEGEN, JAIME REINA, DIMITAR DILKOFF, JUAN MABROMATA, NIKOLAY DOYCHINOV, PAUL FAITH/AFP via Getty Images; [1.1] © iStock/Rich Vantage; [1.2] © iStock/SDI Productions; [1.3] © iStock/Hector Pertuz; [1.4] © iStock/funky-data; [1.5] © iStock/kate_sept2004; [1.6] © Anna Om/Shutterstock

Chapter 2

[2.0] AP Photo/Hassan Ammar; [2.1] Photo by Roger Viollet via Getty Images; [2.2] "Rooftop Party in Brooklyn" by MattHurstis licensed under CC BY-SA 2.0; [2.3] Joe Cavaretta/SunSentinel/TCA; [2.4] "Same sex marriage vote in the Minnesota Senate" by Fibonacci Blueis licensed under CC BY 2.0; [2.5] Michael Simons/123RF

Chapter 3

[3.0] Photo by STR/AFP via Getty Images; [3.1] Rommel Canlas/123RF; [3.2] Andersen Ross/Getty Images; [3.3] © PitukTV/Shutterstock; [3.4] David Grossman/Alamy Stock Photo; [3.5] Tetra Images, LLC/Alamy Stock Photo; [3.6] Michael Dwyer/Alamy Stock Photo

Chapter 4

[4.0] Ringo Chiu via AP; [4.1] © weedezign/Shutteerstock; [4.2] Photo by Gabriele Holtermann/Sipa via AP Images; [4.3] AP Photo/Marta Lavandier; [4.4] © iStock/robertcicchetti; [4.5] "23.TentCity.2000E.WDC.23January2020" by Elvert Barnesis licensed under CC BY-SA 2.0; [4.6] IMG_0386a" by Elvert Barnes is licensed under CC BY-SA 2.0

Chapter 5

[5.0] Stephen Chung/Alamy Stock Photo; [5.1] © iStock/SDI Productions; [5.2] Photo by Jun Fujita/Chicago History Museum/Getty Images; [5.3] Photo by Scott Olson/Getty Images; [5.4] Image by Bayete Stevens, Pixabay; [5.5] AP Photo/Michael Conroy; [5.6] Photo by Mario Tama/Getty Images

Chapter 6

[6.0] AP Photo/Ringo H.W. Chiu; [6.1] Bettman/Getty Images; [6.2] Jetsonorama; [6.3] AP Photo/Lynne Sladky; [6.4] "Silent march to end stop and frisk and racial profiling" by longislandwinsis licensed under CC BY 2.0; [6.5] "Memorial Day 2020 - San Francisco Under Quarantine (49935629483).jpg" by Christopher Michel from San Francisco, USAis licensed under CC BY 2.0

Chapter 7

[7.0] © iStock/siraanamwong; [7.1] RoadPix/Alamy Stock Photo; [7.2] Geoff Forester/The Concord Monitor via AP); [7.3] "Voceros-10" by SLR Imagesis licensed under CC BY 2.0; [7.4] Lyndon Stratford/Alamy Stock Photo; [7.5] © iStock/izusek

Chapter 8

[8.0] Jeffrey Isaac Greenberg 20+/Alamy Stock Photo; [8.1] Rupert Oberhäuser/Alamy Stock Photo; [8.2] Janine Wiedel Photolibrary/Alamy Stock Photo; [8.3] United States Census Bureau, American Community Survey; [8.4] AP Photo/Matthew Brown; [8.5] © Prostock-studio/Shutterstock; [8.6] © iStock/zoranm

Chapter 9

[9.0] © iStock/SDI Productions; [9.1] "High Line @ Night" by lmpicard is licensed under CC BY-ND 2.0; [9.2] AP Photo/Andre Penner; [9.3] © iStock/ljubaphoto; [9.4] Photo by Alex Edelman/Getty Images; [9.5] Fredrick Kippe/Alamy Stock Photo

Chapter 10

[10.0] Mira/Alamy Stock Photo; {Figure 10.1} Redrawn from Gold 1958; [10.1] The Toledo Blade/Jetta Fraser, 2016; [10.2] © Brocreative/Shutterstock; [10.3] © Jacob Lund/Shutterstock; [10.4] Mengwen Cao/Getty Images; [10.5] James Quigg/The Daily Press via AP)

Chapter 11

[11.0] Jeffrey Isaac Greenberg 1+/Alamy Stock Photo; [11.1] Stanford Research Into the Impact to Tobacco Adverstising; [11.2] © West7megan/Dreamstime.com/GetStock; [11.3] © iStock/Juanmonino; [11.4] Shelly Rivoli/Alamy Stock Photo; [11.6] © reddit

Chapter 12

[12.0] MoiraM/Alamy Stock Photo; [Figure 12.1] Adapted from Anna Brown, "The changing categories the U.S. Census has used to measure race," Pew Research Center, Feb. 25, 2020; [12.1] Image courtesy U.S. Census Bureau, Public Information Office (POI); [12.2] © iStock/SDI Productions; [12.3] AP Photo/Matt York,File; [12.4] Photo by Dirck Halstead/The LIFE Images Collection via Getty Images/Getty Images; [12.5] © Helioscribe/Shutterstock; [12.6] © Jennifer Reck

Chapter 13

[13.0] *Legacy Project @ PS250*, by Ellie Balk, www.elliebalk.com. Used with permission of the artist; [Figure 13.1] © Graham R. Gibbs and the University of Huddersfield; [Figure 13.3] © Reck and Fields; [13.1] Everett Collection Inc/Alamy Stock Photo; [13.2] © iStock/Beyond Images; [13.3] © PitukTV/Shutterstock; [13.4] © iStock/nautiluz56; [13.5] Cultura Creative RF/Alamy Stock Photo; [PO 05] Tetra Images, LLC/Alamy Stock Photo

Chapter 14

[14.0] From Ablynx (Infographics XXXXL Part 2), courtesy of ONTWERPBUREAU SOON; [Figure 14.1] Reck and Fields, based on data from Death Penalty Information Center, 2019b; [Figure 14.2] Reck and Fields, based on data from Death Penalty Information Center, 2019b; [Figure 14.3] Reck and Fields, based on data from Death Penalty Information Center, 2019b; [Figure 14.4] Reck and Fields; [Figure 14.5] Redrawn from Perry 2014, p. 447; [14.1] © iStock/Ridofranz; [14.2] Photo by Jeremy Hogan/SOPA Images/Sipa via AP Images; [14.3] Photo by Spencer Platt/Getty Images; [14.4] © RossHelen/Shutterstock; [14.5] (Photo by James Leynse/Corbis via Getty Images

Chapter 15

[15.0] Randy Duchaine/Alamy Stock Photo; [15.1] iStockphoto/SDI Productions; [15.2] © Lamai Prasitsuwan/Shutterstock; [15.3] © iStock/fizkes; [15.4] Randy Duchaine/Alamy Stock Photo; [15.5] Cite Black Women via https://twitter.com/citeblackwomen/status/1195528225868279809; [15.6] Maskot/Getty Images

Index

Page numbers followed by *f* or *t* indicate a figure or table on the designated page